Mental Retardation
in School and Society

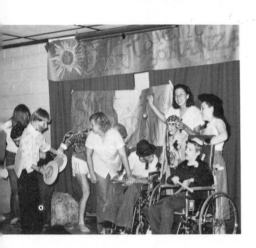

Mental Retardation in School and Society

SECOND EDITION

Donald L. MacMillan
UNIVERSITY OF CALIFORNIA, RIVERSIDE

LITTLE, BROWN AND COMPANY
Boston   Toronto

To Dianne and our sons:
Andrew, John, Daniel, and Paul

Library of Congress Catalog Card No. 81-84230

ISBN 0-316-542725

9 8 7 6 5 4 3 2 1

MV

Published simultaneously in Canada
by Little, Brown & Company (Canada) Limited

Printed in the United States of America

Tonia Noell-Roberts, Photo Research Services

PREFACE

We find ourselves at a time when the quality and quantity of research on mental retardation and the quality of services available to mentally retarded people are at an all-time high. When the first edition of this book was written, the pressures for change and the press for legal rights for the mentally retarded and all handicapped individuals had culminated in passage of Public Law 94-142. Now we have spent several years attempting to implement court mandates and the provisions of the law. While the procedural safeguards in this legislation have helped insure the rights of retarded and other disabled individuals, certain provisions have been found unwieldy when school personnel have attempted to comply with the regulations. Despite some opposition to adhering strictly to some regulations, and predictions that PL 94-142 will be repealed, the major elements of the law—the right to due process, individualized education plans, placement in the least restrictive environment, protection from discriminatory assessment, and parental involvement—have received enthusiastic support. These provisions are now recognized, in principle at least, to constitute good educational practice. As a result, these provisions were retained as organizational themes in this second edition of *Mental Retardation in School and Society*.

The audience for this book continues to be those who have completed a survey course on exceptional children and are now ready to study mental retardation in greater depth. The focus is clearly on the schools. The book is intended for prospective special educators and for other prospective professionals—nurses, physicians, psychologists, and social workers—who will deal with mentally retarded persons in providing them services or when conducting research. Because schools are primary care givers to a vast number of mentally retarded children, adolescents, and adults, an understanding of educationally relevant child characteristics, classification, and issues is helpful in working with educational personnel.

Most textbooks proceed from the severely to the mildly retarded in their treatment of classification schemes, causes of mental retardation, and treatment programs. In this book the sequence is reversed. The reasons for this organization are: First, the majority of persons classified as mentally retarded are mildly retarded and a specific cause of the retardation can be specified in relatively few cases. By considering the biomedical factors known to cause mental retardation first, many introductory students get the impression that there is an underlying biomedical cause in most causes of mental retardation, and that simply is not true. Second, the initial impressions of severe retardation tend to reinforce stereotypes of "the mentally retarded" that students bring to the class—specifically, that all mentally retarded persons are patently disabled, exhibit physical stigmata, are severely retarded, and are the responsibility of physicians. The decision to proceed from the mild to the more severe cases of mental retardation in all discussions in the book was made with the intent of preventing the creation of such misimpressions. Because the response to this organization scheme in the first edition was highly favorable, it was retained in this second edition.

Most programs preparing personnel to work with the mentally retarded include subsequent courses covering the curriculum and teaching methods used with retarded children. Therefore, in this book, the treatment of curriculum and teaching methods is limited in order to emphasize topics that would not be treated elsewhere in the typical course sequence.

The revision required a reconsideration of the topics timely at the time of the first edition. Furthermore, it was necessary to consider whether new issues and trends had emerged and warranted treatment in this edition. In this edition you will find updated information on definitions and prevalence, an entirely new chapter (Chapter 13) on early intervention and mainstreaming, as well as treatment of the recent evidence on community residential facilities as alternatives to institutions. In addition to these new topics, the evidence pertaining to other topics has been updated throughout the entire text.

In preparing the revision it became apparent that some topical areas had received considerable attention in the literature while others had received scant attention. In part, this is due to funding priorities of federal agencies (e.g., research and writing on elements of PL 94-142 abound in the literature as has work on early intervention—both high priority areas of the Office of Special Education). On the other hand, the increased procedural safeguards for protecting human subjects in research have led to a reduction in research on the social psychology of mental retardation and other areas considered "sensitive."

Any effort to survey a subject as broad as mental retardation involves making decisions on emphasis and coverage. Considering the intended audience, the decision was made to limit the treatment of biomedical causes of mental retardation because the educator is concerned primarily with the actual manifestations of mental retardation. However, a basic understanding of biomedical causes is essential for educators to function as part of interdisciplinary teams, and an overview of genetic and physical factors is therefore provided in Chapter 4.

A number of people were helpful in preparing this revision. Some reacted to the first edition, others suggested new areas and/or studies or writings that should be consulted. I would like to thank the following people for their help: Jan Blacher-Dixon, Thomas Cesario, Richard Eyman,

Steven Forness, Jay Gottlieb, Herbert Grossman, Michael Guralnick, Reginald Jones, Kenneth Kavale, Hi Kihara, C. Edward Meyers, Gale Morrison, Arthur Silverstein, Herman Spitz, Ann Turnbull (University of Kansas), James Barnard (University of South Florida), Sandy Alper (University of Missouri/Columbia), Frances Manfredi (Slippery Rock State College), and Ida Jean Windel (State University College at Buffalo). All of these people helped to improve the book, and responsibility for any shortcomings is assumed fully by me.

As in the first edition, Barbara Trumbull was the coauthor of Chapter 4, and I thank her for her diligence in surveying that literature. My mother, Arline MacMillan, handled all typing and preparation of reference material and, as she did throughout high school, corrected my grammar. Two people at Little, Brown and Company were extremely helpful in the production of the book, Mylan Jaixen and Elizabeth Schaaf, and I would like to take this opportunity to thank them. Let me also thank three people who have exerted so much influence over my career in the field of mental retardation, and whose support and friendship I value highly: Reginald L. Jones, C. Edward Meyers, and George Tarjan. I also want to acknowledge the support and encouragement provided me by the administration of the School of Education at the University of California, Riverside—Irving H. Balow and Irving G. Hendrick.

Several people made generous contributions, both personally and professionally, to the photo essays in the book. Thanks go to the Living West and the Life Experience School (page ii, top left; page 585, top right); the Special Olympics (page ii, top right; page 532, middle and bottom); Glen Suprenard, with the assistance of the Child Development Center at the Irving A. Galvin Regional Center, Massachusetts Department of Mental Health, and the Southshore Rehabilitation Center in Quincy, Massachusetts (page ii, middle left, bottom center and right; pages 344–345; page 493, top left, middle, and right; page 580); Claire and Joseph Canning for the classroom photos of their daughter Martha (page ii, middle right; page 510; page 511, bottom right); Mark Seigfried (p. ii, bottom left; page 532, top right); Jane Hotchkiss for the photos of her sister Jennifer and her friend in the part openers and on page 133 (top) and page 533 (bottom left and right); Alan Brightman for the photos taken at Camp Freedom, an educational/residential program for Behavioral Education Projects, Inc. of Cambridge, Massachusetts (page 92); Barbara Crandall, M.D., of the UCLA Mental Retardation Program (page 132); David W. Smith, M.D., University of Washington (page 133, bottom); Judith Sedwick (pages 240–241; page 532, top left and right; page 585, top left, middle, bottom left and right); Christine Reynolds (page 493, bottom left and right); Shoreline Association for the Retarded and Handicapped, Inc. (page 511, top left and right, bottom left); and J. M. R. Audette/Judith Sedwick (page 533, top left).

viii

Finally I would like to express my appreciation to my family for their support and patience over the time this book was prepared. Had it not been for my sons' thoughtful requests to coach their various teams, the revision would have been done a year earlier.

Donald L. MacMillan
Newport Beach, California

CONTENTS

Mental Retardation
in School and Society

PART I

Overview of Mental Retardation

CHAPTER 1

Perspectives

The Education for All Handicapped Children Act (PL 94-142), signed into law in 1975, embodies our nation's comprehensive commitment to the education of all handicapped children. The Act provided equal educational opportunity to some eight million handicapped children. It was passed only after vigorous legal battles to remove the social obstacles that prevented the handicapped from enjoying the rights guaranteed to all citizens. The intent of the legislation is evident in the following passage from the Act itself:

> It is the purpose of this Act to ASSURE that ALL handicapped children have available to them ... a FREE APPROPRIATE PUBLIC EDUCATION and related services designed to meet their unique needs, to assure that the rights of handicapped children and their parents or guardians are protected, to assist States and localities to provide for the education of all handicapped children, and to assess and assure the effectiveness of efforts to educate handicapped children.
>
> (Sec. 601 (3)(c))

The basic rights and protections provided by PL 94-142 are as follows:

1. *The right to due process.* Procedural safeguards were mandated to assure due process in classification and placement in the schools. Parents are

guaranteed access to school records and the right to impartial hearings regarding their child's placement. Parents are also guaranteed the opportunity for independent evaluations of their child.

2. *Protection against discriminatory testing during assessment.* This safeguard ensures that placement will not be made on the basis of a single psychometric instrument, and requires that tests be administered in the child's native language.

3. *Placement in the least restrictive educational setting.* This provision states that handicapped children should be educated in environments resembling, as closely as possible, those in which nonhandicapped children are educated. It is intended to protect the child from the presumed detrimental effects of segregation.

4. *Individualized education programs.* Educators must prepare a written description of each child's program to ensure accountability. These programs must specify (1) the program's objectives, (2) the services to be provided, (3) the program's schedule, and (4) the criteria used to determine the program's effectiveness.

In the years since this bill was passed, educators have found it to be progressive in many respects, but it does present some problems. Chief among them is the amount of nonteaching time teachers must spend meeting the letter and intent of the law. For a detailed analysis of the bill and its major provisions, the reader is referred to Semmel and Heinmiller (1977) and Turnbull and Turnbull (1978b).

PL 94-142 is in many ways a bill of the future, but it is the history of mental retardation that formed it. Mentally retarded persons have been members of every society since the beginning of history. In some societies they have been treated brutally; in other societies they have been treated more humanely and provided with food, clothing, and shelter. References to the mentally retarded have been found in the Therapeutic Papyrus of Thebes (1552 B.C.) and in writings from the ancient period, the Christian era, and the medieval era, indicating an early awareness that certain individuals were *different* (probably mentally ill or mentally retarded).

Every society has had to make conscious decisions about how it would provide for and treat individuals who were unable to adapt to the demands of that society. Prior to 1800 people were aware of the existence of mentally retarded persons but did nothing in the way of systematic study, treatment, or care. While much remains to be done in the field of mental retardation, since 1950 there has been more interest in, and activity on behalf of, retarded persons than during any comparable period of time. Let's consider some of the developments in the United States since 1950 that have influenced our attitude toward mental retardation and our treatment of mentally retarded persons.

DEVELOPMENTS SINCE 1950

A major impetus for change in the treatment of the mentally retarded has come from parents of retarded individuals who did not feel that professionals in the field of mental retardation were making progress rapidly enough. Parents groups had existed before, but in 1950 parents from twenty such groups merged to form the National Association of Parents and Friends of Retarded Children. The name was later altered to the National Association for Retarded Children and then to the National Association for Retarded Citizens (NARC), and in 1980 to the Association for Retarded Citizens–United States (A.R.C.–U.S.). In 1959 NARC had a membership of about 50,000; by 1974 it had grown to nearly 250,000 members, approximately 60 percent of whom were parents, with around 1600 state and local units. While ARC is a nonpolitical organization, it does take positions on governmental policies that concern the mentally retarded.

Parents active in ARC are chiefly from middle- and upper-class homes; their children are mostly moderately or severely retarded. ARC promotes the welfare of retarded persons, research and therapy programs, and a better understanding of mental retardation; it collects and disseminates information and advises and aids parents in the solution of their problems. Before the public schools had established educational programs for trainable mentally retarded children, such classes were created and supported by local chapters. Similarly, efforts by ARC predated those of government agencies in establishing preschool programs, summer camps, and sheltered workshops. It is impossible to assess the influence of ARC on legislation at various levels of government, but it is safe to say that it has been considerable (Roos 1975). Parents organizations are increasingly more involved in court cases to establish the constitutional right of mentally retarded children to an education regardless of their degree of retardation, as in the case of *Pennsylvania Association for Retarded Citizens* v. *Commonwealth of Pennsylvania* discussed in Chapter 8.

The creation of a unified parents organization resulted in lobbying activities at state and national levels that increased pressure to obtain legislation favorable to the mentally retarded. It also became a watchdog to ensure that rights of retarded persons are not denied (e.g., their access to public education) or violated (e.g., by placing them in classes for the mentally retarded without due process).

Parents organizations have helped effect considerable changes in legislation for the mentally retarded. In the late 1950s Congress substantially increased appropriations for research in mental retardation, particularly under the auspices of the National Institutes of Health. The election of John F. Kennedy as president heralded a major upswing in professional involvement, funding, and public awareness of mental retardation; the funding

increases at the federal level were dramatic (Gallagher, Forsythe, Ringelheim, & Weintraub 1975), with corresponding increases at the state and
local level.

In 1961 President Kennedy established the President's Committee on
Mental Retardation, which was made up of professionals and lay people
with an interest in mental retardation. Included in the report of its panel of
experts was the following statement:

> The manner in which our nation cares for its citizens and conserves its man-
> power resources is more than an index to its concern for the less fortunate. It
> is a key to its future. Both wisdom and humanity dictate a deep interest in the
> physically handicapped, the mentally ill, and the mentally retarded. Yet,
> although we have made considerable progress in the treatment of physical
> handicaps, although we have attacked on a broad front the problems of mental
> illness, although we have made great strides in the battle against disease, we
> as a nation have for too long postponed an intensive search for solutions for
> the problems of the mentally retarded. That failure should be corrected.
>
> (President's Committee on Mental Retardation, 1962, p. 196)

On 5 February 1963, President Kennedy sent a message to Congress based
on this report suggesting "a national program to combat mental retardation." Never before had so many resources been directed toward mental
retardation. One member of the President's Committee noted the following
developments at the federal level during or since the Kennedy
administration:

> The construction of university-based Research Centers on Mental Retardation
> and Related Aspects of Human Development; the construction of University
> Affiliated Facilities for the Retarded aimed toward the development of model
> clinical programs and the education of professionals; the construction of Com-
> munity Facilities for the Mentally Retarded; the training of teachers of the
> retarded and other handicapped children; the expansion of maternal, child
> health, and crippled children services, with emphasis on the care of the
> retarded; and the planning of comprehensive services for the retarded in each
> state. Institutional programs were strengthened through demonstration pro-
> jects and inservice training . . . finally a number of other developments, not
> directly focusing on retardation, also benefited the field. The creation of the
> National Institute of Child Health and Human Development, Headstart, and
> the Foster Grandparents Program are good examples.
>
> (Tarjan 1972)

The Head Start program, part of President Johnson's War on Poverty,
attempted to break the vicious circle of poverty by providing preschool
children with experiences they would not otherwise have and that would
help ready them for school. The implementation of Project Head Start did

not result in the kinds of gains originally hoped for, but it did gain support for compensatory education.

In 1966 Congress created the Bureau of Education for the Handicapped. A department of the U.S. Office of Education, its purpose is to coordinate research, training, demonstrations, and service programs for handicapped children, including the mentally retarded. The Bureau's name has recently been changed to the Office of Special Education, and it has played an important role in supporting professional training programs and in stimulating and funding research and demonstration projects.

The enormous increases in monies appropriated on behalf of the retarded in the 1960s attracted professionals from many disciplines to the problem of mental retardation. In addition, the conscience of a nation was awakened—some of the most visible families in the country acknowledged that members of their families were mentally retarded.

The first half of the twentieth century saw a progressive increase in the construction of institutions, creation of special classes for retarded children in the public schools, and progress in terms of more favorable attitudes toward the retarded; but in the 1960s the concern shifted to qualitative issues. Questions were asked about such issues as the quality of life of the mentally retarded and whether their legal rights were being violated through various practices. In other words, the concern shifted from issues of merely providing for the mentally retarded to issues of whether the services being delivered were in the best interest of the individuals being served. This theme emerges consistently in many of the contemporary issues of the field of mental retardation.

Contemporary Trends, Issues, and Problems

Throughout the book you will find that emphasis is given to current issues or problems in the field of mental retardation and to the programs and approaches currently advocated. Some of the questions now before us are empirical issues that require evidence directly bearing on the question. However, in most instances the evidence that would answer the question is lacking or there are contradictory findings. In such cases, the sides of the issue will be presented along with the evidence bearing on it. In other cases the issues are of a philosophical nature and cannot be resolved by means of research, necessitating a clarification of values so that these questions can be answered.

Rights of the Retarded.　A major issue confronting the field of mental retardation concerns the legal rights of the mentally retarded. Cases in which retarded persons in institutions were mistreated or where indiscriminate sterilizations were performed have come to the attention of individuals who have sought redress on behalf of these persons. Let's look at two cases where the rights of the individual were violated.

Kathy, a profoundly retarded child, was twelve years old in 1969. She was unable to speak intelligibly, she could not dress or feed herself, and she was not toilet-trained. Her parents, believing that she would benefit from family support, kept her at home rather than enrolling her in a state institution. They wanted to enroll her in public school classes for the mentally retarded, but the state would not permit children who were not toilet-trained to attend. Toilet training was considered a prerequisite for enrollment in public school trainable mentally retarded (TMR) programs.

Parents of children like Kathy asked why their children should be denied an appropriate education simply because they could not attain the same level of mastery as children with higher abilities. They brought lawsuits against educational agencies to force them to provide appropriate education for severely disabled mentally retarded children, insisting that the Constitution provided for the education of all children regardless of their disabilities.

Juan, an eight-year-old from a Spanish-speaking family, had had little exposure to English before entering school. Upon being enrolled, he was unable to keep up with the other children academically because instruction was provided exclusively in English. The school psychologist, having given Juan an intelligence test in English, found that his IQ was 62 and recommended that he be placed in a class for the mentally retarded. Juan's parents were not initially informed of his placement, but when they realized what had occurred, they took action. They were especially upset that the testing had been done in English and that the test scores were assumed to be accurate; they claimed that Juan had been penalized for coming from a different background than the majority of children taking the test. In court they charged that their right to due process had been violated because they had not been involved in the decision, and that being labeled *mentally retarded* would damage Juan's self-image and hinder his acceptance by other children.

In Chapter 8, some of the important court cases that have corrected abuses experienced by retarded people are analyzed, along with some of the problems encountered in implementing these court decisions.

Intelligence Testing of Ethnic Minorities.   Intelligence tests have been subjected to severe criticism recently. They are implicated in the long-lasting debate over the relative importance of genetic and environmental determination of intelligence and challenged as unfair measures for use with mentally retarded and ethnic minority individuals. In the latter case the critics say the tests consist of items that do not reflect the cultural background of the child coming from a subculture that differs from the dominant culture and that the conditions under which a standardized test is administered depress the performance of the minority child (e.g., a standard test administration could be perceived as threatening by a minority child, resulting in poorer performance than if the administration procedure took cultural differences into account). The testing of intelligence plays a major role in the classification process. It is objected that many ethnic minority children classified as mentally retarded are, in fact, merely different, in the sense that they come from a subculture that promotes different but equally laudable skills that are not tapped on the tests used for purposes of classification.

This issue bears directly on a frequent source of misunderstanding for the introductory student—the meaning of the term *mentally retarded*. For many people the term conjures up an image of a person with physical symptoms that alert the observer that something is wrong. A certain number of the mentally retarded population do exhibit some of these physical signs (called *physical stigmata*), as in the cases of individuals with Down's syndrome (facial appearance that is considered oriental or like Mongolian natives), *hydrocephaly* (characterized by an enlarged head), or *microcephaly* (characterized by a very small head). However, these persons make up a very small percentage of all those classified as mentally retarded. The vast majority have no physical stigmata and show few behavioral signs to an untrained observer. Indeed, many of the mentally retarded are identified as a result of academic problems in the schools, yet they never called attention to themselves through inappropriate behavior prior to enrolling in school and upon leaving school will be responsible citizens, parents, and employees. In this last group of mentally retarded persons (those considered retarded only in the context of the public schools), the minority groups are overrepresented.

The debate over whether intelligence is determined primarily by genetics or by one's early environment has raged for decades. Recent developments that have definitively implicated race with genetics (Jensen 1969) have taken the debate out of the academic arena and into a sociopolitical context. These developments have generated much emotion and increased the sensitivity of an already touchy area—the use of intelligence tests with minority children. An extended discussion of the arguments for and against intelligence tests, along with the existing evidence on this topic, is presented in Chapter 5.

Normalization.   During the last decade there has developed a commitment to the principle of *normalization*, the goal of which is to have mentally retarded individuals live in a fashion that is as "normal" as possible in light of their abilities. Thus far, discussion of this principle has focused on the living conditions for the retarded, with large institutions coming in for the greatest criticism. Operationally, normalization means that the smaller the facility in which the retarded live, the better; that is, small hostel-type residences in the community are preferred over large residential institutions.

The research on alternative residential arrangements is still limited (see the discussion in Chapter 14); however, it is held generally that the institution is too often run for efficiency and for the benefit of those working there instead of for the benefit of the residents. The dormitory arrangement of beds, the large shower rooms and toilet facilities, the uniform dress of the residents, and the sheer size of the facility and resident population are all seen as detracting from the quality of life avilable to the residents.

Mainstreaming.   The principle of normalization has also extended into the educational system, where the term *mainstreaming* has become the educational equivalent of normalization. Until recently it had been traditional to place retarded children in segregated, self-contained classes for the mentally retarded, but the present trend is to integrate retarded children into general education. In other words, retarded children who are mainstreamed are enrolled in a regular class for the major part of their school day. If a mentally retarded student needs special assistance, this assistance is presented in the regular classroom whenever possible. In cases where the needed services cannot be given in the regular class, the child might go to another room in the school building to work with a teacher who has special skills in the area of need. The principle of mainstreaming has received endorsement from most professionals in special education; however, much work remains to be done in developing the skills and techniques required for successful implementation of the principle, which is discussed in Chapter 13 at length.

While the term *mainstreaming* is used widely in the educational literature, most legislation uses the phrase *least restrictive environment* to refer to educational placement of mentally retarded children. The precise meaning of this phrase has yet to be determined, but the general meaning is that a regular class is less restrictive than a self-contained special class, and a self-contained special class in a regular school is less restrictive than a special class for the mentally retarded in a school for disabled children. In general, the intent behind legislation for the least restrictive environment is that educational placement be determined on an individual case basis, that the educational setting most closely approximate that of nonhandicapped children, and that it be one in which the child can function adequately.

Identification of Correlational and Causal Factors.   Behavioral research indicates that there is a close relationship between socioeconomic status and mental retardation. In the early 1960s mild retardation was found to be associated with poverty, thus instigating President Johnson's War on Poverty and programs such as Head Start. Many programs were designed to break the cycle in which poverty begets mildly retarded children who grow up and raise their own children in poverty. During the same period, many behavioral scientists became convinced that the cycle could best be broken in early childhood, before children begin school. In Chapter 13 we will consider the effectiveness of early childhood intervention as a means of preventing mild mental retardation and optimizing development in cases of moderate and severe mental retardation.

Biomedical research has increasingly uncovered genetic conditions associated with mental retardation, physical agents that can damage the unborn fetus and others that can cause brain damage in children, and conditions that lend themselves to various forms of treatment. Mental retardation is a condition that has numerous etiologies, or causes, the overwhelming majority of which are not yet understood, but progress in the biomedical area has been impressive. Even though in the majority of cases no one can point with certainty to what caused the condition, there has been considerable success in identifying high-risk situations. For example, through the analysis of chromosomes, it is now possible to identify husband and wife pairs who carry a risk of having a child with certain forms of Down's syndrome or Tay-Sachs disease. The field of genetic counseling provides such services as identifying high-risk pregnancies and diagnosing, through a procedure known as *amniocentesis*, certain conditions associated with mental retardation early enough in pregnancy to abort the fetus. In addition, research on birth defects has isolated drugs, metals, and other agents (e.g., radiation) that should be avoided by pregnant women because of their proved or suspected toxic effect on the fetus. A discussion of genetic and physical factors as causes of mental retardation is presented in Chapter 4.

An Era of Concern for the Individual

For over a century American society has recognized mental retardation as a social problem. The problem was acknowledged and gradually dealt with in one way or another. Decisions as to what should be done have become increasingly determined in terms of "what is in the best interests of the larger society." At times, the mentally retarded were perceived as a threat to the larger society and the problem was dealt with by excluding them from society—they were sent away from metropolitan centers to isolated institutuions; they were sterilized so they could not reproduce; they were removed from regular educational programs and placed into self-contained special classes. In the cases of institutionalization and special class placement, there was certainly the belief that this was in the best interest of the mentally retarded individuals; however, there was also some consideration given to protecting society in these actions.

Evident in the issues and trends of the past century is an overarching shift in concern from "what is best for society" to "what is best for the individual." An awareness seems to be developing that behind the problem of mental retardation are mentally retarded *people*; furthermore, that these people deserve to be treated with dignity; that they have legal rights that must not be violated; and that they deserve not only to be fed but also to be fed in surroundings that are pleasant; that they deserve not only to be clothed but also to be dressed in a way that reflects individuality. We now realize that mentally retarded people are first and foremost people and only secondarily mentally retarded.

As we move into the last quarter of the twentieth century, concern for mentally retarded people is at its highest level. There is much criticism emanating both from within the ranks of professionals concerned with mental retardation and from outside (as evidenced by court decisions). The field is confronted with numerous unresolved issues and an incomplete understanding of mental retardation. For example, we are constantly reevaluating the definition of mental retardation because we do not have the expertise at present to make the very fine discrimination, on the basis of school performance and intelligence tests, between who should be classified as mentally retarded and whose performance in school and on tests of intelligence is simply depressed by adverse environmental conditions. Many children are problems to teachers because, for whatever reason, they are inefficient learners in the classroom—but should they be classified as mentally retarded?

Despite the gaps in our understanding and the mistakes we make in treatment, it is safe to say that there has never been so much concern for mentally retarded persons, so much research going on to further our understanding of mental retardation, and so much money directed toward the study and treatment of mental retardation as now. A look at the history of mental retardation in society will dramatically support this claim.

HISTORICAL TRENDS AS PRECURSORS OF CONTEMPORARY ISSUES AND PROBLEMS

The history of mental retardation demonstrates clearly that the social climate of a society and a society's attitudes toward the retarded, the unfortunate, and disenfranchised groups play an important role in determining the policies adopted for the care and treatment of the mentally retarded. In addition, it is interesting to trace the recurrence of certain issues and trends in mental retardation and see how the different social climates existing at different times led to the adoption of quite different policies.

Table 1.1 contains a breakdown of the historical periods reflecting different attitudes toward mentally retarded people, and the ways in which these attitudes were reflected in the treatment program. Bruininks and Warfield (1978) divide the history into five periods, while Mercer and Richardson (1975) were concerned only with the period from 1850 to the present, which they break into three periods. Note the rather close agreement between the two sets of authors in terms of emphases from the late 1800s to the present.

A topical presentation rather than a chronology of developments is employed in our discussion of the field of mental retardation to help you see historical trends as precursors of contemporary issues and trends.

Rights of the Mentally Retarded versus Protection of Society

You may wonder why it is necessary to establish the legal rights of the mentally retarded—after all, as citizens they are entitled to the same rights as everyone else. But the mentally retarded have, at various times, been subjected to extreme cruelty and neglect and have not been protected by the legal codes set up to protect citizens from such exploitation and abuse. For this reason it has been necessary to create new legislation to deal with the special problem of ensuring that the rights of the retarded are protected.

Early History.   The extreme of cruelty to the retarded can be seen in the society of the Spartans, who abandoned and killed anyone who was handicapped. Their efforts at extinction may have been prompted by eugenic motives; Greek philosophy stated that the laws of nature dictated that only the fittest survived, so the society may have been applying natural law to

TABLE 1.1 Historical Periods in the Treatment of Retarded Persons

	Bruininks and Warfield's Schema		Mercer and Richardson's Schema	
Period	Sociopolitical Emphasis	Treatment of Retarded Persons	Period and Label	Characteristics
Antiquity–1700 Neglect and Superstition	Varied considerably depending upon the specific historical period.	Characterized by neglect, superstition, harsh and cruel treatment. Little systematic attention given to retarded people. Occasional, infrequent attempts at providing care.		
1700–1800 Awakening Scientific and Humanitarian Interest	Dominated by political and social idealism, with an optimistic view regarding the malleability of intelligence and the importance of assuring equality of people, freedom of thought, and democratic forms of government.	Focus on improvement of the situation of retarded persons with the hope that they could achieve normal functioning and integration into society. Generally small treatment programs located in community settings.		
1880–1925 Era of Pessimism and Eugenic Alarms	Emphasis on application of genetic discoveries and the theory of evolution to understanding social issues; intense economic competition and industrial development. Assumption was that mental retardation resulted from genetic influences and that retarded persons represented a threat to society and social order.	Restrictive treatment with emphasis on protecting society from retarded persons. Sterilization laws, isolated institutions in remote areas, and other restrictive measures prevailed. Rehabilitation and community integration were given much less emphasis than during the preceding period.	1849–1930 Public Menace Cycle	The mentally retarded were viewed as dangerous, immoral, and criminal. Labeling provided a means for either excluding the retarded from schools or for institutionalization and sterilization. Treatment was designed to protect society from a perceived threat.

Period / Cycle	Description	Period / Cycle	Description
1930–1965 Increased Responsibility by Government	Realization, largely resulting from the Depression, that government must assume some responsibility for the welfare of less advantaged persons.	1940–1960 Education-Welfare Cycle	Legislation and services expanded but often were based upon restrictive forms of treatment (e.g., special settings, remotely located institutions, large facilities). Efforts were made to secure funding and establish programs for the mentally retarded (and other handicaps). Increasingly, responsibility for programs was taken by governmental agencies, and the period is characterized as one where programs proliferated.
1965–present Individuals and Human Rights	Growing emphasis on the rights of individuals, along with development of treatment ideologies that de-emphasize effects of labeling and provide treatment through generic services and alternative service models in settings that minimize the separateness of retarded from nonhandicapped persons.	1960–present Civil Rights Cycle	Greatly expanded services, but under conditions of increased self-criticism and experimentation. Models of service stressing integration, individualized planning and treatment, advocacy, and accountability for decisions and programs. Advocates for various retarded subgroups have gone to court to establish and protect the civil rights of the mentally retarded, including the right to a free public education and recognition of due process in the case of ethnic minorities who are labeled.

Adapted from R. H. Bruininks and G. Warfield, "The mentally retarded," in E. L. Meyen, ed., *Exceptional Children and Youth* (Denver: Love Publishing, 1978), and J. R. Mercer and S. A. Richardson, "Mental retardation as a social problem," in N. Hobbs, ed., *Issues in the Classification of Children*, Vol. 2 (San Francisco: Jossey-Bass, 1975).

prevent racial degeneration through the regeneration of those considered defective.

Later, the mentally retarded were not killed outright but they continued to be exploited and treated in a dehumanized way. They were used by the wealthy to perform as fools or jesters; in Rome, Seneca's wife kept a blind imbecile for entertainment. In the courts of France and Germany, the use of *bouffons* and *hofnarren* is well documented; they were often recruited from among the deformed and mentally retarded (Kanner 1964). While the retarded were tolerated by the Romans as diversions or amusements, there is no documentation of any effort to assist them.

With the spread of Christianity and its underlying doctrine of compassion for the unfortunate, for a while at least the plight of the mentally retarded improved; they were provided with clothing, food, and shelter, and the Institutes of Justinian provided guardians for the mentally retarded and for the deaf and dumb. Gheel, a religious shrine in Brabant, was opened as an asylum where private families cared for the mentally ill and mentally retarded.

Tremendous variability characterizes the treatment of the mentally retarded during the medieval era, ranging from treatment as innocents to being tolerated as fools to persecution as witches (Doll 1962); behavior that deviated from the norm was increasingly perceived as caused by Satan.

In the early part of the era the mentally retarded were looked upon with superstitious reverence. Some believed that the utterances of the mentally retarded reflected their unique ability to communicate with the supernatural or were the revelations of "heavenly infants" or "infants of the good God." Tycho Brahe, the astronomer (1546–1601), had for his close companion an imbecile whose speech was carefully listened to as a revelation. In Europe the retarded were allowed to roam unmolested in the streets, which reflected either a belief that they were blessed or at the very least that compassion was the reigning attitude of the times. Various common beliefs came from this notion that the retarded were divinely blessed, such as the Yiddish proverb "A complete fool is half a prophet" and the idea that homes into which the mentally retarded were born were blessed.

With the advent of the period of the Renaissance and the Reformation, however, the plight of the mentally retarded reached an all-time low. The Reformation emphasized personal responsibility, and those who could not take total responsibility for themselves were persecuted and oppressed. A belief in demonism was prevalent and the retarded were often perceived as being possessed. Both Martin Luther and John Calvin denounced the retarded as possessed by Satan. In one of Luther's *Table Talks,* he described a twelve-year-old retarded child. He was disgusted with him, saying, "He ate, defecated, and drooled." Luther recommended that he be taken to a nearby river and drowned, but his advice was not heeded. When asked why he made this recommendation, Luther replied:

He was firmly of the opinion that such changelings were merely a mass of flesh, a *massa carnis,* with no soul. For it is in the Devil's power that he corrupts people who have reason and souls when he possesses them. The Devil sits in such changelings where their souls should have been!

(Kanner 1964, p. 7)

In an attempt to drive out the devil, the process of purgation, or exorcism, was invoked, with the retarded being mentally scourged and physically tortured. Such practices had more impact on those who attempted the purgings than on those who were purged, as a period of protection followed. In the middle of the seventeenth century, St. Vincent de Paul and his Sisters of Charity established the Bicêtre in Paris for the homeless, outcast, and bodily and mentally infirm. But the care of the mentally retarded was still restricted to sheltering, feeding, clothing, and protecting them from abuse; no systematic efforts were yet being made in the scientific study of the condition or in treating, educating, or training the retarded.

Despite a few isolated periods during which compassion was shown the mentally retarded, the historical period prior to 1800 can be best described as one in which people were aware of the presence of severely and profoundly retarded individuals without any real understanding of the condition. Furthermore, beyond simple provisions for survival and protection from brutality by select individual groups, there was no plan for dealing with mental retardation as a social problem. A few isolated events such as the development of a system for educating the deaf by Juan Bonet and the establishment of the Bicêtre in Paris were the first glimmerings of what was to come. While compassion for the less fortunate was emphasized by most religions, and certain groups within various sects began providing shelter, clothing, and food for unfortunates, these efforts can be best described as providing sanctuary for those unable to survive in the competitive society. Once taken into these asylums, there was no treatment, rehabilitation, or education provided, only custodial care. In fact, some of these asylums may have been little better than life in a cruel society. Here is a description of the Bicêtre as it was probably seen by Philippe Pinel, the famous French physician.

The buildings were untenable, the cells were narrow, cold and dripping, unlit and unventilated, and furnished with a litter of straw, which was rarely changed and often infested with vermin. Men crouched there covered with filth, in hideous lairs in which one would have hesitated to confine a beast. The insane, imprisoned here, were at the mercy of brutal keepers, who were often malefactors from the prisons. The patients were loaded with chains and tied with ropes like unruly convicts. This unjust treatment did not quiet them, but rather it filled them with wrath, rage and indignation, aggravating their mental instability, and making the terrible clankings of their chains still more dreadful by their howls and shrieks. When Pinel ordered the chains off these patients in 1792, the commune official in charge of the Hospice des Bicêtre ridiculed the idea, but finally gave his consent remarking that he feared he would be a victim of his presumption. No violence followed their release and better conditions immediately ensued. Two years later Pinel accomplished a similar reform at the Salpêtrière.

(Nowrey 1945, p. 343)

Initial Treatment Programs in the 1800s.   The real beginnings of treatment of the mentally retarded occurred in the early 1800s as the result of a combination of ideology, money, and individuals, albeit on a relatively small scale. The first attempts were carried out by young idealists who went against authorities and the advice of their mentors. Interest spread from Switzerland and France to the rest of Europe and the United States in a short time. Advances were subsequently fostered by another aspect of eighteenth-century individualism—political reform.

It is interesting to note the political leaning of the men who were interested in learning about mental retardation. Itard was known as "Citizen Itard" at the turn of the century. Many of the supporters of Seguin's special classes were Comteans or Saint-Simonists, including Esquirol, Flourens, and Voisin. All these individuals were active social reformers. Samuel Howe, who would play a major role in arousing concern for the retarded in the United States, was a doctor in the Greek revolution of the 1820s, helped Polish patriots, and was instrumental in the establishment of the Perkins Institution for the Blind. Two other Americans who fought for the retarded, Samuel May and James Richards, were abolitionists who volunteered their homes as stations for the Underground Railroad.

Two major cultural developments that increased interest in mental retardation were humanitarian reform movements in Western civilization and increased governmental concern with the spread of endemic cretinism. Even before the French and American revolutions there was considerable discussion of man's relation to man, and indignation was expressed over the neglect and mistreatment of unfortunates—slaves, the imprisoned, and the handicapped. A few physicians went beyond merely speaking out against such injustices and did something. Jacob Rodrigue Pereire (1715–1780) became actively engaged in the education of congenital deaf mutes. In 1749 he demonstrated his methods at the Academie Royale de Belles Lettres of Caen and later presented them at the Academy of Science in Paris. Louis XV asked Pereire to appear at court and was sufficiently impressed to grant him an annual pension of 800 francs. Pereire taught deaf mutes a sign language and invented a device that helped them to calculate. Although Pereire never worked with mentally retarded subjects, he was widely credited as being an inspiration to those who would. [In fact, Barr (1904) stated, "Without Pereire, Itard had been impossible."] Valentin Haüy established the first school for teaching the blind in 1784 in Paris, and in 1801 Itard began working with the "wild boy of Aveyron." Concern for the mentally retarded arose within a general concern for humanitarianism that encompassed the handicapped.

Concern about cretinism was centered in Western Europe. In 1792 Fodéré published a paper on goiter and cretinism that resulted in a grant from Victor Amadeus III, Duke of Savoy to travel and gain more information. It also prompted attempts to identify cretins by census—notably by Napoleon Bonaparte and Charles Albert, King of Sardinia.

In the nineteenth century, industrialization made its impact on society for better or worse. On the one hand industrialization ushered in the exploitation of children as laborers, unsanitary working conditions, and the growth of slums. However, on the positive side it brought a prosperity that could support charitable facilities for the handicapped that would benefit mentally retarded persons.

Early Leaders in the Field of Mental Retardation

Jean Marc Gaspard Itard's (1774–1838) pioneering work with the "wild boy of Aveyron" marks a pivotal accomplishment in the treatment of the mentally retarded. As a young man, Itard enlisted as an assistant surgeon in a military hospital to avoid conscription, and he proved to be a competent physician. He was later assigned to the medical staff of the Institution for Deaf Mutes in Paris, where he became the founder of otology, the medical science of diseases of the ear.

In 1801 the Abbé Bonaterre brought a young "wild boy" of eleven or twelve years to Itard. The boy had been found wandering in the woods by hunters and was capable only of guttural, animal-like sounds. Itard's interest in the child was immediate, possibly because of his resemblance to the "noble savage" described by Rousseau. He attempted to move the boy "from savagery to civilization, from natural life to social life." For five years Itard worked intensively with the boy, named Victor, using intense stimulation and environmental interaction in an attempt to develop speech. Itard finally gave up in frustration, at one point reportedly crying out:

Unfortunate! Since my pains are lost and my efforts fruitless, take yourself back to your forests and primitive tastes; or, if your new wants make you dependent on society, suffer the penalty of being useless, and go to Bicêtre, there to die in wretchedness!

(Davies & Ecob 1959, p. 13)

Despite Itard's failure to civilize Victor, the French Academy of Science in 1806 commended Itard's work. They applauded his persistence and courage and noted how much progress had been made through his "ingenious modes of teaching"—methods that were to inspire many others. Furthermore, the statement acknowledged the scientific contribution of Itard's systematic observations.

Probably more than anyone else, Edouard Onesimus Seguin (1812–1880) influenced the education of the mentally retarded. In 1837 Seguin accepted a chance to work with Itard on the instruction of an idiotic child (the term then in use). Despite the death of Itard one year later, Seguin continued to teach. He was unwilling to wait for medicine to cure the retarded, but rather tried to do as teachers of the deaf and blind did—as he said, to give the retarded "the benefits of education" (Seguin 1843, p. 20).

Seguin established an experimental class for idiots in the Salpêtrière in Paris in 1839, organized a program for idiots at the Bicêtre in 1841, for which space was provided by the French government, and eventually established a school of his own. Seguin's success received considerable attention both within France and in other countries. The Paris Academy of Sciences commended his work; his textbook, published in 1846, was widely recognized; and visitors from other countries were inspired by his success.

The 1848 revolution brought to power in France a new regime that Seguin distrusted and he soon emigrated to the United States, where he rapidly became active in the cause of the mentally retarded. He continued writing, and in 1876 he, Dr. Hervey Wilbur, Mrs. George Brown of the Barr School in Massachusetts, Dr. G. A. Doren of Ohio, Dr. I. N. Kerlin of Pennsylvania, Dr. H. M. Knight of Connecticut, and Dr. C. T. Wilbur of Illinois met and formed the Association of Medical Officers of American Institutions for Idiotic and Feeble-minded Persons, which evolved into the American Association on Mental Deficiency, as we now know it. Seguin was elected the first president of the organization.

Seguin's legacy to the field of mental retardation was invaluable, both methodologically and philosophically. Being a physician, his educational model was a medical one. He firmly held to diagnosis, prescription according to the diagnosis, and summary of the results. His physiological method, according to Talbot (1967), is most closely related to the techniques employed in Montessori schools, fulfilling his hope that his methods would benefit ordinary children. Like Itard, Seguin's influence has been carried through to many present-day efforts.

———

Johann Jacob Guggenbühl (1816–1863), a contemporary of Seguin's, had a career of extreme highs and lows. At the age of twenty, Guggenbühl observed a "dwarfed, crippled cretin of stupid appearance" reciting the Lord's Prayer in front of a way-side cross. The mother said that she had not been able to provide any education for him, but that he had learned the Lord's Prayer and that he went to pray daily at the cross. Guggenbühl wondered what could be achieved with such individuals with systematic treatment. He decided to devote his life to the "cure and prophylaxis" of cretinism.

Guggenbühl established an institution in 1841 near Berne with the purpose of helping his patients through educational, hygienic, and medicinal means. Guggenbühl approached the task with a religious zeal, and his early success was hailed as a major achievement. He was praised lavishly by everyone from psychiatrists to kings. His personal fame and the visibility of his institution, the Abendberg, led to numerous awards and invitations to speak.

But gradually, criticism of Guggenbühl brought about his fall from favor. The major impetus for this came from the British minister to Berne, Gordon, who visited two English patients at the Abendberg in 1858. He described the conditions in a report to the government as deplorable, citing that the death of one patient as a result of a fall went unnoticed for a considerable time. The government ordered an investigation and the report that resulted was devastating. The Swiss Association of Natural Sciences withdrew its sponsorship and the Abendberg was closed.

Attitudes toward Guggenbühl ranged from adulation to criticism for hypocrisy; both extremes were probably unwarranted. At any rate, Guggenbühl was the initiator of institutional care for the retarded and he has had considerable impact on the field of mental retardation.

———

Samuel Gridley Howe (1801–1876) devoted himself to helping the underdog; he served six years as a surgeon in the Greek war of liberation, raised money for refugees, founded the New

England Asylum for the Blind, and smuggled funds to Polish revolutionaries. During this last escapade he was captured and imprisoned in Berlin. Upon his release in 1832 he returned to Massachusetts and founded the Perkins Institution for the Blind, where he developed new techniques for teaching the blind and became famous for his success in teaching Laura Bridgman, who was both blind and deaf. Howe was actively involved with other reformers like Dorothea Dix, Charles Sumner, and Horace Mann.

While his own professional activities were primarily devoted to the blind, Howe championed the cause of the handicapped in general. He chaired a commission in Massachusetts to study the status of mental retardation, which resulted in the establishment of a wing at the Perkins Institution, on an experimental basis, for ten retarded children. In addition, Howe was instrumental in bringing Seguin to the United States. Although he did not work with the mentally retarded directly, his role in establishing support for the mentally retarded in the United States is significant.

Although most of the pioneering efforts of Itard, Seguin, and Guggenbühl lacked understanding of the medical causes of the condition and of the learning characteristics of the retarded population, they were to serve as models for treatment programs for a considerable period of time. Seguin's work was particularly significant, considering the lack of research evidence he had on which to base his practices; some of his principles continue to be used. Talbot (1964) summarized some of the principles as follows:

1. The child should be observed first and the information derived from the observation should serve as the basis of his education.
2. Education deals with the whole child and the things taught the child must be taught as wholes.
3. Activity is the basis and means of learning, and sensory activities are included in activity.
4. Children learn best from real things, and memory for real things is related to the opportunities provided to compare.
5. Every child, regardless of his degree of retardation, has some degree of understanding upon which learning can be built.

(p. 15)

Public sentiment in favor of the retarded enjoyed a high popularity during the Seguin era, but a gradual regression to fear of the mentally retarded occurred during the early part of the twentieth century. Later in this chapter a discussion of institutions will elaborate on the shift in attitude away from the belief common in the last quarter of the nineteenth century that the mentally retarded could be cured. Let us now consider another development that turned public attitudes and led to practices designed to protect society from the imagined potential menace of the mentally retarded.

The Eugenics Movement.   In the late 1800s and early 1900s, several reports were published that purported to show how mental retardation "ran in families." The major thesis of such reports was that the data indicated the hereditary transmission of mental retardation and undesirable social characteristics. Sir Francis Galton expressed concern over the density of the human race given the rate of reproduction among the unfit, and in 1883 presented the concept of *eugenics* as a science that took into account the various factors that allegedly improve the inherent qualities of a race.

In 1875 Richard Louis Dugdale published his study *The Jukes, a Study in Crime, Pauperism, Disease and Heredity,* which reported on a family with a high incidence of imprisonment, dependency on public support, and poor physical and moral standards. The report revealed that one-half of the family located was feeble-minded. Additional data on other families included in the study (the "tribe of Ishmael," the "Zeros," and the "family Markus") all supported the premise that "like begets like"—that is, families stemming from the retarded tend to "decay" and abound with vagrants, the insane, and the mentally retarded.

Possibly the most widely cited report of genealogical tracing was made by Henry Goddard of the Training School at Vineland, New Jersey (1912). He described the case of Martin Kallikak, a revolutionary war soldier who fathered an illegitimate son by a feeble-minded girl and later married and had children by a girl of normal intelligence. Goddard was able to identify 480 descendants of the union with the defective girl—143 of whom were feeble-minded. In the total number there were high incidences of illegitimacy, promiscuity, alcoholism, and criminality. The descendants traced to Kallikak and his wife married into some of the best families of the time and among them were physicians, lawyers, and educators. These findings led Goddard to conclude that feeble-mindedness was hereditary, and he recommended segregation through colonization as a remedy.

Goddard's report was quickly followed by similar studies. A dramatic estimate of the role of heredity in mental deficiency came from A. F. Tredgold of the British Royal Commission in 1908, who estimated that 90 percent of mental retardation was familial in origin. In his book *Twilight of the American Mind,* W. B. Pitkin (1928) expressed the popular belief that something had to be done to prevent "the passing of the great race." The prophets of doom warned against allowing such degeneration to go unchecked.

The rise of the eugenics movement as a result of these warnings brought policies to protect society from the consequences of letting nature take its course. Proponents of eugenics provided a simplistic solution for mental retardation: if the mentally retarded stop having children, the problem will disappear because mental retardation is a result of breeding among defective stock. They went so far as to divest themselves of any responsibility for social problems of the times, rationalizing that slums, for example, are created by the less intelligent and will cease to exist if that group does not propagate. Sterilization laws that provided that the retarded could be sterilized without due process considerations were passed in some states. Another development (although hard to tie directly to the eugenics movement) was the expansion of institutions, which served to get the retarded away from the large metropolitan centers and in which the sterilization of residents was common. The rights of the mentally retarded were relegated to secondary importance and the rights of the larger society were paramount.

A line of thinking similar to that of the eugenics people developed in Nazi Germany, where mental defectives, schizophrenics, and other groups who could "contaminate" the racial stock of Germany were murdered. In the United States, as in Europe, it was believed that through either sterilization or institutionalization the retarded could be prevented from reproducing. Cranefield commented on the eugenics movement as follows:

> Seldom in the history of medicine have so many intelligent and well-meaning men embarked on so vicious and brutal a program with so little scientific foundation for their actions.
>
> (1966, p. 13)

The Need to Protect the Rights of the Retarded. The above discussion demonstrates dramatically how vulnerable the mentally retarded are to exploitation. Their welfare depends on the sway of public opinion and philosophy. Earlier, mention was made of the parents movement in the United States that resulted in educational programs for the mentally retarded. Without such pressures it is unlikely that educational programming for the more severely retarded would have occurred, let alone the recent developments in the courts that established the right to a public education of all retarded children, regardless of the degree of retardation. The mentally retarded depend on the nonhandicapped to guarantee their civil rights and to serve as watchdogs to ensure that these rights, once guaranteed, are not violated. This cause has now been taken up, and will be discussed subsequently in this book.

To understand the origin of current special education programs, it is important to recognize several developments of the late 1800s and early 1900s. Lazerson (1975) emphasized the following as critical factors in the emergence of treatment programs in the United States in the period prior to the civil rights cases of the 1960s and 1970s: (1) the failure of institutions to cure patients, (2) the recognition that it was inefficient to place children with low IQs in the standard curriculum of public schools and the subsequent rise of vocationalism, and (3) the development of intelligence tests as a means of deciding who should enter vocational programs. Let's keep these factors in mind as we consider the historical precursors of current trends in the treatment of the handicapped.

Normalization versus Institutionalization

The number of institutions grew during the nineteenth century, and by 1920 all but four states had at least one institution. In the late 1800s, these institutions perceived their mission to be rehabilitation and education. In fact, many of these institutions were called "schools." The directors of these schools did not try to enroll the most severely debilitated: the director of the Pennsylvania Training School stated that lower-functioning individuals "are hardly admissible applicants" because they would not respond to the treatment program (Royfe 1972). Nevertheless, lower-functioning residents came to constitute a larger proportion of the residents in institutions, until by the turn of the century many institution directors had drastically reduced their estimates of the proportion of residents they expected to become self-sufficient. The next step was to alter the programs in the institutions to permit greater classification by degree of retardation. At the same time, in the interests of "efficiency," institutions became larger. This trend, along with the eugenics scare (described above) and the desire to segregate and isolate "menaces to society," changed the emphasis from education and rehabilitation to custodial care (Lazerson 1975).

Shortly before 1900, with institutions serving a rather severely debilitated segment of the mentally retarded population, debate arose about the treatment of milder, noninstitutionalized individuals. The basic structure of the public school system was being established; it was becoming a tax-supported, tuition-free, age-graded institution. Most states were moving toward compulsory attendance (Lazerson 1975). As we will discuss in the next section, responsibility for individuals with milder mental retardation would fall to the public education system.

The trend toward large, impersonal institutions that provided custodial care continued until about 1950. More recently, psychologists and educators have been questioning whether institutions might in effect be hindering the development of the residents. Evidence on the superior development of retarded persons reared at home compared to others with similar conditions (e.g., Down's syndrome) reared in institutions has been accumulated and interpreted as an indictment against institutions. The exploitation of residents as unpaid workers (Conley 1973) and some instances of physical brutality are two other strong arguments used against institutions. Coupled with the Scandinavian principle of normalization, which advocates the individual placement of retarded persons in settings as close as possible to those in which nonhandicapped persons live, the challenge to the institution as serving a valid function is a serious one. That challenge, its supporting evidence, and the response to such evidence are viewed in Chapter 14.

Mainstreaming and the Special Class

With the beginnings of compulsory public education came a change in the role of education. What had formerly been a privilege for the elite became a more egalitarian opportunity. Children from all social strata were enrolled in public schools, including children from culturally different backgrounds. As Lazerson (1975) has observed, public education was confronted with the problem of educating a large number of children as inexpensively as possible, which led to concern about the efficiency of education. The "marginal" learner became a focus of grave concern. Terman wrote:

> Feebleminded school children are present everywhere. They linger in the third, fourth, fifth, and sixth grades until well into adolescent years. They consume a disproportionate amount of the teacher's time, they drag down the standards of achievement for normal children, they tend to become incorrigible and to feed the never-ending stream of juvenile court cases. . . . Not until the institutional cases have been removed from the public schools, and not until the borderline cases have been placed in special classes, can the work of the school with normal children proceed as it ought. Feebleminded children in the regular classes not only interfere with instruction, they are also likely to be a source of moral contagion.
>
> (1917, p. 164)

Terman's remarks, obviously influenced by eugenic considerations, reflect the prevailing attitude of the time. Others were more constructive. Mealy (1940) quoted another early educator: "Let us do our part to make possible the identification of subnormals early in life so that they may be trained in useful and specific habits up to the limits of capacity, and so that those incapable of profiting from training may be segregated and thus become less of a menace to society" (p. 74).

Public education adopted a corporate-industrial organization in an effort to be more efficient. This model was characterized by centralization, specialization of function, an administrative hierarchy, and cost accounting. Along with this organizational model came a new definition of equality of educational opportunity. This new definition rejected the notion that all children should be exposed to the same curriculum, emphasizing instead that children considered incapable of mastering the highly verbal, abstract curriculum traditionally offered to all children be given more relevant training. This new definition gave rise to vocationalism (Lazerson 1975). The relevance of the standard curriculum for borderline children had been brought into question by studies done in the early 1900s by Thorndike and Ayres, which showed that many such children left school early, frequently repeated grades, and entered dead-end jobs once they left school.

In addition to preventing problems, the creation of special classes was intended to have some positive effects. Semmel, Gottlieb, and Robinson (1979) observed that the creation of special classes was part of a broad transformation of the American school system, paralleling the trend toward general-ability grouping. Educators believed, at least at first, that the ability to categorize and train the handicapped for economic usefulness would benefit society.

Special classes for the retarded were established in Springfield, Massachusetts, Boston, and New York prior to 1900 and, despite failures, by 1905 most of the larger American cities had similar programs. Farber (1968) reports that by 1911 there were public school classes for mentally deficient children in ninety-nine American cities; by 1922 there were 23,000 children enrolled in such classes. During the Depression special class programs declined in number, but after World War II there was again an increase in such programs. In 1948 there were approximately 90,000 children enrolled in special classes, by 1958 there were about 200,000, and by 1963 the number had grown to 400,000 children. By this time the IQ cutoff had risen to 80 or higher.

The increase in special classes after World War II was partly due to the release of resources previously directed to the war effort. However, even as recently as the 1950s there was disagreement as to the responsibility of public education for the group referred to as *trainable mentally retarded* (TMR) children. Parents groups included a large number of middle- and upper-class parents with trainable-level children and only a few parents of *educable mentally retarded* (EMR—mildly retarded), who tend to come from the lower social classes. As one might expect, classes for trainable mentally retarded were established before classes for educable mentally retarded children, even though the latter group is far larger in number. The parents of the mildly retarded were either less aware of their children's special learning needs or less adept politically to get a response from educators to these needs.

The segregation of mildly retarded children in special classes was prompted by concern for the progress of nonhandicapped children in regular grades, but many educators also believed that the mentally retarded could be best served in a special class. It was assumed that the ridicule and frustration that often accompany failure in regular programs were a more serious problem than the disadvantages associated with segregation. The conventional wisdom in the 1950s was that the child would be best served in a special class. In the 1960s, however, a series of investigations failed to demonstrate that mildly retarded children were better off in special classes. These studies, along with the overrepresentation of ethnic minority children in special classes and the greater expense involved, led many educators to question the wisdom of the special class, especially for the higher-functioning EMR children. Currently, the favored approach is *mainstreaming*, the enrollment of EMR children in regular classes, with special assistance provided in the context of the regular program. As you will see in Chapter 13, much work remains to be done before mainstreaming can be implemented successfully.

Intelligence Tests and Their Critics

Differences among individuals had been studied in some detail in the latter part of the nineteenth century by such persons as psychologist G. Stanley Hall in the United States and F. Bartholomai in Germany, who studied the mental abilities of children as they entered school. But psychometrics got its major impetus from the work of Alfred Binet. In 1904 Binet was appointed by the French Minister of Public Instruction to devise a method for identifying children in the Paris schools who were likely to fail in the standard curriculum and therefore should be placed in special programs to suit their needs. Binet invited Théodore Simon to join him in this task.

The project was conducted within the educational environment; hence the constructs measured by the instrument developed by Binet and Simon were shaped by the educational institutions of Europe and North America. Furthermore, the development of the instrument differed markedly from earlier attempts at studying individual differences. The earlier work was limited to comparing specific responses such as reaction time, eye movements, and sensory discrimination. Binet and Simon based their work on the premise that average children achieve certain developmental stages at approximately the same age. Through observation and measurement they were able to establish a scale of ages at which children master certain skills in language, judgment, and other phases of human development.

The first version of the instrument was available in 1905, followed by revisions in 1908 and 1911, the year Binet died. The impact of Binet's efforts has been profound. He provided a reliable means for evaluating a child's mental age, enabling teachers to estimate the child's functioning level in school, and thus providing them with a certain degree of ability in assessing the heterogeneity of a class in terms of response to teaching. Upon testing various populations it became apparent that there were differences of *degree* rather than differences of *kind;* between the normal and retarded groups was a sizable group of borderline cases. For the first time, psychologists and educators were forced out of classifying people as either normal or retarded.

As a result, in 1910 the American Association on Mental Deficiency altered its classification system, which had included only "idiots" and "imbeciles," to include the borderline group, referred to as "morons." The term *moron* was introduced by Goddard and was derived from the Greek word for "foolish," implying a deficiency in judgment. The emergence of the category "moron" for the mildly retarded underscores the importance of considering the context in which mental retardation is identified, what Kanner calls *relativity.* Prior to intelligence tests and mandatory school laws, individuals who were of marginal intelligence were not identifiable. In a rural society, or even in an urban setting, uncomplicated by comparisons to today's cities, such individuals were able to meet the demands of the society and therefore did not stand out as incompetent or different. But when required to attend school, their relative inability to master tool subjects (reading, mathematics, social studies) brought them to the attention of school authorities. With the development of intelligence tests, the proportion of children scoring low shocked many professionals. Here was a new breed of retarded individual: able-bodied, reasonably competent socially, normal looking, but inefficient learners. They were quite unlike those that had been clearly identifiable as retarded in earlier years. These new retarded persons, initially labeled "morons," would later be termed *educable mentally retarded* (EMR) when special classes were established for them in public schools.

The testing movement spread rapidly to the United States. Henry Goddard learned of Binet's work on a trip to Europe. He translated the Binet scale, tried it out at Vineland, and was very impressed with its ability to identify the level of functioning of the children. Goddard's influence on American thinking was considerable, although on occasion he went beyond Binet, as when he interpreted the Binet scale to be a measure of a single unitary factor, the chief determinant of which was heredity; Binet contended that intelligence was malleable and subject to increase.

Although Binet's discoveries quickly prompted a wide range of test development activity, the psychometric movement was not without its critics even in the early twentieth century. There was concern about the loss of unique performance assessment when an individual's performance was reduced to a single score (e.g., mental age), the restriction in the range, the score's use, the possible bad reflection on teaching, and the fact that the tests unduly penalized children with sensory and emotional problems. Nevertheless, by 1915 tests were generally accepted as the method of identifying the mentally retarded. The revision of Binet and Simon's test by Lewis Terman in 1916 became the standard against which all other tests of intelligence would be compared. In that revision Terman introduced the

concept of *IQ,* or *intelligence quotient,* which reflects the individual's brightness *relative* to other individuals, as opposed to the *mental age,* which
reflects the level at which an individual is functioning. The new revision
sparked a heated debate within mental retardation circles about which
index—IQ or mental age—should be used for classification purposes; IQ
became the accepted standard.

With the advent of World War I American psychologists at the Training
School at Vineland, New Jersey, devised two group tests of intelligence for
identifying which draftees should be excluded from service for reasons of
low intellect; they were the *Alpha* for those with sufficient language skills,
and the *Beta,* a nonverbal test. The massive screening of military recruits
with these tests shocked the public, in that a sizable proportion of those
drafted were found unfit for military service due to limited intellectual ability. Particularly high failure rates were found in recruits from certain ethnic
groups and geographic regions.

After 1920 mental testing began to have tremendous influence in the
areas of psychology and education. Questions arose concerning the malle-
ability of intelligence through intervention, the effects of early deprivation,
and the *nature-nurture controversy* [the debate over whether genetic factors
(nature) or environmental factors (nurture) are of greater significance for
the intellectual attainment observed in individuals]. These issues persist to
the present time. As Cronbach (1975) points out, the times and prevalent
attitudes determine the receptiveness of the public (and academics) to a
point of view about testing. For example, he noted that little opposition
arose to the position in the early 1900s that certain immigrant groups (particularly from southern and eastern Europe) were inferior intellectually, but
when Jensen drew a similar conclusion in 1969 (although he did not use
the term "inferior"), the prevailing sentiment was opposed to the idea of a
group's being inferior, and there was little reception of his point. Although
testing instruments provided an objective basis for determining who
should be admitted to certain educational programs, colleges, jobs, and the
like, this was at first seen as counter to the interests of the privileged class
that influenced such decisions—in short, the tests were seen as beneficial
for the lower classes, who could be admitted to such programs if their performance warranted it. At present a prevailing sentiment is that tests are
unfair for children from lower social classes, particularly those of ethnic
minority backgrounds; the tests are blamed for the fact that a disproportionately high number of minority children are classified as mentally
retarded.

It is important to recognize that the results of intelligence tests were
viewed by educators as helpful in making decisions regarding which students to place in vocational programs. These test results provided a fairly
objective measure (or "scientific basis"), which was used to match a child's
ability to a particular curriculum. Because intelligence tests provided the

means of differentiating students, they contributed indirectly to the growth of special classes for mildly retarded students.

Differentiation of the Mentally Retarded

Early writers believed that mental retardation was a single phenomenon, the causes of which were not understood. Paracelsus (1493–1541) is credited with writing the first medical treatise devoted to mental deficiency, primarily a document of religious and humanitarian considerations. It raised questions such as "Why did God allow fools to be born who cannot understand the sacrifice God made for them?" Paracelsus described the fool as having an unspoiled inner soul that, upon death, is freed of all weakness and deformity and guaranteed salvation. He gives a clear description of cretinism and notes that it is found in close association with endemic goiter and that both conditions are common where the water is in some way peculiar (Cranefield & Federn 1963). Around 1602 a Swiss physician, Felix Platter, wrote a description of cretinism that would not be equalled for the following 150 years; around 1614 he wrote another passage that revealed an awareness of milder cases of retardation, usually thought to have gone unrecognized until the development of tests of intelligence in the early twentieth century. Platter wrote:

> In infants this dullness of intelligence soon becomes evident, when they are educated, and forced to learn some things, and especially at the same time when they are taught to read, since only by long and much exertion can they recognize the letters of the alphabet, put syllables together, and form completed words from them.
>
> (Quoted in Cranefield 1966, p. 5)

This passage appears to describe not the severely debilitated children most often described in writings prior to 1900 but children with mild learning problems that only stand out when attempts are made to teach them academic skills.

Mental Retardation and Mental Illness. An examination of the early literature reveals very little in the way of a distinction between mental retardation and mental illness, but there are a few accounts. The definition of Fitzherbert in the *New Natura Brevium* (1534) reflects the same developmental, intellectual, and social dimensions reflected in present definitions:

> And he who shall be said to be a sot (i.e., simpleton) and idiot from his birth, is such a person who cannot account or number twenty pence, nor can tell who was his father or mother, nor how old he is, etc., so as it may appear that he hath no understanding of reason what shall be for his profit nor what for

his loss. But if he hath such understanding, that he know and understand his letters, and do read by teaching or information of another man, then it seemeth he is not a sot nor a natural idiot.

(Quoted in Doll 1962, p. 23)

Another early attempt to distinguish between insanity and mental retardation was by Locke in 1690:

Herein seems to lie the difference between idiots and madmen, that madmen put wrong ideas together and reason from them, but idiots make very few or no propositions and reason scarce at all.

(Quoted in Doll 1962, p. 23)

Thomas Willis (1621–1675) predated Locke and may have influenced Locke's distinction, although he was not much recognized for over a hundred years. In 1672 Willis published a paper entitled "Of Stupidity or Foolishness" in which he made the distinction between mental retardation and mental illness that is considered to be the first clear distinction between schizophrenia and mental deficiency ever written.

Causes of Mental Retardation. Until the middle of the nineteenth century, the words *cretinism* and *mental deficiency* were used interchangeably. For example, Guggenbühl announced that "we may consider as mentally weak and, therefore, on the road to cretinism *all* children who neither at home nor school can be made accessible to the ordinary means of education and instruction." Wilhelm Griesinger, a psychiatrist, objected to this state of affairs when he declared, "Every cretin is an idiot, but not every idiot is a cretin; idiocy is the more comprehensive term, cretinism is a special kind of it."

Between 1866 and 1875 notable breakthroughs in the differentiation of "idiocy" and "insanity" were made (Kanner 1967) and the fallacy of the homogeneity of the mentally retarded and mentally ill was finally laid to rest. In a clinical lecture in London in 1866, John Down spoke on what he called "the Mongolian type of idiocy," now known as *Down's syndrome*. In the same year, Edouard Seguin, unaware of Down's work, described the same condition. Cranefield (1966) expressed annoyance that the term *Down's syndrome* has gained favor when Seguin's description is so concise and accurate and Down's is "presented within the framework of an absurd theory" (p. 10). Nevertheless, Down is commonly credited with the discovery of the condition. Seguin named the condition "furfuraceous cretinism" and described it as follows:

Furfuraceous cretinism, with its milk-white, rosy, and peeling skin; with its shortcomings of all the integuments, which give an unfinished aspect to the truncated fingers and nose; with its cracked lips and tongue; with its red, ectropic conjunctiva, coming out to supply the curtailed skin at the margin of the lids.

(1866, p. 44)

With the new discovery began a search for other types of mental retardation and their underlying causes. In 1877 W. W. Ireland divided the forms of mental retardation into twelve subdivisions, several of which reflected various causes. His system of classification considerably influenced the medical sciences. Before the turn of the century, additional discoveries of specific conditions differing in pathology were discovered. Among these were Bourneville's discovery in 1880 of tuberous sclerosis and the independent discoveries by ophthalmologist Warren Tay in 1881 and neurologist Bernard Sachs in 1887 of what is now known as *Tay-Sachs disease*. In addition, Sigmund Freud conducted his classic studies on the causes and nature of cerebral palsy.

Still, psychiatric and pediatric circles did not accord mental retardation much consideration prior to the mid 1900s. A major impetus for biomedical research in the field of mental retardation came with the discovery of a condition known as *phenylketonuria* (PKU) by Dr. A. Folling in 1934. He showed this condition to be inherited and manifested in an inability to metabolize phenylalanine, a substance found in most proteins, resulting in progressive brain damage and ultimately a severe degree of mental retardation. It was subsequently shown that, if it were detected early and the diet controlled, the condition could be ameliorated. In other words, the degree of mental retardation that would result could be minimized. The point to be emphasized here is that the discovery of PKU attracted researchers to mental retardation; there have been dramatic developments in the identification of inherited conditions and in the screening procedures for some of them, and the entire field of genetic counseling has emerged. Progress has also been made in identifying maternal conditions and agents in the environment related to birth defects. A tremendous amount of money is currently being directed into this line of research and encouraging progress is being made. The major known and suspected biomedical causes of mental retardation are discussed in Chapter 4.

SUMMARY

The overarching theme in the field of mental retardation today is the attempt to protect the individual against abuse. The opposite side of that coin is that we are striving to guarantee the best treatment program available and to deliver that program in a manner that allows the retarded person to retain his dignity. Whereas in the past any efforts were merely to keep retarded persons alive, clothed, and fed, today efforts are concerned with providing them the highest possible quality of life. Clearly the mentally retarded person is in need of treatment that in some cases will be medical in nature, in others educational; either way, that treatment must be delivered in a humane fashion.

A second theme in the field today is the prevention of mental retardation. Biomedical sciences have made advances in uncovering a host of causal agents, tests have been developed to identify persons carrying a risk of having a mentally retarded child, and other tests are available for early detection during a pregnancy. Unfortunately, though, for all the biomedical advances, the cause of mental retardation in most cases cannot be established. Furthermore, in the milder forms of mental retardation there is no demonstrable biomedical cause. Poverty and mild retardation go hand in hand, yet the vast majority of individuals from poor neighborhoods are not mentally retarded. Can mental retardation in such instances be prevented through the modification of the social-psychological conditions associated with poverty? In Chapter 3 we will explore the research to date that has attempted to relate social-psychological variables to mild retardation in an effort to understand what causes this condition.

In the beginning of this chapter it was stated that mentally retarded persons pose a problem to society. Many other different groups pose a problem to society—criminals, the mentally ill, the unemployed, and so on. It is the responsibility of society to seek out people who need help and give it to them. As is discussed in Chapter 2, the problem of defining the population of persons who are to be classified as mentally retarded is a difficult one, particularly with marginal individuals who pose learning problems to teachers in the public schools but who get along quite nicely outside of school. We do not want to deny services to anyone who needs them, and yet we do not want to classify as mentally retarded anyone who is not. The debate over classification and labeling is discussed in Chapter 7.

CHAPTER 2

Definitions, Classification Schemes, and Prevalence

How do we decide who is mentally retarded? Think of the retarded people you have encountered. Did they all share certain characteristics? Did they all have distinctive physical features or patterns of speech that made them appear retarded? Do all retarded people need the same special services? In this chapter we will show that many people classified as mentally retarded differ markedly from common stereotypes, and that they vary dramatically in their needs for special services.

This chapter is divided into three sections. In the first, we consider the consensus definition of mental retardation, some definitions offered in the past, and several contemporary alternatives. Then we consider the various classification schemes used to divide the mentally retarded population into homogeneous groups. Finally, we discuss the prevalence of mental retardation: How many retarded citizens are there, and, according to the classification schemes currently in use, what kinds of services do they need? We will address the problem of definition first.

DEFINITIONS

Professionals have been debating the various definitions and classifications of mental retardation for many years. Their disagreements are not merely academic exercises in semantics. Subtle distinctions, such as whether a definition emphasizes social competence, capacity to learn, or store of knowledge, determine whether a particular child will or will not be classified as mentally retarded. To quote Kuhlman (1924): "Definitions of Mental Deficiency have an extra-scientific interest . . . they decide the fate of thousands of human beings every year and are intimately related to social welfare in general."

We are interested in mentally retarded individuals as people, people with certain problems and needs. Their mental condition may be associated with medical difficulties, educational difficulties, or social difficulties, presenting needs that cannot be met until we identify the retarded individuals. But identifying them is not as easy as it might seem.

The Problems of Definition

There is a subset of the mentally retarded who will always be so classified no matter what definition is used. Members of this subgroup are deficient in the ability to learn and in the knowledge they possess; they evidence gross social maladaptations and frequently have medical problems. But there are also a vast number of marginal children whose plight depends on what definition of mental retardation is being used. These children score on tests of intelligence very close to the IQ cutoff usually thought to separate the retarded from the nonretarded (presently around 70). They may be socially adept in their own neighborhood, but they do not meet the demands of the school in terms of being students. Whether or not such children are classified as mentally retarded will depend on the IQ level adopted in a definition (if IQ is one parameter) and on the importance placed on social adaptability. It will also depend heavily on the setting in which social adaptability is assessed. If the neighborhood is an appropriate setting in which to evaluate social adaptability, these children would not be classified as mentally retarded; however, if the school setting is used, then they would be so classified.

Mental retardation is of interest to professionals in various disciplines— such as anthropology, education, medicine, psychology, and sociology— each with its own concepts and assumptions. Individuals trained in a given field approach problems with the conceptual tools of their discipline. As long as a problem lies clearly in one, and only one, discipline, the use of these unique tools goes unchallenged. However, any attempt to define mental retardation in a way that will satisfy representatives from each of these fields is beset with headaches from the beginning. Which conceptual tools will be employed? To what extent will IQ be emphasized? Must there be pathology underlying the lowered intellectual functioning? Representatives of the various disciplines would respond differently to each question.

Some correlates of mental retardation are of particular interest to specific disciplines; their inclusion or exclusion alters the population that would be defined as mentally retarded. Certain physical traits and diseases found in some cases of mental retardation are of interest to medical personnel; some conditions are inherited and are of interest to biologists. Mentally retarded people are deficient in the acquisition of knowledge and skills, an area served by educators; some run afoul of moral and legal standards established by society, of interest to the sociologist. The problem arises when one group tries to define the conditions for the others.

According to Kuhlman (1941), a further difficulty has been the tendency to include in the definition elements frequently correlated with mental retardation but not *universally* associated with this status. For example, if a definition of mental retardation included as one of its elements brain pathology—since there are many cases of retardation in which brain pathology has been found—the presence of pathology would have to be demonstrated before an individual could be classified as mentally retarded. We know that in the vast majority of cases of mental retardation, brain pathology cannot be shown—hence pathology cannot be an element of the definition.

A satisfactory definition should specify the conditions that must be met before an individual is classified as mentally retarded. The elements of that definition should be shared by all individuals so classified; all individuals not classified as mentally retarded must fail to evidence at least one of the elements of that definition. This is important because the *definition* of mental retardation guides the *diagnostic* procedure; it specifies which elements must be assessed to determine whether or not a child is mentally retarded.

In addition to the difficulty of arriving at a universally applicable definition, those who work with mentally retarded people need a workable definition for differing reasons. Behavioral scientists concerned with mental retardation assume one of two roles: service or research. Those involved in service need a definition that will identify which individuals should receive certain services. Researchers need a definition that provides the parameters of the population they should study in attempts to solve practical problems or to establish general laws of behavior.

Because of problems such as these, no single definition of mental retardation is universally accepted. The definitions offered by the American Association on Mental Deficiency (Heber 1959b, revised 1961; Grossman 1973, revised 1977; in press) have the widest endorsement in the United States. Even these definitions have been criticized, however, as we will see later in this chapter.

The Evolution of Contemporary Definitions

As we noted in Chapter 1, in early times only the most severe forms of mental retardation were acknowledged. Probably the first term used to denote the condition was *idiocy*, derived from the Greek, meaning "people who did not hold public office." In 1838 Esquirol applied the term *imbecility* to the less handicapped cases, the term being derived from the Latin word for weak or feeble (Clausen 1967). Later the term *simpleton* was introduced to denote cases less severe than imbeciles but not quite reaching normality.

Definitions of mental retardation have varied considerably throughout this century, but the general trend has been to include less serious cases in this category. The American Association on Mental Deficiency definition offered in 1961 (Heber 1961) was more inclusive than any previous definition. In 1973 (Grossman 1973) the trend toward broadening the definition was reversed somewhat, but the most recent definition (Grossman, in press) permitted greater inclusivity than the 1973 definition.

Changes in the definition of mental retardation have involved more than its inclusiveness. At different times in history there has been a different emphasis on the importance of causes, manifestations, pathology, social inadequacy, and IQ. From time to time there have been attempts to define mental retardation by a single factor, such as how it is manifested biologically, sociologically, or intellectually. But the definitions most widely accepted today try to incorporate our knowledge of all these factors.

Biological Definitions.   Since physicians were the first group to investigate mental retardation, it is not surprising that the earliest definitions emphasized the biological aspects of the condition. This emphasis resulted in a very narrow definition of retardation, at least by today's standards. For example, Ireland wrote:

> Idiocy is mental deficiency, or extreme stupidity, depending upon malnutrition or disease of the nervous centers, occurring either before birth or before the evolution of mental faculties in childhood. The word imbecility is generally used to denote a less decided degree of mental incapacity.
>
> (1900, p. 1)

Eight years later, Tredgold also emphasized the organic origins of mental retardation, but he added social adaptability as a criterion. His definition of mental retardation was as follows:

> A state of mental defect from birth, or from an early age, due to incomplete cerebral development, in consequence of which the person affected is unable to perform his duties as a member of society in the position of life to which he is born.
>
> (1908, p. 2)

The earliest professionals in the area of mental retardation thus thought the condition was caused by biological problems, which in turn resulted in social inadequacy. This point of view remained influential for many years.

Definitions emphasizing biological criteria—usually linked with social inadequacy—were still being offered after World War II (see Jervis 1952; Penrose 1949).

Social Definitions.   Since mental retardation is a practical problem for society, the majority of definitions have emphasized practical criteria, with considerations such as: Can the individual care for himself without getting into trouble? Such social definitions emphasize the failure of the individual to adapt socially to his environment.

Some who work with retarded persons feel that definitions of mental retardation are incomplete unless they take relativity into account. According to this point of view, a good definition should be applicable to people in a variety of situations; that is, it must recognize that mental retardation is relative to one's surroundings. For instance, it is easier for a person of limited mental abilities to adapt in a rural setting than in a large city because the less complex environment imposes fewer demands for adaptation.

Kanner has pointed out that those who are mentally retarded may achieve considerable success in less complex, less intellectually centered societies. In fact, they may even achieve superiority if they have assets other than those tapped by tests of intelligence. However, such people encounter problems when they attempt to meet the intellectual demands of this society. To quote Kanner:

> Their "deficiency" is an *ethnologically determined phenomenon* relative to the local standards and even within those standards, relative to the educational postulates, vocational ambitions, and family expectancies. They are "subcultural" in our society but may not be even that in a different, less sophisticated society.
>
> (1949, p. 8)

Psychometric Definitions.   Despite warnings that mental retardation was not an absolute condition but one that was relative to its surroundings, the increasing use of intelligence tests, following the work of Binet and Simon, led to attempts to quantify mental abilities and to define mental retardation in terms of IQ. Since they were objective, easy to administer, and readily compared with well-defined normative groups, tests of intelligence seemed to provide a quantitative means for deciding who was mentally retarded.

Over the years, an IQ of 70 has been a popular cutoff point thought to distinguish the retarded from the nonretarded. In 1973 Terman and Merrill, using the 1937 revision of the Stanford-Binet test, found that 5.6 percent of their standardization sample had IQs of 70 to 79, a range classified as "borderline defective"; 2.63 percent of their sample fell into the "mentally defective" category, with IQs of 69 or lower. Wechsler (1955), creator of the

Wechsler Intelligence Scale for Children (WISC), came up with similar results using his tests. In his standardized sample 6.7 percent fell into the "borderline" category, with IQs of 70 to 79; 2.2 percent fell into the "defective" class, with IQs of 69 or lower.

Despite its advocates—such as Hollingworth (1926), Wechsler (1955), and Clausen (1967, 1972)—the use of a psychometric definition of mental retardation has had more critics than supporters. Some critics have objected to any definition that rests solely on the criterion of IQ; others, to any definition that includes IQ at all.

The critics of IQ argue that a child's score on an intelligence test reflects many nonintellectual factors—such as measurement error, emotional factors, and motivational factors—as well as the intellectual factors the test is supposed to measure. Furthermore, they argue, a given IQ cutoff cannot truly discriminate between retarded and nonretarded unless the test's reliability is perfect.

A further criticism of a psychometric definition is that it ignores the relativity of mental retardation to different environments. A child with an IQ of 70 in a class where the mean IQ is 85 would not appear deviant; however, in a class with a mean IQ of 115, this child would probably be unable to compete academically.

As will be discussed later, there is presently a serious challenge to the use of intelligence tests at all in diagnosing mental retardation, particularly with low social status children and minority children. But despite all the criticisms, some states have written IQ levels into legislation to define mental retardation, and in those states a child who achieves an IQ above 70 is excluded from various services for the mentally retarded.

The AAMD Definitions

At the same time that some professionals were advancing a single criterion—biological, social, or psychometric—as a basis for defining mental retardation, others were cautioning against limiting judgment to a single factor. Doll (1941) even suggested that there should be six criteria, all of which he considered essential for a definition of mental retardation: (1) social incompetence, (2) mental incompetence, (3) deficiency of development, (4) constitutional origin (i.e., a biological basis), (5) duration to adulthood, and (6) essential incurability.

As we have seen, people from different professions have tended to focus on different aspects of mental retardation. In 1959 a group of professionals from a number of disciplines—known as the American Association on Mental Deficiency (AAMD)—pooled their ideas and came up with a definition that more or less satisfied them all. The AAMD definition has since been revised periodically to reflect current information and trends, first in

1961 by Heber and subsequently in 1973, 1977, and at the present time (Grossman, in press). The key elements have remained the same, however. They are (1) low general intellectual functioning, (2) problems in adaptation, and (3) chronological age.

The revisions of the AAMD definition have involved changing the level of intellectual functioning used to define eligibility for mental retardation. The 1959 and 1961 definitions were *inclusive* in that they provided a rather high IQ limit (i.e., close to 85), whereas the 1973 and 1977 definitions were more *exclusive*, setting the upper IQ limit close to 70. The most recent definition (Grossman, in press) is a modest compromise, setting the upper limit at 70 but suggesting that this be used as a rough guideline—the limit can be as high as IQ 75 in certain circumstances. In the following section, the most recent definition (Grossman, in press) will be discussed and contrasted with the former definitions in terms of emphases and levels of general intellectual functioning.

Most Recent AAMD Definition.   The definition of mental retardation adopted by the AAMD reads as follows:

> Mental retardation refers to significantly subaverage general intellectual functioning resulting in or associated with impairments in adaptive behavior and manifested during the developmental period.
>
> (Grossman, in press)

This definition consists of psychometric and social inadequacy elements and specifies an upper chronological age for the emergence of the condition. All three criteria must be met before a person can be identified as mentally retarded.

These three elements, and the way the AAMD Manual states they should be measured, should be considered in more detail:

1. *Subaverage general intellectual functioning.* General intellectual functioning is defined as the results obtained on one or more of the individually administered, standardized tests of intelligence. "Significantly" subaverage is defined as an IQ of 70 or below on standard measures of general intelligence. The manual emphasizes, however, that this upper IQ limit (70) is intended only as a guideline and could be extended upward to IQ 75, especially in school settings, if according to clinical judgment the child exhibits impaired adaptive behavior assumed to be caused by deficits in reasoning and judgment.

2. *Impairments in adaptive behavior.* This has proved to be the most difficult element to measure. It is left somewhat vague to accommodate developmental and environmental changes during a person's life. This element refers to significant limitations in the person's ability to meet

the standards of maturation, learning, personal independence, social responsibility, or some combination of these, expected of the individual's age and cultural group. Adaptive behavior can be measured by standardized scales or assessed by clinical judgment.

3. *Developmental period.* This element requires that the condition be identified between conception and the eighteenth birthday.

Adaptive behavior is the most difficult characteristic to measure because societal expectations change as a child gets older. During the preschool years, for example, maturation would be reflected in children's interactions with their peers and in such skills as sitting, crawling, standing, and walking. When the child enters school, learning becomes the major criterion, and in adulthood, social adjustment becomes the standard.

Social adjustment refers to a person's ability to live independently, to hold a job, and to conform to the social standards of the community. Furthermore, to be classified as mentally retarded, a person must be *clearly* subnormal in adaptive behavior. It would be pointless to identify and classify as mentally retarded a person who faces no unusual problems or whose needs are met without professional attention. Some people with an IQ below 70 do well in school and society. Such people are not mentally retarded, and should not be labeled as such.

Unique Elements of the AAMD Definition. The AAMD definition warrants closer scrutiny because it differs significantly from previous definitions in two ways:

1. The diagnosis of mental retardation is made on the basis of *present level of functioning,* with no reference to prognosis for the individual's future status. Unlike Doll's suggested criterion of incurability (1941), classification based on a person's present level of functioning makes it possible to be considered mentally retarded at one point in life and not at another. In comparison to chronological age peers, shifts in the individual's relative standing on either intellectual functioning or adaptive behavior would warrant such reclassification. Such shifts in classification are especially possible for people who are only mildly retarded.

2. The AAMD definition *does not attempt to differentiate mental retardation from other disorders of childhood* associated with impaired intellectual performance, such as autism, brain damage, or learning disabilities. In the past, attempts had been made to establish whether the intellectual deficits were primary or secondary. But with the new focus on present functioning level, such distinctions are no longer necessary.

Rationale for IQ 70.   By adopting a maximum IQ of 70 and stating that it could be as high as 75, the AAMD authors intended to correct a misconception. As they state in the Manual, they believe that IQ 70 should be a commonly accepted guideline, and yet they recognize the need for flexibility in clinical assessment. Previous AAMD definitions (Heber 1961; Grossman 1973, 1977) used −1 and −2 standard deviations (SDs) as the criterion for setting the upper IQ limit. This system implied that a precise score existed, below which all children were retarded and above which no child was retarded. The new definition reflects the position taken earlier, that people should be classified according to need, not according to IQ. Persons with IQs above 70 who need services should not be denied them merely because their IQs are one or two points too high; neither should those with IQs below 70 be given services if they are managing without them. This can be a troublesome problem, particularly in school, where intellectual performance is a prerequisite for success and special educational services may be needed by a child with an IQ of above 70.

The adoption of IQ 70 as an upper limit brought the definition into conformity with the laws of many states and with the international practices advocated by the World Health Organization. The most recent definition represents a compromise between inclusive and exclusive definitions, and thereby avoids two types of problems. When the upper limit is quite high (85) many more people are eligible for services, but the chances that some children will be mislabeled as mentally retarded also increase. By setting a lower IQ limit, the risk of misidentification is reduced, but the possibility of denying services to persons who need them is increased.

Comparison of the Most Recent Definition with Previous AAMD Definitions.   The chief difference between the current AAMD and the Heber definitions (1959, 1961) is that the earlier definitions included a "borderline" category of mentally retarded persons. This category, comprising persons with IQs between roughly 70 and 85, is now considered psychometrically normal. As you can see, the Heber definitions were very inclusive to ensure that all children who needed services would receive them. The earlier definitions set an upper chronological age limit of sixteen years, which has been changed to eighteen years in the more recent Grossman editions (1973, 1977, in press).

In the period between the Heber definitions and the earliest Grossman definition (1973), there were many court cases and debates involving the "erroneous classification" of children, especially ethnic minority children. The inclusiveness of the Heber definition was regarded as one cause of the problem. The first Grossman edition (1973) dropped the upper IQ limit from −1 SD to −2 SDs (that is, from roughly IQ 85 to IQ 70), which provided a more exclusive definition. Moreover, the 1973 version states more explicitly that all three elements of the definition—IQ less than 70, impaired adaptive behavior, and manifested before eighteen years of age— had to be met for a person to be classified as mentally retarded.

Figure 2.1 shows how this system works. (It is assumed that persons under consideration are less than eighteen years old.) Even if children have IQs below 70, making them candidates for the mentally retarded classification, they cannot be so classified unless their adaptive behavior is impaired.

Despite the new guidelines about what constitutes a deficit in adaptive behavior, those who make the diagnosis must still base their assessments on clinical judgment rather than rely on objective measures, particularly in mild cases. Objective measures are available for more severe cases, however (see Meyers, Nihira, & Zetlin 1979).

Alternative Definitions

Although the AAMD definition is widely accepted, it does have its critics. Clausen (1967, 1972) faulted Heber for including adaptive behavior in the definition when it cannot as yet be measured adequately. He contended that, to avoid subjectivity, a measure of adaptive behavior should be developed before this characteristic is included in the definition. As an alterna-

---

FIGURE 2.1   Rationale of AAMD Definition of Mental Retardation with Dual Criteria of Retarded Intellectual Functioning and Adaptive Behavior

INTELLECTUAL FUNCTIONING

		Retarded	Not Retarded
ADAPTIVE BEHAVIOR	Retarded	mentally retarded	not mentally retarded
	Not Retarded	not mentally retarded	not mentally retarded

From H. J. Grossman, *Manual on Terminology and Classification in Mental Retardation.* Reprinted by permission of the author and the American Association on Mental Deficiency. Special Publication series, No. 2, 1973.

tive, Clausen recommended that mental retardation be defined by IQ alone, since the determination is usually made primarily on the basis of IQ anyway. Moreover, he suggested that the upper IQ limit be dropped from -1 SD (Heber 1961) to -2 SDs, a level below which, he argued, adaptive behavior is usually impaired due to low intelligence. This suggestion was incorporated into the 1973 revision, but the revisions continue to include an assessment of adaptive behavior.

Mercer's Social System Alternative.   Mercer (1965, 1970a, 1971b, 1973b) agrees with Clausen that there are no adequate measures of adaptive behavior in cases of mild retardation and that as a result diagnosis relies almost exclusively on measures of intelligence. But from that point they go in opposite directions in terms of what should be done. Clausen says that mental retardation should be defined in terms of intelligence, which can be tested clinically, whereas Mercer feels that the label *mentally retarded* is a socially assigned role and should therefore be defined sociologically.

Objecting to the AAMD's clinical perspective, Mercer argues that the definition is a confusing combination of a medical model and a statistical model. We will explain these constructs before we examine Mercer's proposed alternative.

The *medical model* focuses upon pathology and pathological symptoms. It defines abnormality as the presence of pathology; normality is defined as the absence of pathology. According to the bipolar logic of the medical model, an individual is either sick, unhealthy, or pathological at the one extreme, or free of any pathology at the other.

Two assumptions underlie the medical model: (1) If someone has the symptoms, he possesses the pathology. He *is* tubercular, or he *is* mentally retarded. (2) The pathology can be present even if others around him are unaware of it. That is, a child can be tubercular even if his parents do not know it; or he can be mentally retarded even if his parents or friends do not perceive him as such.

In the *statistical model*, normal is defined in terms of position within a normal distribution (a bell-shaped curve). A test is administered to a sample of individuals and an arithmetic mean and a standard deviation computed; individual scores can then be compared to that distribution. Normal can be defined as some predetermined percentage of the population that score within a certain range. For example, according to the 1961 AAMD definition, normal was defined as those scores falling within one standard deviation of the mean (above and below), or between IQ 85 and 115. About 68 percent of the general population score in that range. In Figure 2.2, which shows the distribution of IQ scores, Row C shows which scores are defined as "normal" and which as "abnormal" if one standard deviation is used. Row D indicates the limits of normality and abnormality as set forth in the 1973 AAMD definition. In this case, a cutoff point of two standard devia-

FIGURE 2.2   Statistical Model for Determining Normal and
Abnormal, Using IQ for the Example

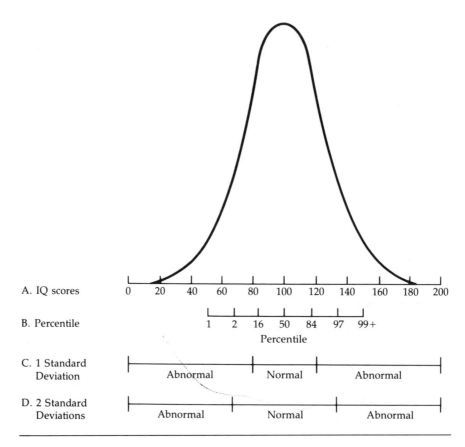

tions extends the range of normality to all scores falling between approximately 70 and 130.

The statistical model in itself is not judgmental; being extreme is neither good nor bad. However, if the characteristic being measured is of social significance, then being at one extreme or the other can carry a value judgment. Such is the case in this society with the characteristic of intelligence: to have a low IQ is considered bad.

To make matters worse, Mercer contends, the medical and statistical models are not separated in the AAMD system. When diagnosis in the absence of pathological evidence must be based upon behaviors alone, Mercer (1970a) warns that there is a tendency to think in terms of one model while using the other. The reasoning goes as follows: low IQ means "bad"; pathology means "bad"; therefore low IQ means pathology.

As an alternative to the clinical perspective Mercer offers the social system perspective, which defines *normal* as appropriate performance according to role expectations. She defines *mental retardation* sociologically, as "an achieved social status in a social system" (1973b, p. 3).

For each status (e.g., teacher, student, police officer) there are defined roles, and a certain type of behavior is expected of the individuals who fill them. Expected behavior varies from status to status. While some flexibility is allowed, all members of the social system share common expectations of how persons of a given status are to behave. Individuals who violate the norms are punished by the group, while those who perform at or above expectation are rewarded. The ultimate punishment that can be imposed for failure to perform at an expected level is removal to a lower and less esteemed status.

According to the social system perspective, in order to be relegated to the status of a mentally retarded person, someone would have to fail to fulfill the role expectations for his assigned status and thus be reassigned to the new (and devalued) status of the mentally retarded person. In Mercer's opinion the study of mental retardation should therefore focus upon such questions as: When and how have people come to be demoted to the status of mentally retarded? What role expectations have they failed to fulfill? Social systems research might explore such questions as how expectations vary according to people's developmental level. During the preschool years, for instance, the role of the child is rather undemanding. During the school years, the role of a student is apparently far more demanding and is one that some children find very difficult to fulfill.

In trying to track down the basis for certain social expectations, Ashurst and Meyers (1973) and MacMillan, Jones, and Aloia (1974) have pointed out that in our schools it is the teachers who set the expectations. They expect certain things of their students based on their age and status, and they evaluate all their students against these expectations. When children are performing far worse academically than their class peers, the teacher may consider them to be failing to fulfill their role expectations as students. To find out why a child is performing poorly the teacher may request a psychological evaluation, perhaps including psychometric tests by which the child's performance can be compared to national norms.

The social system perspective closely parallels the discussion pertaining to adaptive behavior. A definition based on Mercer's model would probably emphasize adaptive behavior and would relegate IQ to a position of lesser significance—in fact, it might exclude it altogether. But the social system and clinical models should not be viewed as alternatives in the identification of the mildly retarded. Rather, they should supplement each other, with the social system model used first and the clinical subsequently. A child who does not fail in the role expectations of a student should not be vulnerable to identification as retarded by means of the clinical model alone. And usually this does not happen. Psychologists are not searching for retarded children by massive screenings with intelligence tests. Children with IQs that would allow placement in an educational program for the mentally retarded are usually left in regular classes as long as they continue to meet their teachers' expectations.

An Educational Alternative.   The Committee on Definition and Terminology of the Council for Exceptional Children, Mental Retardation Division (Kidd 1979) has taken issue with the 1977 Grossman definition, primarily because they feel the −2 SD criterion used in the 1977 version denies services to some children who need them—those whose IQs are slightly above the upper limit. State lawmakers tended to accept the −2 SD standard, but the consensus among educators is that IQ 75 is the upper limit for mental retardation. The adoption of the AAMD definition (in press), which in some circumstances permits identification up to IQ 75, presumably satisfied the CEC–MR committee. Before the revision, however, Kidd and his committee offered the following definition:

> Mental retardation refers to subaverage general human cognitive functioning, irrespective of etiology(ies), typically manifested during the developmental period, which is of such severity as to markedly limit one's ability to (1) learn, and consequently to (2) make logical decisions, choices and judgments, and (3) cope with one's self and one's environment.
>
> (1979, p. 97)

This position reflects the concerns of educators, who since the litigation and legislation of the late 1960s have made a great effort to avoid erroneous labeling—that is, to avoid overinclusiveness. This effort has been reflected in state laws and definitions. The position taken by Kidd and his colleagues in opposition to the relatively exclusive 1977 AAMD definition is contrary to the current opinion, which favors an exclusive definition to avoid erroneous classification, even if that means denying services for children in need whose IQs may be slightly "too high" to be eligible for services for "mentally retarded children."

CLASSIFICATION SCHEMES

Even after we have somehow sorted out those who are retarded from those who are not, our classification problems are not over. If we look at all those we have categorized as retarded, we find that they constitute an unworkably heterogeneous group. Some are able-bodied and others are severely deformed; some are slightly slower than the norm in learning to sit and walk and others may never master these skills; some evidence pathological conditions and others evidence no signs of pathology. Within the mentally retarded category there is great variability with regard to virtually every attribute except mental ability.

A major reason for defining mental retardation is to determine which people are in need of particular services. Yet among the individuals who fit the definition, needs vary considerably. Take, for example, an individual who is profoundly debilitated and in need of life-support systems simply to stay alive. The treatment this individual needs emanates primarily from medical personnel, and any considerations of education, however broadly defined, are of limited significance. At the other end of the scale is a child who poses no medical problem whatsoever yet has been unable to function academically in a regular class and has been classified as mentally retarded. This child's treatment consists entirely of an educational program, with no special consideration given to medical treatment.

The label *mentally retarded* is too unspecific. Classification as mentally retarded is a first step in that it qualifies individuals for services and identifies them for research purposes. But in order to create, within the mentally retarded population, groups of people who need similar treatment, we must further subclassify them.

Various subclassification schemes have been proposed. Just as professionals from different disciplines emphasize different factors in their definition of retardation, they also tend to group individuals on the basis of differing attributes. The educator is more concerned with achieving homogeneity of learning attributes, whereas the physician will desire to group according to medical needs. As you can see from Table 2.1, there are many divergent subclassification schemes being used by different professions for their own research or service purposes. And this table lists only schemes that are related to IQ and behavioral factors; later in this chapter we will take a look at some categorizations based on biological factors.

Special Education Categories

Special educators usually classify the mentally retarded into three categories: the *educable mentally retarded* (EMR), the *trainable mentally retarded* (TMR), and the *severely and profoundly mentally retarded* (SPMR). Until the passage of PL 94-142, which mandated that all children are entitled to a free and appropriate education regardless of their disabilities, the SPMR group was served by nurses or institutional personnel, if at all. Now, for the first time the doors of educational agencies are open to them.

The educational classification system categorizes children according to the severity of their problem. The EMR group has the least severe problems

TABLE 2.1 Terminology and Degrees of Retardation According to Several Definitions of Mental Retardation

Proponents	Generic Term	Intelligence Quotients																				
		95	90	85	80	75	70	65	60	55	50	45	40	35	30	25	20	15	10	5	0
Amer. Assoc. for the Study of the Feeble-minded*	feeble-minded								moron				imbecile				idiot				
Tredgold & Soddy (Great Britain)	mental deficiency							high grade; feeble-minded				middle grade; imbecile				low grade; idiot					
Amer. Assoc. on Mental Deficiency (Heber 1961)	mental retardation (adaptive behavior not included)				borderline mentally retarded			mild				moderate			severe			profound				
Amer. Assoc. on Mental Deficiency (Grossman 1973)	mental retardation (adaptive behavior not included)							mild				moderate			severe			profound				

50

Classification system	General term	dull normal	borderline	mild	moderate	severe	profound
Amer. Assoc. on Mental Deficiency (Grossman, in press)	mental retardation (adaptive behavior not included)		▨ (diagonal hatching)	mild	moderate	severe	profound
World Health Organization	mental subnormality			mild	moderate	severe	
Amer. Psychiatric Assoc.	mental deficiency		mild or slightly mild	moderate	severe		
Wechsler (1949) (WISC)	mental deficiency	dull normal	borderline	mental defective			
Terman & Merrill (1960) (Stanford-Binet)	mental deficiency		borderline defective	mental defective			
Amer. Educators (cited by Smith 1971)	mentally retarded or mentally handicapped	dull normal	educable	trainable		custodial, dependent, or low grade	

*Note that the American Association for the Study of the Feeble-minded was formerly the Association of Medical Officers of American Institutions for Idiotic and Feeble-minded Persons and is currently the American Association on Mental Deficiency.

Adapted from Table 1 in M. Gelof, "Comparison of systems of classification relating degree of retardation to measured intelligence," *American Journal of Mental Deficiency*, 1963, 68:3, 299–301. Reprinted by permission of the author and the American Association on Mental Deficiency.

and the SPMR group is the most severely debilitated, while the TMR group occupies an intermediate position. A range of IQs is associated with each of these categories, but the placement of children in programs must never be made on the basis of IQ alone. Programs for EMR children usually serve children with IQs from 50 or 55 to 70 or 75. TMR programs enroll children with IQs from 25 or 35 to 50 or 55. The IQs of children in SPMR classes are usually below 35.

Each program has a different set of goals and a different set of skills that may be taught in an attempt to maximize the development of those with limited abilities. The categories must remain flexible. If a child placed in a TMR program shows the capability to master the content of the EMR program, then this child should be moved up into an EMR program. Similarly, if an EMR child masters the curriculum of the EMR program rapidly, every consideration should be given to returning the child to the regular educational program.

Practical Distinctions between EMR and TMR. EMR and TMR programs are based on predictions about the different capabilities of each group. EMR children are those who are thought to be capable of learning fundamental academic skills—such as reading and arithmetic—and who, as adults, will be able to be self-sufficient and live independently in society. By contrast, most TMR children are considered capable of mastering only the most basic word and number concepts. As adults they will seldom be self-sufficient or capable of living independently in the community. They will probably require some supervision and financial support. A curriculum designed for the TMR will include activities designed to promote their independence to whatever degree possible (such as mobility in the community) and to train them in social functioning and vocational skills that will enable them to be productive, if not totally self-sufficient, as adults.

Andrew is a ten-year-old black child who has been enrolled in an EMR program for the past two years. Andrew comes from a family of five children who live in a five-room apartment in one of the lower socioeconomic areas of a large midwestern city. His parents both have limited educational backgrounds— his mother dropped out of school at the end of eighth grade after having repeated several grades; his father completed a little over nine years of formal education.

As a preschooler Andrew seemed normal in all regards. There were no complications when he was born and his medical history was quite ordinary, with no serious illnesses or accidents. He got along well with other children his age, and he learned to sit, stand, walk, and talk at approximately the ages considered normal. Physically, Andrew was a very attractive child with excellent coordination, making him quite popular with his peers because he excelled in most sports.

When Andrew was in the first grade it became obvious that he had academic problems. He was unable to keep up with his classmates, particularly in reading. At the end of the year his teacher recommended that Andrew be retained in the first grade, and he was. At the end of his second year in the first grade, he still had educational deficits, but the staff at Andrew's school decided to give him a "social promotion."

Andrew's academic problems were accentuated in the second grade, however, and other students occasionally ridiculed him for his poor academic performance. Andrew began to get in fights. The teacher felt that the fighting was a result of the frustration Andrew was feeling because of his failure and the ridicule. Toward the end of the second grade the teacher conferred with the principal of the school and indicated that she thought Andrew might be better off in an EMR program where there would be less pressure and more individualized attention. The school psychologist evaluated Andrew and concurred that he did qualify for placement in the EMR program since his IQ according to the Stanford-Binet scale was 65. The case was taken before the committee charged with recommending placement in such cases and it was agreed that Andrew should be placed in the special class for EMR children, where he has been enrolled for the past two years.

As one observes Andrew in the EMR program it is obvious that he has to work very hard in academic areas to make any progress. But his behavior problems are no longer apparent; in fact, Andrew is very well liked by his teacher and classmates. At home he gets along well with his brothers and sisters and often plays baseball and basketball with boys two or three years older than himself. He has a paper route and in general is very self-sufficient for a ten-year-old child.

Joanne is an eleven-year-old white child enrolled in a TMR program in the southeastern part of the country. She comes from a family of two children; her sister is thirteen years older and is married with one child of her own. Joanne's mother finished high school; her father completed four years of college and is presently employed as an editor for a large newspaper.

The family lives in an eight-room house in a middle-class neighborhood.

Soon after she was born, it was apparent that Joanne suffered from what is known as *Down's syndrome* (previously it was often called *mongolism*). Her skin was quite dry, her eyelids had the characteristic epicanthic folds, and she possessed other diagnostic signs of Down's syndrome. Before she was released from the hospital, her parents were told of her condition and that she was mentally retarded.

Joanne was slow in developing in almost all areas—walking, toilet training, speaking. Her parents enrolled her in a preschool program for mentally retarded children when she was three. When it was time for her to enroll in public school, Joanne was evaluated and placed immediately in the special program for TMR youngsters, where she has been ever since. Joanne has been given intelligence tests twice since she entered school; in both instances she achieved an IQ of 40. Evaluation of her social development shows her to be functioning at the level of a normal child half her age.

Joanne exhibits a pleasant disposition and seems to enjoy school and her classmates. After school and on the weekends, she is inclined to stay home, watching TV or playing in the backyard. Other children in the neighborhood are cordial to Joanne when they see her outside, but they do not seek her out to play. Her mother reports that parents of much younger children become quite anxious if Joanne plays with them, so she has discouraged Joanne from playing with these children.

If we compare the sketches of Andrew and Joanne, we can see that these children differ dramatically from one another. Andrew, the EMR youngster, is normal-appearing and escapes recognition as retarded unless he is performing academic tasks, where he has problems. On the other hand, Joanne, the TMR child, is readily identified by casual observers in supermarkets, on the street, and in social situations as well as in learning situations. In short, the disability of the TMR child is pervasive whereas the disability of many EMR children is specific only to situations in which they have to perform academically.

Problems in EMR and TMR Placement. In many states EMR and TMR are defined by legislation in terms of IQ ranges. Such definitions run counter to the educational principle of placing the child into the program that is most appropriate for him. IQ should be treated as one, and only one, of the many kinds of information needed to make an appropriate placement.

EMR and TMR should be considered programs rather than crystallized, invariant categories into which children fall once and for all. Some educators (e.g., Dunn 1973) use the terms "general learning disorders" and "specific learning disorders" in lieu of EMR and TMR to soften the distinction between these groups.

Another matter of concern is the notion that the TMR label suggests a prognosis of some degree of dependency throughout life. One could argue that by placing a child in a TMR program, we ensure that he will never be independent, since the educational and vocational programs to which the TMR child is exposed prepare him for a dependent role as an adult. Similarly, one concern over the EMR program is that it restricts the options the individual has when he completes it. Because it is designed on the basis of vocations that, according to the average IQ of workers in particular jobs, are appropriate for the EMR, the EMR person may be prepared for only a limited range of vocations or further educational possibilities.

The Severely and Profoundly Mentally Retarded (SPMR). Until recently, only EMR and TMR children received special education. To be admitted to a TMR program, children had to be toilet-trained and be able to communicate. Children functioning at lower levels were often left to be served by mental health facilities or at the parents' expense in private programs. Recent court cases, however, have broadened the responsibilities of departments of education, requiring them to provide programs for these lower-functioning children. Meyers, MacMillan, and Zetlin (1978) observed that PL 94-142 has brought about a revolution in the meaning of the word *education* as it pertains to the SPMR child. The "education" some of these children receive involves toilet training and instruction in how to dress and chew food. This type of education is a far cry from the education of non-handicapped children and those with less serious disabilities.

Educational systems are now required to classify children into at least three categories. These categories are based largely on the child's degree of disability, although the "best fit" between a child's needs and program components is also considered. It is important to realize that SPMR children are capable of learning; it is just that their learning is more restricted than that of TMR children. Recent demonstration projects and research efforts (see Meyers 1978) have demonstrated that behavioral changes are possible for SPMR children when careful programing is provided. Although this group of children cannot be expected to attain considerable independence, it is possible to improve their quality of life.

Albert is a twenty-six-year-old SPMR person who lives in a large state institution for the mentally retarded, where he has been since he was two. Albert is the second of three children. His parents both hold graduate degrees—his mother, an M.A. in education, and his father, a Ph.D in engineering. The family lives about forty-five miles from the institution where Albert lives; they visit Albert an average of one day a month and take him home for holidays.

Albert's physicians are not sure of the exact cause of his mental retardation. However, during the first three months of her pregnancy, his mother was exposed to rubella (German measles); in addition, during the birth process Albert suffered from a lack of oxygen for about one-half hour. (These conditions often result in mental retardation; see Chapter 4 for a complete discussion of physical factors as causes of mental retardation.)

Within the first two years of his life it became apparent that there was something wrong with Albert. He did not even attempt sitting, walking, and other activities usually developed by the age of two. In addition, he suffered from seizures and was diagnosed as cerebral palsied.

At the age of two Albert was placed in the state institution for the mentally retarded on the recommendation of the family physician. Since the family lived in a small town where there were no medical services or educational programs for the mentally retarded, and since another child had been born into the family, it was thought that Albert might detract from the attention needed by the baby and that he could be better cared for in the institution than at home.

Albert's development has progressed very slowly since that time. Even now his vocabulary consists of no more than thirty words and he seldom speaks in phrases, let alone sentences. His utterances consist of one- or two-word sentences accompanied by gestures. He was not toilet-trained until two years ago and then only by means of an elaborate behavior-shaping project conducted by faculty members from a nearby university. Dressing remains a problem for him, since the cerebral palsy interferes with the motor coordination he needs to tie shoes, button shirts, and put on a belt. Ward attendants must assist Albert in dressing and usually help him when he is eating. His seizures have been controlled through medication, but his frequent respiratory problems have necessitated hospitalization three times during the past year.

Albert appears to be comfortable in the institution. In fact, his parents noticed that Albert was very anxious when he was at home for a recent holiday. The staff at the state hospital considered placing Albert in a foster care home off the grounds but decided against it due to his medical problems and to his limited personal independence.

The "Slow Learners."   Just as there has been increasing recognition that SPMR children need greater educational opportunities, the special educational needs of children functioning above the EMR level have been increasingly recognized. This group of children (roughly IQ 75–90) has at various times been referred to as *dull normal, borderline,* or *slow learners.* Today's special educators, however, regard special class placement as unnecessary for these children because it is too restrictive; giving them a disability label is viewed as dysfunctional. In the 1961 AAMD definition, this group was included as the "borderline retarded" but all definitions since 1973 have not placed these children in any mentally retarded category. In states that have adjusted their criteria to fit the more recent AAMD definitions, these children are not candidates for programs for the mentally retarded. Thus, if these children need special help, it must be delivered under the rubric of a category such as "learning disabled" or "educationally handicapped."

Alternative Classification Schemes

Classification schemes other than the educational model tend to classify differences among the mentally retarded in terms of degree, form, or clinical cause (etiology). The educational model is essentially a scheme that differentiates by degree, but there are schemes that use criteria other than educational need to establish such differences.

Classification by Degree.   Society has long recognized that some retarded people are more severely impaired than others. Terms such as *moron, imbecile,* and *idiot* were once used to denote increasingly severe conditions. These were initially considered technical terms. For the British they designated differential degrees of social adequacy; in the United States they referred to performance levels on tests of intelligence. Initially *idiots* were defined as individuals with mental ages (MAs) below 2; *imbeciles* had MAs between 3 and 7; and *morons* had MAs between 7 and 12. Later these were translated into IQ ranges roughly as follows: idiots, IQ 0 to 25; imbeciles, IQ 25 to 50; and morons, IQ 50 to 70.

Eventually these technical terms crept into everyday speech, where they developed stigmatic connotations. To soften the labels, the Committee on Nomenclature and Statistics of the American Psychiatric Association (1952) used the more neutral terms *mild, moderate,* and *severe.* As was indicated in Table 2.1, these terms were also used by a special subcommittee of the World Health Organization (1954) in its recommendations and by the AAMD Manuals since the 1961 version.

All these groups agree with the principle of subdividing the retarded population according to degrees of measured intelligence. But they differ in their judgment of where the subdivisions fall, and the AAMD stipulates that levels of intelligence are to be used in conjunction with measures of adaptive behavior even though no adequate measures of this factor yet exist.

Classification by degree reflects the recognition that there is a continuum of abilities within the mentally retarded population and the concern that these subcategories should not be thought of as discrete groups. The differences between subgroups are seen as differences in the degree of intellectual functioning—not in the kind of intellectual functioning. When intelligence tests are used to make these differentiations, it is assumed that IQ scores are normally distributed. But people using this kind of classification scheme must recognize that the subdivisions are arbitrary and that consistency is achieved only by adhering to the arbitrary cutoff points.

Classification by Form.   A second approach to classification has been to divide mentally retarded individuals into two groups: those who simply fall into the lower portion of the normal distribution of IQ scores and those whose development has been altered by some pathological condition. But in a confusing variation on this scheme, many reserve the term *mentally defective* for those whose organic deficits have a permanent effect and use the term *mentally retarded* as a nonevaluative term for the entire range.

Earlier writers dichotomized mentally retarded people into *intrinsic* and *extrinsic* groups. *Intrinsic* referred to natural but imperfect development of mental attributes; *extrinsic* referred to the prevention of normal mental development due to adverse factors, such as injury or disease. But, in practice, it is hard to make such distinctions because sometimes there is no way of knowing whether a subnormal condition stemmed from an unfortunate combination of genes (intrinsic) or resulted from some insult (extrinsic). Tredgold (1908), although he used this scheme, recognized that some insults occur during pregnancy, thereby making the retarded condition *congenital,* or existing from birth, but are not necessarily *germinal,* or existing from the earliest period of human development from a fertilized egg.

Lewis (1933) cleared up this matter only slightly and then introduced a new source of confusion. Instead of using the terms *intrinsic* and *extrinsic,* he classified retardation according to its origins as either *pathological* or *subcultural.* By *pathological* he meant all conditions that were organic or biological in origin, conditions in which a destructive process had interfered with normal development. The *subcultural* group, he thought, fell in﹒﹒the lower extreme of the normal distribution because of genetic factors, but he also recognized the role of environment as a possible influence. The term *subcultural* is misleading because some people think it refers to cultural deprivation. Hence Penrose (1949) suggested the term *physiological* and Sarason (1953) the term *garden-variety* as substitutes for *subcultural.*

Probably the most influential work along these lines is that of Alfred Strauss (Strauss & Kephart 1955; Strauss & Lehtinen 1947), who classified mental retardation as either *endogenous* or *exogenous.* The *endogenous* group corresponds to Lewis's subcultural group, in which retardation is a reflection of the individual's overall genetic makeup and in which there is no evidence of neurological abnormalities. The retardation of the *exogenous* group reflects an injury or infection of the brain before, during, or after birth. Strauss suggested that exogenous mental retardation was associated with a characteristic behavior pattern, which included such things as distractibility, impulsiveness, and perceptual disturbances. But many retarded children with known brain damage do not manifest these behaviors, and others for whom there is no reason to suspect brain damage display several of the behaviors Strauss considered characteristic of the exogenous group.

As indicated in Table 2.2, there is yet another classification scheme by form of retardation: Zigler's (1967) distinction between *organic* and *cultural-*

TABLE 2.2   **Terms Used to Denote Conditions in the Mentally Retarded Where Pathology Is Suspected or Present and Where There Is No Known Cause of the Retarded Functioning**

Known or Suspected Pathology	No Known Cause	Source
Extrinsic	Intrinsic	Tredgold (1908)
Pathological	Subcultural	Lewis (1933)
Exogenous	Endogenous	Strauss and Lehtinen (1947)
Pathological	Garden-variety	Sarason (1953)
Organic	Cultural-familial or Familial	Zigler (1967)

familial, or *familial* (see Chapter 3). As in the case of Lewis's term *subcultural,* the term *familial* is semantically confusing. As Zigler uses it, *familial* is supposed to mean "without pathology." But some think *familial* means "hereditary," or "in the family." They thus mistakenly assume that inherited conditions, such as PKU or the hereditary form of Down's syndrome (discussed in Chapter 4), are included in the familial category.

There is now considerable skepticism as to the usefulness of classifying mental retardation by form, due primarily to our current inability to separate biological and psychological forces. Should this later become possible, one might reconsider the usefulness of such a system; as of now it serves little purpose. Inability to identify central nervous system damage may be in some cases caused by a lack of sensitive instruments. Trying to determine whether biological forces have been at work by surveying medical histories for events that correlate with brain damage—such as prolonged high fever—may also be inaccurate. And when dichotomized groups have been compared for behavioral differences, findings have been inconsistent. Despite such current drawbacks to classification by form, numerous studies are still being published that compare retarded children of suspected pathology with those who seem to have developed along generally subnormal lines.

Classification by Cause. Yet another way of subdividing the retarded is to group them according to what apparently caused their condition. In such an etiological scheme most factors are medical, but some psychological factors have recently been added.

The list of specific diseases known to cause or be associated with mental retardation has grown rapidly. In the early years, *cretinism*—retardation caused by a thyroid condition—was synonymous with mental retardation. In the latter half of the nineteenth century Down's syndrome was identified as a separate condition, and in 1934 Folling discovered phenylketonuria (PKU). The identification of many other diseases associated with mental retardation followed.

The most complete listings of diseases associated with mental deficiency have appeared in the AAMD Manuals. The 1961 Manual listed eight groups of causes of mental retardation: (1) infection, (2) intoxication, (3) trauma or physical agent, (4) disorder of metabolism, growth, or nutrition, (5) new growth, (6) unknown prenatal influence, (7) unknown or uncertain causes with structural reactions alone manifest, and (8) uncertain (or presumed psychological) cause with functional reactions alone manifest.

The medical classifications in the 1973 Manual included: (1) infections and intoxications, (2) trauma or physical agent, (3) metabolism or nutrition, (4) gross brain disease (postnatal), (5) unknown prenatal influence, (6) chromosomal abnormality, (7) gestational disorders, (8) psychiatric disorder, (9) environmental influences, and (10) other conditions. This last category includes conditions where sensory impairment (e.g., blindness) alone accounts for slow development or where the etiology is unknown. Under this classification system, as with the 1961 version, the classification is not purely medical. The ninth category (environmental influences) embraces psychological causes and correlates.

The list has not only been extended over time, but it has also been internally modified. For example, Whitney (1949) noted that since 1880 birth injury has been reduced from 14–20 percent to 3–5 percent of live births. While diphtheria and opium were etiological factors in 1880, they were no longer causal factors by the mid-twentieth century. But encephalitis, which was not mentioned in 1880, is now considered a common cause of mental retardation. Improved medical care has all but eliminated certain causes (e.g., the thyroid condition that causes cretinism), while new hazards loom as being potential factors (e.g., pharmacological agents and radiation).

Certain problems arise in etiological classifications. For example, microcephaly, a syndrome characterized by a small conical skull, may be caused by any of three different factors: hereditary factors, massive dosages of radiation to the fetus, or German measles in the early stages of the pregnancy. Thus it is risky to infer the causal agent from the symptom.

Many medical determinations of etiological factors are arrived at through the process of exclusion rather than through positive evidence. In many instances the determination is made on the basis of a medical history, which may not be complete enough for these purposes. As a result of these limitations, many cases are classified as environmental influences (psychological factors) by default. Perhaps the safest way to use etiological classifications is to make retardation the primary diagnosis, with the medical diagnosis as a secondary bit of information when there is sufficient evidence.

PREVALENCE AND INCIDENCE

When there are funds to be allocated to set up mental retardation services and programs, it is important for us to know how many retarded people there are. The problem is, no one knows for sure.

The most obvious way to count heads would be to go across the country, knocking on every door, or even on a representative sampling of doors, asking if any people diagnosed as retarded lived within. But to do so privately would be prohibitively expensive and time-consuming, and the government's usual agent for such chores, the Census Bureau, does not gather statistics on mental retardation. It probably avoids this area for a number of reasons. Among them are problems of definition and the lingering stigma of the label "retarded." Some families might hide information; in the past, some families were even unaware that their children had been diagnosed as EMR and were enrolled in special programs in their schools.

With no direct way to count retarded individuals, researchers have been forced to estimate the prevalence of mental retardation in the general population. But because many factors can bias such estimates, they range embarrassingly broadly from as little as 0.6 percent to as much as 15 percent of the population (Brockopp 1958). Individual survey estimates have ranged from 0.05 percent to 13 percent in 60 studies conducted between 1894 and 1958 (Wallin 1958), but these wide variations seem to be largely a matter of methodology. As Farber (1968) has noted, different investigators have used different procedures for estimating intelligence, have used different cutoff points in the range of intelligence to define *mentally retarded*, have differed in the manner in which the population was screened to uncover cases of mental retardation, and have conducted their surveys in different geographical sections of the country.

In addition to an overall head count, we need to know whether retarded persons are evenly distributed across different low-IQ ranges and in different communities. This information is important because it guides efforts to focus services where they are most needed. But even though it is clear that IQ distribution is unequal, with the majority of retarded individuals being mildly rather than severely retarded, it is hard to judge the differential effects of age, sex, community, and especially race on the prevalence of retardation.

Despite these difficulties, various estimates have been made of the extent of mental retardation as a social problem in this country. In 1970 the President's Task Force on the Mentally Handicapped estimated that 6 million Americans were mentally retarded, with approximately 215,000 in institutions at any particular time and 690,000 in special classes. Five years earlier it was estimated that approximately 5 million individuals in the United States would be diagnosed as mentally retarded at some time in their lives and that some 126,000 more are born yearly (Gardner, Tarjan, & Richmond 1965). Similar estimates came from the Group for the Advancement of Psychiatry (1959) and the President's Panel on Mental Retardation (1962), with the President's Committee (1967, 1969) upping the estimated number who would be considered mentally retarded at some time to 6 million because of increased growth in the general population. According to all these reports, the permanently retarded account for about 3 percent of the total population.

The scope of the problem is underlined in comparisons made by the President's Panel on Mental Retardation (1962): mental retardation affects 10 times more people than does diabetes, 20 times more people than tuberculosis, 25 times more people than muscular dystrophy, and 600 times more people than infantile paralysis. The only health problems that exceed mental retardation in the number of individuals affected are mental illness, cardiac disease, arthritis, and cancer.

There can be no doubt that mental retardation is a social problem of significant proportions. However, although the majority of textbooks cite a 3 percent incidence figure, this estimate is a misleading one. Because of its magnitude, the incidence of mental retardation warrants closer examination.

What Do These Statistics Reflect?

As these statistics indicate, mental retardation is a societal problem of some magnitude. But several major measurements of the extent of the problem have yielded different results, which is quite confusing. Exactly how widespread is mental retardation? Our confusion is due in part to the practice of using the terms *incidence* and *prevalence* interchangeably. This is common in the literature on mental retardation, but it is incorrect.

Morton and Hebel (1979) distinguish between incidence and prevalence as follows: *Incidence* is a measure of the rate at which cases of a condition develop over a specific time period—six months or two years, for example. In other words, incidence figures are measures of the number of *new* cases of the disease or condition. A *prevalence* rate is a measure of the *total* number of cases of a condition at a particular time.

Figure 2.3 shows the relationship between the incidence and prevalence rates of mental retardation. Note that the incidence, or number of new cases, adds to the prevalence rate at any given time. At the same time, however, the prevalence rate is reduced by the cases dropped from the roster of the mentally retarded due to death, decertification, or other circumstances. As we shall see, how long a person is classified as mentally retarded is difficult to establish because of both the higher mortality rates among the severely retarded and sociopolitical factors that influence certification and decertification in cases of mild mental retardation.

The figures cited earlier in this section, such as those of the President's Task Force and the President's Panel on Mental Retardation, reflect *neither* incidence nor prevalence. Instead, these figures are based on estimates of the proportion of the general population that will be considered retarded at some point in their lives. Tarjan, Wright, Eyman, and Keeran (1973) expressed this kind of estimate as follows: "Though 3 percent of the newborn population will be suspected and even diagnosed as mentally retarded sometime during their life, probably during their school years, it is incorrect to assume that at any given time 3 percent of the population is so identified or is apt to be so diagnosed" (p. 370).

In gathering statistics about the scope of mental retardation, one must consider what the statistics are being used for. If we are trying to determine whether a new chemical with widespread use in society is causing an increase in the number of children born with severe mental retardation, we should study incidence. If, on the other hand, we are trying to allocate

FIGURE 2.3   The Relationship between Incidence and Prevalence in
              Mental Retardation

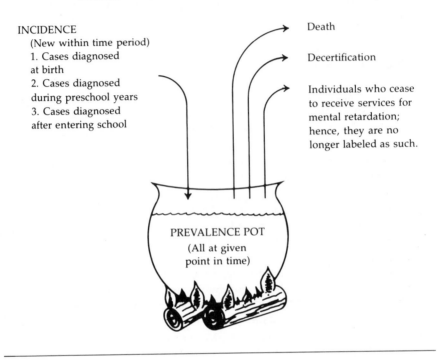

INCIDENCE
  (New within time period)
  1. Cases diagnosed
  at birth
  2. Cases diagnosed
  during preschool years
  3. Cases diagnosed
  after entering school

Death

Decertification

Individuals who cease
to receive services for
mental retardation;
hence, they are no
longer labeled as such.

PREVALENCE POT
(All at given
point in time)

money to programs for different degrees of mental retardation, we would
want to study prevalence.

Definition as a Determinant of Incidence and Prevalence

In addition to some confusion about what is being measured—incidence
or prevalence—the definition of mental retardation being used when a survey is taken will affect its results. The broader the definition, the higher the
incidence and prevalence figures.

For example, if a definition required evidence of central nervous system
damage, the prevalence of mental retardation would be reduced drastically.
Similarly, a survey based on a psychometric definition that defined mental
retardation exclusively in terms of an IQ cutoff score of 85 and ignored the
presence or absence of problems in adaptive behavior would result in an
incidence figure of close to 16 percent, since any persons scoring below IQ

85 would be classified as retarded whether they were having problems or not.

Since the definitions of mental retardation differ from one country to another and from one state to another, one must be cautious in comparing estimates of incidence and prevalence. Further, mental retardation is not a disease entity like chicken pox or tuberculosis; a person does not "have it" except in the context of the community in which he lives. A report of the World Health Organization of the United Nations noted the incomparability of data between countries, and even within the United States:

> Varying estimates have been given in different states of the USA and in Switzerland. For adults the prevalence rates are lower, and the recognition and even the manifestation of mild subnormality in adulthood is dependent mainly on thresholds of community tolerance and the complexity of social life, both of which fluctuate widely. Estimates are thus valid only for the time and place at which they are made.
>
> (1954, p. 9)

As definitions have changed across time from narrow to broader and more inclusive definitions, incidence figures have increased. The first systematic attempt to obtain data on incidence was that of the English Royal Commission of 1904. They estimated that 0.46 percent of the general population was mentally retarded; Lewis (1929) reported 0.86 percent mentally retarded. In the United States, estimates at the beginning of the twentieth century were even lower: from 0.15 percent to 0.20 percent (Clausen 1967). But using a psychometric criterion—performance measured on the Binet scales—Goddard (1911) found that 3 percent of the school population was feeble-minded, and Terman (1919) set the incidence of mental retardation at 2 percent to 3 percent in school-age children.

As Clausen has pointed out, despite broadening of the definition since Goddard's time—in response to the increased complexity of society, improved diagnostic techniques, and a greater sensitivity to the problem of mental retardation—the incidence of diagnosed mental retardation has not increased beyond 3 percent, the rate Goddard found back in 1911.

Recent Estimates

Despite variations among surveys, the 3 percent figure has stuck and is still cited. It is important to realize that most prevalence estimates are based on studies conducted before the onslaught of civil rights cases, which appear to have drastically reduced the prevalence of mental retardation in the states where the litigation occurred. Therefore, it is instructive to consider these later studies since they yielded estimates considerably lower than 3 percent.

Percent Prevalence.   Research conducted in the 1960s and 1970s actually yielded prevalence estimates closer to 1 percent. Tarjan et al. (1973) noted that the "ever-retarded" (i.e., the 3 percent figure) and prevalence estimates are equal only when certain assumptions are made. The first assumption is that the diagnosis is based on a child's having an IQ below 70. This assumption is invalid, since a child must have both an IQ below 70 *and* must display maladaptive behavior to be diagnosed as retarded. The second assumption is that mental retardation is diagnosed in infancy, which is also invalid. The vast majority of cases of mild retardation go unnoticed until difficulties are encountered in school (Mercer 1973a, 1970b; Robbins, Mercer, & Meyers 1967). In fact, only a small minority of cases—the most severely retarded— are diagnosed during infancy or even during the preschool period.

Another problem is that most cases of mild retardation are not diagnosed until the child enters school, and after leaving school these individuals are no longer regarded as retarded. This situation is recognized in the AAMD definitions. Finally, the mortality rate is higher among the mentally retarded. The lower a person's IQ, the higher the likelihood of dying at an early age. Only the mildly retarded have life expectancies that approximate those of the general population.

Estimates of the prevalence of mental retardation made during the 1960s and 1970s consistently yielded a figure close to 1 percent of the general population. As shown in Table 2.3, the estimates of Tarjan and his colleagues (1973) were supported by a study reported by Mercer (1970b, 1973a). The Mercer study was conducted in Riverside, California, which had a population of approximately 100,000 at the time of the study in the mid-1960s. Note how Mercer's data correspond to the Tarjan estimate of 1

TABLE 2.3   Theoretical Distributions Comparing Tarjan's 3 Percent and 1 Percent Prevalence Models with Mercer's Data for a Prototype Community of 100,000

	PMR 0–19	TMR 20–49	EMR 50–69	70+	Total
3 percent (Tarjan)*	100	400	2500	—	3000
1 percent (Tarjan)*	50	200	750	—	1000
Mercer's Data†	42	137	387	404	970*

*Based on Tarjan, Wright, Eyman, and Keeran (1973).
†Persons with IQs above 70 are not included in Tarjan's model. But when Mercer's data were collected, the 1961 AAMD definition had been adopted in California and mentally retarded persons could, and did, achieve IQs above 70. These data are based on clinical nominees only, diagnosed by qualified clinicians. See Mercer (1973b).

percent. It is of particular interest that the actual count was lower in each of the IQ ranges than the number of cases Tarjan estimated would occur. Only if one considers the group with IQs above 70 (at the time of the study IQ 85 was the upper limit in California) does the total prevalence figure approach 1 percent.

Other surveys (e.g., Birch, Richardson, Baird, Horobin, & Illsley 1970) also placed the incidence of mental retardation closer to 1 percent. Heber (1970) noted that in 28 prevalence surveys, although reported prevalence rates ranged from 0.16 percent to 23 percent of the general population, the median rate was 1 percent. The variations can be attributed in part to case-finding procedures and to the geographic regions in which the studies were conducted. One survey, for example, that reported a prevalence rate of over 3 percent was conducted in a rural community in the southeastern part of the United States (Lemkau & Imre 1969).

Variations in Prevalence

Even if we can determine what percentage of the total population in a large social unit such as a state or nation is mentally retarded, we cannot assume that that figure applies to all subunits such as counties, cities, and towns. The diagnosis of mental retardation, especially its mild form, is influenced by several factors, including socioeconomic status, ethnic origin, and the family's educational background. More recently, sociopolitical factors and legislation such as PL 94-142 have called for "nondiscriminatory testing" and provided for parental involvement in the process, which adds more subjectivity to the identification process. As a result, the prevalence of mental retardation must be well below 1 percent given the present climate regarding labeling of the mildly retarded. Variations in prevalence rates probably result from changes in practices for labeling the mildly retarded, since the severely retarded category is not noticeably affected by changes in definition.

Before considering factors associated with variations in prevalence, let's consider the prevalence of severe and profound mental retardation—the group of mentally retarded persons identified early in life who remain so classified for the remainder of their lives in most instances.

Abramowicz and Richardson (1975) used IQ 50 as the upper parameter for defining severe mental retardation. (Note that the AAMD classification has IQ 35 as the upper limit for severe mental retardation.) These authors examined a number of studies of severe mental retaration (IQ below 50) and summarized the findings as follows: "A review of twenty-seven epidemiological studies, nineteen of which may be considered to have reliable prevalence data on severe mental retardation in older children, shows a remarkable consistency in the prevalence of severe mental retardation in children, which approximates 4 per 1000" (p. 37). Eyman and Miller (1978), who based their estimate on the work of Dingman and Tarjan (1960), Tarjan et al. (1973), and Mercer (1973a), used IQ 35 as the upper limit for severe and profound mental retardation and estimated the prevalence to be 1.3 per 1000. The difference in the two estimates can probably be attributed largely to different IQs used to set the upper limit. We will use the 0.4 percent figure of Abramowicz and Richardson, since it corresponds to the IQ 50 that is frequently used to differentiate the two major groups of mentally retarded persons—those whose retardation is caused by biomedical problems and those in whom such biomedical factors cannot be identified as causal factors.

We will now consider the variables associated with variations in prevalence: age, sex, community, state, social class, and race.

Age Variations.   The prevalence of diagnosed mental retardation varies considerably with age, as is shown in Table 2.4. Because the age intervals in the table are not equal, the estimated number of cases is much lower for ages birth to five and twenty to twenty-four than it is for other age groups, especially the group aged twenty-five or older. Most cases below IQ 50 are diagnosed before age five and the high mortality rate of this group results in a lower number of cases beyond age twenty-five. Among the mildly retarded (IQ above 50), a different kind of uneven distribution is found. For this group there is a relatively low prevalence both in the preschool years and in the age periods after school, with an extremely high prevalence dur-

TABLE 2.4   **Estimated Numbers of Retarded Persons in a Community of 100,000 as a Function of IQ and Age Ranges**

	Age (in years)				
IQ	0–5	6–19	20–24	25+	Total
Overall prevalence: 1 percent					
0–19	8	18	4	20	50
20–49	36	70	20	74	200
50+	25	600	25	100	750
Total	69	688	49	194	1000

Adapted from G. Tarjan, S. W. Wright, R. K. Eyman, and C. V. Keeran, "Natural history of mental retardation: Some aspects of epidemiology," from *The American Journal of Mental Deficiency*, 1973, 1977. Reprinted by permission of the American Association on Mental Deficiency.

ing the age period when school attendance is compulsory. The vast majority of children falling into this group come from economically depressed backgrounds and have retardation that is not accompanied by any physical signs. When they leave school, many of them disappear into the ranks of the nonretarded.

Fluctuation in prevalence as a function of age for the mildly retarded should not be interpreted to mean that great numbers of children are misdiagnosed by the schools. Farber (1968) has a different explanation. In comparing prevalence surveys in Maine (Levinson 1962) and Illinois (Farber 1959b), Farber noted a gradual increase by age in the prevalence of mental retardation in the schools. The rate reached a peak (4.25 percent) in Maine at age fourteen and in Illinois at age fifteen (3.8 percent). There was then a sharp decline in prevalence in the late teens. Noting that the prevalence is highest during the early adolescent years, Farber suggested that prior to early adolescence the differentiation of mildly retarded and nonretarded is more difficult; however, with the development of abstract competencies in early adolescence by the nonretarded and the difficulty experienced by the retarded with abstractions, their differences become more apparent and differentiation becomes easier. Upon leaving school many of the mildly retarded are able to function in social settings and occupations that do not require abstract abilities to the extent that their schoolwork did. But it is optimistic to assume that, when they drop off case registers as mentally retarded, these formerly mildly retarded individuals live like the average middle-class citizen. Charles (1957) reported that as adults these individuals usually live in marginal socioeconomic groups.

Sex Variations. In virtually every program serving children with learning and behavior problems, there are more males than females. Mental retardation is no exception: the number of males diagnosed as mentally retarded exceeds the number of females, probably for a variety of interrelated reasons.

In 1929, Lewis reported a prevalence of mental retardation that was 17 percent higher for males than for females under sixteen years of age. The differential was greater below IQ 50, where there were 30 percent more males. Subsequent research has continued to reveal a higher prevalence rate for males in cases with IQs above 50, but the studies yield conflicting evidence for cases below IQ 50. For example, the Onondaga survey (New York State Department of Mental Hygiene 1955) found the following percentages of males for respective IQ ranges: 64.3 percent in the 50-74 IQ range; 55 percent in the 25-49 IQ range; and 45.6 percent in the 0-25 IQ range. The highest percentage of males was found in the mildly retarded range; this finding was also reported by Kirk and Weiner (1959) for Hawaii. The Onondaga data, however, contradicted Lewis's earlier report regarding a larger excess of males in the lowest IQ range. Abramowicz and Richardson (1975) reported a slightly higher prevalence rate for males below IQ 50 that persisted across all ages.

Two kinds of explanations have been suggested for the reported sex differences in prevalence: (1) the greater probability of sex-linked recessive conditions in males and (2) differential environmental expectations for males and females. Levinson (1962) pointed to the frequency of physical deformities and brain damage in the severely and profoundly retarded that result from recessive genetic tendencies in males (see Chapter 4). The recessive genotypes are related to higher mortality rates, and some of these individuals do not live to school age.

A different interpretation was presented by Masland, Sarason, and Gladwin (1958), who emphasized the continued differentiation of sex roles in society. Even within the same family, parents and others shape feminine traits in girls and masculine traits in boys. One trait frequently associated with masculinity has been aggressiveness, which often leads to problems in school. An aggressive, mildly retarded boy probably has a greater chance of being identified as retarded than a mildly retarded girl who is quiet and well behaved.

Community Variations.   The greatest variation by differences in community seems related to urban versus rural residence. In general, rural areas seem to have a higher prevalence rate than urban areas. But we must be careful in drawing conclusions about community size as a factor in prevalence.

Levinson (1962), for example, reported a higher rate for urban school districts, but he noted a greater tendency on the part of rural districts to report more so-called doubtful cases. One possible interpretation of this reversal of the general pattern is that in urban districts, which tend to have more well-developed diagnostic services, the doubtful cases are evaluated and may be identified as mentally retarded. In rural districts these doubtful cases may never be diagnosed formally, due to less well-developed diagnostic services, although they continue to be treated by some as retarded.

Selective migration may be another factor in community variations. According to Farber's 1968 analysis of a survey he made in Illinois (1959b), a small portion of the variation in prevalence rates can be traced to the fact that those who migrate from the country to industrial areas tend to be more intelligent than the remaining rural population. Mentally retarded people are in general less likely to move than normals—less likely to move to a different state (Baller 1936) or even to a different area of a city (Fairbanks 1933). When retarded individuals do move, they are more inclined than normals to merely move from one section of a neighborhood to another.

The urban-rural dichotomy is not the only kind of variation according to community. Even within a single city, localized variations in socioeconomic levels are correlated to variations in the prevalence of mental retardation. By combining Mullen and Nee's 1952 description of the distribution of EMR and TMR children in Chicago with data on the socioeconomic levels of the Chicago communities, Farber (1959a) found that the wealthier the community, the lower the proportion of both EMR and TMR children relative to the total school enrollment. The prevalence of EMR children was even more significantly related to socioeconomic status than was prevalence of TMR children. It has been estimated that a child born and reared in a disadvantaged environment has fifteen times the probability of being classified as mentally retarded as does a child of the same age born and reared in the suburbs (Tarjan 1970; Tarjan et al. 1973). This is particularly true in the cases of mildly retarded children; it is less dramatic, but nevertheless true, for the severely and profoundly retarded. At any rate, it is clear that a disproportionately large part of the need for mental retardation services exists in lower-class communities.

With regard to the severely retarded, Abramowicz and Richardson (1975) failed to find consistent differences between urban and rural prevalence rates. They suggest that this recent development reflects advances in technology and transportation, since early studies reported consistently higher rates of severe mental retardation in rural areas.

State Variations.   The federal requirement that states report the number of children receiving special educational services in each disability category enables us to work with actual counts of children rather than generalizing from prevalence estimates. In Table 2.5, we present the figures reported to the Bureau for the Education of the Handicapped by the various states to meet the PL 94-142 requirements. In the first column are the percentages of school children in each state who are classified as mentally retarded. Note that this figure is not broken down by age, IQ level, program level, or in any other way. It is simply the number of retarded school children divided by the total enrollment in that state. It is interesting to compare the rates, which range from lows of 0.36 percent in Washington, D.C., and 0.66 percent in Alaska to much higher rates in several of the southeastern states such as Alabama (3.89 percent), Arkansas (3.09 percent), and North Carolina (3.39 percent). We assume that such differences reflect a varying sensitivity to civil rights issues in the identification of minority children, and that the differences occur at the EMR level rather than the level below IQ 50. If this assumption is correct, then one could estimate the percentages of retarded school children with IQs above 50 in a given state by subtracting the 0.4 percent expected to have IQs below 50 (Abramowicz & Richardson 1975) from the total percentage. This figure is shown in the second column. The prevalence estimates derived from these figures also vary considerably from state to state. Even though the school years are the period when we would expect the highest prevalence of mild mental retardation (see Table 2.4), we

TABLE 2.5   Percentages of School Children Who Are Mentally
Retarded as Reported by States for 1978-1979

State	Percentage of School Population Who Are Retarded	Estimated Percentage with IQ over 50
Alabama	3.89	3.49
Alaska	0.66	0.26
Arizona	1.25	0.85
Arkansas	3.09	2.69
California	0.80	0.40
Colorado	0.88	0.48
Connecticut	1.13	0.73
Delaware	1.41	1.01
District of Columbia	0.36	—
Florida	1.56	1.16
Georgia	2.52	2.12
Hawaii	0.97	0.57
Idaho	1.74	1.34
Illinois	1.50	1.10
Indiana	1.94	1.54
Iowa	1.85	1.45
Kansas	1.53	1.13
Kentucky	2.69	2.29
Louisiana	1.95	1.55
Maine	1.82	1.42
Maryland	1.05	0.65
Massachusetts	1.88	1.48
Michigan	1.01	0.61
Minnesota	1.52	1.12
Mississippi	2.91	2.51
Missouri	2.06	1.66
Montana	1.09	0.69
Nebraska	2.15	1.75
Nevada	0.93	0.53
New Hampshire	0.98	0.58
New Jersey	1.05	0.65
New Mexico	1.23	0.83
New York	1.04	0.64
North Carolina	3.39	2.99
North Dakota	1.16	0.76
Ohio	2.18	1.78
Oklahoma	2.08	1.68
Oregon	0.73	0.33
Pennsylvania	1.75	1.35
Rhode Island	0.88	0.48

TABLE 2.5   Continued

State	Percentage of School Population Who Are Retarded	Estimated Percentage with IQ over 50
South Carolina	3.79	3.39
South Dakota	0.68	0.28
Tennessee	2.50	2.10
Texas	0.96	0.56
Utah	0.98	0.58
Vermont	0.72	0.32
Virginia	1.65	1.25
Washington	1.20	0.80
West Virginia	2.60	2.20
Wisconsin	1.29	0.89
Wyoming	0.89	0.49
National summary	1.60	1.20

find that states like California, Vermont, and Colorado, as well as the District of Columbia, have extremely low prevalence figures.

Social Class and Racial Variations.   Because a disproportionately high percentage of certain minority groups such as blacks and Hispanics live in lower social class neighborhoods, it is difficult to separate the effects of social class and race or ethnic origin. There is no question that ethnic minority children have been overrepresented in programs of EMR children. In California in 1969, for example, 8.9 percent of the total school population was black, yet the EMR enrollment in 1969 was 27.1 percent black and in 1973 it was 25 percent black. Spanish-surnamed children constituted 15.2 percent of the total California school enrollment in 1969 but accounted for 28.2 percent of the EMR enrollment in 1969 and 23.0 percent in 1973. (Simmons & Brinegar 1973). Such figures were central to the plaintiff's cases in both *Larry P.* v. *Riles* (1972) and *Diana* v. *State Board of Education* (1970), discussed in detail in Chapter 8. Traditionally, minority enrollment in EMR classes has been disproportionately high, to the embarrassment of educators. This disproportionate representation has led to accusations of discrimination in identification practices.

Among severely mentally retarded persons (IQ below 50), the racial differences are not as pronounced, yet there is some evidence of higher prevalence rates of severe mental retardation in lower social class families (Abramowicz & Richardson 1975). Birch et al. (1970) found no significant differences in the prevalence of severe mental retardation among social classes, but he and his associates reported dramatic differences between lower and upper classes for mild mental retardation. In the lower-class portion of the sample, the rate of mild mental retardation was 24.9 cases per 1000; in the upper-class sample, the rate was 0 cases per 1000. Several other studies reported by Abramowicz and Richardson (1975) found slightly higher rates of severe mental retardation in lower-class families, but the researchers noted that these studies were less well controlled than the Birch et al. study (1970).

If IQ alone is considered (and the need for evidence of impaired adaptive behavior to accompany the low IQ is ignored), there are a number of studies that indicate a higher frequency of low IQ among blacks. The Ginzberg and Bray study (1953) showed that among those drafted into the military between the beginning of selective service and the end of World War II, six times as many blacks as whites were rejected on the basis of mental deficiency. But how they were identified is unclear, so there is no way of knowing whether the rejects would qualify as retarded in a prevalence survey. And there is some indication that their disabilities—whatever they were— may have been at least partly related to environmental causes. The rejection rate for blacks was exceptionally high in the Southeast and Southwest, but blacks coming from the Northwest and Far West had a lower rejection rate than did whites from the Southeast and Southwest.

To give another example, Heber (1968) estimated, on the basis of existing evidence, that there is a higher incidence of black children with IQs < 75 than white children at every level of socioeconomic status (Table 2.6). But IQ tests have themselves been accused of a cultural bias; according to this

TABLE 2.6 **Estimated Prevalence of White and Black Children with IQ under 75 by Socioeconomic Status, Reported as Percentages**

Socioeconomic Status	White	Black
High 1	0.5	3.1
2	0.8	14.5
3	2.1	22.8
4	3.1	37.8
Low 5	7.8	42.9

From R. F. Heber and R. B. Dever, "Research on education and habilitation of the mentally retarded," in H. C. Haywood, ed., *Social-Cultural Aspects of Mental Retardation.* Copyright © 1970. Reprinted by permission of the authors.

argument, they may subtly discriminate against children from lower-class backgrounds. It is significant that the disproportions by race that have been found occur almost entirely among those thought to be mildly retarded; among the more severely retarded, there is almost no variation in prevalence according to race. In addition, Heber's data do not prove that more blacks than whites are retarded, because they are based on a single criterion: IQ. Even if intelligence could be measured by tests that were free of cultural bias, the definition of mental retardation requires that impaired adaptive behavior as well as subaverage intellectual functioning be present.

It has sometimes been claimed that psychologists discriminate against minority groups by screening school populations in order to label those with low IQ scores as retarded. But as we have repeatedly noted, a low IQ score does not in itself ensure diagnosis as mentally retarded. In a striking illustration of this point, Mercer (1971b, 1973a) studied 1298 children enrolled in the regular elementary classes in a city of 130,000. When they were given the WISC, 124 of these regular-class children achieved IQs between 57 and 79 (at a time when the AAMD definition was one standard deviation below the mean, or IQ 85). But although the district had well-developed special education programs, none of the 124 had ever been identified as mentally retarded. Of the 124, 8 were whites, 80 were Mexican-Americans, and 36 were blacks. There are at least two possible explanations for the ethnic variations in these findings. First, if minority children who are psychometrically below the IQ cutoff do not evidence impaired adaptive behavior, they are not referred for a psychological evaluation and are therefore not diagnosed as retarded. Second, few white children who qualify psychometrically as mentally retarded escape being labeled as such, while over 10 percent of minority group children who qualify psychometrically go unlabeled. At any rate, there seems to be no basis for the accusation sometimes heard that minority children are sought out by psychologists for labeling; on the contrary, they tend to be overlooked.

Two Distinct Subgroups of the Mentally Retarded

Throughout this chapter we have distinguished between a severely retarded and a mildly retarded group of children, the cutoff between the two groups being about IQ 50. Conceptually, the mentally retarded population can be divided into two distinct (albeit overlapping) subgroups. The more severely retarded, who comprise approximately 25 percent of the total mentally retarded population, are the "clinical types." Persons in this group have some central nervous system pathology, usually achieve IQs in the moderate range or below, have associated stigmata and handicaps, and are frequently diagnosed between birth and early childhood. The second group, the mildly retarded, compose the bulk of the mentally retarded population and appear to be neurologically normal. Persons in this mildly retarded group exhibit no readily detectable physical or clinical signs and appear in disproportionately high numbers in the lowest socioeconomic segments of society.

Zigler (1967, 1977) has suggested that the mildly retarded group, which he refers to as the *familial* mentally retarded, reflects the lower end of a normal distribution: they are merely less efficient in mastering abstract learning. The more severely retarded, however, exhibit intellectual limitations resulting from major chromosomal anomalies or brain damage. Although Zigler acknowledges that the mild group are inefficient learners,

FIGURE 2.4 Frequency Distribution of IQ, Based on a Population of 185,000,000

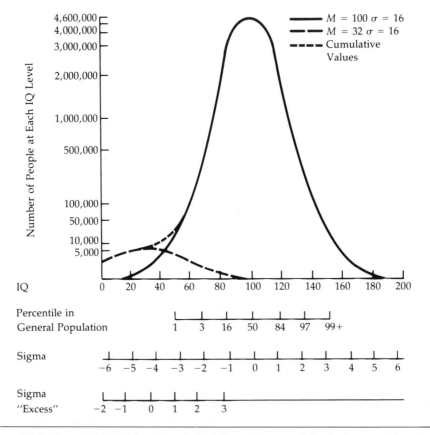

From H. F. Dingman and G. Tarjan, "Mental retardation and the normal distribution curve," from *The American Journal of Mental Deficiency*, 1960, 1964. Reprinted by permission of the authors and the American Association on Mental Deficiency.

he questions the practice of calling everyone who meets the definition of mental retardation by the name *mentally retarded.*

A similar position was taken earlier by Dingman and Tarjan (1960), who based their statements on information about retarded persons in institutions, at home, and in schools, and also on records from various other agencies. Comparing the distributions of IQs for these groups with those of the general population, they concluded that there was an excess of cases in the 0–19 IQ range and in the 20–49 range. As shown in Figure 2.4, the "excess" population formed a hump of its own: a normal distribution of IQs with a mean IQ of 32 and a standard deviation of 16. Clearly these two groups differ in terms of etiology, clinical manifestations, degree of retardation, and prognosis. The wisdom of considering them both "mentally retarded" and differentiating them only by degree has been questioned by Zigler (1977), whereas others (Jastak 1967; Weir 1967) defend the practice of classifying both as mentally retarded.

Evidence of the difference between subgroups is suggested in a study by Roberts (1952). When he analyzed the IQ distributions of the siblings of English imbeciles (IQ < 50) and feeble-minded (IQ 50 to 75), he found that, although they had a higher mean IQ, the siblings of the feeble-minded fell within the same distribution as that of the feeble-minded. However, the siblings of the imbeciles, the lower group, distributed themselves in a manner close to that of the general population, suggesting that the retardation of the imbeciles resulted from some interference in normal development.

SUMMARY

Although the label *mentally retarded* suggests a stereotyped image, it covers individuals as dissimilar as Andrew, who is good at sports and has a paper route, and Albert, who lives in a state institution, where he must be dressed and fed by attendants. Two central problems in finding and treating such varied individuals have been defining what it is they have in common and then separating them into subgroups according to the most significant ways in which they differ. Definition and classification are thus related but opposite processes.

Workers from different professions have tended to focus on single aspects of mental retardation—biological, social, or intellectual—making it difficult for them to agree on a unifying definition that encompasses every unique retarded individual. But after over half a century of debate, workers from many disciplines collaborated on a definition that came closer than ever before to satisfying everyone. The group was the American Association on Mental Deficiency, and their definition came out in their 1959 and 1961 Manuals, with important revisions in 1973 and 1977, and with another forthcoming.

An important feature of the AAMD definition that has been difficult to implement is its inclusion of inadequate adaptive behavior as a criterion for defining mental retardation. There are as yet no totally objective ways of measuring adaptive behavior, especially in relation to different environments. Instead, judgments as to which people qualify for assistance as mentally retarded individuals have for some time been based primarily on IQ levels, although the cutoff point for such assistance has periodically shifted.

In classification, too, intelligence testing has been a major means of grouping mentally retarded individuals into educational programs for people with similar needs. But IQ testing is not a rigid guide to individual capabilities, and those classified as EMR, TMR, or SPMR are sometimes shifted to a different program on the basis of their practical skills.

The educational classifications are not the only subgroups that have been suggested. Mentally retarded people are sometimes theoretically divided for research purposes into groupings according to the degree, form, or cause of their disability. But as is true of every definition and classification scheme yet advanced, each kind of categorization has its disadvantages and its critics.

The prevalence of retardation is the total number of retarded persons in a population divided by the total population. The prevalence of mental retardation in the general population is less than 1 percent. The mentally retarded are not distributed uniformly through the population, however. The distribution varies with IQ range, age, sex, community, state, social class, and race. Higher rates of mental retardation are noted in the IQ range associated with EMR programs, among males, in lower socioeconomic status families, and in certain geographic regions of the country.

These variations in prevalence are probably due to a number of factors, although the descriptive studies establishing these variations do not allow for causal interpretations. Common explanations for the higher rates among males include the possibility of the greater biological vulnerability of the male and the social expectations for higher performance by males. Social class and ethnic origin are so closely interrelated that it is risky to try to establish a connection between race and intelligence. It is apparent that the lower social class or minority child is at greater risk of encountering academic problems in the public schools and being classified as EMR than is a child from the middle-class or white family. But the evidence provided to date indicates that the excess of cases in minorities and in lower social class families is dramatically restricted to the mild, or EMR, range; the disproportion is almost nonexistent in the TMR and SPMR populations.

There is an uneven distribution of prevalence according to IQ scores, with the IQ < 50 group sometimes considered part of a separate distribution because of suspected pathological conditions. The vast majority of cases of mental retardation exist in the mild range, the educable mentally retarded, some of whom seem quite normal in all aspects except school performance. These more-normal children are thought by some researchers to constitute a third possible subgroup.

Most cases of mental retardation cannot be traced to a specific cause, and in the case of EMR children it is rare that a cause can be established. But physical factors, to be examined in Chapter 4, are more likely to be associated with severe retardation; social-psychological factors, to be discussed in the next chapter, are most likely to play a part in mild retardation.

PART II

Causative-Correlational Factors in Mental Retardation

CHAPTER 3

The Social-Psychological Environment

There has long been a feeling that if only we knew what caused mental retardation, perhaps we could cure or at least prevent it. But in spite of biomedical progress in uncovering genetic conditions and toxic agents in the environment that may be linked to retardation, in at least 75 percent of the cases of retardation nothing can be confidently pinpointed as the cause of the condition.

Consider the three groups of mentally retarded persons in the educational classification system, EMR, TMR, and SPMR, remembering that the EMR population is by far the largest of the three. In the EMR population few cases can be traced to a definite cause, although we know that a disproportionate number of these individuals come from families that are in the lower strata of society and often are ethnic minorities. There are a number of factors associated with low social class that could depress intellectual functioning, such as fewer intellectually stimulating experiences and poor language models. But since the vast majority of children coming from such environments are not retarded, we cannot attribute the intellectual retardation that occurs in a minority of cases to these environmental factors alone. In the TMR population the cause is more likely to be known. Typically, one-third have Down's syndrome and one-third have some form of brain damage; in only one-third of this group is there no known cause. In the SPMR category most mental retardation has an organic cause, although it is often difficult to determine specifically. Physical causes of mental retardation will be examined in Chapter 4.

It is in the cause-unknown cases, most of which occur in the predominant mildly retarded category, that attempts have been made to identify possible detrimental factors in the person's environment. But despite some significant correlations that have been established, there is rarely proof of what specific circumstances caused a person to be mildly retarded. Instead there is a whole constellation of factors, both biological and social, found to be *related* to mild mental retardation.

THE NATURE-NURTURE CONTROVERSY

When we try to ferret out causal factors in mild retardation, we run into the classic *nature-nurture controversy.* Some investigators believe that people's intellectual development is affected by their environment (nurture); others claim that development is largely predetermined by heredity (nature). In the biological jargon that will be used occasionally in this chapter, the question is whether or not a person's *phenotype* (his observable characteristics as determined by his experiences and his genetic makeup) is likely to differ much from his *genotype* (his genetic constitution, a construct that cannot yet be measured and can only be estimated).

A century or so ago, psychologists agreed that a person's intelligence was fixed—genetically predetermined at the time of conception. This idea had the support of such influential thinkers as Sir Francis Galton, J. McKeen Cattell, G. Stanley Hall, and three of the early leaders in the intelligence-testing movement—Henry H. Goddard, F. Kuhlmann, and Lewis Terman. Research evidence seemed to support the belief that intelligence was fixed and hereditary; intelligence test performance from one age to another seemed to be rather constant; most tests seemed to correlate rather highly with one another; and close relatives in a family seemed to have similar IQ levels (Hunt 1961).

But as evidence mounted that mild retardation is often associated with certain environmental factors—such as poverty—some investigators came to believe that deprived environments may stunt intellectual growth. This change in belief has led to the notion that *early intervention* by educational agencies in a child's life to provide enriching experiences may be an antidote for cultural deprivation (Hunt 1968). (Although the rationale for early intervention will be discussed later in this chapter, a more detailed examination of programs like Project Head Start will be found in Chapter 13.)

Some supporters of the environmentalist position have even taken the stand that all children are born equal in terms of genotypic intelligence and that any differences that are observed are due to the differential experiences of the children between birth and the time of observation. The reaction to such an extreme environmental view has been a heated debate. Goodenough (1940), for instance, refused to accept the environmentalist notion that children in southern mountain regions had low IQs because their schools were poor. She compared their lot with that of the early New England settlers: "They made schools and it did not require two centuries of residence for them to do so" (p. 329). Zigler (1970b) refers to those who refuse to acknowledge the known role of biological factors in individual differences as "unbridled environmentalists" and writes that "our nation has more to fear" from them than from those who suggest that individual differences are at least partly shaped by genetic differences. The danger, as Zigler sees it, is the false hopes raised by the notion that IQs can be significantly changed:

> It is the environmentalist who emphasizes the plasticity of the intellect, that tells us one can change both the general rate of development and the configuration of intellectual processes which can be referred to as the intellect, if we could only subject human beings to the proper technologies.
>
> In the educational realm, this has spelled itself out in the use of panaceas, gadgets and gimmicks of the most questionable sort. It is the environmentalist who suggests to parents how easy it is to raise the child's IQ and who has prematurely led many to believe that the retarded could be made normal, and the normal made geniuses.
>
> (1970b, p. 83)

This passage should serve to temper extreme expectations that mild retardation could be abolished if poverty and social injustices were wiped out. Intellectual functioning may be influenced by environmental factors, but it is certain that biological determinants are also operative. At the present time precise statements as to the extent to which each contributes are hazardous. Many studies cited in this chapter can be interpreted as proof of either point of view. Since the evidence is mostly descriptive rather than conclusive, we must be careful what we make of it.

Reed and Reed (1965) traced the descendants of the grandparents of 289 mentally retarded persons who lived in a state institution from 1911 to 1918. Over 82,000 descendants were found. It was discovered that, when both parents were retarded, nearly half of their children were retarded. The rate of retardation of the children of normal parents, by contrast, was 0.5 percent. Higgins, Reed, and Reed (1962) reported that the average IQ of children born to two normal parents was 107 and that children with one retarded parent had an average IQ of 90, whereas the average IQ of children born to two retarded parents was 74. It is difficult to dismiss heredity in explaining these findings; although the Reeds are aligned strongly with the hereditarians, a naturalistic investigation such as this simply cannot determine the relative influence of environment. These findings could also be interpreted as evidence of the importance of environment, since retarded parents may provide a poor intellectual environment in which to raise children. Nevertheless, since both heredity and environment influence the development of a child, these findings cannot be taken as *proof* of either position. For a detailed discussion of the role of genetics, see Scarr-Salapatek (1975).

THE COMPLEXITIES OF CULTURAL-FAMILIAL RETARDATION

Environmental factors are most likely to be suspected in the case of *cultural-familial* mentally retarded persons, the largest subgroup in the mentally retarded population. Their condition (referred to in the past as *simple amentia, subcultural mental deficiency, garden-variety mental deficiency, endogenous mental deficiency,* and *familial mental deficiency*) is defined by three criteria, all of which must be present if they are to be classified in this subgroup: (1) the child must be mildly retarded, (2) there must be no evidence to suggest a cerebral pathological condition, and (3) there must be evidence of retarded intellectual functioning in at least one of the parents and one or more siblings (if the child has any) (Heber 1959). The third requirement would seem to eliminate many possible candidates for classification as cultural-familial retarded persons, but, in fact, it doesn't. The majority of mildly retarded children come from lower social strata families and are being raised by at least one parent who is intellectually subnormal.

Two major sets of factors appear plausible to explain cultural-familial retardation. First, it may be due to the child's *genetic draw;* that is, the cumulative effect of genes received from the parents that affect the structure and function of the central nervous system. Second, it may be explained in terms of environmental factors that singly or in combination serve to depress intellectual functioning. Among these environmental variables are poor nutrition, retarded parents, poor medical care, poor language models, low need for achievement, and a host of other factors often associated with low income or poverty.

The highest prevalence of mild mental retardation occurs among people referred to as *culturally deprived, culturally different, culturally disadvantaged,*[1] or some other term that connotes adverse economic and living conditions.

---

[1]The term *culturally disadvantaged* is used here because of its common usage in the literature. It is not in any way meant to devalue a given subculture in the society. But in relation to the dominant culture, the learning experiences in the above described environments do place a child at a disadvantage when he is competing in school or in the higher-status occupations.

Children of high risk are those who live in slums and, frequently, who are members of certain ethnic minority groups. In these high-risk groups there is poor medical care for mother and child, a high rate of broken families, and little value for education or motivation to achieve.

In such high-risk situations it is difficult to isolate possible causal factors. The child's genetic, physical, and social-psychological environments are interwoven at many points. For example, look at the variety of influences that might have interfered with one boy's intellectual development.

Mike is a nine-year-old black child with a tested IQ of 64 who was recently certified as EMR by his school district. His case had been referred to a special education placement committee after he repeated two grades on top of a history of academic failures. Some of the information the committee presented as background material demonstrates the complexity of forces that could have caused Mike's limitations in intellectual functioning.

Mike is the fourth of seven children who live in a three-room tenement apartment with their parents. The family lives in an extremely low socioeconomic status neighborhood: the proportion of residents on welfare there is the highest of any district in this large midwestern city. The neighborhood is entirely black.

While she was pregnant with Mike, his mother did not receive any medical attention. She never went to a doctor and the delivery was performed by a neighbor. Since Mike's father was unemployed at the time, her nutritional intake was very poor. During the fourth month of the pregnancy she hemorrhaged for several days, but no medical services were sought.

As a young child Mike had his share of illnesses. When he had roseola his temperature rose to 105°F and stayed there for three days. As another possible medical hazard, the paint peeling from the walls and ceiling of the family's apartment is lead-base; the parents have never seen Mike eat any of the paint chips, however.

On top of everything else, Mike's family is not the sort to inspire him academically. Two of his older brothers are in EMR classes. Both of his parents dropped out of school before completing junior high school; their academic records had been very poor.

In a high-risk situation like this one, mentally retarded functioning could be caused by one of many possible factors or a combination of several. Mike's retardation could be explained in terms of a poor genetic draw from parents of limited intellectual ability. It could have been caused by conditions present during his mother's pregnancy (her poor nutrition, lack of oxygen to the fetus when she was hemorrhaging, or complications during the delivery). Mike's intellectual functioning might even have been depressed by deprived environmental conditions. Perhaps several of these factors operated in concert to create his retarded condition. The point is that there are many circumstances that could explain the condition, but there is no conclusive evidence that any one acted singly as a causal agent.

Although we do not want to give the mistaken impression that we know what causes mild mental retardation, in this chapter we will try to identify the environmental factors that are correlated with lowered levels of intellectual functioning and look at some different opinions on how great a part environment plays in retarded development.

For purposes of this chapter, the term *environment* will be used to refer to the psychological and social conditions to which the developing individual is exposed and to physical factors that are linked with certain social conditions. The biological aspects of the physical environment will be examined in Chapter 4.

PRENATAL ENVIRONMENT

Perhaps the best place to start is at the beginning, before a person is even born. There are a number of forces to which the unborn fetus is exposed prior to birth, and many of these are sensitive to sociocultural differences in parents. In other words, social factors can affect the physical development of the child prior to birth. For example, a mother from an impoverished home may have had poorer nutrition as her reproductive system matured, poorer nutrition during her pregnancy, and little or no medical attention during the pregnancy. In addition, this woman may have little awareness of toxic agents to avoid, may have a poor state of general health, and may become pregnant repeatedly and into her later reproductive years because she does not practice family planning. Any and all of these factors are related to complications during the pregnancy and can result in prematurity, birth defects, and brain damage.

Scraps of information from many different sources suggest the extent of the relationship between low social status and adverse prenatal environment. For instance, inadequate nutrition in the mother has been implicated in a number of ways. Poor nutrition and health circumstances during her own development are related to the mother's pelvic shape and size in adult-hood. A too-small pelvic opening may complicate delivery. And there may be a nutritional basis for the finding that IQ levels vary according to the time of year when a child is born. Incidence of mental retardation is highest in children born in January, February, and March when these winter months follow extremely hot summers, perhaps because the mother's food intake was reduced during the critical first three months of her pregnancy (Knobloch & Pasamanick 1958).

Studies of twins have been used to demonstrate conditions that may be the effects of inadequate nutrition and a less than optimal uterine environ-ment. On the average, twins score between 4 to 7 points lower on IQ tests than singletons (Vandenberg 1968), and their scholastic achievement is lower as well. This holds true in all social classes, negating the possibility that the finding is due to different amounts of attention given to singletons and twins. Another line of research pertinent to this discussion is that monozygotic (identical) twins are slightly lower in IQ than are dizygotic (fraternal) twins (Stott 1960). All of this suggests that the intrauterine con-ditions are less optimal for twins; and among twins, the environment appears poorer for monozygotic twins. In terms of space and nutrition, twins must share what is available, usually resulting in a prenatal environ-ment that is less favorable than that available to singletons. In fact, Willer-man and Churchill (1967) suggest that nutrient supplies for twins may be inadequate for body and brain development, although one twin usually is harmed more than the other.

The depressing realities of the lower-class mother's life may inhibit fetal development in ways other than nutrition. Those who marry and give birth young often carry a high risk of having retarded children. Pregnancies at early ages, pregnancies at close intervals, a great number of pregnancies, and pregnancies that occur late in the childbearing years are related to pre-maturity, high infant mortality, low birth weight, prolonged labor, toxemia, anemia, malformations, and mental retardation. The mother coming from an environment that is stressful is more inclined to show the psychological factors associated with abnormal pregnancies than are mothers from less stressful environments. Personality traits such as emotional immaturity and negative attitudes towards pregnancy are related to habitual abortion and prematurity. Anxiety has been related to so-called abnormal pregnancies.

Lack of medical care among the poor may have some bearing on the out-come of their pregnancies. Graves, Freeman, and Thompson (1970) note that a woman's decision as to whether or not she will seek prenatal care, and at what stage of her pregnancy, is affected by social, psychological, cul-tural, and economic conditions. Typically, women from lower social classes begin such care later in the pregnancy. There is some evidence that lack of prenatal care is related to prematurity and infant mortality. Prematurity has some bearing on retardation, for, as we will see in Chapter 4, babies born before they are fully developed are more susceptible to central nervous system damage than are full-term babies.

Women from lower social strata frequently have illegitimate children. Studies in Britain (Illsley 1967) and the United States (Monahan 1960) reveal a definite pattern in illegitimate pregnancies: higher than normal rates of complications, prematurity, and fetal and infant loss. As we have seen, poor prenatal care, poor housing, poor nutrition, and the youth of the mother (frequently under twenty) are factors that often lead to conditions resulting in mental retardation; they are also factors commonly associated with illegitimate pregnancies.

The effect of the mother's working during her pregnancy (a situation that is more common in lower-class families by necessity) has also been studied, albeit in a less than precise fashion. Typically the researcher determines how late into the pregnancy the mother worked but neglects to consider what type of work she performed (e.g., hard physical labor versus clerical duties). An expectant mother who is not employed but who cares for a household of ten certainly runs a risk of fatigue equal to, if not greater than, that of a working woman who is a secretary and has only a small apartment and no other children to care for. Graves and his colleagues (1970) therefore concluded that while hard, fatiguing work probably does have an adverse effect on a pregnancy, generalizations about working mothers should not be made without considering the nature of their work.

It is somewhat risky to assume that any group of people that is economically or socially disadvantaged will show a higher incidence of reproductive wastage (birth defects, low birth weight, etc.). There must be factors other than economic ones that account for the higher infant mortality among black Americans, American Indians, and Spanish-Americans, because Jewish foreign-born groups living in equally deprived conditions in the early 1900s had very low infant mortality rates.

But, in general, in lower socioeconomic status environments there is an increased probability that, during the pregnancy or the birth process, adverse environmental influences will exert a detrimental effect on the structural integrity of the child. These adverse effects are a consequence of poor nutrition, poor prenatal care, lack of information, and other conditions that give rise to anxiety and stress. Even in cases of premature birth, which is essentially a biological event, cultural and economic factors are implicated. Women who conceive at young ages, have illegitimate children, have several pregnancies at closely spaced intervals, and are malnourished are more likely to have premature births. All these possibilities are more characteristic of lower-class women.

As far as individual differences in intelligence are concerned, environmental factors to which the fetus is exposed before and during birth are possibly as important as postnatal factors in the social environment—perhaps even more important. If this is so, then advances in medicine, nutrition, prenatal care, and obstetrics may be a more direct course to improving the lot of children coming from impoverished backgrounds than attempts to deal with the postnatal factors (Jensen 1969). Improved maternal care for the economically disadvantaged at the earliest stages of pregnancy might reduce the rate of birth defects. Education would help, too—knowledge about threats to the fetus (e.g., malnutrition, toxic agents) should not be limited to professional journals but should be disseminated to the lower class in understandable terms. Finally, there should be continued efforts to make birth control options available at reasonable costs, since rapid-succession pregnancies and pregnancies late in the childbearing years are associated with a high incidence of birth defects.

Unless such interventions are successful, the number of damaged babies born to the poor may increase. As a result a cycle will be perpetuated in which each new generation will bear damaged children who themselves will have little chance to break out of the cycle.

DIFFICULTIES IN STUDYING THE POSTNATAL ENVIRONMENT

Whether they are more important than prenatal factors to the development of intelligence or less so, postnatal factors are more complicated and have received more attention. After birth, "environment" could mean anything from a family's income and housing conditions to social interaction patterns and classroom climate. But studies of the effect of environment on intellectual development have usually emphasized the stimuli that are closest to the child—toys, books, social contacts.

So much has been written about the relationship between environment and development that it is impossible to review all the relevant literature. As McCandless (1964) notes, this effort would lead one into many disciplines and require an assessment of literature on persons at every stage of development from conception until death. Most researchers have attempted to assess the basic similarities between people's environments. This has resulted in a heavy reliance on the sociologists' notion of social class, or socioeconomic status (SES). Deutsch (1973) observed that SES refers to general groupings of people that are defined essentially in terms of family income and the way it is acquired. Related factors are the status of the major breadwinner's occupation and the level of education.

Since a general SES rating reflects the influence of many environmental variables, research that relies on this measure fails to determine which of the many variables is influencing a particular developmental outcome. According to Bloom (1964), this has led to oversimplified assessments of

environments. We tend to think of an environment in its entirety as good or bad, desirable or undesirable, without determining which specific factors are responsible for a particular outcome. This, in turn, has led to the belief that wealth, high occupational status, and high social position indicate good environments, whereas poverty, unskilled labor occupations, and low social status indicate poor environments. In actuality, however, the situation is a good deal more complicated than this. Low income, for example, does not cause reading difficulties directly; reading problems may instead be related to conditions associated with low income. In a poor family, the parents may work nights and be unavailable to help the child read, or they may communicate to the child that reading is unpleasant or unimportant. The SES is so global that it may mask specific variables such as these that actually do influence specific developmental outcomes.

Specifying Meaningful Variables

Bloom (1964) and several of his students (Dave 1963; Wolf 1964) investigated the use of environmental measurements that were more specific than SES. They rated the home environment, for example, in terms of its quality as an educational environment, a physically healthy environment, and a desirable set of social conditions. These ratings were then related to specific developmental outcomes—height, weight, IQ, and achievement. Bloom found that the rating of the educational environment was strongly correlated with academic achievement and IQ but unrelated to height and weight. Conversely, the rating of the physical and health environment was strongly correlated with weight but showed little relationship to academic achievement.

The Dangers of Class Stereotyping

Interpreting SES ratings or the relationship between SES ratings and developmental outcomes also poses problems, particularly with regard to the meaning of low social class. Zigler (1970a) argued that the study of social class differences in socialization has led to stereotyping of behavior within a social class. Thumbnail sketches of what a middle-class or lower-class person is like, such as those offered by Cavan (1964), emphasize the homogeneity of behavior within a social class and the heterogeneity between classes. Zigler contends that this *modal-man approach* has tended to ignore the variability within a social class as well as the similarities across classes. He argues further that such an approach is not plausible when applied to subgroups of a single society, because of the interaction between members of different social classes.

Cultural variation is probably more accurately represented as variation along a continuum rather than in discrete units. Although in this chapter we are focusing our attention on the lower social class, due to its disproportionate number of cases of cultural-familial retarded persons, we must be careful not to think in terms of class stereotypes. Of the factors commonly associated with the lower-class environment, few are present in every lower-class home and none are present to the same degree in each home. For example, a common stereotyped notion is the following: when compared to middle-class families, lower-class parents have lower expectations for their child. But some lower-class families have quite high expectations for their children; according to Zigler, there is considerable variability within the lower class in the extent to which parents expect achievements such as academic success. Moreover, there is an overlap between lower-class and middle-class parents in their expectations for their children. Clausen and Williams (1963), Elder (1968), and Miller and Swanson (1960) provide extended discussions of the dangers of class stereotyping.

Despite its global nature and lack of precision, social class is still a useful concept. In the research to date, social class has been found to account for considerable variance in studies concerned with intelligence or achievement. Nevertheless, we should aim for greater precision in specifying factors within a social class and representing them as continuous, rather than discrete, variables.

CORRELATES OF SOCIAL CLASS

Despite problems of interpretation and social class stereotyping, we do have some evidence of relationships between features of different class levels and intellectual development, especially in terms of language modeling, factors in the physical environment, and aspects of the psychological environment.

Hess and Shipman (1965), for instance, studied 163 black mothers of four-year-old children to determine the effects of specific parental behavior on particular child behaviors. The mothers were selected as representing four social classes. They were seen twice in their homes and brought once to a university campus where they could be observed interacting with their children. Some observations were: middle-class mothers talked with their children far more than any of the other three groups. Furthermore, the language used by the mothers differed by social class. Those on public assistance used fewer abstract words than did others, and there was a difference among social classes in the use of complex syntactical structures. When mothers were asked to teach a task to their children, the lower-class mothers failed to give their children specific instructions and did not provide them with models. In addition, when their children made errors, the lower-class mothers criticized them; these same mothers were also less inclined to praise successes. Differences also emerged in control systems. When asked how they handled rule breaking, lower-class mothers were more inclined to stress that their children should be obedient in school (status-oriented); middle-class mothers tended to prefer handling these situations on a personal basis and elaborated with explanations.

There is little doubt that, as groups, lower-class and middle-class families differ. However, while a disproportionate number of cultural-familial retarded children come from impoverished environments, the vast majority of children coming from these environmental conditions will never be classified as retarded. This raises two questions for which we have only partial answers: (1) What explains the high prevalence of cultural-familial retardation among the lower social class? (2) If environmental factors are responsible, why do the vast majority of individuals coming from lower social class backgrounds escape the retarded classification?

As we consider the correlates of lower social class, we must keep in mind that, while they are correlates, their role in causing mental retardation is undocumented and their applicability to lower-class environments will differ in degree.

The Language Environment

Studies of the language characteristics of the lower social class have been greatly influenced by the work of Bernstein (1960), a sociologist. Conducting his research in England, he found that lower-class children generally used what he called a *public language code* and middle-class children tended to use a *formal language code*. The public language code involves the use of short, simple sentences, circularity ("You know?"), and a limited use of certain pronouns. Bernstein hypothesized that such a language code restricts thinking. The formal language code uses more elaborate structure and explicit meaning. Building on this background, Jensen (1968) identified a number of environmental situations linked with language development as possible sources of social class differences in intellectual achievement. In the lower class:

1. Early vocalizations by infants are less likely to be rewarded.
2. The child is less likely to have a single mother-child relationship in the early years.
3. There is less verbal interaction and verbal play in response to early vocalizations; hence speech tends to be delayed.

4. In the early stages of speech there is less shaping of speech sounds in which parents reinforce closer approximations to adult speech.
5. Much vocal interaction takes place with slightly older siblings, whose own speech is only slightly more advanced and who do not systematically shape verbal behavior.
6. Auditory discrimination suffers because early listening to language models proceeds through the high-noise background typical of urban and other lower-class environments.
7. Early question asking is extinguished because of a lack of adequate response by distracted parents.
8. The spoken language is less like written language (syntactically, grammatically, logically, etc.) than middle-class speech. Hence there will be less positive transfer to reading and formal writing.
9. Language models are poorer for developing linguistic skills that will transfer to the school setting.

In addition to the direct effect of these variables on the verbal behavior of the child coming from the lower social class, there is some belief that the language characteristics also place limitations on the child's conceptual skills (Bernstein 1960), although evidence has been presented to the contrary (Labov 1972). But in general, socialization in the lower-class home is often lacking in the kind of language modeling and the help with speech development that prepare middle-class children for school activities.

The Physical Environment

Certain physical aspects of the lower-class home have also been related to cultural-familial retardation. In comparison with middle-class households, lower-class households are more likely to have:

1. father absent from the home,
2. crowded living conditions,
3. poorer nutrition and medical care,
4. large family size,
5. dilapidated living environment,
6. high ratio of children to adults.

The effects of such situations are often negative. When living conditions are crowded and family size large, financial, emotional, and spatial resources must all be divided into smaller parcels. Thus there are fewer toys, books, and magazines available in the home that might encourage learning experiences. Furthermore, the lack of finances can prevent travel and other experiences outside of the home (e.g., trips to museums) that provide an experiential basis for school learning.

But the lack of middle-class amenities may also have some positive side effects. For example, the fact that children from lower-class families tend to be closely spaced in age and live under rather crowded conditions with little privacy and few toys almost forces them to learn cooperation. This is one positive trait in which lower-class children seem to exceed middle-class youngsters.

The Psychological Environment

How does the lower-class psychological environment serve to depress academic achievement and IQ? The inadequate language modeling discussed previously is one of the psychological variables thought to be correlated to retardation. In addition, there are a number of variables that may depress the aspiration level of lower-class children, establishing in them an attitude of defeatism.

There are several examples that show how lower-class correlates might affect intellectual development. Inadequate housing can result in an environment that fails to interest children and promote new learning; frequent moves prevent them from making long-term friends. The concerns of the parents over day-to-day survival may preoccupy them, leaving less attention for their children. When their children ask questions, the parents may either fail to respond or suppress the questioning behavior as an interruption.

A variety of psychological dimensions appear to be related to social class differences: quality of family relationships, patterns of affection and authority, expressive styles and reactions to stress, parental expectations for their child, and the child's perceptions of the parents. In addition, lower-class homes tend to be differentiated by a relative lack of stability, and the greater probability that both parents have to be employed.

Zigler (1970a) reviewed the literature on social class variations in behavior and found some more factors that have been shown to differentiate lower-class members:

1. While parents of all social classes wanted their children to be honest, happy, obedient, and dependable, middle-class parents emphasized internal standards (such as honesty, self-control, and curiosity) while lower-class parents emphasized qualities that would assure respectability (such as obedience, neatness, and cleanliness).
2. Lower-class children are more likely to perceive parents and other adults as predominantly hostile; lower-class children also show a greater readiness to experience guilt.
3. Lower-class parents and children are more inclined to vent hostility in overt acts of aggression. But the findings on aggression are mixed; while most studies report higher aggression in lower-class children,

a few find no differences or higher aggression in middle-class children.

4. Middle-class parents appear to emphasize achievement and success striving to their children to a greater extent than do lower-class parents.

If, on top of such achievement-depressing psychological factors, the lower-class child also has parents who are themselves intellectually subnormal, he runs a double risk of cultural-familial retardation. The parents contribute genetically to the child and they also provide the early environment in which the child's intellectual growth is fostered—or squelched. Sarason and Gladwin (1958) suggested several ways in which an intellectually subnormal mother fails to meet the needs of her child. She may be more concerned with her own needs than those of her child and respond to the child's needs in an inconsistent manner—sometimes she gives prompt attention when the child cries; at other times she lets the child cry for extended periods. She is not likely to encourage the child's early responses to the environment and she may even punish the child if they mean more work or trouble for her. Intellectually subnormal women do not necessarily make poor mothers, but in areas like these their children may be especially vulnerable to intellectual stunting.

The Evidence of Environmental Effects on Intelligence

The material we have examined so far in this chapter has been mostly descriptive and theoretical. Although it raises the possibility that early intervention in the preschool years might help to overcome the negative effects of a deprived background, none of the aspects of cultural deprivation have been directly implicated as causes of cultural-familial retardation. We still have not seen any cases in which low IQ was shown to be the result of environment rather than heredity. We have not seen any such evidence because the research that could settle the nature-nurture debate has not, and cannot, be done.

To see how difficult such research would be, let's look at Clarke and Clarke's (1974) suggestion of four possible ways to clarify the relationship between genetics and environment in the determination of intelligence:

1. Children born to two parents of known high IQ could be experimentally placed at birth in conditions of poverty and deprivation and reared by foster parents both of known low IQ for perhaps fifteen years. If they were nonetheless found to be very bright, this would be powerful evidence that heredity was of overwhelming importance in determining intelligence.

2. Children born to two parents of known low IQ could be experimentally placed at birth with parents both known to be bright and brought up in a

stimulating and enriched environment. If they still resembled their true parents more than their foster parents, heredity would be presumed to be the more powerful factor.

3. Children born to two parents of known low IQ could be experimentally manipulated in such a way that the potentially adverse effects of living with their parents would be compensated for. If they nonetheless developed low intelligence, heredity would be considered more powerful than environment.

4. A number of identical twins born to parents of known high (or low) IQ could be separated at birth, one twin remaining with the natural parents and the other twin placed with parents varying from very unintelligent to highly intelligent. If after fifteen the separated twins still resembled each other closely, heredity would be shown predominant.

(p. 165)

Of these four potential sources of evidence, only partial evidence is available on approaches 2 and 3; ethical objections can be raised against perhaps all of them. So we must examine evidence derived from naturally occurring research subjects, such as orphans and twins, and from a few experimental studies.

As you examine these few scraps of evidence, bear in mind that shifts in IQ with time are part of a normal pattern. Both intelligence and achievement appear to develop very rapidly in the early years of life and then slow down or even drop slightly. According to Hunt's (1961) review of the longitudinal research on individual IQ changes, people commonly increase or decrease 15 IQ points or more between the ages of six and seventeen or eighteen. But whether the rapid growth in the preschool years and the shifts during the school years are caused by a predetermined genetic pattern or by the individual's experiences is still not clear.

The Effects of Institutionalization

Understaffed and unstimulating orphanages have been shown to have dramatic adverse effects on children placed in them. Studies made some time ago by the research group at Iowa (Skeels & Dye 1939; Skeels 1966; Skodak 1968; Wellman, Skeels, & Skodak 1940) brought this fact to public attention. In one of the studies, children in an orphanage nursery school were matched with others in the orphanage on the basis of chronological age, mental age, IQ, and length of time in the orphanage. Although all continued to live in the orphanage, half were given five or six hours of school experience and the other half remained in the orphanage environment full time. Investigations first reported that, over a period of three years, those children who received nursery school experience gained in IQ while those who simply lived in the institution without schooling dropped in IQ. But reanalysis of the data on 11 schooled children and 10 control children

(Wellman et al. 1940) showed that both groups dropped in IQ—a drop of 2.2 IQ points for the schooled children and a drop in IQ of 15.6 points for the controls.

The 1939 study by Skeels and Dye had a more dramatic outcome. Despite what we have said about the possible detrimental effects of mentally subnormal mothers, even a retarded surrogate mother may be better than no mother at all, at least insofar as the child's intellectual development is concerned. Skeels and Dye tried placing a group of 13 orphaned children under three years old on wards in an institution for the retarded with female residents. A control group of 12 children were left in the orphanage. On the wards the women patients became attached to the experimental children; they played with the children extensively and provided stimulating materials for them to work with. In the orphanage mental stimulation was lacking, for the adult workers were in contact with the children only when they needed care, and even that contact was kept to a minimum. At the beginning of the experiment, the control group had higher IQs—the experimental group had an initial mean IQ of 64.3 and the controls had a mean IQ of 87. But after being on the wards for some time, all 13 experimental children showed gains in IQ of greater than 7 points (1 increased 58 IQ points; all but 4 increased over 20 points). When the control group who remained in the orphanage orphanage was retested after 21 months to 43 months, all but one showed a decrease in IQ (10 of which were between 18 to 45 points, with 5 dropping more than 35 points). Although there were some methodological problems with the study, the results remain impressive, if not definitive.

All but 2 of the children in the experimental group were eventually adopted, most of them by lower-middle-class couples. All 12 control children, on the other hand, either remained in the orphanage or were placed in state schools for the mentally retarded.

After twenty years had passed, Skeels (1966) and Skodak (1968) followed up the subjects to assess their status as adults. The dramatic differences that existed at the end of the experiment had persisted. The experimental subjects had completed an average of almost twelve years of schooling; the controls had finished an average of only four years of schooling. Occupationally, the 3 males in the experimental group were functioning as a vocational counselor, sales manager for an estate agent, and a staff sergeant in the air force; of the female subjects from the experimental group who were employed, 1 was an elementary teacher, 1 a registered nurse, 1 a licensed practical nurse, 1 a beautician, 1 a clerk, and 1 an airline stewardess. Two were domestics in private homes. In contrast, of the control group subjects, 4 were still residents of institutions and unemployable. Three were dishwashers, 1 was an unskilled laborer, and 1 worked in a cafeteria. One of the men had been in and out of institutions; while he was out, he lived with his grandmother and did odd jobs for her. One worked for an institution where he had been a resident. The only control subject who showed a fairly high degree of adaptation was a typesetter for a newspaper. But he had participated in an intensive stimulation program as part of someone's doctoral dissertation project, and after the initial experiment a matron in an institution where he lived had taken special interest in him.

Spitz's research (1945, 1946a, 1946b) with institutionalized infants supported the findings emerging from the Iowa studies and suggested the plasticity of intelligence during the early years. Spitz studied babies in two kinds of institutions. One institution, which he labeled the "Foundling Home," lacked social attention for the infants and presented little variation in the kinds of stimulation provided. The mothers of these children had come from preferred social backgrounds. In the other institution, labeled the "Nursery," mothers were in a penal institution for delinquents but were allowed to play with their babies daily for the first year. When tested for development, the infants in the Foundling Home were reported to have dropped progressively over the first year of life. In contrast, the babies raised in the Nursery setting advanced progressively up to five months or so, reached a plateau, and then dropped slightly in the last months of the year. Spitz attributed the drop in developmental scores for babies in the Foundling Home to be due to the lack of mothering, or what he called *hospitalism*. The Foundling Home babies, he noticed, tended to suffer from a syndrome he labeled *anaclitic depression*: weepiness, withdrawal, susceptibility to infection, and loss of weight. Factors other than the lack of mothering may in part have been responsible for the differences in development Spitz observed, but Hunt (1961) points out that, whatever the cause, these findings provide little comfort for those who believe in fixed intelligence. The interested reader is referred to a thorough critique of these studies provided by McNemar (1940). A reply was offered by Wellman et al. (1940).

Other studies (e.g., Dennis 1951, 1960; Goldfarb 1945) have been made of the depressing effect of nonstimulating institutions on the development of children. They add further support to the argument that the early social-psychological environment is important for cognitive and social development. In addition to the studies on institutionalization, there have been reports on individual children who are isolated and restricted in very depressing ways—such as being locked in cellars or attics for extended periods of time. All were intellectually stunted, some beyond hope of recovery, but some responded to remedial treatment when they were found (Clarke & Clarke 1974). The effects of this kind of extreme environmental deprivation have been cited in support of the contention that nonstimulating environments can have devastating effects on the cognitive and affective growth of children.

Prior to leaving this set of studies we should note that some critics have not accepted their apparent implications. Originally these early studies on the placement of children into various environments were criticized vociferously by Goodenough (1939). More recently, others have advised against applying blatant generalizations to inner-city children. And Jensen (1969) has cautioned against impulsive interpretations of the IQ (or Developmental Quotient, in the cases of the Bayley or Gesell Developmental Scale for tapping fine motor coordination) increments. For example, a tempting interpretation is that the initial IQ differences in the Skeels and Dye (1939) study explain the differences in adult status reported by Skeels (1966). However, it may also be that the initial program gave confidence to those involved that the children were adoptable. Other interpretations of the significance of these studies will be presented later along with some discussion of their significance for cultural-familial retardation.

Studies of Relatives

In addition to the institutional studies, individuals have also been compared with their relatives to see if they have similar intellectual abilities. Studies by Illingworth (1966) and Haywood and Tapp (1966), for instance, have computed correlations between children and their natural parents and children and their foster or adoptive parents to see which was stronger, nature or nurture. One of the most extensive reviews of this literature is provided by Erlenmeyer-Kimling and Jarvik (1963). In Table 3.1, which summarizes their analyses, there are considerable ranges in the correlation coefficients. As Clarke and Clarke (1974) have pointed out, this could be due to differences in how the studies were set up, genetic and environmental differences in the populations studied, or both.

The correlations summarized in Table 3.1 have traditionally been interpreted as strong support for the position that heredity is more important than environment in determining intelligence. Figure 3.1 shows the median values of correlations for unrelated children, siblings, fraternal (dizygotic) twins, and identical (monozygotic) twins when they are either (1) reared together or (2) reared apart. Whether siblings, for instance, are reared apart or together, they show the same similarity in IQ. Hunt (1961), however, interpreted these studies as revealing the importance of the environment. He focused on studies of identical twins who were reared apart. Since monozygotic twins come from the same ovum and therefore share the same set of genes, any differences they show in IQ can be assumed to be due to differences in their experiences or environment. One study (Newman, Freeman, & Holzinger, 1937) included 19 pairs of identical twins who had been separated when they were anywhere from six months to six years old. In 7 cases there were differences between the twins of 10 IQ points or more, with 1 pair differing by 24 points and others by 19, 17, and 15 points. Hunt (1961) points out that when we consider that the twins were placed into similar socioeconomic environments, resulting in considerable uniformity in the way they were probably raised, their discrepancies in IQ are even more remarkable. If reasonably modest differences in the environ-

TABLE 3.1   Correlations for Intellectual Ability: Obtained and Theoretical Values*

Correlations between . . .	Number of Studies	Obtained Median r†	Theoretical Value 1‡	Theoretical Value 2§
Unrelated Persons				
Children reared apart	4	−.01	.00	.00
Foster parent and child	3	+.20	.00	.00
Children reared together	5	+.24	.00	.00
Collaterals				
Second cousins	1	+.16	+ .14	+ .063
First cousins	3	+.26	+ .18	+ .125
Uncle (or aunt) and nephew (or niece)	1	+.34	+ .31	+ .25
Siblings, reared apart	3	+.47	+ .52	+ .50
Siblings, reared together	36	+.55	+ .52	+ .50
Dizygotic twins, different sex	9	+.49	+ .50	+ .50
Dizygotic twins, same sex	11	+.56	+ .54	+ .50
Monozygotic twins, reared apart	4	+.75	+1.00	+1.00
Monozygotic twins, reared together	14	+.87	+1.00	+1.00
Direct Line				
Grandparent and grandchild	3	+.27	+ .31	+ .25
Parent (as adult) and child	13	+.50	+ .49	+ .50
Parent (as child) and child	1	+.56	+ .49	+ .50

*Jensen's table relies heavily on the Erlenmeyer-Kimling and Jarvik (1963) analysis but also includes additional studies reported by Burt (1966). The validity of Burt's data is currently in question.
†Correlations not corrected for attenuation (unreliability).
‡Assuming assortative mating and partial dominance.
§Assuming random mating and only additive genes; i.e., the simplest possible polygenic model.

From A. R. Jensen, "How much can we boost IQ and scholastic achievement?" Reprinted by permission of the *Harvard Educational Review*. Copyright © 1969 by the President and Fellows of Harvard College.

ments can result in IQ differences of 24 or 19 points between monozygotic twins, Hunt argues, think of the differences that might occur if such twins were placed in environments that differed dramatically. But Hunt's hopes notwithstanding, it still seems risky to interpret differences as evidence for or against environmental effects on intelligence. Scarr-Salapatek (1975)

**FIGURE 3.1   Median Values of All Correlations Reported
in the Literature up to 1963 for the Indicated
Kinships**

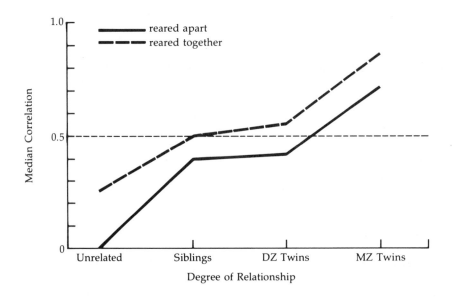

From Jensen 1969, adapted from Erlenmeyer-Kimling and Jarvik, "Genetics and Intelligence: A Review,"
Science **142** (December 1963): 1477–79, copyright © 1963 by the American Association for the Advancement of Science.

observed that our failure to account for variations in IQ in terms of environment may be due in part to our inability to measure environment very
accurately.

Studies of Adoptions

A variation on studies of relatives are studies that examine the relationship between an adopted child's IQ and the IQs of the child's biological and
adoptive parents. Willerman (1979) examined four major adoption studies:
Burks (1928), Leahy (1935), Scarr and Weinberg (1978), and Horn, Loehlin,
and Willerman (1979). It was concluded that the environment accounted for
little variation in the IQ scores of the children. This result was surprising
since children are selectively placed in adoptive homes that would tend to
enhance the correlation between environment and the child's IQ. In these
four major studies, however, environmental measures accounted for less

than 10 percent of the variation in IQ. Moreover, the IQ correlations between the adoptive child and other children raised in the same home were very low.

These studies do not support the notion that placement in different environments results in different phenotypic outcomes. Table 3.2 gives the IQs of adopted children as a function of the biological mother's IQ. When the biological mother had an IQ of less than 95, none of her offspring had an IQ of over 120; conversely, when the biological mother had an IQ of over 120, none of her offspring had an IQ of 95 or lower. If the home environment was a powerful determinant of IQ, one would expect fairly high correlations between unrelated children reared in the same home, and one would expect a lower correlation between biological mothers' IQs and those of their children when they were raised in someone else's home. The adoption studies contradict these expectations, and although they don't prove the heredity position, they clearly do not support the environmental position.

THE DYNAMICS OF ENVIRONMENTAL EFFECTS

Now that we have examined some of the relationships that have been found between environment and intelligence, we will finally look at some theories of how the relationships work. As spokesmen for the two sides of the nature-nurture controversy, we will use Bloom to represent the environmentalist point of view and Jensen to speak for the power of heredity.

Bloom: The Rationale for Early Intervention

Bloom's analysis of the effects of environmental factors on intelligence has been most influential on the thinking of psychologists and educators. His conclusions are frequently cited as the rationale for early intervention.

TABLE 3.2   **IQ of Adopted Child as a Function of the Biological Mother's IQ**

Biological Mother's IQ	Mean IQ of Children	Child's IQ ≥ 120 %	Child's IQ ≤ 95 %
IQ of 95 or less (27 cases)	102.6	0	15
IQ of 120 or above (34 cases)	118.3	44	0

Based on J. M. Horn, J. C. Loehlin, & L. Willerman, "Intellectual resemblance among adoptive and biological relatives: The Texas Adoption Project," *Behavior Genetics*, 1979, 9, 177–207.

In his book *Stability and Change in Human Charactersitics* (1964), an excellent piece of scholarship, Bloom argued that intelligence develops rapidly during the first few years of life. Then the pace gradually slows and becomes highly stable after age eight. We can predict 50 percent of the *variance in IQ* for the group at maturity. Variance refers to differences in IQ in a group of scores for different individuals. These differences (the *variance*) can be explained partially by the differences that existed in IQ when these same subjects were tested at age four—but not all of the differences at maturity (age seventeen or eighteen) can be attributed to the IQ differences at age four. The *explained* variance (explained in terms of IQ differences at age four) and *unexplained* variance (due to factors other than IQ differences at age four) can be separated statistically. It is found that about 50 percent of the differences in IQ at maturity is "explained" by IQ differences at age four; the same analysis of IQs at age eight reveals that 80 percent of the variance in IQs at maturity can be explained by IQ differences at age eight. Environmental effects (whether beneficial or detrimental) are maximized during the critical period when a particular characteristic is undergoing its greatest growth. The significance of the quality of the environment is least during the period of least growth. In the case of intellectual development, environmental intervention has the greatest impact if it is provided during the preschool years, before the age of four. Variations in environment would probably have relatively little impact after age eight.

Bloom envisions environmental variations as a continuum from good to bad, with *good* meaning "abundant" and *bad* meaning "deprived." A normal environment is somewhere between these two extremes, but Bloom only attempts to consider the effects of the two extreme kinds of environments. According to his theory, the quality of the environment has a simple linear relationship to the development of intelligence. The better (more abundant) the environment, the closer an individual comes to performing at the level set by his biological limits. The more deprived the environment, the greater the extent to which intelligence is depressed. By the age of seventeen, an individual's IQ could theoretically differ by up to 20 IQ points, depending on whether he had been raised in a deprived or an abundant environment. If the child spent only part of his first seventeen years in either a deprived or an abundant environment, the effect would be less, depending on how old he was at the time. Bloom claims that these hypothetical estimates compare well with data from intervention programs initiated at various ages.

Jensen: Environment as a Threshold Variable

Jensen (1969) rejects Bloom's theory that the quality of the environment has a linear influence on intellectual development. He thinks the environment functions as a *threshold variable*. By this he means that a certain mini-mal quality of environment is necessary for normal intellectual develop-ment. Above this threshold, however, variations in the environment do not cause major differences in intelligence. What constitutes an environment below the threshold level? According to Jensen, a subthreshold environ-ment consists of extreme sensory and motor restrictions such as those described in the Iowa studies of earlier institutions and in the reports of children hidden in attics or closets by their parents without human or sen-sory stimulation for years. He is very specific in stating that he does not consider the culturally disadvantaged's characteristic lack of middle-class amenities to constitute a subthreshold environment. Jensen contends that the conditions present in culturally disadvantaged environments are totally unlike those described in the early orphanage studies.

From Jensen's perspective, dramatic IQ changes of over 20 IQ points could be predicted in cases where children are removed from extremely deprived environments to favorable environments, particularly when the child is reasonably young. On the other hand, children moving from cul-turally deprived to middle-class environments would not be expected to show IQ rises of 20 points or more, since the culturally deprived environ-ments are above the threshold necessary for normal intellectual develop-ment. The following analogy may clarify this point:

> The environment with respect to intelligence is thus analogous to nutrition with respect to stature. If there are great nutritional lacks, growth is stunted, but above a certain level of nutritional adequacy, including daily requirements of minerals, vitamins, and proteins, even great variations in eating habits will have negligible effects on persons' stature, and under such conditions most of the differences in stature among individuals will be due to heredity.
>
> (Jensen 1969, p. 60)

According to Jensen, available evidence supports his skepticism about early intervention. When children were removed from the extreme depri-vation of orphanages and attic isolation and placed in adequate environ-ments, their IQs rose rapidly and the sizable IQ gains were permanent. But when culturally deprived children are given enrichment experiences, the IQ gain is typically meager (less than 10 points); it is usually lost soon after, and in subsequent school years the children's IQs typically decline.

Reaction Range

The concept of the reaction range has been used extensively to explain the interaction between heredity and environment. Scarr-Salapatek (1975) explains that the reaction range model (Figure 3.2) attempts to demonstrate

**FIGURE 3.2   Scheme of the Reaction Range Concept
for Four Hypothetical Genotypes**

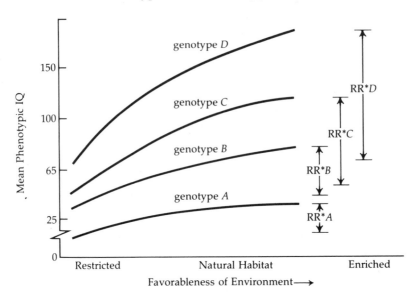

*The phenotypic range of each genotype is indicated by RR. Genotype *A*, which achieves a very low phenotypic IQ under excellent conditions, is not part of the normal IQ range. The other curves represent genotypically unique responses to the changing favorableness of the environment.

After Gottesman, 1963. From A. R. Jensen, "How much can we boost IQ and scholastic achievement?" Reprinted by permission of the *Harvard Educational Review.* Copyright © 1969 by the President and Fellows of Harvard College.

how quantitatively different phenotypes can result from the same genotypes under different environmental conditions. This model argues against the position that heredity sets limits for potential development and that environment determines the magnitude of the development. Note in Figure 3.2 how the same restricted or enriched environment has different effects on different people according to their genotypic makeup. The possible range of reactions is greater for some genotypes (e.g., genotype D) than for others (e.g., genotype A). According to the reaction range concept, persons with lower inherited or genotypic intelligence are likely to have smaller reaction ranges; as a result, their ultimate level of ability is influenced less by environmental factors than is the ultimate level of children with higher genotypic intelligence.

The reaction range concept has several provocative implications. The same genotypes, for example, can yield different phenotypic IQs due to the influence of different environments, and the same phenotypic IQ can be arrived at from different genotypes. In other words, many different heredity-environment combinations can result in the same IQ. Monozygotic twins are of interest in studying these ideas because they possess the same genotype, but, if reared in different environments, they have been exposed to somewhat different environmental forces.

Jensen (1969) contends that the dynamics of the relationship between heredity and environment are far more complex than some have suggested. In supporting the notion of reaction range, he argues that the influence of environment on development may differ in persons who vary in genetic makeup. Moreover, he challenges the argument that for every unit of increase in the quality of the environment there will be a corresponding improvement in development. Instead, Jensen argues that environment acts as a threshold variable: below a certain qualitative level there will be adverse effects on development, but once a certain quality of environment is present, any further increments in the quality of the environment will not yield increased benefits for development.

The concept of reaction range is an effort to explain the interplay of environment and heredity in determining phenotypic IQ, but the reader should appreciate the complexity of the process. Although ardent environmentalists portray the child as a passive organism subjected to environmental influences, the work of Bell and Harper (1977) clearly indicates that children also influence the environments in which they are placed. A bright child, for example, may be very responsive to a parent's attempts to teach a skill. Similarly, such children may create stimulating environments for themselves since they find a wide range of activities interesting. Less able children are unlikely to provide the same responsiveness, and as a result they fail to encourage their parents' efforts to stimulate them. This is not to deny the environment's influence on children; it is, rather, to recognize that children differ in their ability to recognize how an environment can be used in stimulating ways.

THE IMPLICATIONS FOR SPECIAL EDUCATION

Although the nature-nurture controversy has not been settled and probably never will be, the points made by those who believe in the strength of inherited intellectual endowment must temper our optimism about curing or even preventing mild retardation by providing high-risk children with environmental enrichment. Social class differences are correlated with differences in intellectual functioning, but whether this is the result of environment or heredity or both is still unclear. It is one thing to argue that environmental variables play a role in creating individual differences, but yet another to argue that environmental events can depress intelligence sufficiently that the individual of potentially normal IQ would be retarded.

But despite uncertainties about the extent to which environment affects intellectual development, there is evidence that it has at least some effect. Almost everybody agrees that extreme sensory and physical deprivation has devastating effects, particularly when it occurs in the early period of development. In most cases the damage can be partially undone by providing an enriched environment. The practical question that remains is whether enrichment programs are of much help to the mildly retarded who do not come from subthreshold environments.

From the social scientist's point of view, early intervention may not solve everything, but it is the only tool we have. By the time we ecounter a child with subaverage intellectual functioning it is too late to do anything about the genetic makeup of the child. From a programmatic perspective the question becomes this: How can we enhance the effectiveness of this child's functioning? We are not going to be able to realign a child's central nervous system; instead, we must identify ways of maximizing that child's achievement, adaptation, and social skills so that the child can be as successful as possible. In this respect the environmental variables are the elements available for manipulation.

In addition to trying to design programs to help individual children, social scientists are also concerned with the long-term goal of preventing cultural-familial retardation. To some degree this means creating so-called good environments in which children will be raised. To date, very little can be said with certainty regarding what constitutes a good environment for intellectual development. We tend to equate goodness of environments with the American middle-class home. But this kind of stereotyping does not satisfy the need to specify which variables within the lower class are related to specific outcomes such as IQ. Social isolation, cruelty and neglect, institutional upbringing, adverse child-rearing practices, and separation experiences are known to be detrimental to the child's development (Clarke & Clarke 1960). But if we are ever to prevent cultural-familial retardation— if this is possible—we must gather more specific proof about which environmental variables are related to which intellectual outcomes in children.

SUMMARY

This chapter summarized a considerable body of literature bearing on the role of the social-psychological environment on the development of intelligence. Despite some areas of disagreement, the following points are supported by the analysis in this chapter.

In most cases of mental retardation, no specific cause can be identified. But many of the mildly retarded (EMR) have been found to come from low socioeconomic status environments. This observation has led to considerable speculation that environment plays a role in the development of intelligence. In the case of retardation, there is thought to be a possibility that adverse environments can depress intelligence sufficiently to be seen as a cause of mild retardation. Bloom and Hunt are frequently cited as spokesmen for this point of view.

In considering environments we must not overlook the effect of the prenatal environment on the ultimate intellectual level achieved by a child. Adverse prenatal environmental conditions (e.g., poor maternal nutrition, oxygen deprivation, toxic agents) have been shown to have deleterious effects on the developing fetus. Low socioeconomic status is associated with potentially harmful prenatal influences and care. For instance, prematurity, which is related to mental retardation, is more common in children born to mothers of low socioeconomic status.

In drawing relationships between social class and environmental effects thought to be related to retardation, we must be careful to avoid class stereotyping. That is, we must not assume that there is homogeneity within a given social class—in actuality there is considerable variability with regard to most characteristics other than income. Studies of environments and their effect on intellectual development should specify environmental elements (e.g., emphasis in the home for achievement) and relate these to specific outcomes (e.g., achievement). This approach would be more productive than approaches that use global measures of environments (e.g., social class).

There appears to be a consensus among investigators regarding the detrimental effects of extremely deprived environments in which sensory and-motor stimulation is restricted. The effects of such environments on children exposed to them are adverse and quite dramatic.

Investigators disagree on the extent to which environments described as "culturally deprived" affect intellectual development. Evidence that does exist appears to lend itself to competitive interpretations, two of which were developed herein. Bloom hypothesizes a linear relationship between the "goodness" of an environment and the extent to which an individual in such an environment would approach his optimal development. To the contrary, Jensen suggests that low social class environments are adequate in that they do not deprive individuals reared in them by means of sensory and motor restrictions. He postulates that environments serve as a threshold variable; beyond that threshold, additional increments—in the form of enrichment programs, for instance—do not yield substantial additional benefits.

At present, professional sentiment seems to favor a position suggesting that the environment is more important than heredity as a determinant of intellectual development. But it would be too extreme to suggest that all differences in intellectual performance are due to differences in the environments in which individuals are raised. Such a position ignores the ample evidence on the importance of heredity. Researchers like Zigler and Jensen warn against unwarranted faith in the power of the environment to make the retarded normal.

CHAPTER 4

Genetic and Physical Factors

We do not yet know what causes mental retardation in the majority of cases, but it has been shown that certain physical and genetic factors do cause mental retardation, and others are suspected to cause retardation under certain circumstances. However, as we saw in the last chapter, the percentage of cases in which a precise cause can be specified is quite small. Stern (1973), for example, contends that in half the cases of mental retardation, no etiological diagnosis can be made; in a broader context, Wilson (1974) estimated that only 30–40 percent of identifiable cases of developmental defects (of all kinds) have known causes.

Although we are rarely able to look at a given case of mental retardation and attribute it to a single cause, advances in the biomedical sciences have enabled us to understand the variety of factors that can have mental retardation as a consequence. Advances in the study of genetics have uncovered conditions that are transmitted genetically and are implicated in mental retardation. We are learning more about the effects of malnutrition and disease on the fetus and the child. And research on chemicals in the environment and drugs has led to a greater understanding of the potential damage that can be done to the fetus if they are ingested by the mother, or to the central nervous system if ingested by the child.

In this chapter consideration is given to known genetic and environmental factors that cause mental retardation before, during, and after birth. These causes can be separated into two groups:

1. *Genetically determined conditions in which mental retardation is one of the consequences.* The condition, or weakness, is established before birth as a result of genetically transmitted information. In some cases mental retardation is always a consequence; in others there may be a vulnerability created that can indirectly result in mental retardation if the individual is not protected from certain environmental agents.
2. *Damage to the central nervous system.* This can occur during the prenatal, perinatal, or postnatal periods. The specific dynamic whereby the central nervous system is injured varies tremendously. In some cases there is a defect in the development of the neural tube; in others, insufficient oxygen supply to the brain, direct trauma, or toxic agents in the blood.

For the sake of clarity we have tried to separate heredity and environmental factors. Hereditary factors are those that exert their influence before and at conception; environmental factors are those that exert their influence after conception. But there is often overlap between the two kinds of factors. It is known, for instance, that some environmental factors in the parents' experience can cause mutations in the genetic information before conception. To facilitate the study of known causes of and contributing factors in mental retardation, the time sequence described by Penrose (1966) will be used.

BASIC CONCEPTS OF GENETICS

The study of genetics has revealed the importance of *genes* in directing and controlling human development and life processes. In some instances recent advances have enabled us to identify subtle underlying genetic causes of mental retardation.

Sometimes mental retardation is an inevitable consequence from the moment of conception, such as in Down's syndrome. In other cases the genetic makeup of the child creates vulnerability to certain environmental forces; however, if protected from these particular environmental factors, the child may develop more or less normally. This is the case in conditions such as galactosemia and phenylketonuria (PKU), in which children inherit a defect that prevents the proper metabolism of specific substances.

Before examining in detail the genetic basis for Down's syndrome and PKU, we must build up some background information about how genetic transmission works. Keep in mind that while our concern is with mental retardation, which is a *phenotype* (the manifested characteristics of the individual at a given time), the *genotypes* (the genetic constitution received from one's parents) underlying the phenotype of mental retardation are many. It is also important to remember that the genotype is a set of potentialities and not a set of predetermined characteristics (Kaplan 1971).

Chromosomes

In living cells the central portion is called the *nucleus*. It contains all the genetic material, called the *chromatin*. During the complex process by which randomly donated genes from the parents join at conception, the chromatin aligns itself into threadlike bodies called *chromosomes*. In the normal body cells of the child, which will develop according to the genetic information in the chromosomes, there will be a total of 46 chromosomes, 23 from each parent. Each pair carries unique information.

Twenty-two of the chromosome pairs are called *autosomes*, with each one duplicated. There is one pair of sex chromosomes, which is duplicated in the female (XX) but not in the male (XY). Figure 4.1 on page 132 shows the pairs of chromosomes found in the nucleus of a normal cell; the photograph is called a *karyotype*. The pairs of chromosomes may be referred to by the numbers[1] 1–22, from the largest to the smallest, with the twenty-third pair being designated as duplicates in the female (XX) but not in the male (XY).

Within the chromosomes are genes that contain the chemical codes necessary to direct cell functions such as protein synthesis. Genes opposite each other on the paired chromosomes may carry the same information for a certain trait, in which case they are referred to as *homozygous*. If the genes at the same location on the two chromosomes differ in terms of the information for a given trait, they are referred to as *heterozygous*.

Dominant and Recessive Genes

In the heterozygous situation, when the aligned genes indicate a different trait (color of eyes, for example), only one trait will be manifested. It is described as *dominant*, since one gene dominates the other. A dominant

---

[1]With technical advances, the particles that comprise the chromosome can be stained with dyes and photographed. Hence it has become possible to identify specific chromosomes by number. Previously the chromosomes were identified by groups (before banding procedures enabled the precise differentiation now possible) and were designated by letters A through G. The reader may encounter sources where the chromosomes are referred to by letter designations instead of numbers.

gene determines the phenotype no matter what its partner is. Other genes are called *recessive*. A recessive gene donated by one parent will not determine the phenotype unless it is matched by a recessive gene from the other parent at the same location on the paired chromosome. Hence recessive genes have less chance of being manifested.

There can be several genotypes that result in a similar phenotype. If both parents contribute various combinations of dominant and recessive genes that might cause conditions involving mental retardation, what are the probabilities that the offspring will be affected? Figure 4.2 shows the child's chances of inheriting a disorder from one parent, in the case of dominant genes, or from both parents, in the case of recessive genes. If one parent possesses the trait and it is dominant, there is a 50 percent risk that each child will manifest the defect. In recessive traits, if both parents carry the harmful gene, for each child born there is a 25 percent chance that that child will manifest the defect, a 25 percent chance that the child will not inherit the gene in any form, and a 50 percent chance that the child will receive a single defective gene and become a carrier of the condition but will not manifest it.

Autosomal dominant traits are those carried on the autosomes as dominant genes and therefore manifested in one or perhaps both parents. Cases in which autosomal dominant traits determine conditions involving mental retardation are relatively uncommon. Persons affected with the severe conditions caused by dominant traits usually die before childbearing age or are so severely afflicted that they do not reproduce.[2]

Autosomal recessive traits—in which neither parent manifests the trait but both carry it recessively—seem to be more common as causes of mental retardation than dominant autosomal traits, although their incidence of manifestation (both parents contribute the recessive gene) is estimated to be less than 1 in 10,000. Since both parents must carry genes for the recessive trait before the offspring can be affected, there has been much research interest in the detection of carriers. Such research has two goals: to identify and inform the carrier parents of the probabilities of their children's being affected and to detect affected fetuses early in gestation. Although many of the recessive gene traits are innocuous (e.g., blue eyes), a variety of conditions involving mental retardation have etiologies described as autosomal recessive (Grossman 1973).[3]

---

[2] Several cases where autosomal dominant traits result in mental retardation include Huntington's chorea, tuberous sclerosis, myotonic muscular dystrophy, and craniofacial dysostosis. The interested reader may want to consult a text that goes into more detail on specific conditions, such as these, that exemplify autosomal dominant traits.

[3] Conditions associated with mental retardation transmitted by means of autosomal recessive genes include hyperglycinenemia, infantile cystinosis (Lignac-Fanconi syndrome), maple syrup urine disease, galactosemia, Tay-Sachs disease, Hurler's disease, Pompe's disease, Marquio's syndrome, and metachromatic leukodystrophy. The reader can consult other sources for a detailed discussion of these conditions.

FIGURE 4.2 How Dominant and Recessive Inheritance Work

Dominant Inheritance

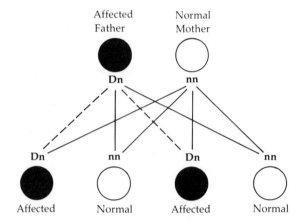

Each child's chances of inheriting either the **D** (dominant faulty gene) or the **n** (normal gene) from the affected parent are 50%.

Recessive Inheritance

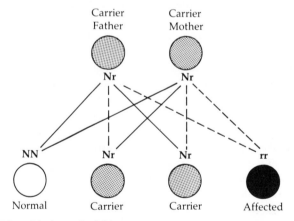

The odds for each child are:
    a 25% risk of inheriting a "double dose" of **r** (recessive faulty gene) genes that may cause a serious birth defect
    a 25% chance of inheriting two **N**s (normal genes), thus being unaffected
    a 50% chance of being a carrier like both parents

Sex-linked Chromosomes

In autosomal dominant and recessive conditions resulting from the matching of genes on the first 22 chromosomes, it makes no difference which parent donates which genes. But the sex of the transmitting parent and of the child is significantly related to outcomes affected by the twenty-third pair, the *sex chromosomes*. The sex chromosomes determine the sex of the child: the mother always contributes an *X*; however, the father may contribute an *X* or a *Y*, resulting in either an *XX* (female) combination or an *XY* (male) combination. The *Y* chromosome is essentially barren of genes, with its principal function being the establishment of the sex of the child; the *X* chromosome carries other genetic information in addition to the sex trait.

Genetic pairing on the sex chromosomes poses a greater risk for male offspring than for female. For a daughter, dominant and recessive conditions follow the same laws of inheritance as they do on the other 22 chromosome pairs. Since a female has two sex chromosomes with a full complement of genes, a recessive gene she inherits from one parent will be manifested only if she inherits a matching recessive gene from the other parent. This is not true for a male. If he inherits a defective gene from the mother (i.e., on the *X* chromosome), it will be manifested since the *Y* chromosome with which it is paired is barren of genes and has nothing to counteract the effect of the trait. The two *X* chromosomes tend to protect the female from forms of mental retardation carried on the sex chromosome;[4] she will only manifest recessive sex-linked traits if both parents are carriers, an uncommon situation. Sex-linked conditions are therefore found far more often in males than in females. For instance, colorblindness, which is transmitted on a sex-linked basis, is approximately sixteen times as common in males as in females.

Figure 4.3 illustrates how sex-linked inheritance works and shows the probabilities of an offspring's being affected. Notice that the example is for a recessive trait and that the odds differ according to the sex of the offspring.

Mutation

Occasionally, new forms of specific genes appear; these new forms are called *mutant genes*. They may be caused by factors such as radiation, viruses,

---

[4] Among the conditions associated with mental retardation transmitted according to sex-linked inheritance are Duchenne's muscular dystrophy, Renpenning syndrome, Lesch-Nyhan syndrome, and Hunter's syndrome. There are some conditions referred to as *sex-limited conditions*, in which the abnormal trait is found on the autosomes, but the phenotype differs between the sexes.

FIGURE 4.3   How Sex-linked Inheritance Works

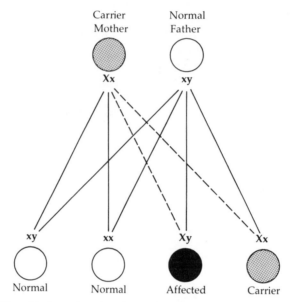

The odds for each *male* child are:
   a 50% risk of inheriting the faulty **X** and the disorder
   a 50% chance of inheriting normal **x** and **y** chromosomes
The odds for each *female* child are:
   a 50% risk of inheriting one faulty **X**, to be a carrier
   like the mother
   a 50% chance of inheriting no faulty gene

and some chemicals. For instance, LSD has been reported in some studies to have caused mutations, but other studies have failed to replicate these findings. Such factors may alter the genetic code before conception occurs or early in embryonic development. Since these mutant genes may be dominant or recessive, they follow the normal laws of inheritance.

Aberrant Chromosomes.   Aberrant chromosomes are those with abnormal numbers or structures. Aberrations may involve either the autosomes or the sex chromosomes. One of the most common aberrations is called *trisomy*. It occurs when improper cell division results in three matching chromosomes instead of the normal two. Down's syndrome, for instance, is known as *trisomy 21*, since a person with the condition invariably has three of the twenty-first chromosomes. Figure 4.4 on page 132 shows the karyotype of a person with Down's syndrome; contrast this with the normal chromosomal alignment shown in Figure 4.1. There are three ways in which aberrant chromosomes may develop: *meiotic nondisjunction, translocation,* and *mosaicism.*

Nondisjunction. Chromosomal aberrations can happen even before conception. When the sperm cell or egg is being formed there can be an error in its chromosomal distribution. Sometimes when the sex cell is dividing by the process referred to as *meiosis,* the chromosomes are not equally divided between the two new cells being formed. One of the new cells gets an extra complement of whatever chromosome did not divide evenly. The resultant body cells that will develop in the offspring will all have an excess of that chromosome. Figure 4.5 shows the process whereby nondisjunction in the formation of an egg, which unites with a normal sperm, leads to an offspring with trisomy 21.

Translocation. In another possible chromosomal abnormality, all or part of one chromosome may mistakenly attach itself to another chromosome—either its partner or one of a different pair. This can happen to any chromosome, but the most common ones involved are groups 13–15 and 21–22 since these chromosomes are constricted near the end rather than in the middle (see Figure 4.1). In approximately one-third of the cases of translocation, one parent is a genetically balanced carrier[5] of the translocation, as opposed to situations where the error occurs in the formation of the egg or sperm or in the first cell division after conception. The balanced carrier has an excess amount of chromosome 21; i.e., one set of chromosomes has a double dose of chromosome 21. Through one of these three processes the offspring has three of chromosome 21 instead of the normal pair.

Mosaicism. The third kind of chromosomal abnormality occurs after conception, and the genotype is more complex than in the other two. As the fertilized egg begins to divide, an error occurs in the chromosome distribution. A nondisjunction of one of the chromosomes occurs, with one of the new cells receiving three of the chromosomes of that number and the other receiving only one of them. The latter cell dies off, leaving only the cell with trisomy to continue dividing. If this error occurs on the first cell division, all body cells will have trisomy for that chromosome number, and the phenotype will resemble cases where the error occurred before conception. However, if the first cell division is normal, and the faulty distribution occurs during the second division, then two of the new cells will be normal. But in the two new cells resulting from the abnormal split, one cell has

---

[5] A parent who carries some abnormal gene pattern; the abnormality is not manifested in the parent.

**FIGURE 4.5   How Faulty Chromosome Distribution
During Meiosis (Nondisjunction) Results in a Child
with Down's Syndrome**

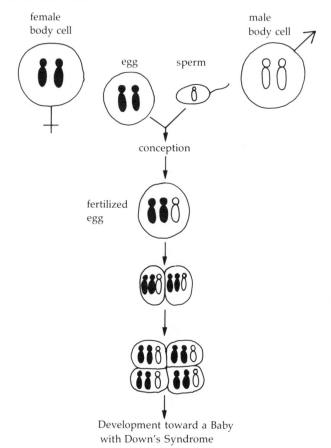

faulty chromosome distribution*

female
body cell

male
body cell

egg   sperm

conception

fertilized
egg

Development toward a Baby
with Down's Syndrome

*can also occur in the development of the sperm

trisomy and the other has *monosomy* (only one chromosome of a certain number). The monosomy cell dies off leaving three cells—two normal ones and one with trisomy. Hence the body cells of the mosaic individual vary; some are normal, with 46 chromosomes, and others have 47 chromosomes. The consequence of this is somewhat unusual. Since determination of which cells will become what parts of the body (such as organs) occurs very early in development, the specific phenotypic characteristics that show up will depend on which parts of the body got the cells with trisomy. Since the presence of abnormal cells is not consistent throughout the body, when chromosome studies are made of possible mosaic individuals, various tissues should be sampled. Skin is reported to have a greater proportion of these abnormal cells than other tissues, but a skin sample gives no clue to whether the condition exists somewhere else (Bunker, Morris, Lynch, Mickey, Roderick, Van Pelt, & Fornot 1972).

SOME GENETICALLY TRANSMITTED DEFECTS

As we have seen, genetically carried defects can show up for a number of reasons: mutations, defective genes on the sex chromosomes, abnormalities in chromosome duplication during cell division, and matching of recessive traits in two parents who are carriers. The last two situations account for most cases of genetically based mental retardation, so we will examine in greater detail their effects on the intricate process of human development. As an example of chromosomal aberration we will look at what happens in Down's syndrome; as examples of recessive matching we will look at PKU and a few other recessive conditions.

Down's Syndrome

Down's syndrome, formerly often called *mongolism,* was one of the first forms of retardation to be differentiated from cretinism (see Chapter 1). The physician Langdon Down first distinguished the condition in 1866. Down's syndrome will be used to exemplify mental retardation resulting from chromosomal aberrations. We should note, however, that there are many other such conditions that result in mental retardation. They are much rarer than Down's syndrome, however, so you are less likely to encounter them.[6]

Of all the conditions associated with mental retardation, Down's syndrome is probably the most familiar to the lay public. It is the cause of approximately 10 percent of all cases of moderate and severe mental retardation. Interestingly, we have recently seen a decline in the incidence and an increase in the prevalence of Down's syndrome. Formerly, the incidence was estimated to be 1 per 600 live births, but recent evidence sets the incidence at closer to 1 per 900 live births (Hansen 1978; Stein & Susser 1977).

---

[6] Cases of chromosomal aberrations that result in mental retardation are considered in some detail in several sources, including Bergsma (1973) and Smith (1970), which the interested reader should consult. Other than trisomy 21, the two that occur most often in mental retardation are trisomy 18 and trisomy 13.

The reduction in incidence is probably due to a decline in birth rate among older women, the development of more reliable birth control techniques, improved prenatal diagnosis, and the availability of therapeutic abortion. During the same period, medical advances have improved the chances that affected children will survive and increase their life expectancy. These advances have resulted in higher prevalence rates.

The Known Causes. All children with the phenotype of Down's syndrome possess extra genetic material in the twenty-first chromosome. This condition, known as *trisomy 21*, is most commonly the result of nondisjunction, an error in the distribution of chromosomes when the sperm or the egg is being formed. Translocation and mosaicism, two other cytogenetic aberrations, also result in the pathology of Down's syndrome, but they account for far fewer cases.

In Down's syndrome caused by translocation, the location of a chromosome is in the wrong place. In such cases maternal age is not a factor, as it is in nondisjunction. But while the incidence of Down's syndrome caused by translocation is relatively low, the risk of having a Down's syndrome offspring if one or both parents is a balanced translocation carrier is considerably greater than in other chromosomal aberrations. The exact probabilities vary according to which chromosome groups are involved. Table 4.1

TABLE 4.1 Recurrence Risks of Types of Translocation Down's Syndrome

Down's Syndrome Child's Karyotype	Parents' Karyotype		Risk per Pregnancy	
	Father	Mother	Down's Syndrome %	Carrier %
D/G translocation involving chromosomes 13–15 and 21	carrier	normal	2	60
	normal	carrier	30	33
	normal	normal	low	low
G/G translocation involving chromosomes 21/22	carrier	normal	low	50
	normal	carrier	low	11
21/21	carrier	normal	100	0
G/G translocation	normal	normal	low	low

shows the probabilities of having a Down's syndrome offspring or a carrier, depending on which chromosome is involved with chromosome 21 in the translocation. In cases where the father is the carrier, the risk is considerably lower than the 33 percent theoretical risk, probably because the sperm carrying the defect is unlikely to fertilize the egg. Also notable is the rarer case where the translocation involves only the chromosome 21 pair ($^{21}/_{21}$), in which case the probabilities for subsequent offspring having Down's syndrome are 100 percent.

The third kind of Down's syndrome, the mosaic form, occurs when trisomy happens after cells have begun to multiply, giving some cells the normal 46 chromosomes and some 47 because of trisomy. The physical characteristics of a mosaic Down's individual will depend on which cells have the trisomy 21. As a result, the features of mosaic Down's individuals vary; often they are not as striking as the cases resulting from nondisjunction or translocation. In addition, the degree of mental retardation they suffer is less than that encountered in the former cases.

In overall population terms, the incidence of Down's syndrome of a mosaic type is only 1 in 3000. But the risk of recurrence is greater than for the other genotypes. When the mother has a mosaic karyotype, the chances of recurrence are 1 in 10. Kirman (1970b) has observed that often mothers with mosaic karyotypes were themselves born to mothers of advanced age.

Parental Age.   For some time we have known that older women are more likely to give birth to a Down's syndrome baby than younger women. Miller and Erbe (1978) reported that the incidence of Down's syndrome births among twenty-year-old women is 1 in 2000, whereas for women over forty-five the incidence is 1 in 20. Of course, women under thirty-five bear far more children than those over thirty-five, so the vast majority of Down's syndrome babies are born to women under thirty-five. Nevertheless, the risk is far higher for older women. Table 4.2, which summarizes several large-scale investigations, clearly demonstrates the relationship between maternal age and risk. In the United States during the last thirty years, there has been a marked reduction in the number of women over age thirty-five choosing to have babies (Stein & Susser 1977). In addition, Hansen (1978) reported that women over age 35 terminated their pregnancies more frequently than did younger women. These trends have reduced the number of Down's syndrome children born to this age group (Abroms & Bennett 1980). Hansen (1978), examining the effect of the 1970 liberalization of abortion laws in New York on the birth rate of Down's syndrome children, noted a reduction of 20 percent between 1971 and 1975. Although this change in legislation concerning abortion corresponded to the decline in the number of Down's syndrome children being born, one cannot rule out the possibility that birth control, attitudes toward childbearing, and other changes noted at the beginning of this section contributed to the decline.

TABLE 4.2 Maternal Age-Specific Incidence of Down's Syndrome Births in Prospective Studies of 120,000 Pregnancies (Number of Cases/Number of Live Births)

Study Population	⩽ 19	20–24	25–29	30–34	35–39	40–44	⩾ 45
WHO* study, Czechoslovakia	2/2281	8/8493	5/5291	4/2619	2/972	3/200	1/14
WHO study, Northern Ireland	1/1812	2/8943	3/7455	5/4742	7/3011	5/1080	4/91
Jerusalem Perinatal Study	2/1101	6/6522	8/7465	12/5543	11/2708	12/773	2/136
Coll. Perinatal Project, white	1/4029	11/8870	4/5091	5/2624	4/1340	4/342	0/16
Coll. Perinatal Project, black	3/6859	4/7956	2/4523	4/2531	6/1291	10/321	1/12
Average incidence†	0.56	0.76	0.74	1.66	3.22	12.52	29.74

*World Health Organization.
†Per 1000 live births.

From H. Hansen, "Decline of Down's syndrome after abortion reform in New York State," *American Journal of Mental Deficiency*, 1978, 83, 185–188.

The increased risk to older women has long been attributed to the greater risk of nondisjunction in aging ova. Another factor currently being examined is the increased risk resulting from exposure to environmental hazards, particularly radiation. Stein and Susser (1977) reviewed investigations conducted in Baltimore, London, and Winnipeg that demonstrated that increased exposure to radiation raised the chances that a woman would bear a Down's syndrome baby. The risk was even higher in older women in all three studies. The London study was particularly noteworthy in that it showed an increased risk to women exposed to radiation more than ten years before their babies were conceived.

Traditionally, the relationship between maternal age and Down's syndrome has been emphasized, but paternal age has also been implicated recently. It is estimated that the extra chromosome originates in the sperm between 20 and 30 percent of the time. Abroms and Bennett (1980) reported that taking paternal age into account improves investigators' ability to predict the occurrence of Down's syndrome independent of maternal age. Thus far, however, the evidence supports this relationship primarily in fathers aged fifty to fifty-five. The relationship may exist in younger fathers, but we won't know for certain until more research has been completed.

It is of interest to note that relatively few trisomy conceptions are carried full-term and delivered. Figure 4.6 shows that somewhere between 60 and 67 percent of all trisomy 21 conceptions are spontaneously aborted. In this

FIGURE 4.6   Survival Model for Down's Syndrome: Conception through Childhood

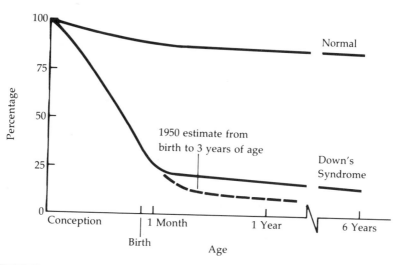

From Z. A. Stein and M. Susser, "Recent trends in Down's syndrome," in P. Mittler, ed., *Research to practice in mental retardation: Biomedical aspects,* Vol. III (Baltimore: University Park Press, 1977, p. 52). Reprinted with the permission of the International Association for the Scientific Study of Mental Deficiency.

respect, there are no apparent differences between older and younger women (Stein & Susser 1977).

Physical Characteristics.   You can usually identify a Down's syndrome child just by appearance alone, for the extra copy of chromosome 21 has a marked effect on physical features. Down's children are quite similar to one another in appearance, usually to the extent that differences in their physical symptoms are not noticed. The number and nature of physical symptoms are apparently not related to the degree of retardation.

The most apparent physical characteristics of Down's syndrome involve the face; it has a flat appearance because the nose is small and has a low bridge. Most obvious are the eyes of the Down's individual; they have an upward slant with folds of skin at the inner corner of the eye (called the *epicanthic folds*). The iris of the eye often has colored spots (called *Brushfield spots*). Visual problems—particularly refractive errors and crossed eyes—are common.

The back of the skull tends to be flat and the ears unusually small, especially the lobes. In addition, the upper rim of the ear often folds over. The tongue often appears to protrude because the mouth is small and the roof of the mouth short. In addition, with increased age the surface of the tongue becomes furrowed. Dental abnormalities are common. The relatively small and unusually shaped teeth tend to erupt late and position themselves irregularly. Gums tend to become inflamed and to recede, and teeth are often lost. The hair of the Down's syndrome individual tends to be sparse, fine, and straight; its coloration tends to be fair compared to that of parents or siblings. The neck of a Down's syndrome individual is broad and quite short, with loose skin on the sides and back of the neck. The skin tends to be dry and mottled, with dermatological problems being prevalent.

Other characteristics are found on the hands and feet of persons afflicted with Down's syndrome. The hands tend to be small with the fingers short; the little finger is unusually short and curves inward instead of being straight. Across the palm of the hand there is usually a single crease (called a *simian crease*) instead of the normal two. A crease runs between the first and second toes, and the space between them is wider than normal. Finally, the muscle tone of the Down's child is noticeably poor in infancy, although it tends to improve with age.

Many of these characteristic features can be readily observed in Figure 4.7 on page 133, which shows a child with Down's syndrome. Since they are usually pronounced and noticeable, the characteristic physical symptoms make it easy to diagnose Down's syndrome, but they also increase the visibility of the child as different when he is seen in public. Because of the high visibility of Down's syndrome and because it accounts for the greatest number of cases of mental retardation in which a definite cause can be established, the stereotyped image of a mentally retarded person in the mind of the lay public is that of a person with Down's syndrome.

Health Problems. In addition to their distinctively different appearance, Down's syndrome children and adults have certain characteristic health problems. In some individuals there are congenital abnormalities of body organs, such as defects in the structure of the heart. Respiratory problems have been reported to be the primary cause of death; they are due in part to characteristic lung abnormalities (Crome & Stern 1972). Even when lung trouble is not severe, Down's syndrome individuals often are susceptible to upper respiratory infections.

Certain biochemical abnormalities have been found in Down's syndrome individuals. There are low serum calcium levels, low rates of vitamin A absorption, and low stores of vitamin B_6. The incidence of leukemia is relatively high (Conen & Erkman 1966; Kirman 1970b). And bone and nervous tissue defects that resemble defects reported in the offspring of animal mothers who were experimentally fed a diet deficient in fat-soluble vitamins have shown up in Down's patients (Sobel, Strazzulla, Sherman, Elkan, Morganstern, Marius, & Meisel 1958).

Along with all their other possible physical defects, Down's syndrome children have unusuallly small skulls and brains. However, no specific structural brain abnormalities have been identified (Olson & Shaw 1969).

Behavioral Characteristics. Developmentally, the gap between Down's syndrome and nonretarded children is negligible during the first year, but it gradually widens with age. By about age four or five, the rate of development of Down's syndrome children slows and the gaps become dramatically wider (Cornwell & Birch 1969; Lodge & Kleinfeld 1973; Zeaman & House 1962a).

Gibson (1978) observed that the development of Down's syndrome children is quite variable—they are not a homogeneous group in terms of learning, personality, or other behavioral dimensions. Gibson provides an extensive examination of the behavioral literature pertaining to Down's syndrome children, noting that failings in the research preclude definitive statements about similarities and differences between Down's syndrome children and nonretarded children or other retarded children who do not have Down's syndrome.

Attempts have been made to identify specific processes in learning in which Down's syndrome children differ from other retarded children. Those factors that are particularly weak in Down's children are:

1. tactile perception (Belmont 1971),
2. higher-level abstract reasoning and conceptual abilities,
3. auditory perception.

When they are working on tasks that are not highly abstract or conceptual, the deficit of Down's syndrome children appears less pronounced.

While chromosomal aberrations do place rather low limits on the potential development of Down's syndrome children, they are somewhat responsive to environmental variations. Seagoe (1964), Hunt (1967), and Butterfield (1961) have described the growth of specific Down's syndrome individuals who have been provided with extensive stimulation. In addition, attempts have been made to minimize the decline in the rate of development during the early years. We will not know how successful such efforts have been—in the long run as well as the short run—until they are evaluated more thoroughly.

The personality of Down's syndrome individuals has too often been characterized in stereotypic terms. Many observers have the impression that all Down's syndrome patients are alike, perhaps because they all look so much alike. All the people with Down's syndrome are often lumped together with such remarks as, "They are good mimics" and "They love to shake hands."

The most frequent generalization is that all Down's syndrome individuals are good-natured. They are often referred to as "happy puppy" or "Prince Charming." But hard evidence on the personality characteristics of the Down's syndrome individual is lacking. As Belmont (1971) noted, one can find evidence in the literature for and against the stereotype of an even disposition. There does appear to be less severe emotional disturbance among the Down's syndrome population than is found among individuals with the same degree of mental retardation but with differing etiologies. As in any other group of people, however, there is considerable inherent variability in the personalities of Down's syndrome individuals. Furthermore, their personalities are affected by the environmental influences they are exposed to. If parents deny that their children are retarded and push them to compete in areas for which they are ill equipped, the children very well may become aggressive and disagreeable. Compare the profiles of Brad and Carol.

Brad is a nine-year-old Down's syndrome boy who lives at home with his parents and younger sister. His condition was diagnosed immediately after birth; chromosome tests revealed that the Down's condition resulted from a nondisjunction situation. The parents sought out professional help from a mental retardation center at a major university near their home. There they learned what to expect from Brad in the way of development and were given suggestions regarding the kinds of experiences and stimulation that would promote his maximum development and yet not prove frustrating.

At the age of two-and-a-half, Brad was enrolled in a preschool program for mentally retarded children; he attended from eight to twelve in the morning, five days a week. In conjunction with the preschool program, the mothers were instructed in the nature of mental retardation and the development of mentally retarded children. They were also provided with concrete suggestions for dealing with problems that might arise in the neighborhood (such as teasing) and in the home (such as embarrassment of siblings and mastering developmental tasks like toilet training).

Now that he is nine, Brad is enrolled in a TMR program in the public school. His social acquaintances are mainly other mentally retarded children he encounters in school, but his parents have encouraged his playing in the neighborhood under the supervision of his mother. Although his parents say he can be stubborn, he is generally easy-going and pleasant and gets along with his sister, who is three years younger. His sister has already gone beyond Brad in terms of language, physical skills, and social skills. But she appears not to be embarrassed by her brother's condition and readily brings her friends in to play.

Brad's parents involve him in all family affairs, take him out to eat at restaurants, and generally treat him as normally as possible given his intellectual limitations. But it has been necessary to restrict some of their activities since Brad is prone to respiratory infections.

In general, however, the parents have accepted the situation and are attempting to provide a healthy environment for Brad and his sister. They are concerned about how to plan for Brad as an adult and his plight should anything happen to them.

———

Carol is an eighteen-year-old Down's syndrome girl who lives at home with her parents. She is an only child, born when her parents were in their late forties. For some reason the diagnosis of Down's syndrome was not made until Carol was over two years old, despite the fact that her features were clearly those of a Down's child. When told that their child had Down's syndrome, her parents would not accept the diagnosis, particularly her mother. She was convinced that her daughter was not mentally retarded and went to a succession of physicians seeking a different diagnosis.

Carol was kept at home, where she was protected by her mother. Other children were occasionally allowed to play with Carol in her home, but her mother berated them if they wanted to stop playing with her or got into arguments with her.

When it was time for Carol to begin school, her mother insisted that she be placed in a regular kindergarten class. Her request was granted after a long and heated exchange with school officials. At the end of kindergarten the school again recommended that Carol be placed in the program for the mentally retarded. Again her mother refused, and she was placed in the first grade, where she became the object of ridicule of the other children. The teacher objected to the fact that Carol was not toilet-trained because she had to deal with her wetting or soiling every day. Carol's mother insisted that these were merely "accidents" and that she was toilet-trained. She hired a tutor to work on reading with Carol, but little progress was made.

By the end of the first semester Carol's mother was at the elementary school daily. According to school officials she interfered constantly, catching the teacher during her breaks to discuss Carol and reprimanding children who she felt were picking on her daughter. One day Carol undressed in the restroom and came walking out in the hall naked. This prompted the principal to insist that she be withdrawn from school unless the parents would place her in the program for the mentally retarded if her psychological workup warranted such placement. Since that time Carol has been enrolled in programs for the TMR and EMR in six different elementary schools. She was enrolled in the EMR program on a trial basis when her mother argued that she was much brighter than the TMR children.

By now Carol is very aggressive; she taunts and teases other children constantly. Her behavior has made her a problem in the TMR program and she has had difficulty in any situation involving cooperative work or play. Her teachers are concerned that she will be unable to function in a sheltered workshop later on because she causes trouble so frequently.

The prognosis is poor for Carol. Her parents are approaching seventy and both are in poor health. It is very tempting to attribute her aggressive behavior to her mother's treatment, but regardless of the source, it will prove a problem in placing her in any setting where cooperation in living or working is required.

Prevention.   Although patient efforts by parents and educators can help children with Down's syndrome, another approach is to focus on preventing the problem. Sells and Bennett (1977) provide a broad review of developments in medicine that may help prevent mental retardation in some cases. One area in which advances have been made is prenatal diagnosis. Couples who have already had one Down's syndrome child should consult a genetic counselor for careful genetic studies to determine their risk of having another one. If they decide to have another child, new methods of prenatal diagnosis enable them to determine whether the pregnancy will produce a Down's syndrome baby or a normal one. This diagnosis, made early in the pregnancy, enables the couple to consider the option of abortion. *Amniocentesis,* a test of the fluid surrounding the fetus to check for many kinds of abnormalities, is now commonly offered to pregnant older women and to those who are known balanced carriers of a chromosomal translocation.

The number of Down's children born could also be reduced if women in their childbearing years avoided radiation. Women who have been exposed to infectious hepatitis may also prove to be high risks, as the virus causing infectious hepatitis has been reported to cause chromosomal abnormalities in human tissue. In Australia, variations in the incidence of Down's syndrome have been found to correspond to the incidence of viral hepatitis.

Finally, trends mentioned earlier, such as birth control techniques, reduced frequency of childbearing by older women, and liberalization of abortion laws, coupled with the advances in prenatal diagnosis, offer some promise of reducing the incidence of Down's syndrome.

Phenylketonuria (PKU)

Although Down's syndrome has long been recognized, the discovery of phenylketonuria (PKU) as a cause of mental retardation happened relatively recently. In 1934 a mother of two children brought her retarded children to Dr. Asbjörn Folling, a Norwegian physician, for a diagnosis. The mother reported that there was a peculiar odor, musty or haylike, that clung to the two children constantly. During routine tests Dr. Folling took a urine specimen and found that when he added ferric chloride, the solution turned green instead of the usual red-brown color. Dr. Folling hypothesized that the problem involved a disturbance in the metabolism of the amino acid phenylalanine and that this abnormality was causing the mental retardation apparent in the children. To determine whether the metabolic disorder was in fact causing the mental retardation, Dr. Folling surveyed the patients in a large nursing home and a local school for the mentally retarded. He found eight more individuals who had the same symptoms.

The article Folling published about his discovery fostered interest in mental retardation among physicians and scientists who previously had not been very interested in retardation. In the research that followed, there were several attempts to establish the prevalence of PKU among institutionalized retarded persons and to estimate its prevalence in newborn infants.

We now have proof that the basic inherited problem in PKU is a deficiency of liver phenylalanine hydroxylase, an enzyme necessary to metabolize phenylalanine to tyrosine. Phenylalanine is an amino acid found in dietary sources of protein such as milk. Because it cannot be metabolized properly, phenylalanine builds up in the blood. These high serum levels of phenylalanine are toxic to the brain, causing damage in much the same way as poisons. When the condition is not controlled, PKU seems to cause abnormalities in the nerve cells of the brain (Berman 1971; Woolf 1970).

The phenotype of individuals with PKU varies widely from normal appearance and IQ in the normal range to various degrees of mental retar-

FIGURE 4.1
Chromosomes of a
Normal Male

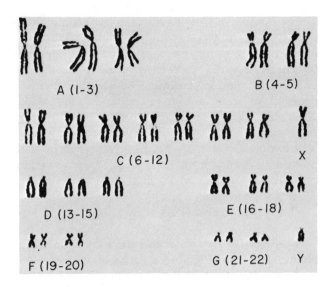

FIGURE 4.4
Chromosomes of a
Down's Syndrome
Male (Trisomy 21)

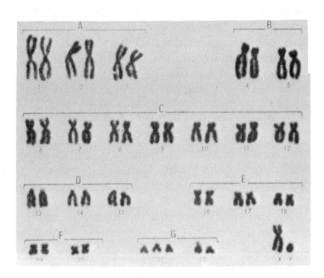

FIGURE 4.7
Jennifer, a Down's
Syndrome Child

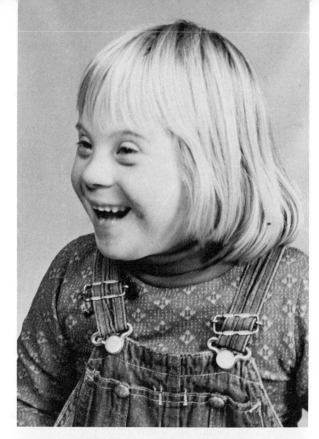

FIGURE 4.9
This three-year-old
is a fetal alcohol
syndrome child.
Some of the
characteristics of
the condition that
she manifests are
mental deficiency
(IQ in the 60s),
growth deficiency,
small eye slits, and
a small mid-face.

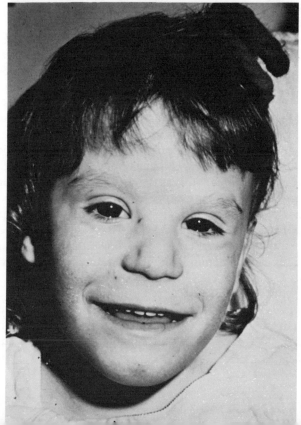

dation accompanied by eczema, reddish hair, and a mousey odor to the urine. In some cases PKU patients have seizures, vomiting, hyperkinesis (overactive behavior), head-banging, and behavior disorders.

PKU is transmitted genetically as an autosomal recessive trait (see Figure 4.2 for how inheritance of the condition works). Note that both parents must be carriers of the condition in order for the offspring to manifest PKU. Mothers with PKU provide an intrauterine environment containing high levels of phenylalanine and ketones, which result in early and severe mental retardation for their offspring. However, mothers who are PKU *carriers* have children who are normal at birth, with the damage coming after they are born as a result of their own metabolic disorder.

Hsia (1971) has pointed out that some children whose mothers have PKU are retarded but do not have PKU. To further confuse things, there are two forms of PKU—one is the more common form we have referred to so far, and the other is called *hyperphenylalaninemia without phenylketonuria* or *time-variable phenylalaninemia*. This second, less common form occurs as a mutation that produces an enzyme deficiency similar to the one responsible for PKU. Both kinds are transmitted as simple recessive traits, but they have different effects on phenylalanine levels in the blood. Children without PKU, but whose mothers have hyperphenylalaninemia, seem to have more severe symptoms than those with PKU. In such cases, mental retardation, microcephaly (small skull circumference), and congenital defects are frequently found.

Physical and Behavioral Characteristics. If PKU goes untreated, mental retardation is the result in the vast majority of cases. Knox (1972) reported that very few of these persons achieve IQs above 50, and most score well below that. Earlier, Lyman (1963) estimated that 64 percent of PKU individuals who went untreated score in the IQ 0–20 range, 23 percent in the 21–40 range, 10 percent in the 41–60 range, 2 percent in the 61–80 range, and 1 percent in the 81–100 range. There have been cases of untreated PKU where the individual was not mentally retarded, but these are rare.

In addition to the characteristic low IQ, certain clinical signs have been frequently noted in cases of untreated PKU. Wright and Tarjan (1957) grouped these signs into mental defects, neuromuscular abnormalities, behavioral deviations, and somatic changes. Factors present in a sizable proportion of cases were low IQ, seizures, and behavioral deviations such as emotional instability, aggressiveness, temper tantrums, and schizophrenic outbursts. In general, Wright and Tarjan wrote, "None could be described as friendly, placid, or happy" (1957, p. 407).

Physically, PKU children often have fair skin (since the tyrosine they are unable to make is important in the formation of skin pigmentation), blond hair, and blue eyes. They may have eczema of the skin and underdeveloped tooth enamel. In addition, microcephaly is reported in close to 50 percent of the cases.

Detection.   Although the physical signs of PKU are often subtle, the disorder must be detected early—as untreated PKU usually results in mental retardation. If it is detected early, a dietary treatment can be instituted to limit the damage. Although urine testing with ferric chloride was used initially in the diagnosis of PKU, a blood inhibition assay test developed by Guthrie has proven to be more reliable. This test, which is currently in use, involves drawing a blood sample from the heel of the child and culturing it. Debate is continuing about what level of phenylalanine in the blood should be considered a positive screening result (Hansen 1977; Sells & Bennett 1977). Hansen (1977) reported on two large-scale projects in which 86 and 94 percent of the infants who had positive screening tests were found not to have PKU upon further testing. Proper timing of the blood test is critical. The blood test requires that the child spend at least 24 hours during roughly the third or fourth postnatal day on a diet of protein. Many babies have been discharged from the hospital by this time. The rate at which blood phenylalanine levels elevate appears to be slower in females than in males, which increases the risk of false negative results. False positive results are most common among infants with low birth weight and among those of nonwhite ethnic origin (Hansen 1977).

To determine accurately whether a child has PKU, the diagnostic procedure must be repeated under certain circumstances: during the neonatal period with children who are nonwhite, have low birth weight, or are female; if the child has had insufficient time to build up phenylalanine levels in the blood; when a child is breast-fed, since the protein content of the milk is very low and might escape detection; and under certain other circumstances. Follow-up tests are suggested at six weeks or six months to determine whether a false negative reading was obtained on the initial test. Today many states require initial testing of all newborns, but parents may have to request follow-up tests by their pediatrician.

Tests may reveal that certain individuals are only carriers of PKU. While they will be unaffected by the condition, this information will be an important warning of possible problems in their offspring if their mates are also carriers of PKU. Siblings of PKU children can even be tested to determine whether they are carriers. Tests to detect carriers have been developed by Knox and Hsia.

Incidence.   As mass screening of infants for PKU has increased, so have estimates of the incidence of PKU in the general population. For example, in 1939 Jervis estimated that 1 in every 25,000 newborns was affected. Later, however, he dropped the estimate to 1 in 12,500. A seven-state study conducted by Hsia in 1971 reported an incidence of 1 in 20,000, with an incidence of variant conditions of 1 in 50,000; if the classic and variant PKU conditions are lumped together, the incidence is approximately 1 in 13,000. Most current sources report an incidence somewhere between 1 in 13,000 and 1 in 20,000.

Hsia notes that the incidence of PKU varies in different ethnic groups, an observation that brings into question the cost of screening all newborns. PKU is highest among whites: Ireland and eastern Scotland have very high rates, and high rates are reported in West Germany, Canada, Israel, and the United States. Ashkenazi Jews, however, have an extremely low incidence. While he questions the need for PKU screening among such low-risk populations, Hsia suggests that multiple testing for several of the 50 known harmful genetic defects of metabolism would be financially and medically beneficial (Hsia 1971, p. 112).

Treatment.   In spite of the controversy regarding screening procedures, PKU should be detected and treatment begun as early as possible. The prognosis with early treatment is very encouraging. The treatment consists of a diet of a formula low in phenylalanine along with solid food and vitamin supplements. By limiting the intake of phenylalanine to the amount essential for cell growth and replacement, it is hoped that phenylalanine buildup that results in progressively more severe symptoms will be prevented. Information on the effectiveness of dietary treatment continues to accumulate. Increasingly, the data suggest that the need for phenylalanine varies during growth and development (Kirman 1971). Holtzman, Welcher, and Mellits (1975) reported that the excessive restriction of phenylalanine intake impairs normal growth; they conclude that intermediate blood phenylalanine levels should be maintained. Another problem is that infection and breaks in diet can alter phenylalanine levels between medical checkups. Careful monitoring of blood levels of phenylalanine is therefore essential. A diet restricted too severely may in itself result in retarded growth and possible mental retardation (Berman 1971, p. 118; Woolf 1970, p. 34).

Despite the dangers, a low-phenylalanine diet may have dramatic results. Woolf reports alleviation of behavior problems within 48 to 72 hours after a special diet is started. He reports calmness in hyperkinetic children, improved attention span, greater alertness, and greater responsiveness (Woolf 1970, p. 35).

The overall effectiveness of the dietary treatment is still being evaluated. Dobson, Kushida, Williamson, and Friedman (1976) found that four- to six-year-old children with treated PKU had IQs 5 points lower than those of their unaffected siblings. The treated PKU children achieved a mean IQ of 94. Although this is far superior to the typical progress of untreated PKU children, who are usually severely retarded, it appears that the treatment minimizes damage rather than leading to normal development. If the special diet is initiated after damage has been done, there are still beneficial effects: eczema tends to clear up, seizures are reduced, and behavior and motor performance are improved (Anderson, Siegel, Tellegan, & Fisch 1968; Knox 1972).

There is some disagreement in the literature regarding whether or not PKU patients can eventually go off the low-phenylalanine diet. Holtzman et al. (1975) present some evidence that school children who discontinued the diet were not affected cognitively, but Berry, Butcher, Brunner, Bray, Hunt, and Wharton (1977) report that ending dietary control raised phenylalanine levels to high levels, which brought about behavioral changes that interfered with school learning. Hence, the conservative position seems to recommend that the diet be continued throughout the school years. Another problem with dropping the diet concerns PKU women of childbearing age. Although treated PKU women have normal or near-normal intelligence, Sells and Bennett (1977) report that the vast majority of children born to these women will be mentally retarded even though the children won't have PKU. This is because the high phenylalanine concentration and metabolites in the blood of the mother no longer on the diet damage the brain of the fetus. To avert this problem, these women must be reidentified and placed on the diet again.

Other Recessive Traits

PKU is only one of the ways in which an inherited enzyme deficiency may interfere with total body function, causing mental retardation as well as other problems. There are many other metabolic disorders caused by recessive genes. Some, such as Tay-Sachs disease, are inevitably fatal; others, such as hypoglycemia, can be treated if they are properly diagnosed.

Some of these other recessive traits are found among individuals with a common background. When the group of possible marriage partners is small, there is an increased likelihood that defective traits will be transmitted to successive generations. One such condition, Tay-Sachs disease, is peculiar to the Ashkenazi Jews, a small group from a specific area of eastern Europe. Many of them are carriers of a recessive genetic defect that causes improper lipid metabolism, degeneration of the brain, progressive deterioration of nervous tissue, and finally death. Carriers of the recessive gene can be identified, and massive screening programs have been conducted among the Ashkenazi Jewish population in various parts of this country. Although the risk of a Tay-Sachs baby is 1 out of 4 in each pregnancy if both parents are carriers, many couples will risk pregnancy anyway. The chances are 3 out of 4 that the baby will not have Tay-Sachs disease; if it does, amniocentesis will reveal the condition and therapeutic abortion can be considered.

If a newborn baby has hypoglycemia (a metabolic defect that keeps blood sugar levels abnormally low and therefore depresses brain functioning) possible causes include a number of recessive genetic traits. Among these are glycogen storage disease, glycogen synthetase deficiency, hereditary fructose intolerance, and galactosemia. Low blood sugar may also be found in infants with tyrosinemia and maple syrup urine disease (Cornblath 1967, p. 60). Since there are so many different possible causes, the physician has a tremendous responsibility for thorough testing in order to make an accurate diagnosis and properly treat a child with hypoglycemia.

PRENATAL ENVIRONMENTAL FACTORS

According to the National Foundation, March of Dimes (1975), mental retardation of prenatal origin is the most common of all birth defects. In 1974 it affected an estimated 1,170,000 individuals in the United States under the age of twenty. Some such conditions are not manifested until later in life, in which case a diagnosis cannot be made immediately following birth. For example, tuberous sclerosis is a late-appearing birth defect that does not manifest clinically detectable symptoms until the child is about three years of age.

Birth defects are not caused solely by genetic conditions. Many factors other than genetics can negatively influence the development of the fetus prior to birth, and some of them are preventable. Ongoing research is being done to study the relationship between specific factors in the prenatal environment and specific congenital abnormalities. At present, some prenatal environmental factors have been shown definitely to cause certain birth defects. Even more factors are suspected of causing birth defects, but research evidence is not available to confirm a precise cause-and-effect relationship. Nevertheless, we hope that, in order to provide children with an optimal opportunity for healthy development, women who are in the childbearing years will understand the importance of avoiding, whenever possible, any influence suspected of being detrimental to the fetus.[7]

In light of the rapidly accumulating evidence on possible sources of danger to the fetus, the most obvious preventive measure is to improve the quality of the pregnant woman's daily life. Often environmental factors have already had an adverse affect on the embryo before diagnosis of the pregnancy is made. At this point it is often too late to begin avoiding the factors suspected of causing or known to cause birth defects. Those factors that have been linked with mental retardation include inadequate nutrition, maternal infections,[8] chemicals in the fetal environment, radiation and ultrasound, chronic maternal conditions, and blood incompatabilities.

---

[7] Precisely speaking, the embryo is the developing human in the first three months (trimester) of pregnancy; the fetus is the developing human from three months after conception to birth. In this text the word *fetus* is used to refer to the developing unborn child in general, at any stage. When our meaning is limited to the first trimester of pregnancy only, the word *embryo* is used.

[8] Some of those maternal infections related to mental retardation in the offspring are *Herpesvirus hominis*, the flu, *Coxsackievirus* group B, rubella, infectious hepatitis, herpes zoster, and poliomyelitis. While these do not appear to cause congenital malformations, they can result in abortions and stillbirths (Sever 1970).

Prenatal Nutrition

The importance of nutrition at virtually every stage of development is now recognized. Adequate nutrition is especially important to women during their developmental years and during pregnancies, for it has a profound effect on the prenatal development of their children. But although we will focus in this section on the importance of nutrition during pregnancy, this is not the only period when people should pay attention to what they eat. Poor nutrition does not just mean starvation, although this is, in fact, a common condition for much of the world's population. People can be malnourished even if they have plenty to eat, because adequate caloric intake is not the same thing as good nutrition.

The mother's general eating habits, physical health, and genetic makeup will greatly influence fetal development. If she is to provide a healthy environment for the fetus, her diet must provide the essential nutrients for both herself and the fetus. Her body must be able to metabolize her diet into materials they can both use. The placenta must be properly implanted, healthy, and functioning properly if it is to transport nutrients and oxygen to the fetus. Furthermore, the placenta must produce necessary enzymes and hormones and transport carbon dioxide and other wastes from the fetus to the maternal circulation. If these conditions are not met, the oxygen and nutrients necessary for cell growth, differentiation, and maintenance are not likely to be delivered to the fetus and damage could result.

Richardson (1977) has noted the need for continuing research into the relationship between malnutrition and mental development. The results of research in this area are difficult to interpret because mental development is influenced by three closely related variables: nutrition, social setting, and biological circumstances. It is nearly impossible to attribute a problem in mental development to malnutrition alone. Richardson also reported that the critical growth spurt of the brain extends from the third trimester of pregnancy through the second year of life; it does not end in the sixth postnatal month, as was previously believed.

The importance of considering the interaction of nutritional and social variables was also stressed by Susser, Stein, and Rush (1977) and Chase and Crnic (1977). The Susser et al. (1977) research supports the concept that brain growth continues through two years of age. The possible primary and secondary effects of undernutrition on development and the psychological and environmental factors important to an understanding of impairments in cognitive functioning are portrayed in Figure 4.8.

Fetal Malnutrition from Other Maternal Causes. In some cases the fetus is unable to get the nutrition it needs no matter what the mother eats. Studies of placentas, for instance, have indicated that sometimes vascular insufficiency in the mother limits the blood supply to the fetus, thereby

FIGURE 4.8   Schematic Representation of the Interrelations
              between Primary Effects of Undernutrition,
              the External Environment, Psychological Factors,
              and Secondary Effects of Undernutrition

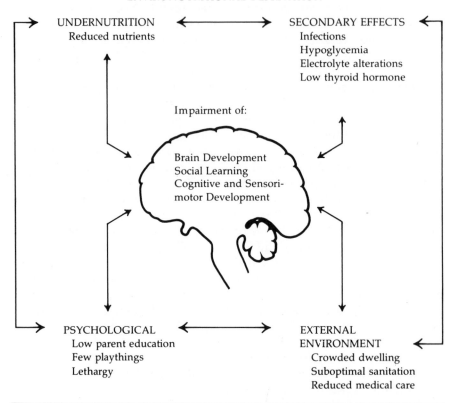

ENVIRONUTRITIONAL DEPRIVATION

UNDERNUTRITION   SECONDARY EFFECTS
Reduced nutrients   Infections
                                        Hypoglycemia
                                        Electrolyte alterations
                                        Low thyroid hormone

Impairment of:

Brain Development
Social Learning
Cognitive and Sensori-
motor Development

PSYCHOLOGICAL   EXTERNAL
Low parent education   ENVIRONMENT
Few playthings   Crowded dwelling
Lethargy   Suboptimal sanitation
                                        Reduced medical care

From H. P. Chase and L. S. Crnic, "Undernutrition and human brain development," in P. Mittler, ed., *Research to practice in mental retardation: Biomedical aspects*, Vol. III (Baltimore: University Park Press, 1977, p. 338). Reprinted with the permission of the International Association for the Scientific Study of Mental Deficiency.

depriving it of oxygen and nutrients. This may happen if the mother has toxemia (an abnormal level of toxic substances in the bloodstream), in which case the limited blood supply results in a small placenta, small fetal organs, and a low birth weight (Winick 1970).

Chronic maternal illnesses such as diabetes, anemia, thyroid deficiency, and hypertension may interfere with the nutritional status of the fetus.

Organ size and development are affected and the possibility of prematurity is increased. Prematurity due to maternal illness increases the risk of mental retardation to the infant. The specific problems of the premature infant include *hypoxia* (limited oxygen to the tissues), *anoxia* (total lack of oxygen), and *hypoglycemia* (low blood sugar). If a baby must be delivered surgically because of some maternal illness, it is likely to be immature. There is a risk of respiratory distress, resulting hypoxia, and a high incidence of *hyperbilirubinemia* (breakdown of red blood cells and release of a chemical, bilirubin, that may be toxic to the brain).

Infants carried by diabetic mothers are at a higher risk of dying before or soon after birth than are infants of nondiabetic mothers. In severely diabetic mothers, vascular changes limit nutritional exchange through the placenta. Infants are born either small for their gestational age or large and edematous (puffy and swollen with fluid). In addition, hypoglycemia is commonly noted in these infants. Whether the diabetic process causes impaired intelligence other than that associated with hypoglycemia is open to question; however, the prematurity, respiratory distress, and hypoglycemia that are common in babies born to mothers with chronic illnesses are certainly capable in themselves of causing neurological insults.

Prevention. Mental retardation due to malnutrition can often be prevented. Even in parts of the world where nutritionally adequate food and dietary supplements are available and people can afford them, social and cultural factors and uncaring attitudes may influence dietary habits to the extent that fetal deficiencies result. Although we sorely need further research on the complex nature of dietary habits, education should help to convince people to be more careful about what they eat. Research evidence may be used to educate the public as to the need for a lifetime of good nutrition, early and consistent medical care, supervision during pregnancy, and proper postnatal nutrition. The choices they personally make will influence not only themselves but also generations to come.

Good nutrition is important for optimal development. In many parts of the world, however, particularly in developing countries, people cannot meet even their minimal nutritional needs. Using data from many studies, Chase and Crnic (1977) made the following recommendations for improving conditions for children in impoverished countries:

1. Provide pregnant women with nutritional supplements—minerals, vitamins, protein, and sources of calories.
2. Provide nutritional supplements to lactating mothers. Postnatal nutrition is important to brain growth, which is rapid into the second year of life.

3. Encourage breast-feeding, particularly during the first six months of life when adequate nutrients are necessary for normal brain growth. This is particularly important in areas where adequate nutrition is not available or is beyond the means of the family.

4. Provide vegetable protein fortified with amino acids for pregnant and lactating mothers in countries where the need to obtain protein from vegetable sources is critical (in developing countries).

Alcohol

In the early 1970s, a fetal alcohol syndrome was described by Jones, Smith, Ulleland, and Streissguth (1973). Certain symptoms were found consistently among children born to chronically alcoholic women and the symptoms were definitely attributable to alcohol rather than other variables such as maternal nutrition, age, or race (Jones, Smith, & Streissguth 1974). One symptom of this syndrome is prenatal and postnatal growth deficiency. The linear growth rate of children with fetal alcohol syndrome is 65 percent that of normal children, and the weights of these children are 40 percent less than normal. Microcephaly is frequently present, even when the small stature of these children is considered. Recent evidence indicates that the IQs of these children tend to fall in the moderate to mild range of mental retardation. Some have IQs as high as 65, which is higher than was previously estimated. Other problems include fine motor dysfunction and distorted facial features such as a short nose, long upper lip, very thin lips, short eye openings, drooping eyelids, and a flat face (see Figure 4.9 on page 133). Fusion of the cervical vertebrae is common, as are curved digits, joint abnormalities, and fewer palmar creases than normal.

It is clear that alcohol freely crosses the human placenta (Waltman & Iniques 1972), but the means by which toxicity affects the fetus and the reasons for variations in susceptibility are not clear at present. There is, however, considerable evidence of some kind of cause-and-effect relationship. In one study (Jones & Smith 1974) a mother had 7 normal children before she became an alcoholic. Subsequently, she had 3 spontaneous abortions and 1 child who manifested the symptoms of fetal alcohol syndrome. The records of the Collaborative Perinatal Research Study contain case histories of 23 women who were chronic alcoholics (Jones et al. 1974). Of the children born to these women, 4 died in the perinatal period, 6 evidenced features of fetal alcohol syndrome, and the remainder had less severe physical problems and mental retardation.

Jones (1980) has summarized even more recent findings regarding fetal alcohol syndrome. He reported that cardiac defects occur in half of the affected persons. Respiratory distress is another common problem. The incidence of these symptoms is twice as high among chronic heavy drinkers as among moderate drinkers and nondrinkers, but the symptoms are not found consistently enough to justify being described as a syndrome (Ouellette, Rosett, Rosman, & Werner 1977). Jones (1980) also summarized recent retrospective studies conducted in Seattle, Boston, and Loma Linda, California, reporting that 40 percent of the offspring of chronically alcoholic women who continued to drink during pregnancy were victims of the syndrome. A Swedish study of female alcoholics found that 33 percent of their children exhibited symptoms of fetal alcohol syndrome, 33 percent demonstrated some of the symptoms before the age of two, and the remaining 33 percent were normal.

Although the influence of maternal alcoholism is not yet clearly understood, the evidence suggests that sexually active women of childbearing age should drink moderately. Women who are trying to conceive and pregnant women should not drink at all.

Air and Water Pollution

Air and water pollutants have been suspected of causing nervous system damage as well as genetic damage, cardiovascular problems, and cancer. Lead is one of the contaminants known to be deposited in the body over a period of years; it is known to cause neurological damage, including mental retardation, lethargy, listlessness, and seizures. In addition to inhaling airborne lead pollution, children have sometimes eaten lead-base paint chips. Other pollutants that affect the central nervous system are asbestos, chlorines, fluorides, nickel, and mercury. These often come from industrial sources, but people are sometimes exposed to them even in their own homes. Recently, for instance, reports have been published of severe poisoning of the fetus due to maternal inhalation of phenylmercury fumes from latex paints and lead fumes from lead-base paints during pregnancy.

Mercury, too, has recently been linked with fetal damage. In Iraq during 1972, wheat was contaminated with antifungal mercury compounds; when this wheat was eaten by pregnant women, the fetal blood levels of mercury were found to be equal to those of the others in all but one case. As an apparent result, severe brain damage was reported in several of the infants (Casarett & Doull 1975). Similar isolated incidents in which mercury-contaminated foodstuffs seemed to cause prenatal and postnatal brain damage have been reported. The neurological symptoms vary from severe to moderate and have included seizures, blindness, retardation, and death. The use of such compounds does increase the amount of food produced by protecting crops, but the very real possibility of food contamination poses a threat to the safety of consumers and their offspring.

Maternal Infections

The placenta often protects the fetus from the mother's diseases, but in some cases protection is ineffective. Prenatal viral infections sometimes cause fetal defects, including mental retardation. Three maternal infections that are important causes of fetal disease are rubella virus, *cytomegalovirus* (syphilis and toxoplasmosis), and *Herpesvirus hominis*, a viral infection that can infect the brain of the fetus or newborn, possibly causing permanent damage or death. The severity of fetal involvement depends on the stage of gestation when the fetus is affected, the severity of the maternal infection, and the type of infection. In some cases a viral infection may not cause severe symptoms in the mother, yet severe damage may result in the fetus. Such is the case with rubella virus.

Rubella. One of the most common maternal infections involving the fetus is rubella (German measles), a relatively mild form of measles that has very serious consequences for the infant whose mother is either exposed to it or who contracts it.

The disease may be extremely destructive to the fetus because its developing tissues are so susceptible and its immune system so immature. The ultimate effects of the infection depend on what tissues are involved. During the first trimester of the pregnancy, the virus damages the tissues of the newly developing organs—and it is during this period of gestation that the central nervous system is developing. The rubella virus may live in the fetus for months, resulting in the involvement of many developing tissues and organs (Vernon 1969a).

In the report of his research into the results of prenatal rubella infection, Vernon concluded that only "a relatively few" postrubella children showed severely impaired performance on intelligence tests (1969b, p. 2). But on the Bender Gestalt, the rubella children evidenced more so-called soft signs of neurological dysfunction than did a contrast group of genetically deaf children. And behavior disorders were more common among postrubella children than among the contrast group of deaf children.

The greatest tragedy of the rubella syndrome is that it is preventable. The mother can develop immunity to rubella before conception and thereby prevent this infection from ravaging her children before they are born. She can develop resistance to rubella in one of two ways: (1) she may be exposed to the virus, stimulating antibody production, or (2) she may be artificially immunized with rubella virus, which also stimulates antibody production. The antibody level in the bloodstream is referred to as the antibody *titer*; it can be measured in a laboratory test of a blood sample. Laws in some states now require blood testing for immunity to rubella before a marriage license is issued in order to provide the couple with information about the woman's immunity level in the hopes that she will become immunized, if necessary. If the antibody titer is high enough to protect each fetus, the test is merely reassuring. But if the antibody titer is too low, the woman may choose to be immunized. It is extremely important, however, that she not become pregnant for at least three months afterward because the virus will be present in her body and would involve the fetus.

Approximately half of the pregnancies where rubella is contracted during the first trimester involved infection of the unborn child (Cooper & Krugman 1966). Sequelae (symptoms that follow exposure or the condition) of the prenatal infection include hearing deficiencies in at least half of the infants affected, mental retardation, microcephaly, hydrocephaly (increased volume of fluid within the skull, resulting in a large head), cerebral palsy, blindness, seizures, orthopedic problems, jaundice, and cardiac defects. It is not uncommon to encounter combinations of these problems in a single child who was affected by rubella virus. While deafness is the most common symptom, the children exposed to rubella prenatally during the 1964 epidemic were more frequently affected by mental retardation than had been true in preceding epidemics of rubella.

Young children are also being immunized against rubella to prevent them from contracting the disease and thereby exposing a woman who does not yet know she is pregnant or a woman soon to be pregnant. There is some question as to whether immunization of young girls will generate long-lasting antibody responses that will protect them during their entire childbearing years. In addition, there is some evidence to suggest that during a pregnancy a woman has greater difficulty fighting off rubella infection.

Despite these possible limitations of immunization, public education and public action are still the two major defenses against another rubella epidemic and the resultant rubella syndrome.

Other Viruses. Cytomegalic inclusion disease (cytomegatovirus) is another viral infection known to involve the fetus severely. It produces no demonstrable illness in the mother but the infant suffers severe symptoms. Inclusion-bearing cells may be identified microscopically in infected tissues. The infant may have any or a combination of the following symptoms: microcephaly, anemia, jaundice, enlarged liver and spleen, hydrocephaly, cerebral calcification, varying degrees of mental retardation, deafness, cataracts, and convulsive disorders. On the other hand, some children show no significant sequelae.

Herpesvirus hominis has been implicated in meningoencephalitis (inflammation of a layer of tissue that covers the brain), microcephaly, and cerebral calcification, among other symptoms (Sever & White 1968). Unlike rubella and cytomegalovirus, the virus is thought to be acquired during delivery as the baby passes through the birth canal. Sells and Bennett (1977) reported that 40 to 60 percent of all babies delivered to women with active primary herpes infection become infected. The babies of such mothers should be delivered by cesarean section.

Syphilis. Interest in venereal diseases has increased because of the recent dramatic increase in incidence. As a result, a considerable amount of information has been disseminated to the public. In the past, syphilis was the cause of a significant number of fetal deaths; when children of syphilitic mothers were born alive they were frequently mentally retarded. While treatment techniques and detection methods for syphilis have now improved, the result has not been a reduction in the number of cases. In 1970 the U.S. Public Health Service statistics included a 22 percent increase in *reported* cases of congenital syphilis.

The spirochete bacterium that causes syphilis is spread by sexual contact. In an infected mother, the organism crosses the placenta and, after the eighteenth week of gestation, invades the fetus as it develops. Damage involves the developing tissues of the nervous and circulatory systems. The consequences to the fetus include miscarriage, stillbirth, mental retardation, cataracts, heart defects, and deafness. Additional findings frequently include dental deformities, enlarged liver and spleen, kidney disease, skin eruptions, bone deformities, and small size for the period of gestation.

Prevention of fetal involvement with syphilis is possible. In most states, before a marriage license is issued, evidence of a blood test negative for syphilis must be presented. Even if this test is negative, subsequent sexual relations with someone infected with syphilis can result in infection. The outward symptoms are not dramatic and even without treatment these symptoms subside. But the infection remains. Hence a woman can be infected with syphilis and be unaware of it, and she can conceive without suspecting that she has syphilis. Blood testing for syphilis in prenatal care is therefore advisable so that cases of syphilis can be detected and treated. Early treatment with antibiotics can cure the infection in the mother and prevent damage to the fetus, for little or no damage will occur before the eighteenth week of pregnancy. But once damage is done it is irreversible.

Toxoplasmosis. Toxoplasmosis is a protozoan parasite infection relatively unfamiliar to the general public. It is spread in raw meat and cat feces. Maternal infection is mild, but the disease is devastating to the fetus. It can cause convulsions, blindness, hydrocephaly, microcephaly, feeding problems, and damage to the nervous system. Desmonts and Couvreur (1974) have shown that less than half of the infections occurring during pregnancy affect the fetus; only primary maternal infections contracted during the first two trimesters are likely to damage the fetus.

Women who want to conceive or who know they are pregnant are therefore encouraged to cook meat thoroughly and to avoid contact with materials that may be contaminated by cat feces, such as litter boxes and flower beds. Antibody studies of maternal blood may indicate whether a mother has been exposed to toxoplasmosis. These baseline readings should be taken as early in the pregnancy as possible for comparison with later readings in order to ascertain whether the exposure occurred before or after conception; if readings elevate, the exposure took place sometime during pregnancy. Exposure prior to conception is not dangerous.

Radiation

Radiation has long been known to cause genetic mutations. It may also interfere with cell division early in the pregnancy, resulting in retarded or otherwise abnormal growth of the brain and other organs. The most direct consequences of maternal exposure to radiation are leukemia and other cancers, which generally appear before the child reaches age ten (National Research Council, National Academy of Sciences 1972). Radiation may also cause mental retardation, microcephaly, or both when the mother is exposed to massive doses of radiation for cancer treatment (Murphy 1928), therapeutic pelvic irradiation (Rugh 1958), or disasters such as the atomic bomb blasts at Hiroshima and Nagasaki (Wood, Johnson, & Omori 1967). Sells and Bennett (1977) report that exposure to radiation during pregnancy increases the risk of spontaneous abortion and raises the frequency of chromosomal abnormalities in the aborted fetus. It also increases the risk of Down's syndrome, especially in the late reproductive years.

Low-level doses of radiation come from many sources, including television, glow-in-the-dark watches, x-ray equipment, and even natural rock formations. The major dangers occur to expectant women who work where radiation is present or who are patients receiving radiation treatment. A number of factors determine the doses of radiation received during radiation treatment, such as (1) type of x ray, (2) speed of the film, (3) thickness of the table, and (4) size and weight of the woman.

Although we cannot say for sure what amount of radiation will cause mental retardation, we do have evidence of which factors are related to the degree of threat. In terms of susceptibility, the more immature the cells, the more sensitive they are to radiation damage (Regulatory Guide 8.13, 1975). The Atomic Energy Commission (1975) reported that the embryo is particularly sensitive to radiation in the first trimester, when radiation will increase the chances of malignancy and detectable somatic mutations in organ-forming cells, resulting in deformities. During the first trimester, the fetus is most vulnerable, and is still highly vulnerable during the remaining prenatal period. The child is less vulnerable in early childhood and less yet during late childhood.

Most of the radiation we receive comes from medical sources, so carelessness on the part of medical personnel cannot be tolerated. Radiation should not be administered unless indisputably warranted, especially during pregnancy. Particular attention should be paid to shielding the gonads, both of children and adults. Additional care should be exercised in controlling equipment that gives off radiation. In 1968, federal legislation was passed to regulate equipment, but it was not fully implemented until 1974; moreover, these regulations only applied to new equipment, because of the high cost of replacing substandard machines. Even today substandard equipment may be used until it is sold or moved to a new office.

PERINATAL FACTORS

During birth, the child is compressed by strong muscular contractions and squeezed through the narrow birth canal. But despite the potential traumas to the infant during this passage and the stress on the mother, everything usually proceeds without incident and the child survives the experience without any measurable consequences. There are, however, potential hazards to the child during this perinatal (birth and newborn) period. Fortunately, some of them can be anticipated and prevented thanks to new diagnostic tools and careful management of labor and delivery.

High-risk Pregnancies

The identification of high-risk pregnancies can alert medical personnel to perform tests and employ techniques that minimize the dangers to the mother or infant. High-risk pregnancies include those in which:

1. the mother is under twenty or over forty years of age;
2. there is the combination of low economic status and closely spaced pregnancies;
3. the expectant mother has a history of miscarriages, stillbirths, premature infants, and previous children with significant birth defects;
4. the expectant mother has a chronic condition such as diabetes, hypertension, or alcoholism;
5. the mother has Rh negative blood or her blood is otherwise incompatible with that of the fetus.

Risk is also increased when the placement and the condition of the placenta impede the flow of oxygen to the fetus or result in accumulated fetal waste. Separation of the placenta, implantation near the cervical os, infarction (a blood clot in the vessels of the placenta), diminished maternal oxygen, and decrease in uteroplacental blood flow may create an oxygen deficit for the fetus and thereby cause brain damage (Assali, Brinkman, & Nuwaybid 1974).

In other cases maternal pelvic disproportion may increase the risk of vaginal delivery sufficiently to warrant surgical intervention. For example, if the baby's head is too large for the cervical opening, there may be hemorrhage, separation of the placenta, or precipitous delivery, all of which can damage the baby. Abnormal positioning of the fetus (breech or transverse presentation) increases the risk of injury or suffocation, unless the infant can be turned by the physician to a head-first position.

Signs of toxemia during the pregnancy increase risk to the fetus and call for careful medical supervision. Changes in blood pressure alter the availability of oxygen and nutrients to the fetus. Such pregnancies may result in fetal asphyxiation, low birth weight, and stillbirths. First pregnancies, poorly nourished mothers, and mothers of low economic status are at highest risk for developing toxemia.

Fetal Monitoring

In addition to carefully supervising high-risk mothers, doctors can also keep track of how the fetus is doing. A variety of new techniques have been developed for detecting certain fetal abnormalities. Amniocentesis can be performed if genetic defects are suspected or if the maturity of the fetal lungs is to be evaluated for possible delivery before term. Amniotic fluid is obtained by going through the anterior wall of the mother's abdomen, a procedure of low risk when performed by a skilled physician. This fluid can be analyzed for amino acids, hormones, enzymes, and metabolic products to detect a variety of disorders. Chromosomal studies may also be undertaken.

Another procedure used in prenatal diagnosis is *fetoscopy*, a procedure that enables the physician directly to observe the fetus in utero. It involves the surgical introduction of an endoscope into the uterus. Ancephaly and hydrocephaly may be diagnosed in this way, and in the future it appears possible that this technique may be used to take samples of fetal tissue.

Indirect views of the fetus for prenatal diagnosis can be obtained through use of x rays, amniography, and ultrasonography. There is concern over the exposure of the fetus to radiation through x rays. But newer equipment reduces the amount of radiation to which the fetus is exposed. Ultrasound involves the bouncing of a sound wave through the abdomen and recording the densities of tissues as shadows; in this way it is possible to determine placental placement. Ultrasound and α-fetoprotein levels can be used in the detection of central nervous system deformities.

The analysis of maternal blood and urine has made it possible to detect fetal sex, some genetic defects, toxemias, and many infections. Monitoring of the mother's blood for abnormal biochemistries during labor is now possible. Continuous recording of fetal heart rate during labor also provides helpful information to the physician. Head compression, uteroplacental insufficiency (as in toxemia, diabetes, and Rh isoimmunization), umbilical cord compression, and immunity of the autonomic nervous system may be detected by studying the variability and deceleration patterns of the fetal heart rate (Hon 1974).

Early detection of abnormalities and distress permit the physician to attempt to alleviate the distress, prepare for an abnormal infant, or abort the fetus.

Perinatal Factors Related to Central Nervous System Damage

Although it is always hard to establish definite cause-and-effect relationships in mental retardation, certain conditions and traumas occurring at birth are known to increase the risk of mental retardation. Those we will consider here are prematurity, physical trauma, asphyxiation, seizures, hypoglycemia, infection, complications in which fetal red blood cells are destroyed, and maternal sensitization.

Prematurity.   Premature delivery has a variety of causes and results, none of them beneficial for the baby. In general, the immature infant is more susceptible to neurological insult, has a higher mortality rate, and is at greater risk of succumbing to sudden infant death syndrome than is a term baby (Behrman 1973). There is a high relationship between prematurity and low social class, maternal age, heavy cigarette smoking by the mother, and poor nutrition. In the United States the incidence of prematurity is higher among nonwhites than among whites (Babson & Benson 1966).

Research on prematurity is complicated by the fact that the term *prematurity* may refer to a number of different conditions. It may mean a gestational age of under 37 weeks, a birth weight of under 2500 grams, or low birth weight for gestational age. Within each of these definitional parameters there are two more groups: (1) those who have been developing quite normally but are delivered prior to full term and (2) those delivered close to full term but whose growth has been adversely affected during gestation. Most of the research evidence available does not differentiate between these two groups but simply compares children of low birth weight, for example, to children whose birth weight was above 2500 grams. But distinctions between the kinds of prematurity may make an important difference in some research results. For instance, the Collaborative Perinatal Study (Niswander & Gordon 1972) reported that the perinatal death rate for infants with low birth weight was about 25 percent higher than that of infants with higher birth weights. When these figures are broken down into (1) low birth weight children who simply were born before term as contrasted with (2) those who were slow to mature, the evidence seems to indicate that while the slower-developing infants had lower neonatal death rates than did the preterm infants, their developmental problems emerged later and were quite marked.

Physical Trauma.   Physical trauma during birth may cause damage to the brain. This can occur during labor and delivery as a result of the position of the infant or the instruments and the techniques used in delivery.

Symptoms of neurological damage may be clearly identified at birth or may be manifested only as the child grows. Symptoms vary from severe retardation, paralysis, and convulsions to various forms of cerebral palsy, mild perceptual problems, and hyperkinetic behavior.

Asphyxia.   During some deliveries, the infant becomes unconscious or even dies from lack of oxygen. Fetal distress may begin before labor, during labor and delivery, or postnatally. When Behrman (1973) analyzed the major causes of death among 1000 births where infants weighed over 1000 grams, he concluded that anoxia (lack of oxygen) was the major cause of death, followed by prematurity with no abnormality identified, and then by identifiable malformations. Behrman also reported increasing evidence of areas of infarction in the cerebral cortex and neurological disturbances in children who survive periods of hypoxia (limited oxygen) during the perinatal period. But it is not yet clear what duration of hypoxia will result in neurological damage.

Although we cannot always determine what causes asphyxia, some known causes have been identified. They include toxemia, pelvic disproportion, placental separation, infarction, hemorrhage, maternal supine positioning, prolonged labor, overdosage of oxytocin (a hormone chemical used to induce or stimulate labor), and use of depressants, narcotics, sedatives, or anesthesia (Behrman 1973, p. 44). Damage from the latter causes is often preventable. For reasons of safety to the infant, current medical management of labor now depends upon medication much less than it did in the past. Active participation by prepared parents is encouraged by many physicians, and classes for expectant parents are widely offered.

In addition to decreased use of pain-relieving drugs, asphyxia can sometimes be prevented by careful monitoring and medical management. During the prenatal period, the fetus is able to adapt to hypoxia with an increased heart rate; this increases the flow of blood to its heart and brain.

Because of this reaction, the fetal heart rate can be monitored to detect distress; fetal blood samples can also be taken to check for fetal acidosis (highly acidic body chemistry).

Amniocentesis can also provide evidence that the lungs are too immature to function properly, in which case delay of delivery of the infant could be encouraged to prevent the complications of severe respiratory distress.

Seizures. Neonatal seizures are often caused by anoxia and birth trauma. Such trauma may be due to fetal presentation, cephalopelvic disproportion (the infant's head is proportionately much larger than the mother's pelvis), or an accident in handling the infant.

Neonatal convulsions occur in between 5 and 10 per 1000 live births (Jabbour, Danilo, Gilmartin, & Goulieb 1973). Since they are associated with high mortality rates, diagnosis and treatment of the underlying cause of the seizures are of paramount importance.

Hypoglycemia. Although we have talked about hypoglycemia before, it is worth looking at again here, because it often shows up during the perinatal period and because there is much current interest in the condition.

Symptoms of hypoglycemia that may appear after birth include lethargy, weak cry, tremors, convulsions, cyanosis, poor muscle tone, irregular respiration, feeding difficulties, and rolling of the eyes. But these symptoms are not unique to hypoglycemia and careful diagnosis is essential.

The relationship between prolonged hypoglycemia and central nervous system abnormalities has been emphasized by Cornblath (1967). For instance, early studies indicated that children with a history of hypoglycemia achieved lower scores on intelligence tests than matched control children. But 10 percent to 15 percent of newborns with hypoglycemia also have underlying pathology (e.g., intracranial hemorrhage, birth defects, infections such as toxoplasmosis and cytomegalic inclusion disease), which complicates the picture. Diagnosis of the type of hypoglycemia and the possible underlying factors is essential for proper treatment and decreased risk of brain damage.

Many possible causes of hypoglycemia have been identified. External factors such as low environmental temperature may precipitate symptoms of hypoglycemia and of respiratory distress. Premature infants are particularly susceptible to such insults.

Some hypoglycemia conditions are due to decreased glucose output from the liver. The store of glycogen may be limited because of prematurity, prenatal malnutrition, starvation, severely low body temperature, liver disease, an abnormality in glucose formation in the liver, or an abnormality in its release from the liver. Glycogen storage diseases (von Gierke's disease, Andersen's disease, Cori's disease, galactosemia, inherited fructose intolerance, adrenal insufficiency) may be the underlying causes for the failure.

Maternal diabetes, erythroblastosis (damaged red blood cells in the fetus due to blood incompatibility between the mother and baby), Beckwith-Wiedemann syndrome, or tyrosinemia (inborn error in metabolism) may cause infants to utilize more glucose than would be expected in a normal infant. An excess of insulin (hyperinsulinism) may result from maternal ingestion of tolbutamide or genetic syndromes (such as maple syrup urine disease) or may occur when intravenous feedings of hypertonic glucose are stopped. Hypoglycemia from causes not yet understood may be related to cyanotic congenital heart disease (in which the child turns purplish-blue due to lack of oxygen), central nervous system pathology, ketotic hypoglycemia (abnormal level of ketone bodies resulting from incomplete metabolism of sugar), or idiopathic hypoglycemia (hypoglycemia of unknown cause).

Toxemia interferes with the nutrition available to the fetus, and as early as 1959, Cornblath reported a high incidence of hypoglycemia in infants born to mothers with toxemia during pregnancy. Currently he reports an incidence as high as 50 percent (Cornblath 1967, p. 58). He also identified maternal kidney disease, heart disease, chronic infection, and heavy cigarette smoking as factors increasing the risk of neonatal hypoglycemia.

The amount of cerebral nervous system damage done by a specific duration and degree of hypoglycemia cannot yet be specifically measured. The complexities of etiology, prevention, diagnosis, treatment, and prognosis of individuals with symptoms of hypoglycemia require an alert and well-informed medical staff and underscore the need for continuing research into possible prenatal intervention and possible genetic engineering to prevent such neurological insults.

Infection.   Infection can cause neurological damage during the prenatal, perinatal, and postnatal periods. During the perinatal period, symptoms of fetal infection that began prenatally may become obvious. Prenatal rubella, polio, and varicella (chicken pox) viruses and other organisms such as parasites may cause encephalitis (inflammation of the brain) and meningitis (inflammation of the brain-lining membrane) in the newborn.

Aseptic meningitis is caused by infectious organisms, usually viruses, that enter the fetus before birth. The organisms affect some infants little or not at all, but in others there is extreme involvement of the central nervous system, respiratory system, and circulatory system. A large proportion of the infants who survive are mentally retarded and have seizures and neuromotor disabilities.

Bacterial meningitis is a much more common infection. It may be contracted during labor, delivery, or soon after birth. Gotoff (1973) reported 50 percent mortality among newborns contracting bacterial meningitis. Among those who survived, 30 to 60 percent had residual problems, such as mental retardation, hearing loss, seizures, neuromotor problems, and speech defects. Proper medical management of pregnancy, labor, and delivery, as well as high-quality newborn nursing care, can do much to prevent the problem of infection. Careful techniques, particularly hand washing, limit cross-contamination. Airborne infections can be partially controlled by monitoring the health of the staff responsible for infant care. Since prevention is possible in some cases, retardation, deafness, and death are a high price to pay for carelessness in these matters.

Kernicterus.   The most serious complication of hemolytic disease (destruction of red blood cells) in the newborn is called *kernicterus,* or *bilirubin encephalopathy.* It occurs when red blood cells are destroyed rapidly and the liver is unable to keep pace by metabolizing bilirubin (the breakdown product of hemoglobin), creating an oxygen deficiency. Unconjugated (free, not bound to red blood cells) bilirubin in the blood causes neurological damage. The extent of damage depends on the maximum amount of bilirubin in the plasma.

Symptoms include jaundice (a yellowish coloration of the skin and the sclera of the eyes resulting from hyperbilirubinemia, or excesses of bilirubin in the bloodstream) and toxicity of the brain cells, which results in rigidity or spasticity. Neurological damage in the newborn can include severe retardation, deafness, and spasticity. Although lower bilirubin levels do not have such severe consequences, they may result in perceptual impairment, delayed speech development, hyperactivity, and learning difficulties (Behrman 1973).

A variety of conditions may produce hyperbilirubinemia and kernicterus. Defects in the red blood cells, deficiencies of certain necessary enzymes, and disorders of the hemoglobin may be congenital. Toxins or infection (such as toxoplasmosis, rubella, syphilis, or cytomegalic inclusion disease) may contribute to the development of hemolytic anemia. Salicylates (such as aspirin) and sulfa drugs may act in the plasma to increase the unconjugated bilirubin and thereby increase the risk of neurological damage. Fetal conditions such as hypoxia, acidosis, and hypoglycemia increase the chances for bilirubin to remain unconjugated and cause neurological damage. Premature infants are more susceptible to damage and at lower plasma levels than term infants.

Some of these conditions are preventable. But with kernicterus, once damage is done, it cannot be reversed. However, intervention may prevent further damage.

Maternal Sensitization.   Blood incompatibility and consequent maternal sensitization is another hemolytic disease that can lead to mental retardation. The most publicized and most common form of blood incompatibility is Rh incompatibility. While many red blood cell antigens may cause an antibody reaction, Rh and A-B-O factors are the most common groups to elicit antibody reactions in the mother and hemolytic anemia in newborns.

If a mother is Rh negative (a homozygous condition for the recessive gene determining Rh blood type), she may become sensitized against Rh positive blood cells. This can happen if she has a blood transfusion of Rh positive blood or, more commonly, if Rh positive blood cells from a fetus reach her circulatory system during labor and delivery. Her system responds by producing an immune response of antibodies to destroy the Rh positive blood cells. If blood leaks from a fetus occur in a subsequent pregnancy—and this usually happens—her system produces antibodies to the fetus's Rh positive blood. When the mother's blood with the antibodies to Rh positive blood cells enters the fetus's circulation, it releases bilirubin and destroys the Rh positive blood cells. The bilirubin level reaches toxic levels in the fetus because of the inability of its immature liver to metabolize the bilirubin. Damage to the brain results.

A-B-O incompatibility between mother and fetus can result in isoimmune hemolytic disease (allergy to one's own blood) even in the first pregnancy, depending on the antibody potential in the maternal serum. The mother with type O blood will produce anti-A and anti-B antibodies; type B mothers will produce anti-A antibodies when exposed to the specific antigen. Exposure of fetal and maternal blood usually occurs during labor and delivery, a limited time span that should minimize exposure of the infant to maternal antibodies. However, one characteristic of women with type O blood warrants attention. They produce anti-A antibodies with low molecular weight that, among other things, cross the placenta during the pregnancy. This characteristic is extremely dangerous to a fetus with type A blood, because the mother's anti-A antibodies will destroy its type A blood cells, leading to the same bilirubin buildup and brain damage in utero as occurs in Rh incompatibility.

If the antibody titer of the mother rises during the pregnancy, it is an indication of seepage of the fetal and maternal blood. Amniotic fluid analyses may reveal the presence of bilirubin; but in performing the amniocentesis, the doctor must be careful to avoid damaging the placenta and sensitizing the mother. If there is evidence of increasing bilirubin levels, severe neurological damage can be prevented by intrauterine blood exchange. Blood exchange may also be carried out during the neonatal period; this procedure is recommended when bilirubin levels exceed 20 milligrams of bilirubin per 100 milliliters of blood. In the past, transfusions have resulted in saving the fetus, but residual brain damage sometimes occurred anyway.

Today sensitization can be avoided in Rh factor cases. Within 72 hours after delivery of an Rh positive baby, an Rh negative mother is injected with gamma globulin. The gamma globulin seems to destroy the Rh positive fetal blood cells in the maternal system and thus stops the antibody production. It should be noted that this injection (commercially known as RhoGAM) must be used by an Rh negative mother after delivery of an Rh positive baby of any stage of gestation.

In addition to RhoGAM injections for the mother, bilirubin levels of infants are evaluated at the first signs of jaundice. If the concentration of bilirubin is kept below 20 milligrams of bilirubin per 100 milliliters of blood, complications such as kernicterus can be avoided. Phototherapy (placing the child under lights) can now be used to decrease the bilirubin level and eliminate jaundice, the transient form of which is not uncommon in newborns. The jaundice is considered transient if it appears after three days of life, because it is usually readily controlled.

POSTNATAL FACTORS

During the postnatal period, the phenotype of mental retardation will be manifested, regardless of what caused it. Some manifestations of mental retardation are evident right at birth, in which case the degree of retardation is quite severe. In other cases genetic defects may be suspected and even identified early (as in Tay-Sachs disease) but not show up until later in the child's development.

In this section we will look at two general kinds of conditions that are manifested during the postnatal period: (1) those that began prenatally or perinatally but do not become evident until the postnatal period and (2) those caused by hazards after birth that impede normal development. In the latter case some of the same environmental factors that can harm fetuses before birth can damage children afterward as well. Environmental factors such as severe malnutrition, asphyxia, trauma, infections, and toxins continue to affect the developing child and can cause retardation. It is important to keep in mind that the very same causal factor will have slightly different effects on the child depending on the age at which it occurs. In general, the earlier the injury occurs, the more generalized the effect.

Conditions That Manifest Themselves Later

Before we discuss factors limited to the postnatal period, we will look at conditions that begin during the prenatal or perinatal period but are not identifiable at birth. In such cases developmental lags may not be noticeable until later.

Abnormalities of the nervous system observed after birth are the result of abnormal fetal development. Microcephaly, cranium bifidum (separation of hemispheres of the brain), and some forms of hydrocephaly, for instance, are caused in the first 175 days of gestation (Gabriel 1974, p. 126). Diagnosis of such cerebral defects may be made prenatally or postnatally but usually occurs sometime before the first birthday. Surgical intervention can sometimes minimize the damaging condition. In some cases of hydrocephaly, a direct route can be provided surgically for the large quantity of cerebrospinal fluid to drain into the general circulation, relieving the abnormal pressure on the brain and the resulting damage it would cause. Surgical intervention, however, is not without its hazards; the side effects of anesthesia, infection, and blood clotting are among the possible complications.

Some other conditions that develop postnatally into mental retardation are metabolic disorders such as PKU, maple syrup urine disease, Hurler's disease, and galactosemia. Although the symptoms of these conditions are progressive, dietary intervention may be beneficial in some cases.

Late-appearing mental retardation may also result from endocrine dysfunctions, such as hypothyroidism or neurocutaneous disorders (abnormal blockages of fluid bathing the central nervous system; e.g., tuberous sclerosis). In hypothyroidism, the degree of intellectual impairment varies. While treatment with thyroid medication improves physical growth, it is questionable whether it improves mental functioning. In tuberous sclerosis, the age of onset of symptoms is an important factor. Menkes (1974) reported that approximately one-third of the patients do not become mentally retarded, although they may have skin lesions, tumors in other organs, and seizures. When mental retardation does occur, the impaired intellectual functioning does not become evident until late childhood. It is the result of tumor growth and increased intracranial pressure.

In Tay-Sachs disease, symptoms of neurological degeneration are not apparent at birth. But because of the inherited enzyme deficiency, a lipid-soluble substance accumulates in the neurons and gradually the number of cortical cells diminishes. In the white matter, myelination (the sheathing of the nerve cells of the central nervous system) stops and demyelination (the breakdown of that process) occurs. Cells involved in the transmission of impulses from the retina to the brain can also fill with lipid. As this process progresses, the neurological symptoms become more severe. An infant may become restless and irritable; by about one year of age, activities previously learned are lost. Poor muscle tone progresses to spasticity, and convulsions and blindness develop. Head size may increase. Death by the age of two or three is inevitable at this time. Like other lipid-storage diseases, Tay-Sachs disease demonstrates the pattern of a progressive, degenerative condition that results in mental retardation.

Malnutrition

Turning to environmental factors that may cause damage in the postnatal period, nutritional deficiencies in the child are clearly associated with mental retardation. But poor nutrition is invariably associated with other factors (e.g., social status, incidence of infections, prenatal and perinatal factors) known also to be associated with mental retardation, complicating the task of isolating causal relationships. Some specific deficiencies, however, have been shown to cause specific neurological consequences. For example,

1. iodine deficiency can cause cretinism;
2. protein deficiency, which can limit brain growth or normal development, can result in Kwashiorkor. (*Kwashiorkor* means "deposed child"; it is characterized by dry skin, rash, potbelly, edema, weakness, irritability, and digestive disturbances.)
3. vitamin A deficiency may cause increased intracranial pressure;
4. vitamin B_6 deficiency can cause seizures;
5. vitamin B_{12} deficiency may result in mental retardation, spasticity, and weakness;
6. vitamin D deficiency can cause convulsions.

Although these conditions require severe undernutrition for them to occur, they show that a poor diet can have destructive consequences.

In addition to dietary lacks in the food that is eaten, some nutritional deficiencies can be caused by metabolic effects. For example, hypocalcemia and hypomagnesemia can be produced by hypoparathyroidism and prematurity and may result in convulsions and mental retardation.

Trauma

Trauma has been mentioned repeatedly as a cause of neurological damage. Asphyxia is the most common form of trauma. When it is partial and lasts over a long period of time, the brain swells (this swelling is called *edema*). Swelling diminishes the blood supply to the brain, resulting in a lack of oxygen. Intracranial bleeding and blood clots also interfere with the oxygen supply to the brain.

Sometimes injuries contact the brain directly, as when a fractured bone pierces the brain or an object such as a knife pierces the skull and brain. In addition to the original destruction of nerve tissue, there may be secondary damage as well from lack of oxygen due to hemorrhage, thrombosis (clot or obstruction), or edema. Hematomas (accumulations of blood) may occur between the skull and the membranes of the brain itself after an injury. The nature of the damage to the brain depends upon a number of variables, including the amount of intracranial pressure created, duration of the pressure, the size of the hematoma, and the rate at which it formed. Symptoms vary according to the rate of its development and the areas of the brain involved.

In closed head injuries, damage may be caused by one of these factors: (1) a blow when the head is not moving, (2) a blow when the head is moving into a stationary object, or (3) a tearing or twisting action that may damage the brain stem. Secondary damage in such cases may be caused by cerebral edema and hematoma. Coma may result from the increased intracranial pressure, and epilepsy may be a residual symptom of the injury.

The two most common causes of severe head injury in young children are automobile accidents and child abuse. Deceleration accidents are particularly severe: an automobile or motorcycle stops when it hits a stationary object, but the soft tissue of the brain continues at 60 or 70 miles per hour until it hits the skull. Battered children are those who repeatedly suffer severe injury intentionally inflicted by another person or persons. The physical and psychological damage is a very real possibility. And because abused children are repeatedly returned (for lack of testimonial *proof*) to the parents, from whom they often receive the beatings, the chances of suffering such damage are considerable.

Infection

Infections of the central nervous system may also increase intracranial pressure. Severe bacterial meningitis, for instance, often results in mental retardation. The severity of the effects is influenced by the person's age, the extent of the infection, the length of time before treatment, and the medication used in treatment.

Brain abscesses can be caused by blood infections, middle ear infections, and wounds of the brain and are related to some problems of the heart. Residual problems resulting from brain abscesses include mental retardation, hydrocephalus, and seizures.

Many of the organisms that invade the nervous system can cause residual neurological symptoms. Residual mental retardation and seizures may develop after roseola (scarlet fever), a common childhood illness. Rabies and Rocky Mountain spotted fever can also cause severe neurological damage.

Postinfectious encephalomyelitis (inflammation of the brain and some covering tissue) may occur as a complication of mumps, measles, whooping cough, and chicken pox. Krugman (1977) reported that encephalitis occurs in 1 or 2 of every 1000 cases of morbilli (regular measles) but the rate varies from epidemic to epidemic. Sixty percent of those who get encephalitis recover completely, 15 percent die, and 25 percent show evidence of brain damage, including mental retardation. Encephalitis is an uncommon complication after vaccination for these diseases, but the whooping cough vaccination results in a rather high incidence of encephalitis and residual retardation.

Chemicals

The final group of postnatal factors that can cause brain damage is toxins in the environment. The effects of poisoning vary. All organs of the body are not equally susceptible to toxic chemicals in the body. The barrier that seems to protect the brain in some instances does not protect it in others. The immature brain is more vulnerable than the mature brain. In addition, specific areas of the brain differ in their sensitivity to specific toxic chemicals. Norton (1975) attributes this difference to the biochemistry of the cells and to the degree of vascularization (amount of blood vessels to an area). If nerve cells die, their function may be continued by other cells, but the dead cells are not replaced.

Chemicals that are toxic to the central nervous system do their damage in one of two ways: they cause some form of anoxia, or they act on specific structures. Carbon monoxide, severe barbiturate poisoning, and cyanide are among the known causes of anoxia; the process may be acute or chronic. As examples of damage to specific structures, direct damage to the brain and peripheral nerves may be caused by organic mercury and isoniazid (a medication used to arrest tuberculosis), whereas only peripheral damage is caused by dissolved organic phosphates.

Pesticides.   Neurologic damage may also be a residual effect of pesticide poisoning. Pesticides are of concern as an occupational hazard to those in the chemical industry and in agriculture. Among the chemicals most commonly identified as causing occupational diseases are organic phosphate pesticides, some hydrocarbon pesticides, herbicides, fertilizers, fungicides, phenols, and sulfur and organomercury compounds (Murphy 1975). Convulsions, irritability, and dizziness are among the symptoms of poisoning with DDT and organophosphate insecticides such as TEPP and endrin. Methyl bromide poisoning may result in depression, phobias, paranoia, and even death.

Drug Abuse.   Although many drugs have legitimate medical uses, improper use of prescription drugs and over-the-counter patent medicines, as well as unsafe combinations of drugs, may cause serious complications, sometimes death. Contamination and inconsistent dosage are two of the hazards of taking drugs obtained illegally.

Many drugs commonly abused—stimulants, depressants, and hallucin-ogens—affect the nervous system. Psychotic behavior and hyperactivity are possible symptoms of chronic amphetamine use.

LSD has been reported by Casarett (1975) to increase the incidence of chromosomal damage. Chronic use of LSD may cause a variety of other symptoms, including impaired intellectual functioning. Casarett suggests that this may be due to organic brain damage, although the evidence at this time is inconclusive.

Permanent brain damage is caused by chronic sniffing of glue containing toluene. Chronic inhalation of solvents can cause degeneration and cerebral edema. Sniffing gasoline may cause lead encephalopathy. Methanol (wood alcohol) may cause poisoning when inhaled, ingested, or absorbed through the skin. Degeneration of nervous tissue, among other tissues, causes symptoms of delirium, unconsciousness, and coma before death.

Barbiturates, commonly used and abused, may cause impaired intellectual functioning if used chronically, according to a 1950 study by Isbell that was summarized by Casarett (1975). There are many other serious symptoms involving the respiratory and cardiovascular systems.

Metals

Heavy metals are particularly damaging to the nervous system. Lead, arsenic, and mercury poisoning are among the most common causes of brain damage.

Lead ingestion has been a recognized pediatric problem for over fifty years. Close to 50 percent of the weight of paints and plaster once used in slum dwellings was lead. As these dwellings deteriorated, flaking and peeling of paint and plaster was common, and infants and young children inhaled and ate sizable quantities of it.

Paints used for furniture and toys that children chewed once had lead in them, too. More recently, the main source of lead poisoning has shifted: now it comes from air pollution. Chow and Earl (1970) reported that 98 percent of the lead in air coming from exhaust of automobiles is either inhaled by persons in areas of high air contamination (near highways) or contaminates the soil. Massive screening programs have shown that 10 percent of the children tested have levels of lead in their systems that are considered toxic. The sources of available lead seem to be more commonly found in poorer neighborhoods, where proximity to heavy traffic and the presence of peeling lead-base paints are most likely. The relationship between retardation and lead poisoning is therefore confused by the social-psychological factors also common to low social class environments. But it is important to remember that low social class environments encompass a number of physical threats that may in part account for the higher incidence of retardation in these settings.

Many of the symptoms of early lead poisoning are not dramatic. The individual may become irritable, constipated, and pale and tired from anemia. With increased ingestion of lead, vomiting and convulsions occur. Repeated exposure is common because the source of lead often remains available.

In severe lead poisoning, edema of the brain causes convulsions, visual disturbances, a form of communicating hydrocephalus, and lead lines in the gums or anus or both. Blindness, spasticity, and convulsions may be residual symptoms.

Mercury poisoning is another hazard that can cause mental retardation and other problems. In the past it was believed to be a hazard only to certain occupational groups who worked in close proximity to metallic mercury vapors (such as miners and felt-hat workers). Recently, however, other forms of mercury have been identified as causes of damage. In Japan a factory was dumping waste products containing methyl mercury into a creek. The wastes were eaten by shellfish, which were then caught by fishermen and eaten. The fishermen and their families soon evidenced symptoms of mercury poisoning, particularly the young children, who in some instances developed cerebral palsy and lowered intelligence. In a United States case, families who ate pork from hogs that had been fed grain contaminated with mercury were found to be adversely affected. We know now that organic mercury used in some fungicides can be carried by foodstuffs (such as grains); if the food is consumed while it is still contaminated, mercury poisoning can occur.

Those most susceptible to mercury poisoning are the unborn, but devastating effects have also been reported in young children and adults. The effects of mercury poisoning include mental retardation, blindness, convulsions, poor muscle tone, and seizures. Among the Japanese families of the fishermen, there were symptoms such as memory loss, imbalance of gait, visual effects, and emotional instability.

At present, the sources of mercury poisoning are being identified. Steps are being taken to reduce contamination of water (such as Lake Michigan and the Swedish coastal waters) and foodstuffs by restricting sewage contamination and phasing out fungicides containing mercury.

It is evident that many environmental factors may cause mental retardation. Some controls exist to protect the individual from known hazards in food, air, the working environment, and commonly used products. But constant reassessment of the protection of the public and continuing search are extremely important.[9]

[9] For readers with a limited background in biology or those interested in more detail concerning genetic factors, several sources are recommended: Allen, Cortazzo, & Toister 1971; Stern 1973; Thompson & Thompson 1973.

SUMMARY

In this chapter we considered the wide variety of genetic and environmental influences impinging on the developing human that may cause mental retardation.

Genetic information causing retardation may be carried on the autosomes or on the sex chromosomes; it may be manifested in dominant or recessive traits, or through mutations or chromosomal aberrations. Although retardation from a dominant gene is rare—since people who manifest such conditions usually die before they can reproduce—recessive traits and chromosomal aberrations are common.

Down's syndrome, a familiar form of mental retardation, results from any of three different kinds of chromosomal aberrations: nondisjunction, translocation, or mosaicism. The people it affects have many distinctive physical characteristics, but their personalities may differ depending on how they are brought up. While attempts to normalize Down's syndrome patients have met with limited success, a more fertile approach to the problem is to try to prevent it. Genetic counseling is especially advisable for couples in which the mother is nearing the end of her reproductive years, for such women are at high risk of having Down's syndrome babies.

PKU is an example of a recessive genetic trait that causes mental retardation. Infants who receive the defective gene from two carrier parents are unable to metabolize phenylalanine, an amino acid. It builds up to a toxic level in the blood, poisoning the cells of the brain. There are different forms of PKU with different degrees of damage. The condition can be detected early through urine or blood tests of the infant; if it is diagnosed early, PKU children can be put on a special low-phenylalanine diet that allows them to develop almost normally in terms of intelligence. Other recessively carried genetic traits that may cause mental retardation include Tay-Sachs disease and hypoglycemia.

Turning to environmental factors, we first looked at what could affect the fetus even within the uterus, and we found that there are many factors that can invade its environment. Most are traceable to the mother, and it is sometimes in her power to prevent them: poor nutrition, toxic chemicals, radiation, drugs, alcohol, and infections such as rubella, syphilis, and toxoplasmosis fall into this category.

Most infants survive the trauma of birth with no ill effects. But for some it is a time of severe distress that can result in neurological damage. Some infants are born premature—either too small or too immature to carry on normal life functions and withstand stress. Some sustain physical injuries during the birth process; some are cut off from their oxygen supply; and some have seizures. Hypoglycemia and infection may show up during the perinatal period, weakening and endangering the baby. The infant's red blood cells may even be attacked by antibodies from the mother if their blood is incompatible; or the blood cells may be destroyed by the baby's own deficiencies, as in the case of kernicterus.

Mental retardation does not always show up at birth. Some conditions develop gradually, and some are not even caused until later in life. In Tay-Sachs disease, the baby may progress normally at first but then begin to backslide in development, losing skills previously gained, as the brain fills with fluid. Postnatal factors that may cause mental retardation include severe malnutrition, asphyxia, head injuries, infections, exposure to toxic chemicals, and drug abuse.

PART III

Assessment

CHAPTER 5

Intelligence and Issues in Testing

DEFINING INTELLIGENCE

What is intelligence? Is it using big words and being clever with figures? Is it the ability to find your way around in a strange place? Is it the capacity to learn, or the capacity to act rationally? What characterizes the people you think of as intelligent?

Most of us find it easier to make intuitive judgments about how intelligent our acquaintances are than to define what intelligence is. The same thing is true of professional educators and psychologists. Even though their work often involves making distinctions among people according to their level of intelligence, they are hard pressed to define the basis for their decisions.

Educational psychologist Arthur Jensen (1969) admitted the scientifically embarrassing truth: intelligence is easier to measure than to define. Even in the earliest grades of school, students come to know who among themselves are the most intelligent. They infer this from observing the effects of the force we call *intelligence*, as some children master tasks with greater ease or speed than others. Teachers make the same observations. And by recognizing that one child is more intelligent than another, they can predict on a forthcoming task which child will master it faster. But even though it often seems easy to tell who is smart and who is not, educators and psychologists must find ways of making such judgments objectively rather than subjectively, for the course of a person's life may depend on them.

One thing that makes intelligence such a slippery thing to define is our tendency to think of it as a real entity such that, the more you have of it, the smarter you are. As Eysenck (1973) puts it:

> The man in the street, and often the unwary psychologist too, thinks of intelligence as something really existing "out there"; something which the psychologist may or may not recognize successfully, and measure with more or less success. In these terms it would make sense to argue about whether a particular test "really" measures intelligence. Such reification is utterly mistaken; there is nothing "out there" which could be called intelligence. . . . Intelligence [is a] concept, and concepts only exist in the minds of scientists; they are useful or useless, appropriate or inappropriate, in terms of their success in enabling us to form generalizations, discover invariances, and predict future events.
>
> (p. 1)

Intelligence, then, is not an entity that exists but a hypothetical entity or force that is used by scientists to explain certain types of behavior.

Some scientists feel that you can measure and study intelligence without trying to define it (Eysenck 1973; Tyler 1965). Others have labored to come up with a definition of intelligence that everyone could agree on, to ensure that all researchers would be measuring and studying the same thing (see Burt 1955, 1968; Cronbach 1975; Guilford 1967; Matarazzo 1972; Miles 1957; and Stoddard 1943 for discussions of the various definitions that have been suggested). Three definitional themes occur commonly: (1) the capacity to learn, (2) the totality of knowledge acquired, and (3) the adaptability of the individual, particularly to new situations. But no single definition has ever received the total support of all who deal with intelligence.

Attempts to get a handle on intelligence go back to ancient writers such as Plato, Aristotle, and Cicero, continue through the nineteenth-century work of Sir Francis Galton, and are still being made by more recent scientists like Charles Spearman, Cyril Burt, and J. P. Guilford. The early approach was first to define intelligence and then select items or tasks that appeared to tap the content or operations included in the definition. However, the type of intelligence test we use today was developed initially to solve a practical, not a theoretical, problem: the problem of overcrowding in schools.

At the beginning of the twentieth century, the schools in Paris were overcrowded and many of the children in school were not able to profit fully from schooling. Hence the charge to Binet and Simon in 1905 was to develop an instrument that would predict accurately those children who would fail in school; they were to be taken out of the crowded regular schools and placed in special schools.

The tests designed by Binet and Simon over seventy years ago are still in widespread use, with some minor revisions but few substantive changes in the basic instrument (Mussen, Conger, & Kagan 1969). Points that should be noted about their work are therefore still valid:

1. The Binet-Simon tests, and those based upon them, had their origins in schools and are shaped by the educational content and methods of instruction used in European and North American schools (Jensen 1969). As such, the types of learning tapped are restricted to predicting the success an individual will have in a traditional school.
2. The Binet-Simon tests, unlike their predecessors, bore a relationship to real life criteria of behavior as one would rate it on a "bright" to "dull" continuum (Jensen 1969). A child's rank order in a class was found to correspond rather closely to the impressions of teachers and others as to who was brighter than whom.
3. Since the Binet-Simon tests and those derived from them are called "intelligence" tests, it is necessary to distinguish between the specific educationally related skills tapped by these tests and the somewhat ambiguous term *intelligence* used in layman's parlance (Tyler 1965).

Because the Binet-Simon tests worked, because they were found to predict school achievement even though there was no adequate definition of the trait they measured, the resultant trend toward considering practical problems was one probable reason for the decline in the search for a definition of intelligence. Another reason was that theoretical differences between test constructors came to have little practical effect: even though two test constructors might be a great distance apart in their conceptual definitions about what intelligence is or the nature of the test, their instruments were very similar in that they were related to the same practical outside criterion—predicting school success.

Perhaps the most useful definition of intelligence is therefore a roundabout one: intelligence is the trait measured on intelligence tests. This concept will not necessarily correspond to what the term *intelligence* means in everyday language. And as Jensen (1969) has pointed out, the constellation of abilities tapped by tests of intelligence would probably be markedly different if the content and instructional techniques of education were noticeably different from what they were, and still are. For our purposes, then, intelligence is the trait measured by intelligence tests, which are based on abilities needed in today's schools.

The necessity of tying intelligence test items to what goes on in the schools has made intelligence testing a focal point for criticism from civil rights advocates. Since the number of minority children who score within the ranges considered mentally retarded has been unusually high, critics say that the tests are loaded against minority children and that those who score low are not necessarily retarded. As a result, PL 94-142 has been passed, calling for nondiscriminatory testing that will not treat children from culturally different backgrounds unfairly. This mandate raises a new problem (which will be explored in detail later in this chapter): How can we devise tests that are fair and at the same time related to academic outcomes in the public schools?

WHAT DO INTELLIGENCE TESTS MEASURE?

You should not conclude from what we have just said that tests of intelligence tap only insignificant correlates of school achievement and nothing else of consequence in a broader psychological sense. But on the other hand, we should be careful not to read too much into scores derived from such tests. As Mussen et al. have noted (1969), American parents are anxious about their child's IQ and may attribute more importance to this trait than to any other individual characteristic. They seem to feel that IQ is one of *the* fundamental determinants of success in life. Different researchers have suggested different ways of looking at how broad a range of capabilities intelligence tests really do measure. All agree that intelligence tests tap only certain kinds of mental abilities.

General Factors versus Specific Factors

Some theorists regard intelligence as a *unitary* phenomenon; some regard it as a highly *specific* one. The foremost advocate of the former position was the British psychologist Spearman (1927), who postulated that there is a unitary general (g) factor underlying all intellectual operations. This point of view is shared by Jensen (1969, 1979), who argued that tests that tap "higher mental processes" (rather than characteristics such as sensory acuity or reflex behavior) correlate positively and substantially with one another. As Jensen stated, one of the most striking and solidly established phenomena in all of psychology is the ubiquitous positive correlation among all tests of mental ability, no matter how diverse the mental skills or content tested, when obtained in an unselected, or representative, sample of the population (1979, p. 16). In a battery of tests, one test might consist of arithmetic problems, another of verbal analogies, and yet another of spatial relationships. Although they are seemingly different tests, the individuals taking them tend to score at approximately the same level on all three. The existence of a g factor, common to all tests, was proposed to account for this high interrelationship. Spearman described it as "the ability to educe relations and correlates." Jensen (1969) represents the essence of this g factor as "cross-modal transfer": recognition of a stimulus initially presented in one modality (e.g., auditory) when it is presented in a different modality (e.g., visual).

At the other extreme are those who believe that intelligence is a function of highly specific (s) abilities and that general intelligence is merely the totality of these s factors. This approach was initially proposed by Thorndike (1925) and extended by Guilford (1956). Thorndike rejected the idea of a g factor of intelligence and instead concluded that there are a number of different specific intelligences, which group into roughly three categories: abstract, mechanical, and social intelligence.

These two positions have important implications for mental retardation. Those suggesting a g factor would view mentally retarded individuals as low in the g factor and predict a consistently low performance across all kinds of tasks that entail higher mental processes. By comparison to average-ability children, mentally retarded children would be thought to possess substantially less general intelligence. On the other hand, those who agree with the theory of s factors would accept the idea that a mentally retarded child could be high on some factors (e.g., social intelligence) and low on others (e.g., abstract intelligence). If we adapt the theory of s factors to what goes on in school, we would attempt to identify areas of strength and exploit them to the benefit of the child. On the other hand, if we operate from a g factor position, we would assume an across-the-board deficit and gear instruction at a consistently low level across various areas.

Fluid and Crystallized Intelligence

A different distinction has been put forth by Cattell (1963). What he calls *fluid intelligence* refers to the mental brightness or adaptability of an individual that exists independent of experience and education. *Crystallized intelligence* is the direct result of experience and education, consisting of knowledge and skills. Obviously, crystallized intelligence depends on fluid intelligence; but when individuals who are high in fluid intelligence are restricted in experience or education, they will show less crystallized intelligence. Fluid intelligence peaks in late adolescence or early adulthood, whereas crystallized intelligence is thought to increase gradually throughout life.

Genotypic and Phenotypic Intelligence

Scarr-Salapatek (1975) and Jensen (1969) are among those who used the terms *genotypic intelligence* and *phenotypic intelligence* to distinguish the genetic factors that determine a particular trait (genotype) from the measurable expression of that trait (phenotype). The genotype is determined at conception and is not alterable, but the phenotype results from the interaction of the genotype with physical and social forces with which the developing child comes into contact. Measured intelligence is a phenotypic trait, not a genotypic one. As we saw in Chapter 3, differences between phenotypes are influenced to a considerable extent by stimulation or deprivation in the environment, as well as by the innate capabilities and reaction range of the genotype.

THE MEASUREMENT OF INTELLIGENCE

In any effort to measure a trait such as intelligence we must consider two properties of the proposed test instrument: reliability and validity. The *reliability*[1] of a test refers to the extent to which a person would obtain the same relative score in retaking the test. In other words, is the test consistent in measuring the trait that it measures? The *validity* of a test is the degree to which a test measures what it purports to measure, the extent to which a test does the job for which it is intended.[2] The scores of children who take an intelligence test should correspond to their relative brightness. One way to check the validity of intelligence test results is to compare them with achievement test scores, for the two are significantly related. High-IQ children are also high scorers on tests of achievement.

There are many instruments on the market that assess intellectual functioning. The ones most often used in the field of mental retardation are the Stanford-Binet and the Wechsler scales (Wechsler Intelligence Scale for Children–Revised, or WISC-R; Wechsler Adult Intelligence Scale, or WAIS). These tests are administered individually to reduce the chance that performance will be depressed by reading problems or trouble in following directions.

The Stanford-Binet

The Stanford-Binet includes items tapping memory, perception, information, verbal ability, and logical reasoning. At the lower levels there are

---

[1] For a detailed discussion of test reliability and the ways it is established for a test, see Anastasi (1961), Cronbach (1960), Sattler (1974), or Silverstein (1970).

[2] Three types of validity have been distinguished in *Standards for Educational and Psychological Tests and Manuals* (APA 1974): content validity, construct validity, and criterion-related validity. The reader may want to consult this source, as well as Anastasi (1961) and Cronbach (1960) for a detailed discussion of the construct of validity.

a number of manipulative and pictorial items; they tend to be of either a complex sensorimotor type or a simple verbal type. Moving to successive levels of the test, the Stanford-Binet becomes increasingly verbal in nature, with vocabulary being tapped at all levels in one form or another, until by the adult level the tasks are highly abstract and verbal in nature.

When tested, a child is administered six items for succeeding age levels until he fails all the items at a single age level. At this point the test is stopped. Originally, the child's score was converted to a mental age (MA), which was then compared to the child's chronological age (CA). Later, the intelligence quotient (IQ) was calculated as follows:

$$IQ = \frac{MA}{CA} \times 100$$

Currently, scores are converted to a deviation IQ (a standard score), using tables available to the examiner in the test manual. Note that giving the test result as a single score reflects a conceptualization of intelligence as a general factor.

Wechsler Scales

The Stanford-Binet mixes different types of questions at each age level. The Wechsler scales, by contrast, are divided into two portions: a verbal scale and a performance scale. Each scale includes five subtests, for a total of ten subtests. The verbal scale of the WISC-R contains the following subtests: information, comprehension, arithmetic, similarities, vocabulary, and an alternate, digit span. The performance scale subtests are picture completion, picture arrangement, block design, object assembly, coding, and an alternate, mazes. Scores on each of the subtests are converted to IQ scores by use of tables. The test yields three IQ scores: a verbal IQ, a performance IQ, and a full-scale IQ.

Comparison of the Stanford-Binet and Wechsler Scales

The Stanford-Binet and the WISC scales are far and away the most commonly used individual tests of intelligence.[3] In addition to differing from one another in structure and scoring, there are other factors that determine their usefulness with the mentally retarded.

[3] The reader may wish to consult Buros (1972) or Meyers (1971); courses that cover test content may also be beneficial. In the recent Manual (Grossman 1973), the Stanford-Binet and Wechsler scales are recommended along with the Cattell Infant Intelligence Scale and the Kuhlmann-Binet for use with very young or severely retarded subjects.

Until the publication of the Wechsler Preschool and Primary Scale of Intelligence (WPPSI), the Wechsler scales were of limited usefulness with children under age five. Furthermore, the IQ scales for the WISC-R and WAIS only go down to IQ 45, limiting their usefulness with mentally retarded subjects functioning at the lower levels. The Stanford-Binet, on the other hand, is a more sensitive instrument for very young children and for individuals functioning at low mental ages (IQ tables go down to age two). Hence if you were trying to assess the level of intellectual functioning of children under five years of age or individuals in the severe range of mental retardation, the Stanford-Binet would be the preferred instrument.

The organization by content areas characteristic of the Wechsler scales appeals to many examiners since it does not require the frequent shifting from one type of task to another that is necessary when administering the Stanford-Binet. Others prefer the WISC-R over the Stanford-Binet because the WISC-R results in an s factor profile that indicates in which subtests the individual shows relative strengths and weaknesses and because the WISC-R gives separate verbal and performance IQs. We must exercise caution, however, in attributing significance to differences in verbal and performance IQs unless they differ by 25 IQ points or more (Wolfensberger 1958). Furthermore, the low reliability of individual WISC-R subtest scores renders comparisons among subtest scores hazardous. We should therefore corroborate any such differences with evidence from outside the testing situation.

THE STABILITY OF INTELLIGENCE

Those who work with the mentally retarded often have to make inferences about the course of development that can be expected for specific individuals. Parental concerns and educational decisions often necessitate that we estimate the level of intellectual functioning that a given child can be expected to achieve at later points in life. Intelligence tests give us an intelligence quotient (IQ) that, according to the reliability evidence, would be highly stable if the same test were to be administered a month later. However, in planning for a mentally retarded child (or any child), we need to be able to make predictions with some certainty about five years from now, ten years, and so forth. In this section we will examine the evidence on the stability of IQ over time and consider the most pertinent forces that are liable to exert influence on fluctuations in IQ.

The longitudinal data that bear on the question of stability or constancy of IQ are derived from testing children who fall at many points along the IQ continuum. The data reported are not, for the most part, based on mentally retarded populations. We must consider this when generalizing from these studies to various subgroups of the mentally retarded. For example, in the case of profoundly retarded children (IQ < 25) there will be very little shift in IQ, particularly upward, because of the biomedical causes of the arrested mental development and the environmental conditions to which the child will probably be exposed. Some exceptions to this general statement have been reported, most of which occurred when the subjects were infants.

Attributes of Stable Characteristics

In this section we will use as criteria for judging stability the attributes of stable characteristics that have been specified by Bloom (1964). First, he contends that, empirically, a stable characteristic is one that is *consistent* from one point in time to another in a predictable way. That is, individuals can change both quantitatively and qualitatively with regard to a given characteristic, but those changes must be predictable to some minimum degree. Bloom illustrates this with height: it does change from birth to maturity, but from measurements at about age three or four we can predict with considerable accuracy the relative height of the child at maturity.

A second attribute of a stable characteristic is that it is *nonreversible*. A change in the trait will not be lost at a later point in time—hence development is additive and cumulative. Height meets this criterion (at least until old age) but weight does not. An individual can diet to lose or gain weight.

Bloom raises the question of how changes in the rate of growth fit into the picture of stability. Intelligence, like height, is a characteristic that appears to grow rapidly at first and then slow down. We do not yet know whether less than normal growth at one period of development can be compensated for at a later point in time.

As we turn to consider the stability of intelligence it is important to remember that IQ scores are not points on an absolute scale (like weight, height, or temperature) but instead indicate the individual's relative standing with regard to the normative population. Hence the means of analyzing the degree of stability of IQ is by correlating intelligence test scores at one point in time with the scores of the same individuals at a second point in time.

Correlations versus Shifts in Absolute IQ

In surveying the literature related to the constancy of IQ we encounter the question approached in two different ways: (1) analyzing correlations between intelligence test scores over a period of time (e.g., Bloom 1964; Jensen 1969) and (2) analyzing shifts in absolute IQ for a given individual over time (e.g., Ebert & Simmons 1943; Honzik, Macfarlane, & Allen 1948). These two methods provide us with very different kinds of information; we can draw different conclusions about the stability of intelligence depending on which kinds of data we consider.

Shifts in absolute IQ tend to confuse the issue of stability. Tyler (1965), for instance, listed several reasons why a child's obtained IQ may vary considerably from year to year, reasons that are unrelated to stability of intelligence. First, different tests tap different abilities; if a different test is used at the two test administrations, differences in the results are likely. Second, even when the same test is used both times, the items at different levels tap different aspects of intelligence. Third, at lower levels, perceptual-motor items predominate, but as one progresses to higher test levels the test becomes more highly verbal, and here educational deficits would take their toll.

Another major problem inherent in analyzing absolute shifts in IQ reported in extant studies pertains to the differences in variability for different tests and even for different ages on the same test in the case of the Stanford-Binet. Many studies were conducted before the most recent revision of the Binet (Terman & Merrill 1960) was available; the older Binet form had different standard deviations at different age levels. For age six the standard deviation was 10 points. A child taking the test at six years of age could score one standard deviation above the mean and achieve an IQ of 110. If the child was administered the test again at age nine, when the standard deviation was 16 points, and again scored one standard deviation above the mean, an IQ of 116 would be assigned. The apparent increase in IQ is a statistical artifact, not a true change in IQ relative to age group.

It may be more useful to examine correlation coefficients (the extent to which individuals maintain their same ranking in the group over time) than to look for indications of stability in statistics of absolute IQ shifts. For example, look at the cases in Table 5.1. On the first and second testings there are sizable shifts in absolute IQ, but a correlation coefficient would show a perfect positive correlation (1.00) because the subjects remain in the same rank order. The correlation coefficient reflects the degree to which the rank order remains the same but tells us nothing about fluctuations in absolute IQ.

Longitudinal Evidence on the Stability of Intelligence

Using correlation coefficients, Bloom (1964) has analyzed the major longitudinal studies that have followed the same children for periods of time ranging from five to twenty-one years. Intelligence tests were administered to the children at several different times, enabling us to gauge the stability

TABLE 5.1   Fictitious Data on IQ Testing of Five
Children Over Time Where a Perfect
Positive Correlation Exists for Ranks*

	First Testing			Second Testing	
Child	IQ	Ranking	Child	IQ	Ranking
A	148	1	A	129	1
B	136	2	B	120	2
C	130	3	C	116	3
D	105	4	D	112	4
E	100	5	E	110	5

*Note: The correlation coefficient for IQ scores = 0.937.

of their intelligence. Bloom concluded from his analysis of these studies that intelligence is a developing function and the stability of measured intelligence increases with age. Stated differently, we can be more confident in making predictions about intelligence when these predictions are based on tests taken when a subject is older. Several studies warrant closer inspection.

Projects at the University of California (Bayley 1949; Honzik et al. 1948) followed 40 children from the Berkeley community. While these subjects were representative of the Berkeley population, they were considerably above the national average in intelligence. Several findings are noteworthy. First, infant tests administered during the first year or year and a half were found useless in predicting IQ at later ages (in fact, there was a slight inverse relationship between the scores). Honzik et al. (1948) reported that prediction of later IQ from IQ at age two is better than chance, but correlations become much higher when IQ is taken at later ages. The second major finding of these projects was that the degree of relationship between IQs at different ages depends on two factors: the age at which the first test is administered and the length of time between test administrations. For example, the older the child when the first test was administered, the greater the relationship with the IQ at a later age. In general, from age six on there is a definite predictive value in the IQ over limited periods of time.

This does not mean that intelligence stops developing when a child is six. Even with very high correlations between IQ *rank* at youth and maturity, there is room for considerable fluctuation in individual cases. For example, Honzik et al. (1948) found changes in IQ by as many as 50 points during the school years. Changes of greater than 30 points were found in

9 percent of the cases and of 15 or more points in 58 percent of the cases. Only 15 percent of the subjects changed by fewer than 10 points. It should be recalled, however, that these absolute shifts in IQ are in part due to factors other than true shifts in cognitive ability. For example, the preschool items tend to be of a perceptual-motor type, whereas the items at age eighteen are almost exclusively verbal and abstract. But the shifts in IQ do also reflect the fact that intelligence is a developing construct and not a static one.

The correlations of IQ at different ages and IQ at maturity, as reported in several longitudinal studies, are shown in Figure 5.1. The Bayley (1949) data reveal especially clearly the rapid increase in correlations between IQ at early ages and IQ at age seventeen. The most rapid increases occur before age four, the less rapid increases after age four. After age eight the relationship of IQ score with IQ at age seventeen should be extremely high (Bloom 1964, p. 61).

Bloom (1964) concluded that since intelligence develops most rapidly during the early years, the time at which environmental effects are most likely to affect IQ comes before age eight, with the greatest impact occurring before age five. The converse of this conclusion is that exposing a child to a dramatically different environment after age eight would have relatively little effect on IQ. This theory highlights the importance of the early years of life and suggests a critical, or sensitive, period in the development of intelligence.

Most people accept Bloom's critical period theory. But another of his conclusions has been criticized as misleading. Bloom wrote:

> Put in terms of intelligence at age 17, from conception to age 4, the individual develops 50% of his mature intelligence, from ages 4 to 8 he develops another 30%, and from ages 8 to 17 the remaining 20%.
>
> (1964, p. 68)

Jensen (1969) rightfully criticized this interpretation, pointing out that half of the *variance* in adult intelligence can be predicted by age four or five. This does not mean that the four-year-old child has half of the total intellect that he will possess at age seventeen, but only that the correlational analysis allows one to explain 50 percent of the variance in IQs at age seventeen by the IQ at age four.

Despite some confusion over Bloom's predictions, it is safe to draw these conclusions from the longitudinal data: intelligence is a relatively stable human characteristic; as age increases, this characteristic becomes increasingly more stable; the correlations of IQ at two points in time increase as the age of initial testing increases and as the interval between testings decreases.

**FIGURE 5.1 Correlations Between Intelligence at Different Ages
and Intelligence at Maturity**

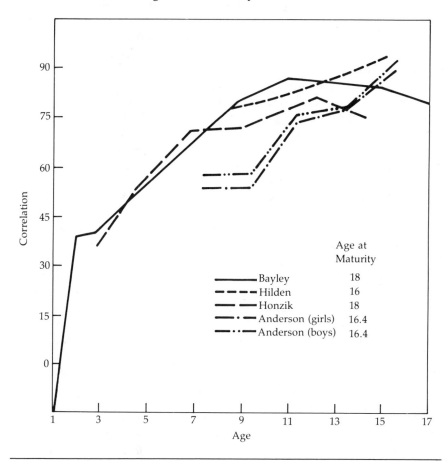

From B. S. Bloom, *Stability and Change in Human Characteristics.* Reprinted by permission of John Wiley & Sons, Inc., copyright 1964.

Individual Variations in IQ.   As we noted earlier (see Bayley 1949), researchers found that, despite very high correlations between IQ at two points in time, there was considerable fluctuation in IQ scores for individual subjects (Ebert & Simmons 1943; Honzik et al. 1948). The investigators at the University of California attempted to identify some of the factors that might account for these changes. Note that when one refers to changes in IQ they can be changes in either direction; some subjects' IQs increased while others' decreased.

Bayley (1954) reported that the most clear-cut relationship existed between a child's mature IQ and the educational level of the family. The child from a home with high educational achievement is more likely to show an increase in IQ; the child from lower educational level families will probably show a decrease.

The longitudinal study conducted at the Fels Institute in Ohio (Sontag, Baker, & Nelson 1958) was designed to answer the question, What *kinds* of children are likely to have increases and decreases in IQ over time? It was found that in the ascending group boys predominated, whereas girls predominated in the descending group. This suggested sex difference has been reported elsewhere (Bayley 1968; Bayley & Oden 1955; Ebert & Simmons 1943; Moore 1967). Furthermore, in a study of poor black children, it was reported that as a group boys were less likely to have decreases in IQ than were girls (Roberts, Crump, Dickerson, & Horton 1965).

The Fels data revealed several personality correlates of changing IQ between ages three and twelve. During the preschool years, those children characterized as independent and competitive tended to be IQ gainers, a finding that was true for both sexes. During the elementary school years, IQ gainers were independent, self-initiating, problem solving, and scholastically competitive. Several personality attributes of the children during their preschool years (aggressiveness, self-initiative, and competitiveness) were predictive of IQ gains during the school years. These findings were based on ratings, but the results were confirmed with projective testings (Kagan, Sonta, Baker, & Nelson 1958). A concise summary of these studies is found in the McCall, Appelbaum, and Hogarty (1973) monograph.

The fact that data collected in the same longitudinal studies show high correlations over time and also reveal individual changes may seem to be contradictory, but it is not. The high correlation coefficients indicate that the subjects tend to remain in about the same rank order. What the correlation coefficient fails to reveal is that individuals within the group are shifting in absolute IQ, but shifts affecting the relative standing of subjects in the group do not occur in enough cases to lower the correlation coefficient.

Growth of Intelligence in the Retarded.   The evidence reviewed thus far on the stability and growth of intelligence has been based on data collected on nonhandicapped populations. But how does the stability and growth of intelligence in the mentally retarded population compare to that of normals? Although far less research has been conducted on this question, several relevant studies have been undertaken.

Goodman (1977b) stated that it is commonly assumed that the IQ gap between retarded and normal persons widens with age. Fisher and Zeaman (1970), in a review of over thirty studies, reported that most authors found spontaneous decline in IQ with age in retarded persons. But before we accept this conclusion, we should consider the possibility that the research contains some flaws in sampling that may have biased the findings. First, there is frequently a loss of subjects in research using institutionalized subjects. The more able residents are released from institutions more often, so by the end of the study the less able cohorts—the residents who were not released—are being measured. Second, in studies of institutionalized subjects, a decline in IQ with age may reflect the depressing effect of an institutional environment. It cannot be assumed that the decline in IQ would have occurred if the subjects were living in a more stimulating environment.

Goodman and Cameron (1978) found that the IQs of young retarded children are more stable than those of normals. The stability was found to be greater among lower-IQ than among higher-IQ retarded children, however. In fact, the greatest fluctuations in IQ occurred among children with IQs between 51 and 80. Of significance in this study was the finding that intellectual growth in retarded children is proportional to that of younger normal children of the same mental age. That is, a retarded child with an IQ of 50 will progress about half as much in a given period of time as a normal child of the same mental age whose IQ is 100. In addition, Goodman and Cameron found that the retarded child continues to grow intellectually for more years than the normal child, diminishing the gap between the two groups. Such findings suggest that the mental development of retarded populations is delayed rather than halted. This is consistent with the findings of Fisher and Zeaman (1970), who reported that the retarded as a group do not achieve their highest mental age levels until age thirty-five.

Figure 5.2 depicts four hypotheses presented by Fisher and Zeaman (1970, p. 152) to explain how the mental growth of the retarded contrasts with that of normals:

Hypothesis I: Mental age (MA) in retarded people progresses linearly until about age sixteen and then stops. The *rate* at which it progresses is slower than that of normals, the slowness of the rate being determined by the degree of retardation. The final level achieved is lower for the retarded.

Hypothesis II: The retarded accumulate MA at a slower rate than normals, but ultimately they achieve the same upper limit. As Fisher and Zeaman put it, the retarded have a longer MA "growing season," as MA continues to progress after chronological age (CA) sixteen.

Hypothesis III: The retarded have a *shorter* MA growing season—MA ceases to grow well before CA sixteen—so they peak early and at a lower level than normals.

Hypothesis IV: The retarded have a slower growth rate than normals and MA growth continues after CA sixteen, but the ultimate level of MA achieved is lower than that of normals.

FIGURE 5.2 Four Hypothetical Growth Rates for MA in the Retarded Compared to Traditional MA Growth in Normals

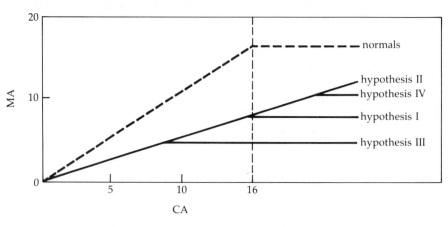

Adapted from M. A. Fisher and D. Zeaman, "Growth and decline of retardate intelligence," in N. R. Ellis, ed., *International Review of Research in Mental Retardation,* Vol. 4. Reprinted by permission of the authors and *Academic Press.* © 1970.

Data reported by Fisher and Zeaman (1970), Demaine and Silverstein (1978), Goodman (1976), and Silverstein (1979) are useful in assessing these hypotheses. Fisher and Zeaman (1970) reported that the intellectual growth of mentally retarded subjects at all levels is slower than that of normals; borderline and mildly retarded persons, however, were found to have a longer growing season. The growth of intelligence leveled off among the profoundly retarded before age fifteen and among the severely retarded by age twenty-five. Mild and borderline subjects, however, did not achieve their highest MAs before age thirty-five. A decline in MA was found in all groups after age sixty, with the higher-functioning groups falling off the most. The research of Silverstein (1979) and Demaine and Silverstein (1978) was consistent with these findings with one exception. Silverstein (1979) reported that higher-functioning retarded subjects have a shorter growing season, which contradicts the findings of the other researchers cited.

Goodman (1976) also reported no decline in IQ in the early adult years. She found slight increases in full-scale IQs with age. In addition, she introduced some provocative ideas regarding the growth of intelligence in retarded persons, noting that we need to discover the traits associated with low IQ that influence whether IQ reaches a plateau early, progresses normally, or continues to progress for a longer than normal period. Her data revealed a longer growing season that continues well into adulthood. This suggests that the development of some mentally retarded persons is delayed rather than deficient. In institutionalized populations, she found that verbal IQ is more susceptible to the influence of environment than performance IQ.

These findings provide the most support for Hypotheses II and IV given above. That is, the mental progress of the mentally retarded is linear from early childhood until about age sixteen, at which time the degree of retardation comes into play. Among the severely and profoundly retarded, the evidence suggests that intellectual growth reaches a plateau, whereas the growth of the mildly retarded continues beyond the time when it usually stops among normals, especially in the performance area. More research will be necessary to determine which personal or environmental factors influence the length of the intellectual growing season of mentally retarded persons.

No significant differences between males and females were found by Fisher and Zeaman (1970) or Demaine and Silverstein (1978). In addition, Fisher and Zeaman (1970) found no dramatic differences between diagnostic categories such as Down's syndrome and retardation resulting from other causes. This finding led them to conclude that the etiology of retardation is unimportant. Demaine and Silverstein (1978) found similarly shaped growth curves for Down's syndrome and a comparison group of children with retardation from other causes; however, the comparison group was consistently higher in MA than the Down's syndrome group.

As for IQ, it is not clear whether this measure of intelligence remains stable or not in retarded people. According to Fisher and Zeaman (1970), between ages five and sixteen the IQs of the mentally retarded drop off dramatically, since the gradual increase in MA is not enough to offset the increase in chronological age. The IQ becomes quite stable between sixteen and sixty years, with the higher-IQ retarded (borderline and mild) showing some gain in IQ with age. Other studies have reported a spontaneous decline in IQ with age both for institutionalized retarded subjects (Silverstein 1966a; Sloan & Harmon 1947; Zeaman and House 1962b) and for mountain children of lower than average IQ (Chapanis & Williams 1945; Wheeler 1932), suggesting that institutionalization alone cannot be blamed for the drop. But other studies of retarded populations found no decline in IQ with age (Collmann & Newlyn 1958; Throne, Schulman, & Kaspar 1962).

There are not many longitudinal studies on retarded populations to compare with studies like the Berkeley and Fels projects for normals. But the Fisher and Zeaman (1970) study points to some ways in which the growth of intelligence in the retarded differs from that of normals. However, before we can draw any sound conclusions about growth and stability of intelligence in retarded individuals, we need more evidence on mildly retarded subjects who were not institutionalized, to determine whether the trends noted by Fisher and Zeaman in institutionalized people still hold true.

INTERPRETATION OF THE IQ

So far we have dealt mostly with theoretical issues: What do intelligence tests measure? How can intelligence be measured? And does what intelligence tests measure remain stable? As we turn to practical considerations that arise in the administering of intelligence tests, we run into more theoretical issues. These concern interpretation of the tests.

Perhaps the hottest debates revolve around racial differences in tested IQ. Some minority groups do average lower than normal scores, but we are not sure why this is so. Some attribute the poorer showing to genetic differences, greatly angering those who claim that environmental deprivation or unfair tests are to blame. Any suggestion that there are ethnic differences now meets with great resistance. Critics of intelligence tests now appear to have captured public sympathy, and minority groups are increasingly vocal in their opposition to the use of the tests. However, as in most issues, truth does not reside exclusively on either side. Cleary, Humphreys, Kendrick, and Wesman (1975) noted that the responsible and fair use of psychological tests does not depend on a solution of the heredity-environment issue. To the teacher and psychologist it is of little importance whether a child's learning problem or low IQ is due primarily to genetic or environmental causes; the information that is useful is the prognosis for future school learning. Cleary et al. went on to state that all ability tests (including intelligence tests) measure current performance—there is no known way to measure innate capacity or potential. Any inference from an IQ that suggests a judgment as to a child's capacity is unwarranted.

Remember, too, that semantic confusion has tended to cloud the racial differences issue, for the layman's vague concept of "intelligence" is not the same as the meaning psychologists and educators give the word: the ability to do well in school. It is quite possible to have good street sense but a low tested IQ. The fact that educators' and psychologists' concept of intelligence is highly school-based is reflected by the content of intelligence tests—they are highly verbal in nature. In fact, the verbal scale of the WISC is even more highly related to school achievement than is the performance scale. However, this correlation reduces the efficiency of the test to predict in nonschool settings, particularly those for which abstract verbal skills are not a prerequisite for success. To further ease tensions in the racial differences controversy, Meyers (1971) suggests that we think of performance in classrooms on tests in terms of a "difference" model rather than a "deficit" model—that is, low performance may represent a difference in background rather than an inferiority.

It is legitimate to question whether today's schools teach—and today's IQ tests measure—the kinds of skills most useful in today's world. This should be the focus of attempts to determine whether intelligence tests are unfair to minority groups. But despite the lack of any conclusive evidence on the unfairness of intelligence tests, circumstances surrounding the use of the tests may make them unfair. Any child may be unfairly treated when the test is inappropriately administered, scored, or interpreted. Meyers, Sundstrom, and Yoshida (1974) have discussed in some detail the evils inherent in inappropriate practices (e.g., irresponsible procedures such as testing a bilingual child in English and testing a child who does not feel well) and slipshod write-ups by psychologists. Similarly, the report by Cleary et al. (1975) supporting responsible and fair use of psychological tests also condemns various misuses of aptitude tests.

Assuming adequate administration and scoring, there are still potential problems in the interpretation of the IQ, particularly in cases of mild retardation. The psychologist and teacher must know what information about the child is contained in the IQ, and, furthermore, they must be on guard against attributing more to the IQ than is warranted.

Test-Trait Fallacy

Tryon (1979) warned against interpreting test scores as if they were direct measures of a person's enduring generalized characteristics, or *traits*. He points out that a psychological test score is derived from the responses a person makes to a set of standard stimuli for the purpose of predicting responses to similar, naturally occurring stimuli in other settings. Responses to items on an intelligence test are predictive, for example, of responses to items on standardized achievement tests or examinations used in school. Test scores do not, however, reveal a person's basic qualities. Tryon gives examples of how certain test editors and publishers advertise their products as if their tests do measure some enduring quality of the person tested.

Tests of intelligence are standardized stimuli to which a child responds under standardized conditions; the resulting scores are descriptions of these responses. The scores permit us to make predictions about a child's performance in certain other kinds of measures—school tests and achievement tests—but the scores must not be interpreted as measures of a person's basic traits.

Performance versus Capacity

In any testing situation we can infer that children know any answer they get correct. But when children do not respond correctly to a question, we cannot infer that they do not know it—only that they have not performed. There are many reasons why children might fail to answer correctly when capable of it. In interpreting the results of intelligence tests, we must not confuse the observation that children "did not" respond correctly with the inference that they "cannot."

Cole and Bruner (1971) observed that competence is not tapped when ghetto children are required to perform in a manner that is inconsistent with past experience. In their article the authors relied heavily on the work of Labov (1972), who demonstrated that children can have considerable reasoning and debating skills in their own environments, yet when tested in a more standard situation, tend to be defensive, misinterpret questions, and seem motivated toward a different end than being correct.

Bortner and Birch (1970) reviewed considerable research that demonstrated that children possessed concepts that they were unable to use in standard testing situations. If the instructions or materials were altered, the children were suddenly responding correctly. For instance, there are age-specific tendencies to respond differentially to physical attributes, functional attributes, and class membership. We often obtain a response in terms of current child priorities: for instance, shown a copper pan and a scissors and asked how they are alike, a young child might answer "They are both shiny" or "They both have handles" rather than the highest-scored response, "They are both metal." Even though children know the other answers, they may not offer them unless we exhaust their repertoire of responses—something not done on standardized tests of intelligence. Clearly, we can only discuss *performance* when describing a child's behavior on intelligence tests—inferences about *capacity* are unwarranted.

Permanence of the Condition

Just as we cannot infer capacity from intelligence test results, we also cannot infer that a tested IQ is permanent. As we saw earlier in this chapter, there is room for considerable fluctuation in IQ *score* despite the high correlation in IQ *rank* over time. Whether a child is classified as retarded or gifted, the longitudinal studies have shown great individual variations in IQ scores over time—the most dramatic changes coming at critical periods (i.e., when that trait is undergoing its most rapid change) and when there is a marked change in environment (from one extreme to another). In the case of the mildly retarded there should be periodic reviews to determine whether the classification for each child continues to be appropriate.

Use in Placement Decisions

A final consideration in interpretation of the IQ is especially important in placement decisions for mildly retarded children: the IQ alone must never be the sole reason for placement. Some test manuals recommend that a certain percentage of a population—usually the lowest 2 or 3 percent by IQ scores—be used as a guide for identifying retarded individuals. As Meyers (1971) warns, this is a dangerous assumption and such directions should be ignored.

Meyers further warns against obtaining exploratory IQs or using low-ranking test performance as a signal to further test a child for possible placement in classes for the mentally retarded. Many children with IQs below a given cutoff function adequately in regular classes and should never be considered for special classes unless they have encountered learning problems of a rather severe degree in the classroom.

Particularly in the case of mildly retarded children, we must not lock children into a program (e.g., a program for the educable mentally retarded) on the basis of a single IQ score. Instead, IQ should be supplemented with other evidence pertaining to a child's functioning. As you will remember, the definition of mental retardation provided by the American Association on Mental Deficiency requires evidence of both low intelligence and impairments in adaptive behavior (Grossman 1977). Children should be reassessed periodically to determine whether changes in performance warrant alterations in programing. IQ scores should be only one of many types of information used to make that decision.

In summary, the intelligence test provides valuable information about a child if it is used appropriately and if the results are interpreted judiciously. We have discussed several common misconceptions about what these tests measure, misconceptions that can lead to misinterpretations and bad decisions. For more information on the use and misuse of intelligence tests and the judicious interpretation of scores, see Cleary et al. (1975), MacMillan and Meyers (1980), Meyers, MacMillan, and Yoshida (1974), Scarr (1978), and Jensen (1980).

INTELLIGENCE TESTING OF THE MINORITY CHILD

Even when the utmost caution is exercised in administration, scoring, and interpretation, there is concern that the use of intelligence tests with minority children is still discriminatory, for a variety of reasons.

Much of the criticism leveled at special education programs for mildly retarded children has focused upon the disproportionate number of minority children classified as mentally retarded and, more specifically, on the means whereby they were so classified. Litigation brought on behalf of ethnic minority children has hammered at the use of standardized intelligence tests for classification purposes, charging that these tests discriminate against children coming from cultural backgrounds that differ from the background and experiences of middle-class white youngsters (Cohen &

DeYoung 1973). The legal decisions pertaining to the mildly retarded and the alleged denial of due process will be reviewed in Chapter 8 of this book. The debate over the use of intelligence tests with minority children also rages in the professional literature (see *American Psychologist*, 1975, vol. 30, for the Report of the Ad Hoc Committee on Educational Uses of Tests with Disadvantaged Students). We cannot hope to resolve the issue in this book, but we will try to give an overview of its complexity and the arguments surrounding it.

The simplistic manner in which the issue tends to be argued (and, in fact, the simplistic manner in which the issue has been discussed in court cases) fails to do justice to the problem. No reasonable person can deny that administration of standardized tests has on occasion been shabby and that children have been abused as a consequence. The research evidence on the various subissues is simply incomplete and inconclusive, and some of the issues are philosophical ones for which all the empirical evidence in the world will not prove conclusive.

Even though it is hard to draw a conclusion as to whether intelligence testing should or should not be used with minority children, it is important that teachers familiarize themselves with both sides of the issues at stake. The teacher is typically a member of admissions and dismissal committees, where the decision of placement is handled. All too often the teacher sits quietly while other people present the evidence on a child's intellectual functioning. In order to represent the interests of the child in question, the teacher must be familiar with the arguments about intelligence testing and the evidence bearing on those arguments. If the child happens to be a minority child from a cultural background that differs markedly from the middle class, then the points raised by critics of the use of intelligence tests must be introduced and considered.

Intelligence tests do allow certain predictions to be made about minority children as well as other children. The critics do not deny this. Nonetheless, they recommend discontinuance of the tests because they feel that when all factors are considered, the results are more negative than positive. On the other hand, defenders feel that the tests are of too much benefit to stop using them because of their abuse by some insensitive individuals. This is not to say that intelligence tests are perfect instruments with no faults nor that intelligence tests are inherently bad and of no use whatsoever.

History of the Criticism of Intelligence Tests

Intelligence tests have been criticized ever since they were introduced in 1905. Meyers (1971) has described the early and continuing criticism stemming from massive and often impersonal screenings in achievement tests, tests for college admission, and the like. One frequent criticism has been that after psychologists secure a score, they become fatalistic about the trait. That is, instead of considering the trait amenable to modification through changes in experience, psychologists come to see the trait as stable and unalterable. Bijou (1966) and White (1970) have discussed this long-noticed problem in detail.

After World War I, social scientists noted that there were racial differences in IQ scores, with some groups scoring higher than others. Brigham (1923, 1926), for instance, made racial comparisons based on Army IQ data and concluded that racial differences in intelligence did exist. Such findings were popularized in periodicals of the day. Although social conscience was not then ripe for accepting countercharges by immigrants and the poor, Brigham did retract his contentions in 1930.

Following World War II, intellectual ability came to be seen as a valuable commodity, and education expanded tremendously. Merit scholarships appeared, career guidance grew, and entrance into prestigious colleges and universities became more competitive. One apparently humane response to this growth was a widespread attempt to place on an objective basis decisions as to who would be awarded scholarships and who would be admitted to colleges. The use of intelligence tests seemed to provide a way to do this. Proponents of testing advocated the tests as an impartial, objective means for assessing intellectual ability, as contrasted with making decisions about applicants on the basis of their parents' political influence or station in life. It is ironic that the very groups who were supposed to benefit from the use of tests rather than other criteria—the poor and those from racial minorities—are the very ones who now oppose testing on the grounds that it is discriminatory.

How did this shift occur? It seems as though the more that tests determined the life chances of the population, the more they became a focus of anxiety. Although testing was first seen as an alternative to choices made on the basis of influence, objections were raised to the elitism and meritocracy that some perceived to develop out of this trend toward reliance on testing. Testing that singled out the most intelligent for preferential treatment seemed somehow undemocratic.

By the 1950s the tests were under heavy fire. Eells, Davis, Havighurst, Herrick, and Tyler (1951) charged that existing tests tended to underestimate the abilities of the lower class. Their argument was that items on the tests (particularly verbal items) artificially depressed the ranking of lower-class children. They claimed that if tests were devised with "fair" items, poor children would rank higher. Accordingly, new tests were devised and the early reports indicated that the poor children did, in fact, rank higher on these tests. Subsequent investigations with these *culture fair tests*, however, revealed as much social class difference in performance on these tests as on the traditional tests of intelligence. Furthermore, the culture fair tests did not predict school success nearly as well as the traditional tests. The result was that the movement to develop culture fair tests gradually lessened. But it left an awareness that the public schools—and traditional tests of intelligence that predict success in those schools—are biased toward the dominant culture in this society. According to Cronbach (1975), there is now a sense that certain reasoning abilities in lower-class children could be capitalized upon if formal schooling were redesigned to be less verbal and less culture-laden.

Despite this accommodation of two points of view, the issue is by no means settled. In 1969 Jensen stirred things up again. After reviewing the literature on IQ testing, Jensen published a paper in which he suggested (in addition to some other, less inflammatory ideas that we have already mentioned) that the difference in IQ scores between blacks and whites in the United States was a matter of basic genetic differences. Segregationists praised him, while blacks and integrationists were outraged. In the furor that followed, students called for Jensen's dismissal from the University of California at Berkeley faculty and some social scientists proposed that all research on racial differences be stopped. Some overzealous advocates of segregation grabbed onto Jensen's analysis as evidence to support the proposal that public policy be altered in light of "racial differences." Others supported Jensen's academic freedom to study possible racial differences despite the unpopular conclusions he had reached through his analysis. Both sides have oversimplified his position, which we will not argue here, but the fact of the controversy remains.

In trying to explain why Jensen could run into so much criticism for saying essentially the same thing that Brigham was able to say in the 1920s, Cronbach (1975) spoke of *Zeitgeist,* the prevailing public sentiment:

> The public of the twenties was sour on immigrants; hence, Brigham's racial comparisons were popular and his critics got little hearing. In the 1970s a proposal merely to do research on ethnic differences is howled down. Jensen scorned the Zeitgeist and became a target of scorn himself.
>
> (pp. 11–12)

In addition to the controversy that still rages over *jensenism*—racial comparisons with inferences as to the relative importance of heredity and environment in determining intelligence—new fuel has been added to the fire by civil rights advocates. They claim, for instance, that it is unfair even to compare one group with another. For instance, if a test used only whites in its standardization sample, its norms should not be applied to inner-city black children. In diagnosing mental retardation especially, there is a feeling that inappropriate norms set up unfair standards for culturally different children and result in racial discrimination by placing disproportionate numbers of minority children in low educational tracks or in classes for the mentally retarded.

Questionable standardization norms and possible ethnic bias in testing have become the basis for a number of court cases challenging placement of minority children in EMR classes. These cases are described in some detail in Chapter 8. In the vast majority of these cases, the court has upheld the allegation that the tests discriminate against or are culturally biased against certain ethnic minority children. In the remainder of this section, we will consider the research evidence (as opposed to the legal evidence) bearing on the areas in which unfairness is now alleged: the items, or content, of intelligence tests, standardization procedures, and sources external to the test that might introduce bias when used with ethnic minority children. First, however, we will consider some of the terms used in discussion of the testing of minority children.

Concepts and Terminology

Jensen (1980) has provided a thorough, comprehensive review of the concepts and empirical data related to the issue of bias in mental testing. Although his book is rather technical in places and requires a basic understanding of statistics, many of the topics examined relate to our discussion. The terminology used in this discussion has been the subject of close examination since 1970.

Discrimination.   Three common interpretations of the word *discriminate* appear in the literature: (1) to treat unfairly because of an individual's group membership, (2) to treat differently, and (3) to show a reliable difference between individuals or groups. It is important to specify in which way the term is being used when we contend that "Intelligence tests discriminate." The third definition means that a test must discriminate what it claims to measure. A yardstick, for example, that does not discriminate between Kareem Abdul-Jabbar and Willie Shoemaker is a useless instrument for measuring distance. By the same token, a test of intelligence that fails to discriminate (in the sense of showing a reliable difference) between gifted and retarded children is likewise a poor tool.

Psychometric instruments can discriminate at several different levels: (1) within an individual, as when a child is a good reader but a poor mathematician, (2) between individuals on a particular ability, as when Billy is a better reader than John, or (3) between the averages of groups, as when girls are better than boys on vocabulary tests. The discrimination is said to be *incidental* when the test is not designed primarily to differentiate between groups and when it discriminates among individuals in each of several groups. An example of a test of this sort would be one that indicated that girls do better than boys on vocabulary tests and also indicated which boys had better vocabularies than others. Thus, as we examine the empirical data to determine whether they discriminate against blacks, we must ask whether such discrimination is incidental and therefore yields important information about specific black children, or whether the test yields lower test scores for blacks in general.

Bias. This general statistical term refers to a systematic under- or over-estimate of a population parameter based on measures of samples from the population. In psychometrics, the criteria for establishing test bias are *predictive validity* and *construct validity*. To establish a test's construct validity, we examine both *external* and *internal* criteria. External criteria are examined by considering the relationship between test scores and external criteria independent of the test. We could, for example, examine the relationship between IQ and other external criteria such as school marks or teacher ratings of intellectual ability. To establish internal criteria as biased, we would statistically examine the test data themselves. This would involve assessing reliability, item discrimination between high and low scorers on the total test, the extent to which items intercorrelate, and other item statistics. To determine the predictive validity of a test, we examine the relationship between test scores and the outcomes we hope to predict. This relationship is tested among various groups (e.g., blacks and whites, males and females) to determine whether the test scores predict as well for one group as another. A discussion of the statistical procedure for testing predictive validity is beyond the scope of this book; detailed explanations can be found in Cleary et al. (1975) and in Jensen (1980, Chapter 9).

Another kind of possible bias, *situational bias,* refers to influences in the test situation independent of the test itself that may lead to systematic bias in test scores. The sex, age, or race of the person administering the test, the child's level of maturation, and the relaxed or threatening atmosphere of the testing situation may affect one group of children differently than another, leading one group to score lower than the other.

Jensen (1980) describes several general concepts of how tests are biased against minority groups and contends that all of them are fallacious and unscientific. He refers to these concepts as the *egalitarian fallacy,* the *culture-bound fallacy,* and the *standardization fallacy.*

Egalitarian Fallacy. This concept is based on the assumption that all populations or groups are equally endowed with any trait or ability presumed to be measured by any test. According to this belief, there should be no differences between ethnic groups on any test; if groups are found to differ in the distributions of their test scores (e.g., mean differences or differences in variance) the test is assumed to be biased. Using this assumption as a basis, an unbiased test would be defined as one that yields reliable differences between individuals but does not yield reliable differences between groups.

Culture-bound Fallacy. This fallacy occurs when one person subjectively examines items on tests and judges certain items to be "culture-bound"—that is, to be unfair to someone taking the test who is from a culture other than the dominant middle-class culture. Specific items frequently cited as being unfair to minority children include the following:

1. Who wrote Hamlet?
2. What should you do if a child much smaller than yourself tries to pick a fight with you?
3. A child is shown a picture of a comb with a tooth missing and asked what is missing.

Jensen (1980) points out that although certain items may discriminate unfairly between groups, subjective inspections are not the correct means for establishing unfairness. The bias of test items must be established through objective psychometric and statistical criteria, which were mentioned previously as the means of evaluating the *internal* criteria for construct validity.

Standardization Fallacy. This concept refers to the belief that because a test was standardized on one population, such as middle-class whites, it is necessarily biased or unfair when used with a different population, such as blacks or Hispanics. This is a common criticism of the Stanford-Binet and earlier versions of the Wechsler tests, because they were originally standardized on a white population. It is true that before a test standardized on one population can be used with a second population, it must be determined whether that test is reliable and valid for the second population. This determination should involve an empirical examination of the test's appropriateness for the second population, not the ipso facto argument that a test standardized on one population is automatically biased when used with another population.

Predictive Validity

Considerable research has addressed the issue of predictive validity of intelligence tests for minority children (Cleary et al. 1975; Jensen 1980; Flaugher 1978; McNemar 1975). Although much of the research and writing is highly technical, involving procedures for relating IQ scores to criterion measures for different groups, the results clearly suggest that the predictive validity of tests varies for certain outcomes among certain distinct groups. After analyzing data on the use of intelligence tests among different cultural groups, Cleary et al. (1975) concluded that an intelligence test is fair when used to predict academic success. But we should not automatically conclude that it is equally fair for predicting social success in the neighborhood, marital success, or any other outcome.

Williams (1972b) has approached this topic from a slightly different angle. He found that when the bias is either present in both the predictor (the IQ test) and the criterion (academic success) or absent in both the predictor and criterion, the correlation will be high. However, whenever the bias is present in only one (either the predictor or criterion), the correlation is low. The correlation for whites is high when one compares IQ with school achievement, because bias is absent on both measures. For blacks the correlation is high but for a different reason: bias is present on both measures. Hence Williams argues that the high correlations found between IQ and academic achievement for whites and blacks are high for different reasons.

Jackson (1975) used Williams's logic as an argument against the way Cleary et al. (1975) treated the issue of fairness. According to Jackson, the mode of statistical analysis used by Cleary et al. masked the role of the bias that operates in the case of blacks but not in the case of whites. Merely improving administration and limiting interpretation of the tests, as Cleary et al. had recommended, is not enough, according to Jackson. Speaking for the Association of Black Psychologists, he stated that the tests themselves would have to be changed.

Williams (1972a) had already experimented with a black-oriented test he had devised: the Black Intelligence Test of Cultural Homogeneity (BITCH).[4] He administered the culture-specific test to 100 black and 100 white children ranging from sixteen to eighteen years of age. Each group was equally divided into low and middle socioeconomic status. Although Heber, Dever, and Conry (1968) had reported that the incidence of IQs below 75 was higher for black children than for white children at every socioeconomic level based on standard IQ tests, Williams reported that on his BITCH test, black subjects had reliably higher scores than whites. This led Jackson (1975) to speculate about the possible interpretation of these results as evidence for a "white intellectual deficit" model.

BITCH is probably predictive of something (e.g., success in some aspect of the subcultural setting of black youngsters). If that is the goal of intelligence testing, then the BITCH test is probably superior to the Stanford-Binet or WISC. However, as noted by Humphreys (1975), knowledge of street vocabulary is interesting but as of yet has not been studied seriously as predictive of anything of social consequence. The fact remains that the

---

[4]An example of the type of questions in BITCH is: "What is Mother's Day?" The correct response is "the day the checks arrive for Aid to Dependent Children every month."

dominant culture in the United States is the middle class and the values held therein. As a result, the criterion variables against which intelligence tests are validated are culture-bound. It will be difficult to develop a new type of test that can predict socially relevant outcomes and yet not be influenced by the skills valued by the dominant culture. While subcultures within the society may develop different kinds of skills than those valued by the dominant culture, these skills often are not related to success in the larger society. They do not lead to success in school, and in turn are not sought after in the prestige occupations; as a result they may be useful within the subculture but not in the dominant culture.

Jensen (1980) concluded that the predictive validity of mental ability tests is generally the same for blacks and whites. In other words, research indicates that we can predict academic outcomes for blacks about as well as we can for whites. When bias occurs, the systematic error tends to *favor* blacks—we tend to predict higher academic performance levels than blacks actually achieve. By using the norms developed on whites to predict on the basis of IQ scores the academic outcomes for blacks, we find that we tend to *over*estimate the performance of blacks.

Critics of intelligence tests (Goldman & Hartig 1976; Mercer 1973) frequently argue that standardized achievement tests are a poor criterion for establishing the predictive validity of intelligence tests because standardized intelligence and achievement tests are somewhat interdependent— they measure many of the same things. Critics contend that a more telling criterion would be school marks, and studies show that the correlation between IQ and school marks is relatively low (Gerard & Miller 1975; Goldman & Hartig 1976). A more recent study by Messé, Crano, Messé, and Rice (1979), however, indicates a strong predictive relationship between mental ability scores and classroom performance. Messé et al. also found that mental ability test scores predicted just as well for lower socioeconomic status children; if anything, the mental ability test scores overpredicted these children's academic performance.

The research has fairly consistently indicated that the predictive validity of test scores is equal for black and white children. As MacMillan and Meyers (1980a) note, however, a child's success in school in the upcoming year is predicted better by the child's success in the current year than by the results of a test battery. In other words, a child's marks in third grade are predicted better by the second-grade marks than by test results. This is because factors other than academic aptitude influence academic success and are relatively stable from year to year, factors such as emotional health, motivation, support of family members, extent of academic assistance at home, absence of chronic illnesses, and similar influences. All in all, the existing literature provides little support to the argument that predictive validity of intelligence tests is different for blacks and whites.

Construct Validity

A second criticism of standardized tests of intelligence is that the test content is biased against children coming from backgrounds other than the white middle class. This relates to the culture-bound fallacy described by Jensen (1980). It is argued that an assumption underlying standardized tests is that all children have had equal exposure to the material tapped on the test, so that differences in performance can be attributed to differences in the children's abilities to profit from the exposure. But in the case of children coming from cultural backgrounds that differ from that of the middle class, the child often has not been exposed to the same experiences. The tests tend to tap only the experiences of the middle-class child. They never tap experiences that the inner-city child has had but the middle-class child has not.

Earlier in this chapter, we listed several items frequently noted as evidence that tests are culture-bound. Williams (1970) argues that a child's response to a question such as "What should you do if a child much smaller than yourself tries to pick a fight with you?" depends on the neighborhood the child lives in. In many black neighborhoods, it would be suicidal to walk away, but the response "fight back" would be scored as an error.

The points raised by Williams and by Hewitt and Massey (1969) are not denied by defenders of the tests. Instead, they would note that the problem with IQ tests lies not so much in the bias of the content as in the interpretation of the score. The problem, as they see it, is that some people interpret intelligence test performance as a measure of overall capability. Certainly no one should infer that some children have less gray matter or are inferior when they have had experiences that interfere with getting correct answers on a test. Instead, interpretations must be restricted to the setting in which the test is predictive—the school. But it can be argued that the content bias in the test is also present in the schools. That is, a child coming from a culturally different background will encounter difficulty in school, since the school and its content are derived from the same middle-class perspective that is inherent in the test.

Another source of confusion in discussions of the validity of minority testing is the common assumption that minority children are most handicapped in the verbal sections of tests, for these are the parts that seem to be most heavily culture-laden. But the evidence does not consistently bear out this assumption and may even disprove it. According to Sattler's (1970) review of the evidence, results for the WISC show that the nonverbal parts (labeled *performance*) are as difficult, if not more difficult, for black children than are the verbal portions of the tests. Teahan and Drews (1962) found that junior high black children in the South scored higher on the performance scale than on the verbal scale; but for Northern blacks, achievement on the two scales was comparable. Caldwell and Smith (1968) reported higher verbal than performance scores for Southern black children. Other comparisons of verbal and performance scales (Atchison 1965; Hughes & Lessler 1965) for retarded black children reported advantages on the verbal scale. Higgins and Sivers's (1958) comparison of performance on the Stanford-Binet (verbal) and the Raven's Progressive Matrices (nonverbal) revealed that white and black youngsters who were all from low socioeconomic status backgrounds did comparably on the Stanford-Binet, while the black children did worse on the Raven's than did the white children. Hence while many people have looked at the items on the verbal and performance scales, superficially analyzed them on cultural loadings, and come to the conclusion that verbal items are necessarily more culturally loaded, this assumption is unwarranted—in fact, the opposite view seems to have garnered more empirical support.

Jensen (1970a) recommends that, in order to analyze the Stanford-Binet and WISC tests for cultural bias, we should break them down into smaller pieces than the verbal and performance chunks. Looking at specific items and subtests, he notes that certain kinds of items (e.g., digit span, block design) do not appear to have the same status bias as other items. He suggests further that there are no extremely fair or extremely biased tests. He thinks it better to represent them on a continuum of various degrees of culture loading.

As noted earlier, however, bias must be established through psychometric examination rather than subjective scrutiny. Sattler (1979) concluded that "numerous studies indicate that the construct validity of the WISC and WISC-R, as well as other standardized intelligence tests, is as similar for Black children as it is for White children" (p. 5). Similarly, Jensen (1980) concluded after examining a variety of internal psychometric features of tests that white, black, and Mexican-American children tend to show the same internal consistency on items. Moreover, comparisons between whites and blacks failed to substantiate charges of differential difficulty on items judged to be culturally biased. Social class differences were also unrelated to performance. In fact, differences between blacks and whites were consistently greater on items believed to be less culturally biased than on items believed to be culturally biased. The rank order of item difficulty for whites was found to be highly similar to the rank order of item difficulty for blacks. In general, Jensen's analysis revealed that items that discriminate individual differences in general mental ability for whites also differentiate general mental ability for blacks.

The contention that the content of individual tests of intelligence is biased against minority children is not supported by empirical data. The evidence is much clearer for comparisons of blacks and whites than it is for comparisons of Hispanic and white children, since there is less evidence bearing on the Hispanic child. Nevertheless, the available evidence indicates that the content is fair for Hispanic children as well.

Standardization Data

Mercer (1973a) and others have criticized the use of standardized tests of intelligence with ethnic minority children in cases where the test developers have failed to include ethnic minority children in the standardization sample. The argument put forth is that it is unfair to compare the performance of a black or Spanish-surname youngster to standards developed exclusively with white children, who are, as a group, of slightly higher social class than the national average. In normative testing, a given child's performance is compared to norms established by administering the same instrument to a sample of individuals. The sample on which the norms are established must be representative of the population in general for the norms to be valid. For example, if we measure the height of a ten-year-old child and find that the child is six feet tall, how can we determine whether that is tall, short, or average? Here is how it is done: over time a representative sample of ten-year-olds has been measured and norms established; we can then look at the resulting chart to determine how this child's height compares to that of ten-year-olds throughout the nation.

It is only logical to assume that norms for IQ should be developed in the same way as norms for height: through representative sampling. But this has not been the case. For the Stanford-Binet test, the standardization sample in 1937 consisted of 3184 native-born white subjects ranging in age from one and a half to eighteen years and divided equally by sex. The sample included a disproportionate number of urban subjects, and the subjects tended to be above average in socioeconomic status.[5]

The WISC standardization sample consisted of 2200 white children ranging in age from five to fifteen years. Equal numbers of male and female subjects were tested and the sample was broken down with respect to geographic location, urban versus rural residence, and parental occupation. The sample also included 55 mentally retarded subjects from institutions and special classes in public schools.

When Mercer (1970b) tested 1298 children in a medium-size California school district with the WISC, she found discrepancies for three ethnic groups: white children had a mean IQ of 110.3 with a standard deviation of 14.0; black children had a mean IQ of 92.9 with a standard deviation of 14.2; Mexican-American children had a mean IQ of 93.9 with a standard deviation of 19.9. While these data may not be accurate for the nation as a whole, they do point up the vulnerability of the minority children to being classified as mentally retarded when they may be just slightly below the aver-

---

[5] The third revision of the Stanford-Binet did not include a restandardization. Instead, more current data (collected between 1950 and 1954) were checked against existing standards for the 1937 revision. As a result, the best 122 items from the previous revision, Forms L and M, were selected to constitute the 1960 revision.

age for their ethnic group. This would mean that a higher proportion of minority children would be placed into special EMR classes than one would expect based on their proportions in the larger society. This has in fact been the case. But Cleary et al. (1975) noted that while the *proportion* of blacks qualifying for a low track in school will be greater than for whites, there will be a larger *number* of whites qualifying due to the greater absolute number of whites.

Defenders of the tests note that item selection during standardization should be investigated for different groups. Test developers, they argue, should examine item correlations and analyze items separately for different groups to ensure that the items have the same rank order difficulty across subgroups, have similar reliabilities, and have similar construct and predictive validity. This practice is known as *scaling*. Jensen (1980), however, maintains that scaling of scores is an unimportant issue in standardization, since the final goal is to give different numerical values (IQs); scaling, he says, will not in any way affect the relative standing of persons in their subgroups, nor will it affect the relative difference between one group and another. A change in scaling only presents differences within a group or between groups on a different numerical scale, which is analagous to translating a distance expressed in feet to meters.

The distribution of IQs among blacks has about the same standard deviation as the distribution among whites, but the mean IQ among blacks is lower by about one standard deviation. But what, if anything, should educators do about this? Educational decisions are not made on the basis of group comparisons, they are made for individual children. There is little doubt that in our society and educational system today, whether or not intelligence tests are used, whether or not they are adjusted for sociocultural factors to yield "corrected" IQs, black children are not succeeding as well as white children. The reasons for this tendency cannot be explicated precisely; certainly social class, poverty, and similar factors are implicated. Sattler (1979), a strong defender of intelligence tests, had this to say about them:

> If they are to partake in our country's development, children will need to have certain cognitive skills. These skills are not white skills. They are not black skills. They are not middle-class skills. They are simply skills needed by literate people. It is a myth to say that intelligence tests are biased; culturally loaded, yes, culturally biased, no. If one accepts the myth that intelligence tests are biased, then one also must accept the fact that our Western civilization is biased. And this I refuse to do. I am not willing to condemn our civilization's tools, such as mathematics, language, nonverbal reasoning, memory, social comprehension, conceptual thinking, and perceptual organization. Intelligence tests measure these abilities, and they measure them equally well in black children and in white children.
>
> (p. 9)

Bias Introduced by Situational Factors

So far we have been dealing with general charges of bias in intelligence tests. But some specific ways in which individual children's culturally different backgrounds may lower their IQ scores have also been suggested. The area of greatest concern is the biracial testing situation, usually one in which a white examiner tests an ethnic minority child. Many variables may operate to depress the performance of the child in such a situation. Some of these variables are seen to reside within the examiner—such things as stereotyped ideas about ethnic minorities. Others are differences between the minority child and white middle-class youngsters—in terms of motivation, anxiety, and attitude toward the examiner. And finally, some reside in a lack of communication due to a poor matchup in backgrounds.

Language as a Factor.   Critics of intelligence testing of minority children often cite language differences as a possible source of bias. The major contention of critics is that the examiner's unfamiliarity with a dialect other than standard English may serve to lower a child's IQ score. The way in which this operates differs for the city black child who speaks "black English" and for the bilingual youngster who comes from a family that speaks a language other than English. It is the children from Spanish-speaking families (Puerto Rican or Mexican-American) who are most often referred to in discussions of the problems of the bilingual.

There is no current consensus on the extent to which nonstandard English affects a child's performance in IQ testing. Some people feel that the language of the ghetto black child is deficient; others feel that it is simply different. The theory that ghetto black children are verbally deprived is held by several noted scholars (e.g., Bernstein 1967; Hess & Shipman 1965), according to Samuda (1975). But this position has been strongly challenged by Labov (1971) and Baratz and Baratz (1970).

While we cannot settle this argument, we can examine questions that pertain to intelligence testing: Do children who speak a dialect have trouble being understood by the examiner? Can they understand what is being asked of them by the examiner? Has the ghetto black child's exposure to the verbal content of the test been equal to that of a middle-class child?

To find out whether these potential problems do indeed hamper ghetto black children on IQ tests, black examiners (Quay 1971) tested four-year-old black children on the Stanford-Binet in both standard English and dialect and under two incentive conditions (tangible and social reinforcers). They found that it made no difference which kind of incentive they used. And the black children responding in dialect tended to be bilingual in their understanding of both standard English and dialect. But while the black examiners understood the children's responses, there is no way of knowing whether other examiners could have done so. As noted by Meyers et al. (1974), research on the ability of different ethnic groups to understand dialects is anything but conclusive.

Jensen's (1980) analysis of these data failed to support the contention that children who speak black dialect cannot understand verbal test items or instructions given orally. In Quay's studies (1971, 1972, 1974), the Stanford-Binet was translated into black dialect and then administered to inner-city black children in both black dialect and standard English. The study failed to reveal significant differences in IQs related to the form of the test administered.

Jensen (1980) did find, however, that bilingual populations tended to score significantly lower on verbal portions of tests than on performance sections, which raises questions about the construct validity of intelligence tests when used with bilingual populations. He noted, however, that this does little to impair the predictive validity of the tests in short-term predictions of academic achievement, since the language difficulty encountered on the test will also occur in the child's learning in classes where English is spoken and on achievement tests administered in English.

Sattler (1970) reviewed the literature on translations of standardized tests into Spanish and concluded that any such attempt is fraught with hazards. In one study (Keston & Jimenez 1954) the Stanford-Binet was administered in both English and Spanish to fourth-grade bilingual Mexican-American children. Scores for the group as a whole were significantly higher on the English version. Sattler noted that the Mexican-American child who is bilingual does not speak the formal Spanish that was used in translating the test but rather a version that is contaminated by intrusions from English. And Spanish equivalents of English words are sometimes more difficult, sometimes easier.

When the WISC or Stanford-Binet is translated into Spanish, it becomes a "hybrid of neither culture." The validity and reliability of the test must be reconsidered, and the examiner must be aware of the possibility that the bilingual child may not have mastered either Spanish or English to the extent that a monolingual child has mastered his native tongue. The bilingual child's capability may even be mixed. For example, a bilingual child taught in an English-speaking school may not be sure of the vocabulary of science in Spanish since he used only English in this context. Hence, the child may be fluent in conversational Spanish, yet may be more comfortable using English in discussions of scientific matters.

The Child's Opinion of the Test and the Examiner. How children feel about being tested and about who is doing the testing may have a significant effect on their scores. Sattler (1970) cited work going back as early as 1913 in which the race of the examiner was thought to affect the performance of black examinees. He wrote that this fear was heightened in the case of Southern blacks:

> They may show fear and suspicion, verbal constriction, strained and unnatural reactions, and a facade of stupidity to avoid appearing "uppity." They may also score low to avoid personal threat.
>
> (p. 169)

Katz and his associates (Katz 1964, 1968; Katz, Epps, & Benjamin 1960; Katz & Greenbaum 1963; Katz, Henchy, & Allen 1968; Katz, Robinson, Epps, & Waley 1964) ran a number of experiments in this area in the 1960s. One experiment (Katz, Roberts, & Robinson 1965) was designed to test the hypothesis that children's performances are depressed when they feel a threat of evaluation on a dimension considered important, such as intelligence. In the experiment, college students were tested by black and white examiners on a digit symbol task. When told by the white examiner that the task was a measure of hand-eye coordination, the subjects did better than when told it was a measure of intelligence.

Katz and his colleagues (1968) also tested the theory that black children are fearful of failing as a result of their earlier negative experiences with white adults, a factor that also will depress performance in a biracial testing situation. They reported that black youngsters responded to verbal reproof by a black examiner with increased effort to gain approval, but they perceived the criticism of white examiners as expressions of dislike.

Although Katz's findings are widely cited, their significance has been questioned. Meyers and his associates (1974) noted that generalizations from this work to individual intelligence testing may be hazardous since the tasks employed in these studies do not correspond to those on the Stanford-Binet or Wechsler scales, and the kinds of evaluative comments made during testing in the 1968 study are violations of recommended testing protocol. Furthermore, for most of their studies, Katz and his associates tested college students, who differ dramatically in terms of age and IQ from children referred for possible EMR placement. Nevertheless, the Katz research must sensitize us to possible sources of bias. And Barnes (1974) has pointed out that the mood of black people has changed, possibly making examiner-examinee variables even more potent than they were when Katz studied them in the 1960s.

In the 1970s, a complex dynamic involving a covert hostility held by the child toward the examiner has been hypothesized as a possible bias factor in test results for black children (Barnes 1974; Leland 1971; Meyers et al. 1974). It is believed that when children anticipate failing, their feelings of being victimized are aroused; these lead to hostile feelings. Since the children know that they cannot express these feelings toward the examiner directly, they manifest them in indirect ways, one of which is nonpartici-pating resistance.

Differences in motivation between low socioeconomic status black and middle-class white children are also suggested as inhibitors to maximum performance on standardized tests. Due to their differential experiences, inner-city black children are not as inclined to be achievement-oriented as white children; they do not feel as comfortable in a testlike situation in which adults question them. But the test situation is something the middle-class children have experienced frequently, so they know: (1) it is not threatening and (2) in such a situation you are to do your best. In working with culturally deprived preschoolers (both white and black), Zigler and Butterfield (1968) likewise observed the desire on the part of low socioeco-nomic status children to terminate the unpleasantness of the testing situa-tion by giving responses like "I don't know" that hurried the examination along. It has also been suggested that low and middle socioeconomic status children differ in their individual reinforcer preferences. Lower-class chil-dren are less motivated to be correct. Instead, they appear to be more ori-ented to the social aspects of the test situation than to the test items them-selves (Leland 1971; Zigler & Butterfield 1968).

Despite all the ways in which it has been shown that racial tension could affect the IQ scores of black children, analyses of extant studies using stand-ardized intelligence tests have failed to demonstrate that the race of the examiner adversely affects the IQ scores of black children (Sattler 1970, 1973; Jensen 1980; Shuey 1966). Sattler (1979) claims that twenty-four of twenty-eight studies related to the examiner's race indicated that race is an insignificant factor. It is even possible that a biracial testing situation may *improve* performance. When Bucky and Banta (1972) analyzed the atmo-sphere during biracial testing, they found that the white examiner–black subject combination was equal to or better than black–black pairs on all measures except one (physical contact).

The research on white examiner–black child relationships is inconclu-sive; the research on testing relationships with Spanish-surname children is almost nonexistent. In this area we have to rely heavily on extrapolations from experimental studies that usually use tasks other than those on the standardized intelligence tests.

Those who try to explain the lowered test performance of Spanish-sur-name children (in both IQ and achievement) frequently point to social and cultural circumstances that are believed to depress their performance (Hel-ler 1966; Manuel 1965). For example, it is suggested that Spanish-surname children have a lower need to achieve (Ramirez, Taylor, & Petersen 1971) and a low level of aspiration (Heffernan 1955), and that they tend to view interpersonal relationships as an attempt by one person to control another (Ramirez et al. 1971). If these generalizations are valid, the traits they describe could lower performance on intelligence tests due to an inappropriate motivational set and a tendency to perceive the testing situation as a threatening event. Research on this topic and the effects of such traits on performance in individual tests are lacking.

It is often charged that Spanish-surname children are at a disadvantage in the testing situation and in school since they are taught to be cooperative, while success in school depends on competitiveness. Madsen and his associates (Kagan & Madsen 1971; Madsen & Shapira 1970) have investigated cooperative and competitive behavior in Mexicans, Mexican-Americans, urban black Americans, and white Americans. In the first study they found that Mexican-American boys (ages seven to nine) tended to be less competitive than Mexican-American girls and both sexes of black and white children. However, all three groups of American children were found to be highly competitive in comparison to the sample of village children from Mexico, who were found to be cooperative. These findings were essentially confirmed in their 1971 study, in which the seven- to nine-year-old subjects were found to rank as follows in terms of cooperation: Mexicans, Mexican-Americans, and Anglo-Americans.

Ramirez and Gonzalez (1971) have criticized the use of standardized intelligence tests with Spanish-surname children because these children's cognitive style is primarily relational, while good performance on the tests requires an analytic style. They may be right, but the data reported in their article do not support their assertion.

Examiner as a Source of Bias.   After reviewing the literature on how a child's ethnic background could affect IQ test performance, Meyers et al. (1974) suggested that perhaps race in itself is not the dimension that needs further study. They propose that research into certain modes of interaction by the examiner that could prompt negative behaviors might be more profitable.

Examiners may be a source of potential bias through a "self-fulfilling prophecy" dynamic. If they hold stereotypes about black and Spanish-surname persons, they are liable either to communicate to the child that they expect poor performance or not to credit the child for close responses. In either case they can cost the child IQ points and thereby depress the score. A second source of examiner bias is the possibility that pretest information (such as knowing that a child has been referred for possible EMR placement) develops an expectancy in the examiner that could cost the child a few points. This sort of thing may be crucial in borderline cases. But research evidence on both of these possibilities is extremely limited.

Sattler (1970) discussed the possible effects of stereotypes held by a white examiner towards a Mexican-American child and stereotypes held by the child towards the white examiner. The evidence he reviewed indicated that if either one holds a negative stereotype, the rapport essential to testing will be damaged. Simmons (1961) described the white-held stereotype of the Mexican-American: unclean, prone to drunkenness, criminal, deceitful, of low morality, musical, romantic, and having a love of flowers. Mexican-Americans, conversely, tend to think of whites as stolid, cold-hearted, distant, conceited, insincere, ambitious, and industrious. Whether and how these stereotypes operate in the testing situation have not been determined. However, Madsen (1964) concluded from a study in south Texas that, although the two ethnic groups are aware of differences that divide them, feelings of resentment arise from a lack of understanding on both sides.

As for the possibility of an examiner's scoring or perception of the child being influenced by previous knowledge of what the child is "suspected of," it has been suggested that when psychologists test children for possible placement in special programs (such as those for the mentally retarded or gifted), they should do so blindly. This is what is commonly done in medical research on medications when a placebo group is used as a control: subjects receiving and delivering the medications are unaware of (i.e., blind to) the contents of the pill they are receiving, to keep them from biasing the research by their expectations.

Meyers et al. (1974) concluded that the findings of research that tried to test the effect of expectations on test outcomes are inconsistent. In these studies the prospective "tester" was typically told that the child to be tested was high or low in ability; sometimes the "scorer" was also told in advance that the child was considered to be a person of high or low ability, in order to determine the effect of the description on the child's score. Some of the studies showed that the labeling altered scores in the direction expected, with higher scores for favorably described subjects and lower for those described as low. But other studies reported that the labeling made no difference in test scores. Meyers et al. (1974) offered the following possible reasons for the inconsistent results: (1) extreme descriptions as gifted or retarded may have been recognizably unrealistic given the abilities of the child during testing; (2) some studies employed children, while others used tapes or printed information; and (3) the experience of the tester or scorer varied from graduate students to experienced professionals.

CONSEQUENCES OF PROHIBITING THE USE OF INTELLIGENCE TESTS

The critics of intelligence tests have considerable support, and one option available is to prohibit the use of intelligence tests. In California the legislature voted twice to prohibit the use of group mental ability tests in schools, but twice the governor vetoed the bills. More recently it was decided that intelligence tests should not be used for purposes of identifying mentally retarded children in California. Some of the consequences of such actions may harm the minority children they were supposed to benefit as much as or even more than IQ testing had harmed them.

Obtained in a standard manner, an IQ for a child has more behavioral correlates than any other psychological measure now available (Kohlberg & Zigler 1967). Its predictive value helps us to provide appropriate special help for students who are likely to fall behind. Without IQ tests we might have to wait three or four years to find out what the test could tell us now: whether a child is going to have academic problems. Of the alternatives that have been suggested—subjective evaluations of children by interviewers or their teachers, academic grades, tests of qualities other than intelligence, diagnostic tests, and mastery tests—none is as reliable a predictor of academic success as the standard intelligence tests.

The California decision to prohibit the use of intelligence tests for purposes of placement as mentally retarded is frightening because it opens the door to subjectivity. Unless the legislature decides completely to prohibit the classifying of children as retarded, diagnosis is going to depend exclusively on subjective impressions: the teacher of the regular class "thinks" the child is retarded, the psychologist "thinks" the teacher's impression is right, and so on. Many children may be misdiagnosed as retarded, while many others who need help may be overlooked. Some school psychologists point out that the state has taken away from them the one means of *preventing* EMR placements. In cases where everyone else was certain that the child was retarded, the psychologist could block EMR placement if the child had an IQ above some limit.

If the IQ tests are discontinued it will be more difficult to identify and encourage low achievers—students who are not performing well but who score high on intelligence tests. The teacher may conclude that such students' low performance is all they are capable of. Programs will be hard to evaluate, and educational opportunities will come to depend more heavily upon ancestry and influence. As Sattler (1970) put it, curriculum decisions "would be based less on evidence and more on prejudice and caprice" (p. 186). In short, bias and discrimination could actually increase as a result of not testing.

Reactions to the moratorium on intelligence testing in California have been mixed. Some psychologists have hailed it as an endorsement of their competence and judgment, saying that they are now free to use whatever criteria they judge appropriate (except intelligence tests) to make determinations of mental retardation. A more frequent reaction, however, is that prohibiting testing will prove disadvantageous to the black and Hispanic children in the state who are having academic difficulty.

MacMillan and Meyers (1980) noted that, although the prohibition of intelligence tests in diagnosing mental retardation may reduce certain types of erroneous placements, other erroneous placements will occur through the use of subjective evidence that is frequently unreliable and subject to misinterpretation. Such evidence can no longer be contradicted by an IQ score that is above the mandated upper limit. Teacher judgment, for example, is notoriously unreliable and inaccurate. In a massive study by Lewis (1947), for example, teachers were asked to identify the mentally retarded and gifted children in their classes. This study involved 455 schools in thirty-six states. The teachers successfully identified only 12 percent of the children who scored below 70 on an intelligence test. Moreover, of the children identified by the teachers as mentally retarded, 26 percent achieved IQs above 90.

Possibly even more misguided is the naive assumption that prohibiting the use of intelligence tests will improve the educational plight of minority children who have been overrepresented in EMR classes. As Scarr (1978) noted, the prohibition of testing is unlikely to reduce drastically the proportion of certain minority students in EMR programs or other special help programs. Neither will adding points to the mental test scores. The test of the success of education is not the predictor, IQ, but the criterion being predicted, academic achievement. MacMillan and Meyers (1980) wrote that "*not* giving mental tests at seven, eight, or nine years of age cannot retroactively correct the academic failure experienced at ages five to seven" (p. 146).

The frustration experienced by children from disadvantaged backgrounds may be intensified by the recent trend across the country of requiring students to pass proficiency exams to graduate from high school and in some states to progress from earlier levels of school. Unlike all other students, special education students are not required to pass these criterion-referenced tests to progress or graduate. Milton C. Gordon reported in *Newsweek* (October 22, 1979) that in North Carolina, a state with a high prevalence of mental retardation, 18 percent more black high school juniors failed the math test than whites. This case points up the prospect that minority children who are denied special help will find out at graduation that such help was needed. Denial of special education *because* a child comes from a minority is a highly discriminatory practice, one that may eventually be challenged in the courts.

This being the case, why do efforts to prohibit intelligence testing receive so much popular support? Perhaps one explanation is that many proposals to eliminate testing are really attempts to eliminate the *function* supported by the test. For example, critics attack testing as a contributor to homogeneous grouping, placement and labeling of EMR children, or honors programs.

We seem upset with the information that the test gives us: there will be a disproportionately high academic failure rate among ethnic minorities. But with or without the test, there is going to be this higher failure rate in schools as long as they continue teaching the content presently taught, using the instructional strategies now employed, valuing and rewarding the behaviors now rewarded, evaluating success the way they do, and employing teachers from the backgrounds they now recruit them from. Negative emotions now focused on intelligence testing might be more appropriately directed at the school and the larger society.

SUPPLEMENTS TO INTELLIGENCE TESTS

The standardized intelligence tests have long been criticized, especially in their use with minority children. Some critics have advocated the prohibition of intelligence testing, but as we have seen, elimination of the tests may create more problems than it solves. In a less emotional attack, psychologists have expressed concern over the limited range of skills tapped by conventional tests. This concern has led to the development of tests and procedures to supplement the intelligence test, changes that have coincided with attempts to make the interpretation of the tests more culture fair.

Limitations of the Assessment of Intelligence

Some of the criticism of traditional psychometric assessment has come from behaviorists. They argue that the nonspecific descriptive categories (e.g., mentally retarded, gifted) that are used and the kinds of information provided to the teacher are not of as much benefit for programing as are descriptive data on the relationship between behavior (such as responses) and the environmental events (specific stimuli) that control it. They feel that this is the kind of information needed most if the behaviors are to be increased or decreased. Hence the behavioristic orientation suggests a vastly different role for the psychologist than administering psychometric tests and classifying people according to existing categories (e.g., mentally retarded). Instead, the psychologist would engage actively in the description of behavior and the designing of environmental interventions to promote development in children whose behavior is in need of modification.

From a somewhat different point of view, intelligence tests have been criticized on the grounds that they serve primarily to classify individuals (as mentally retarded or gifted, for instance) but provide little useful information to teachers that pinpoints areas of relative strength or weakness. The IQ score tells the teacher how a child will compare to other children of lower or higher IQs on school learning tasks, but it does not provide the information that enables the teacher to select appropriate materials or instructional strategies to promote the student's growth. In short, the intelligence test tells us that a child is likely to fail in school, but it does not tell *why* the child will have difficulty.

In assessing cognitive abilities, the intelligence test fails to distinguish between *product* and *process*. Test items are either passed or failed, reflecting a product orientation. The examiner can only determine whether or not the child can provide the correct answer; the test is not designed to allow the examiner to identify *how* the child arrived at the answer.

Furthermore, the examiner is often prohibited by the guidelines for administering the test from probing to find out whether the child could provide the correct answer. Sigel (1965) used the example of a question from the WISC mentioned previously: the child is asked to tell the examiner how scissors and a copper pan are alike. If the child responds that they are both made of metal the examiner must score this response as a 2, while if the child says they are both household utensils, a lower score of 1 must be assigned. Sigel contends that both reponses reflect a categorical response and that furthermore the child who said they are both household utensils might know that they are both made of metal and might say so if asked "Tell me another way in which they are alike." Sigel argued that the tests, as presently designed, tap the preferred mode of responding for a given child (since only one response is given) and thereby limit our understanding of the child's intelligence. He noted in addition that children who provide unconventional answers are penalized in the scoring, even though the response may be correct.

Psychologists can now use diagnostic tests that have been developed to fill in some of the gaps left by intelligence tests. Among the most widely used of these tests, which are presumed to assess underlying basic abilities, are the Frostig Developmental Test of Visual Perception (Frostig, Lefever, & Whittlesey 1964) and the Illinois Test of Psycholinguistic Abilities (Kirk, McCarthy, Kirk 1968). But like the intelligence tests, the diagnostic tests have also been subjected to criticism (e.g., Mann 1974; Rosenberg 1970).

Other supplements to standardized intelligence testing appear promising. One new approach is to consider personal cognitive styles; the other is to take into account the child's degree of adaptation to the environment.

Cognitive Styles

Consistent with the observation that the way a person organizes the perceptual and conceptual world is important to our understanding of the person's cognitive functioning, the literature in psychology and education has reflected a growing interest in what have come to be called *cognitive styles*. The construct of cognitive style refers to the consistent ways in which different individuals select and organize environmental information or data (Keogh 1973).

The rubric "cognitive style" has come to include processes studied by several research groups. Each has used different research techniques and emphasized different aspects of perception and information processing (Coop & Sigel 1974). Although the research groups have not studied the same psychological processes (Kagan & Kogan 1970), they have all been concerned with the variety of ways in which individuals perceive, analyze, and process stimuli (Keogh 1973). In an attempt to provide a definition of cognitive style that incorporates the specific emphases of the various groups working in the field, Keogh (1973) wrote, "cognitive style refers to individual consistencies in information seeking and information processing across a variety of problem-solving situations" (p. 84).

Three Kinds of Preferred Styles.   Kagan, Moss, and Sigel (1963) looked primarily at the child's *preferences* for using a particular style of categorization (Coop & Sigel 1974). The major modes used by individuals in attempts to sort objects have been described in some detail by Sigel (1961, 1965) and are summarized here.

1. *Analytic-Descriptive:* The individual preferring this style separates the environment into discrete units, and when asked to form groups, tends to use objective physical attributes. Two subclasses of this means of categorization have been described: (a) *part-whole,* where the label denotes parts of the stimuli (e.g., "They all are flat on the right side," or "They all have on hats"), and (b) *global,* where the label denotes the total attributes (e.g., "They are all men," or "They are all round").

2. *Relational-Contextual:* Individuals exhibiting this style prefer to create categories on the basis of functional or thematic interdependence between elements. They do not look for any single kind of element—things belong together only because they are somehow related to each other. For example, a horse and wagon belong together "because the horse pulls the wagon" (a functional basis), or a boy and a dog belong together "because the boy is training the dog to do tricks" (a thematic basis).

3. *Inferential-Categorical:* The individual who prefers this style forms categories on the basis of inferred characteristics of the stimuli. Any one element can singly exemplify the concept or the basis for the grouping. Among the subclasses of this grouping preference are: (a) *functional,* where objects are grouped on the basis of their inferred use (e.g., tools "are all used to build with"), (b) *class naming,* where a taxonomic class label is used (e.g., animals, furniture, clothing), and (c) *attribute selection,* where only one attribute is inferred (e.g., "They are all happy," "They run by motors").

Conceptual Tempo. Kagan has focused on the relationship between analytic style and sex and age (Kagan, Rosman, Day, Albert, & Phillips 1964). He has also stimulated extensive research on the impulsivity-reflection, or conceptual tempo, construct (see Kagan & Kogan 1970 and Keogh 1973 for reviews). The reflective child tends to delay, inhibit, survey alternatives, or process slowly, while the impulsive child exhibits a more rapid response tempo. Reflective responders are reported to obtain more correct responses, while impulsive responders make more errors, since their responses are unconsidered.

Considerations of tempo as a behavioral characteristic of the atypical learner are promising, but it remains to be seen whether the impulsive style (which is associated with high error rates) is a determinant of inefficient performance or an outgrowth of repeated failure. Thus far, attempts at modifying the tempo of retarded learners (e.g., Duckworth, Ragland, Sommerfeld, & Wyne 1974) have met with success in reducing errors, although far more research is needed before any definitive conclusions can be reached. Nevertheless, research with nonretarded subjects (e.g., Kagan, Pearson, & Welch 1966; Yando & Kagan 1968) has succeeded in teaching children to take more time before offering solution hypotheses. And some evidence (Debus 1970; Michenbaum & Goodman 1969) indicates a reduction in errors as a result of modifying conceptual tempo.

Field Articulation. Another approach to cognitive styles is represented by the work of H. A. Witkin. It differs from the approaches of Kagan and Sigel in that, instead of personal preference for selecting a response, the research taps one's *ability* to perform a particular task (Coop & Sigel 1974). Although this work covers a broad area (Faterson & Witkin 1970), the field articulation construct, commonly called *field independence-dependence* (FID), has received the most attention. Keogh (1973) described these two perceptual styles as follows:

> FID refers to individual differences in modes of perception. Subjects able to overcome the influence of a surrounding perceptual field by differentiating or distinguishing parts from the whole are described as "field-independent"; those more influenced by context or background are termed "field-dependent." Ability to disembed, i.e., to maintain a set against field influences, is considered not only the essence of the FID dimension but also the main characteristic of a general perceptual style.
>
> (p. 88)

While there is no explicit value judgment made regarding these two perceptual modes, Keogh (1973) observed that, implicitly, field independence is the more differentiated psychological condition and is the mode associated with success in school and society. Variables that have been found to influence the mode an individual uses include age, sex, and personality.

Diagnosis of Cognitive Styles. Keogh (1973) has noted that for children with learning problems, standardized psychological tests serve only to confirm a suspicion (i.e., the IQ confirms that the child is functioning at a retarded level); they do not provide an understanding of the child or the conditions under which the child does or does not perform on learning tasks. In addition to supplementing the IQ score with measures of individuals' preferred or actual styles of problem solving, Gardner (see Gardner, Holzman, Klein, Linton, & Spence 1959; Gardner & Moriarity 1968) has recommended testing cognitive controls, while Broverman (1960) has considered assessing conceptual versus perceptual dominance. Bruner's work (Bruner, Goodnow, & Austin 1956) on focusers and scanners provides another way of analyzing problem-solving styles employed by children. But these theoretical positions have not been extended to the exceptional child and have not generated the quantity of research or the testing instruments that have resulted from the work of Kagan or Witkin.

In the diagnostic situation examiners can broaden their understanding of the child's intellectual functioning by looking not only at the IQ score but also at some functional aspects:

> How does a child approach a new task? What kind of information does he seek and rely on? What strategies does he apply in seeking solutions? How rapidly does he make decisions? Are his errors perceptual or intellectual?
>
> (Keogh 1973, p. 99)

The answers to some of these questions can be found in the WISC, if subtest scores are further broken down. According to the research of Witkin, Faterson, Goodenough, and Birnbaum (1966), retarded youngsters do have consistent rather than erratic cognitive styles, but how they go about solving problems is often masked by test scores that reflect their low verbal comprehension. Witkin, Dyk, Faterson, Goodenough, and Karp (1962) therefore recommend dividing the total WISC into three more factors consisting of:

1. Verbal-Comprehension Factor: Vocabulary, Information, and Comprehension;
2. Attention-Concentration Factor: Digit Span, Arithmetic, and Coding;
3. Analytic Factor: Block Design, Picture Completion, and Object Assembly.

Such an approach would reveal information about the relative strengths of specific children, making it possible for us to design educational programs that match their problem-solving styles.

Other tests exist that can elicit information about cognitive styles, but there are problems with some of these instruments. For example, the exchange between Kagan and Messer (1975) and Block, Block, and Harrington (1974, 1975) should be read prior to using the Matching Familiar Figures Test, the most common means of measuring conceptual tempo. Similarly, the tasks used by Witkin to assess FID (i.e., Rod and Frame Test, Witkin Embedded Figures Test) are also subject to some criticisms (see Keogh 1973). Nevertheless, the cognitive style construct is worth consideration as a supplement to evaluation procedures.

SUMMARY

Intelligence is an elusive concept. We have no workable definition of it, but tests such as the Stanford-Binet and the Wechsler scales can pin down an individual's level of mental functioning in areas that will be important in determining success or failure in school. This is all that is meant by "intelligence" in discussions of intelligence testing.

Even when experts are careful to limit their interpretation of intelligence test outcomes to statements about a child's present level of functioning on school-related tasks, they are unable to agree on precisely what it is they are measuring. Some claim that intelligence tests should indicate the child's general level of mental functioning—as in the single IQ score of the Stanford-Binet. Others feel that people often have strengths in one area and weaknesses in another, requiring an intelligence score that is broken down into specific subscores for different kinds of skills (as provided for in the Wechsler scales).

Another question in intelligence testing is "How stable is the IQ?" Research has shown that individuals' intelligence does vary during their lifetimes. Typically it grows rapidly during the early years and then tends to level off after about age eight. This growth pattern may not be typical of retarded people, however. The intellectual functioning of retarded individuals seems to grow more slowly than that of normals, peaking a good bit later and at a lower level.

The biggest problem in intelligence testing is the unusually high number of children from low socioeconomic status minority groups who fall within the retarded range in IQ scores. Some blame this fact on genetic differences, some blame environmental deprivation, and some blame bias in the content and administration of the tests themselves. Even though the tests were originally thought to eliminate subjectivity and bias in placement decisions, many people now think the tests themselves discriminate against those whose background differs from that of the middle-class majority. But success in school is still measured against standards set by the middle-class majority and their values, which are closely related to material success in the larger society. This is of small comfort to minority groups, as is the knowledge that classification as mentally retarded entitles children to special services. The label still carries a stigma, and no one wants to be called retarded if they are not.

In addition to the controversy over racial differences in IQ scores, some psychologists are dissatisfied with IQ tests since they reveal only the product but not the process of a child's thinking. Rather than abolish IQ testing altogether, thus ensuring a return to the old subjectivity, some researchers have come up with new kinds of tests that can be used to supplement the IQ test.

CHAPTER 6

Diagnosis, Placement, and Parental Reactions

The process whereby individuals come to be classified as mentally retarded is different for EMR than for SPMR and TMR children. In this chapter we will look at three principal factors in the diagnostic process for each group: (1) Who makes the diagnosis? (2) What kinds of information are used to make the diagnosis? (3) At what age is the child diagnosed as mentally retarded? Then we will consider the effect of the diagnosis on the child's parents—the tremendous emotional reaction to the birth of a recognizably handicapped child, as well as the psychological resistance to being told that a preschool or school-age child is mildly retarded.

Differences in the diagnosis of EMR and SPMR or TMR children have been summarized by MacMillan and Meyers (1979). Generally, more severe retardation is diagnosed at birth or shortly thereafter. These diagnoses are made by medical personnel almost exclusively; the school later accepts the diagnoses.

Seventy to 85 percent of all diagnoses of retardation are made by educational personnel—teachers, school psychologists, and placement boards—after the child enters school. These diagnoses are usually of mild retardation, which is by far the most common form of retardation. The demands of schools have been implicated as "causes of mild mental retardation," since these children were capable of meeting the demands placed on them before they entered school.

Intelligence tests are not subjected to the same kind of criticism in the diagnostic process for TMR and SPMR as they are for EMR. In nearly every case we do not need an IQ score to tell that a Down's syndrome child, for instance, is retarded. But as we saw in the last chapter, the use of standard intelligence tests reveals that an unusually high number of minority children fall within the range that puts them at a risk of being labeled mentally retarded. Because this result is so controversial, it suggests a basic question: Why is it desirable to diagnose a child as mentally retarded anyway?

In the case of mildly retarded children, many special educators have argued that more harm than good is done by diagnosing a child as mentally retarded. On the other hand, few would question the desirability of diagnosing retardation early in a case where treatment can be initiated to minimize the degree of mental retardation (as in the case of PKU). These two situations should be judged separately, for the kinds of evidence one relies on in making the diagnoses in the two cases are different: one is of a biomedical nature and the other is of an educational and psychological nature. Furthermore, the treatments that will be instigated are also quite different: one is medical and dietary while the other is educational.

The assumption underlying diagnosis is that it enables us to institute an appropriate treatment program and make a prognosis of what to expect in the future. For example, if we can diagnose that a child is microcephalic, we can in most cases tell the parents with certainty that the child will be mentally retarded throughout life and during that time will require a certain amount of supervision. In the case of PKU, diagnosis makes it possible to begin dietary treatment to minimize the degree of retardation. However, the comparative precision found in the diagnosis of biomedically based cases of mental retardation is lacking in the diagnosis of mild mental retardation. With most mildly retarded individuals, there is no physical sign of retardation, the long-range prognosis is hazardous, and the evidence on which the diagnosis is made (e.g., educational failure and IQ) is under attack. Furthermore the treatment (some form of special education) is of questionable benefit, for it has not been shown to be of great value to some who have received it.

We will not try to draw any conclusions about the value of diagnosing EMR children, for this is still an area of professional disagreement. But we will try to show what goes on in such diagnoses.

DIAGNOSIS OF EMR CHILDREN

The great majority (between 70 and 85 percent) of children classified as mentally retarded have not been diagnosed as such by the time they get to school. These children, by and large, are able-bodied youngsters who during the preschool years walk and talk at about the same age as other children. They get along well with neighborhood children and usually are not regarded by their parents as anything but normal. In these children, the label *mentally retarded* will arise in the educational context—via academic failure, often underscored by behavior problems. Children who are identified as retarded after arriving in school are likely to be only mildly retarded; they are unlikely to continue in the status of mentally retarded after leaving school, for in all other settings their behavior is likely to be adaptive.

EMR children are not usually detected until they enter school because their appearance is normal, they have no physical disabilities, and they have not been involved in academic activities. Although they are slow academic learners in school, they may excel in nonacademic endeavors. Upon leaving school, they are no longer identifiable in society, as they join the ranks of the unskilled and semiskilled labor force. The EMR, thus, resemble their nonretarded peers more closely than they do the more severely retarded. As a result, many professionals question the appropriateness of labeling EMR children mentally retarded, since the label is associated with images of the more severely retarded and related negative reactions (Hollinger & Jones 1970). Others argue that regardless of what they are called, these children need special educational help to avoid continuing academic failure and social ridicule (MacMillan & Meyers 1980a). Zigler (1977) argues that the EMR should not be called *retarded*, but that they should be given the services necessary to optimize their chances for success in the school setting.

In addition to the issues surrounding testing, labeling, and treatment of the EMR, there is an obvious misunderstanding of the process by which the schools identify mildly retarded children. School psychologists are sometimes portrayed as searching for retarded children through the widespread and indiscriminate use of intelligence tests. While there have been cases reported in which the psychologist was essentially a "score-getter," it is grossly unfair to present isolated cases as the rule rather than as the exception (Meyers, Sundstrom, & Yoshida 1974).

The fairness of intelligence tests for ethnic minority children was discussed in Chapter 5, and the benefits and detriments of labeling EMR children and segregating them in special classes will be considered in Chapter 7. In this section we will examine the theories and processes involved in diagnosing mental retardation in the schools. We will discuss traditional practices, but the reader should note that these practices will have to be modified to accommodate the provisions of PL 94-142. This law mandates that testing be "nondiscriminatory" and that due process and parental involvement be ensured to a far greater degree than was true previously. These requirements are designed in part to avoid erroneous classification of children as mentally retarded.

Criteria for EMR Diagnosis

We will begin our description of the process by which EMR children are identified by asserting that it is not a hunt for a certain percentage of the total school population. Recalling the Bureau of Education for the Handicapped figures presented in Chapter 2, you will remember that the prevalence varied considerably from state to state. Clearly, the criteria for EMR identification are different in different states. Prevalence figures cannot be used as a guide by a school district to set policy. School officials cannot decide that a certain percentage of their enrollment will be classified as mentally retarded and then attempt to find that percentage of retarded children. Similarly, individual schools cannot simply establish an arbitrary IQ cutoff and then administer tests to determine which children fall below that cutoff (Ashurst & Meyers 1973).

Keep in mind that EMR categorization is not accomplished by intelligence test scores alone. This is a popular misconception, one that has been publicized by the position of the plaintiff in court cases such as *Larry P*. v. *Riles* (1972), but it is simply untrue (Ashurst & Meyers 1973; MacMillan, Jones, & Aloia 1974; MacMillan & Meyers 1980; Meyers et al. 1974; Sattler 1979). Those who contend that children are placed on the basis of IQ alone are either unaware of the diagnostic process or so intent on condemning the process that they overstate their cases. Before a child is labeled as EMR and placed in an EMR program, the child (1) has evidenced severe and persistent academic failure in regular classes and (2) has achieved an IQ below the mandated cutoff for the state in which the child attends school.

Diagnosis as retarded is not intended as a form of punishment or discrimination. Mildly retarded pupils are identified primarily for educational reasons: to get these children out of the regular program where they are frustrated by repeated failure, to get them into an EMR program, or to provide them with extra help so that they can be successful in the regular program. Historically, programs for the EMR were created as a means to provide an academic education for certain children who were normal in every sense except that they were very slow learners. The impetus for classifying these children as retarded came from legislation for mandatory special education. The formulation of clinical guidelines (usually in terms of IQ cutoffs) provided a way to justify the excess costs (over the monies given every district per pupil) for each child so classified. Moreover, mandated IQ scores serve as a state accountability measure to prevent capricious labeling of children as EMR.

Despite its intent the specification of IQ guidelines has caused some confusion. According to Mercer (1973a), who has written the most detailed analysis of the labeling process in the schools, there are two perspectives in which mental retardation can be considered: (1) the clinical perspective and (2) the social system perspective. The clinical perspective is characterized by the simultaneous use of a *medical model* (pathological-normal dichotomy) and a *statistical model* (bell-shaped curve). Mercer contends there is frequently confusion in the clinical perspective when the medical and statistical models are used in close proximity. An IQ that falls on a distribution below the cutoff for mentally retarded ("abnormal" according to the statistical model) is often interpreted within the context of the medical model as "pathological." Mercer suggests that this problem can be avoided through use of the *social system model*. In the social system model, mental retardation is considered in a community setting, since it is in the context of a social system that mental retardation occurs.

Before we explain her recommendation any further, we should note that Mercer's argument applies principally to cases of mild retardation. The medical or defect model is probably appropriate for the more easily identified retarded children (e.g., Down's syndrome), but it is not appropriate for the mildly retarded.

According to Mercer (1973a), the social system allows individuals to continue in the status of normal until they consistently fail to meet their role expectations. The role expectations for children change as a function of their developmental level. Even at a given developmental level, these role expectations vary from one situation (e.g., the classroom) to another (e.g., the neighborhood). Hence it is conceivable that some individuals can meet the role expectations at one developmental level and not another, or in one setting and not another. We have observed that the role expectations for preschool children are met by the vast majority of future EMR students, but the role of the student appears to be a difficult one, which EMR children do not fulfill in the regular program. The postschool years again present a role opportunity that is more easily mastered than that of student.

Mercer (e.g., 1965, 1970b, 1971b, 1973a) writes about the clinical and social systems perspectives in a way that suggests that they are an either-or proposition. She characterizes the schools as operating exclusively from the clinical perspective. This is probably true in the case of school psychologists, but a *combination* of social system and clinical perspectives is in fact operative in the overall situation. As we look at the steps in the diagnostic process, we can see that the initial referral by the classroom teacher reflects the social system perspective, while the psychologist later uses the clinical perspective to confirm or disprove the teacher's concern.

In a telling critique of Mercer's argument, Goodman (1977a) characterized Mercer's position as "diagnosticism," in which mental retardation is viewed as an entity within the person, not as a set of behaviors stemming from many causes. Goodman also argues that Mercer's attempt to uncover "real" cases of retardation and to differentiate them from "apparent" retardation is irrelevant to educational programing, since instruction is not affected by a knowledge of the origin of retarded functioning. Educators are not concerned with diagnosing etiology; they attempt, rather, to ascertain a child's current level of functioning and to deliver the most appropriate educational instruction once the level of functioning is determined.

Mercer's Eight Stages

Mercer (1973a) noted fairly consistent stages that children pass through in becoming classified as educable mentally retarded. If the decision at each stage was negative, the child took another step toward being classified as EMR; if the decision was positive at any stage, the child remained as a regular student outside of the special education program. Statutes in California have changed since publication of Mercer's book, but the stages she identified are probably still valid in most states, although use of intelligence tests and parental involvement may vary. Figure 6.1 summarizes and illustrates the stages identifed by Mercer.

Enrollment in Public School (Stage 1). This may appear to be an obvious step, but Mercer found that parochial schools almost never identify children as possibly mentally retarded. In one district only two children out of an enrollment of 2800 children in the Catholic parochial schools were labeled as mentally retarded. In an attempt to discern how many children enrolled in private schools would qualify psychometrically as retarded, Mercer administered group tests of intelligence and then gave the Stanford-Binet to any child who scored below IQ 90. With this procedure, 27 children of the 2800 (or about 0.1 percent) were found to achieve an IQ of 70 or lower. But there was no administrative mechanism in the private schools for identifying and placing EMR children, so Mercer concluded that while enrolled in private schools, children incur little, if any, risk of being identified as mentally retarded. She noted that white male children who are at risk of being labeled retarded in the public schools (below age-norm) can be removed from risk by being enrolled in the private schools. No mention was made of the opposite possibility: that very low achieving children who would be troublesome to teachers may be expelled or otherwise pressured out of private schools into the public schools, where they are at risk of being labeled. But, in general, if the child is enrolled in a private school, the probability of being labeled as mentally retarded is dramatically reduced.

Normal Student in the Regular Classroom (Stage 2). It is almost never apparent that EMR children are mentally retarded when they first arrive in the public school. Hence their educational careers begin with enrollment in regular primary grades as so-called normal students. Within the primary classroom, however, children are differentiated and sorted into groups for reading and math. Further sorting may take place when accelerated or remedial classes are established. Although some statuses are more highly

FIGURE 6.1 Achieving the Status "Mentally Retarded" in the Public Schools

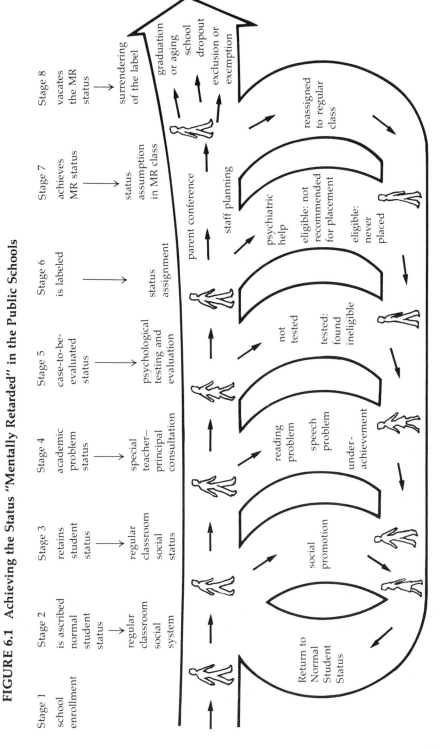

Stage 1
school enrollment

Stage 2
is ascribed normal student status → regular classroom social system

Stage 3
retains student status → regular classroom social status

Stage 4
academic problem status → special teacher–principal consultation

Stage 5
case-to-be-evaluated status → psychological testing and evaluation

Stage 6
is labeled → status assignment

Stage 7
achieves MR status → status assumption in MR class

Stage 8
vacates the MR status → surrendering of the label

graduation or aging
school dropout
exclusion or exemption

parent conference
staff planning
psychiatric help
eligible: not recommended for placement
eligible: never placed
reassigned to regular class

reading problem
speech problem
under-achievement

not tested
tested: found ineligible

social promotion

Return to Normal Student Status

Adapted from J. R. Mercer, *Labeling the Mentally Retarded*. Copyright © 1973 by The Regents of the University of California. Reprinted by permission of the University of California.

valued than others (e.g., highest reading group versus lowest reading group), all of these statuses are within the regular classroom and all students holding these statuses are normal.

Retained Student Status (Stage 3).   Some students deviate from the class norms sufficiently that they are retained at a given grade level. Nevertheless, even when retained a child holds the status of a normal child. Mercer found that 62.5 percent of the children who were in special classes at the time of her study had repeated at least one grade prior to being placed. However, this was more likely to have occurred for Mexican-American children than for white children. Like the cultural-familial retarded children, the retained child tends to come from a lower socioeconomic status background. But while Mercer saw retention as the first step toward being labeled as mentally retarded, the majority of children who are retained are never classified as mentally retarded.

Children who perform at a level well below the class norm may be considered for removal from the regular class and reassignment to a special education class. The classroom teacher plays a focal role in proposing that a certain child be considered for either retention or special education placement. This role will be discussed more fully later in this chapter. The points to be emphasized here are that (1) the standards applied by the teacher to determine whether a child deviates sufficiently to warrant such action vary from teacher to teacher and (2) the social system perspective is operative here, albeit in an imperfect manner, since the child's level of functioning is compared to the teacher's role expectations for a student.

Referral by the Principal (Stage 4).   Children who cannot meet the teacher's expectations after being retained one year are at a critical juncture, since schools prefer that children be kept with their age peers. The options available to the teacher boil down to social promotion or referral for a psychological evaluation. Usually the teacher consults with the principal regarding this pivotal decision. If the principal decides not to refer a child for a psychological evaluation, the child cannot be labeled as retarded since most, if not all, states require a psychological workup prior to placement in any special education program.

Several findings are noteworthy about this process. First, there is a consistent decline in referrals for psychological examinations beyond grade four. Second, there are dramatic differences in referral rates in different schools (Robbins, Mercer, & Meyers 1967), with the major difference being the size of the elementary school. The referral rate was lower in larger schools; children in larger elementary schools are therefore at a lower risk of being classified as mentally retarded.

Mercer reported no socioeconomic status bias and only a very slight ethnic bias in the children referred by the teacher-principal team to be given a psychological evaluation. There exists, however, a chance that the reasons for referring minority children differ from the reasons for referring majority children.

Psychological Testing and Evaluation (Stage 5). State guidelines usually require that before children can be formally classified by the schools as mentally retarded each must receive an individual test of intelligence given by a licensed psychologist or psychometrist. However, psychologists do not test every child referred for a psychological examination by the teacher and principal. Mercer found that about 30 percent of the children referred were not tested, a decision by the psychologist that meant that these children could not be classified as mentally retarded. While there was no difference between tested and untested children on the basis of sex or ethnic origin, two factors did differentiate the two groups. The first was the reason for referral: those cases in which special education evaluation was specified were tested 9 times out of 10; when there were unspecified reasons for referral (such as academic difficulties), 7 in 10 were tested; and referral for behavior alone reduced the chances of being tested to 4 in 10. The second factor that differentiated the tested from the untested was the person making the referral: children referred by the teacher-principal team were most likely to be tested, followed by children referred by parents or relatives, and then by community agencies, in that order.

At the time of Mercer's study (1973a), the IQ cutoff for placement eligibility in classes for the mentally retarded was approximately IQ 80 in California. When children referred to school psychologists were given standard intelligence tests, significantly more Mexican-American and black children scored below IQ 80 than white children; furthermore, of those children scoring below 80, a disproportionately greater number came from lower socioeconomic status families. It is Mercer's contention that the ethnic and social class distributions for children who are referred for testing are similar to those of the general population but that the use of the intelligence test as a screening device accounts for the disproportionately high number of ethnic minority and low social class children who are ultimately placed in special classes for the EMR.

Children who were placed in EMR classes represented an excess of black and Mexican-American youngsters (over their proportions in the populations in the school district) and fewer white children than were expected. Furthermore, there were higher incidences of placement for males and children from lower socioeconomic status families.

Labeling and Placement (Stages 6 and 7). Subsequent to the psychological evaluation, the case is referred to an admissions and dismissals committee. The committee usually includes the regular class teacher, special education teacher, psychologist, administrator (principal), and a physician or nurse. They consider the case and decide what is in the best interest of the child in question.

Some children who are evaluated psychologically and are eligible for an EMR class on the basis of IQ score are still not placed in an EMR program by the committee. Mercer (1973a) found that only 64 percent of children with an IQ of 79 or below were placed in EMR classes. The individuals that went unplaced at this point tended to be white or female or both, to come from higher social class homes, and to be referred to the psychologist for reasons other than consideration for possible classification as EMR. Interpretation of this observation will be discussed later in this section in the light of the findings of Ashurst and Meyers (1973).

Vacating the Mentally Retarded Status (Stage 8). Vacating the status of a mentally retarded person is the final stage in Mercer's labeling process. This step is common in the case of EMR students. It exists primarily, if not exclusively, in the context of the schools. Hence when children leave school they usually cease to be considered retarded. Among the most frequent reasons for leaving school are graduation, dropping out, or expulsion. The role expectations for individuals outside the school are mastered more readily and they no longer exhibit maladaptive behavior as they did in school, since the inabilities in abstract reasoning so apparent in school learning cease to be important for performance in certain occupations and in social interactions.

Some EMR children vacate the status of mentally retarded while in the schools, although this has been found to affect fewer children than has leaving school. Some EMR children exhibit improved academic performance in the EMR class, are referred for reevaluation, and are found no longer to warrant EMR placement. These children are reassigned to a regular class and reassume the status of a normal student. Also, EMR children may return to normal status in the transition between elementary school and junior high school. In the transition EMR children will often find their way into regular programs and function adequately. There is no formal reassignment into a regular class; it simply occurs without planning and is allowed to continue if noticed later because the child performs adequately. Finally, recent court decisions and legislative actions have modified guidelines for defining mental retardation in some states, resulting in large numbers of EMR children vacating the status of mentally retarded students—in this case often despite continued academic problems on the part of some students.

However, the reader should keep in mind that most EMR students do vacate the status at some time—most commonly when they terminate their public school education.

A Different View of the Clinical Perspective

Mercer (1973a) emphasizes the ethnic disproportion in EMR classes. Some critics regard this disproportion as evidence that the identification process is unfair and that intelligence tests are bad since they are responsible for the high prevalence of minority children in EMR programs. On the contrary, Ashurst and Meyers (1973), who studied the same project through the Pacific State Hospital as Mercer did (1973a), emphasized that EMR children are not found by means of surveys with intelligence tests. They are actually found initially through failure in their regular class (social system); the teacher's suspicion is either confirmed or unconfirmed through psychological testing (clinical perspective); and finally a decision is reached regarding placement by the admissions and dismissals committee after it reviews evidence from both sources plus additional evidence (such as a physical examination) in order to decide what is best for that child.

There are many children who achieve an IQ below the existing IQ cutoff employed in any given state who are never referred or tested. For example, Mercer (1971a, 1971b) found that 126 children out of a random sample of 1298 regular class children scored below IQ 80 (57 with IQ below 74) but had never even been referred by the classroom teacher. These children had fulfilled the role of student in the social system and had never been clinically evaluated.

According to Ashurst and Meyers, the clinical perspective is not an evil one. The psychologist's clinical perspective and the action of the admissions and dismissals committee may actually *prevent* children from being labeled as retarded, even though the teacher suspects retardation. Ashurst and Meyers (1973) analyzed 269 cases of children referred by teachers and principals as suspected mental retardates. In what they saw as a three-step process—teacher referral, psychologist determination, and placement—five different results were identified along with the number of cases for each:

1. teacher referred, psychologist labeled, child placed (86 children);
2. teacher referred, psychologist labeled, child not placed (63 children);
3. teacher referred, psychologist did not label, child not placed (116 children);
4. teacher referred for reason other than suspected mental retardation, psychologist labeled, child placed (1 child);
5. teacher referred for reason other than suspected mental retardation, psychologist labeled, child not placed (3 children).

It is noteworthy that of the 269 children referred by teachers for suspected mental retardation, only 86 were placed in EMR classes; in 116 cases the psychologist's clinical perspective prevented the placement; and in 63 cases, despite confirmation of the teacher's suspicion by the psychologist; the children were left in regular programs by decision of the placement committee. These statistics hardly demonstrate a railroading of children into EMR classes. Once the psychologist had certified the children's eligibility for classification, factors such as sex, IQ, and ethnic origin were not found to be related significantly to the committee's final decision. The only significant variable was the presence of a disciplinary problem: over half of the children whose retardation was complicated by behavior problems were not placed in EMR classes.

One major concern over the clinical perspective is its unfairness to ethnic minorities and low social class children. However, Ashurst and Meyers (1973) reported greater agreement between teacher and psychologist in the following cases:

1. in cases of white children than in cases of ethnic minority children;
2. in cases of girls than in cases of boys;
3. in cases where disciplinary problems are not mentioned in the referral than in those where they are;
4. in cases coming from schools with high proportions of white children than in those with high ethnic minorities;
5. in cases referred in the early grades than those referred in later grades.

It is ironic that school psychologists, who have been criticized for their insensitivity to minority children, apparently try in many instances to prevent placement of minority children regarded as retarded by classroom teachers. Recent court cases such as *Larry P.* v. *Riles* (1972) prohibit the use of intelligence tests to place EMR children in California, but Ashurst and Meyers's data suggest that the prohibition may result in *greater* proportions of minority children being classified as EMR.

Popular assumptions to the contrary, the clinical perspective in diagnosis is not a cold-hearted method of segregating everyone who does not meet narrow standards of acceptability. It is, rather, a process in which all pertinent information, including IQ, is considered in making the best educational decision about the placement and instruction of a particular child.

New Directions in EMR Diagnosis

Several new trends in the diagnostic processing of EMR children have occurred in response to court cases, PL 94-142, and the resulting hesitancy on the part of educators in identifying minority children as EMR. PL 94-142 has made good clinical practices a matter of law.

PL 94-142 contains *protections in evaluation procedures* (PEP), which are provisions for nondiscriminatory assessment. Their purpose is to protect the child from biased testing and to provide a more comprehensive evalu-

ation of the child, one that includes parental input and that leads to placement in and the design of an individualized educational plan. To prevent
violation of due process and inappropriate classification, parental involvement is required at every step of referral, assessment, placement, and planning. There is also a provision for a review process designed to correct
placement or plans for placement that are inappropriate or inadequate. In
essence, PL 94-142 attempts (1) to prevent children from being railroaded
into EMR programs and (2) to protect children from culturally different
backgrounds from capricious and inappropriate testing and misinterpretation of test results. These provisions are expensive and time-consuming to
implement; they may not fare well when balanced against the taxpayer
revolt, which has reduced the number of educational personnel available
to implement such provisions.

The issue of bias in testing was considered in detail in Chapter 5, so we
will not discuss it here except to say that the issue is complex (Jensen 1980;
MacMillan & Meyers 1977) and very emotional. Court decisions have been
contradictory, with Judge Peckham in San Francisco ruling that intelligence
tests are biased against blacks and Judge Grady in Chicago ruling that the
tests are not culturally unfair. Interestingly, Judge Grady considered the
importance of criteria other than IQ in EMR placement, whereas Judge
Peckham viewed the IQ as the primary, if not sole, criterion in such placement. Nevertheless, California school personnel are prohibited from using
the intelligence test in the diagnosis of EMR children, but in Illinois the
tests continue to be used. The important point is that the courts influence
the diagnostic process differently from state to state, which leads to some
inconsistency in the diagnostic process.

Several authors (MacMillan & Borthwick 1980; Meyen & Moran 1979)
have noted a trend away from the diagnosis and placement in special education programs of mildly retarded children. This observation is supported
by state prevalence data (shown in Table 2.5), which reveal very low prevalence rates for EMR children in certain states (e.g., California, Colorado,
Michigan, New York). There are probably many reasons for this development, but several reasons seem obvious. First, the public school personnel
responsible for diagnosis are reluctant to identify any but the most obvious
cases out of fear of litigation. This seems particularly true with minority
children. As a result, the children currently enrolled in EMR classes are
generally far more debilitated than those formerly found in these classes
(MacMillan & Borthwick 1980).

Meyen and Moran (1979) explain another reason these children are not
being identified. The identification begins with the regular class teacher,
but these teachers are not initiating referrals. By now these teachers have
had experience with the PL 94-142 guidelines and realize that even if they
refer the child they are likely to continue to have responsibility for the
child because of the principle of *least restriction*. If they initiate a referral,

they have to participate in a conference to certify the child's eligibility for
EMR programs. If the child is certified, the teacher will have to participate
in extensive conferences with parents, plan an individualized education
plan, and evaluate the child's progress, which involves maintaining extensive records. After this additional work, the teacher often finds that the
child will continue in the teacher's class because it is the least restrictive
alternative. The teacher may regard the resource help available as minimal
and not worth the additional responsibilities taken on once the child is
certified.

The reduction in the number of EMR children in many states indicates
that PL 94-142 may be a two-edged sword. Educators currently seem preoccupied with avoiding erroneous classification, but Congress, in drafting PL
94-142, stated that there are many handicapped children throughout the
United States participating in regular school programs who are prevented
from having successful educational experiences because their handicaps go
undetected (Section 601).

New Directions in Testing

Among children achieving IQs in the 60s and 70s there are at least two
distinct groups: (1) children who are inefficient learners in all situations and
(2) children who are inefficient learners of abstract material, but who are
"street wise" or otherwise demonstrate the ability to learn efficiently in
some nonschool activities. Mercer has frequently used the distinction
between "stupidity" and "ignorance" to differentiate the truly retarded
child (stupidity) from the child who is not cognitively deficient but who
performs poorly on an intelligence test due to a lack of experience, or at
least of experiences that match those tapped on the test of intelligence
(ignorance). Recall that earlier in this chapter we discussed Goodman's
(1977a) position that such distinctions are irrelevant in educational planning. Two experimental learning approaches, those of Jensen and Budoff,
claim to make this distinction, as does Mercer's System of Multicultural Pluralistic Assessment, or SOMPA (Mercer 1977; Mercer & Lewis 1977).

**Jensen's Theory of Primary and Secondary Familial Mental Retarda-
tion.**   Arthur Jensen is probably known to the public from the debate generated by his *Harvard Educational Review* article "How Much Can We Boost
IQ and Scholastic Achievement?" (Jensen 1969), in which he argues that
efforts to increase IQ and achievement have failed because the assumption
that these are determined primarily by environmental factors is invalid.
However, it is often overlooked that his research has for years focused on
the learning abilities of low socioeconomic status (low-SES) children. Jensen (e.g., 1963, 1968) was impressed with the performance of low-SES chil-

dren on certain laboratory learning tasks. In some areas their scores were often significantly higher than the level of performance of middle-class children of comparably low IQ and often even comparable with the performance levels of children with IQs in the normal range. Yet on other learning tasks (particularly those requiring verbal mediation), these same low-SES retarded children performed at the same approximate level as their middle-class retarded peers and considerably below the performance levels of the normal children.

Jensen developed what he learned about performance on the various learning tasks into a theory of primary and secondary familial mental retardation (1970b). In this paper he proposed that there are two levels of learning abilities. Level I, or *associative abilities*, is tapped by tests such as digit span and serial learning. Level II, or *cognitive abilities*, is tapped most heavily by tests such as Raven's Progressive Matrices and Cattell's Culture Fair Tests. According to Jensen, Level II abilities seem to depend in part upon Level I abilities. Jensen suggests that Level I abilities are distributed similarly for low-SES and middle-SES populations but that these two social classes differ in the development of Level II abilities (Figure 6.2). Since many manual jobs and social success depend more heavily on Level I abilities, it is possible to succeed in those settings while failing in a scholastic environment, which requires abstract, conceptual abilities.

Jensen (1970b) hypothesizes that there is a weakness in both Level I and Level II abilities in the severely and profoundly retarded. Within the mildly retarded range an individual can be diagnosed as mentally retarded on the basis of being (1) low on both Level I and Level II, (2) low on Level I but not on Level II, or (3) low on Level II but not on Level I. Since the second possibility (2) is never observed, Jensen therefore draws a distinction between these factors:

1. Primary Familial Retardation—deficiency in Level I and Level II,
2. Secondary Familial Retardation—deficiency in Level II.

Jensen suggests that mildly retarded children of the secondary type are able to be taught through techniques designed to maximize Level I abilities, the area in which they are strong. Such an education will be useful in getting a job afterward, for secondary familial retardates are unlikely to be perceived as retarded once they leave school.

If Jensen's theory is valid, it has important implications for diagnosis and educational programing. Before you draw your own conclusions, consult Jensen's work (1968, 1970b) along with some of the criticism of the two levels of abilities he described (e.g., Cronbach 1969).

Budoff's Learning Potential Hypothesis.   Budoff and his associates (Budoff 1967, 1970; Budoff, Meskin, & Harrison 1971) have made an attempt

FIGURE 6.2   Hypothetical Distributions of Level I (solid line) and Level II (dashed line) Abilities in Middle-class and Lower-class Populations

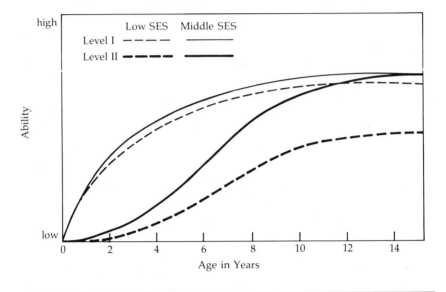

From A. R. Jensen, "A theory of primary and secondary familial mental retardation," in N. R. Ellis, ed., *International Review of Research in Mental Retardation,* Vol. 4. Reprinted by permission of the author and Academic Press. © 1970.

to predict those EMR children who will profit from scholastic instruction. Both Budoff and Jensen agree that children falling within the mild range of mental retardation according to IQ scores do not constitute a homogeneous group. In Budoff's terms some are *educationally* retarded but not mentally retarded, while others are essentially unintelligent.

Budoff and his associates (1971) feel that an intelligence test taps, in part, a child's prior school experiences, but failure on the test has been interpreted to mean an inability to reason on all tasks. The fact that most children identified as EMR do fail scholastically seems to verify the validity of assuming that their reasoning is limited in all tasks. However, Budoff (1970; Budoff et al. 1971) explains that failure both in the classroom and on intelligence tests can be blamed on the highly verbal nature of the intelligence tests and the academic curriculum.

As an alternative to the intelligence test, Budoff and his associates (1971) offer a *learning potential* (LP) assessment procedure. This procedure consists in testing the child with nonverbal reasoning problems (e.g., copying geometric designs with blocks, using modified Kohs blocks), then instructing the child on the principles relevant to the task and testing the child on the task again. In short, the LP assessment gauges the child's ability to profit from tutorial experience, an idea suggested by Vygotsky (1962).

Three distinct patterns of response to this assessment procedure have been identified for children in the IQ range of 60 to 79:

1. *High Scorers:* These children grasp the principle during the initial testing and perform at a level comparable to children with higher IQs.
2. *Gainers:* These children perform poorly at the time of initial testing but improve considerably after instruction.
3. *Nongainers:* These children, like the gainers, do poorly on the first administration of the task. But unlike the gainers, they do not profit from the instruction.

In an earlier study with institutionalized EMR children, Budoff (1967) reported a tendency for gainers to come from poor homes and disorganized family units; the few middle-class subjects were nongainers. Budoff hypothesized that the LP assessment may be useful in uncovering abilities that can determine occupational success, since it taps nonacademic abilities.

Budoff and his colleagues (1971) used the LP assessment procedure to predict performance in a specially designed laboratory science program in electricity. The curriculum was highly motivating and it emphasized manipulation of materials and minimized reading and formal explanation. The LP profiles were found to be better predictors of performance than either IQ or class placement (special or regular class). The difference between EMR and normals on the posttest became clear when they were required to give verbal explanations of electrical phenomena—the EMR children, regardless of LP status, did poorly. Budoff interpreted these findings as evidence that high scorers and gainers are *educationally* retarded rather than mentally retarded.

The attempts at differentiation among the mildly retarded are still at the experimental stage, but they seem to have support in the frequent clinical observation that some of these children seem much brighter than other of their IQ equals. The children from poor economic circumstances or ethnic minority backgrounds are often seen as more adept socially and in nonacademic learning situations than are their middle-class peers of comparable IQ. Jensen's work with levels of learning abilities and Budoff's LP assessment procedures offer provocative experimental bases on which further research can proceed.

Mercer's SOMPA. The System of Multicultural Pluralistic Assessment (SOMPA) includes an extensive battery of measures, some of which are administered to the child and some of which are solicited in parent interviews. The system assesses medically related information, such as physical dexterity and visual and auditory acuity; it also requires an inventory of health history. In addition, it includes a measure of sociocultural background (the Sociocultural Scale), the WISC-R, and the Adaptive Behavior Inventory for Children (ABIC). The ABIC assesses the child on scales in six areas of development: community, family, schools, peers, earner/consumer, and self-maintenance. The ABIC is one of many scales available for measuring adaptive behavior.

The IQ a child achieves on the WISC-R is compared to national norms to yield a *school functioning level* (SFL). The IQ is also compared with pluralistic norms derived from children of the same sociocultural, socioeconomic, or racial and ethnic background to determine how the child compares to sociocultural peers. The pluralistic norms enable the clinician to correct or adjust the IQ score according to a series of equations to yield an *estimated learning potential* (ELP). ELP scores for middle-class children tend to be about equal to WISC-R IQs, but for lower-class children the ELP scores tend to be higher.

Research investigating what ELP scores predict and whether ELP correlates more highly with significant educational outcomes than IQ is currently under way (see Oakland 1980; Reschly 1979; *School Psychology Digest* 1979). Mercer's norms were based on a California sample, rather than a representative national sample, so local norms may have to be established (Oakland 1980; Reschly 1979). In a recent study, Oakland (1980) found highly significant correlations between WISC-R IQs and achievement; correlations between ELP and achievement were lower. Thus, IQ appears to be a better predictor of scholastic success. Precisely how the ABIC and ELP can be used in education has yet to be demonstrated. At present, the SOMPA system might reduce the number of minority children eligible for EMR programs, but whether this is in their best interest remains to be seen; it will probably depend on the availability of alternative programs to meet their learning needs when they are no longer eligible for EMR-related services.

DIAGNOSIS OF TMR AND SPMR IN THE FIRST YEAR

Unlike the subtle deficiencies that make it difficult to diagnose mild mental retardation, the most dramatic cases of mental retardation are often obvious to physicians at, or soon following, birth. The physical symptoms of conditions like Down's syndrome, microcephaly, and hydrocephaly alert the obstetrician who delivers the baby or the pediatrician who first examines the baby that the child has problems. In addition, routine tests such as the one mandated in many states for phenylketonuria (PKU) soon provide information to the physician that a problem may exist. Even when the characteristic physical symptoms of mental retardation do not lead to a causal explanation (such as Down's syndrome), individuals who can be diagnosed during the first year include those who have severe damage to the brain accompanied by seizures or gross delays in motor development. For example, the pediatrician can usually detect abnormal neurological conditions at birth in the initial examination. Based on what is noticed, the pediatrician will alert parents to the possibility of mental and physical abnormalities, recommending that these conditions be kept under surveillance.

In summary, children diagnosed as retarded at birth or during the first year of life tend to be those with either the most obvious physical symptoms or gross developmental lags (Gardner, Tarjan, & Richmond 1965). They are identified almost exclusively by physicians, usually pediatricians. Finally, the parents have little, if any, time to prepare themselves psychologically for having a mentally retarded child.

Initial Parental Reactions to Early Diagnosis

The parents of a mentally retarded child must come to understand their child as a human being and plan for the child as a parent would plan for any child. But consider the suddenness of the shock for parents whose baby is diagnosed as retarded early in life. During a pregnancy, parents develop an expectation of what the child will be like (Ross 1964). They may envision the cultural stereotype of the "ideal child," combined with what has been communicated by their own parents. The child the parents imagine has attributes that will allow him or her to compete favorably in society. It also has special meanings to the parents. The child may signify a product of labor, something the mother has made; when the product is defective, the mother may internalize feelings of depreciation. A baby may also signify a gift to the husband, mother, or father; Ross particularly emphasized the possibility that the mother sees the baby as a gift to her own mother to make up for the hypothesized rivalry between them for the father's attention. The value of the gift when it is defective is obviously reduced, leading to a sense of worthlessness or guilt. Further, if one has adopted a religious posture that the child is a gift from God, a handicapped child can be seen as punishment for sins. Still other parents have babies not because they expect great things from them or see them as gifts, but because they think society expects it. From this point of view, as Zuk (1962) pointed out, to be a parent is a good thing; however, to be the parent of a defective child is a bad thing.

With the birth of a child that is mentally retarded, the parents' expectations of a normal child are shattered and, in addition, the parents are suddenly confronted with a child with special needs who will need supervision for his or her entire life. The anxious fears experienced by every

prospective mother ("What if my baby isn't normal?") are realized, whereupon the parents often enter a period of mourning over the loss of the
anticipated perfect baby and begin to prepare themselves to cope with the
crisis of a birth of a defective child. At the same time, the threat to one's
self-worth typically creates anxiety on the part of the parents, and anxiety
calls forth defense mechanisms to protect the self from further damage.
Therefore, it is common for parents to manifest both anxiety and guilt as
well as grief. Some specific studies have been made of these reactions.

Grief.   Solnit and Stark (1961) interpreted the birth of a defective child
within the psychoanalytic framework. They suggested that, with the birth
of a defective child, the parents have lost the anticipated healthy child; it
is this lost child for whom the parents grieve. In some cases a chronic state
of mourning can result. But interpretation of the parents' grief as neurotic
rather than normal has been challenged on the grounds that little evidence
supports it (Wolfensberger 1967). Taichert (1975) reported that the stages of
grief and mourning experienced by parents of severely retarded children
resemble those experienced by parents of dying children.

Guilt.   Parents almost invariably perceive their child's mental retardation with a profound sense of shock, but Carr (1974) reports that writers
have taken as fact the notion that parents of retarded children also feel
guilty, reject their children, or overprotect them. Roith (1963) pointed out
that no matter what a parent does, some professional is liable to interpret
it as a result of guilt feelings.

Wolfensberger (1967) provided a number of reasons why guilt may be
observed so frequently. In response to the oft-asked question "Why did this
happen to me?" a parent can find many possible reasons—such as poor prenatal care or carelessness during pregnancy. The event may also be seen as
a punishment by God for prior transgressions—frequently for sexual acts
such as premarital and extramarital sex (possibly due to the close connection
between sexuality and reproduction). Even when intercourse occurs within
marriage, parents may feel guilty about it (Ross 1964; Tisza 1962; Zuk 1962).
This guilt remains latent if they give birth to normal children; but with the
birth of a handicapped child, the guilt may surface. Another possibility is
that parents resent these children since they will require considerable time;
but since this resentment is not allowed to surface, the parents feel guilty
about their real feelings towards the child. Guilt may also arise when the
child was unwanted and turns out to be retarded—a phenomenon observed
in cases where mothers admitted to attempts at abortion or when the parents feel homicidal impulses towards the child.

It is important to recognize that these are all just psychoanalytic theories
and that the common generalization that most parents of retarded children
feel guilty is not supported by research evidence (Boles 1959). Roith (1963),

for instance, reported that 94 percent of mothers responding to a question-naire said they did not feel guilty or think that they had been at fault in causing their child's condition.

Although we cannot confirm the existence of guilt, Wolfensberger (1967) feels that it is still worth consideration. He takes the unique position that, while most writers imply that guilt is without a reality basis and that parents should never feel guilty, as they did not cause the condition, in some instances guilt may be an appropriate reaction. He uses as an example a case in which a mother's attempted abortion probably did cause the retardation. Drawing an analogy to a drunken driver who causes an accident, Wolfensberger asks whether we should attempt to minimize such a person's guilt feelings. And even when there is no reality basis, Wolfensberger (1967) wrote:

> Perhaps a bit of guilt may go a long way in motivating a parent to provide the extra attention, effort, and even love a retarded child may need. Perhaps it may prevent premature institutional placement, thus serving for the welfare of the child, society, and perhaps even the family, and instead of being alleviated, some parents may need to be helped to a realistic and manageable dose of it.

> (p. 331)

Similarly, Wright (1960) observed that in some instances overprotection can be the result of real love for the child rather than guilt, and she recommended that parents do whatever they feel will benefit their child, since no matter what they do they are apt to be criticized for it.

Anxiety and Defense Mechanisms.   Like guilt, the anxiety felt by parents who have been told that their baby is retarded must be dealt with. For in trying to protect themselves from pain, the parents may use defense mechanisms that may harm their child in the long run.

In the *denial* form of defense, the parents try to deny that a problem exists. They insist that the child is not mentally retarded, saying that if others would give the child a chance, the child would prove not to be mentally retarded or would outgrow this stage with time. One way the parents can maintain the effectiveness of such denials is to avoid having to make comparisons with nonretarded children of the same age. Or they may apply undue pressure on the child to achieve in order to validate denial of the reality of the condition. Another parental reaction is to criticize the physician who made the diagnosis as incompetent and look for a different physician who will tell them what they want to hear. This "shopping around" will be discussed in more detail later, but the important point here is that the professional must guard against supporting such denials by holding out unrealistic hope, promising unlikely cures, or minimizing the condition when it is severe. Taichert (1975) reported a case in which a woman took her daughter to seven different facilities for evaluation, denying the diagnosis of mental retardation and claiming that the child was emotionally disturbed and would be helped if she could only get psychotherapy.

In *projection*, the parents recognize their child's condition but avoid taking responsibility for it by projecting the blame for this terrible thing that is happening to them onto someone or something else. They might blame the obstetrician for poor practice or blame the child's defect on the mother's drinking during the pregnancy. This effort is often related to a search for the cause of the retardation; it may even lead husbands and wives to blame one another's family heredity for the child's handicap. The problem with the prolonged search for a cause is that, in most instances of mental retardation, a specific cause cannot be provided; and while the search goes on, little is being done to benefit the child or the family.

Sublimation is a third defense mechanism, one in which the energy generated by the anxiety is directed into a socially useful activity. Undoubtedly, organizations that have been established on behalf of retarded children are a beneficiary of this defense mechanism.

Other defense mechanisms have been discussed in detail by Ross (1964). Some reactions can be harmful to the child—such as *acting out* of hostility toward the child. For example, the parents may be overly rigid in restricting a child's diet or may administer a series of painful exercises to the child. Others, such as *rationalization*, may lead the parents to make peculiar sour grapes statements like "At least he won't be drafted," or to use other means of implying that they are glad their child is not normal. These defense mechanisms do not exist alone in most cases but in combinations. Anxiety over the condition of the child is at the base, and it must be dealt with by the professionals if the parents are to be assisted in coping realistically with this crisis.

The way in which the physician presents the diagnosis of mental retardation to the parents is critical in helping them to adjust to the fact of their child's retardation. But since the conference with parents when the diagnosis is made during the first year is similar to the conference when the diagnosis is made slightly later, we will not consider this subject yet. First, we will look at the diagnostic process in cases where the condition is not apparent at birth but comes to the attention of the parents and authorities over the next few years.

DIAGNOSIS BETWEEN AGES ONE AND FIVE

Cases of mental retardation that are not diagnosed during the first year of life are those that are not immediately apparent. For example, there may not be the telltale symptoms, as there are in Down's syndrome or hydrocephaly, that suggest an immediate examination for the possibility of mental retardation. Compared to individuals diagnosed at birth, the child diagnosed during the preschool years is more normal in appearance and does not deviate so markedly from a normal child in mastering the developmental tasks of early childhood. In general, children diagnosed as mentally retarded during this period of time fall into the moderate range of retardation, roughly IQ 35 to 50 (Gardner et al. 1965; Wright & Tarjan 1963).

Awareness of the Problem

Prior to age five, parents may notice a delay in their child's acquisition of speech, toilet training, ambulation, or ability to construct sentences. Usually these delays are troubling enough to the parents that they seek an explanation. In other cases, it is the physician who, through routine examinations or in taking the child's developmental history, notices marked delays in the acquisition of these skills and brings them to the parents' attention. Diagnosis at this stage of development is usually made by the pediatrician but occasionally by a psychologist.

Parents often focus their attention on a narrow aspect of development when they first become aware of the child's problem. They will describe the child's destructiveness, shyness, inability to get along with peers. Or they may suspect deafness when the child is slow to develop a speaking vocabulary. Either because they do focus on specifics or because they are fearful of the label *mental retardation,* they approach the physician or psychologist aware of the existence of a problem, but often they are deluded by the reassurances of family and friends that the child will grow out of it. Hence the mental set of the parents in seeking help is one of concern mixed with a touch of denial as to the seriousness of the problem.

Diagnostic Workup by the Pediatrician

The probability that a specific causal diagnosis can be made is low in cases that have not been diagnosed during the first year of life. The pediatrician must make a very careful examination and exercise care in pinpointing mental retardation as the correct diagnosis. The reason for this caution is that the manifestations that lead parents to bring the child in for examination (e.g., delayed speech, slow habit training) can often be explained by factors other than retarded intellectual development. For example, the presence of cerebral palsy, emotional problems, or visual or hearing problems can depress performance on learning tasks and can be confused with mental retardation due to the similar symptoms manifested. On the other hand, some of the syndromes commonly associated with mental retardation (e.g.,

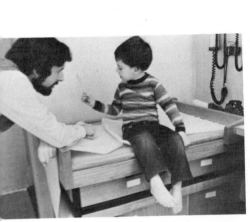
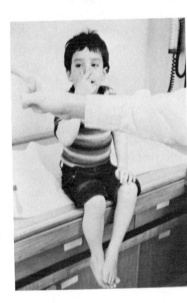

hydrocephaly, Klinefelter's syndrome) may or may not result in mental retardation (Gardner et al. 1965). And Illingworth (1961) noted that in cases where delayed motor development is a prime symptom, care must be exercised in diagnosis because some children with considerable delays in general maturation during the first year later develop quite normally.

Gardner and his associates (1965) noted that the physician is often accustomed to acting in crisis situations with speed; when dealing with a possible cause of mental retardation the doctor may feel compelled to provide a rapid diagnosis. But the consequences of a premature diagnosis may be harmful to parents and child alike. Therefore, a complete workup is recommended (Gardner et al. 1965; Wright & Tarjan 1963).

History Taking. The physician obtains information from several sources in order to understand the child's behavior. Typically the major sources are: the developmental history, the social history, and the medical history. The parents can usually provide a description of the child's development by comparing the child to other siblings regarding habit training, language development, and age of sitting, standing, and walking. By comparing the child to developmental norms, the physician is able to assess current level of development and attempt to project future rate of development.

In addition, the physician attempts to gain an understanding of the quality of social interaction in the family. Is there reason to suspect a lack of environmental stimulation, or are there apparent problems in parent-child interactions? These factors, rather than limited mental ability, could explain delayed development.

Finally, a medical history is taken to find out whether there were any biomedical factors that could have led to complications. Included here would be these factors: (1) pertinent genetic information, (2) experiences of the mother during the pregnancy, (3) problems during labor, (4) episodes in the life of the child, such as infections and accidents, (5) any history of seizures, and (6) progressive developmental or neurological deterioration (from Gardner et al. 1965, pp. 8–9).

Physical Examination. In addition to the history taking, the physician conducts a physical examination during which an attempt is made to assess the child's *current functioning*, which can be compared to developmental norms for children of the same age. The physical exam serves two purposes. First, it provides the physician with evidence on how this child compares to others on the mastery of skills (e.g., speech, locomotion, memory). Second, it provides a baseline on each of these behaviors against which later examinations can be compared.

During the physical exam the physician is alert to certain symptoms commonly present in certain conditions associated with mental retardation.

Specifically, a check is made for facial disproportions, characteristic abnormalities of the eyes and external ear, skin condition, and abnormalities of the fingers (sometimes associated with certain chromosomal disorders). Routine laboratory tests can be run for PKU, and other procedures may be helpful, such as blood sugar examinations, skull x rays, and electroencephalograms.

Psychological and Sociocultural Evaluations. The third kind of information that is useful in making a diagnosis can be obtained by psychologists. Their assessment of the child's intellectual functioning can give an estimate as to the degree of impairment, information that the physical examination cannot provide. To make this assessment they use the standardized tests of intelligence, usually supplemented with other clinical instruments and observations. The pediatrician may also wish to have a social worker visit the home in order to gain insight into the forces influencing the child and the family. This information might help to explain the child's functioning, or it may be useful later in planning for an alternate placement and educational program.

More and more medical centers now include representatives of various professions who are familiar with mental retardation. When the pediatrician is reluctant to make a definitive diagnosis of mental retardation, a referral can be made to a specialist in mental retardation. However, in cases of mental retardation diagnosed in the first five years of life, the pediatrician is a central figure in the diagnostic process and usually makes the diagnosis based on developmental and physical evidence. If the physician finds that there are serious developmental lags in several areas, the main concern is whether the slow development is due to mental retardation or other factors that are not related to intellectual ability.

CONVEYING THE DIAGNOSIS

Once the diagnosis of mental retardation is made, the task facing the physician is to communicate the diagnosis to the parents in a manner that will allow them to cope realistically with the problem. The central problem in the diagnostic interview—which is about the same for individuals diagnosed at birth as for those diagnosed during the preschool years—is anxiety on the part of *both* the parents and the doctor.

Wright and Tarjan (1963) note that the physician can be anxious about communicating the diagnosis to the parents because of past experiences with the mentally retarded, attitudes toward social incompetence, difficulties in making value judgments, or fear of dealing with the parents' questions. Similarly, Spock (1961) and Zwerling (1954) spoke of the anxiety on the part of the pediatrician provoked by the diagnosis of mental retardation.

Benjamin Spock (1961) described the anxiety experienced by a physician in conveying the diagnosis of mental retardation to parents. He described how he dreaded being the one required to confirm the fears of the parent, and how guilty he felt—as though he was the one who created the problem. To cope with his own anxiety, he put on his "professional face" and delayed telling them that their child was retarded by dragging out the medical history and the findings of the physical exam. Once he had to tell them that their child was mentally retarded, he resorted to talking in theoretical terms, emphasizing that their child, like all children, would need loving parents who would provide this child with companionship, training, and appropriate playthings—although he or she would probably never be cured. Spock reminisced that he probably failed to reconcile to the parents the positive approach he described with the gloomy demeanor in which he presented the approach, because his demeanor conveyed to them how tragic he really thought the situation was. He went on to describe how he treated a case in which the child was diagnosed as having Down's syndrome, whereupon he recommended, as was conventional then, that the child be placed in an out-of-home residence, ideally before the parents ever saw the child. This was based on the belief that lack of contact would prevent attachment to the child. Moreover, Spock reported that the thinking then was that this would permit the parents to provide a more cheerful and attentive atmosphere for their other children.

The stalling tactics described by Spock are not the most humane approach to breaking the news. According to Carr (1974), three factors will determine how constructive the interview is: timing, what is told, and how it is told.

In terms of timing the rule of thumb seems to be this: the quicker the better. In cases of Down's syndrome children, the condition is recognizable at birth, and the evidence indicates that parents told early are more satisfied than those told later (Berg, Gilderdale, & Way 1969; Carr 1970a; Drillien & Wilkinson 1964). Most mothers stated strongly that they wanted to know the diagnosis as soon as it was definite. It is critical to convey the diagnosis to parents quickly to minimize the period of distress that occurs before they begin to deal constructively with their child. Beck (1959) observed that since parents' readiness and expectancy for help are aroused during the diagnostic interview, the physician must not delay helping them formulate a plan of treatment.

What do you tell the parents? They want the *truth* (Carr 1974; Kanner 1962; Wolfensberger 1967). Weaknesses in this area result more from professionals' anxieties, which make them want to delay giving bad news, than from conscious attempts to deceive parents. Mothers have indicated that they felt bitter when they were given false reassurances, when information they asked for was withheld, or when they were actually lied to (Hutton

1966; Tizard & Grad 1961). A study by Kramm (1963) indicated that 62 percent of the parents of retarded children had been told their child was normal or had been told nothing. Yet over a third of the physicians who had told the parents their child was normal admitted, when contacted later, that they knew the child was retarded.

Lipton and Svarstad (1977) found that the ability of clinicians to be frank and informative was related to several factors: (1) The severity of the diagnosis. Clinicians were more frank and informative when the child was severely retarded. (2) The clinician's perception of the parents' level of emotional adjustment. Parents judged to be average or above average in emotional adjustment received more information more directly. (3) The clinician's difficulty in conveying the diagnosis. Communication was easier when this difficulty was not encountered. (4) The clinician's experience in the field of developmental disabilities. Those with more than four years' experience were better sources of information.

We find many reports of deplorable practices by physicians in reporting the diagnosis of mental retardation to parents. Most research has focused on reporting the diagnosis of Down's syndrome. Zwerling (1954) reported that one physician told parents that "retardates make nice pets around the house." Another informed a parent over the phone that the child was a "mongolian idiot" (Koch, Graliker, Sands, & Parmalee 1959). Pueschel and Murphy (1976) reported that this term was used to describe the Down's syndrome child in 5 percent of the cases they examined. They also found that in two cases out of 414, the parents were actually told of their child's condition by mail.

Koch et al. (1959) reported that among the major complaints of parents were the physician's abruptness, hurried handling of the case, lack of interest, and hesitancy to communicate. According to Kramm (1963), 67 percent of the parents of retarded children said they felt they had been treated harshly at the time the diagnosis was made and conveyed to them. More recently, Pueschel and Murphy (1976) found that 25 percent of the parents surveyed felt that their physician had been abrupt or blunt, but nearly half of the sample reported that their physician exhibited sympathy and understanding. It is to be hoped that bad practices and insensitivity will disappear as physicians become more sensitive to the need for careful counseling. This will require the teaching of new levels of awareness about mental retardation and how to handle it in medical school curricula.

While most writers suggest that little information other than the diagnosis itself should be presented at the initial interview, Carr (1974) disagrees. He finds that parents also want to know about the prognosis, how to handle the child, and what expectations to hold for the child.

The question of how the diagnosis should be presented depends on the severity of the condition and an assessment of the parents and family characteristics. Carr (1974), in summarizing extant evidence, suggests that the doctor should (1) take time, (2) be sympathetic toward the parents, and (3)

answer all questions fully. Tizard and Grad (1961) have noted that sometimes the parents may be unable to formulate the questions they want
answered, and the professional may have to present even more information
than asked to provide. It also seems to be important that both parents attend
the diagnostic conference (Ayrault 1964; Gardner et al. 1965; Wright & Tarjan 1963). If both are present, it will not be necessary for one parent to break
the news to the other. Having them both present also avoids the possibility
that one parent will misinterpret what is said and pass along inaccurate
information to the other. Pueschel and Murphy (1976) found that 76 percent of the time only one parent was present, generally the mother. So,
although it is recommended that both parents be present, this is apparently
seldom the case.

How much advice should the professional give the parents? The parents'
right to decide their own destinies was expressed by Sheimo (1951), while
Jensen (1950) lists the three major errors the medical profession commits in
regard to diagnosing mental retardation as follows: delay in defining the
problem, false encouragement of parents, and too much direct advice on
issues such as institutionaliztion. Although the professional is concerned
with prognosis for the child, care should be taken not to be either overly
optimistic and raise unrealistic hopes for the parents or unduly pessimistic.
Some parents who had been given the impression that their retarded child
would never be able to accomplish anything (Raech 1966) stated that they
wished that professionals would present the positive side (what the child
will be able to accomplish) rather than give the impression that the child
will be a "vegetable" (Carr 1974).

PARENTAL REACTIONS TO SPMR AND TMR DIAGNOSES

We have looked at the diagnostic interview from the point of view of the
concerns and anxieties of the professional; for the parents, the news that
their child is mentally retarded may be met with profound shock. While
shock is considered by most writers to be a universal reaction in the first
weeks after the disclosure, Wolfensberger (1967) cautions that this assumption is based on clinical observations of middle- and upper-class parents
only whose children are quite low in functioning. According to Wolfensberger, many emotions have been noticed in the parents' initial reaction,
such as anguish, disbelief, hopelessness, mourning, self-pity, and sorrow.
Some authors emphasize the few predominant reactions, others the diversity of reactions evident in parents. Dalton and Epstein (1963) observed that
parents may be at the same time "depressed about their disappointment,
guilty about their responsibility and ambivalence, angry about the narcis-
sistic injury done to them, and anxious about the child's future."

Stages Parents Pass Through

Parents of the retarded are not a homogeneous group, and it would be surprising if their emotions were not diverse and complex. But out of the diversity of reactions, some writers have found evidence of recurrent patterns—predictable stages in adjusting to the impact of a retarded child. As you can see in Table 6.1, the authors differ regarding the number of stages parents pass through, the order in which they appear, and the nature of the concern at each stage, but there are several consistent themes that emerge.

Several authors note an initial period where the parents are disorganized as a result of getting information that they were unprepared for and with which they cannot cope. Boyd, Egg, Gardner and his associates, Grays, Hay, and Koegler all acknowledge either a shock or withdrawal reaction, a distortion of the situation, or self-pity. When the parents already suspect that something is wrong with their child and search for an explanation, the diagnosis may serve only to confirm their suspicion. In such cases the description of "shock" is probably an overstatement, but it probably does apply in cases diagnosed at birth.

Gradually, the parents are seen to react against the information received—feeling guilty, distorting information, protesting, and so on. All of these reactions may be included in the phase of "reintegration" posited by Gardner et al. in which parents begin to work through their original self-centered reactions.

A search for information then appears in several of the schemes (Grays, Koegler, Rosen, & Hay). In this stage the parents attempt to educate themselves concerning causes, solutions, significance of diagnostic information, prognosis, and so on. Here the shift is finally made from self-concern to concern for the child.

If this progression continues, the parents ultimately accept the child and work on what is best for the child. The reaction is now reality-based. It may also broaden out to work on behalf of the spouse and siblings (Boyd 1951) or on behalf of retarded children in general (Egg 1964). The stages posited by Blodgett begin at this point—acceptance—and go on beyond it to constructive action.

"Shopping Around" Behavior

One phenomenon noted frequently in the literature on parental behavior is "shopping around." Parents may make repeated visits to the same or different professionals without resolving their problems (Anderson 1971). There is no general rule as to how many visits a parent must make before being considered a "shopper" (Keirn 1971). And there is no current consensus as to the reasons for this behavior.

Traditionally, professionals have portrayed shopping behavior as a

TABLE 6.1 Stages Passed Through by Parents in Adjusting to a Retarded Child

Boyd (1951)	Egg (1964)	Gardner et al. (1965)	Grays (1963)	Koegler (1963)
1. Self-pity 2. Concern for child and condition of child 3. Concern broadened to include spouse and other children	1. I-centered 2. Child-centered 3. Community-centered	1. Emotional disorganization 2. Reintegration 3. Mature adaptation	1. Guilt and shame 2. Knowledge and understanding 3. Acceptance 4. Help for child	1. Shock 2. Disbelief 3. Fear and frustration 4. Intelligent inquiry

Kanner (1953)	Blodgett (1957)	Rosen (1955)	Hay (1951)	
1. Inability to face reality 2. Disguise reality 3. Maturely face the actuality of the child's retardation	1. Parents accept the disability 2. Make long-range plans 3. Work on their feelings and attitudes	1. Awareness of the problem 2. Recognition of its nature 3. Search for a cause 4. Search for a solution 5. Acceptance of the problem	1. Bewilderment 2. Suspicion 3. Shock 4. Protest 5. Education 6. Acceptance	

response to repressed guilt, which is manifested in overprotecting the child. In attempting to absolve themselves of guilt the parents project blame for the child's condition onto the professional (Stewart 1978). Professionals who hold this point of view resent what they see as an attempt to manipulate them. They see it as maladaptive, costly, and disruptive to the family, and they feel that it diverts energy that might otherwise be directed toward helping the child.

On the other hand, Keirn (1971) suggests that the term *shopping parents* may reflect a negative bias that ignores the parents' request for help. They may be looking for assistance in handling specific problems (e.g., behavior management); going to other professionals may reflect their need for different services or dissatisfaction with true inadequacies in the assistance they received from former doctors.

Anderson (1971) has written that the failure to work through one's initial feelings helps establish shopping behavior. Sometimes this failure is not the parents' fault, for sometimes they are not told that their child is retarded. In some instances the professional focuses on a secondary problem (e.g., cerebral palsy) and does not determine that the child is retarded. In other cases the professional diagnoses the retardation but fails to convey the information to the parents. In yet other ambiguous cases, the professional suspects that the child is retarded but cannot give a definite diagnosis. But according to Anderson, the most common situation is one in which the professional diagnoses mental retardation and attempts to inform the parent but is not heard by the parents.

Shopping may differ in terms of what the parents are shopping for. In some cases parents may seek someone who will tell them what they want to hear—that is, someone who will tell them that the child is not mentally retarded. In others the parent may be seeking a "cure," although this is usually a false hope. In yet others parents are seeking help for a specific problem and feel they should go to a psychologist instead of their pediatrician for assistance in working on specific behaviors.

Much remains to be learned about parent shopping. Little is known, for instance, about what kind of parents (e.g., income level) shop more, whether shopping is less pronounced in parents of children diagnosed at birth, or why parents with long histories of shopping suddenly stop shopping. These and other questions pertaining to shopping need to be answered before this phenomenon will be understood. Until it is, it seems questionable to lump all cases of doctor changing under the negative term *shopping*. There is a real need for careful and truthful early counseling and caution on the part of professionals in labeling parent behavior when it may be information seeking of a very legitimate type (Keirn 1971).

The professional tendency to be critical of parents or to try to psychoanalyze them may interfere with giving them the kind of help they need in dealing with the diagnosis. Wolfensberger (1967) observed that professionals have tended to view parents as problem-ridden, anxious, and maladjusted. He notes that, traditionally, the *parents* have been approached as patients with a problem of their own. In the same vein, Carr (1974) quotes a parent's dismay at the impertinence of the experts who convey the feeling that parents can do nothing right. Parents are fortunate if they can find a professional who can help them cope with the realities of their situation. Wolfensberger (1967) sums it up: "The parents, as is apparent over and over, want counsel on child management and facts about retardation. The professionals often want to give them therapy."

Later Reactions

Long after the initial diagnosis of mental retardation is made, parents may continue to experience their initial emotions. New problems, such as ridicule by neighborhood children, may add to parental feelings of anxiety, guilt, disappointment, and grief. Bryant and Hirschberg (1961), in a review of the continuing causes of parental concern, identified the following situations as especially troublesome: (1) suspicion of the diagnosis, (2) parental guilt and hostility, (3) a sense of hopelessness, (4) acute illness, (5) neighborhood rejection, (6) sexual problems when the child reaches puberty, and (7) problems concerning placement.

In addition, all parents of retarded children experience problems associated with having a child who requires more attention for a longer period of time than other children. Some retarded children need care 24 hours a day, and parents may be in a state of perpetual exhaustion from heavy lifting, bathing, dressing, and frequent visits to health and educational facilities. As we will discuss in Chapter 13 the parents of retarded children may have to play a major role in facilitating the placement of their child in regular classes, a role that parents of nonhandicapped children need not assume. The health of the retarded is often precarious as well.

Given these problems, it is not surprising that many parents feel frustrated and ambivalent. The parents resent the child's greater need for help, but they genuinely love and want to protect their child. Furthermore, the child cannot rationally be blamed for the problem. The result is a vacillation between these approach and avoidance tendencies. Schild (1964) argues that the ambivalence is never entirely resolved; each new crisis stirs up these same feelings. Others (e.g., Roos 1963) contend that ambivalence provides an alternate explanation for the apparent overprotection shown retarded children by some parents, which is otherwise interpreted in terms of an underlying rejection of the child.

Grebler (1952) suggested that parents are frustrated by the retarded child. The child is slow to reach developmental levels, such as walking, talking, or toilet training; the parents also sense that the family line is stopped with this child. Financial demands and difficulty in obtaining services may increase their frustration.

These problems are compounded by societal insensitivity to handicapped children. Parents who regard the child as an extension of themselves may suffer a loss of self-esteem and feel ashamed (Roos 1978). These parents are not immune to people who point out their children in a supermarket or laugh at them in a restaurant when they do not "act their age." In reaction, they may withdraw to avoid exposing their child and themselves to these experiences, or they may become more determined to confront others' ignorance.

Greer (1975) contends that society subtly tells parents of disabled children that they are expected to be "superparents." These parents sometimes sense that others are watching them and judging whether they are carrying out their duties, which results in a "goldfish bowl" existence that takes its toll in energy, strength, and courage. Only the strongest parents can cope with a life in which the level of stress is high and the rewards for parenting are diminished. Most need respite and contact with other parents of handicapped children or professionals for relief and help.

The professionals who work with the parents of retarded children often have opportunities to help them cope with their problems but are unsure how to proceed. In addition to physicians, psychologists, and social workers, those in a position to help include teachers. While the diagnosis of the more severe forms of mental retardation usually occurs before a child comes to school, a teacher in a TMR program may encounter parental behavior that reflects continuing attempts to cope with the diagnosis. It is not unusual for parents to explore alternatives with the teacher for coping with problem behaviors exhibited by the child or problems arising in the neighborhood.

Readers interested in the experiences of parents of children with various handicaps are referred to the excellent book by Turnbull and Turnbull (1978a).

COUNSELING AT DIFFERENT CRISIS STAGES

In helping parents with adjustment problems, it is important to know what kind of basic crisis they are experiencing. Farber (1960b) hypothesized two different kinds of crisis reactions to the diagnosis of mental retardation: (1) tragic crisis and (2) role organization crisis. The tragic crisis was observed in higher socioeconomic families and was precipitated by the diagnosis. It resembled bereavement in the sense that expectations for life careers were shattered; the child was not going to be the doctor or lawyer hoped for. The parent reacted to this crisis with symptoms of nervousness.

The tragic crisis appeared early and persisted for some time. What Farber called *role organization crisis* was found more commonly among the lower classes and occurred well after diagnosis. This crisis was precipitated by the parents' inability to cope with the child over a prolonged period. A common complaint among mothers in this group was their own poor physical health.

Wolfensberger (1967) isolated three crises experienced by parents of severely retarded children, crises that are generally related to the age of the child. His unique treatment incorporates much of the evidence on parental reactions and suggests ways to deal with them. He notes that these crises may be experienced simultaneously or at different times; some parents will experience all three types of crises while others may experience none of them.

Novelty Shock Crisis

The first crisis is likely to occur at the time of diagnosis, and it is most probable in the case of unsuspecting parents. At the time of birth, parents expect a perfect child—not just a normal child (Solnit & Stark 1961). They hold notions regarding talents, future occupations, and so forth for the expected child. The arrival of a baby that upsets these expectations is met with the novelty shock crisis. When parents are told that their newborn has Down's syndrome, they are shocked because their expectations are so greatly at odds with the actual characteristics of their newborn child.

The crucial dimension in this crisis is not so much the diagnosis of mental retardation as the shattering of parental expectations. Wolfensberger (1967) cites cases in which parents were shocked by the diagnosis of mongolism (the term used at the time to denote Down's syndrome) when they did not even know what the term meant.

Value Crisis

The second type of crisis hypothesized by Wolfensberger (1967) occurs when mental retardation is unacceptable in the parents' minds because the condition or its manifestations run counter to the parents' value system. For example, the fact that this child will never be self-sufficient or will not be successful academically may be a source of anguish to parents who value these accomplishments. An example of the value crisis is seen in the writings of Abraham (1958) and Frank (1952), which describe the impact of a retarded child on families of academically oriented persons who valued achievement and education.

The reaction of parents who experience the value crisis involves some form of rejection. In mild forms this rejection might be manifested as over-protection or ambivalence; in an extreme form it can lead to rapid institutional placement and the denial of the child's existence. This crisis is thought to persist for long periods of time, perhaps even for a lifetime.

Reality Crisis

The third type of crisis occurs when the family is faced with additional problems, such as when a child requires inordinate amounts of care and supervision or when needed professional services are not available. The determinants of such crises are often external to the parent, as when a retarded adult is judged dangerous or when sexual behavior is viewed as unacceptable by the community.

Compared to the novelty shock crisis and the value crisis, the reality crisis tends to come later in the life of the retarded person and to center around situations that are real reasons for concern.

Wolfensberger (1967) suggests that viewing parental or family reactions to mental retardation as different kinds of crisis responses enables the professional to identify what kind of help parents need most. He wrote:

> Parents in novelty shock need primarily information and support; those in the value crisis need prolonged counseling or personal therapy; those in reality crisis require practical, down-to-earth help.
>
> (p. 337)

SUMMARY

The course of diagnosis of mental retardation differs markedly depending on the degree of mental retardation. The EMR child is diagnosed in the schools by educational personnel; since the majority of cases of retardation are in the EMR range, the schools are therefore the major agencies for classifying mentally retarded individuals. Academic failure is the first clue in EMR diagnosis; if the impaired intellectual functioning it suggests is confirmed by psychometric testing, a placement committee may decide to place the child in an EMR program. But when the teacher refers the child for academic problems that are found not to be intellectual in nature, the psychologist's clinical perspective can serve to prohibit labeling of the child as retarded. The common portrayal of the school psychologist as a case-finder who uses IQ as the sole basis for diagnosis of EMR children is generally inaccurate. But, on the other hand, the process is not error free. If PL 94-142 is to be implemented, due process concerns and safeguards must be established at each step of the diagnostic process.

Diagnosis of TMR and SPMR children follows an altogether different course. The physician takes a primary role in this process and relies more heavily upon medical and developmental history than on psychological evidence, although it may play a secondary role in confirming or supplementing the suspicion of mental retardation. Conveying the diagnosis properly is of the utmost importance so that parental reactions that would interfere with the needed treatment for the child can be avoided.

Various parental reactions to the diagnosis of TMR and SPMR children have been identified and categorized. But specific reactions probably vary according to such factors as the age of the child, the presence of additional handicaps, and the extent to which parents were aware of a problem before the diagnosis was conveyed. Some reactions may be counterproductive; others may be genuine attempts to do what is best for the child.

PART IV

Special Issues in Diagnosis and Placement

CHAPTER 7

The Mentally Retarded Label and Attitudes Toward Labeled Persons

When we classify and label children as mentally retarded, are we helping them or harming them? This question has been hotly debated in professional circles and has been a major issue in court cases concerning mildly retarded children, as we will see in the next chapter. Some critics charge that the mentally retarded label has detrimental effects on children that may persist throughout their lives. The empirical evidence, however, fails to support such allegations; in some instances the label actually appears to protect the labeled person.

The evidence for and against classifying and labeling is complex and inconclusive. Although it does not demonstrate convincingly that calling attention to people with intellectual deficiencies by giving them special treatment is always a bad thing, the controversy over labeling should make us all more sensitive to its potential hazards: by labeling people as retarded, we may place additional burdens on them that will make it more difficult for them to gain acceptance, or we may increase whatever feelings of depreciation they had without the label.

We may never know the extent to which these fears are valid. Although much research has been done in this area, it often fails to consider or control all the variables that may modify the effect of a label on the individual who bears it. It is especially difficult to distinguish between the actual effect of the label and the behavioral limitations that led to the labeling in the first place.

In this chapter, we will consider the empirical evidence regarding labeling and its influence on attitudes toward persons labeled mentally retarded. The attitudes of nonretarded people toward the mentally retarded *may* be altered by labeling, but attitudes and their sources are extremely complex. The study of attitudes is becoming progressively more important, because attitudes influence the extent to which the retarded benefit from society's resources. Positive attitudes increase the likelihood that more resources will be made available; negative attitudes do the reverse. The trend toward deinstitutionalization and mainstreaming also requires that we consider the attitudes of nonretarded citizens and their effect on the chances that the retarded child's reentry into society and the public schools will be successful. In segregated classes or institutions the retarded can take refuge from negative attitudes and behaviors, but in society and regular classrooms retarded children are exposed to their nonretarded peers. Contact with nonretarded persons gives them a chance to break down negative stereotypes and promote more favorable attitudes, but it also permits the retarded to exhibit inappropriate behavior and thereby intensify negative attitudes. Exposure per se is neither good nor bad—the outcome depends on the quality and nature of the experiences of the retarded and nonretarded alike.

PROS AND CONS REGARDING CATEGORIES

Although we have repeatedly used the word *labeling*, it is not the same thing as classification or categorization. According to Professor Nicholas Hobbs of Vanderbilt University, author of voluminous reports (1975a, 1975b) on a huge project on classification of exceptional children that was supported by nine HEW agencies:

> By *classifying* we mean the act of assigning a child or a condition to a general category or to a particular position in a classification system. There is an unfortunate but persistent tendency to transpose the label of a condition to the child. "Retardate" is one of the most objectionable forms.
>
> By *labeling* we mean to imply more than the assignment of a child to a category. We intend to include the notion of public communication of the way the child is categorized; thus, the connotation of stigma is present.
>
> (1975b, p. 43)

When we classify people we put them in some conceptual category; when we label them we use the name of that category in talking about them. The purpose of classifying seems obvious, but perhaps it is not; the purpose of labeling seems questionable, but as we will see later, its effects may not be altogether negative.

Possible New Categories

Classification has traditionally been thought to serve a purpose. In special education, children have in the past been separated into categories—blind, deaf, mentally retarded—on the assumption that they could not be taught together, that what they were taught and how they were taught would have to differ. But some have questioned the need for this kind of division (Cromwell, Blashfield, & Strauss 1975), and there is a new trend toward noncategorical special programs that do not distinguish between people who are blind, learning disabled, or educable mentally retarded for instructional purposes (MacMillan 1973b). Even under the traditional separation of these categories, there is little difference in the teaching techniques found in programs for EMR and learning-disabled children. Some professionals have therefore argued that the distinction between such groups is not valid for instructional purposes and that they should be reclassified under a single large category: "children with special learning needs" or "exceptional children." This approach is not truly noncategorical; it might better be called "new categorical."

An opposite approach would be to divide children with special needs into smaller categories than are now used. We have identified a variety of subgroups within the EMR category:

1. Bilingual children (e.g., Chicano, Puerto Rican) who need accommodation in the area of language but who are not genotypically defective or retarded.
2. Children from environments that are described as impoverished because they are lacking in materials or experiences considered beneficial to a child in adjusting to school. Again, these children are not genotypically retarded.
3. Children who have developed failure sets—that is, who have poor self-concepts and expect to fail before they even attempt a task.
4. Children of dull-normal ability with so much emotional overlay that their performance in school and on the intelligence test is depressed below the district cutoff.
5. Children who received a poor genetic draw or suffered prenatal, perinatal, or postnatal damage resulting in lowered cognitive capacity. These children are genotypically retarded.

(MacMillan 1971b, p. 5)

We could specify additional subtypes, but the point is that no single program would maximally benefit all these children. They are alike only in their failure to achieve academic success in regular classrooms, but they differ greatly in their needs for special education and in their social characteristics. According to critics of ethnic minority group testing, some may not even be retarded; their placement in the category may be based on tests and judgments that are biased and invalid. But faced with the academic failure they have in common, we could handle the considerable differences between EMR children in two possible ways: (1) develop specific programs for the various subgroups or (2) go to a broad category and attempt to accommodate the differences by individualizing instruction to meet individual needs.

Potential Benefits of Categories

Granted that the present category of EMR—or of "retarded"—may need to be either refined or broadened, what are the advantages to categorization in general?

One of the principal arguments for categories is that they relate diagnosis to treatment. An accurate diagnosis, and subsequent classification, should lead to the most efficient treatment program. If we diagnose and classify a metabolic disorder such as PKU, we can begin specially designed dietary treatment. In this case classification is beneficial to the individual because it leads to effective treatment. As noted by Hobbs (1975a), this treatment-oriented role of classification is most obvious in cases of physical disorders or disease. In such cases classification does not add to the problem: calling a fractured bone *broken* has never widened a fracture, and diagnosing spots as *measles* has never increased the number of spots on a child. However, in cases of mild mental retardation in which classification is based on inferences from psychological evidence, the effectiveness of the treatment—special education—is questionable and the categorization may theoretically make some of the child's problems worse.

In addition to relating diagnosis to treatment, categories have served as rallying points for special interest groups (Gallagher, Forsythe, Ringelheim, & Weintraub 1975). In most cases interest groups such as the California Association for Neurologically Handicapped Children and ARC organize on behalf of a specific group of handicapped youngsters. Frequently, members of such groups are parents of children in that category. Drawn together around a particular category, these volunteer groups work to get improved services for their particular category. Such special advocate groups have been extremely influential in getting legislation passed, providing services, and raising money. We wonder whether parents of a Down's syndrome child would work as diligently in an organization for "children with special learning needs" if this meant that all handicapped children would share equally in the benefit. Would such a rallying point perhaps seem too diffuse?

The use of categories is also tied to the passage of legislation to aid handicapped people. For decades legislators have been taught to think in terms of categories. Federal agencies with mandates to serve handicapped children are organized along the lines of the classic categories, probably because legislation was pushed by special interest groups working on behalf of specific categories. The legislator geared to supporting legislation for the mentally retarded, blind, and deaf might be less responsive if these traditional categories were suddenly changed. Gallagher et al. (1975) illustrate the sharp increases in funding for the handicapped achieved over the past fifteen years (for mental retardation, an increase from slightly over $200 million in 1965 to over $600 million in 1971 across all agencies in HEW), contrasted to the failure of funds given to programs for general education to filter down to the handicapped. Table 7.1 shows the figures for four such general education programs. On a state level, too, special education administrators are concerned that sudden changes in labeling practices would decrease resources for handicapped children. It is little wonder that some professionals fear that the abolition of categories would mean a vast cut in the resources available to the handicapped. They would prefer instead to retain labels as a means of ensuring that funds would go to those for whom they were intended.

Finally, categories are essential for research purposes (Hobbs 1975a). We need to know whether a specific diet or a specific teaching technique benefits one category of children and not another. If we ignore categories, the differential effects will be masked in research results. At least for research purposes, then, categories should be refined rather than broadened or abolished. Hobbs (1975a) therefore argues for more precise categories and for more accurate ways of identifying which children fit which categories.

Potential Detrimental Effects of Categories

One must weigh the possible benefits of classification against the pitfalls in the same process—there are dangers and they must be avoided whenever possible. Although classification for purposes of treatment is useful for physical problems, it may not do as much good in cases of mild retardation and certain other categories (e.g., emotionally disturbed). Critics who ques-

---

TABLE 7.1   The Proportion of Funds That Reached Handicapped Children in Four Federally Funded Programs

Legislative Authority	Handicapped Proportion (Percentage)
Title I ESEA (Culturally Disadvantaged)	2.4
Title III ESEA (Innovative Programs)	3.5
Vocational Education Amendments	1.0
Cooperative Research Act	5.0

J. J. Gallagher, P. Forsythe, D. Ringelheim, and F. J. Weintraub, "Finding patterns and labeling," in N. Hobbs, ed., *Issues in the Classification of Children*, Vol. 2 (1975). Reprinted by permission of Jossey-Bass, Inc.

tion the treatment given to an EMR child look for evidence that the treatment has led to improved achievement, uplifted feelings of self-worth, and the like. When these benefits cannot be shown, they argue that the classification does not relate to a beneficial treatment and should be terminated.

In addition to the paucity of positive evidence that treatment for mild mental retardation is helpful, there is the theoretical danger that in classifying people as mentally retarded we are excluding them from so-called normal society. Hobbs (1975a) pointed out that a case could be made that the primary function of classification is to protect the community by classifying those who are different or deviant. When we read that exceptional children are classified so that they can be taken care of, according to Hobbs this rationalization:

> can and should be read with two meanings: to give children help and to exclude them from the community. . . . Categories and labels are powerful instruments for social regulation and control, and they are often employed for obscure, covert, or hurtful purposes: to degrade people, to deny them access to opportunity, to exclude "undesirables" whose presence in some way offends, disturbs familiar custom, or demands extraordinary effort.
>
> (pp. 11, 21)

While classification as mentally retarded opens doors to certain services, it also closes doors to certain opportunities. If children are classified as mentally retarded, they may therefore develop less fully than if they had not been labeled because of the limitations of the programs in which they are placed.

While it may be necessary to exclude some individuals from the larger society for their own benefit or for the benefit of society, as in the case of severely destructive individuals, it is essential that we guard against legitimatizing the practice of getting individuals out of the way in the name of providing treatment. Citing two extreme cases, Hobbs (1975a) noted that in Nazi Germany in regard to Jews, and in the United States during World War II in regard to Japanese-Americans, classification and labeling were used to feed the private fears of the public.

A major concern of professionals in the field of mental retardation is that some children may be labeled mentally retarded because they are difficult or merely different, not because they have general intellectual limitations. In such cases, labeling children as mentally retarded may be used to justify excluding them from regular class placement and the opportunities available to the nonhandicapped. Special services may be of little or no benefit to children erroneously labeled.

Research on the effects of labels on mentally retarded persons is exceedingly complex. Guskin (1978) has offered an extensive discussion of the theoretical framework of this work, and he has suggested several alternative formulations that might better explicate the relationship between labeling and outcomes. The interested reader should consult Guskin's work for an excellent analysis and comprehensive review of research.

DEVIANCE THEORY: THE HYPOTHESIZED EFFECTS OF LABELING

According to sociologists (e.g., Rowitz 1974), mental retardation should be seen in the larger perspective of social organization as a manifestation of deviance labeling (Becker 1963; Erikson 1964; Kitsuse 1962; Lemert 1951, 1967, 1972; Rubington & Weinberg 1968). From this perspective, "deviance refers to an attribute(s) of an individual or some action(s) by an individual which is regarded as objectionable in a particular social setting" (Glaser 1971). The sociological perspective emphasizes that deviance is relative rather than absolute. As Becker (1963) noted, the society creates deviance by setting up rules; the individual who breaks them is classified as an "outsider," or "deviant." Consequently, the deviant, whether retarded or delinquent, is only an outsider when so labeled by the society. Or as Erikson (1964) put it, deviance is not seen as "a property *inherent in* certain forms of behavior; it is a property *conferred upon* these forms by audiences which directly or indirectly witness them" (p. 307).

Deviance theory has four important tenets: (1) deviance exists only when the group judges behavior exhibited by the individual to be rule breaking; (2) the individual whose behavior is judged to be deviant is formally labeled and removed from the normal patterns of interaction within the society; (3) once an individual is labeled formally, a definite role is assigned and expectations set as to how the person will behave; and (4) removal of the labeled person from the social group represents an almost irreversible act. We will group the first two and last two tenets together for further examination.

Rule Breaking and Removal

Hobbs (1975b) described a process called *boundary marking,* which serves the society by setting limits on what kinds of behavior can be tolerated. When behavior goes beyond these limits it threatens the group identity, and to allow it to go unsanctioned would ultimately be destructive to the social unit. To prevent this from happening, the society institutes certain sanctions for behaviors that go beyond these limits; these barriers serve to distinguish "us" from "them." There is a whole range of sanctions that can be invoked, all of which serve to create barriers between the deviants and the normals. The most extensively studied sanction is the removal of

deviants (e.g., placement in institutions), by which means the society protects itself from the deviants.

Sociologists have studied this process in treatment of criminals, mentally
ill individuals, and the mentally retarded. In general, the research on the
sociological perspective to labeling has tested narrow forms of antisocial
behavior (Yoshida 1974). But conclusions drawn about one kind of deviance
cannot be applied to another. Each form of deviance is thought to require
quite different treatments and have different consequences as a result of the
degree of the threat posed to the society. Furthermore, it seems unlikely
that one can extrapolate from studies in which the mentally retarded were
institutionalized to speculate about the effects of physical segregation in a
special class for the EMR. But removal is practiced even on mildly retarded
individuals. Even when they are not physically separated, official labeling
of children as mentally retarded increases the *psychological* distance
between the threatened individuals (society) and the labeled (Hobbs
1975b). And retarded children are often set apart from other children (in
institutions or special classes), a separation that can permit or even encourage the denial of their humanness.

The Effects and Irreversibility of Labeling

In studies of deviance from the sociological perspective, little significance is attached to the behavior that leads the individual to be classified as
deviant; the main focus is the extent to which being labeled affects subsequent behavior. Labeling is seen to affect both the labeled and the labelers.
The significant others in a social system expect the mentally retarded to
behave in certain ways, to do certain things and to be unable to do other
things. As a result of these expectations these people behave differently
toward mentally retarded persons than they would have if they had not
been labeled. The deviant, in turn, undergoes progressively negative experiences—labeling, public degradation, institutionalization, stigmatization—until the label may become a self-fulfilling prophecy (Dexter 1956,
1958, 1960).

This progression leads into the final tenet of deviance theory: due to the
differential treatment accorded to the individual as a result of the label, it
becomes virtually impossible to return to the normal patterns of social
interaction. Erikson (1964) put it as follows:

> An important feature of these ceremonies in our own culture is that they are
> almost irreversible. Most provisional roles conferred by society ... include
> some kind of terminal ceremony to mark the individual's movement back out
> of the role once its temporary advantages have been exhausted. ... A circular-
> ity is thus set into motion—which has all the earmarks of a "self-fulfilling
> prophecy," to use Merton's fine phrase.
>
> (pp. 16–17)

The evidence bearing on whether or not this really happens will be considered later in the chapter; the point here is that, within the theoretical framework of the sociological perspective, there is a feeling that deviance is *caused* by labeling, since the label puts a negative status on the individual as being inferior or morally unfit (Davis 1972).

Limitations of the Sociological Perspective

Guskin (1978) and Yoshida (1974) noted certain limitations of the sociological perspective on labeling as it applies to the mildly retarded. Guskin noted that this perspective developed in large part out of the sociological study of crime, in which deviance was defined as rule breaking. Society was said to create deviance by establishing rules, the breaking of which is considered deviant. This situation is not parallel with the "rule breaking" of a child who fails to meet the expectations for normal students and scores under 70 on a test of intelligence. Another criticism of the sociological perspective is that it ignores the history of the person prior to being labeled (Akers 1968; DeLamater 1968; Gibbs 1969; Stoll 1968). As Guskin (1978) puts it, the theory does not deal adequately with the deviant behavior that leads to the labeling. The sociological perspective is not concerned with variables that influenced the development of the behavior judged deviant, nor is it concerned with behaviors that do violate group norms yet go undetected and unlabeled. Rowitz (1974) does not consider the latter cases to be worth considering because they are not officially recognized as deviant; however, Yoshida (1974) points out that such individuals may be labeled informally.

A second series of criticisms has been leveled at the assumption that all members of the social group hold the same role expectations set for the particular deviant and reinforce only role-appropriate behavior (Gibbs 1969; Gove 1970; Yoshida 1974). That is, is there a unique role expectation for EMR children held by everyone in the public schools, and are they all consistent in reinforcing the same behaviors? Do regular classroom teachers and special education teachers hold the same expectations for EMR children? There has been no systematic study of this question of the universality of expectations for the different groups of deviants (Gove 1970; Mankoff 1971), including the mentally retarded (Meyers, Sundstrom, & Yoshida 1974).

The issue of irreversibility was criticized severely by Gove (1970) when he analyzed studies of the placement of mentally ill individuals in institutions. He wrote:

> In summary, the studies reviewed, while in no way denying the existence of the processes outlined by the societal reaction theorists, suggest that mental hospitalization does not necessarily or even typically lead to a prolonged occupancy of the mentally ill role.
>
> (p. 882)

If the effects of the mentally ill classification are reversible, what about EMR classification? Rowitz (1974) has stated that if individuals are labeled, there is an assumption that they are deviant for 24 hours a day and that they will always be deviants. But according to an analysis of the labeling literature, this is not so. The fact that different demands are made in different social settings (e.g., school versus neighborhood) disproves the notion that a deviant is always and everywhere considered a deviant. This argument has been essential to the attempts to provide a definition for mental retardation (Grossman 1977; Heber 1961); the feeling now is that mental retardation can only be defined in terms of the environment in which the individual is functioning.

Even though there are weaknesses in the sociological perspective, it makes the point that labeling has an effect on an individual. But the dynamics of how this works seem to be far more complex than the sociological perspective indicates.

THE MENTALLY RETARDED LABEL: ITS IMPACT ON CHILD OUTCOMES[1]

When we are looking for evidence that has a bearing on how labeling affects a child we often run across dogmatic statements about the "harmful, lifelong labels" being pinned on children (Catterall 1972, p. 95) and claims that labels are attached "indelibly to the individuals, often resulting in scapegoating" (Reynolds & Balow 1972, p. 357). In the courts as well as in some of the literature, such notions are taken as fact. To the extent that being classified as mentally retarded can result in involuntary hospitalization, sterilization, a loss of civil rights, and so forth, we can hardly challenge the assertion that being classified as retarded does have an impact. However, implicit in the debate surrounding special class placement of mildly retarded children is the contention that the effects are not the legally intended ones; there is an assumption instead that being labeled somehow results in devaluation of the self or lowered performance. Our discussion of the literature focuses on labeling's effects on adjustment and achievement.

The fact that the labeling effect has been cited in court cases in which the defendants made no attempt to prove that labeling had a *beneficial* effect is not proof that labeling is necessarily detrimental and long-lasting. Evidence of labeling effects is still too tenuous to support any such conclusions.

The debate over labeling is hardly new. Maslow (1948) discussed the dangers inherent in labeling, and his ideas were later extended by Rotter

---

[1]This section of the chapter relies on a review of research for a 1974 article by MacMillan, Jones, and Aloia. The author wishes to acknowledge the conceptual input and interpretation contributed by the coauthors of that paper.

(1954) when he decried the entire categorizing process. Later, Zigler and Phillips (1961) provided an incisive critique of the positions on diagnostic classification in the mental health field. However, the current debate over the issue is focused upon the mildly retarded child who is hypothesized to be detrimentally affected by being labeled.

Confusion in Identifying the Issues

In addition to the basic problem of determining what people would have been like had they not been labeled, research on labeling is subject to confusion arising from other sources.

According to Guskin (1978) the current interest in labeling grew out of a social attitude of identification with those rejected by the larger society: minority groups, the poor, the mentally ill, and the mentally retarded. Associated with this attitude has been a tendency to attribute the problems of these groups to society and its institutions. Whereas earlier writers attributed problems to individual attributes, recent writers often hold society directly responsible for the deviance in the form of the very agencies and services developed to address the problems. Thus, intelligence tests, special classes, and institutions are viewed as causes of the problems of mental retardation rather than as solutions to these problems. Hence, the labeling issue is often confused with concerns such as the effects of segregation, the specific curriculum, and other issues related to the use of special classes to meet special educational needs.

The labeling issue has also become submerged in the debate over the present process for classifying children as mentally retarded. The work of Mercer (1970b, 1971a, 1971b, 1973a), for instance, clearly documents the process whereby children are identified and classified by the public schools, but sheds no light on the detrimental effects of the label on any significant outcomes except in the form of anecdotal notes. Usually the concern over the identification process centers on the use of intelligence tests with ethnic minority children and only tangentially touches upon the effects of labels on children. When the effects of labeling are not isolated from such issues, nothing of value can be extracted from the debates.

Another problem is that within the labeling issue there may be two separate phenomena worthy of study. One is mislabeling—what is the effect of a label on a child who does not deserve it? The other is appropriate labeling—what is its effect on a child? Does a label only damage when it identifies children as less able than they really are? Or do labels always hurt? Do they always lower performance no matter what the circumstances?

An additional problem is the failure of many investigators to specify the nature of the outcomes that will be adversely affected by the label. There are two ways in which labels might affect outcomes: a direct influence on self-concept or an indirect influence through triggering expectations on the parts of others. In studying the direct effect of the label on some aspect of the self, we could hypothesize that when children recognize that they have been labeled mentally retarded, they view themselves more negatively. In such a case we would expect to find an individual having a lower self-concept, being more self-derogatory, having a lower level of aspiration, or otherwise manifesting devaluation of self-worth as a direct result of being labeled. In the hypothetical indirect effect, significant others in the child's environment (teachers, parents, peers) react differently to children if they are labeled than they would were they not labeled. They thus assist the labeled child in fulfilling the prophecy of poor performance connoted by the label.

Efficacy Studies

Much of the research into the direct effects of labeling is based on studies that compare EMR children in a special class to children who score in a similar IQ range (usually IQ 60 to 75) but who, for a variety of reasons, were never placed in an EMR program. Comparisons of children in these two settings are referred to as *efficacy studies*, since they presumably evaluate the efficacy of the two administrative arrangements for educating mildly retarded children. But the results of such studies do not really tell us much about labeling because there are differences between these groups of children that have nothing to do with labeling. Usually the children left in regular programs and not identified as EMR have evidenced either superior academic achievement or superior adjustment; this is why they were not classified. Comparisons of the adjustment or achievement of the two groups are therefore specious because the outcome is already obtained by the way the groups were created. It is therefore hazardous to attribute any differences found to the fact that one group was labeled mentally retarded and the other was not.

According to several excellent reviews (Bruininks & Rynders 1971; Guskin & Spicker 1968; Kirk 1964; MacMillan 1971b; Quay 1963), efficacy studies have methodological weaknesses as well as selective bias in the formation of the groups. For one thing, there are too many uncontrolled variables. Look at the ways in which children in a special EMR program differ from comparable IQ children in a regular class. One group is labeled mentally retarded while the second is not; one group has teachers who have special training; the curricula the children are exposed to differ dramatically; one group is physically segregated for much of the school day; the teacher-pupil ratio differs markedly between the two settings; and the peer groups are dramatically different. If we do in fact find differences between the two groups, to which of these factors, or combination of factors, can we attribute the differences? Another methodological problem is the question-able nature of the instruments used to measure adjustment (Gardner 1966).

Despite the methodological flaws inherent in most such studies (the Goldstein, Moss, & Jordan 1965 study being an exception), the results indi-cate that the children who were labeled and placed in a special class were superior to the regular class children in terms of adjustment. It is therefore paradoxical that these studies are sometimes cited as evidence of the detri-mental effects of the mentally retarded label. As we concluded in our study:

> The efficacy studies, in general, do not support the deleterious effect of label-ing no matter how they are viewed. In fact, given the majority of these studies which indicated better adjustment (however that was assessed) for the special-class children, the interpretation of deleterious effects of the label is hardly appropriate to the data.
>
> (MacMillan et al. 1974, p. 245)

Evidence of Direct Effects on Various Outcomes

On top of the problems in comparing groups, there tends to be lack of agreement among efficacy studies as to what outcomes are supposedly affected by labeling. Comparisons among studies are therefore impossible in most instances; in one study the investigator measured self-concept; in another the measure of adjustment was how often classmates chose the labeled child for some activity. Even more confounding is the fact that two studies that measured self-concept did so with different instruments (Schurr, Towne, & Joiner 1972). We will therefore group the various kinds of outcome measures into several categories and consider them separately: (1) the child's reaction to being labeled, (2) self-concept, (3) peer acceptance, and (4) postschool outcomes (a variety of adult indices of adjustment, such as marital adjustment and employment).

Reaction to Being Labeled.   Extant research reveals that labeled chil-dren and their parents do not like the child's being called mentally retarded. As Dunn (1968) put it, the label "mentally retarded" is not worn as a badge of distinction. Mercer (1973a) described the parental belief that programs for their children are discriminatory against minority children and are educational dead ends. Gozali (1972) contacted former EMR stu-dents to get their perceptions of the programs and reported that 85 percent felt the special class was degrading and useless. However, these reactions are not to the fact of being labeled only but to the overall educational experience. Furthermore, we can only speculate as to how these individuals would have judged a regular class experience given the likelihood of aca-demic or social failure that led to their initial referral to the special classes.

In several studies R. L. Jones (1971a, 1971b, 1972, 1973a, 1973b) examined the reactions of EMR high school students to being labeled and segregated. He found that many tried to avoid being identified as a member of the EMR class, lying about their course work and resorting to various techniques to avoid being found out. Some EMR subjects reported that labeling or special placement had altered their friendships, made it difficult to date, or hurt their chances for jobs. Jones's results lend themselves to differing interpretations. One could take these responses as valid and conclude that labeling and segregation are harmful to children. A competitive interpretation is that the social ineptness of these high school students would have surfaced regardless of labeling and placement and that their responses represent an attempt to rationalize their failures by placing the blame on something other than themselves. And even though students—and parents—seem to think that the label hurts them, we will have to look at real evidence of its effect on feelings of self-worth, on peer acceptance, and on postschool outcomes to see if this is so. The problem is that studies that have been made of these kinds of evidence are themselves contradictory and inconclusive.

Self-concept. Some opponents of labeling hypothesize that, as a result of being called mentally retarded, labeled children come to see themselves as worth less than if they had not been labeled. Gardner's (1966) review revealed vast differences in the way self-concept was measured in various studies, and he and others (e.g., Jones 1973a) have questioned the validity of many of these measures. Usually the investigators measured self-concept after the individual had been labeled for some time. Such a procedures does not allow one to attribute lower scores to the label alone. Many other things happened to these individuals before they were labeled, and labeling usually carries with it all sorts of other consequences (e.g., special class placement, segregation).

The evidence on devaluation of self as a consequence of labeling is mixed. Some of the studies reported lowered self-concepts in the labeled groups (Borg 1966; Jones 1973a; Mann 1960; Meyerowitz 1962), while others found just the opposite (Drews 1962; Goldberg, Passow, & Justman 1961). One article (Bacher 1965) reported no differences between the groups.

Despite the methodological problems in most of this research, one series of studies is of particular interest because the researchers assessed self-concept at several points in time, including a measure taken right before the individual was labeled and placed in a special class (Schurr, Towne, & Joiner 1972; Towne, Joiner, & Schurr 1967). Children were tested on a self-concept of ability test before they learned that they were being classified as EMR. Subsequently they were tested at four times during the first year of EMR status. The result: children evidenced more favorable self-concepts after being labeled and placed than they had prior to learning they were going into the EMR program. The more favorable self-concept rose with

EMR placement and stayed high until the end of the first year, when it fell slightly. The sample of children were followed and seven were ultimately returned to a regular class and delabeled. They were tested for self-concept prior to their return and then one year later. It was reported (Schurr et al. 1972) that the self-concept score was significantly lower one year after delabeling and return to the regular class than it had been just prior to delabeling.

These results suggest that labeling and placement in an EMR program may inflate the self-concept of mildly retarded children—probably by changing the reference group from regular class peers to EMR classmates.

Peer Acceptance.   Another hypothesis is that labeling children reduces their popularity or results in their being selected less often by peers for various activities. Frequently the case against labeling comes from efficacy studies and is based on sociometric evidence. In sociometric studies children are asked to name children in their class that they would want to work with on a project or to be friends with, or to fit some description provided by the experimenter. Since sociometric techniques seldom have any real or implied consequences, Gottlieb (1975b) suggests that they should be interpreted as measures of how much the selector likes or dislikes the individual being rated. Such procedures are often used to indicate the social ranking of the retarded child in a class or school compared to the nonretarded children.

The results of sociometric studies are difficult to interpret because the standard is quite different for an EMR class than for a regular class. For example, does being moderately accepted by classmates in an EMR class indicate higher, lower, or the same degree of acceptance as being moderately accepted in a regular class by higher-ability children?

One thing that has been found is that there is a consistent relationship between intelligence and peer acceptance (Dentler & Mackler 1962). Regardless of whether a person is placed in a regular class, a special class, or an institution, the more intelligent, the greater the acceptance by peers. But this may not have anything to do with labeling.

Wilson (1970) has argued that children are not rejected because they are labeled but because they exhibit behaviors that are objectionable. He wrote:

Teachers trying to help retardates win better sociometric status will want to remember that retardates are generally unacceptable because of bothersome, inappropriate, or antisocial behavior including bullying, fighting, misbehaving, showing off, swearing, lying, and cheating . . . or simply an absence of positive likable traits and behavior.

(p. 240)

These conclusions are supported, in part, by the early research of Johnson (1950) and Johnson and Kirk (1950), who studied the social position of low-

IQ children in regular classes where they were *not* labeled mentally retarded. Even though they were not labeled, these children were not popular because they did things the other children objected to. Even when they try to be likable, retarded children may be rejected. As Edgerton (1967) has pointed out, the mildly retarded child may seek out attention and affection to a greater degree than nonretarded children, but the seeking behavior may be so inept that the retarded child may drive away even those who are initially receptive.

Are acceptance and rejection two extremes of a continuum or are they separate processes? Recent findings on Project PRIME (Gottlieb 1975a) suggest they are separate processes and that *rejection* is highly related to misbehavior while *acceptance* is related to cognitive variables. Yet numerous studies represent them on a continuum, with retarded students tending to be rated by peers at slightly above the average rating. Miller (1956) interpreted such findings to indicate "mild acceptance," despite the fact that such a rating is reliably lower than that received by nonretarded peers.

Interpretation of peer ratings is further complicated by the investigators' failure to control the referent of the individual doing the rating. For example, we speculated that a peer may perceive a retarded child only in terms of what that child does in the classroom (e.g., he cuts and pastes). Hence his low rating of that child may reflect rejection of children who cut and paste rather than read and write, independently of how the child is labeled. For these results to support the opponents of labeling, one would have to isolate the role of the label as a determinant of the peers' ratings.

Increasingly, the evidence suggests the possibility that labeling may actually benefit retarded children in terms of peer acceptance. This supports Guskin's (1963a) earlier observation:

> The role concept "defective" probably leads to certain privileges as well as punishments, including the absence of demands for self-supporting and protection, and the acceptance of certain unusual behaviors contrary to normal for nondefective individuals.
>
> (p. 332)

Seitz and Geske (1977) reported that mothers who observed children in free play with their mothers actually rated labeled retarded children higher on interpersonal attractiveness than they did unlabeled retarded children. Foley (1979) showed fourth graders a videotape of children labeled normal, learning disabled, or mentally retarded. The fourth graders rated the children higher when they were labeled mentally retarded than when they were labeled either learning disabled or normal. The children may have been giving answers they thought would please adults, or their responses may reflect a "protective function" whereby a different standard is applied for evaluating the behavior of a child known to be handicapped. Two studies (Budoff & Siperstein 1978; Siperstein, Budoff, & Bak 1980) examined the effect of the mentally retarded label when applied to children portrayed as either academically competent or incompetent. Sixth graders rated labeled children higher than unlabeled children; the child who was unlabeled and academically incompetent received the most negative ratings of all, particularly from sixth-grade boys. In the study by Siperstein et al. (1980) the label *mentally retarded* and the idiomatic label *retard* were compared. It was again found that the mentally retarded label protected the child who was portrayed as academically incompetent but appeared normal, whereas the label *retard* failed to protect the child even when portrayed as academically incompetent. The investigators noted, however, that these ratings may reflect feelings of sympathy and that these children would not necessarily accept the retarded. Kurtz, Harrison, Neisworth, and Jones (1977) examined the effect of labeling on the behavior of adults reading a story to children who were either labeled or unlabeled. They reported a "positive bias" resulting from labeling, in which the adults showed more "immediacy"— touching, forward leans toward the child, greater eye contact—while reading the story to the labeled children.

The issue of a possible protective function of labels was examined by Gibbons and Gibbons (1980) and by Gibbons, Sawin, and Gibbons (1979). In the 1980 study, the effect of the label *institutionalized* was examined. It was not found to influence ratings of traits such as friendliness, but the raters tended to favor the unlabeled when indicating how much social contact the rater would want with the person. The 1979 investigation assessed the influence of the mentally retarded label on the explanations adults gave for the successful or unsuccessful performance of children. They reported a "patronizing effect": when the labeled child failed, the raters reduced the blame for the failure, and when the labeled child succeeded, the raters gave the child less credit for the success. The authors concluded that these patterns of attributing both success and failure could be detrimental to the development of retarded children.

A series of studies by Gottlieb and his associates (Goodman, Gottlieb, & Harrison 1972; Gottlieb & Davis 1973; Gottlieb, Hutton, & Budoff 1972) has shown that, while EMR children integrated into regular classes are rejected more often than their nonretarded peers, the integrated EMR children are also rejected more often than EMR children segregated in special classes. Gottlieb (1972) explains these surprising results as follows:

> Non-EMRs maintain a dual set of standards as to what constitutes social acceptance. Integrated EMRs who were never defined as being retarded insofar as the normal children are concerned may be perceived by the latter as "normal." As such, they (integrated EMRs) are subject to the same standards of behavior as other normal children.
>
> (p. 19)

In other words, the children who are labeled are held to a lower standard and may be accepted, while the integrated (nonlabeled) children are held to the higher standard and may be more actively rejected by nonretarded classmates.

Gersch and Jones (1973) found similar results even for TMR children: sixth-grade nonhandicapped students gave higher ratings to TMR children when they were labeled mentally retarded than when they saw the same children under an unlabeled condition.

As we see it, one function of the label seems to be to put behavior into perspective. Nonhandicapped children are more likely to accept behavior they consider strange if they know *why* a child is acting that way; they may think to themselves, "Oh, he acts that way because he is retarded." The retarded label thus serves to reduce the dissonance between expected and actual behavior because it prompts the nonhandicapped child to use a different standard by which to judge the behavior. Use of the label may even make the difference between avoidance and social interaction: nonretarded children may interact with children known to be retarded even though they would have avoided them if the children were unlabeled. This need to explain bizarre behavior may have happened to you. Have you ever encountered in a grocery store a child who looks to be six or seven years old but who is really a very large four-year-old? You would probably think this child unusually immature because you compare the child's behavior to your ideas of what a seven-year-old does. But if you knew that the child carried a "four-year-old" label, you might accept the behavior as appropriate (applying a standard for four-year-olds) instead of condemning it.

Postschool Outcomes.   One fear of those who say labeling is detrimental is that it is difficult, if not impossible, to shed the label. But for the subgroup of retarded children over whom the controversy rages (mildly retarded children of ethnic minority or poor background), this assumption may be especially shaky. As we have seen, the term *six-hour retarded* can be used to describe the many EMR children who are only seen as retarded wtihin the school context. They were not seen as deviant before they came to school, are not perceived as deviant in nonschool contexts during their school careers, and will not be perceived as deviant once they leave school via graduation or dropping out. If this is a valid description, how can we say that being labeled and placed in a special class has lifelong effects?

How valid is the assumption that mildly retarded people tend to "disappear from the rolls of retardation" (Haywood 1971, pp. 7–8)? This conclusion has been reached by many (e.g., Goldstein 1964; Guskin & Spicker 1968; Kirk 1964) who have reviewed the literature on postschool adjustment of the EMR. Early follow-up studies of former EMR class students (Baller 1936) found that the majority were self-supporting (Baller, Charles, & Miller

1967). Similar findings were reported by McIntosh (1949) in Toronto, where 37.8 percent were earning at or above the average for the city. If one breaks down the EMR subjects into high, medium, and low subgroups, success is found to be more prominent in the higher-ability subjects. Charles (1966) resurveyed Baller's (1936) original group and reported that almost all subjects in the middle and high group were employed, while 16 percent in the low-ability group needed some help. The greater success of the higher-ability EMR students in securing employment seems to be a consistent finding (Collmann & Newlyn 1957; Kennedy 1966). But at least one investigator found that the majority of former EMR students were *not* self-supporting. A study by Miller (1956) reported the dismal news that only 30 percent of the former EMRs surveyed were employed and the vast majority of these were earning very low wages.

The evidence on the postschool adjustment (such as marital success) of former EMR pupils leads one to conclude that they do not do as well as their nonretarded peers (Goldstein 1964; Guskin & Spicker 1968; Wilson 1970). But when compared to children of comparable IQ who remained in a regular class, there is some evidence (Peck & Stephens 1964; Porter & Milazzo 1958) that the EMR-labeled group was *superior* on postschool adjustment measures.

Labeling alone does not determine success, for it operates in conjunction with certain personality and work-habit variables. The fact that an individual is not prompt, misses a lot of working days, dresses sloppily, and argues with coworkers must be at least as potent as former labels in determining whether or not an individual is fired. However, the label may interact with personality factors so that a person labeled mentally retarded who engages in nonproductive personality-related behavior is more likely to be fired than a nonlabeled individual who engages in the same behavior. Furthermore, Edgerton (1967) has found evidence that former residents released from an institution were detected and reacted to negatively by people who had no way of knowing that they had ever been labeled and institutionalized. But no systematic study has yet been conducted on what specific behaviors it is that the society at large reacts to negatively.

While the evidence on former EMRs indicates that their occupational status is below that of average-IQ persons, it still reveals a rather favorable adjustment in light of the limited ability of these individuals. In other areas, too—self-concept and peer acceptance—the evidence is hardly supportive of the notion that labeling has a lifelong devastating effect. It does not prove, on the other hand, that labeling has a beneficial effect either. If a negative effect does exist, it probably consists of an initial and persistent devaluation of self and attempts to cover up their past status. Such an effect is difficult to demonstrate experimentally—and thus far it has not been demonstrated.

Hypothesized Indirect Effects of Labeling

Conclusions about how labeling directly affects a child are unwarranted, but what about the hypothesized indirect effects? According to some observers, the label may color how others see retarded persons indirectly affecting them in a negative way even if the label itself does not.

The labeling of children and their separation from the regular education program is thought to lead teachers to differential expectations for their performance (Yoshida, 1974). This culminates in what Merton (1948) termed the *self-fulfilling prophecy*.

There are two ways that the indirect effect could work (MacMillan et al. 1974). First, individuals who know that a child is retarded communicate it to that child, who internalizes the information and comes to feel devalued as a person. A second possibility is that individuals who know a child is retarded behave differently toward that child than they would if they did not know about the child's classification.

Dexter (1956, 1958, 1960, 1964) has argued forcefully that much of the retarded behavior displayed by the labeled individual is determined by expectations of others. For example, he wrote:

> There is a distinct possibility that many mental defectives become concrete social, legal, or economic problems simply because of the direct or indirect consequences of [labeling]. The indirect consequences of the high valuation placed upon such (academic) skills manifest themselves in discrimination and prejudices against the "stupid" which leads them to acquire a negative or hostile self-image of themselves and therefore to live according to a self-definition of themselves as worthless and contemptible.
>
> (1958, p. 920)

Many have voiced similar concern over the possibility that, once assigned the label *mentally retarded*, the child is socialized to play that role and meet the lowered expectations of the retarded status (Christophos & Renz 1969; Dexter 1956, 1958, 1960, 1964; Gallagher 1970; Johnson 1969; Jones 1973b; Larsen 1975; Mercer 1970b; Riscalla 1974). The role of expectation is currently used as an argument for abolishing the special class. But according to Yoshida's (1974) incisive analysis of this literature, while the arguments for the labeling effect are plausible, the theory that the EMR label affects expectations "is based more upon a philosophical position than valid empirical data" (p. 4).

The role of the teacher in determining a self-fulfilling prophecy has been the most widely studied and debated. The teacher is the central figure in the child's school day and, as an agent of the school, introduces the curriculum, socializes the child to cultural norms, and evaluates the child's social and academic performance (Dreeben 1967; Parsons 1959). The teacher's expectations may initiate a self-fulfilling prophecy, according to the following theoretical process:

> (a) Labels bias the teacher's perception of the child's capabilities on certain dimensions in academic work; (b) these perceptions are translated into observable behavior; (c) those behaviors communicate expectancies to the child; (d) the child then behaves according to the teacher's definition; (e) those behaviors are consistent with the original perception, and (f) the process is again initiated.
>
> (Meyers et al. 1974, p. 19)

However, if a link in this chain is broken, the process whereby a self-fulfilling prophecy comes to operate would be destroyed.

Although there is little research evidence to indicate how often the full cycle is established, we can imagine that it does get started in some instances. The teacher has some information about certain children (e.g., they are EMR) before they first come to class, and this foreknowledge may trigger certain expectations. But these expectations are probably modified in many cases as a result of the teacher's repeated evaluations of these children in the classroom, tending to disrupt the cycle.

Expectations: Good and Bad. An impression often left by the discussions of expectation research is that it is bad to set expectations for children; however, as noted by Meyers and his associates (1974), this need not be the case. They suggest that labels can serve a supportive function when they set realistic goals that children are able to accomplish. Because of their preparation and experience, special education teachers may set expectations for achievement for their classes that are lower than those held for regular class children, yet these expectations may be realistically optimistic for EMR children in terms of where to begin instruction, how rapidly to proceed, and what materials and strategies to rely upon in teaching these children. However, at certain points and under certain circumstances, these expectations can become dysfunctional if they go beyond performance to actually limit behavior. Meyers and his associates (1974) cite the possibility that the label may be so potent as to lead the teacher to deny gains achieved by an EMR youngster. Denial of the possibility that the child can make such gains possibly sets into motion the feared dangers of a self-fulfilling prophecy. It is crucial that the teacher revise expectations in light of new information rather than establish static expectations.

One test of this process was reported by Yoshida and Meyers (1975). Regular elementary teachers and teachers of EMR classes were shown a video tape of a black elementary-age student who was portrayed as either a sixth grader or an EMR student. The tape showed four testings of the child on concept formation tasks. After each test presentation the teachers were asked to estimate his future achievement on similar tasks. It was reported that the expectation scores given by the teachers who were told he was an EMR child were no lower than those given by teachers who thought he was a normal sixth grader. Instead, the teachers increased their predictions on each trial, indicating that they did revise expectations based on new information. Similar results were reported by Foster, Ysseldyke, and Reese (1975) for the emotionally disturbed label and by Salvia, Clark, and Ysseldyke (1973) for the mentally retarded label; all these studies demonstrated that the label did not inhibit the teacher from revising expectations as more information was made available.

Siegel (1967) reviewed a series of investigations (conducted before the onslaught of studies on the "Pygmalion effect," discussed below) that clarify how people adapt their behavior on the basis of cues received from direct contact with a retarded person. In research, an adult was asked to interact verbally with institutionalized retarded children. The verbal interaction was taped and later analyzed. The retarded children selected were usually either high or low in verbal ability, but the adults were not informed of this. The results generally indicated that adults adapted their language to the language ability level of the retarded child with whom they interacted. Adults who interacted with low-ability children usually used more redundant language than adults who interacted with children of high ability.

The Pygmalion Effect.   Rosenthal and Jacobson (1968) ran an experiment on the potential *positive* effects of teacher expectations that greatly excited educators. The study related teacher behavior to falsified descriptions of children. It reported dramatic gains on tests of general ability for a randomly selected group of children portrayed to the teachers as likely to show significant intellectual growth in the near future.

The impact of that one study on education has been profound, to the dismay of those who critiqued the study. Thorndike (1968), for example, wrote:

> Alas, it is so defective technically that one can only regret that it ever got beyond the eyes of the original investigators! Though the volume may be an effective addition to educational propagandizing, it does nothing to raise the standards of educational research.
>   In conclusion, then, the indications are that the basic data upon which this structure has been raised are so untrustworthy that any conclusions based upon them must be suspect. The conclusions may be correct, but if so it must be considered a fortunate coincidence.
>
>   (pp. 708, 711)

Other critiques (Elashoff & Snow 1971; Snow 1969) have been similarly devastating. Despite its methodological flaws, the Rosenthal and Jacobson

(1968) study has stimulated numerous attempts to replicate their findings (Claiborn 1969; Dusek & O'Connell 1973; Fleming & Anttonen 1971a, 1971b; Goldsmith & Fry 1971; Jose & Cody 1971; Kester & Letchworth 1972; Meichenbaum, Bowers, & Ross 1969; Mendels & Flanders 1973; Silberman 1969; Sorotzkin, Fleming, & Anttonen 1974). But these studies have failed to provide substantiating evidence for Rosenthal and Jacobson's hypothesis (Gozali & Meyen 1970; Soule 1972).

Complexity of Expectation Effects.   Meyers and his associates (1974) and Yoshida (1974) have suggested several possible reasons for the failure of many investigators to show an expectation effect, negative or positive. First of all, they noted the short time used in most of the studies—it may take a longer time for this expectation effect to show up in student behaviors such as reading. Another potentially crucial factor that may have mitigated the effect is that in most studies the contrived information was given to the teacher *after* the teacher had interacted with the children without the bias treatment. By this time the teachers might have already established their own expectations for the children, as has been shown in a series of studies (Brophy & Good 1970; Dusek & O'Connell 1973; Good & Brophy 1972; Kranz, Weber, & Fishnell 1970; Mendoza, Good, & Brophy 1971). In such cases the plausible contrived information might not have been accepted by the teachers since it was contrary to the expectations they had already set by interacting with the children.

Both Meyers and his colleagues (1974) and Yoshida (1974) noted that in studies where teachers were unfamiliar with the children, the probability of an expectation effect taking place was increased. For example, several studies (Beez 1970; Rothbart, Dalfen, & Barrett 1971; Rubovits & Maehr 1971) have used teachers, volunteers, and college students who were given information that certain children were high or low achievers prior to any contact with the students. The results showed a consistent pattern in which labels presented prior to contact with the students resulted in a biasing effect on the behavior of the tutors.

The research to date on labeling and expectations suggests that reactions to the mentally retarded are influenced more by individual behavioral characteristics than by a label (Guskin 1978). The research reviewed in this section suggests that the retarded child's competence, physical attractiveness (Aloia 1975), social and antisocial behavior, and other characteristics influence how others react. These factors may interact with the label, but labeling alone does not seem directly or indirectly to influence the reactions of nonretarded children or adults. It remains to be shown how this extends to classrooms in which the teacher deals with many students over a long period of time. Most of the studies reviewed were of very brief duration, unlike a classroom situation in which teachers receive frequent ongoing feedback that apparently causes them to modify expectations.

FACTORS THAT MODIFY THE EFFECTS OF LABELING

The fact that the evidence reviewed fails to provide conclusive evidence that the mentally retarded label has detrimental effects on children cannot be interpreted to mean that there are not detrimental effects. It only proves that the instruments that are employed to measure outcomes are insensitive and that researchers are unable to control the effect of the label across subjects doing the rating. Labeling may have an effect but it probably influences different children in different ways. The impact of labeling may range from none at all on any possible outcome measure to rather profound effects on many outcome measures. To predict how a child will be affected by labeling we must identify the variables involved. These variables include the child's prelabeling history, for it may be as important as, if not more important than, the postlabel career of the individual in determining outcomes.

Looking at the extremes of individual variation we might find on one end a very bright adolescent with a history of academic success who if labeled retarded would probably shrug off the label, and on the other end a profoundly retarded hydrocephalic child with an IQ below 10 who would not be able to comprehend the significance of the label. At these extremes, labels like *mentally retarded* have no effect whatsoever on any outcome measure. However, as we move from these extremes toward the mildly retarded we might expect to find cases in which (1) individuals do comprehend that the label has negative overtones and (2) their histories of success and failure in various situations are not sufficiently positive to enable them to discredit the label. In borderline cases the label might exert sufficient influence (either directly or indirectly) on the individual to depress performance below the mentally retarded cutoff level.

Prelabeling Experiences

The sociological perspective focuses upon the formal label as the explanation or cause of lower potential achievement and ignores the child's earlier experiences. But as noted in Meyers et al. (1974), a child's career is an accumulation of diverse experiences, many of which shape and affect achievement and attitudes. When a child is classified as mentally retarded and placed in a special class, we cannot discount the importance of past history. This is particularly true in the cases of children who first come to the attention of the regular classroom teacher *because of* poor academic achievement and adjustment. When such children have already fallen behind their age peers, we might presume that a sense of difference has developed even before they are formally labeled.

As noted by Guskin, Bartel, and MacMillan (1975), the prelabeling careers of children who will be labeled mentally retarded differ. Some display physical or psychological characteristics that alert others to the fact that they are different very early in their lives. Others become labeled when parents actively solicit a label in order to get services. In other cases neither the child nor the parents are aware that there is a problem until an agency labels the child. These different patterns may produce different effects when labeling takes place.

For instance, imagine a child who, prior to being formally labeled, has been ridiculed by peers (and even by insensitive parents and teachers), informally labeled *stupid* or *dummy,* and isolated socially at school and in the neighborhood. Such a child's self-concept would have suffered so much abuse before labeling that it would be surprising if the label would lead to any further depreciation of the self. On the other hand, a child who has not faced ridicule and has not failed repeatedly may have a self-concept that is sufficiently positive and stable to resist any such mortifications.

A partial explanation of the history of failure typical of EMR children can be found in the motivational studies of Zigler (see Balla & Zigler 1979). Many EMR children expect failure before they even attempt a task, probably because they have failed so often in the past. Whether this pattern of failure develops before labeling, after labeling, or both is unclear. The point is that the extent to which children's self-concept, peer acceptance, academic achievement, and other characteristics have been depreciated before labeling varies from child to child. In testing children on any measure three years after labeling, it is impossible to attribute relatively low scores exclusively to the label and experiences since the time of labeling.

Multiple Labels

In many cases where children are labeled EMR they are simultaneously classified with other labels such as *culturally deprived* or *culturally disadvantaged, delinquent,* or *poor.* The use of multiple labels has been discussed at some length with regard to black children (Rivers, Henderson, Jones, Ladner, & Williams 1975) and probably extends to other minority groups as well.

Are the problems of a child carrying more than the EMR label compounded compared to those of a child who is only labeled EMR? Similarly, is the effect of multiple labels a function of the specific combination of labels (e.g., is *retarded-culturally deprived* more debilitating than *retarded-delinquent*)? Or are certain labels so potent as to override any additional labels?

There is some evidence from which to speculate. Jones (1972), for instance, reported that labels such as *culturally disadvantaged* are distasteful to those who carry them. Hence in the case of a multiply labeled child we must be sensitive to the possibility that an effect such as a lowered self-concept could be due either to one of the labels alone or to some combination of the specific labels.

Formal versus Informal Labeling

In most of the discussion regarding labeling there has not been a distinction between formal labeling (that done by recognized agencies in the community) and informal labeling (that done by peers and other individuals with no authority to institute any programmatic treatment). There is one obvious difference: formal labeling leads to decisions about placement and treatment, whereas informal labeling does not. However, does one lead to greater devaluation of self than the other? Does one cause greater rejection by peers? These differences have been studied.

We know that the retarded child's peers are often cruel in attaching informal labels. Goldstein (1963) likened this process to formal labeling: "In all justice we cannot close our eyes to the fact that the retarded child in the regular class can be and frequently is labeled by his peers in much the same way as children in special classes" (p. 52). Jones (1972) asked special class teachers what terms were used by age peers to describe their EMR students. Among those terms reported were *dumb, dumb bunny, dum-dum, retard, Z, eddie,* and *dodo.* Would the formal label attached by an amorphous body like the school have as great an impact as such informal labels attached by one's peers?

The labels *retard* and *institutionalized* were mentioned earlier in this chapter in discussion of studies by Siperstein et al. (1980) and Gibbons and Gibbons (1980), but these studies did not provide direct evidence on the relative impact of formal and informal labels. Recall, however, that the mentally retarded label protected children who were normal in appearance and who were portrayed as academically incompetent, but the idiomatic label *retard* failed to provide such protection. We might speculate that cruel informal labels are applied to children by peers in response to offensive personal behaviors such as bullying and swearing, but this must await further investigation.

The literature on child development clearly documents the gradual orientation to one's peer group in the later elementary school years; this orientation increases throughout secondary grades. Would the effect of peer labeling become stronger at the same time? We do not yet know.

Attacking the question from a different angle, Tarjan (1970) asked whether the ease of shedding a label once the individual is removed from the status of mentally retarded (as when an EMR child leaves school) depends on who made the original diagnosis. In contrast to the results of

Mercer (1973a) and those of Edgerton (1967), Guskin and his associates (1975) concluded that the diagnosing agency does make a difference. According to these studies it seems to be far easier for a former special class EMR to pass for normal than it is for a child who has been in an institution. But who did the labeling is not the only possible explanation; the formerly institutionalized children may have been more debilitated in the first place, and that is why they were placed in institutions.

Even though we cannot yet say how potent informal labeling is, we cannot assume that formal labeling takes place in a vacuum and is the only factor causing self-devaluation. Informal labeling goes on, too, and may exert as much and sometimes even more influence on certain outcomes.

Responses to Labeling Events

When the label *mentally retarded* is attached, there are a variety of responses that can be made by the individual or on behalf of the individual. While there has been no systematic research on these responses, several that can be identified would conceivably alter the impact of the label on the individual (Guskin et al. 1975; MacMillan et al. 1974). Parents may respond to labeling defensively by trying to find a cure for the condition, or they may acquiesce to the condition in a fatalistic manner. The retarded individuals themselves can either accept or deny the validity of the label. They or their parents might attack the labeling agency ("What do they know?") or might even systematically challenge the label through legal and political means. Another response to the label is to attempt to ignore it; when children are called names ("retard"), they can ignore it or reply with a similar epithet.

The underlying concern in the response issue is that the labeling of a child as mentally retarded may lead to what Dunn (1968) called "mortifications of the self." But on the contrary, Edgerton and Sabagh (1962) reported that labeling and placement in an institution resulted in certain aggrandizements of the self for higher-ability retarded individuals since it gave them a peer group of lower-ability individuals with which to compare themselves. Labeling may not cause mortification in some children from minority families and low socioeconomic status backgrounds either, for such families frequently deny the accuracy of the diagnosis. As Edgerton and Sabagh explained:

This nonacceptance may have been facilitated by several circumstances. For instance, the entire family of the retarded person may have been rejected and mortified by the community at large and feel the need to protect its members against the onslaught of "authorities." Many of the mentally retarded come from families of low socioeconomic status, and family members may have had humiliating experiences with law enforcement or welfare agencies. Such a family will protect its members against those who "accuse" them of mental retardation, and may not even believe that the accused actually is retarded, since his intellectual level may not be much below that of his relatives. To them, this may simply be another instance of discrimination against the whole family.

(pp. 265–266)

The circumstances described above might lead to an immunization against any mortification of the self, in which case the label would have far less effect than in a case where the child accepts the label as accurate. Even when the family does not rally to the defense of the child and deny the accuracy of the label, the child may deny it. Again, the effect of being labeled would be minimized. These considerations seem important in determining the impact of the mentally retarded label on the child, but thus far they have received little attention.

Situational Variables

Also unresearched are other situational variables that might alter the impact of the label. Is the child institutionalized when the label is applied? Does the kind of program make any difference? Is one label less potent than another? Do different communities respond differently to a child's labeling as retarded?

Although these questions have not been researched, we can at least speculate about them. In the matter of the type of program, for instance, we might speculate that any treatment that designates certain children as "different" will target them for differential acceptance by their peers regardless of how benign the treatment appears to professionals. Hence mainstreamed EMR children who go to a resource teacher may be perceived by classmates as different; despite the attempt to integrate them into a regular program, stigmata may be attached to the treatment independent of the label or class affiliation.

In considering the specific label employed, we know that some states label the mildly retarded as EMR, whereas others use the term *slow learner*. In Britain the term *educational subnormal* is used, and in Norway EMR children are called *children in need of help*. Does the specific label alter the effect? There is some evidence, mentioned earlier, that *slow learner* does not have as great a potency as *mentally retarded* in the minds of the American public. But when attitudes towards the Norwegian "children in need of help" were contrasted with the attitudes toward United States children classified as EMR, it was found that attitudes were more favorable toward the children labeled as EMR (Gottlieb 1972). However, it is unclear whether this means that Norwegians are less tolerant or that their label is more potent.

Yet another variable is the community in which the child lives and the value it places on intellectual attainment. In communities where intellectual pursuits are valued highly, the fact that certain children are labeled may have a profound effect on their acceptance and ability to achieve success in that setting. In a community where intellectual pursuits are not valued as highly, labeled children may be able to be successful in activities that do not involve intellectual behavior. A lack of academic prowess and being labeled mentally retarded may not be devastating if these children can demonstrate competence in other ways seen as important by the community in which they live.

Specificity versus Generality of the Hypothesized Effect

In addition to considering variables within and outside the child that determine the effect of the label, there is a need to study whether a specific outcome (e.g., self-concept) is affected only in the school setting or whether it generalizes to settings other than the school, such as the playground, home, neighborhood, or community. For example, if a child dropped in self-concept as a direct consequence of being labeled mentally retarded by the school, would self-concept in althletic settings or social settings also drop?

Mercer's (1973a) findings demonstrate that the vast majority of EMR children are labeled in the school context, but the research we have already reviewed fails to demonstrate a drop in self-concept as a consequence of labeling. There is thus little foundation for this theoretical question, but for the sake of the argument we will assume temporarily that labeling does cause a drop in self-concept.

Sentiment seems to favor the assumption that the effects are very pervasive, permeating all aspects of a child's life and persisting well beyond the school years. But look again at Mercer's (1973a) study. She found that many children with low IQs, poor academic performance, and poor adaptive behavior in the school context still show highly adaptive behavior in their homes and neighborhoods. These results are usually interpreted to mean that since these children function so well in the home and neighborhood they should not be considered mentally retarded in the school setting. But there is another way of looking at these findings: if the effect of the label given by the schools is supposedly so potent and its effects so generalized, then why is this large proportion of EMR children adapting so well in the contexts of home and neighborhood? The assumption of a generalized effect may be as unfounded as the assumption of a specific one.

ATTITUDES TOWARD RETARDED PERSONS

Will nonhandicapped persons accept retarded persons in the community and in regular classrooms? Today's trend toward normalization and mainstreaming gives this question, which is of theoretical interest in the labeling controversy, critical practical importance as well. We believe that people's behavior toward the retarded is basically consistent with the attitudes they express toward them. The study of attitudes is also important because the public's attitudes toward the retarded determine the extent to which the public supports programs and funding for programs. In addition, residents of the community play a major role in determining whether the severely and moderately retarded can be placed in the community and whether they will be accepted if they are. As mildly retarded children are returned to regular classes, the attitudes of regular class teachers and nonretarded peers will be crucial.

Some Basic Concepts in the Study of Attitudes

Definitions of the term *attitudes* usually stress attempts to measure a person's set of predispositions for responding in a particular way to a specified class of objects or people. Attitudes have three components: the cognitive, the affective, and the conative. Gottlieb and Corman (in press) wrote that "The cognitive component is sometimes called the perceptual, informational, or stereotypic component of an attitude. The affective component concerns people's feelings of liking and/or disliking, while the conative component concerns behavioral intentions or behavior *per se.*" Attitudes develop gradually through experience. They begin to crystallize at the start of the school years, but children are apparently unable to differentiate the cognitive, affective, and conative components until the middle elementary school years.

Gottlieb and Corman (in press) provide an interesting discussion of how direct and indirect experiences affect attitude formation. When two persons have a *direct experience* with each other, each person forms an impression of the other. The impression is initially based on physical appearance and the behavior observed. Whether the attitude we develop from a direct experience is favorable or unfavorable toward a group such as the retarded depends on several factors, including the frequency of contact, the duration of the interaction, and the intensity of the relationship. More frequent contacts and contacts of longer duration increase the likelihood of having more favorable attitudes toward the retarded. The siblings and parents of retarded persons, who have had intense contact, have more favorable attitudes toward the retarded than does a nonselect group of persons without such contact. In addition to direct contacts of this sort, we have *indirect experiences* with mentally retarded persons through TV promotional ads, books and shows dealing with retarded people, lectures, and other sources. Gottlieb and Corman (in press) characterize indirect experiences as those in which we are passive participants who are not actually having personal contact with a retarded person.

Problems in Measuring Attitudes

Gottlieb's (1975b) excellent analysis of research on attitudes toward the mentally retarded yielded mixed results. Studies dealing with nonretarded peers' attitudes indicated that the retarded are rejected (Heber 1956; Johnson 1950; Johnson & Kirk 1950), but other studies suggest that they are tolerated (Lapp 1957). One study (Bruininks, Rynders, & Gross 1974) suggests that acceptance is higher among same-sex peers. Studies designed to test whether increased contact with retarded people leads to more favorable attitudes also yielded mixed results. Jaffee (1966) and Gottwald (1970) report more favorable attitudes among those having contact, but others report more negative attitudes among those having contact (Goodman, Gottlieb, & Harrison 1972; Gottlieb & Budoff 1973). What accounts for these discrepant findings?

The apparent confusion in these findings is in part due to the ways in which the particular researchers collected the evidence. Some used younger subjects than others; the severity of the retardation also varied. Some retarded subjects had physical stigmata; others were not obviously retarded. As Gottlieb (1974a) points out, attitudes toward retarded persons may vary as a function of age and the severity of the retardation, and a critical analysis of these studies should consider these factors when comparing results. In addition, the presence or absence of physical stigmata could account for different attitudes.

Another important difference in research studies is how the concept of mental retardation—more technically, the *referent*—is defined. We know, for example, that attitudes are more favorable toward the mildly retarded than toward the severely retarded (Gottlieb & Siperstein 1976). When we consider the many ways in which the referent has varied, it is not surprising that the findings have varied. Some of the referents used in various studies are listed below.

1. An abstract label of *mental retardation* (Hollinger & Jones 1970).
2. The label *mental retardation* plus a brief statement: "They will never be able to read better than about fourth grade level and will always be like a nine-year-old child" (Meyers, Sitkei, & Watts 1966).
3. A specific mentally retarded child the rater knows (Bruininks et al. 1974; Goodman et al. 1972).

4. A brief description of a hypothetical mentally retarded person (Guskin 1963b).
5. A video tape of a mentally retarded person (Gersh & Jones 1973).

The point is that differences in results may be due to differences in the methodologies used to assess attitudes. But despite the inconsistencies, the research indicates that certain factors are related to attitudes and changes in attitudes.

Public Attitudes toward the Retarded

Potter (1971) noted that the use of a single label—*mentally retarded*—to cover both biological and social-psychological cases of lowered intellect confuses public attitudes. The term *mentally retarded* evokes an image of a multihandicapped retarded child with physical stigmata (Hollinger & Jones 1970; Meyers 1973; Meyers, Sitkei, & Watts 1966). According to Guskin (1962, 1963a, 1963b), such stereotyped images are commonly applied to all who are retarded, for people tend to think in terms of what Zigler (1970a) called the *modal man:* they tend to perceive all individuals who share some designation (e.g., mentally retarded, culturally deprived) as possessing identical attributes. In the case of mental retardation, people think of the biologically impaired retarded person with physical stigmata, severe or profound retardation, and an extremely poor prognosis, even though the vast majority of mentally retarded individuals have no observable stigmata.

In addition to stereotyping, another source of confusion concerns the possible spillover from other labels, especially the label *mentally ill* (Haywood 1971; Hollinger & Jones 1970). Since the word *mentally* is common to both, many people attribute characteristics of the mentally ill to those who are mentally retarded. This apparently has a negative effect, for in comparison to other terms for handicapped persons (e.g., slow learner, educationally handicapped), the term *mentally retarded* is viewed more negatively by the lay public.

No one disagrees with the notion that the public does hold negative stereotypes and attitudes toward the mentally retarded. However, whether these attitudes change when people get feedback on the accuracy of their stereotypes and how strongly children are affected by negative attitudes are as yet unanswered questions.

Gottlieb (1975b) noted that the public holds numerous other misconceptions regarding mental retardation, including the belief that retardation is a disease and that sterilization is the best solution to the problem (Winthrop & Taylor 1957). Furthermore, when responding in the abstract to labels, the public holds more positive attitudes toward the concept "slow learner" than the concept "mentally retarded." According to Hollinger & Jones (1970), the term *mental retardation* carries a connotation of physical disability and severe mental debility. Belinkoff (1960) described how reluctant parents were in a real situation even to discuss enrolling their children in a program titled "Mental Retardation Project," but when the project was renamed "Special Education Project" parents became more willing to discuss the possibility.

Factors Related to Public Attitudes toward the Retarded. There has been some effort to identify which characteristics of members of the public are related to positive or negative attitudes toward the retarded. Gottlieb (1975b) reported that the characteristics receiving the most attention in such studies have been the rater's sex, age, educational level, social class, and extent of contact with retarded people.

In general, women express more favorable attitudes toward the retarded than do men (Harasymiw 1971). However, no sex difference was found when people were asked questions pertaining to the social worth of retarded persons (Gottwald 1970). Gottlieb and Corman (described in Gottlieb 1975b) found that women held a more positive general stereotype of the mentally retarded, but they found no sex differences on three other factors: segregation in the community, segregation in school, and negative stereotype.

Most of the research on the relationship of age differences and attitudes reveals that younger subjects hold more positive attitudes than do older subjects (Gottwald 1970; Hollinger & Jones 1970).

Data on educational level are mixed. While Gottwald (1970) found that the higher the educational level (and knowledge about retardation), the more favorable the attitudes, Greenbaum and Wang (1965) reported the opposite. Two investigations studied the relationship between educational level of employers of retarded persons and attitudes. Phelps (1965) found more favorable attitudes on the part of the more highly educated employers, yet Cohen (1963) reported just the opposite—less favorable attitudes by the more highly educated. Hence no definite trend is apparent in the evidence relating educational level to attitudes in the general public.

Gottlieb (1975b) considered three studies on social class differences and concluded tentatively that lower social class individuals hold more favorable attitudes than do middle- or upper-class individuals. But one study (Gottwald 1970) found no social class differences.

Finally, the research on the effect of the degree of contact with the retarded on attitudes fails to support the belief that contact fosters more positive attitudes. In fact, Phelps (1965) found that the more experience a personnel officer had with retarded workers, the less likely the officer was to hire a retarded person.

Attempts to Improve Public Attitudes.   Normalization and mainstreaming have been accompanied by attempts to improve public attitudes toward retarded persons. But we don't yet know what is the best way to go about this, and some of our efforts may even have been counterproductive.

One idea has been that by exposing nonhandicapped people to retarded people we will engender more positive attitudes toward retardation. Typically, exposure has come in the form of a tour of an institution. Results are mixed, partly because, as Gottlieb (1975) commented, a tour can be of high or low shock value; it can be given to groups who differ markedly in areas such as the intensity and direction of their initial attitudes, what conditions they observed on the tour, and so on.

Cleland and Chambers (1959) studied the effect of such a tour on attitudes of high school and college students. Attitudes toward the *institution* improved; in fact, after the tour students were more likely to favor institutionalization of the retarded. Kimbrell and Luckey (1964) found that those who took such a tour became more negative toward the retarded residents as a consequence of the tour; at the same time their attitudes toward the institution improved slightly. The improvement in attitude toward the institution was also reported by Sellin and Mulehahay (1965). Gottlieb (1975b) summarized the typical shifts in attitude as a consequence of such tours:

> It appears that attitudes toward the patients became more negative while attitudes toward the institution became more positive. This combination of attitudes toward the patients and the institution is easily interpretable if one considers that the more likely people are to believe that retarded people have a limited prognosis and should be segregated, the greater will be their belief that institutions are necessary to achieve these ends.
>
> (pp. 108–109)

Peer Attitudes Toward the Retarded

Most of the research on peer attitudes toward the mentally retarded consists of sociometric studies of mildly retarded children in the school setting (MacMillan & Morrison, in press). In many studies, attempts have been made to relate a type of administrative arrangement (such as a regular class or a special EMR class) to acceptance, but more recent research considers the characteristics of the retarded child and the nonretarded raters and also the correlates of social status.

When low-IQ children remain in regular grades, the evidence is consistent that they enjoy lower social status than do higher-IQ children (Heber 1956; Johnson 1950; Johnson & Kirk 1950; Miller 1956). Miller (1956) pointed out that while the low-IQ children were not accepted, neither were

they overtly rejected. The reasons for nonacceptance appear to be the undesirable behavior exhibited by the low-IQ children rather than low IQ per
se.

Direct comparisons have been made of EMR children in special EMR
classes and regular class children of comparable IQs who in most cases have
not been diagnosed as EMR (e.g., Thurstone 1959). This type of comparison
has revealed that those in special classes are rated higher by their special
class peers than are IQ-equal children rated by their regular class peers. Different groups of peers used different frames of reference (MacMillan &
Morrison, in press), however, which makes these findings hard to interpret.
Differences in achievement are less pronounced in the special class, and
different criteria may be used to select friends in these two settings, as will
be discussed later.

When retarded children have been integrated into regular classes there
has been some hope (e.g., Christophos & Renz 1969) that the attitudes of
nonretarded children toward retarded individuals in general would
improve as a result of the contact. The results of studies bearing on this
hypothesis (Goodman, Gottlieb, & Harrison 1972; Gottlieb & Budoff 1973;
Gottlieb & Davis 1973; Iano, Ayers, Heller, McGettigan, & Walker 1974)
have, in general, found no support for the hypothesis. On the contrary,
integrated EMRs tend to be more rejected by nonretarded peers than are
EMR children segregated in special classes.

Meyerowitz (1967) compared neighborhood relationships of segregated
EMRs and those in regular classes, groups that were matched for social class.
Regardless of educational placement these children were isolated socially
in their neighborhood. So the apparent lack of acceptance of the retarded
children in the school setting appears to extend to the neighborhood; moreover, the lack of acceptance is independent of the educational placement of
the mildly retarded child.

Different educational arrangements have little impact on the general
finding that EMR children are accepted less than nonretarded children.
This line of research does not, however, consider the influence of the characteristics of the person doing the accepting or rejecting (Gottlieb 1975b).
Several studies indicate that lower social class nonretarded children are
more accepting of EMR children than are more affluent nonretarded children (Bruininks et al. 1974; Goodman et al. 1972; Gottlieb & Budoff 1973).
Care must be exercised in interpreting this finding, however; it could mean
either that the lower-class nonretarded persons are more accepting or that
the lower-class EMRs are less deviant in their social skills. The willingness
of nonretarded peers to accept the retarded is also influenced by their popularity (Siperstein & Gottlieb 1977) and sex. A series of factors related to the
total class composition such as modal level of achievement, classroom climate, and teacher reinforcement patterns may also affect acceptance
(MacMillan & Morrison, in press).

Several characteristics of retarded children being rated may also influence whether they are accepted. These include academic competence, physical attractiveness (such as the absence of the physical stigmata associated with Down's syndrome), socioeconomic status, and possibly other factors such as race, which would be influenced by the racial composition of the class in which the retarded child is enrolled. The many factors related to the social status of mentally retarded children in regular grades, including the characteristics of the target retarded child, the rater, and classroom variables, are displayed in Figure 7.1 (MacMillan & Morrison, in press).

A different approach to studying the social status of the mentally retarded is exemplified by the research of Gottlieb, Semmel, and Veldman

---

FIGURE 7.1   Alternative Model for Research on Sociometric Status in Special Education

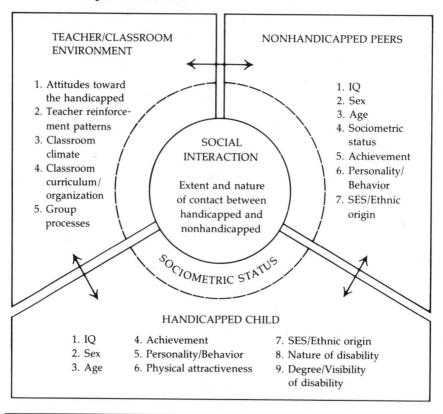

TEACHER/CLASSROOM ENVIRONMENT

NONHANDICAPPED PEERS

1. Attitudes toward the handicapped
2. Teacher reinforcement patterns
3. Classroom climate
4. Classroom curriculum/ organization
5. Group processes

SOCIAL INTERACTION

Extent and nature of contact between handicapped and nonhandicapped

SOCIOMETRIC STATUS

1. IQ
2. Sex
3. Age
4. Sociometric status
5. Achievement
6. Personality/ Behavior
7. SES/Ethnic origin

HANDICAPPED CHILD

1. IQ	4. Achievement	7. SES/Ethnic origin
2. Sex	5. Personality/Behavior	8. Nature of disability
3. Age	6. Physical attractiveness	9. Degree/Visibility of disability

Adapted from "Sociometric research," in *Attitude and attitude change in special education,*" R. L. Jones, ed. (Reston, VA: Council for Exceptional Children, 1982). Reprinted by permission of the Council for Exceptional Children.

(1978) and MacMillan and Morrison (1980), in which investigators studied the correlates of social status. Gottlieb et al. (1978) examined the correlates of social status of mildly retarded children integrated into regular grades and reported different patterns of correlates for acceptance and rejection. Both peer and teacher perceptions of the target child's cognitive competence were related to acceptance scores, whereas peer and teacher perceptions of misbehavior were related to rejection. In other words, acceptance appeared to be determined by the child's cognitive and academic status, but rejection was determined by whether the child was regarded as a behavior problem. MacMillan and Morrison (1980) replicated this study in a self-contained special class in which the raters were retarded peers, not nonretarded classmates as in the Gottlieb et al. study. MacMillan and Morrison found a different pattern of correlates of acceptance and rejection, which seems to suggest that the qualities that lead to acceptance or rejection in a special class are different from the qualities that lead to acceptance or rejection in a regular class. Hence, we cannot assume that the child with the highest social status rating in a special class would be the child most likely to be accepted in a regular class. The likelihood of acceptance in the regular class could be improved by selecting children in the special class who rate highest in cognition and achievement (Gottlieb et al. 1978).

Attempts to Improve Peer Status. Since the evidence indicates that the retarded are not well accepted, we might expect that efforts would be made to improve their peer status. However, few studies have been reported that attempt to do this (Gottlieb 1975b). One such attempt (Chennault 1967) involved group activities in which EMR children with low status participated with high status EMRs. Those from the lower group who took part achieved a significant increase in social status as compared to EMR children who did not participate. McDaniel (1970) also involved EMRs in square dancing and basketball with nonhandicapped students, while a control group simply engaged in regular classroom activities. Those who participated were reported to be either more accepted or more rejected than the control group; contact in some cases resulted in higher rejection.

The difficult task confronting a teacher in a class that includes a mentally retarded child is to structure learning activities such that the retarded child is an integral part of the group and not on its periphery. Ballard, Corman, Gottlieb, and Kaufman (1978) reported on an effort in which teachers, through inservice training, involved the retarded child in group work in a mainstreaming class, thereby improving the child's social status. This intervention lasted approximately thirteen weeks, which is considerably longer than most experimental interventions. This project demonstrated that improvement is possible when the teacher provides the structure necessary for the child to be accepted by nonretarded peers. Two other studies (Lilly 1971; Rucker & Vincenzo 1970) also improved the social status of EMR children by involving them in activities with other children, but in these stud-

ies the improvement in social status disappeared some time after the experimental involvement.

Teacher Attitudes Toward Retarded Students

While there are a number of professions involved in the diagnosis and
treatment of mentally retarded individuals, most research on the attitudes
of professionals toward the retarded has focused upon teachers.

Teacher attitudes toward retarded children have taken on added importance since publication of the Rosenthal and Jacobson (1968) work on expectations, since it seemed to demonstrate that a positive teacher expectation
can boost the retarded child's achievements. There is a parallel concern that
negative teacher expectation can lower achievement. Despite the methodological flaws inherent in the expectation research, it is legitimate to be concerned about the possibility that teachers transmit their attitudes to retarded
children or their peers and that this in turn might affect social status or
performance (Lapp 1957).

You might expect that special education teachers would have more favorable attitudes toward retarded children since they know more about retardation and have chosen to work with such children. There seems to be little
doubt that special education teachers have more factual knowledge (Efron
& Efron 1967; Semmel 1959), but there are mixed findings regarding attitudes. Efron and Efron (1967) reported more favorable attitudes by special
education teachers than regular class teachers; however, Greene and Retish
(1973) and Semmel (1959) found no differences between special education
and general education teachers. Another study (Alper & Retish 1972) evaluated attitudes of prospective teachers before and after student teaching.
While no significant changes in attitude were found for special education
and secondary school candidates, regular elementary teachers expressed
more negative attitudes toward retarded children after completing student
teaching. Siperstein and Bak (1980) summarized the relationship between
knowledge and attitudes as follows: *"knowledge of mental retardation is necessary* for teachers to have a positive attitude toward retarded children, *but
it is not sufficient* to ensure that their attitude will be positive" (p. 210).

Shotel, Iano, and McGettigan (1972) studied attitudes of teachers toward
various types of children, including the emotionally disturbed and the
retarded, in schools that had special classes and resource rooms. In schools
where resource rooms were used, 37 percent of the resource teachers
favored this approach for retarded children at the beginning of the year.
The percentage dropped to only 13 percent following one year of experience in such a program, with the teachers preferring emotionally disturbed
over mentally retarded children. Gottlieb (1975b) noted that this finding is
inconsistent with the findings of Jones and Gottfried (1966) that teachers

expressed a preference to teach mildly retarded over emotionally disturbed children. In the latter study, the fact that the teacher responses were not based on personal experience but stated preference only may help to explain the inconsistency.

As mainstreaming becomes more commonplace, the attitudes of regular classroom teachers become more important. In Chapter 13 we will consider in more detail the attitudes of regular class teachers toward mainstreaming. To improve negative attitudes, we need more evidence on the effectiveness of direct and indirect experience and other possible influences.

SUMMARY

There have been many claims in the courts and in professional literature that spotlighting children's intellectual weaknesses by labeling them mentally retarded and segregating them in a special classroom or taking them out of the regular classroom at times for special help has a devastating and long-lasting effect on self-concept, peer acceptance, and postschool chances for success. But our review of the literature fails to support this argument.

Categorization is supposed to be a useful way of dividing into groups people who need similar treatment. But it is possible that our current categories should be changed, either to include many kinds of handicapped children under the same heading since they already receive the same kinds of education, or to break the present category of EMR down into subgroups whose needs differ. Even though they may need revision, categories do function peripherally to focus volunteer efforts, legislation, and research.

On the negative side, categorization of the mildly retarded may not do them much good in terms of academic improvement. And segregating them from the nonhandicapped may be doing the retarded a disservice. According to the sociological perspective, retardation is a relative condition *created* by society. People are deviant only when they fail to measure up to socially established norms. Once stigmatized, started toward a self-fulfilling prophecy, and removed from normal society, they may never make their way back in. It is important to recognize that this deviance theory is only a theory, for the evidence that this process really happens is very shaky.

According to the opponents of labeling, children don't like being called *mentally retarded*; the label lowers their self-concept and peer acceptance and decreases their chances for success once they leave school. But some studies have demonstrated the opposite: although children clearly do not like to be formally labeled, the effects they cite may only be rationalizations for failures they would have had even without the label. Instead of lowering, their self-concept may in fact rise after they are placed in an EMR program since they now look better in comparison to their classmates. Their acceptance by their peers, too, may rise because the label *retarded* helps to explain their previously unacceptable behavior. Once they leave school, mildly retarded people won't do as well as nonhandicapped people in finding jobs and making successful marriages, just as they were never as well-accepted as normal students in school. But there is some evidence that those who were labeled EMR and placed in special classes may have a slight edge over people of similarly low IQ who were never labeled and given special class help.

It has been hypothesized that even if labeling doesn't hurt children directly it can hurt them indirectly by biasing the perceptions of others. It is theoretically possible that negative teacher expectations can limit a child's performance and that teacher optimism can raise it. But although Rosenthal and Jacobson found evidence of a positive "Pygmalion effect," no one has ever been able to reproduce their findings. And experiments that have tried to test the effect of negative teacher expectations have shown that, no matter what label children carry, teachers tend to revise their expectations based on what they learn about them from working with them for a long time.

A number of variables have been isolated that may influence what impact labeling has on children. They include children's prelabeling experiences, whether they carry more than one stigmatic label, whether they are informally called names like "stupid" by their peers, whether they are formally labeled retarded by the school, how they and their families react to the labeling, what label is used, and what kind of community they live in. We do not yet know what the impact of each variable may be and whether labeling affects children only in school or in all aspects of life. Without such knowledge we cannot make any blanket generalizations about labeling that can safely be applied to all who are labeled.

Because we are now trying normalization and mainstreaming as vehicles for treatment of retardation, it is critical that retarded individuals meet with acceptance in the community. As the problem now stands they are probably not very well accepted, and we don't know how best to go about improving their image. We would think that increased exposure to retarded individuals would help to overcome the negative public stereotype of the retarded person as someone with severe disability and physical stigmata. But this has not necessarily been the case. Some experiments that increased contact between retarded and nonretarded people actually increased rejection of the retarded individuals. Education is another possibility, but some studies show that more educated people are more rejecting. Even among teachers, those who have been trained in dealing with mentally retarded persons may be no more positive toward them than general education teachers who have not had this training.

CHAPTER 8

Litigation

Categorization procedures and treatment programs for the retarded were not challenged in the courts until the early 1970s. Since then, however, legal inquiries have been made as to the validity of the identification process and the possibility that institutions and special classes are mere holding functions that do not meet the needs of the retarded. Some of these issues had already been debated at length in professional journals and conferences, but little change in practice had resulted from these professional debates. It was not until the issues were taken to the courts that any substantial changes were made. Recent court decisions defining the rights of the retarded have had a profound effect on the identification process for mildly retarded children and on access to educational programs for more severely retarded individuals.

The fact that restrictions are being imposed on delivery of services to the retarded has a great impact on what professionals dealing with these children can and must do. Changes in practice are forthcoming, but not necessarily changes that professionals feel are beneficial. The courts have not relished moving into the fields of medicine, psychology, and education, but they expressed the sentiment that they have no choice. As Judge Wright explained in *Hobson* v. *Hansen:*

> It is regrettable, of course, that in deciding this case this court must act in an area so alien to its expertise. It would be far better for these great social and

political problems to be resolved in the political arena by other branches of government. But there are social and political problems which seem at times to defy such resolution. In such situations, under our system, the judiciary must bear a hand and accept its responsibility to assist in the solution where constitutional rights hang in the balance.

Some critics have questioned the wisdom of judicial intervention in such cases, arguing that the courts have no responsibility for implementing the changes and do not comprehend the problems their decisions cause (Cohen & DeYoung 1973). But some decisions have been passively accepted by the professionals. Some special educators have voiced the belief that the changes ordered by the courts are desirable and that what the courts have done in a relatively short period of time would have taken a long time to achieve through other channels. Because of this feeling, special educators have not come forth to argue against some of the charges leveled at special education, even when they knew that the so-called facts being introduced had little, if any, backing in the research evidence. By their silence, they were indicating that philosophically or morally they believed in the plaintiff's case regardless of the quality of the evidence being cited in court to support the allegations.

This chapter is not an exhaustive review of cases pertaining to the mentally retarded. Instead, it is a selective review of several landmark cases that have had a great impact on special education. For excellent reviews that cover the court cases in some detail, see Cohen and DeYoung (1973), Hobbs (1975a, Vol. 2, Part 5), Kindred, Cohen, Penrod, & Shaffer (1976), Kirp (1973), Turnbull and Turnbull (1978b), Weintraub (1975), and issues of *Mental Retardation and the Law.*

LEGAL RESTRAINTS

The treatment of retarded individuals has made its way into the courts because it involves issues that can be seen as legal restraints. The fact that some individuals are classified as mentally retarded carries with it consequences that frequently handicap them. In a way, mentally retarded persons are relegated to second-class citizenship in the eyes of the law since they are not entitled to all legal rights and privileges of other citizens. Detailed accounts of the legal restraints on the handicapped have been provided by Brakel and Rock (1971) and Hobbs (1975b).

Among the restraints discussed by Hobbs were involuntary hospitalization, compulsory sterilization, prohibition of marriage, removal of children, and declaration of legal incompetence. As of 1971 a mentally retarded person could be committed involuntarily to a hospital in 37 states. Hobbs noted that such commitment can occur without a fair hearing and does not require the kinds of evidence necessary to convict an individual of a crime. Furthermore, there is no guarantee to these individuals that they will be provided with needed treatment. Hence persons who are classified as retarded can be placed in a hospital for a lifetime with few procedural safeguards, not even the ones guaranteed to criminals.

Twenty-one states had laws providing for compulsory sterilization of the mentally retarded in 1971. Public recognition of this possibility was stirred up by national media coverage of the case of two sisters in Montgomery, Alabama, who were sterilized without informed parental consent. Hobbs reported that of the 21 states with such laws, only 5 required the patient's permission. He raised the question as to how often release from a state institution was made contingent upon the patient's agreeing to be sterilized before release.

Marriage is prohibited for retarded persons in 41 states; when it occurs, it can be legally voided. Furthermore, in 41 states no parental consent is required for the state to remove children for adoption when one parent has been classified as retarded.

In most states one person can request that the courts declare another person legally incompetent. This decision is made on the basis of a simple hearing, seldom requiring a jury or guaranteeing the right to legal counsel. One bit of evidence often introduced in such a hearing is a label (such as *retarded*) attached during childhood. Once an individual is declared legally incompetent, virtually all civil and social rights are withdrawn and the person assumes the legal status of a minor, which often means that the person cannot execute legal documents, initiate litigation, vote, or hold office. Furthermore, in most states it is illegal to issue a driver's license to anyone officially classified as mentally retarded.

Even when individuals have been rehabilitated, they are still restricted by such laws, which may, as Hobbs put it, "handicap the handicapped beyond the limits of reason, necessity, and justice" (1975b, p. 159). But while the use of blanket laws to cover all individuals who are similarly classified is unduly rigid, it is often necessary and reasonable to restrict or classify those of limited judgment or special educational needs. As Hobbs pointed out, we should not forget in considering court cases about specific abuses that, in general:

1. Legal restraints on the liberties of people are necessary and reasonable in the interest of society (people who cannot see should not be allowed to drive automobiles).
2. The classification of children is ordinarily undertaken with constructive intent, usually to get some kind of special help for them. Nonetheless, there

is no gainsaying the further fact that gross abuses of individual rights (of due process, for example) occur with intolerable frequency and that categorization and labeling can be instrumental for the legitimization of abuse.

(1975b, pp. 156–157)

LITIGATION ON BEHALF OF CHILDREN

Investigations into the legal status of the handicapped have highlighted the importance of *due process* considerations. While it may now be desirable to classify children in order to obtain services for them, classification must be done with the recognition that it may have undesirable consequences in the future. Safeguards must be instituted so that the chances of abuse can be minimized and so that the children are protected from arbitrariness and a disregard for their civil rights. Since the mentally retarded frequently are those least able to protect themselves from such abuses because they are handicapped, poor, or uneducated, we must be extremely cautious not to overlook their rights.

Regardless of how blatantly a person's rights are violated, the courts cannot intervene until a lawsuit is filed. If abused persons are children, they are not able to file suits in their own behalf. Unless a child's parent or guardian is willing and able to bring suit on behalf of the child, the violation of the child's rights is beyond the scope of the court's power. Hobbs (1975b) contends that parents have tended to be uninformed as to what constitutes an abridgment of their child's rights during classification; moreover, parents often cannot gauge the appropriateness of a given treatment or determine the success of the treatment. Furthermore, many parents decide against going to the court because of the time and energy required to see the case to its completion.

Recently, lawyers and legislators described by Blatt (1972) as "the new heroes of special education" have championed the rights of exceptional children through class action suits and legislation designed to provide equal opportunity for education and safeguards to protect children's civil rights. The resulting court mandates and laws are necessary, but so far they have been insufficient to bring about substantial changes (Hobbs 1975b; Kirp, Kuriloff, & Buss 1975). What changes are made ultimately depend on the ability and willingness of those charged with implementing the new mandates and laws.

The problems of implementation will be discussed later in this chapter; we will first consider the changes and decisions in specific court cases. They fall into three main categories, those pertaining to: (1) treatment in residential facilities, (2) the right to education and the responsibility of states to allocate funds for such programs, and (3) identification and segregation of mildly retarded children. In the first two categories, the rights of the more severely retarded have been emphasized; the last category pertains primarily to ethnic minority children and low social class children.

Cases Pertaining to Treatment in Residential Facilities

Several suits have been brought recently against state agencies in an attempt to improve the services provided to handicapped children. Some degree of success has been achieved, but opinions differ as to the impact of these decisions. Cohen and DeYoung (1973) claim that they establish clear recognition of the rights of the retarded, but Burt (1975) thinks the decision in *Wyatt* v. *Stickney* (1971) may be only a hollow victory.

The issue addressed in *Wyatt* is whether institutionalized mentally retarded children have a constitutional "right to treatment." Due to a budgetary cutback in the state of Alabama, a staff reduction was ordered in state residential facilities for the mentally retarded by the Department of Mental Health. A lawsuit against this cutback in services was brought on behalf of mentally ill patients and eventually extended to include residents of the Partlow State School and Hospital for the Mentally Retarded.

Wyatt was a landmark case because it was the first time the courts stated that the institutionalized mentally retarded have a constitutional right to rehabilitation. Although the constitution does not explicitly prescribe a right to rehabilitation, the right follows from guarantees of due process (Fourteenth Amendment) and from the prohibition of cruel and unusual punishment (Eighth Amendment). The legal arguments in this case are quite interesting. Halpern (1976) characterized the civil commitment of mentally retarded persons to institutions as government incarceration of a person who has committed no crime. Since these persons have committed no crime, it follows that they are not confined for punitive purposes, but if no rehabilitation is offered, the incarceration is indistinguishable from penal confinement. To quote the court, "Adequate and effective treatment is constitutionally required because, absent treatment, the hospital is transformed into a penitentiary where one could be held indefinitely for no convicted offense" (Halpern 1976, p. 391). In other words, the justification for allowing the state to institutionalize the mentally retarded is that they cannot care for themselves without special rehabilitation; if they do not receive rehabilitation, institutionalization is unjustified. As Halpern (1976) stated in relating another case to *Wyatt*, "For the mentally retarded people who are committed to institutions, the purpose for which classification is made is to provide habilitation. If the mentally retarded are confined without habilitation, all semblance of rationality of the classification purportedly based on the need for habilitation disappears" (p. 395).

The evidence heard in *Wyatt* led the court to conclude that Partlow was a warehousing institution with an atmosphere of psychological and physical deprivation, incapable of providing treatment and rehabilitation. The court found conditions that would violate the prohibition of cruel and unusual punishment for convicted criminals, and persons in this group had committed no crimes whatsoever. The conditions included physical deprivation, overcrowding, unchecked violence by employees against residents and residents against each other, the abuse of restraint and solitary confinement, inadequate diet, and insufficient sanitation, physical exercise, and medical and psychiatric care.

The judge issued an emergency order directing that steps be taken to protect the physical safety of the residents. These steps included the hiring of 300 additional employees within thirty days, providing for fire safety, and having a team of physicians examine the drug program for every patient. The court's decision included a statement supporting the position that the mentally retarded should not be taken from the community and placed in large institutions *at all*, stating that they should be placed in the "least restrictive habilitation setting feasible."

The institution subsequently admitted to the lack of a rehabilitation program, whereupon the court set up machinery to establish sets of standards for adequate rehabilitation, including the right to an educational program regardless of the degree of retardation and accompanying handicaps.

Similar cases have sought to remedy inhumane and inadequate treatment of retarded patients in residential facilities. In *Ricci* v. *Greenblatt* (1972), the Belchertown State School for the Retarded in Massachusetts was charged with failing to provide adequate treatment. Restraining orders were issued by the court requiring that patients' medical needs be assessed, that a prohibition on hiring be lifted, and that comprehensive treatment programs be established.

In a lawsuit filed in New York (*New York State Association for Retarded Children, Inc.* v. *Rockefeller* 1972), conditions in the Willowbrook State School were challenged. Among the charges were widespread physical abuse, overcrowded conditions and understaffing, inhumane and destructive conditions, extended solitary confinement, and a virtual absence of therapeutic care. The court was asked to set minimum standards and to order the state to meet standards, which it did. Burt (1975) noted that in the Willowbrook case, unlike *Wyatt*, the court did not uphold the constitutional right to treatment for institutionalized retarded residents but did support their constitutional right to be protected from (state-imposed) harm.

In analyzing these court decisions, Burt (1975) noted several problems. The *Wyatt* decision is under review, and a number of federal district courts faced with similar cases have failed to follow the same line of reasoning as the *Wyatt* court. In *Wyatt*, the allegation that the institutionalized retarded have a constitutional right to treatment led to the decision that conditions at Partlow had to be "improved." This kind of vague directive is not going to bring about dramatic changes on behalf of the mentally retarded residing in state institutions. And Burt argued that the court ignored a major issue— whether a "large-scale, geographically remote, full-time residential institution can beneficially affect the lives of its residents" (p. 300).

The *Wyatt* decision did invoke a principle that will be encountered frequently in laws and educational programing, that of "the least restrictive setting." In this regard the court said that patients are to be placed in the least restrictive setting in which rehabilitation can be accomplished. As Burt noted, this standard is cloudy and elusive; it did seem to preclude placing borderline or mildly retarded persons in the institution, but did not require development of community facilities that would enable more severely debilitated persons to stay in the community.

In addition to the potential problem of defining what the least restrictive setting is in individual cases, the decision that mentally retarded persons have a constitutional right to treatment raises a new question: If the state owes institutionalized retarded children such things as medical services, clothes, and food, then why does it not owe the same to every child? We will consider the problem of the expense of treating retarded children later when we discuss the difficulty of implementing these court decisions.

In contrast to Burt's pessimism about the effect of the right-to-treatment cases, Cohen and DeYoung (1973) foresee that these cases will serve as prototypes for cases across the country and that the outcomes of all such cases will be an increase in qualified personnel and possibly a mandating of educational programs in residential facilities. However, as Burt pointed out, we must not assume that the temper of these initial decisions necessarily dictates the direction subsequent decisions will take. He wrote: "We thus cannot assume that a new era of judicial solicitude for retarded children has arrived" (1975, p. 294). Furthermore, some court decisions will result in greater changes than others (Kirp et al. 1975).

Halpern (1976) suggested that judicial attention to these problems may raise more questions than it answers. Once the court has decided that the community is the preferred setting for serving the mentally retarded, we must consider whether society has the ability to generate the community services necessary to provide for them. In Chapter 14, we will discuss the extent to which this has occurred. Will society accept the retarded in its neighborhoods, supermarkets, and parks? Can we alter society's attitudes toward the mentally retarded, even those who are severely debilitated and who possess physical stigmata, who were formerly placed in institutions?

If court decisions persist in favor of the plaintiffs, the implications for treatment of the severely and profoundly retarded are obvious. Standards will be imposed and professionals in institutions will have to meet them. Treatment programs (recreational, educational, physical, vocational) will have to be established or upgraded at some cost to taxpayers. How will administrators of the large institutions react to these changes? Their feelings will probably be mixed. On one hand the decisions enable them to hire personnel that they were previously blocked from hiring by budgetary decisions; on the other the mandated program changes have allowed them little time for planning.

While the direction of the right-to-treatment cases cannot be seen for sure until subsequent decisions are made, there can be little doubt that the courts are going to continue to determine the practices of the residential institutions to some extent. In addition, since the courts are alerted to the potential abuses to residents who live in inadequate institutions, it seems safe to predict that advocates for the retarded will be going to the courts for relief when they feel the rights of the retarded in institutions are being violated.

Cases Pertaining to the Right to Education

While the three cases we discussed in the last section established the right of retarded persons to humane basic care in institutions, other suits have tried to establish the principle that they have the right to be educated in the public schools no matter how severe their retardation. In the past, special education programs in the public schools of most states have had minimum behavioral standards that a child had to meet before being enrolled in a TMR program. These often included requirements that the child be toilet-trained and able to communicate basic needs. Children functioning at lower levels were excluded from public education. Their parents had to seek out private programs or programs of treatment provided by state agencies other than the department of education (such as a department of mental health). The essential charge brought against public education is that handicapped children who are excluded from school or whose entrance is postponed are being subjected to discriminatory practices. Abeson, Burgdorf, Casey, Kunz, and McNeil (1975) note that some state constitutions contain reasons whereby the state (e.g., New Mexico) can deny educational services. Other states specify programs for certain categories of exceptionality (e.g., blind, mentally retarded), but children who are classified into one of the categories not enumerated or who fall into more than one category (e.g., a deaf and retarded child) can be denied access to public education.

For many years the exclusion of large numbers of handicapped children from public education went unchallenged. But these practices too have been challenged in the courts, with the *Pennsylvania Association for Retarded Children (PARC)* v. *Commonwealth of Pennsylvania* (1972) case being the most notable.

PARC. The *PARC* case was described by Burt (1975) as a landmark in the litigation against state agencies to improve services for the retarded. The legal theory behind the *PARC* decision is that excluding retarded children from public education is "unconstitutional invidious discrimination" (Burt 1975, p. 294) and that the retarded through exclusion are being denied equal access to educational opportunity.

For years Pennsylvania required that all children between the ages of eight and seventeen attend school, but any child judged by a school psychologist to be "unable to profit from further school attendance" or "uneducable and untrainable" was excused (i.e., excluded) from the schools. The result of these clauses was that severely retarded children were relegated to institutions or their homes. In 1971 PARC filed a suit charging that the exclusion of severely retarded children from the public schools was unconstitutional, as it represented a denial of equal protection. PARC further charged that assignment of children to programs for the retarded, unless preceded by notice and the opportunity for a hearing, was a denial of due process. The court never ruled on the basis for the constitutional claims, for the case was settled prior to a decision through a consent agreement (Kirp et al. 1975).

The signing of the consent agreement by both parties established the "right to education" for all of the retarded children of the Commonwealth of Pennsylvania, with the court indicating that all children can benefit from education and have a right to an education. In the assessment of Hobbs (1975b), the consent agreement forced structurally conservative institutions to take on the major internal tasks of reorganization, reorientation, and reordering of priorities. The agreement specified the following:

1. Within 90 days the state was to locate and identify all retarded children of school age not in school and to begin teaching them no later than September 1972.
2. It provided for medical and psychological evaluations for all children previously excluded to determine the "most appropriate placement."
3. Every child located and evaluated was to be placed in a free public program "appropriate to the child's capacity."
4. All children in special classes for the mentally retarded were to be reevaluated to determine the proper placement.
5. The State Department of Education was required to submit a plan describing the range of programs available, what was needed to assure all retarded children the appropriate program, and arrangements for financing these programs and recruiting teachers.

In order that the court could oversee the implementation of the court action, two masters were appointed: Dennis Haggerty, a Philadelphia attorney and former PARC officer, and Herbert Goldstein, professor of special education at Yeshiva University.

The court did not define "appropriateness" as used in the consent agreement. But it did specify that regular class placement was preferable to placement in any special program. Furthermore, it allowed that parents who were displeased with placement recommendations for their children could request a hearing before an impartial officer (Kirp et al. 1975).

Despite the profound changes ordered in the *PARC* case, it contained some elements that Burt (1975) found disturbing. One was the way in which a remedy was sought. According to Burt, the court did not resolve a dispute between contesting parties but instead "ratified an agreement between advocates for children's services and professional service agencies to raid state treasuries for greater funds on behalf of their shared clientele" (p. 296). That is, the state department of education (the defendant in the case) was not really attempting to defend the charges against Pennsylvania but rather agreed with the plaintiff (PARC) that funds should be allocated to support programs for the severely retarded.

Burt also noted a potential danger in the legal theory advanced—that excluding retarded children from public schools is a wrongful inequity. He argued that if only total deprivation of education is found wrong, then any minimal educational program would satisfy the court's decision. Issues of the quality of such programs would have to be decided subsequently.

Another principle of the PARC case pertains to equality. The state is now funding public education for some children and refusing it to others (the severely retarded) on the grounds that it is more expensive and difficult to teach severely retarded individuals and the attainments likely for these children are far more modest than for less handicapped children. As Burt (1975) noted, this rationale makes sense if the public commitment to education is to develop the "excellence of the few"; however, this commitment is not explicitly espoused by the state. For more details about the issues in PARC you can consult Burt (1975).

Related Cases. Several other court decisions have also established the right to education for retarded children, but none has approached the *PARC* decision in terms of publicity or impact.

In *Wolf* v. *Legislature of the State of Utah* (1969), a suit brought on behalf of two TMR children excluded from school, the court ruled that education is a fundamental and inalienable right guaranteed by the United States Constitution. In effect this ruling made education mandatory for all children in the state of Utah, regardless of their level of intellectual functioning. It thereby invalidated clauses used to justify excusing (excluding) certain children from attendance.

In Wisconsin two exclusion cases were heard in 1970. One, *Doe* v. *Board of School Directors of the City of Milwaukee* (1970), resulted in a temporary injunction that prohibited placing retarded children on waiting lists for special education classes. The other, *Marlega* v. *Board of School Directors of the City of Milwaukee* (1970), placed restrictions on the system in the exclusion of children from school for medical reasons, thereby protecting the due process rights of the children. In *Marlega* the court established that a due process hearing must include the following:

1. specification of the reasons for recommending exclusion;
2. a hearing prior to the exclusion;
3. the right of the child to be represented by counsel as well as to confront and cross-examine the witnesses;
4. a stenographic record of the hearing;
5. a written final decision that specifies the reasons for exclusion;
6. a specification of alternatives available to the child within public education.

(Cohen & DeYoung 1973, p. 273)

Even if such a hearing ends in a decision that exclusion of a certain child is legitimate, the last clause establishes the ongoing responsibility of public education for that child's education.

Another case, *Mills* v. *Board of Education of the District of Columbia* (1972), was quite similar to *PARC*. Both were designed to establish the constitutional principle of the right to education in public schools for children previously excluded as uneducable. And both sought to require due process hearings prior to placement in special programs. However, the *Mills* case was brought on behalf of a broader spectrum of excluded children than those in the *PARC* case. *Mills* included incorrigibles, the physically handicapped, and the emotionally disturbed in addition to the mentally retarded. In essence, the *Mills* case sought to establish the right to a public education for all children regardless of their disabilities or behavioral symptoms (Kirp et al. 1975).

The judge in *Mills* supported virtually every point requested by the plaintiffs. His decision supported the right to public education and established the need for a hearing prior to exclusion or classification. However, the judge did not see fit to appoint masters to oversee implementation of the decision as had been done in Pennsylvania. Public support for the education of the excluded was extended to include tuition grants if adequate programs were not available in the public schools. The decision was to be implemented immediately.

In summary, the cases reviewed here reflect a consistent finding by the courts that the right to a publicly supported education is a constitutionally guaranteed right. This right cannot be denied individuals because of their level of functioning or because of the cost to schools of providing a free and appropriate public education. Furthermore, the decisions establish due process safeguards to prevent children from being railroaded out of school or into special education programs they do not need. These decisions clearly provided the conceptual basis for the drafting of PL 94-142 and its "zero reject" provision. Turnbull and Turnbull (1978b) noted that the zero reject concept is intended to prevent (1) exclusion of some or all handicapped children from the schools, (2) exclusion of some handicapped children while others with the same handicap are given schooling, and (3) exclusion of all persons with certain handicaps while persons with different handicaps are served. We now have litigation precedents (e.g., *PARC*) and legislation (PL 94-142) that mandate a free and appropriate public education for *all* handicapped children.

Cases Pertaining to Placement Procedures

While the exclusion cases try to get severely retarded children *into* special education programs, other cases try to keep mildly retarded children *out* of them, particularly ethnic minority children. The primary issue in such cases is that the process used to assess mild retardation is inappropriate, leading to inappropriate educational placement and thereby exposing the individual to stigmatization and progressively inadequate educational development (Meyers, Sundstrom, & Yoshida 1974).

The rights-to-treatment-and-education suits admit that their plaintiffs are mentally retarded and seek to get the state to assume responsibility for them, but the cases pertaining to placement allege that normal children are being classified as mentally retarded as a result of biased tests. The state is accused of committing sins of omission in the former cases and sins of commission in the latter.

At least two kinds of constitutional violations are charged in the placement cases: equal opportunity and denial of due process. The contention is made that children placed in special education classes are denied equal educational opportunity because their options are reduced (e.g., the opportunity to go on to college is eliminated) and because the quality of the EMR program is poorer than that of the regular class. The denial of due process arises out of the use of the tests alleged to be biased and the lack of parental involvement and hearings prior to placement.

Arguments Against Placement.   The most common criticisms leveled against placement procedures have been summarized by Cohen and DeYoung (1973) and Sorgen (1976).

1. *Tests used are biased and inappropriate.* This argument holds that the intelligence tests tap a life-style (white middle-class) that is alien to many children. Furthermore, the tests are heavily weighted with verbal items that tap a child's familiarity with the English language. As a result these tests do not reflect the true learning abilities of children of racial and cultural minorities.

2. *Test administraton is often performed incompetently.* Essentially, this contention focuses on the tester's insensitivity to nontest factors (such as
   the child's anxiety, and language and cultural differences). Although
   these factors may affect the score on an intelligence test, they may not
   be taken into consideration by testers in interpreting the meaning of
   IQ scores for placement decisions.
3. *Parents are not involved.* Plaintiffs argue that children are frequently
   tested and placed in special programs without parental awareness or
   consent. Furthermore, parents have not been allowed to be heard
   before a decision is made. Instead they are often contacted to obtain
   their agreement to a decision that has already been made.
4. *Special education programs are inadequate.* The major arguments presented under this rubric are that placement is essentially permanent
   and the programs are ineffective in terms of educational, vocational,
   or personal outcomes.
5. *Placement is stigmatizing.* The final argument holds that improper placement in special classes causes irreparable personal harm. Labeling is
   seen as harmful to self-concept and remaining with the individual for
   a lifetime.

It must be pointed out that while these charges have proved convincing
in courts of law, most cannot at present be supported by empirical evidence.
While a lawyer can find a study to support each allegation, the comparison
of all extant research on the topic will not clearly support several of these
arguments. For example, the discussion of intelligence testing in Chapter 5
does not provide unequivocal support for the position that intelligence tests
are inherently biased. Extended reviews of the efficacy studies cited in
Chapter 7 (Bruininks & Rynders 1971; Christophos & Renz 1969; Guskin &
Spicker 1968; Kirk 1964; MacMillan 1971b) all conclude that all such comparisons of regular and special classrooms lack sufficient control of variables
to warrant many definite conclusions. If anything, the studies reveal a fairly
clear-cut finding that the adjustment of children in special classes is superior to comparable-IQ children in regular classes. The instruments used to
measure adjustment are suspect, and how the lawyers use the efficacy studies to conclude that the special class children are worse off is perplexing.
Furthermore, the empirical evidence on the postschool adjustment of special class EMR children versus regular class children of comparable IQ
reveals superior postschool adjustment of the special class children (Goldstein 1964). Similarly, the conclusion that labeling children mentally
retarded has detrimental and lifelong effects is confusing and is not supported by empirical evidence.
    The evidence bearing on some of the alleged misplacement charges does
not provide clear-cut support for either the plaintiffs or the defendants. It
is apparent in reading the accounts of lawyers (e.g., Kirp 1973; Kirp 1974b)
that the literature pertaining to these issues has not been exhaustively

reviewed but rather used selectively where a specific reference supports a point they want to make. While this procedure seems wrong to the social scientist, it is the way that evidence is considered by the courts in deciding cases, as will be discussed later in this chapter.

Background Cases.   Reviews of the placement cases usually begin with the well-known United States Supreme Court decision in *Brown* v. *Board of Education* (1954), in which the court declared that racially segregated education is inherently unequal. It thereby invalidated the old "separate but equal" doctrine, reasoning that racial segregation denies the constitutional right to equality of opportunity. A countersuit, *Stell* v. *Savannah-Chatham County Board of Education* (1963), challenged the *Brown* decision by presenting psychological and educational evidence that segregation was more beneficial for black children than was desegregation. In denying the appeal the court ruled that *"Brown* had established as a matter of *law,* rather than as a matter of *fact,* that segregation is inherently unequal" (Cohen & DeYoung 1973).

Following the attempts to define the legal rights of children in regular programs, the focus has broadened to the handicapped. The first case challenging the use of tests to place school children came in *Hobson* v. *Hansen* (1967). It was alleged that the Washington, D.C., schools placed children into one of four tracks on the basis of test performance and that once a child was placed in a track it was extremely difficult to be reassigned to a different track. Judge Skelley Wright ruled that this represented a violation of the equal-protection clause of the United States Constitution and ordered that the tracking system be abolished. The *Hobson* decision carried over the principle of the *Brown* decision—the tests used for placement were considered biased because they resulted in segregation of pupils by race and socioeconomic class.

A similar case was brought against the Pasadena schools in California in *Spangler* v. *Board of Education* (1970), which challenged ability grouping on the basis of performance on a group test of intelligence. A group of black students charged that the practice of ability grouping resulted in a racial imbalance within the facilities of the Pasadena school district. These charges were not contested by school officials (Cohen & DeYoung 1973). The decision was that group tests of intelligence are a faulty basis for educational placement.

Diana **and** *Larry P.*   These two cases, heard in California by the same judge, were important in limiting the means by which ethnic minority children could be labeled EMR. The first case, *Diana* v. *State Board of Education* (1970) was brought on behalf of nine Mexican-American children, age eight to thirteen, who had been placed in EMR classes; two years later a parallel case, *Larry P.* v. *Riles* (1972), was brought on behalf of black children similarly placed. The cases were both concerned with testing for EMR placement. In 1980, Judge Robert Peckham ruled on *Larry P.*, making permanent his injunction against the use of intelligence tests in the placement of black children in EMR programs (see MacMillan & Meyers 1980a).

The overrepresentation of Mexican-American and black children in special EMR classes in California had been recognized for some time by educators. A group of professionals, some of whom had themselves been classified as EMR, had already criticized procedures leading to what they saw as unfair labeling (Meyers et al. 1974, p. 7). Similarly, school psychologists had already been warned to be cautious about recommending special class placement when low test scores were due to experiential differences or language differences. But even though professionals in California were aware of the disproportions and related issues, their awareness did not change the situation. No substantive changes were being made within the system.

Among the allegations in *Diana* were the following: (1) individual intelligence tests are inappropriate for Spanish-speaking children, (2) the quality of the education received in EMR classes is poor, and (3) children suffer irreparable injury as a consequence of grossly inadequate education and the stigma of the mentally retarded label. Affidavits filed in the case described deplorable educational programs in certain schools. Parents recounted how the children in EMR classes were used to cut grass, provide free janitorial service, wash buses, and even to leave school to work as farm laborers. Such practices were indefensible and clearly violated every principle of decency, let alone constitutional rights. However, the use of individual tests of intelligence was to be the major target of *Diana*.

Whereas earlier cases had focused on the inaccuracy of *group* testing, the claim made in *Diana* was that the Mexican-American children had been improperly placed in classes for the mentally retarded on the basis of biased *individual* test results. It was argued that these children achieved low scores on these tests not because they were mentally retarded but because they came from different cultural backgrounds. According to the plaintiffs, individually administered tests of intelligence were developed for and normed on middle-class white samples, and they are inappropriate for use with individuals from other backgrounds. Furthermore, the English language was used exclusively in testing children, regardless of their language preference. All of the plaintiffs spoke predominantly, or exclusively, Spanish.

The *Diana* case was settled out of court, with the issuance of six mandates:

1. All children whose primary language is other than English shall be tested in both their primary language and in English.
2. These children shall be tested only with tests or sections of tests that do not depend on such things as vocabulary, general information, and other similar unfair verbal questions.
3. Mexican-American and Chinese-American children already in classes for the mentally retarded must be retested in their primary language and must

be reevaluated only as to their achievement on nonverbal tests or sections of tests.

4. Each school district is to submit to the state, in time for next school year, a summary of retesting and reevaluation and a plan listing special supplemental individual training which will be provided to help each child back into the regular school class.

5. State psychologists are to work on norms for a new or revised IQ test to reflect the abilities of Mexican-Americans so that in the future Mexican-American children will be judged only by how they compare to the performance of their peers and not the population as a whole.

6. Any school district which has a significant disparity between the percentage of Mexican-American students in its regular classes and in its classes for the retarded must submit an explanation setting out the reasons for this disparity.

(Ross, DeYoung, & Cohen 1971, pp. 7–8)

An Analysis of *Diana* and *Larry P.* The primary consideration in these cases was the alleged bias of intelligence tests against minority children. The decisions fail to address several other important educational issues. The court failed to take into account the fact that the children in question were identified through persistent and severe academic failure in regular classes before any psychometric testing was performed. MacMillan and Meyers (1980a) wrote: "We are compelled to fault the court for not looking upstream, as it were, to inquire why so many minority children were brought into the assessment process to start with" (p. 138). In other words, is it the fault of the intelligence test that minority children are failing in the standard curriculum in our public schools? Will prohibiting the use of tests somehow advance the achievement of minority children?

Whether or not the content or norms of intelligence tests are biased, the tests permit more or less equally accurate predictions of academic success among various subgroups; in fact, the verbal section, although it superficially appears more biased, predicts academic success better than the performance section. Nevertheless, in *Diana* the court called for the use of "nonverbal tests or sections of tests" in the reevaluation of children in EMR programs. This practice, along with the use of Spanish translations, is inconsistent with research findings about the usefulness of test results in predicting academic achievement. Note that the best predictor of future achievement is past achievement, in part because of academic aptitude and factors that tend to be stable from year to year such as emotional health, motivation, the example and support of family, and the extent of academic assistance at home. Banning intelligence tests will not alter the predictability of achievement from one year to the next. A child who is failing needs some *special* help. Whether that means EMR placement will depend on the needs of the particular child.

A related fact is that during the period of the initial hearings (about 1970–1972), there were more minority children experiencing academic difficulty in California schools than white children. Most schools had few alternatives to EMR placement for providing special help. School districts had made some EMR placements on a temporary remedial or compensatory basis until state auditors complained. Groups such as school psychologists had requested that compensatory education programs be initiated, but only token funding was provided, so that marginal learners were denied a special program less restrictive than EMR. Thus, a child with marked learning difficulties could not receive help without being labeled EMR. School personnel reluctantly labeled borderline children EMR, considering it the "least objectionable" alternative. Had Judge Peckham focused on the lack of intermediate alternatives between special class EMR placement and remaining in regular classes without help, he could have advanced the cause by encouraging the funding of compensatory programs.

Another concern of the court in these cases was the overrepresentation of minority children in EMR classes. In *Larry P.* Judge Peckham insisted that the overrepresentation of black children cease; in *Diana* he had made a less forceful ruling, requiring school districts to explain ethnic disproportions beyond a certain generous allowance if such disproportions continued (Meyers et al. 1974). These requirements suggest that subcultures vary little in educationally relevant traits, but the rationality of such a suggestion is questionable. It denies the realities of our many subcultures, forcing educators to ignore the principle that education should be based on the child's needs, not on quotas. MacMillan and Meyers (1980a) wrote: "We cynically wonder when we should take steps to increase the proportion of EMR students from ethnic groups that have typically ben *under*represented in EMR" (p. 147).

Judge Peckham's decision on *Larry P.* was made final some eight years after the initial hearing in 1972. MacMillan and Meyers (1980a) noted that the opinion described the identification process, programing, and children enrolled in 1972 and ignored the changes that had occurred in California in the interim. Judge Peckham's opinion was an inaccurate portrayal of special education in 1979 in several ways. Between the two hearings the following changes had taken place:

1. The upper IQ limit for EMR was dropped from one standard deviation below the population mean to two standard deviations below the mean.
2. The politicization of EMR identification resulted in extreme caution on the part of school personnel in identifying minority children as EMR (see the state prevalence data reported in Table 2.5).
3. The provisions of PL 94-142 and the California Master Plan for Special Education were instituted and strictly adhered to by school personnel.
4. Between 1969 and 1972, somewhere between 11,000 and 14,000 EMRs were decertified and dropped from California EMR enrollment.

5. The 1981 EMR population in California included a sizeable proportion of moderately retarded children, some of whom had physical stigmata. These children were seldom found in EMR classes prior to the *Diana* case. The current EMR population in California is clearly a far more debilitated group than the EMR population of 1972 (MacMillan & Borthwick 1980).
6. The referral of mildly retarded learners has dropped drastically. This is probably because teachers must devise individualized education plans, provide documentation, and attend many meetings. Meyen and Moran (1979) contend that the time these requirements take makes teachers hesitant to refer mild cases, since they are likely to keep the child in their class and be burdened with extensive paperwork but not get services to help them teach the child.

Learning problems cannot be legislated or mandated away. Whether the children in question should be called *mentally retarded* is debatable, but the fact that they will continue to have academic problems unless they receive special help is not. Testing never helped educators in their central problem, teaching children certain skills and attitudes. As a result of *Diana* and *Larry P.*, however, we must be sensitive to the possibility that some services will be denied to California children because they are members of certain minority groups. As MacMillan and Meyers stated in a summary of their concerns:

> There must be hundreds if not thousands of ill-served school children as a consequence of *Diana* and *Larry P.* . . . California is incongruously second low among 51 states with D.C. in proportion of pupils in programs for the mentally retarded. Few in the schools question that fear of litigation has been the principal reason after the lowering of the maximum qualifying IQ score some years ago. Now, given that severe drop in EMR enrollments and given the fact that each placement was initiated with severe academic failure, resistant to simpler remedial steps, one has to believe that there are many, many children without adequate help. Some of those back in regular class will again be kept busy with crayons and scissors.
>
> (1980a, p. 147)

***PASE* v.*Hannon*: A Contradictory Decision.**   After the *Larry P.* case in San Francisco, an identical case was heard in Chicago by Judge John Grady. In *People in Action on Special Education (PASE)* v. *Hannon* (1980) a parent group, People in Action on Special Education (PASE), initiated a class action suit against the Chicago School system on behalf of two black children. The plaintiff charged that these children, who had mild learning problems, had been inappropriately placed in special classes on the basis of low IQ scores derived from culturally biased instruments.

Judge Grady's decision in *PASE* is diametrically opposed to Judge Peckham's decision in *Larry P.* Grady concluded that individual tests of intelligence, when used in conjunction with other criteria, do not discriminate against black children in the identification and placement process. Although many of the same expert witnesses testified in both cases, the two judges came to different conclusions regarding the role of IQ, the validity of IQ for black children, and the function of special classes. In addition, the validity of IQ testing was established differently in the two cases. Judge Grady did not regard IQ as the sole or primary basis for identification. In stating his opinion, Judge Peckham repeatedly referred to special classes as a "dead end," whereas Judge Grady assumed that special classes were designed for children who were not benefiting from the regular curriculum and who needed a slower pace, repetition, and concrete teaching. Finally, although defenders of intelligence tests were probably pleased with the *PASE* decision, many were concerned with the means by which Grady decided the validity issue (Armstrong 1980). Judge Grady essentially dismissed the expert testimony and examined the tests item by item himself. He concluded that there were eight items on the WISC and WISC-R and one item on the Stanford-Binet that were biased against black children. Judge Peckham, on the other hand, concluded the tests were biased because they were not normed for black children. He also repeatedly expressed concern in his opinion that intelligence tests do not measure a child's potential.

We will have to await appeals of these cases, possibly to the Supreme Court, to resolve the contradictory decisions. We can only hope that children's educational careers will not become political pawns in a fight between two factions over the comparatively unimportant issue of test bias.

THE BASIS FOR LEGAL DECISIONS

Although scientific evidence fails to demonstrate conclusively that intelligence tests, special class placement, and the retarded label are necessarily undesirable, the court decisions we have reviewed seem to support these assumptions. To understand how this can happen we must look at how lawsuits work.

The Burden of Proof

For a plaintiff to win a lawsuit it must be proved that the plaintiff has suffered or will suffer damages as a result of what has been done. This is more easily proved in the right-to-treatment and the right-to-education cases than in those concerned with placement. To win a placement case the plaintiff would have to demonstrate that certain negative consequences resulted from placement in an EMR program. This would be very hard to do; it is difficult to specify the precise negative consequences of placement and even more difficult to measure them with any degree of precision.

Although the burden of proof is supposed to be on the plaintiff, there are legal ways of easing the burden of proof. It has been suggested that the courts view certain classifications, such as mental retardation, as "suspect categories" when they seem to either deprive a child of educational opportunity or alter the educational process for some children (Burt 1975; Hobbs 1975b). As a consequence the burden of proof is sometimes shifted to the state, which must justify the differentiation of these children. Where there is a class of persons that has been designated by the courts as "suspect," or when a right is denied that is explicitly or implicitly guaranteed by the Constitution, the courts will invoke "strict scrutiny." This places a heavy burden on the defendant, who must then show a "compelling state interest" for the classification. When the classification system results in disproportionate representation of a minority group, the imbalance can be used to challenge the classification system on the basis that it involves unconstitutional racial discrimination (Kirp 1973).

When there is no suspect class involved, the test used is whether a rational relationship exists between the classification and the objective of the state. In such instances the burden of proof lies with the plaintiff, who must show that the relationship between classification and objective is not permissible or that the objective itself is questionable.

In *Hobson* v. *Hanson* (1967) and *Larry P.* v. *Riles* (1972) the court saw the cases as similar to de facto racial segregation cases. The burden of proof was shifted to the defendant in both cases. In *Larry P.*, for example, once the court was convinced that (1) intelligence tests were the primary basis for placement in EMR classes and (2) there were disproportionately high numbers of black children in EMR classes, it fell to the State of California, the defendant, to demonstrate the rationality of this method of classification. In such cases a decision against the state does not necessarily mean that the contentions by the plaintiff could be proved or have been proved; it only means that the defendant did not present a convincing case for the rationality of the challenged classification system.

In all probability, neither side in *Diana* or *Larry P.* could have proved its case or defended extant practices using empirical evidence. The evidence is all too often based on data obtained in studies that can be faulted on methodological grounds. Therefore, the posture of the courts was critical in determining the outcomes.

Law or Evidence?

Think back to the *Stell* case. It challenged the *Brown* decision by submitting educational and psychological evidence alleged to show that black children benefited more in segregated than desegregated settings. In the appeal the court ruled that *Brown* had established as a matter of *law* rather than as a matter of *fact* that segregation was inherently harmful. As this case demonstrates, some social science evidence runs contrary to current moral and ethical beliefs, and decisions must be made on the basis of values rather than evidence. Even though the *Brown* decision stimulated an extensive debate over the relationship between facts and values, with charges that some of the evidence used was questionable, Cahn (1955, p. 159) pointed out that the court determination was made on the obvious and evident proposition that segregation is cruel to black children. On the other hand, Clark (1969) argued that the *Brown* decision was made largely on the basis of evidence; he de-emphasized the role of policy or values.

A different posture yet is assumed by Lochner (1973). He contends that "facts do not necessarily compel conclusions," so the contribution of both facts and values should be recognized. He notes that even if children were born with a trait that would allow social scientists to predict with 95 percent certainty that they would commit a felony by age eighteen, society would probably not allow them to be institutionalized at birth. Because some of these individuals would never commit a felony, social values would not allow the decision.

It might seem that deciding whether a decision is based on value or fact is irrelevant, but this factor may become important after the decision is put into effect. Whenever cases like *Brown, Diana,* and *Larry P.* are decided, they are followed by an attempt to evaluate whether desegregation is good, usually by collecting social science evidence. If *Diana* and *Larry P.* were decided on the basis of values, then subsequent evidence that the children affected do better or worse in achievement, or have higher or lower self-concepts, does nothing to support or undermine the "goodness" of the original decision. On the other hand, if the decision was based on evidence, and if subsequent evidence did not support the decision, it might be time to reconsider the decision.

THE IMPLEMENTATION OF COURT DECISIONS

The first step in changing practices through the courts is to achieve a favorable decision on behalf of the plaintiffs. In the cases we have reviewed this has been achieved. However, the impact of these decisions on the lives of the retarded ultimately depends on the implementation of the decisions. The impact of *Brown*, for example, has been tremendous, but even today, three decades after the Brown decision, the fight over racial segregation continues and full compliance has not been achieved (Hobbs 1975b).

Difficulties in the implementation of the decisions in *PARC, Wyatt,* and *Diana* have already arisen and others are anticipated (Hobbs 1975b). The implementation problems are discussed at length by Kirp et al. (1975).

After *PARC, Mills,* and *Wyatt*

In Pennsylvania the Right to Education Office's program to locate retarded children was far-reaching. However, the masters had to pressure the Philadelphia schools to get compliance, and many retarded children in institutions still are not receiving an education.

According to the *PARC* decision, all children in special programs were to be reevaluated. This turned out to be costly and difficult since the evaluation involved more than simply administering an intelligence test. The effort required that additional teachers be recruited, classrooms located, and special curricula developed. In an interview Herbert Goldstein, one of the masters, said he felt that the results of the litigation (testing, finding, and placing) were a series of procedural facades; there had been no substantive change in the educational programs in Pennsylvania.

The problems in implementing *Mills* were very similar to those in *PARC* except that there were no masters observing the process. This meant that the details of implementation, and its evaluation, were left to school officials who were often responsible for the state of affairs that led to the filing of the suit in the first place.

On top of the problems inherent in implementing the decisions that were to have widespread effects on the school systems in Pennsylvania and Washington, D.C., there was professional resistance to the mandated changes. At some hearings prior to placement, parents were coerced into accepting the school's placement decision, a clear violation of the intent of the mandates. In Pittsburgh, abandoned school buildings were reopened to accommodate the previously excluded children; although this enabled an easy means of compliance with the agreement, it was probably in violation of the agreement's intent. The school superintendent in Washington, D.C., increased the special education budget by only 7 percent, so the major problem in implementing *Mills* was a lack of resources. The net result was a reduction of 40 special education positions. Probably the most blatant resistance resulted when top-level school administrators encouraged parents of nonhandicapped children to file countersuits against the school system to prevent them from diverting any more money to special education (Hobbs 1975b).

In 1981, the *Wyatt* decision was still being implemented in Alabama. A panel of experts was overseeing the process and reporting on progress to the court.

It should be kept in mind that the implementation of these decisions and those related to identifying minority children is costly. *PARC, Diana, Larry P.,* and other decisions concerning education are on a collision course with the taxpayer revolt. The provisions of these decisions, many of which are also required by PL 94-142 and parallel state legislation, are viewed by some as "special privileges" for the handicapped. We hear parents of nonhandicapped children, for example, saying that they believe *every* child in the public schools should have an individualized education plan—not just the handicapped. We must wait to see whether all the provisions of these cases will be implemented, how much the public is willing to pay for the implementation, and whether the personnel responsible for implementation will remain faithful to the spirit as well as the letter of the decisions.

Toward Full Implementation

If court decisions concerning mental retardation are ever to be fully implemented, some conclusions drawn by Hobbs (1975b) based on a subcommittee report (Kirp et al. 1975) are worth looking at. Hobbs points out that court mandates rely on others to implement them, that the mandates most readily implemented are those that do not require much organizational change, and that resistance arises primarily from the perceived threat to the current institutional and social structure and to individuals who are functioning easily within that structure rather than from resentfulness or malevolence.

If full implementation of court objectives is to be achieved, Hobbs urges that the following steps be taken. First, he recommends that intense and lasting pressure to change be combined with systematic incentives rather than simply requiring that changes be made. Second, the court should appoint overseers to encourage and direct completion of the implementation. Third, resources that are called for by the mandate (personnel, money, etc.) should be provided. Finally, the commitment of administrators of institutions involved must be obtained. Hobbs claims this commitment can come only when administrators are assured that the needs of their institutions have been considered in the creation of the mandated orders that they are called upon to implement.

These features seem essential if the intent of the court decisions is ultimately to benefit retarded individuals. Without them the legal rights of the mentally retarded are going to be recognized repeatedly by the courts, but the impact of these decisions is unlikely to be recognizable on the front lines where services are rendered directly to the mentally retarded.

Impact of the Courts on Professionals

One of the major problems in implementation is that policy is being made by one institution for another. Those individuals who are ultimately involved in service delivery—and presumably these are the people with the greatest expertise in dealing with retardation—are not deciding how to identify the mentally retarded in the schools, which individuals can benefit from an educational program, and what kind of treatment should be delivered. Instead the courts are making these determinations, and the professionals are being handed procedural regulations not of their own making. The extent to which professionals disagree with the mandates is unclear. On the one hand they did not truly defend existing practices in the courts; one might interpret their silence to mean agreement with the position of the plaintiffs. However, the resistance of professionals to implementation of the *PARC* and *Diana* decisions indicates opposition at least to the specific requirements if not to the general intent of these decisions.

On top of their resistance to specific provisions, practitioners seem to feel that the timetables the courts have given them for implementing the decisions are unrealistic. Furthermore, the courts do not seem sensitive to the realities of securing the additional resources needed to implement the mandates. The orders have called for immediate and substantial changes, a burden that falls mostly on the shoulders of professionals.

Educators, psychologists, physicians, and others working with the handicapped must also realize that they will be operating under the scrutiny of the courts, who will be watching practices that pertain to the rights of retarded individuals. Cohen and DeYoung (1973) speculated about the likelihood that in future court cases money damages may be asked, as has occurred in malpractice suits against physicians and lawyers. This would probably require that specific responsibility for the harm be established— in the person of the psychologist, teacher, or physician.

AN INTERPRETATION

Through the litigation on behalf of the handicapped, special education and school psychology have been subjected to a very close examination— and this examination is good. However, Cohen and DeYoung (1973, p. 279) note that children have been "whipsawed" between various points of view and are concerned with what is being done *to* children by those claiming to be working *for* them. Whether the courts perceive parents groups, school personnel, and the like as adversaries in court is interesting to consider— but everyone, the courts included, should be concerned with what is best for the children in question. This is not as troubling in regard to the right-to-treatment and right-to-education cases as it is in the cases on placement.

Although the courts decide cases on a legal basis, their decisions depend on the demonstration that certain practices represent violations of individual rights, for which the use of social science evidence is critical. But are lawyers expert enough in the complexities of retardation to evaluate the validity of the evidence? Do they cite all the known evidence or only the pieces of research that support their case? This is crucial if the true concern is what is best for the children. Scarr (1978) noted that although judges know little about the technical construction of intelligence tests, the appropriate administration and interpretation of the tests, or the issues of inequality that bring plaintiffs and defendants to court, it is judges who will decide how, when, and on whom intelligence tests will be used. She also contends that it is precisely because there is no scientific consensus regarding the worth and fairness of intelligence tests that the tests are at the "doubtful mercy of the legal system" (p. 325). Professionals who are concerned with the mentally retarded must continue to argue for decisions—whether through the courts, legislation, or educational policy—based on the needs of the mentally retarded, not on political expediency.

The fact that cases such as *Diana* have been resolved in favor of the plaintiffs seems to lead some to conclude that the *evidence* supports the allegations involved in the case, that is, that intelligence tests are biased against minority children, that special classes are less effective than regular classes, and that the label "mentally retarded" has a detrimental effect that persists into adulthood. None of these points has been conclusively demonstrated empirically. Since the evidence is not conclusive in either direction, the side that must prove its case is bound to lose. As we have seen, the burden of proof in these cases was usually shifted from the plaintiffs to the defendants. Had the plaintiffs been required to prove their allegations, they would probably have been unable to do so.

SUMMARY

Despite professional recognition of occasions of abuses and unfair practices in the classification and treatment of mentally retarded individuals, little was done to change the situation until the courts moved in. The courts have recently been asked to try three kinds of lawsuits: those in which people acting on behalf of severely retarded individuals fight for their right to adequate treatment in institutions, those in which advocates for severely retarded children fight to keep them from being excluded from public education, and those in which advocates of children classified as EMR fight to have them removed from this classification. The court's right to intervene in such cases is clear, because a person categorized as retarded may lose many legal rights.

Lawsuits involving the right to treatment, such as *Wyatt* v. *Stickney* (1971), seemed to go a long way toward improving degrading conditions in institutions. But they may not lead to substantive reform. And they have failed to give much consideration to alternatives to institutionalization, aside from a vague provision in *Wyatt* that placement should reflect the least restrictive environment for an individual.

In the right-to-education cases, the *PARC* decision stands out as a landmark. It ordered a major overhauling of the practices by which Pennsylvania schools accepted or excluded retarded pupils, including reevaluation of all children already in special classes. Other right-to-education cases have asserted that education is everyone's constitutional right—a right that cannot be denied because of severe retardation—and have specified due process provisions to protect individual rights at every step of the placement process.

As in the right-to-treatment and right-to-education cases, the courts have until recently *(PASE* v. *Hannon)* consistently ruled in favor of the plaintiffs in cases about the right of minority children *not* to be placed in EMR classes. The burden of proof in these cases has fallen on the defendants, and the empirical evidence does not conclusively support one position or the other, so it has proved very difficult for defendants to document their cases. Because these cases have hinged on the rather minor issue of the tests used for placement, the courts have not considered the broader issue of why a disproportionate number of minority children fail in general education and are eligible for the assessment process in which the intelligence test has played a role. Regardless of the ultimate disposition of the *Larry P.* and *PASE* cases, the courts and the educational system will ultimately have to address this broader question, since the use (or prohibition) of intelligence tests when a child is eight or nine does not influence the academic failure that initially led to the child's being considered for special education placement.

In addition to the problems caused for individual children when they are shifted for political rather than personal reasons, the court mandates have proved difficult to implement. Among the problems are professional resistance, hurried timetables, insufficient funding, and inadequate supervision. A potential problem that may someday concern you is that lawsuits on behalf of mentally retarded individuals may begin to name specific professionals as defendants and sue for damages. This possibility complicates decision making, for despite the current political sentiment against labeling minority children as mentally retarded, the advantages of special class placement might outweigh the disadvantages for some children.

PART V

Characteristics of Mentally Retarded Persons

CHAPTER 9

Adaptation and Adjustment

What happens to mentally retarded children as they grow up? Do they lag far behind their normal peers in social skills like talking and playing? How do they express sexual urges that develop as they reach biological maturity? As adults are they able to find jobs, support themselves, marry, raise children? Or must they live apart from the normal community, as semirecluses in their parents' homes or as residents of institutions?

The answers to these questions are complex, as are the answers to most questions about retardation. Individual variations in the degree and type of retardation, the environmental setting, and the availability of caring, helpful people make it impossible to draw broad generalizations about the social lives of retarded persons. But in evaluating the success of special programs, we must try to determine whether the programs help retarded persons master the skills necessary for independent living. Although studies of the efficacy of special classes and compensatory education programs such as Project Head Start invariably try to measure gains in *achievement* or *aptitude* through the use of standardized tests of achievement or intelligence, *social competence* is really the outcome of interest (Zigler & Trickett 1978). As Berry and Gordon have written, "The acid test of mental deficiency is not, and should not be, scholastic educability, but this power of fending for one's self in life, or an adaptability to the environment" (1931, p. 5). In their excellent discussion of whether social competence or IQ should be the important evaluative index in early childhood programs, Zigler and Trickett (1978) suggest that the following molar criteria should be considered: (1) incidence of juvenile delinquency, (2) incidence of teen-age pregnancy, (3) incidence of child abuse, either as a victim or a perpetrator, (4) being in school rather than out, (5) being in the appropriate grade for age, (6) being in a regular classroom rather than a special education classroom, and (7) being self-supporting rather than on welfare (p. 796).

Measuring social competence is difficult (Zigler & Trickett 1978). As a first step, we must consider which behaviors retarded children have trouble mastering and which behaviors prevent them from living independently in society. The behaviors that indicate to parents that a SPMR or TMR child is lagging behind developmentally are different from the behaviors that alert teachers to possible mental retardation in EMR children. The EMR, TMR, and SPMR all exhibit problems in adaptive behavior. The EMR child, although reasonably adept socially, has trouble mastering academic tasks. The TMR or SPMR child lags behind on many other kinds of tasks as well, such as walking, talking, and social play with peers.

After analyzing the forms of childhood maladaptation, we will consider the social adaptation of mentally retarded individuals once they finish school or leave an institution for the mentally retarded. In that section we will look at attempts to measure adult standards of adjustment. Although the standards employed usually consist of self-sufficiency, marriage, and lack of trouble with law enforcement officials, some attempts have been made to find more subtle information about the quality of life enjoyed by retarded adults in our society.

ATTEMPTS TO ASSESS ADAPTIVE BEHAVIOR

As we have repeatedly noted, diagnosis of mental retardation now requires evidence of both low intellectual functioning and inadequate adaptive behavior. According to the AAMD Manuals (Grossman 1973, 1977, in press; Heber 1959b, 1961), the term *adaptive behavior* refers to the effectiveness and degree with which individuals meet the standard of self-sufficiency and social responsibility expected of their age and cultural group.

Our present ideas about adaptive behavior trace back to the notion of social competency, an extension of the biological concept that if the biological organism does not adapt, it will not continue to survive. In the social sciences this biological concept has been expanded to explain the need for organisms to adapt both cognitively and socially to the social environment if they are to be rewarded for their behavior and even allowed to continue as members in the social unit.

Another definition of adaptive behavior, offered by Meyers, Nihira, and Zetlin (1979), reads as follows:

> Adaptive behavior at the very least refers to a subject's typically exhibited competencies in adjustment to the culture as expected for his/her age level, in or out of school. To be adaptive in behavior presupposes that one possesses the potential to be adaptive, but the degree and quality of actual adaptive behavior are not identical with potential.
>
> (p. 433)

Coulter and Morrow (1978) summarized ten definitions commonly used by government agencies or associations and concluded that they had two elements in common: (1) socially defined standards of performance and (2) the extent to which the person meets these standards. The standards most commonly employed were independence or autonomy and social responsibility.

There have been many attempts to define and measure social competency or adaptive behavior [see Meyers et al. (1979) for a comprehensive review of existing scales]. In 1953, Doll defined social competency as "a functional composite of human traits which subserves social usefulness as reflected in self-sufficiency and in service to others" (p. 2). And back in 1936, the Vineland Social Maturity Scale (VSMS) was developed to assess social competency. Essentially, the Vineland Scale attempts to ascertain the degree to which children have mastered skills expected at certain ages in the family and the community: Can they tie their own shoes? Can they count change? The major emphasis is upon self-reliance and social responsibility. The VSMS consists of eight categories of behavior: general self-help, self-help in dressing, self-help in eating, communication, self-direction, socialization, locomotion, and occupation. The earlier age levels are heavily weighted with self-help items; the adult levels are more heavily weighted with items concerning self-direction, socialization, and occupation. Other scales also have been used in attempts to assess social competency in the retarded, such as the Cain-Levine Social Competency Scale (Cain, Levine, & Elzey 1963). A new scale, the AAMD Adaptive Behavior Scale (AAMD ABS) (Nihira, Foster, Shellhaas, & Leland 1969) will be described in detail after we note the variables that it attempts to encompass.

Developmental Lags

Inadequate adaptive behavior is often first noticed by the parents of retarded children. Comparing their progress with that of their peers, parents may be alarmed to notice that their children are dropping behind. Warren (1968) has suggested several areas in which markedly delayed development compared to age peers may be an indication of retardation:

1. *Motor development:* sitting, walking, hopping, and running
2. *Psychomotor development:* fine motor tasks such as holding a pencil, drawing a circle or square, writing own name
3. *Speech development:* first word, use of phrases and simple sentences
4. *Development of "common sense":* a marked lack of judgment concerning safety, poor use or understanding of money, inability to travel independently
5. *Academic development:* noticeable problems in letter and word recognition and numerical concepts

In the preschool and school years, delay is again gauged by comparing the child to age peers. But in late adolescence and adulthood, the individual is compared to standards held by the society.

Degree of Deviation

Traditionally the mentally retarded have been thought to differ from their nonretarded peers with regard to social competency in two ways. First, the retarded are thought to develop social competencies at a slower pace. For instance, while a normal child may be expected to walk alone at one year of age, the retarded child would be expected to master that skill at a later age, depending on the degree of retardation. Second, the social competency of a retarded adult would fail to reach the ultimate level achieved by nonretarded peers. Meyers and Nihira (1975) referred to this double impairment as a "slower and lower" development of social competence.

This slower and lower development, though often observed, is hard to measure. As Clausen (1967, 1972) has noted, even though various adaptive behavior scales are available, none is really adequate. As a result tremendous subjectivity enters in when we try to measure a child's adaptive behavior. Furthermore, the AAMD Adaptive Behavior Scale, the Cain-Levine Social Competency Scale, and the VSMS are not appropriate for use with the mildly retarded, whose maladaptation often extends only to academic problems. If some of the newer instruments are used (e.g., the Public School Version of the AAMD ABS reported by Lambert, Windmiller, Cole, and Figueroa in 1975), the question arises as to how much deviation from the age-norm is sufficient to indicate that this individual has impaired adaptive behavior. The problem is further compounded when the child in question comes from a different subculture, for which the usual norms may be inappropriate.

Environmental Demands

Comparison of possibly retarded children with other children their age is complicated by environmental variables. As Meyers and Nihira (1975) have pointed out, social maturity is not an absolute, internal competence but rather a response to the demands of the environment. An individual's success or failure can only be measured in terms of that environment. A sixteen-year-old child living in New York City may be expected to understand subway schedules, know the fare for a particular ride, and know how and when to transfer trains, but for a child living in a rural community the inability to master these subtleties does not surface because the environment does not expect or demand such skills. Of two children with IQs of 67 living in these differing environments, the urban child might be classified as retarded and the rural child not, as long as adaptive behavior is included as one dimension of the definition of mental retardation (Clausen 1967, 1972). This dimension has long been recognized, for in 1931 Berry and Gordon defined mental deficiency as an individual's inability "to react to his environment in the manner regarded as normal by the average member of society" (p. 5). And even back in 1858, Samuel Howe wrote that retarded persons "can only be measured by a sort of sliding scale with a standard adapted to different localities and conditions of society" (p. 18).

In a widely cited book, Havighurst (1972) outlined the developmental tasks that American boys and girls are expected by the culture as a whole to master. But he emphasizes that expectations differ for boys and girls and for different social classes. He also points out the need to allow subgroups to establish individual priorities in defining what is normal. According to Havighurst, we must consider what the specific subculture expects a child of this sex and of this social class to be able to do at this developmental level. Mercer (1965, 1973a), too, decries the application of a standard from the dominant culture to subgroups that systematically differ from the dominant culture.

Behavioral Aspects of Adaptation

In laying the groundwork for the AAMD Adaptive Behavior Scale, Leland, Nihira, Foster, Shellhaas, and Kagin (1968) identified three basic forms of individual adaptation to the environment:

1. *Independent functioning*, defined as the ability of individuals to accomplish successfully those tasks or activities demanded by the general community, both in terms of critical survival demands for that community and in terms of the typical expectations for specific ages.
2. *Personal responsibility*, defined as both the willingness of individuals to accomplish those critical tasks they are able to accomplish (generally under some supervision) and their ability to assume responsibility for their personal behavior. This ability is reflected in decision making and choice of behaviors.
3. *Social responsibility*, defined as the ability of individuals to accept

responsibility as members of a community group and to carry out appropriate behaviors in terms of these group expectations. This is reflected in levels of conformity, socially positive creativity, social adjustment, and emotional maturity. It was further analyzed in terms of the acceptance of some level of civic responsibility leading to complete or partial economic independence.

In summarizing the work done on the AAMD ABS, Leland (1973) pointed out that in evaluating independent functioning, the question is, Can the individual perform certain tasks? Independent functioning is closely tied to age expectations. If a five-year-old child does not accomplish on time what is expected of a five-year-old child, a social difficulty is created. But the expectations of peers and parents may vary. Peers may expect behavior at odds with the expectations of the adults in that environment (e.g., underage drinking). And some tasks that are age-related in childhood become less indicative in adulthood. Leland points out that whereas locomotion, for instance, is carefully considered in assessing the adaptive behavior of a four-year-old, it becomes of secondary importance in adulthood if other aspects of adaptive behavior are sufficiently developed, as in the willingness of the public to overlook the physical handicaps of President Franklin D. Roosevelt.

In considering personal responsibility, the question is, Will individuals do what they can? If people do what they are capable of doing with a minimum of supervision, they demonstrate personal responsibility. If others feel that they cannot be trusted, they may be given no choice in the matter—they may be ordered to brush their teeth, bathe, and engage in other activities. If compelled to do these things by external coercion rather than self-motivation, then they fail to demonstrate personal responsibility. Judgments about an individual's degree of personal responsibility are important in deciding whether the person can be trusted—to stay alone in the house, to go on an errand, to associate with younger children, and so forth.

Social responsibility is supposed to be a product of maturation. With increased age individuals are expected to comply with the demands of the community, such as laws concerning safety and decency. If they are unaware of regulations or choose not to follow them, they become undesirables, and the community may decide that it will not tolerate their behavior.

Visibility

According to Leland (1973), personal responsibility and social responsibility take on added importance as a person grows up. As long as individuals are motivated to do what they can and are aware of social regulations, they can cope in the society. However, if they fail on either dimension, the individuals become highly visible as an annoyance. At that point the society steps in with efforts to remove the annoyance from its midst, through institutionalization or other means.

The criterion then for adaptive behavior in the context of the larger society is whether or not the behavior can be, and will be, tolerated by the community. If the nature and degree of deviation are tolerated, individuals remain in the larger society and are not considered retarded regardless of their level of intellectual functioning. However, if individuals do not show personal responsibility and are constantly dependent on others around them or if they must be constantly supervised because of a lack of social responsibility, then the community will insist that they be cared for at a more specialized level, in which case they will probably be identified as mentally retarded.

As Leland sees it, society is not influenced by the formal definitions. Instead it operates in a manner consistent with Mercer's (1973a) social system perspective. If individuals fulfill role expectations they are normal; if not, "the promiscuous use of the word 'stupid' reflects society's judgment" (Leland 1973, p. 95).

Adaptive Behavior Scales

There are many scales for measuring various domains of adaptive behavior. Due to space limitations, we cannot describe all of these scales; the interested reader can consult Meyers et al. (1979). Note especially the charts on pages 438–45, in which 17 adaptive behavior scales are summarized. Information is included on the population for whom the scale is appropriate, the behavior domains, standardization groups, normative data, reliability, and validity.

Meyers et al. (1979) contrast the measurement of adaptive behavior (as accomplished with adaptive behavior scales) with the measurement of intelligence. Following are some characteristics of adaptive behavior measurement:

1. Adaptive behavior emphasizes everyday behavior rather than thought processes.
2. The behavior measured is valid in its own right (e.g., dressing competence). There is no need to infer a trait from the score.
3. Adaptive behavior assessments are usually secured by an informant rather than the person whose adaptive behavior is being assessed.
4. Adaptive behavior scales are not normed on a general population. They are referenced against the population for whom they are designed—the mentally retarded.

The AAMD Adaptive Behavior Scale.   In judging social competence the alternative to using informal social judgments of visibility is to use a comprehensive professional instrument to measure social adaptation. Nothing yet developed can measure all the complex variables in social maladaptation, but the AAMD Adaptive Behavior Scale (Nihira et al. 1969) is the best instrument we have. The AAMD ABS resulted from a project under the auspices of the American Association on Mental Deficiency conducted at Parsons State Hospital and Training Center beginning in 1965. Those working on the project first developed a behavior rating scale. It provided a quantitative description of the individual's skills and habits pertinent to maintaining personal independence. Second, the project focused on identifying behavior domains in terms of environmental demands imposed upon retarded persons (Nihira 1973).

A revised AAMD ABS was published in 1974 and consists of two parts. Part I consists of items that evaluate developmental skills in 10 domains related to independent functioning in daily living; these 10 domains are subdivided into 21 subdomains. Table 9.1 shows the breakdown of Part I of the ABS according to its major rubrics.

TABLE 9.1   AAMD ABS, Part I: Domains and Subdomains of Adaptive Behavior

Domain	Subdomains
Independent Functioning	eating, toilet use, cleanliness, appearance, care of clothing, dressing and undressing, travel, general independent functioning
Physical Development	sensory development, motor development
Economic Activity	money handling and budgeting, shopping skills
Language Development	expression, comprehension, social language development
Numbers and Terms	—
Domestic Activity	cleaning, kitchen duty, other domestic activities
Vocational Activities	—
Self-direction	initiative, perseverance, leisure time
Responsibility	—
Socialization	—

In Part II of the ABS (Table 9.2), an attempt is made to assess the extent to which the retarded person evidences maladaptive behavior. Nihira (1973) explains that although behavior norms do exist in various social environments (such as home and school), there are degrees to which deviations from those norms will be tolerated. He observes that in assessing the degree of sexually aberrant behavior, we must remember that a female member of our society has traditionally been expected to conform to certain norms concerning sexual behavior, but the society tolerates some deviation from these same norms by males. Behavior norms are sometimes the same for all social groups, but sometimes they vary for one sex or for different social groups in the extent to which conformity is required. Although the AAMD ABS evaluates how subjects adapt to their particular environments, it does not appraise environment per se and no adjustment for the complexity of the environment is made. This is a definite weakness of the instrument.

The AAMD ABS is administered in one of several ways. An individual familiar with the person being considered, such as a parent, can fill out the scale, or an interviewer can ask the questions of a caretaker or teacher. The ABS can also be filled out in the context of an interview, in which case the information can be obtained more informally.

The AAMD ABS has been standardized on institutionalized retarded persons in the United States, although attempts have been made to obtain

---

TABLE 9.2   AAMD ABS, Part II: Domains of Behavior Related to Personality and Behavior Disorders

Domains

Violent and Destructive Behavior
Antisocial Behavior
Rebellious Behavior
Untrustworthy Behavior
Withdrawal
Stereotyped Behavior and Odd Mannerisms
Inappropriate Interpersonal Manners
Unacceptable Vocal Habits
Unacceptable or Eccentric Habits
Self-abusive Behavior
Hyperactive Tendencies
Sexually Aberrant Behavior
Psychological Disturbances
Use of Medications

---

norms for retarded persons living in the community (Nihira 1973). The Public School Version of the AAMD ABS (Lambert et al. 1975) is appropriate for individuals with suspected mild retardation in school settings. The Public School Version was standardized on four groups: children in regular classes in grades two through six, and EMR, TMR, and Educationally Handicapped (special class and learning-disabled) children. In each group, the children were approximately equally distributed by socioeconomic status, sex, and ethnic origin (total sample = 2618).

Adaptation to the School

Until the development of the Public School Version of the ABS and the ABIC (see discussion of Mercer's SOMPA in Chapter 6), adaptive behavior scales were of little use in identifying EMR children because none could be used to measure the adaptive behavior or social competency of the mildly retarded.

Mercer (1973a) noted cases where children placed into EMR classes were adapting in their neighborhood quite well, sometimes as adolescents holding down jobs that demanded fairly high degrees of skills. She interpreted this observation as an indication that such individuals were inappropriately classified as retarded; from the social system perspective, these children were fulfilling the roles assigned to them. Furthermore, the AAMD Manual (Grossman 1977, in press) emphasizes that both intellectual functioning and adaptive behavior must be substandard for a person to be classified as mentally retarded.

But adaptation can be understood only in the context of environmental demands (Nihira 1973). When children's IQs are sufficiently low to make them candidates for the status of mentally retarded and they demonstrate adequate adaptation in their homes and neighborhoods but inadequate adaptation in school, where do they fit? Schools must often make this kind of decision, for compared to the environmental demands of the home, neighborhood, and the occupational world, the demands of the school are the most difficult for the child with an IQ between 55 and 75 to meet, with successful performance in school relying more heavily on IQ than it does in the other settings. Since the AAMD's definition of mental retardation fails to give any guidelines for cases in which diagnosis hinges on the contextual setting for the assessment of adaptive behavior, school personnel have had to use their own judgment. In other settings people recognize the right of society to tolerate deviations from the norm up to a point; when the deviation goes beyond that limit, the society no longer has to tolerate it and can require treatment at a specialized level. This is precisely what the schools have done in saying that a child who deviates in achievement or deportment behaviors to an extent that cannot be tolerated warrants treatment at a specialized level. But in the absence of official guidelines and in the face of public concern over labeling, the schools have been criticized for making such distinctions.

How Assessments of Adaptive Behavior Are Used

Parents seek help for their children because they cannot talk, are not toilet-trained at age eight, cannot manage their own affairs, or are self-destructive. The schools consider children for EMR status because they are not adapting academically or socially. The schools must make judgments about degrees of maladaptation because, beyond the importance of measurement of adaptive behavior for diagnosis, it is highly important in terms of programing. No one seeks help for a child who has no trouble adapting but has a low IQ.

To create a better fit between individual abilities and environment, three adaptive strategies have sometimes been used (Nihira & Shellhaas 1970):

1. Some effort may be made to alter existing behaviors of the individual, or develop new behaviors, to satisfy existing environmental demands.
2. The individual may be shifted to an environment that tolerates the existing behaviors.
3. An attempt may be made to alter the environment so that its requirements are more congenial to the individual.

The first strategy is the most common one, with attempts to alter behavior taking the form of special education or rehabilitative programs. Treatment should address the precise areas in which the individual was not adapting. If individuals can be taught to be adaptive in those areas that led to the initial referrals, then they will presumably be tolerated by the environmental unit—home, neighborhood, or school—that initially judged them to deviate too markedly to be retained. In the case of the EMR child, reading and other academic skills may have to be modified. In the case of the TMR child, problems in adaptation will encompass more dimensions, including learning, social, and vocational skills. Nevertheless, the TMR program for that child should focus on ameliorating, to whatever degree is possible, specific behaviors that interfere with adapting to society. The SPMR individual typically poses a medical problem in addition to the problems in adaptation; moreover, the prognosis for ever achieving any degree of self-sufficiency is poor. Typically the treatment program for SPMR individuals entails developing self-help skills (toileting, dressing, eating), but release from a closely supervised program of treatment is seldom considered.

In some cases modification of the maladaptive behavior is unlikely, due to the degree to which the behavior deviates or the numerous areas in which it occurs. In such cases the second alternative—placement into an environment that can tolerate these behaviors—is advised. This is what happens to most profoundly retarded and many severely retarded persons; they are placed in an institution. (To a lesser extent it is also what happens to an EMR or TMR child placed in a special class.)

Even when individuals are placed in an institution, some degree of social competency may be helpful to them (Dingman 1973). Some of the research of Edgerton (Edgerton & Dingman 1964a; Edgerton, Tarjan, & Dingman 1961) has demonstrated rather skilled manipulation of social situations by retarded persons living in institutions for the mentally retarded. Dates were arranged between patients, lookouts posted, and meetings scheduled for certain times and at unsupervised locations. Even though some patients were unable to tell time, they still managed to arrive at the arranged place on time. Edgerton and his associates (1961) reported one patient who developed a car-washing operation on the hospital grounds.

For former patients of institutions for the mentally retarded, it is the ability to get along socially that determines their success in avoiding trouble with society once they leave the institution. Dingman (1973) described how some former patients move from community clinic to community clinic, getting social workers to find them inexpensive housing, money, and other help. Obviously, these individuals were able to use the system to full advantage. Edgerton (1967) noted that the ability to ask questions is a major aid to adapting to society when the person cannot read newspapers, do basic arithmetic, and so on.

The third alternative requires that the original environment, in which context the individual's behavior was initially judged maladaptive, become more lenient in its definition of what it will tolerate. To date, few examples of this approach exist; however, this alternative is involved in both normalization and mainstreaming, discussed later in this book. In both of these modes the individual is being retained in a more normal environment (the community and the regular classroom), which of necessity will have to become more tolerant of behavior that has heretofore been judged deviant.

The litigation concerning right to treatment and right to education (see Chapter 8) and the subsequent legislation require that the educational system be accountable for the progress of all children. This responsibility is embodied in the individualized educational plan (IEP) and individualized program plan (IPP). The progress of SPMR and some TMR children is difficult to assess in some of the dimensions emphasized in the educational or rehabilitative program. Accountability measures for these children may require not only a statement of the client's current status but a statement of the child's progress over some period of time—a year, perhaps. These assessments may use adaptive-behavior-scale domain scores or questions such as "How many clients enrolled in your program to teach self-grooming can brush their hair at the end of the program?" The AAMD ABS is currently the tool used most often for comparing different treatments (Eyman, Silverstein, & McLain 1975; Nihira & Mayeda 1977).

Development of Adaptive Behavior

Nihira (1976) plotted the developmental trends from age four to sixty-nine for the three forms of individual adaptation evaluated in Part I of the ABS: personal self-sufficiency, community self-sufficiency, and personal-social responsibility. This was done for each of five levels of retardation— borderline, mild, moderate, severe, and profound. Graphs of the results are shown in Figure 9.1. Note that all three forms of adaptation vary with the level of retardation. The following developmental trends are especially noteworthy:

1. *Personal self-sufficiency:* Except for the profoundly retarded, the development is characterized by a rapid growth spurt during the early childhood years followed by slower growth during adolescence. Growth levels off in early adulthood and then remains stable until old age.
2. *Community self-sufficiency:* The borderline, mildly retarded, and moderately retarded develop more slowly during early childhood and accelerate rapidly during late childhood. Development levels off in late adolescence. Among the severely and profoundly retarded, growth is slower but relatively constant throughout the life cycle.
3. *Personal-social responsibility:* The borderline and mild group develop rapidly during late childhood and reach a plateau during late adolescence. The moderate and severe groups grow rapidly during early childhood and more slowly during adolescence, reaching a plateau in early adulthood. The profoundly retarded grow at a slow but constant rate throughout the life cycle.

The growth curves for the three highest functioning groups of retarded persons are very similar to those plotted by Bloom (1964) for IQ (shown in Chapter 5). There is a definite relationship between adaptive behavior and intelligence in the mentally retarded—borderline and mildly retarded children master most of the skills tapped by adaptive behavior scales at about the same age as nonretarded children; the moderately and severely retarded master them later; and the profoundly retarded master them much later, if at all.

FIGURE 9.1   Development of Adaptive Behavior for Five Levels of Mental Retardation: Mean Factor Scores for Ten Age Groups

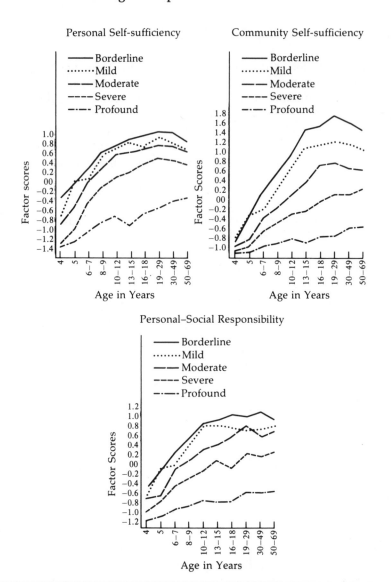

From K. Nihira, "Dimensions of adaptive behavior in institutionalized mentally retarded children and adults: Developmental perspective," *American Journal of Mental Deficiency,* 1976, **81,** pp. 221, 222. Reprinted by permission of the author and the American Association on Mental Deficiency.

EVIDENCE OF ADULT ADJUSTMENT

We might get some idea as to the effectiveness of the treatments provided for the mentally retarded by studying the extent to which those treated adjust as adults to societal demands. What percentage of retarded children will as adults be capable of functioning independently and escaping identification as mentally retarded? If we can identify those dimensions of behavior that are critical for successful adjustment as an adult, that information can be fed back into the treatment program so that the program will promote those behaviors.

Follow-up studies are plentiful for two types of programs: special classes for EMR children and institutions. In most instances studies have focused upon occupational adjustment (Do they have jobs? How long have they held these jobs? Are they on public assistance?) and personal adjustment in the society (Are they married? Can they care for their own needs? Do they avoid trouble with the law?). In general, the results show that for EMR persons the environmental demands for adults in our society are far more easily met than are the environmental demands of the school. But some investigators show more optimistic results than others.

Differences between the results of various studies may be partly blamed on the fact that our society is changing. Modernization may be increasing the problems for adjustment of the mentally retarded. For example, urbanization is increasing and the extended family is dying out. In the rural setting the extended family often allowed retarded adults to receive necessary support and direction, while at the same time offering small jobs that they could perform. In the large city the retarded adult is at a marked disadvantage. Today's minimum wage laws frequently operate against the employment of retarded persons, whose output may not be worth the minimum wage. Some service jobs that the retarded used to perform have now been taken over by machines. Such factors have made it more difficult for the moderately retarded to obtain employment and to be even partially economically self-sufficient.

Another factor to consider is that advances in medicine have increased the life expectancy for retarded persons; in the past many succumbed to illnesses that can now be treated. As a result there are now greater numbers of retarded persons reaching adulthood.

Adjustment of Retarded Persons Who Attended Special Classes

Research on the postschool adjustment of retarded children who attended special classes is somewhat dated, largely because of the movement toward mainstreaming and the requirement that an individualized education plan be devised for all handicapped children. As a result of these

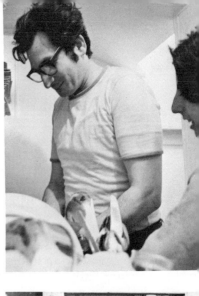

"We worked in the same workshop—at the Jewish Vocational Service.... In a way I guess that's how we met.... Our parents were quite shocked [when we got engaged].... We said that we wanted to get married, that we wanted each other and we loved each other very much, and that we don't want to split.

"My mother always had herself in—you know, how can I say it—she always brought herself forward to me. She never, you know, she always helped me, she never stood in a hole, or in a cubbyhold, and just watched me. She always helped me.... And that's what I love about my mother.

"I went to a lot of schools.... I stayed back quite a lot of times.... I couldn't keep up with the kids. See, that's my problem, I couldn't keep up. They put me in a special class when I was twelve.... I went to high school, and I was in a special class.... I graduated when I was twenty.... They had to push me, I had a very hard time.... They used to call me a nok-nok, and a retard, and all kinds of names.... A nok-nok is somebody that's supposed to be up here. And I'm not up there, I'm not crazy.... Well, I was told that anybody that says that to somebody else has something wrong with them."

"I had a job ... for thirteen months. I was housekeeping ... on the ward.... They dropped me off the program. But now I'm getting help from a cousin of mine that I know. They're testing me first, and after that they'll give me a job I would like."

"I worked in a nursing home. I had two different jobs and I got laid off from both of them. I found out that I can't cope with pressure, and I can't understand the different things that they ask me to do.... I get all nerved up.... It's in my head. I can't grasp. There's just some things that I can't do. Going out on a job, working for someone—it's not easy. I have too many ups and downs. They call it a ... minimal neurology, something, some big word, and it means that I have too many ups and downs. I want to find out what's making me click, what's causing all this— just to see why I can't work.

"The only thing that worries me is about children—about having children.... We want to have two kids, a boy and a girl ... and a dog and a cat.... We both had operations on our eyes. When you have a child, the eyes could be cross-eyed.... For me it's oxygen—it damaged some of my brain cells. With him it wasn't oxygen ... we don't really know.... He's not working. When he's going to be working, when he's going to bring home enough money, that's the time we can talk about it, and make a decision. That's what we're waiting for. I'm not in any rush.... I want my child to be able to do things, to be able to think on her or his own, and be with other people— and just to have a good life, that's all.

"Everybody's happy [for us]. And they wish us the luck all the time.... When you're living with a person, ... sometimes you have to realize ... that you're not alone, I'm with him! ... and it's nice. As long as we love each other that's all that matters."

developments, the special class program is no longer able to be specified, as each child's program is individually tailored and therefore does not constitute a single "treatment" that can meaningfully be compared to an alternative educational placement. Let us here consider the evidence from past years in order to gain insight into the quality of life experienced by former special class students as they move into adulthood.

Follow-up studies of special education graduates have focused almost exclusively on EMR children as opposed to TMR children. One exception is the extensive follow-up of 520 adults who had attended special TMR classes in New York City (Saenger 1957). As has been the case in many TMR programs, prerequisites for enrollment in these classes had included basic self-help skills. The subjects were located as adults and interviews were conducted with their parents. In general, Saenger's (1957) results suggest that the former TMR class members were leading satisfying lives and that their families were pleased with their adjustment. Approximately 66 percent of the subjects were living in the community, 26 percent were in institutions, and 8 percent had died. Saenger reported that about half of those residing in the community were happy and content. Most of the subjects (73 percent) were not employed and there was considerable variation in the extent to which they helped around the house. Nevertheless, parents indicated that in the majority of cases they enjoyed a very good relationship with the retarded person. Few TMR individuals in the community represented any problem in terms of delinquent behavior. In summary, the Saenger follow-up of a select group of moderately and severely retarded TMR students in adulthood suggests that many TMR students will achieve adequate degrees of success in living at home, but few will achieve economic self-sufficiency.

The Optimistic View of Former EMRs. In studies of the adult status of former EMR children, the general impression is that the vast majority disappear into the larger society and escape identification as mentally retarded beyond their school careers. In his major review of research pertinent to social and occupational adjustment of the retarded, Goldstein (1964) drew several generalizations concerning the mildly retarded. First, most of the mildly retarded avoid the attention of authorities and are capable of meeting the demands of the environment for normal adult functioning. For all intents and purposes, they cease being retarded when they leave school. Second, the mildly retarded are more vulnerable to adverse economic conditions than are their nonretarded peers. Recession often means unemployment for them, while in prosperous times the mildly retarded may be able to share in the material indices of success (such as homes and automobiles). Third, the occupations held by the mildly retarded as adults tend to be those considered the least prestigious on occupational status scales.

Three of the follow-up studies of EMR graduates done prior to 1960 contrast the retarded subjects to normals who were in school at the same time

TABLE 9.3   A Comparison of the Findings of Three Studies on the Basis of Social Adjustment

	Fairbanks; 1931 (1933) Locust Point, dist. Baltimore, Md. General employment 122 (72 males, 50 females) 90 (39 males, 51 females)		Baller; 1935 (1936) Lincoln, Neb. Severe depression 206 (126 males, 80 females) 206 (126 males, 80 females)		Kennedy; 1948 (1948) Millport,* Conn. General employment 256 (159 males, 97 females) 129 (80 males, 49 females)	
Study: / Locale: / General Economic Conditions: / Number of Mentally Retarded: / Number of Controls:	MR	Controls	MR	Controls	MR	Controls
Employment Status						
Gainful Employment	95%	96%	20.00%	50.00%	75.00%	65.6%
Temporary Employment	—	—	71.00%	44.00%	10.30%	29.6%
Never Employed	5%	4%	9.00%	—	14.70%	4.8%
Economic Status						
Owns Home	30%	24%	—	—	9.20%	13.0%
Married Status						
Married	79%	58%	42.86%	54.95%	51.60%	45.0%
Dependency and Relief						
Relief Received	25%	7%	38.46%	15.58%	86.20%	65.5%
Kinds of Aid						
Cash	27%	0%	—	—	64.90%	56.6%
Work Relief	13%	0%	—	—	70.10%	64.5%
Court Records						
Never Arrested	75%	90%	57.14%	89.61%	78.90%	94.6%
Jail Sentences, etc.	—	—	9.69%	1.43%	2.42%	—

*Fictitious name

Reprinted from H. Goldstein, "Social and economic adjustments" in H. A. Stevens and R. Heber, eds., *Mental Retardation: A Review of Research*, p. 239, by permission of The University of Chicago Press. © 1964 by The University of Chicago.

347

(Baller 1936; Fairbanks 1933; Kennedy 1948). Table 9.3 shows some pertinent data from these studies. Goldstein (1964) noted that the Baller study was conducted at a time of severe economic depression, in part explaining the lower employment rates reported. In general, Baller painted a bleaker picture of the lives of retarded adults than did Fairbanks or Kennedy. Charles (1953) followed up Baller's subjects in Lincoln, Nebraska (locating 77 males and 50 females of the original 206) 16 years later, at which time the data for these subjects were more comparable to Kennedy's.

In addition to differing economic conditions, the three studies differ in the kinds of communities they surveyed and the kinds of jobs the EMR graduates could find in the face of increasing mechanization. But despite differences among the studies, they indicate that, at least in good times, as many (and perhaps even more) people who were classified as mildly retarded during childhood marry and own their own homes as people from the same backgrounds who were never classified as retarded.

We must be careful not to make too much of these apparent results. For one thing, the comparison of former EMR to nonretarded persons who were in school at the same time raises some serious methodological questions (Goldstein 1964). The Fairbanks study, for instance, reported as retarded many subjects who would not be classified as retarded today because their scores are above current cutoff levels. Of those retested as adults, 3 were retarded (mean IQ 66), 24 were dull-normal (mean IQ 89), 50 were of normal intelligence (mean IQ 100), and 4 were superior in IQ (mean IQ 118) (Farber 1968, p. 170). Even so, comparisons of these former EMR class members with the control group revealed a higher incidence of broken marriages, a slightly higher rate of sex delinquency, greater dependency on others, poorer living conditions, and less movement to the better parts of the city (Fairbanks 1933). Baller (1936), too, found that his retarded sample had a higher frequency of court records and imprisonment and had a higher proportion on relief roles.

When Charles (1953) later followed up the 206 retarded subjects studied by Baller, he found that at the ages of thirty-six to forty-nine years, a lower proportion of them had married than the norm for the population of Lincoln, Nebraska as a whole. In addition, he characterized their marriages as generally unstable. Their offspring, however, were in most cases not considered mentally retarded in the schools (two were institutionalized and two had been in special classes). While Charles thought that the IQ scores achieved by the so-called retarded subjects while in school were artificially affected by language problems, behavior problems, and delinquency, the group as a whole was still functioning at a marginal level. But he gave an optimistic summary of his results, concluding:

> The studies of the social adjustment of persons judged to be mentally deficient present a fairly bright picture, suggesting that many, if not most such persons,

can find a happy and useful life in the community, if given understanding and guidance.

                                                           (1953, p. 19)

Some years after Charles followed up Baller's original (1936) study, the same subjects were contacted again (Baller, Charles, & Miller 1967; Miller 1965). At the time of the third follow-up, the majority of the retarded subjects were self-supporting.

The Pessimistic View of Former EMRs.   Heber and Dever (1970) challenge the optimistic outlook. They contend that former EMRs do not do as well as nonretarded persons from the same socioeconomic background. As evidence they point out that former EMRs abound in occupations characterized as unskilled and service-oriented (Strickland & Arrell 1967), whereas nonretarded persons from the same adverse economic background are primarily employed in clerical, semiskilled, or skilled vocations (Peterson & Smith 1960). The Dinger (1961) and Peterson and Smith (1960) studies show that nonretarded females outearn former EMR males by over $1000 per year in median annual incomes. Comparing the median annual income of former EMRs (females, $1002; males, $2837) to the poverty figure adopted by the President's Council of Economic Advisors in 1963 ($3000), Heber and Dever ask how the picture can be called "fairly bright." They point out that if the question of employment is judged by the percentage of subjects who are employed full time or are self-supporting, the data will tend to paint a fairly bright picture. But if we consider income derived from that employment in comparison to nonretarded samples, the data show the economic status of the retarded as marginal.

After Heber and Dever's analysis, another study (Gozali 1972) was published that supported their conclusions. For this study 72 individuals were selected from 218 male EMRs who had participated in a work-study program from 1964 to 1966. Of the 56 who were located, 25 percent were unemployed, 45 percent were married and maintained their own household, and 55 percent were unmarried and living with their parents or guardians. The average income of those employed was $3145 per year. Since inflation of the cost of living had raised the poverty level above the 1963 figure of $3000, an income of $3145 was still substandard.

Interpretations.   Interpretations of the above results are conflicting. Some writers interpret these results to indicate that former EMRs melt into society and adjust economically and socially as well as nonretarded persons from the same social class. And it would appear that former EMRs do adjust to a certain extent. In the majority of cases they avoid designation as mentally retarded as adults, they find work unless economic conditions are poor, they marry and raise families, and they provide housing and food for their families.

However, these same results can be interpreted to reflect a poor adjustment, particularly if we look at degrees of adjustment. Former EMRs appear at the lowest points on scales of social and occupational adjustment. That is, if we go beyond the simplistic consideration of whether or not the person is employed and look at the nature of the job and the income received, we see that the degree of adjustment is relatively poor—the former EMR does not compare favorably to the nonretarded person coming from the same social class. Furthermore, the degree to which marriages are satisfying reveals a very different picture than we would obtain from simply asking whether or not the individual is married. Qualitatively, the life of the former EMRs as a group is not comparable to that of the general public or even to that of their immediate neighbors.

The Effect of Special Classes on Adjustment. In the current debates over the efficacy of special classes and the possible negative effects of labeling, the adjustment evidence has been considered in two ways: (1) to demonstrate that these children should not have been classified as retarded by the schools, since they adjust well as adults and (2) to determine whether the special program has equipped these individuals to adjust to community life as adults better than a regular educational program would have. These two interpretations tend to be opposite sides of the same coin: if the former EMRs adjust well as adults, some will argue that they never should have been classified as retarded by the public schools, while others will contend that the reason they adjusted so well as adults is the special training they received. Conversely, if adjustment as adults is poor, one faction will contend that the reason is that they were labeled and segregated in school, and the opposition will contend that without special education their adjustment would be worse yet. Such arguments just go in circles. In reality, it is impossible to evaluate the benefits of specialized training from the foregoing studies since the control groups were not retarded.

Some other studies have been more to the point. One study (Porter & Milazzo 1958) compared former EMR special class students with a group of comparable-IQ students who attended regular classes. They found that as adults those who attended special classes were better adjusted (e.g., marital success, recreational interests). This finding is consistent with other similar studies (e.g., Peck & Stephens 1964). However, we must exercise caution in interpreting such differences as being caused by educational placement alone. While the EMR and regular class children may be comparable in IQ, there is good reason to suspect they differ on other attributes since one group was classified and the other was not. Nevertheless, it is rather difficult to explain superior adult adjustment of former EMRs in terms of anything other than special education, for the initial distinction beween them and the control group was probably that the EMRs had *less* adequate adaptive behavior.

To get some insight into the beneficial or detrimental effects of special education, some investigators (e.g., Gozali 1972; Jones 1971b, 1972, 1973a) have sought the perceptions of the special education students themselves. Jones found that students currently enrolled in EMR classes resent labeling and placement and consider such placement to have adverse effects on social relationships (e.g., dating) and on opportunities for postschool job placement. Apparently when former EMR students view the same experiences as adults (Gozali 1972) their perceptions do not become any more favorable; rather, they are quite negative about the whole experience. However, as Gozali observed, "It is possible that the very same students would have considered most of the available educational programs as being inadequate . . ." (1972, p. 35).

The question is still open to debate. Marginal individuals enrolled in special education and rehabilitative programs as children and adolescents will probably adjust marginally as adults. We can only speculate whether they would have been better off without these programs and labeling or whether they would have needed greater public assistance and supervision. With the dramatic cutbacks in the number of children currently being identified as EMR in response to political pressures, we may get some insight into these questions by following current marginal children in regular classes who in the past would have been classified as EMR. The social and economic community into which they will progress will differ from that of the 1950s, 1960s, and 1970s, but comparisons with the older studies will be interesting.

Adjustment of Patients Who Left Institutions

Research on the community adjustment of mentally retarded persons who left institutions has taken two different directions. The earlier work (roughly prior to the mid-1970s) studied a host of variables (e.g., intellectual level, personality, diagnostic category) that might be predictive of success in the community (Heal, Sigelman, & Switzky 1978; McCarver & Craig 1974). Retarded subjects in these evaluations tended to be released from the institution because it was believed they could adjust. Typically, adjustment meant that these retarded persons were on their own, with the support of family or other benefactors. The more recent research has considered adjustment in the community in terms of living in some type of community residential facility (CRF) such as a foster care home, halfway house, or group home. Hence, the more recent work examines the efforts to deinstitutionalize many retarded persons, in contrast to the earlier research, whose subjects were released because they were thought capable of living independently or semi-independently in the community. In this section we will examine the earlier evidence on community adjustment of subjects released, and in Chapter 14 we will consider the evidence on the success of deinstitutionalization and alternative residential alternatives.

Just as the data on former EMRs can be interpreted optimistically or pessimistically, the success or failure of former residents of institutions is also open to debate. In general, the early studies tended to take the optimistic point of view that while moderately retarded subjects do not achieve tremendous occupational and personal successes in the community, they do adjust and become self-sufficient and able to cope with the demands of society. But studies conducted since the 1960s have painted a far less rosy picture.

The Optimistic Early Studies.   Attempts at following up the careers of former residents of institutions for the mentally retarded can be traced back to Fernald (1919). Of the 1537 persons discharged over a 25-year period, 612 had been readmitted to some type of custodial institution. Of the 90 females found living in the community, 58 percent showed no problems, while 42 percent had records of sexual, alcohol, or theft problems. The one factor that differentiated the adjusted from the maladjusted was that individuals in the former group typically had someone who had taken an interest in them. The males who remained in the community (64 percent) appeared to have adjusted better than the female population, but having someone to assist the retarded person was still an important factor. Those who held jobs were the higher-ability individuals; the jobs they held were predominantly unskilled labor. Goldstein (1964) noted that release of most of the patients followed by Fernald had not been recommended by the institution. These patients nonetheless functioned fairly well in the community. We can only speculate as to how well a more capable group of patients might have done.

Other studies (Foley 1929; Matthews 1922; Storrs 1924) that followed Fernald indicated that a sizeable proportion of severely and moderately retarded persons could make a satisfactory adjustment outside the institution. But such follow-up studies usually contained serious methodological flaws that make conclusions hazardous (see Goldstein 1964 and Windle 1962 for discussions of the procedures employed). As Heber and Dever (1970) noted, the studies cannot be compared with each other because they differed in the extent to which the following outcomes were evaluated: occupational status, income, police records, and marital status. In addition, the studies varied in terms of what constitutes adjustment, the sampling procedures, the length of time subjects were institutionalized, and the length of time since release.

After reviewing the studies, Goldstein (1964) concluded that they supported only one broad generalization:

> The probability is that the majority of higher grade mentally retarded inmates of public institutions will make a relatively successful adjustment in their communities when training, selection, placement, and supervision are all at an optimum.

(p. 229)

This conclusion refers basically to subjects with IQs above 50. Above that point the retarded tended to perform as well as nonretarded employees at unskilled jobs, in which job success seems more related to personality factors than to IQ. A few other facts can be extracted from the early studies. Heber and Dever (1970) noted that maximum occupational adjustment seemed to occur in a person's late twenties. Goldstein (1964) observed that individuals released from institutions tended to be placed in urban rather than rural settings. He also noted that once in the community, retarded persons have not been inclined to participate in civic and social events to the degree that the general population does.

The Pessimistic Later Studies.   Heber and Dever (1970) have challenged the conclusion that the early studies demonstrate a favorable adjustment of formerly institutionalized retarded persons. They point out the vulnerability of this group to economic recessions and argue that comparing their occupational success to that of nonretarded persons performing the same jobs is inappropriate because the nonretarded individuals are probably only marginally employable for reasons other than IQ or they would not be functioning in these unskilled occupations. Furthermore, they point out that the studies often use the absence of legal infractions as an indication of social adequacy, yet the released retarded subjects generally live in low social class neighborhoods with high crime rates, making comparisons with local norms inadequate. Heber and Dever's critique of the early studies has been supported by evidence gathered by Windle (1962) and Edgerton (1967).

Certainly one of the most sophisticated studies on discharged institutionalized patients is that of Windle (1962). He followed up four groups of former Pacific State Hospital patients who were residing in the community: (1) patients on vocational leaves, (2) patients on leave to their homes, (3) patients on unauthorized leaves, and (4) a group of lower-ability patients who were placed in family care. This last group were on leave for differing reasons that do not bear directly on the issue at hand. However, of the 200 subjects falling into the other three categories, approximately 70 percent failed in the community and were returned to the institution within four years. Persons on unauthorized leaves were returned especially rapidly: over 80 percent were returned within 200 days after leaving, usually with some help from the authorities.

The two remaining groups (home leave and vocational leave) are of particular interest here. After approximately two years, close to 60 percent of both groups had been returned to the hospital. Their failure is especially significant because these groups were not selected at random; instead they were selected from all patients as the best bets to make it in the community.

Table 9.4 shows the main ways in which these former patients failed to adjust in the community. Of those on vocational leave who were returned to the hospital, the most common failures were, in descending order, (1)

TABLE 9.4   Percentage of Failures for Various Reasons by Type of Leave

Reason for Failure	Vocational Leave (N = 27)	Home Leave (N = 49)	Family Care (N = 71)
Patient's Actions	**92%**	**83%**	**44%**
Antisocial Behavior: crimes, sexual misbehavior, pregnancy, minor antisocial actions	14%	63%	4%
Intolerable Behavior: unhygienic, untidy, temper, hyperactive, destructive, sleeping problems	0%	0%	21%
Inadequate Interpersonal Relations: jealousy, disrespectful, quarrels, dominates	26%	2%	7%
Inadequate Work Performance: cannot take orders, anxiety, poor self-evaluation	30%	2%	3%
Voluntary Return and Escape	18%	6%	3%
Mental Illness: commitment to mental hospital, psychotic, depressed	4%	10%	6%
Health Medical problems, seizures, or too much care required	**4%**	**2%**	**21%**
Environmental Lack of Support Parental disinterest, home closed, parental interference, community objection	**4%**	**15%**	**35%**

C. Windle, "Prognosis of mental subnormals," from *The American Journal of Mental Deficiency* (1962). Reprinted by permission of the publisher and author.

inadequate work performance, (2) inadequate interpersonal relations, (3) voluntary return where the patient initiated the action, and (4) antisocial behavior. By comparison, of those who were returned from home leave, the great majority were returned for reasons of socially unacceptable behavior—sexual misbehavior, crimes, and so on.

Windle (1962) pointed out that the frequency with which antisocial behavior occurred in home leave as contrasted with vocational leave could be explained in terms of a closer scrutiny of the individuals selected to go out on vocational leave. Such leaves were denied in instances where antisocial behavior was seen as a possible problem. Another possibility is that families may have resisted returning their child until a major incident forced them to act to avoid police intervention.

We can draw several conclusions from Windle's (1962) findings: the results run counter to the optimism noted in the writings prior to 1960; they are consistent with them only in the finding that factors independent of IQ appear to determine success and failure; the reasons for individual failures seem to vary as a function of the type of leave granted.

Another study of the movement of patients in and out of Pacific State Hospital was done by Edgerton (1967). He studied intensively 48 persons who had been formerly released by the hospital because they had been successfully rehabilitated. It is important to note that these subjects had been initially selected as having a good prognosis; they had already been sent out several times with varying degrees of success, and by the time Edgerton (1967) studied them, they were considered "successes" and discharged from Pacific State Hospital. They were released at a time of unparalleled prosperity in the United States. The original sample of 110 had a mean IQ of 65 and a mean CA of 35 years. The final sample of 48 were chosen because they lived within a reasonable distance from the researchers.

Edgerton and his staff spent considerable time with each of the subjects, interviewing and observing them in order to characterize their lives. The vivid picture they drew is anything but optimistic.

On virtually every index of economic and social functioning, Edgerton's subjects were found on the extreme lower end of the continuum. They lived in extreme poverty, residing in slum areas under deplorable conditions. Economically, they were experiencing difficulty with debts that had accumulated. They had little job security and possessed few marketable skills. They were economically successful only to the extent that they escaped starvation and had a roof over their heads; but by any qualitative considerations it would be hard to consider this group successfully adjusted.

The single most important factor that consistently emerged was the extent to which these individuals depended on benefactors. These benefactors assisted the retarded in coping with day-to-day living tasks and in passing for normal by denying their mental retardation. Benefactors—frequently spouses—were typically of normal intelligence and were of assistance in carrying out those activities requiring literacy or the use of numbers and symbols (such as telling time or reading instructions). We can get some idea of the frequency of such dependency and the extent to which it was needed from Edgerton's estimate that only 3 of the 48 subjects could be judged as independent and that without the support of their benefactors 20 subjects would have been returned immediately to the institution.

Heber and Dever (1970) concluded that Edgerton's subjects traded the protective environment of the institution for survival in the community only through the support provided by a benefactor. They also speculated that the possible reason for the failures of these same individuals on earlier releases may have been the lack of a benefactor rather than any real differences in skills or attitudes.

Edgerton (1967) emphasized the extent to which the former patients directed their energies toward dealing with the burden of having been classified as mentally retarded. They constantly had problems trying to convince others that they were normal; of equal importance were their attempts to convince themselves that they were normal. According to Edgerton, these individuals could not admit to themselves that they were, or ever had been, retarded; the stigma was too great and the threat too powerful. Only in denying their mental retardation could they maintain a sense of personal worth.

Edgerton's subjects were contacted again to determine the effects of time and changes in life situations on social adaptation (Edgerton & Bercovici 1976). The findings of that follow-up do not conclusively support the notion that the passage of considerable periods of time improves the social adaptation of retarded persons. Of the 30 subjects followed up, 8 were considered to be better adjusted than they were in 1960–61, while 10 were believed to be more poorly adjusted. More important was the finding that within each of these categories (better adjustment, worse adjustment, same adjustment) there was diversity. For example, one person judged to be very competent in 1960 was found to be even better adjusted in 1976; however, so were some individuals considered highly dependent in 1960.

The lives of the mentally retarded are anything but simple—they are quite complex and changeable. There were several noteworthy changes in the lives of Edgerton's subjects as a whole. First, less time and energy was expended on passing as normal than had been noted in the initial study. The former patients still had not forgotten that they had been retarded, but it was no longer a preoccupation with the majority of them. Second, the subjects were less dependent on benefactors than they had been in the first follow-up (either because of less need for the benefactor's help or because the benefactors were less available). Finally, the lives of these individuals appeared more devoted to recreation, hobbies, leisure, good times, friends, and families—they were concerned with enjoying life and most saw their lives as more enjoyable than at the time of the initial contact.

Family Interest. Given the apparent importance of the benefactor shown by Edgerton's (1967) study, the interest of the family could be critical if the most likely benefactor for a released retarded person is a family member. According to a study by Farber (1968), once families have placed a child in an institution their interest varies. Some families visit frequently, have the child home on holidays, and in other ways maintain interest and contact. Others avoid contact with the child and the institution.

Several researchers have looked for reasons why family interest varies. Downey (1965) found that education was a significant variable; the educational level of the parents was inversely related to interest in their institutionalized retarded child. According to Downey, families with high educational attainment tend to consider their retarded child as "inhuman" and do not consider that child to be a family member of full status; lower-education families are more inclined to consider their institutionalized child as a family member of full status who happens to be living away from home (Farber 1968).

Farber (1968) found that the interest of a family in their retarded child is related to the probability that the child will be returned home. And the probability of release is in turn related to family characteristics as well as to the individual's characteristics. Since families from different social classes place their retarded children in institutions for different reasons (see Chapter 14), the patterns of release also differ for the social classes (Mercer 1965). Farber (1968) found that lower-class residents of institutions tend to have higher IQs and are institutionalized later than is true of middle- and upper-class residents. The lower-class residents are also more likely to be released. Among the lower-class residents, children whose placement was by an official agency were more likely to be released than were those whose families were instrumental in their placement. Furthermore, children who were released from the institution tended to have mothers and siblings with lower educational attainment. While only 33 percent of the released residents had mothers who attended college, 66 percent of the mothers of residents not released had attended college (Mercer 1965). Farber concluded that these data suggest that the mentally retarded child poses a greater threat to the middle-class family than it does to the lower-class family.

Variables Predicting Release and Adjustment. Family interest and attitudes do appear to be related to the probability that a patient will be released; they may or may not bear on the issue of how well these individuals adjust once they are released. This dimension has not yet been studied, for release and adjustment are two separate processes with two sets of known variables:

1. *The release process:* What are the factors related to the probability that an institutionalized retarded patient will be released—and given a chance to succeed on the outside? Among the factors found to be related to this decision are IQ level, age at time of admission, physical disabilities, social class of the child's family, and the interest of the family in the child while the child is in the institution.
2. *The adjustment process:* Once released, what are the factors related to the degree of success that individuals will achieve in the community? Among the known factors are IQ level (above IQ 50), age at time of release, type of leave granted, and presence of a benefactor.

These findings may not be applicable to institutional residents today. With the current emphasis on community placement of the retarded, the residents of institutions are a more debilitated group than the population studied in the past. For example, the proportion of residents in institutions for the retarded with IQs above 50 is far lower now than it was in the early 1950s. On the other hand, the findings of Edgerton (1967) seem pertinent to any efforts to normalize moderately and severely retarded persons. To the extent that benefactors determine success or failure, it might be helpful to involve professionals or paraprofessionals in a benefactorlike role, at least in the early periods following a retarded person's release from an institution.

SUMMARY

In asking what becomes of retarded children as they grow up, we find that social competence is the chief measure of success in our society. Whether retarded individuals achieve it or not seems to depend both on their own characteristics and on outside circumstances.

Identification of the child as retarded comes about because of problems in adapting to the environment, usually because of a lack of skills. Various scales have been devised to assess common areas in which retarded children have difficulty. But although these scales take into account the fact that the demands of society change with age and differ by sex, they are unable to measure the subtle differences in expectations within cultural subgroups. And they are inappropriate for measuring academic failure, often the only kind of social incompetence manifested by children classified as EMR. In the absence of any totally accurate measures of adaptive behavior, perhaps the best thing we have to go by is whether an individual is judged retarded by the individual's own community. The overall criterion would then be whether or not an individual's behaviors are tolerated by the community.

If certain persons are judged socially incompetent, what can we do to help them fit better into society? There are three possible opinions:

1. Modify their behavior so that they can meet the demands of their environment and be considered adaptive.
2. Remove them from the original environment and place them in an environment that is adjusted to their level of functioning. In milder forms of deviation, this is a special class; in more extreme forms, it is an institution. In either case there should be programmatic elements designed to modify behavior in order for the child to move back into the original environment.
3. Alter the original environment so the individual exhibiting the mal-

adaptive behavior can be tolerated. This alternative as yet remains untested, but in efforts toward mainstreaming and normalization it will be the preferred approach.

Treatment is considered successful if individuals can return to their original environment and function independently. This is easiest in the case of the EMR since their maladaptive behavior usually is only academic; when they leave school the larger society does not appear to place the same emphasis on abstract learning and they can usually function adequately. But there is no way of knowing whether their success is caused by the treatment or by innate abilities. And although some studies emphasize that former EMRs disappear into the community as self-sufficient adults, others point out that their quality of life is very poor.

When former residents of institutions for the retarded are released and later studied for indications of adjustment, the conclusions drawn depend on what criteria are used to measure success. Finding that, at least in prosperous times, the majority were able to find jobs, marry, and buy homes, Goldstein (1964) concluded that the higher-IQ residents of institutions will probably make a relatively successful adjustment in their community. However, Heber and Dever (1970) contend that the conditions under which the "successfully adjusted" former institutional residents live are frequently so depressing as to raise doubts as to their success. And a very different portrayal of the quality of life enjoyed by patients released from institutions is depicted by Edgerton (1967) from the one that emerged from the follow-up studies conducted prior to 1960. Edgerton's subjects were the most qualified patients in the institution and were sent into the community in a period of unparalleled prosperity in the United States, yet they survived only marginally, and apparently largely because of the support of benefactors. In fact, consideration of Edgerton's (1967) results leads to the conclusion that independent living by former institutionalized patients may be far less dependent on personal differences in IQ and vocational skills and more a function of whether someone of normal intelligence takes an interest in the retarded persons and assists them in meeting societal demands as well as provides personal support. It is possible that treatment in the form of teaching self-help, and vocational skills is of little value unless provision is also made to have someone help retarded persons when they are returned to the community.

CHAPTER 10

Learning and Cognitive Characteristics

The mentally retarded are, as a group, inefficient learners. This characteristic more than any other differentiates them from their nonretarded peers. If retarded individuals are to learn the skills and knowledge that will assist them in life, their teachers must somehow compensate for their inefficiencies in learning.

Children with average and above-average ability often learn with little guidance from teachers, but mentally retarded people (particularly the more severely retarded) are not very self-educable. In order for them to learn, considerable structure must be imposed on the learning process.

Learning theories and laboratory research evidence can suggest possible directions for teaching the mentally retarded. But theories of learning applied to the mentally retarded (Meyers & MacMillan 1976) often disagree with each other, and laboratory research evidence may not be applicable to the classroom because the materials, the conditions of learning, and the students may be different in the two settings.

For an excellent review of research on the cognition and learning of mentally retarded persons, we recommend Norman Ellis's book (1979) about basic research, especially the chapters that deal with the use of behavior modification with retarded subjects. In addition to the Ellis book, there are chapters or articles by Butterfield and Belmont (1977), Heintz & Blackman (1977), Schonebaum and Zinober (1977), and Weisz and Zigler (1979) that also review extensive bodies of research literature pertaining to cognition and learning in retarded subjects. The most current research can be found by examining the research journals.

Despite the vast literature on learning and cognition in the mentally retarded, there is little practical information available. Very few studies have specifically considered which teaching techniques work best for retarded students. In many instances, we must extrapolate from research evidence derived in contrived laboratory situations, and this kind of extrapolation can be risky.

We begin this chapter with a review of preliminary concepts and background information. We then discuss theoretical and laboratory research undertaken to determine how retarded children differ from nonretarded children on learning and cognitive tasks. We conclude by considering the research on learning and teaching in the school setting—how to teach reading and arithmetic to retarded children.

LEARNING

Learning can be defined as change in behavior due to experience, as distinguished from change in behavior from maturation, growth, or aging. The term *learning* covers a complex array of activities. An infant learns to recognize the mother's face, a two-year-old learns to walk, a child learns the value of money, and an adolescent learns algebra. Despite the differences in these situations, certain laws and principles of learning have emerged from research, and some general statements can be made regarding how people learn (Keller 1969).

Informal Learning

Teachers and parents often think of learning exclusively in terms of behavior changes that occur as a result of formally structured experiences: the teacher uses an instructional strategy to teach reading, the parent sits down with the child to teach sewing. Much learning, however, occurs in an incidental manner. A child learns attitudes toward reading tangentially to the lesson being taught. Parents are appalled when their child uses swear words, only later to recognize that the child may be imitating something overheard from them.

With retarded children it is particularly important to recognize that children learn much new behavior independent of structured exercises that parents or teachers design in order to teach a particular skill. Being careful of what is informally taught can be a tricky matter. For example, parents pay attention to behavior emitted by their children that the parents hope to weaken or terminate. Assuming that they can do so by attending with a frown or a negative comment, the parents fail to realize that the attention itself (despite its apparent negative tone) can actually serve to strengthen, or reinforce, the behavior it follows. On the other hand, those charged with caring for the retarded often perceive their role as one that entails putting up with bizarre or inappropriate behavior, since they attribute this behavior to the retardation; so they ignore the behavior and do nothing to weaken it. Either way, parents and attendants may be inadvertently teaching retarded children to behave in ways that are inappropriate, thereby hampering their acceptance in society. Much of the evidence on the effectiveness of operant conditioning (e.g., Gardner 1971) indicates that undesired behaviors are sometimes inadvertently reinforced.

Learning versus Maturation

We pointed out before that learning as a result of experience is different from behavior change due to maturation. But in some cases experience and maturation do produce the same results. We suggest that certain behaviors may be "outgrown"; instead of trying to eradicate them, we could simply wait for the behaviors to change with the passage of time. Consider the frustration and failure involved when a parent tries to teach a ten-month-old child how to walk. Most ten-month-old children are simply physically incapable of walking. It is therefore important to determine whether a child is sufficiently mature to respond to teaching or whether a specific behavior will be altered with time as the child matures.

On the other hand, the retarded child's maturation may sometimes have to be guided. In attempting to plan educational experiences for a retarded child the teacher must be careful not to assume that a retarded child has learned certain things incidentally. Retarded children demonstrate a lower propensity for attending to relevant stimuli (Zeaman & House 1979), and they tend not to have acquired the skills and knowledge possessed by children of the same age whose intelligence is normal. It will often be necessary to confirm whether a retarded child has certain knowledge commonly acquired incidentally by normal children as they grow up; if the child does not have this knowledge the teacher will have to teach these prerequisite skills in a formal manner before proceeding with the intended lesson.

Learning and Performance

When questions are asked of children and they provide the correct responses, it is reasonable to infer that they have *learned* the information requested. But when they do not respond correctly we must be cautious in drawing inferences. Their failure to respond correctly may be due to any number of factors other than the inefficiency of their learning. They may not want to answer the question; the incentive for answering correctly may not be sufficiently desirable to make it worth their while. For example, in a preschool program for disadvantaged children described by Zigler (1968), children were asked their names on the first morning. Few children answered. But when they were told that unless the teacher knew their names the teacher might miss them when juice and cookies were passed out, suddenly all but one "learned" their names. Until the teacher made it worthwhile, the children did not *perform* even though they had *learned* their names.

This distinction between learning and ability (or competence and capacity) is pointed out in two excellent articles (Bortner & Birch 1970; Cole & Bruner 1971). These articles note that performance levels are only partial indicators of a child's learning or capacity. Yet we frequently encounter interpretations of performance levels as direct indicators of that child's capacity. By changing the materials used for testing, training procedures, task organization, social circumstances, and incentive conditions we can often influence performance levels of the child.

Careful interpretation of the performance of retarded children does not lend itself to conclusions that the retarded *cannot* do certain things. Instead, failures only mean that they *did not* perform on those specific tasks under existing incentive conditions and with the specific tester. Change in any one of these circumstances *might* result in successful performance.

HOW LEARNING IN RETARDED PERSONS IS STUDIED

Mental retardation is a rather new field of study for behavioral scientists. It was in the mid-1950s that the amount of behavioral research in mental retardation increased dramatically (Ellis 1969). At first the research was designed to answer practical problems (such as diagnosis and psychometric evaluation); the newer work has increasingly dealt with learning, motivation, memory, and other concepts derived from general psychology.

With this abundance of data from research efforts, some attempts have been made to organize findings from isolated studies into theoretical formulations about retarded development. Later in this chapter we will examine the applications of general learning theories—operant behaviorism, Piaget's cognitive-developmental theory, social learning theory, and observational learning—to how retarded individuals learn and might be taught. But first we will examine the research models and strategies that have been used to determine how the learning process differs for mentally retarded and normal individuals.

Developmental versus Difference (or Defect) Models

Two contrasting models have been offered to explain the cognitive development of retarded children. The *developmental model* suggests that the cognitive development of the retarded child of IQ 50 or so is delayed or slow, but essentially normal. The *difference* (or *defect*) *model* contends that the cognitive development of retarded children progresses differently than the cognitive development of nonretarded children. For an extended discussion of these models, see Ellis (1969), Milgram (1969) Schonebaum and Zinober (1977), and Zigler (1969; 1973).

A developmental approach assumes that, at least for mildly retarded persons, formal cognitive processes are identical to those of more intelligent individuals except that (1) there is a slower progression through the stages of formal cognitive development and (2) the upper stage of cognitive development achieved by the retarded will be lower than the ultimate stage of cognitive development achieved by an individual of average intellect. Figure 10.1 illustrates this model.

Zigler (1969), who wrote an article supporting the developmental model and criticizing the difference model, contends that the mildly retarded rep-

---

FIGURE 10.1   Developmental Model of Cognitive Growth

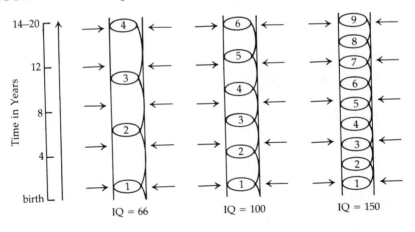

The single vertical arrow represents the passage of time. The horizontal arrows represent environmental events impinging on the individual, who is represented as a pair of vertical lines. The individual's cognitive development appears as an internal ascending spiral, in which the numbered loops represent successive stages of cognitive growth.

E. Zigler, "Development versus difference theories of mental retardation and the problem of motivation," *American Journal of Mental Deficiency*, 1969, **73**. Reprinted by permission of the publisher and author.

resent a group whose intellectual development is determined largely by normal polygenic considerations; they progress from lower to higher developmental levels in the same sequence as normals. The only differences are the *rate* at which the individuals progress through these stages and the upper *level* of achievement. Retarded cognitive development, Zigler says, is like a short person's height. The short individual develops at a slower rate and does not reach the same level at maturity as people of normal stature; but in kind and form of typical growth, the short and the retarded are no different from normals. Bloom (1974) has reached a similar conclusion.

People holding a difference or defective position (e.g., Weir 1967) argue that there are differences in retarded cognitive development that go beyond mere rate and ultimate level achieved. Zigler's position would suggest that if a retarded person and one of normal intellect could be equated in terms of their theoretical level of cognitive development (the retarded person would have to be older than the normal one), they would behave exactly the same on cognitive tasks. But the difference theorists would argue that differences in IQ (e.g., IQ = 66 versus IQ = 100) carry with them qualitative differences in the way information is processed.

Those who oppose the developmental model can themselves be divided into difference theorists and defect theorists. According to the difference theorists, the greater the IQ difference, the greater the degree to which the individuals differ qualitatively. According to the defect theorists, there is a discontinuous relationship with IQ. Below a certain IQ some processes differ qualitatively from the functioning of those above that IQ; but above the IQ cutoff there are no qualitative differences between retarded and normal people. The IQ cutoff used in theories of retarded versus normal development is IQ 50, with no one denying that individuals functioning below this level may differ markedly from normal people. The academic debate centers on mildly retarded people whose functioning is a result of normal polygenic inheritance and its interaction with environmental forces (Zigler 1969).

Arguing on behalf of those who feel that cognitive functioning of mildly retarded people is different from that of normal people, Ellis (1969) responded to Zigler's criticisms of the difference theory. Ellis felt that Zigler unfairly criticized the difference orientation by implying that all difference theorists inappropriately extrapolate from organic retardation to cultural-familial retardation and assume that there is a physiological basis for postulating a difference. Ellis contended that difference from the norm can be either behavioral or physiological, and a difference model may be appropriate in either case. Retarded persons, he argued, exhibit retarded behavior, and that defines them as different. In the future they will continue to exhibit behavior different from that of normal people, for at present we do not possess techniques for normalizing the behavior of retarded persons. Because there are behavioral differences between retarded and nonretarded persons, Ellis contended, the task confronting the psychologist is to describe these differences. Ellis also rejected Zigler's contention that a difference orientation treats the retarded as a homogeneous group. As Ellis observed, a selected sample of retarded persons might be rather homogeneous in IQ but not in etiology or socioeconomic status.

Research on the progress of the retarded through Piaget's cognitive stages generally supports the "similar sequence" hypothesis, which states that both nonretarded and retarded children traverse the same stages of cognitive development in the same order. The groups differ only in the rate at which they progress and the level of functioning they ultimately attain. The severely retarded sometimes do not reach the higher-level stages. Reviews by Weisz and Zigler (1979) and Woodward (1979) indicate that, except for subjects who have brain wave abnormalities, the data tend to confirm the similar sequence hypothesis.

The debate between developmental and difference theorists is still only an academic exchange. But the positions have profound implications for how retarded children should be taught. If, as the developmental model suggests, retarded children in EMR classes are employing the same cognitive strategies as younger normal children, teachers in training need not take special courses on methods for teaching content to the retarded. EMR teaching methods and materials could be those routinely used for younger children. However, if the difference position is valid, we should investigate unique teaching methods for this group of children that are destined to compensate for or circumvent their inefficiencies in learning.

Research Strategies

In order to resolve the developmental-difference debate and put its implications into practice, careful research is required into how retarded children learn and into comparisons of retarded and normal functioning in specific cognitive areas. If you are considering doing this kind of research, note that there is a professional consensus about conducting such research: you must be careful not to include subjects with IQs below 50 along with subjects with IQs above 50, unless they are considered as separate groups.

The advantages and disadvantages of various methods of conducting research on learning and cognition in retarded subjects are discussed by many authors (including Baumeister 1967b; Denny 1964; Ellis 1969; MacMillan, Meyers, & Morrison 1980; and Winters 1977). Denny (1964) and Winters (1977) describe three popular designs in detail. In Type I, retarded persons are compared with a group of average intelligence of equal mental age (MA). In Type II, retarded persons are compared with a group of average intelligence of equal chronological age (CA). In Type III, two contrast groups of normals, one of equal MA and one of equal CA, are matched with a retarded sample. Table 10.1 shows these designs and notes the sources of the differences in the two groups in each type, if any. Note that the results of Type I and Type II strategies can yield several interpretations. In Type I (groups equated on the basis of MA), differences probably result from differences in IQ. In this design, however, the retarded sometimes perform significantly better than normal children on tasks dependent on chronological age rather than level of cognitive ability. Similarly, in Type II (groups equated on the basis of CA), differences between the two groups could be explained in terms of either lower MA or lower IQ among the retarded sample. Design Type III is preferred by both Denny (1964) and Winters (1977), since it allows the researcher to determine whether differences exist only when (1) the CA-equated group differs but the MA-equated group does not or when (2) both groups of nonretarded subjects perform reliably higher than the retarded sample. The second situation would indicate that the difference is due to IQ differences unrelated to, or independent of, chronological age.

TABLE 10.1   Common Sampling Designs for Learning Studies and Interpretation of Findings If Differences Emerge

Design Type	MR and Normal Samples Equated on Basis of:	Differences in Performance May Be Due to Differences in:	Differences Found Exhibit the Effects of:*
I	MA	IQ (or CA if MR sample performs better)	low IQ
II	CA	MA or IQ	low MA/low IQ
III†	CA and MA (2 contrast groups)	IQ (if both nonretarded samples score higher); MA (if only the nonretarded CA-equated group scores higher)	low MA–low IQ or the more basic low IQ

*If the results of the study indicate that the retarded group is performing at a lower level than the normal group, the differences are probably due to the traits listed.
†Two retarded groups could be compared with one nonretarded sample, or two nonretarded samples could be compared with one retarded sample. The latter practice is usually followed because of the greater availability of nonretarded subjects.

Reprinted from M. R. Denny, "Research in learning and performance," in H. A. Stevens and R. Heber, eds., *Mental Retardation: A Review of Research*, p. 101, by permission of The University of Chicago Press. © 1964 by the University of Chicago

RESEARCH FINDINGS ON LEARNING CHARACTERISTICS

Researchers have found that there are some areas of relative difficulty for the retarded in learning and performance. Whether the evidence supports the developmental position of Zigler (1969) or something more like a difference or defect position is open to debate. But it is important for those who teach retarded individuals to be aware of the problem areas in learning that have been identified. If they know which content and process areas have a high probability for causing difficulty, teachers can anticipate and accommodate likely problems as they design their instructional strategies.

In general, learning involves paying attention, organizing the incoming stimuli, remembering, and recalling from memory what is needed to solve a particular problem. We will consider these dimensions separately—although they overlap at many points—with special attention to areas in which there is enough evidence for us to make some statements about the learning and performance of the mentally retarded. But before we consider the specific research results, we will discuss the differences between basic and applied research in an effort to caution the reader about extrapolating too readily from laboratory research to educational and rehabilitative teaching situations.

Basic and Applied Research

By basic research we mean studies typically conducted under highly controlled conditions in a laboratory or laboratorylike situation. MacMillan and Meyers (1980b) characterized basic research as involving highly molecular types of learning such as nonsense syllables, paired associates, digit span, and other tasks that permit the experimenter to control the stimuli and neutralize any previous experience the subjects might have had with the stimuli. Such tasks are usually administered to subjects on a one-to-one basis in situations in which extraneous stimuli such as noise and visual distractions are highly controlled. Basic researchers also attempt to select subjects who are relatively homogeneous in IQ, adaptive behavior, social class, and other variables that might influence performance.

When this situation is contrasted with that of the teacher, we realize that the *match* between experimental conditions and classroom conditions is quite poor. A teacher usually teaches tasks that are quite molar in nature, tasks on which previous experience definitely affects the rate of learning. In the classroom there is noise in the corridors, on the playground outside, and from other children in the class. Moreover, the teacher frequently teaches small or large groups but rarely has a chance to teach on a one-to-one basis. Finally, the class is usually heterogeneous in every respect except IQ. As a result of these factors, teachers must be extremely cautious about trying to apply basic research evidence in classroom instruction. Some of this research may have implications for the classroom, but the teacher must act on these findings carefully.

The first body of evidence we will consider concerns attention, memory, and rehearsal strategies, and is derived from laboratory research. Although this research has identified differences between retarded and nonretarded subjects, the implications of such differences in educational and rehabilitative programing for retarded persons are not yet clear. In the next section of the chapter, we will consider research attempts to discover differences in the way retarded children learn academic tool subjects such as reading and arithmetic. It is important to note that there is much more basic research on the learning and cognitive characteristics of the retarded than there is on ways to instruct retarded children in acquiring academic, vocational, and social skills in the home or classroom environment. In the latter areas, there is a paucity of research evidence.

Attention

A systematic study of discrimination learning in retarded children led Zeaman and House (1963) to conclude that retarded children are deficient in attention. Discrimination learning requires the subject to examine stimuli that differ in several dimensions (e.g., position, shape, and color) and select one of the stimuli. The key to discrimination learning is the ability to select the dimension in which the discrimination is to be made (e.g., color). Zeaman and House's original attention theory was presented in 1963, but it has been modified in subsequent writings (Fisher & Zeaman 1973; Zeaman & House 1979) to reflect more recent research findings.

In the earlier version of the theory, Zeaman and House (1963) observed that retarded subjects had trouble focusing on the dimension in which the discrimination was to be made. Once they zeroed in on the salient dimension, however, their instrumental learning proceeded at a rate comparable to that of normals. This is illustrated in Figure 10.2. Discrimination learning was seen to involve two stages. In Stage 1—the *attention* phase—the learning curve remains horizontal, with correct responses occurring at a rate similar to the rate that would occur by chance. In Stage 2, the learning curve rises sharply as the subject starts attending to the relevant dimensions of the stimulus. The lower the mental age, the greater the number of trials necessary in Stage 1 before instrumental learning begins.

According to Zeaman and House (1963), the longer line before the slope ascends indicates that retarded subjects have greater difficulty in attending to the relevant stimulus dimensions in the discrimination tasks. Their performance requires a greater amount of time and practice before it begins to improve, but once it does it improves at a rate comparable to normals.

FIGURE 10.2   **Learning Curves for Discrimination
Learning in Relation to Mental Age (MA)**

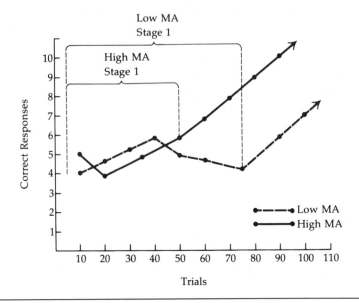

From C. D. Mercer and M. E. Snell, *Learning Theory Research in Mental Retardation*, p. 97. Reprinted by permission of the Charles E. Merrill Publishing Company. Copyright 1977.

Despite this similarity in what they called *second stage learning*, Zeaman and House found two important differences in the first stage. For one thing, retarded subjects attended to fewer dimensions than normals; this is detrimental if the key stimulus is not among those attended to. And normal subjects are more likely to attend to dimensions that have been critical to solving similar problems in the past and to ignore those dimensions that are irrelevant. (The reader should not generalize these findings to EMR individuals, however.)

Zeaman and House (1979) revised the theory in light of subsequent findings to accommodate (1) the effects of feedback and (2) the implications of "multiple-look" discrimination learning findings. In the multiple-look investigations, subjects were reinforced for focusing on certain dimensions of the stimuli. For example, Zeaman and House (1979) present the following discrimination: RED SQUARE versus GREEN TRIANGLE. Some children saw both cues (color and shape) and, because of previous reinforcement, had a strong preference for the triangle over the square and a weaker preference for red over green. These children selected the green triangle because of their strong preference for the triangle. Thus, the *cue* associated with the probable reinforcement for shape (in this instance) influences the attending behavior. It is recalled from memory, which we will discuss in the next section. Feedback was also found to play an important role in attending. When Fisher and Zeaman (1973) updated the theory, they acknowledged that both *learning* and *retention* were important in attention. Learning rate (the slope of the curve) is unrelated to intelligence, but retention is definitely related to intelligence. Zeaman and House (1979) also noted that *breadth of attention*—the number of dimensions to which a learner can attend simultaneously—is related to MA and, thus, to mental retardation. Mentally retarded children cannot attend to as many dimensions simultaneously as normal children.

Zeaman and House (1979) have suggested several remedial procedures for the attention deficit they found in retarded subjects, and they have demonstrated the usefulness of these procedures empirically. They suggest that in teaching discrimination to retarded students teachers should (1) use three-dimensional objects, (2) sequence tasks in an easy-to-hard progression, (3) emphasize the relevant dimensions (such as color), (4) alternate the novelty of either the negative or positive stimuli, (5) avoid failure, and (6) establish a "set" to focus relevant dimensions.

While some have interpreted Zeaman and House's findings of inattention in discrimination learning to suggest a general inability of retarded subjects to attend, this conclusion awaits further research. And as Baumeister (1967b) has pointed out, the term *attention* in the context used by Zeaman and House does not pertain to the degree to which a subject perseveres on a task. A subject may work diligently on such a task and still perform poorly if the subject attends to the wrong dimensions.

Turnure (1970b) has challenged the attention deficit position of Zeaman and House; he has explained seemingly inattentive behavior in terms of the retarded child's history of failures in problem solving. Turnure suggests that retarded children have learned to seek out cues from the environment rather than the task (e.g., looking for approval in the experimenter's face while performing a task instead of concentrating on the task) to find correct solutions to problems. This problem-solving strategy (known as *outerdirectedness*) may appear to reflect inattention to a task, but retarded children may have found that it yields a higher probability of success than if they attend to the dimensions inherent in the task itself.

Memory

Memory is essential in the application of learning to problem solving. Efficient learning requires that one be able to recall previous experiences so that they can be adapted to fit the demands of new situations. Thus, retarded children must be able to formulate the initial learning set if they are to adapt. But learning alone, although it is a prerequisite of adaptation, is not sufficient. Retarded children must also be able to remember what they have learned and apply the learning to new situations.

Traditionally, the mentally retarded have been considered to have poor memories. This conclusion is based on comparisons of the number of items such as words and numbers recalled by retarded and nonretarded subjects. Detterman (1979), however, questions the validity of such simple comparisons, arguing that the differences between the two groups could be explained by task difficulty, past history, and a host of other factors. Recent research has considered the processes or strategies employed in remembering. Why do the retarded remember inefficiently? Interest has focused on the following aspects of the memory process: (1) the retarded child's inefficiency in organizing incoming stimuli, (2) the retarded child's inefficient use of rehearsal strategies to retain input and transfer it from short-term to long-term memory, and (3) the retarded child's inefficiency in gaining access to remembered information that bears on current situations. Keep in mind that another dimension of memory is the ability to attend effectively to incoming stimuli, which was dealt with in the previous discussion of the attentional problems studied by Zeaman and House (1979).

A host of memory models have been advanced to explain the inefficient memory functions of the mentally retarded (Belmont & Butterfield 1977; Campione & Brown 1978; Ellis 1963, 1970; Fisher & Zeaman 1973; Spitz 1970). Although most of these models have some elements in common, they vary considerably, reflecting the particular interest of the theorist and the kinds of stimuli used in the study. The most common elements in these theoretical models of memory are:

1. Attention
2. Input Organization
3. Strategy Selection—such as visual imagery or clustering
4. Short-term Memory—learning will soon be forgotten if not rehearsed
5. Rehearsal Strategy—for converting to long-term memory
6. Long-term Memory
7. Retrieval—the strategy for recovering information needed in the present situation from the long-term memory

Although this is a gross oversimplification of the various models, the research has tended to fall into these categories. Let us now consider some of this research in the following sections.

Input Organization.   Once a child attends to a task the next step in the successful solution of a problem is to make sense out of the stimuli presented—in other words, to *decode* the input. From the information-processing perspective, the process of learning can be broken down as follows:

1. Arouse (person is alerted)
2. Attend (attention is given to a specific stimulus)
3. Input (file into appropriate hold area)
4. Hold (hold for permanent storage)
5. Recall (retrieve material from temporary file, if necessary)
6. Storage (put into appropriate permanent file)
7. Recall (retrieve material from permanent file, if necessary)

(Spitz 1966, pp. 52–53)

At any of these steps information can be lost. Spitz (1966) has found evidence that retarded subjects are less efficient than normals at Step 3 (categorizing the mass of incoming data into chunks). As a consequence they overload their capacity quickly. It may be that their performance is hampered either by a very inefficient organizational strategy or else by no attempt at all to organize input.

Can teachers organize information in advance to help retarded students learn it? Some suggested organizational strategies that teachers can provide for retarded students include grouping, mediators, and learning sets. These strategies are often used spontaneously by people of normal intelligence, increasing their learning efficiency, but they may not be used without prompting by retarded students.

Grouping and Concept Usage. In laboratory tasks one of the simplest ways to structure material so that retarded children can remember it is to group it spatially. This effect has been demonstrated in studies using digit span as the task (Harris 1972; Jensen 1965; MacMillan 1972a; Spitz 1966).

In tests of intelligence the tester typically reads a sequence of digits (e.g., 8, 3, 5, 9) and the subject is asked to recall these digits in the proper order. Jensen (1965) demonstrated that the delay between the presentation and the recall (e.g., 10 seconds intervening) requires self-rehearsal if performance is to be maximized. The studies with retarded subjects have tried to determine how the digits could be presented to increase the chances for self-rehearsal.

Spitz (1966) showed that if digits are presented visually, spatial grouping facilitates their recall by retarded subjects. For example, if instead of displaying the digits as 8 3 5 9, the experimenter showed them as 83 59, the subject was asked to remember two *bits* of information (eighty-three and fifty-nine) as opposed to four bits of information (eight, three, five, and nine). This facilitative effect of spatial grouping was not found for normals.

Spitz found that spatial grouping helped older EMR subjects (CA = 12) but did not benefit a younger group of EMR subjects (CA = 9). We attempted to replicate Spitz's finding and did in part (MacMillan 1972a). In a subsequent study (MacMillan 1972b) we did not require the retarded children to respond verbally to the grouped digits (e.g., 41) as a couplet (e.g., forty-one), and hence some subjects called back 41 as 4 and 1. In this study spatial grouping alone did not improve the performance of EMR children. In an attempt to clarify the relative importance of spatial grouping per se, we conducted an additional study (MacMillan 1972b) that showed that EMR subjects performed best when digits were both grouped and called as couplets. They performed worst when digits were ungrouped spatially and called as single integers; spatially grouped digits called as single integers fell in between. Interestingly, spatial groping tended to affect *adversely* the performance of nonretarded subjects, suggesting that the imposed grouping strategy (two digits) interfered with their spontaneous strategy (possibly by hundreds).

In laboratory tasks other than digit span, a correct response may again be facilitated by some form of grouping. Stephens and his associates have run a series of experiments (Stephens, Nopar, & Gillam 1971; Stephens 1972; Stephens 1973) in which subjects were presented with a variety of stimuli that lent themselves to grouping. The groupings could be by (1) physical similarity (such as size or color), (2) function, in which stimuli are grouped according to what can be done (cake and carrot can both be eaten), (3) concepts, in which members of the same classification are grouped together (bird and horse are both animals), or (4) sentential equivalence, for stimuli that could fit together in a plausible grammatical structure (The *boy* hits the *ball*). In general, the investigators found that as children increase in MA they shift from grouping on the basis of physical similarities to grouping according to function. This progression was reported for both normal and EMR subjects (Stephens 1972) when equated for MA. With age the EMR sample showed slightly less adequate mastery of functional processes within the environment, but the procedure used might have tapped a preferred response instead of assessing the full capabilities of the subjects. When the tasks were structured in an attempt to find out whether the children were capable of using higher-order organizational strategies, the level of performance improved for both nonretarded and EMR groups (Stephens 1973). The Stephens studies on equivalence formation thus suggested similar developmental trends for retarded subjects and for normals—as MA increased, both groups evidenced more advanced grouping strategies.

Although retarded subjects are capable of forming concepts under structural laboratory conditions, they may not use the concepts spontaneously on unstructured tasks. According to several authors (Blount 1968a; Bruner, Goodnow, & Austin 1956), a distinction should be made between *concept usage* and *concept formation*. Concept usage refers to the application of previously acquired concepts to a task, whereas concept formation refers to the formation of a new concept during the experimental situation. Most tasks used in laboratory attempts to assess the conceptual abilities of the retarded tap concept usage abilities. The experimenter typically presents a task that determines (1) whether children have encountered the concept in their experiences and (2) whether they can use the concept to organize a set of stimuli.

One approach to studying concept usage that has received considerable attention is called *associative clustering*. The experimenter compiles words or pictures that are examples of several concepts or categories (e.g., food, animals, body parts):

Food	Animals	Body Parts
bread	cat	arm
milk	horse	head
soup	bear	thumb
cake	goat	leg

These words (or pictures of objects) are then randomly ordered and presented to subjects, with no clues that they fall into several categories. The subjects are then asked to recall as many of the items as they can. Bousfield (1953) noted that in recalling the items, normals tend to cluster them spontaneously according to membership in a particular category—they recall the "food" items in a group, then the "animals," and so on. They seem to impose this structure on the material, enabling them to store it systematically. But subjects who do not possess the concept will not be able to structure the stimuli efficiently; their inadequate concept usage is revealed when they recall the items in an unclustered fashion.

Attempts to study clustering in retarded samples pose some problems (see Spitz 1966). But several findings bear mention:

1. Retarded subjects tend to cluster and to recall less than do CA-equal normals (Stedman 1963).
2. Only where very low MA subjects are included is clustering related to MA or IQ (e.g., Rossi 1963); otherwise no significant relationship emerges.
3. Retarded subjects tend to insert items of a particular category that were not on the list. If this is adjusted, they tend to perform at about the level of equal-MA normals.

Spitz (1966) concluded that retarded subjects appear to use rote memory to recall these lists as opposed to a more systematic organization. Their storage and retrieval systems thus appear to be active but there is little to suggest an efficient input organization at the time of storage.

Will retarded subjects use input organization strategies spontaneously once they have been taught? Spitz and Gerjuoy (Gerjuoy 1967; Gerjuoy & Spitz 1966) suggested an answer to this question when they investigated sorting and clustering in fourteen-year-old institutionalized retarded subjects of two ability levels (high mean IQ = 72.04 and low mean IQ = 52.95).

Of the 20 subjects in each group only 2 of the low-ability sample sorted words by categories, while 14 of the high-ability sample did so—although both groups had been shown how to do so two weeks earlier. When the same words were presented visually in an already clustered format and the subjects were asked to recall the words, there was no difference between the two ability groups—neither group's responses were clustered according to the presented conceptual structure. Gerjuoy and Spitz interpreted this as a reflection of a lack of spontaneous use of these categories, or clusters, since the subjects had possessed the concepts on earlier trials.

Spitz (1966) tested the effect on recall of two procedures used to promote clustering for retarded subjects. First, the list was given with all words in a category *presented clustered* (as opposed to randomly presenting the words). A second procedure presented the words in random order, but when testing for recall the experimenter asked for "all the animals you remember" *(requested clustered)*. Both of these procedures improved the performance of institutionalized retarded subjects significantly over performance under standard procedures. Inducing the retarded subjects to organize the material did have a facilitative effect on recall.

It would appear that retarded children have acquired spontaneous concepts and when prompted to employ them can do so to advantage in organizing material in a hierarchical fashion. But without external prompting retarded subjects appear to resort to inefficient organizational strategies or rote memorization.

Another kind of inefficiency in concept usage that differentiates retarded children from normals of the same mental age concerns the frequency with which they verbally label concepts they have identified (Blount 1968a; Stephens 1966a, 1966b). In one study Blount (1971) reported that while EMR children used the same number of spontaneous concepts as equal-MA normals, the retarded children were less able to verbalize the relationships than were normals.

There are also qualitative differences between the concepts used spontaneously by retarded and normal samples. In general, the retarded have been observed to generate more concrete, as opposed to abstract, concepts (Spreen 1965a, 1965b; Stephens 1972, 1973).

Short-term Memory.   Ellis (1963) originally attributed the weakness of retarded subjects in short-term memory to the rapid deterioration of a *stimulus trace*, a hypothesized brief circuit in the brain. He speculated that the stimulus trace is both briefer and less intense in the retarded, which is characteristic of the generally poor integrity of their central nervous systems. This physiological speculation has not yet been confirmed. Increasingly, researchers are turning to behavioral studies to explain the short-term memory weakness of the retarded.

Investigators have identified inefficiencies in rehearsal strategies by retarded subjects that explain their relatively poor performance on tasks requiring short-term memory (Butterfield, Wambold, & Belmont 1973; Ellis 1970; Frank & Rabinovitch 1974). Mentally retarded persons are not inclined to rehearse spontaneously the information they are attempting to hold. Rehearsal training procedures have been shown to improve the performance of retarded learners (Belmont & Butterfield 1971; Brown, Campione, & Murphy 1974); however, the benefits of such training tend to be rather short-term.

Atkinson and Shiffrin (1968) explained the distinction between structural features and control processes. They hypothesized that information is either lost from short-term memory or transferred to an intermediate status—short-term store—in which information transformation takes place. In short-term store, information can be either forgotten or transferred to a long-term storage area, where it remains more or less permanently. These theorists considered the strategies a person initiates (e.g., schemas, coding techniques, mnemonics) to be crucial to memory, since they are the means by which information is converted from short-term to long-term memory. Glidden (1979) has reviewed the literature on spontaneous strategies used by retarded persons and the effectiveness of training the retarded to use strategies to increase memory. She notes that the techniques used to teach strategies in the laboratory need much work before they can be used in applied settings with durable results.

Rehearsal Strategies.   One means by which information is believed to be remembered for a short time is through the use of various rehearsal strategies. As noted previously, this is also thought to be a means of transferring information from the short-term to the long-term memory. If you ask people how they "think to themselves," they can often be quite specific about how they remember telephone numbers, names of people, capitals of states, and so on. Some people, for instance, remember the lines of the treble clef in music by using the sentence "*Every good boy does fine.*" The normal individual connects stimuli and responses by means of psychological processes that facilitate learning, retention, or understanding. Psychologists refer to these processes as *mediators* because they lead to some psychological activity that mediates between stimuli and responses (as opposed to immediate response to stimuli, like the reflex action of withdrawal from a hot stove). Although imagery has received some attention as a mediator capacity (see Taylor, Josberger, & Knowlton 1972), the most studied of the various types of processes serving this function are verbal mediators, that is, any verbalized means (spoken or silent) to facilitate performance.

We have concluded from the evidence on mediators that when experimenters imposed mediators on preschool-age nonretarded children, they had no major facilitating effect; but by first grade children can be substantially assisted by various strategies (Meyers & MacMillan 1976). Nonretarded children above age fourteen spontaneously use various mediating strategies without being instructed to do so and can be hampered if an unfamiliar strategy is imposed. Retarded children appear to go through the same sequence, although they require more time to do so.

The study of mediators has become involved with an approach to the study of verbal learning called *paired associates learning* (PAL). In this technique two words are typically presented together and then the subject is asked to supply one word when only the other is given. Much verbal learning normally takes this form. If you learn to speak a foreign language, for instance, you may be given a foreign word paired with its English equivalent ("la femme"—"the woman") and then given the foreign word alone and asked what English word it should be paired with.

Prehm (1966), Mordock (1968), and Kaufman and Prehm (1966) discuss how PAL studies and other kinds of verbal learning research can be set up with retarded subjects. The PAL research with retarded subjects has revealed several distinct characteristics. When mildly retarded subjects are equated with normals on the basis of MA, differences in performance appear to be due to differences in the materials used in the research (Cantor & Ryan 1962; Jensen 1965; Ring & Palermo 1961). If the pictures used are easily associated (e.g., toothbrush—comb), the mildly retarded perform comparably with normals; however, if dissimilar objects are associated (e.g., pipe—comb) the performance of the retarded subjects is lower (O'Connor & Hermelin 1963a; Rieber 1964). The most apparent interpretation of these findings is that IQ interacts with meaningfulness of the associational pairs. For lower-IQ children the material must be meaningful and easily associated if their performance is to approach that of normals (Lyman 1963; Spitz 1966).

Mediators have become linked with the PAL research in studies testing the effect of providing mediational aids for retarded PAL subjects (Jensen & Rohwer 1963a, 1963b; MacMillan 1972a; Milgram 1967). It was hypothesized that if the retarded subjects did not spontaneously generate verbal mediators to facilitate retention of an association (e.g., hat—table), then their performance might be facilitated if the experimenter provided a sentence linking together the two words (e.g., The *hat* is on the *table*). According to the evidence from these studies, the hypothesis is true: the retarded subjects do not appear to use organizational strategies spontaneously by generating verbal mediators—or if they are spontaneously generating mediators, they are apparently inefficient ones. But if the experimenter provides the verbal mediators, the retarded tend to be able to use them to advantage. Retarded subjects can even make up their own mediating sentences if the experimenter asks them to do so and they can use these sentences to improve their PAL performance. But their own sentences appear to be less efficacious than those provided by experimenters (MacMillan 1972a; Milgram 1967). Mediating sentences provided by the experimenter have less effect on the performance of normal subjects than of retarded subjects.

In other mediational research, discussed in detail by Heatherington and McIntyre (1975) and Stevenson (1972), some investigators (e.g., Taylor et al. 1972) have recently studied imagery as a mediational tool to facilitate performance. And Turnure and his associates (Turnure, Larsen, & Thurlow 1973; Turnure & Thurlow 1973, 1975; Turnure & Walsh 1971) have studied the effectiveness of various verbal elaboration strategies (compound sentences, complex sentences, paragraphs). They report that the paragraph elaborations result in fewer errors than sentences; more complex linguistic structures in the paragraphs also appear beneficial, especially if the elaboration connecting the pairs is meaningful and reasonable.

Although these approaches have proved successful in facilitating learning in retarded subjects in laboratory situations, as Spitz (1966) has noted it remains to be shown whether it is worthwhile to teach the retarded to use mediational techniques on a continuous basis and whether doing so would improve their general level of performance.

Long-term Memory. Research on long-term retention has been severely criticized by Belmont (1966), who reported that all of the research studies except one had serious methodological flaws. In another review, Prehm and Mayfield (1970) concluded that the retarded are deficient in long-term retention. Detterman (1979) reported that even when retarded persons have information in their long-term memory, they appear less able to make use of it.

Another line of research evidence suggests that although the retarded may take longer to learn a task to the criteria of the experiment, they retain it as well as the nonretarded. The extra learning could consist of the requirement that the retarded overlearn the material to five criteria—that is, perform the task correctly five times rather than once (Vergason 1962). However, the retarded tend to have difficulty selecting which strategy best fits the demands of the task. The strategy that would enable long-term storage may therefore elude the retarded subject. Even if the teacher provides the strategy for the retarded person and overlearning takes place, there is some doubt that the learning will be transferred to situations that are not exactly like the original learning experience (Shif 1969; Spitz 1963). The distinction of importance in this case is between long-term memory and generalization. Retarded individuals appear capable of retaining certain experiences if a training procedure is provided; however, the extent to which they can generalize that experience to somewhat different, new situations seems questionable.

Conclusions about Memory. That the retarded have inefficient memories is evident, but the reasons for this deficiency remain elusive. Belmont and Butterfield (1977) and Campione and Brown (1978) attribute memory problems to a deficiency in the ability to employ appropriate strategies. Even when retarded persons possess the strategies, they tend to be inefficient in selecting the appropriate one to fit the demands of the situation. Despite the similarities in the positions of these writers, their theories differ in some respects. Campione and Brown contend that there may be unalterable structural differences between normal and retarded subjects; Belmont and Butterfield consider this view a position of last resort, to be considered only after all other alternatives have been discredited.

Spitz's Position Regarding Reasoning

After conducting numerous investigations on the learning and memory of the mentally retarded, Spitz (1979) concluded that the distinguishing feature of mental retardation is a deficit in *reasoning*, not learning and memory. Spitz observed that retarded persons are not inclined to use organizational strategies in most novel situations, and that information stored in an unorganized fashion is more difficult to retrieve. In other words, Spitz feels that retardation is most evident in problems involving "thinking and reasoning."

To study the reasoning of the retarded, Spitz (1979) used game problems of logic and strategy. He found that retarded persons not only perform more poorly than CA-equal normals on these tasks, but that they perform substantially below the level of MA-equal normals, who are considerably younger. Spitz notes that retarded subjects can perform higher than college students on tasks requiring stereotyped responses, and that they perform like CA-equal normals on certain other tasks. On logical and reasoning tasks, however, the mentally retarded perform at lower levels than MA-equal normals.

To solve logical problems, a person must be able to use what Spitz (1979) calls *logical foresight*, which is the ability to make "complex correct inferences about the consequences of an act" (p. 134). This ability consists basically in being able to look ahead and consider possible "if–then" conditional situations. Spitz's games required the use of logical foresight; his results suggest that mentally retarded children have an MA lag of from one and a half to four years, depending on the game used. The important point is that, with training, retarded children can use strategies, but when confronted with novel situations they *do not* use them. According to Spitz, the evidence indicates that the results of strategy training are task-specific and of short duration. A pessimistic interpretation of the research on learning and reasoning is that the problems of the retarded are caused, not just by inefficient rehearsal strategies, but by inefficient strategies of many kinds.

Language Behavior

The critical role of language in problem solving and learning has long been recognized. The fact that retarded individuals show weakness in language should come as no surprise given the definition of mental retardation (Sitko & Semmel 1973). The operational definition of mental retardation usually entails some language deficit criterion, and intelligence tests become increasingly weighted with verbal components at the higher levels. Poor academic performance and subaverage intellectual functioning are heavily loaded with language factors. But although difficulty with language causes people to be classified as retarded in the first place, it is possible that these central language problems can be dealt with. Language therefore continues to be a major area of attention in mental retardation, even though it is in language-related areas that retarded individuals are most restricted.

A number of excellent reviews of language behavior in retarded subjects have appeared in the literature, and you are encouraged to consult them for a more intensive treatment of the topic (Blount 1968b; Jordan 1967; Ludlow 1980; Olson 1970; Rosenberg 1970; Sitko & Semmel 1973; Spradlin 1963a).

Language Characteristics. Although much of the earlier work on linguistics and psycholinguistics in the retarded does not reflect contemporary developments, several consistent findings emerge (Sitko & Semmel 1973). There is a higher incidence of speech problems (e.g., articulation, voice), difficulties that are most pronounced in the more severely retarded. Speech problems are found in quite high proportions of samples of institutionalized retarded persons. It is of interest to note that the disorders are of the same kind found in nonretarded populations. In addition to articulation problems Spradlin (1968) identified the following language areas in which the retarded have trouble: limited vocabulary, inadequate auditory discrimination, and poor grammatical structure.

Lenneberg, Nichols, and Rosenberger (1964) monitored the language development of Down's syndrome children over a three-year period and concluded that language develops in retarded children the same way it does in nonretarded children. Its unfolding depends on biological maturation, which follows regular stages (Lenneberg 1967). The difference in the development of language is the *rate* at which it develops in the retarded—it does so more slowly (Rosenberg 1970). The rules of grammar are acquired by the vast majority of retarded persons but again at a slower rate (Graham & Graham 1971). Hence except for the profoundly retarded, the differences in the language of retarded and normal individuals appear to be quantitative rather than qualitative.

Verbal Control of Behavior. Much of the current thinking on the role of language in mental retardation can be traced to the work of the noted

Soviet psychologists Pavlov, Vygotsky, and Luria. It is important to recognize that they define mental retardation, or oligophrenia, as a consequence of pathology of the nervous system and thereby exclude all the mildly retarded and some portion of the moderately retarded who are subsumed under our classification system.

Luria (1959, 1961, 1963) postulates that there are two signaling systems for processing stimuli. The first signaling system consists of direct environmental stimuli whose physical properties (color, shape, size, etc.) can be discerned. As the child gains experience with parents and others, a second signaling system develops—a system using language, which allows for abstraction and conceptualization. Luria (1961) demonstrates how this second signaling system emerges and becomes dominant in normal development and enables active modification of the strength of stimuli bombarding the child. Children were shown the following figures in color:

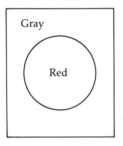 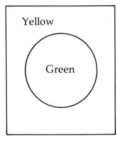 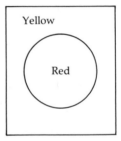

Younger children (CA 3–5) indicated that the circle is the stimulus dimension of greatest force; yet by giving the child verbal instructions the experimenter can enable the weaker component (the background) to predominate by naming its color. For example, in the third figure the experimenter said, "The plane can fly when the sun is shining and the sky is yellow." The background colors were now found to predominate over the central figures. Luria (1961) also demonstrated that there is one point (CA 2½–3 years) when language can *initiate* motor behavior but still cannot serve to *inhibit* the behavior.

Through experimentation Luria has come to characterize the performance of the retarded as follows:

1. Connections between stimuli are acquired more slowly.
2. Responses to verbal signals show more generalizations to words that sound similar (e.g., cat–hat) than to words that have similar meanings (e.g., cap–hat) (Luria & Vinogradova 1959).
3. Retarded subjects demonstrate a deficit in the ability for language to *inhibit* motor behavior, a limiting, regulatory role of language.

The essence of Luria's findings is that the second signaling system is under-developed in retarded persons, particularly as it serves to regulate behavior. Moreover, the verbal and motor systems are dissociated from one another.

An extension of this line of research has been conducted by two British psychologists, O'Connor and Hermelin (1961, 1963b). Their research was designed to explore coding behavior (translation of stimuli from one modality to another without changing the meaning). For example, a subject is presented with an auditory stimulus of three taps of a pencil. The subject is asked to recognize the same stimulus (i.e., three) in either the same modality (auditory) by tapping *once* or in a different, or *cross*, modality (e.g., verbal) by saying *"one."* The evidence of O'Connor and Hermelin suggests that the performance of the severely retarded is facilitated by the cross-modal conditions. If the stimulus and response items were to be in the same-sense modality, the retarded gave more stereotyped responses (i.e., mimicked responses, or three taps instead of the one requested) than when the modalities were different. O'Connor and Hermelin hypothesize that when cross-modal techniques are used, retarded individuals are forced to translate the stimulus from one type of sensory image to another, resulting in a specific association between language and images that improves recognition.

Attempts to replicate the O'Connor and Hermelin results in the United States (Hinshaw & Heal 1968; Lucas 1970) have failed to support the benefits of cross-modal coding. Instead, the *same* modality appeared beneficial if the visual modality was used; presentation and recognition in the auditory modality resulted in the lowest of the same-modality scores.

An interesting finding that parallels rather than duplicates the finding that cross-modal transfer is beneficial to retarded subjects is the discovery that retarded subjects are better than normals at reverse discrimination tasks. In reversal procedures the initial discrimination may be on the basis of color and the second on the basis of size (or some other feature). Retarded subjects learn the reversal more rapidly than normals (Kendler & Kendler 1959; O'Connor & Hermelin 1959), presumably because normals have to extinguish the verbalized set while the retarded subjects do not because they never verbalized the set for the initial discrimination.

After studying the results of the comparative studies on discrimination learning, Denny (1964) drew the following conclusions about the apparent lack of verbal control over motor behavior in retarded subjects:

1. Retarded persons are less inclined to verbalize the discrimination; hence they are able to solve reversals as quickly as, or more quickly than, normals.
2. Retarded persons are less able to inhibit the influence of direct stimuli when the response is to be in the same modality as the stimulus.

3. The effectiveness of verbal instructions that were originally effective fades with time.

It is noteworthy that the research on verbal control of behavior summarized in this section has been restricted to children in the moderate range or lower, while the Soviet work involved only children with pathology. For those who work with children in this range, the research suggests several implications:

1. There is a need to repeat instructions frequently.
2. Children should be encouraged to verbalize what they are doing motorically.
3. With the more profoundly and severely retarded, emphasis should be placed upon language development and relating speech to overt motor behavior.

Language Strategies.   The organizational strategies used by retarded children to process linguistic data, an area that had received scant attention, were studied in 1973 by Sitko and Semmel. They tried to figure out how, under what conditions, and how efficiently the retarded organize linguistic material. Much of Semmel's earlier work (Semmel 1967, 1969; Semmel, Barritt, & Bennett 1970; Semmel, Barritt, Bennett, & Perfetti 1968; Semmel & Bennett 1970) and a 1972 study by Sitko and Semmel tested a hypothesized difference in the strategies used by EMR children to process linguistic information.

Semmel (1967, 1969) contends that there are two principal strategies by which children process linguistic information. The more primitive *sequential-associative*, or *syntagmatic*, strategy is characterized by associations such as dog–bark or red–apple. The association is one that is typical of sequential organizations of words in sentences. Somewhere between six and eight years of age, children of normal intelligence show a shift in their word associations from the sequential-associative type to associations that are alike in their grammatical form class (e.g., dog–cat, red–black). This second kind of strategy is called a *paradigmatic*, or *hierarchical*, strategy. EMR children were found to employ primarily the sequential-associative strategies, while nonretarded children were reported to use both sequential-associative and hierarchical strategies. Sitko and Semmel (1973) write that sequential-associative strategies develop as the result of the child's direct experiences with language. In comparison:

Hierarchical grammatical and semantic strategies are more abstract, frequently taking the form of rules governing the permissible relationships between linguistic units. Because the generality of such strategies makes them more powerful tools for generating and processing language, they are probably related to more proficient language behavior than are sequential-associative strategies.

(p. 228)

Semmel (1967) speculates that this observation does not appear to reflect an incapacity in the linguistic competence of the EMR. Instead, it may be a reflection of something else:

> Perhaps the retarded child operates primarily on the surface structure of language and derives relatively little from the base structure of linguistic constructions. He is therefore relatively more dependent on the frequency of occurrence of linguistic forms and patterns as he experiences them in his natural language environment.

(p. 43)

Strong support for Sitko and Semmel's position comes from two studies with EMR children (Semmel et al. 1968; Semmel et al. 1970). In the first study public school EMR children who were tested on word associations gave fewer paradigmatic associations than did normals of the same CA, while institutionalized retarded subjects gave the fewest paradigmatic associations. Public school EMR and normal subjects equated on MA were similar in their paradigmatic responses. In the second study the same subjects were given four-word sentences with a word deleted at various positions in the sentence (this method of testing is called the *cloze procedure*; e.g., The boy _____ home. The boy ran _____.) Given the tendency of retarded children to use sequential-associative strategies, it was predicted that the EMR children would do best when the blank was at the end of the sentence. The words preceding the blank should cue their strategies, so that the solution would be less dependent on grammatical cues. This prediction was confirmed, with EMRs doing as well as equal-MA normals in completing blanks at the ends of sentences.

From their research on linguistic strategies Sitko and Semmel (1973) have drawn tentative conclusions for teaching the retarded:

1. It may be more useful to group EMR children for instruction according to organizational and processing characteristics than to use existing global psychometric variables (e.g., MA).
2. Teachers might try to modify the sequential-associative strategy by attempting to move the child toward hierarchical strategies. This might help to increase memory capacity.
3. Present approaches to teaching reading to EMR children (e.g., the phonic analysis approach) ignore the communicative nature of read-

ing and the relevance of the linguistic context—elements that are especially important to children who cannot yet deal with isolated words as embodiments of grammatical concepts.

4. As Agard (1971) has suggested, the underlying competence for developing hierarchical strategies is available in EMR children but is not being used.

Implications of the Learning Research

In general, the research on the learning and performance of the retarded suggests that they are slower at mastering tasks than children of average and above-average intelligence. However, the differences that appear tend to be quantitative rather than qualitative, and when organizational strategies are provided, retarded individuals (except the profoundly retarded) tend to benefit. The research thus supports Zigler's (1969) developmental position more than it supports a difference or defect model.

A major factor that emerges in studies of a variety of learning tasks is the apparently inefficient use of language by retarded children as an aid to problem solving. The language of the retarded, while adequate for communication, lacks an appreciation or awareness of deep structure—concepts seem less embellished, hierarchical organization appears limited, language and motor behavior appear dissociated. Retarded children are not inclined to use verbal strategies spontaneously to organize input or to mediate responses.

Despite the learning inefficiencies that show up in retarded children, the fact that they are capable of improving their performance if certain strategies are provided makes the outlook for teaching retarded children an optimistic one. Although few attempts (e.g., Agard 1971) have been made to bridge the gap between basic research and pedagogical application, we at least have some general principles to go by. Clarke (1958), for instance, gives a list of principles for working with retarded subjects below IQ 50 that may be useful with children above IQ 50 as well:

1. Make available the appropriate incentives and goals.
2. Break up tasks into components, which should be taught separately but in sequence.
3. Require correct responses prior to teaching the subsequent component in the sequence.
4. Use distributed practice rather than massed practice.
5. Use overlearning by means of thorough practice beyond initial mastery.
6. Encourage children to verbalize their behavior while making the response.

7. In the initial stages of learning, stress accuracy rather than speed.
8. Carefully organize for the child the material to be taught.

SCHOOL LEARNING

It is easier to grasp the notion that information should be carefully organized for retarded students than it is to know *how* to organize specific learning units for them. In teaching a social studies unit on the local community, for instance, which pieces of information should be taught? What organizational scheme should be used? We should be very cautious in generalizing from basic research studies of learning in retarded children to making specific classroom decisions about what should be taught and how. On the other hand, we should be sensitive to material that does lend itself to organization in order to assist children to see ways in which they can organize material or else to organize it for them. And at least in two content areas—reading and arithmetic—there are some scraps of research evidence on the most effective ways of teaching retarded children.

Reading

Not surprisingly, teaching reading to retarded children has received the most attention. As we have seen, difficulty in using language as a learning tool is often the basis for their poor academic performance. If reading disability is defined as a discrepancy between actual and expected level of achievement, then it is apparent that reading disabilities are at least as serious a problem with mentally retarded learners as with nonhandicapped learners. DeHirsch, Jansky, and Langford (1966) estimated that the incidence of reading problems in the general school population was approximately 30 percent. Kirk (1940) estimated that reading problems are at least as prevalent among the mentally retarded.

In this section we will consider several basic questions in teaching reading to mentally retarded children. First, which retarded children can, or should, be taught reading? Second, how great is the discrepancy between actual and expected reading achievement, based on the mental age of the child? And third, what methods are most effective in teaching reading to the mentally retarded?

Who Should Be Taught to Read?   While it may be possible to promote mechanical reading in a sizeable proportion of the mentally retarded, it is debatable whether the time and energy required in some cases is as well spent on reading as on developing social and vocational skills. Such a position was summarized by Gunzburg (1965) as follows: "It is realized that mastery of reading or spelling results very often in the acquisition of a meaningless skill which cannot be put to good use because of the trainee's mental limitations and that teaching time is out of proportion to results" (p. 331). This observation is particularly germane to the education of TMR children, for whom skills other than reading are more critical to their independent functioning as adults. On the other hand, the EMR population appears quite capable of reading. For those who do not learn to read, Dunn and Capobianco (1954) have noted that it appears that failure to learn to read mechanically is, in most cases, more dependent on the lack of motivation, drive, persistence, adequate teaching, etc. than on intelligence, once a minimal IQ of, say, 50 has been established.

Even children below IQ 50 can learn to read at least the cautionary signs needed for their own protection or for independent functioning in the community (e.g., stop, exit, men, women). Higher levels of reading are to be expected for EMR students, with Kirk (1940) providing the following guidelines by IQ levels: IQ 50–59 will achieve between first- and third-grade levels; 60–69 between second- and fourth-grade levels; and 70–79 between third- and seventh-grade levels. These expectations should be considered as only crude guidelines, for children with lower IQs than 50 have been found to read as long as the material was meaningful and familiar to them (Gunzburg 1965). Gunzburg (1970) has noted that practically all the research on reading in the mentally retarded is concerned with developing the mechanical skills of reading; reading comprehension has received much less consideration. He observed that more effort has been devoted to promoting "barking at print" or simply recognizing words, with less effort directed at developing comprehension skills.

It appears reasonable to conclude that reading can, and should, be taught to EMR students and probably should take a rather high priority in the EMR curriculum. For TMR children, consideration should be given to individual cases. In deciding where to place curricular emphasis, the belief that all children should be taught to the limits of their capacity should be weighed against the costs. If undue time is devoted to reading it will be at the expense of teaching other skills that might be of greater importance to the adult adjustment of the specific child.

Reading Achievement.   The extent to which retarded children read up to their capacity has achieved considerable research attention over the years. Dunn and Capobianco (1954) analyzed eleven studies that related reading achievement to mental age and concluded that, in general, mentally retarded children in special classes read below mental age expectation. But in three studies the subjects read at, or above, expectation, leading Dunn to believe that if special attention is given to reading skills in EMR children, we might anticipate their achievement in reading to be at or beyond their mental age.

Research suggests that for mentally retarded children, progress in reading is related to the emphasis placed on reading in the curriculum. Dunn and Capobianco found the conclusions of the research on the rate of progress to be conflicting. But they observed that under typical conditions the rate of progress in reading parallels the progress made in the growth of mental age. This is approximately three-fourths of the rate of an average-ability child, or three-fourths of a school grade on a test of achievement in one year's time. But when mentally retarded students are given intensive instruction, rather marked initial gains have been noted. Dunn and Capobianco observed that as reading age begins to exceed mental age, the rate of this progress might be expected to cease.

When Kirk (1964) compared the findings on the relative achievement of mentally retarded children to that of average and gifted children, he concluded that the retarded children achieve closer to their mental age than do superior children. He interpreted this finding as a result of the fact that superior children are not pressured to achieve up to their capacity since, on the basis of their chronological age, they are already accelerated.

After a review of the same literature, Quay (1963) reached a different conclusion. She concluded that the actual achievement of retarded children is different from what one would predict on the basis of mental age. This discrepancy occurred in all areas of study except arithmetic computation. In drawing inferences from these studies, Quay (1963) wrote:

> A tentative conclusion based on a synthesis of these results is that a relationship exists between type of placement and achievement discrepancies. Institutionalized retardates tend to show retardation in all academic areas; special-class retardates show no retardation on arithmetic computation but are retarded in all other skill areas. Regular-class retardates show no academic retardation except, as shown by one study, in some areas of reading comprehension.
>
> (p. 681)

It is important to realize that such findings may be due largely to the curricular emphases in these settings. That is, the curriculum for retarded children in regular grades emphasized tool subjects such as reading and arithmetic. In the special class at the time of the studies, the curriculum emphasized social and prevocational skills (see Chapter 12). Children in institutions may not have received any educational programing. The point is that the curriculum a child is taking will influence in which areas the child performs well.

Methods of Teaching Reading. No conclusive answer can yet be given to the question of how to teach reading to mentally retarded children. Kirk (1964) wrote:

> The research on teaching methods has not clearly demonstrated the superiority of one method over another. The phonic method has its advocates, while

others report success with varied methods. It is likely that the enthusiasm of the experimenter for one method is a determining variable. It is also likely that retarded children can learn by various modes of presentation, provided the methods are presented systematically and enthusiastically.

(p. 79)

Pope and Haklay (1970) contrasted the "sight-word" approach with techniques that emphasize sound and symbol, such as linguistic and phonic methods. While research evidence fails to demonstrate the advantage of one over the other for use with mentally retarded children, Chall (1967) concluded that approaches relating sound to symbol would be preferable for use with children from low socioeconomic status backgrounds (a very common situation for EMR children). The sight-word approach requires children to figure out words, and children from deprived backgrounds will not have other books or adults around to assist them when they have difficulty with a word.

In addition to the two major approaches described above, Kirk (1933) achieved an equally rapid learning rate with the kinesthetic approach (described in detail by Fernald in 1943) as with a sight method for teaching word recognition. And he found that the kinesthetic approach resulted in considerably better retention. Sentiment seems to favor the phonic approach and other methods that emphasize decoding, but as Kirk (1964) noted, there is no conclusive evidence of its superiority. It is interesting to note that the conclusion drawn in the section on learning research—that there is not a qualitative difference in the learning of the EMR—is apparently valid here as well. The teaching methods used with normals are equally applicable to EMR students and all appear to be viable, particularly if the instructor is enthusiastic in the belief that they will succeed. But there is a need for additional research that goes beyond the mechanical aspects of reading and concerns itself with comprehension (Pope & Haklay 1970).

Arithmetic

Compared to reading, far less research has been conducted on the arithmetic abilities of the mentally retarded. Yet arithmetic skills are essential for the TMR as well as the EMR if they are to function independently in society. An adult in this society must be able to tell time, determine comparative sizes, and understand monetary values. Nevertheless, there is little educational research pertaining to the teaching of arithmetic skills to the retarded. What has been studied can be subdivided into the relationship between mental age and arithmetic achievement and processes, and the efficacy of methods of teaching arithmetic.

Arithmetic Achievement and Processes. The research evidence indicates that in arithmetic *computation* mentally retarded individuals achieve close to their mental age (Cruickshank 1948b, 1948c; Dunn & Capobianco 1954). But in arithmetic *reasoning*, when compared to normal students of comparable mental age, retarded subjects are considerably behind their mental age peers. Dunn and Capobianco point out that arithmetic reasoning depends on both reading and reasoning, two areas of difficulty for the mentally retarded.

Kirk (1964) reviewed the literature on arithmetic processes and observed that the differences that do emerge might be as much due to teaching and testing methods as to differences between mentally retarded and nonretarded subjects. One widely cited study (Cruickshank 1948c) compared normal subjects to mentally retarded subjects on three different kinds of problems. In the first type of problem, the necessary facts for the solution of the problem were embedded in superfluous information. The second type of problem contained only the necessary facts for the solution in verbal form; the third type of problem consisted of the computational facts (e.g., 3×4 =). The retarded students did significantly worse on the first two types of problems, but on the third type—in which computational facts alone were presented—the retarded students performed much like the normal subjects. As mentioned earlier, the first two types of problems involve both reading and reasoning, and the poorer performance by the retarded subjects could be due to either factor. In examining the behaviors of retarded students as they tried to solve math problems, Cruickshank (1948a) reported that they exhibited an excess of primitive habits (e.g., counting on their fingers), made careless mistakes, and committed errors in reading as they went about solving arithmetic problems.

One other line of research on the arithmetic performance of the mentally retarded showed some rather surprising results. Comparisons of brain-damaged and non-brain-damaged retarded subjects fail to reveal any systematic differences (Kirk 1964). Although there is a widespread belief that brain-damaged individuals have perceptual problems and problems in abstract reasoning, the logical conclusion that they would exhibit more problems in arithmetic is simply not supported by the evidence.

Methods of Teaching Arithmetic.   Evidence on the efficacy of various means of teaching arithmetic is almost nonexistent. Kirk (1964) reported one study (Costello 1941) comparing three methods of teaching arithmetic: (1) an experience method, (2) an adaptation of the Montessori techniques, and (3) a conventional approach (verbal presentation). The experience method resulted in the greatest gains, followed by the Montessori method and the conventional method, in that order.

If students are to achieve adequate number concepts, they apparently need to develop a number vocabulary linked to situations they will encounter in everyday life (Cruickshank 1946; Silverstein, Auger, & Krudis 1964). For example, they need a vocabulary dealing with length, weight, volume, and time. While the development of these vocabulary terms as prerequisites to computation or reasoning problems has not been evaluated, we might speculate that mastery of such terms could minimize the inefficiency exhibited by retarded subjects on reasoning tasks.

Brown and Dyer (1963) compared teaching arithmetic by applying it to a work situation to conventional teaching methods. They reported that the group taught mathematical concepts in the work situation made significant increases. These findings correlate with Costello's (1941) findings that the experience method, in which arithmetic was taught through real life situations, was most effective.

Based on these very few studies, it seems desirable to teach arithmetic in a fashion that facilitates transfer to the real life situations in which the retarded child will have to apply these skills. Nevertheless, the evidence is so limited that any conclusions at this time are hazardous.

USING LEARNING THEORIES WITH RETARDED STUDENTS

The learning of the retarded generally follows the same principles as the learning of the nonretarded, so it seems practical to consider several theories of learning that may be useful guides to teaching retarded students. Mercer and Snell (1977) examined a number of learning theories and tried to draw from them concrete suggestions for teaching. Some theories, such as operant behaviorism, had many specific implications for teaching; others, such as social learning theory, led to very few concrete suggestions.

We have grouped a number of current theories under the rubrics of operant behaviorism, cognitive-developmental theories, and social learning theory (Meyers & MacMillan 1976). This grouping combines specific theorists who share similar theoretical postures on learning but who emphasize slightly different dimensions in learning. In addition to discussing these three theories, we will also look at the theory of observational learning. After each theory is examined, its implications for work with retarded persons will be discussed.

No one theory accounts for all types of learning. Certain theories are appropriate for explaining certain forms of learning. For example, operant behaviorism appears to be the most appropriate learning model to explain (and suggest procedures for teaching) those learning tasks that are readily sequenced and for which the response made by the child can be readily defined. Teaching children to sit at their desks, for instance, is better explained by operant theory than by one of the cognitive theories. On the other hand, more complex abstract learning (e.g., learning the law of gravity) is less well explained by operant theory. There are internal mental operations that mediate between a particular stimulus and a response, a process that is posited by cognitive theorists but ignored by operant theorists.

We cannot uncritically apply a single theory to all forms of learning and expect it to be equally appropriate. Scholars in children's learning have based their conclusions upon selected research, often research that involved the specific form of learning with which they were concerned. For the practitioner trying to apply these theories to children it is essential first to analyze the type of learning desired (e.g., sensorimotor, habit skills, conceptual tasks) and then look to the various theories to determine which theory best explains the particular form of learning involved. For teaching complex sequences, as would be involved in toilet training, athletic skills, or dressing behaviors, the operant approach described by Skinner (1953) appears most appropriate. But in developing hierarchical concepts, one of the cognitive-developmental theories would probably be preferable to operant behaviorism.

Operant Behaviorism

By far the most influential theory of learning in the field of mental retardation is operant theory. It began with the work of Skinner (1938), evolving through several transitional stages (MacMillan & Morrison 1980) to the form in which it is currently used in the education of retarded and other handicapped children. The operant theory has influenced general educational practices with retarded children (MacMillan & Morrison 1979) and has been applied effectively in the education and treatment of the severely and profoundly retarded (Schroeder, Mulick, & Schroeder 1979; Whitman & Scibak 1979), especially in the development of self-help skills and attempts to terminate self-destructive behavior. The most ambitious extension of this approach was Bijou's (1966) attempt to explain mental retardation in terms of operant constructs.

Concepts in Operant Behaviorism. Operant theory hinges on the description of the relationship between the behavior of the individual (i.e., *responses*) and environmental events (i.e., *stimuli*) that exert control over the responses made by the individual. According to operant behaviorists, there is no need for positing intervening variables such as mind or internal states of the individual unless they can be measured in some objective manner.

Stimuli are differentiated in terms of their function (how they exert control over responses). Some stimuli precede the response in the temporal relationship and exert control over the response. Stated differently, in the presence of certain stimuli (called *discriminative stimuli*), a particular response is more probable than it would be in the absence of those stimuli. For example, the chain of responses required to make an automobile go into motion are more probable in the presence of a green traffic light than in the presence of a red light. The green light is said to be a discriminative stimulus in that it cues the individual that a particular response or set of responses is appropriate. A major problem in mental retardation is that while the retarded person can make a desired response, the response is often not under the control of the appropriate discriminative stimuli. The task of the teacher, then, is to bring the response under the control of appropriate discriminative stimuli and to lessen the probability of its occurrence in the presence of inappropriate preceding stimuli.

The major attention of applied behaviorists has been given to stimuli that *follow* responses. According to the law of effect, a response will be strengthened or weakened as a result of the consequences it has on its environment. Behaviors that lead to consequences that are desirable will be strengthened, while those that lead to consequences that are undesirable to the individual will be weakened. The function of the consequence can only be determined by its effect on the behavior it follows, not on the basis of what the teacher thinks the consequence will do to the behavior. Three types of consequences can be identified: (1) reinforcing stimuli, (2) punishing stimuli, and (3) neutral stimuli. These effects can take several forms. Following a response, some environmental event (stimulus) is presented, which may do one of four things:

1. Strengthen the response it follows, because it is a pleasant or desired stimulus; this stimulus is said to be a *positive reinforcer.*
2. Lead to the termination of a noxious stimulus, and hence serve to strengthen the response it follows; this stimulus is said to be a *negative reinforcer.*
3. Lead to the presentation of a noxious stimulus, which serves to weaken the response it follows; this stimulus is a form of *punishment.*
4. Lead to the withdrawal of a desired stimulus, which serves to weaken the response it follows; this stimulus is another form of *punishment.*

A fifth kind of effect can be called a *lack of function.* This occurs when a *neutral* stimulus follows a behavior and has no effect on either weakening or strengthening it.

In addition to the antecedent stimuli, the response, and the consequences that follow responses, behaviorists are concerned with the *contingencies* that interrelate these three elements. Contingencies are the conditions under which a specific consequence will be presented. They are planned by the individual in control of the situation, who decides what discriminative stimuli and what acceptable response must be present before the planned consequence will be given (either reinforcing or punishing). When behaviorists analyze and manipulate the environment in an attempt to modify behavior (the response), they explicitly control both stimuli and consequences to shape the desired response. They thus pay attention to both the elements that precede and the elements that follow the response:

discriminative stimuli → response → consequences

For a more detailed discussion of the concepts of operant behaviorism, you can consult Bijou and Baer (1961), MacMillan (1973a), and Reynolds (1968).

Application to Mental Retardation.   Operant behaviorists view mental retardation somewhat differently than do cognitive theorists. They reject traditional categories, considerations of etiology, and circular explanations for poor performance (e.g., it is because the child is mentally retarded). Instead they view limited behavior or poor performance in terms of the child's faulty previous learning or lack of learning and go about manipulating the environment in such a way as to foster learning.

In an attempt to foster appropriate learning, behaviorists attempt to (1) provide the right situational cues, thereby increasing the likelihood of the desired response, (2) select consequences that are effective for that individual child, and (3) relate the stimuli to the desired response by exerting control over these contingencies. Since the control of contingencies is the key to a successful behavior modification program, the term *contingency management* is used to describe the role played by the teacher or therapist.

Possibly the healthiest element in behaviorism is the behaviorists' unwillingness to set limits on what can be learned by a retarded child. In the new behavior modification programs we see severely retarded children learning things that were thought ten years ago to be beyond their capabilities. The behaviorists view a lack of learning not as a problem within the child but as a reflection of the tutorial inadequacies of the individual designing the intervention.

Implications.   This description oversimplifies the concepts and intricacies involved in operant behaviorism, and you are encouraged to go into greater depth in one of the suggested sources. But our review should provide sufficient detail to allow you to consider how you would proceed with teaching the mentally retarded from the operant point of view in order to maximize learning.

The following guidelines are a result of some of the implications that would flow from this theoretical orientation:

1. Consistently present situational cues that control the desired classes of responses (i.e., attention to the teacher) in order to facilitate learning.
2. Identify consequences that are effective for individual children and avoid the assumption that a certain stimulus (e.g., praise) will be universally successful with all children.
3. Make these effective consequences contingent upon the response's meeting a predetermined standard. In the early stages of learning you may wish to reinforce a gross approximation of the goal behavior. However, gradually require closer and closer approximations to the goal behavior prior to giving the reinforcer. This approach gets at the

heart of taking children from where they are and moving them to
more acceptable levels of performance. Just as the sculptor shapes a
final product from a hunk of clay, the teacher shapes polished behaviors from very crude approximations.
4. Reinforce even slight improvement; you should not wait for perfec-
   tion before delivering reinforcement.
5. Identify activities that a child enjoys, which can then be used as reinforcers for behaviors that you want but that the child is less inclined
   to perform (Premack 1959).
6. Deliver consequences promptly after the behavior is emitted, particularly in the early stages of learning.

The teacher within the behavioristic framework is continuously
involved in research. The paradigm is provided, but the teacher must constantly analyze the relationship between responses and environmental
stimuli to determine whether a particular consequence is exerting the
desired effect over the response, whether the response is being controlled
by the desired discriminative stimuli, whether the steps involved in shaping more complex behavior are too small or too large, and whether adjustments need to be made. These elements must constantly be reevaluated as
a behavioral intervention program is going on.

In Chapter 12 we will consider some of the specific behavioristic programs that have been used with retarded individuals in attempts to develop
self-help skills, to reduce self-destructive behavior, and to modify classroom
behaviors.

Piaget's Cognitive-Developmental Theory

Cognitive-developmental theorists view children quite differently than
operant behaviorists, primarily because they emphasize the processes performed by the individual. That is, the cognitive-developmental theorist
attributes to the learner the ability to make generalizations, inferences, discoveries, and transformations. As a result, a teacher operating from this perspective will promote learning in a fashion far different from the operant
behaviorist, who views the child as a responder to appropriate stimuli. The
teacher using a cognitive-developmental approach guides the child and
provides opportunities for discovery of principles and insights.

The cognitive theorist places importance on the environment but would
argue that mental development undergoes a self-directed growth:

Development is dependent upon experience; practice does not necessarily
accelerate it but lack of an environment suited to the stage of the learner will
handicap it. Growth is marked by stages which occur in an inexorable

sequence, each a necessary prelude to the next and absorbed into the next. The pace of growth will vary among children for both natural and cultural reasons.

(Meyers & MacMillan 1976)

Piaget contends that mental development occurs as a natural interactive process of the child with the environment—every experience is one in which the child copes with adaptation. In fact, Piaget characterizes intelligence as an adaptive process wherein the child is forced to adapt to situational reality while the environment is at the same time being modified by the structure the child imposes on it (see Flavell 1963; Hunt 1961; Piaget 1950; or Piaget & Inhelder 1969 for extended discussions of the theory).

Concepts in Piaget's Theory. Two processes are central to Piaget's theory: *assimilation* and *accommodation*. Assimilation refers to the adaptation of the environment, or the child's perception of the environment, to the child's existing system. A person can only understand or interpret the environment in terms of existing mental structures, and novel experiences are more or less forced into these systems. The complementary process, accommodation, refers to the necessary adaptation of existing mental structures to reality. Existing mental structures are never so flexible as to allow infinite amounts of assimilation, so it is necessary that these mental structures be modified in light of new experiences. In every intellectual act, both assimilation and accommodation operate. They serve to enrich or broaden existing mental structures as well as to force the individual to develop new mental structures when existing ones cannot account for a new experience.

Since adaptation gets out of equilibrium because of new experiences and challenges perceived by the child, the continuous development due to assimilation and accommodation is called the *equilibration process*. The child is constantly stirred by new challenges perceived within the level of competence. The child masters these challenges, increasing competence to a point where still higher-level challenges are brought within the realm of the child's abilities. *Equilibrium* exists when the processes of assimilation and accommodation are in balance—the individual and the environment are interacting without either one predominating. For example, children's play activities often represent assimilation situations in which the child forces reality to fit existing mental structures (a stone is a ball, a stick a gun). But when children imitate (talking like a movie star, carrying a football like O. J. Simpson), the process of accommodation dominates. In either case there is a lack of equilibrium since either assimilation or accommodation predominates.

In Piaget's theory the behavior pattern, or *schema*, is used as the unit of analysis; schemas are seen as the structures of the individual's mental equipment. But although schemas are defined in behavioral terms, Piaget does not specifically exclude underlying structures that control the behaviors. Schemas are characterized by their tendency to be repeated when the individual is confronted with a similar situation; the more they are repeated or rehearsed, the better integrated, more stable, and more enduring they become. Another characteristic of schemas is their tendency to interlock or combine with one another to form more complex schemas. When an infant begins to look for things heard, for instance, the infant is coordinating visual and auditory schemas. Woodward (1963) noted how total reorganization of schemas occurs, wherein some that were independent are combined or coordinated while others become more differentiated and are later recombined.

Application to Mental Retardation.   Inhelder (1968) and Woodward (1963, 1979) attempted to relate Piaget's theory to mental retardation. They noted that Piaget's orientation shifts attention from what the retarded cannot do to what they are doing. After reviewing the research on the application of Piaget's theory to retarded subjects, Weisz and Zigler (1979) concluded that the mentally retarded pass through the same stages of development in the same order as normals, albeit at a slower pace. Thus, the age at which retarded children reach the Piagetian stages will be later than for normals, and any age-specific expectations will need to be adjusted. The rate of progress is determined by the degree of retardation; more severely retarded persons will reach a particular stage at a later age than the less severely retarded. Nevertheless, it is still important to provide the retarded with an environment that allows them to interact with people and objects on a level appropriate to their stage of development.

One hypothesis advanced is that the ultimate stage achieved in the Piagetian scheme may be a function of the level of retardation. Profoundly retarded persons, for instance, may never achieve above the sensorimotor stage. Inhelder (1968) suggested the following scheme for equating the ultimate developmental level with the classification level:

a. *Severely and profoundly retarded:* fixate at sensorimotor stage
b. *Moderately retarded:* fixate at preoperational intuitive stage
c. *Mildly retarded:* fixate at concrete operations stage
d. *IQ 70 to 85:* will only be capable of the simpler forms of formal operations

Piagetian theory has also provided the basis for the development of assessment instruments for very young children (Uzgiris & Hunt 1975). These instruments have been used with some success with the severely and profoundly retarded (Wachs & DeRemer 1978). Wachs and DeRemer found that object permanence and foresight on the Piagetian tasks were reliably related to self-help skills, an important component of adaptive behavior.

An extensive longitudinal study at Temple University compared EMR children (IQs of 50–75) and normals on a variety of Piagetian tasks (Stephens, Mahaney, & McLaughlin 1972; Stephens, McLaughlin, Hunt, Mahaney, Kohlberg, Moore, & Aronfreed 1974). The retarded subjects showed very minor deficiencies on some moral judgement items, but performance on the other items was the same for retarded and nonretarded subjects. On the measures of cognitive development, the retarded and nonretarded subjects progressed at similar rates.

Some tentative evidence (Carlson & MacMillan 1970; MacMillan & Carlson 1971; MacMillan & Lucas 1971) may suggest qualitative differences in the veracity of the schemas of the retarded. Compared to normal children, retarded children appear to establish schemas that they are less able to articulate and that are more susceptible to countersuggestion by the experimenter. This may suggest the impact of a less well developed verbal system on Piagetian measures.

Implications. Operating from a Piagetian orientation, several recommendations are offered to maximize the learning of the retarded. Remember that in this theory, development is attained by children on their own terms; rather than teaching directly the teacher provides materials with which the child can interact. While Piaget is opposed to theories that regard the child as a passive receptor of environmental stimuli, he is equally opposed to maturational theories that ignore the importance of experience (Woodward 1979). Some direct implications are as follows:

1. In theory, there is no problem in motivation. Since children select their activities in terms of what is challenging to them, there is no need for extrinsic reinforcement.
2. A child is always prepared to learn something. But it is important to assess a child's readiness to learn a specific task, as we do not want to push too early or too fast.
3. When a child is found to be performing at a particular developmental stage, we should provide the objects that allow the child the opportunity to develop the schema.
4. Social interactions are of great importance. Adults influence the development of concepts and reasoning by way of the feedback they provide in affirming or denying the statements of the child. Similarly, interaction with peers represents a chance to compare one's ideas to those of others, noting similarities and differences.
5. While a Piagetian purist would oppose any attempt to hurry children through stages, other cognitive theorists (e.g., Bruner 1966; Gagne 1965) would structure activities in an attempt to promote more rapid development.
6. In selecting instructional objectives and activities, we should present children with opportunities to manipulate physical and social reality

in order to anticipate what would happen if certain changes occurred—e.g., require the child to reverse a process (if 3 + 4 = 7, what is 7 − 3?); have the child classify and order objects according to different dimensions (height, then color, function, and so forth). Excellent readings on this point are provided by Furth (1970) and Schwebel and Raph (1973).

7. Curricula should be planned in a manner that places specific content at appropriate grade levels, and experiences should be carefully planned and ordered within subject areas. The overall curriculum should reflect the idea that:

Behavior patterns of type A, when coordinated, differentiated, and recombined through activities with objects, can give rise only to behavior patterns of type B; these in turn can develop only into those of type C.

(Woodward 1963, p. 299)

Social Learning Theory

Several different movements use the title "social learning theory," but they all emphasize the social context in which learning takes place and highlight the importance of the evaluation of one's performance by *significant others* (e.g., parents, peers, and teachers). In classroom situations the social learning theorist would emphasize pupil–pupil interactions and pupil–teacher interactions rather than instructional strategies. Focus would be placed on the manner in which others reinforce or punish responses.

It is interesting to note the imposition of external criteria for success that so often occurs in a classroom. Before entering school, and in activities outside of school, children participate in activities that are noncompetitive. When children roller-skate or ride bicycles they set their own criteria for success. However, if a child agrees to a bike race with a friend, there is a new criterion for success, and it is imposed externally. In the first instance failure is not terribly damaging, as the child can revise criteria or shift activities. However, criteria are not easily revised when they are externally imposed.

Concepts in Social Learning Theory. We will consider here the social learning theory (SLT) of Rotter (1954), particularly as applied to the mentally retarded by Cromwell (1963) and Mercer and Snell (1977). This theory assumes that a person's interactions with a meaningful environment are directional in nature: the person moves toward objects (*approach behavior*) or away from objects (*avoidance behavior*).

The basis for approach and avoidance behavior changes with age. Cromwell (1963) postulated different motivational systems dominant at various stages. The earliest one is a hedonistic system, in which the child approaches objects that are associated with pleasurable events and avoids objects and situations that have been associated with noxious objects or events. In Cromwell's terms this motivational system is called the *pleasure-approach and pain-avoidance system*. Gradually this system is superseded by a more mature system wherein the child exhibits approach behavior not so much to gain pleasure but to demonstrate competence or effectiveness. Avoidance behaviors in this more mature system are carried out with the intent of avoiding situations in which behavioral competence is threatened. Cromwell terms this latter motivational system the *success-approach and fail-ure-avoidance* (SA-FA) *system*.

Before children can conceptualize success or failure, however, they must perceive themselves in control of event outcomes, as opposed to seeing event outcomes as the result of chance or fate. Bialer (1960) constructed a measure of what he called *locus of control* that tapped the extent to which individuals see themselves in control of events around them (internal locus of control) or see event outcomes as being decided by chance or fate (external locus of control). With increased CA and MA, individuals come to exhibit an increasing internal locus of control.

One concept of the social learning theory that is especially applicable to mental retardation is the concept of *expectation* of success. There are two kinds of expectation: (1) *situational expectation*, developed through reinforcement in the specific situation under study, and (2) *generalized expectation*, developed from reinforcement in other situations and generalized to the situation under study. Because of the frequency with which retarded persons fail in varied situations, we would anticipate that they would hold a low generalized expectation unless their environments have been adapted to prevent failure experiences.

The final concept we will consider in social learning theory is that behaviors are interrelated and sometimes interchangeable. Rotter (1954) noted that distinctly different behaviors may be emitted in an attempt to attain the same goal or reinforcement. One behavior may be substituted for another if each leads to the same goal (such as love or affection). The probability that an individual will exhibit a specific behavior depends on the perception of whether that behavior will obtain the goal.

Application to Mental Retardation.   The most comprehensive reviews of research applications of social learning theory to retarded subjects are those of Cromwell (1963) and Mercer and Snell (1977). Although these reviewers generally concede that retarded persons appear to have a higher generalized expectation of failure, the evidence supporting this assumption is not completely conclusive. Nevertheless, expectations for children are often based on chronological age or appearance—on how old they look. As a result, societal expectations of the retarded are usually too high, and retarded children experience a series of failures. This history of failure is thought to be reflected in a higher avoidance tendency than that which occurs among nonretarded children. This belief, buttressed by some tentative research findings, led Cromwell (1963) to postulate the SA-FA motivational system, in which the retarded are characterized as "failure-avoiders." It is important to recognize that it is the excess of failure typically encountered by retarded children that accounts for their higher generalized expectation of failure, avoidance behavior, and the like. These characteristics are *not* inherent in the condition of mental retardation. In fact, children of normal intelligence who fail excessively for reasons other than lowered intellect (such as learning disabilities) would be expected to show similar characteristics.

Retarded children shift from the hedonistic motivational system to the SA-FA motivational system at a later chronological age than do normals; they also exhibit an external locus of control for a longer time than do normals. Some of the research reviewed by Cromwell (e.g., Gardner 1958; Heber 1957) suggests that for normal children mild degrees of failure tend to result in increased effort; retarded subjects, on the other hand, do not increase their effort after mild failure. However, experimental failure may not be perceived as failure by retarded subjects. For example, while to the experimenter a test score of 60 percent wrong is failure, the retarded child may see it as success since this child seldom has gotten 40 percent correct on similar tasks. In fact, since the same degree of failure may be perceived quite differently by children with markedly different histories of failure (e.g., retarded and gifted children), mild failure may be more disruptive to gifted than retarded children because it contrasts with their general experiences.

A major concern with retarded children is that they use an excess of energy in avoidance behavior. After repeated failure in socially imposed tasks, the child can resort to (1) noninvolvement, (2) token observance of tasks, or (3) reducing the sense of failure by not competing. Note that each of these avoidance behaviors is an impediment to cognitive growth in the Piagetian scheme described earlier. Instead of attempting tasks that are challenging (i.e., those that require adaptation), the retarded child avoids such tasks and experiences if they are perceived as sources of potential failure. The initial deficit is thereby compounded, resulting in a cumulative deficit phenomenon similar to that described for culturally different youngsters.

Implications.   While social learning theory does not bear directly on how instruction should proceed, it has very definite implications for structuring the social milieu in which the instruction would take place:

1. Teachers and parents should maintain a fundamental optimism toward retarded children. They should structure situations so that the

failure set of these children can be reversed or at least neutralized, attempting to maximize success for the child and providing immediate interpersonal support if the child fails.

2. Care should be exercised in the selection of tasks for the child, with the intent of assuring a high probability of success. Additional devices—such as the use of prompting techniques—heighten the chances of success.

3. Parents and teachers should remain sensitive to their own expectations for the retarded child lest they come to expect failure and inadvertently communicate it to the child. They might do so either in an affective sense or through setting trivial goals for the child.

4. Teachers should be alert to the ways in which specific children exhibit avoidance behavior, as they will want to intervene with techniques such as *shaping* (reinforcing any approximations of the task) to get the child on-task when the child is avoiding failure. In addition, when a child has experienced large doses of failure in specific situations (such as arithmetic), the teacher may attempt to avert immediate avoidance reactions by changing the situation in novel ways. For instance, the teacher might avoid teaching arithmetic by way of textbooks or worksheets and have the child calculate batting averages instead.

Observational Learning

Recently, appreciation has been renewed for the significance of imitation in the development of children. The new interest is not merely academic, as observational learning has been shown to be an effective tool in modifying behavior. Partly out of concern for the effect of the media—particularly television—on behavior, considerable empirical data have been generated about what is variously called *imitation, modeling,* or *learning through observation.* Probably the most extensive research on this form of learning has been conducted by Bandura (1965, 1969).

Concepts in Observational Learning. One need only watch children to verify that they learn a great deal through modeling, often to the dismay of parents. It has been shown empirically that allowing children to observe violence increases the likelihood that they will exhibit aggression with friends. At present there is agreement that observational learning occurs, but there is disagreement as to the theoretical explanation for this phenomenon (consult Bandura 1969; Holt 1931; and Miller & Dollard 1941 for discussions of three differing explanations).

Several phenomena have escaped earlier investigators. First, imitation may be long delayed; considerable time may pass before there is an appropriate opportunity to emit behavior previously observed. Second, reinforcement does not appear necessary; the child can learn without any trials, although reinforcement of the newly learned behavioral sequence will increase the probability of its being emitted.

In comparing modeling with operant conditioning, Bandura (1965) noted that operant procedures have considerable strength as means of promoting performance but are most useful when the individual already has that response in the behavioral repertoire. He saw modeling as preferable to operant procedures when a new response is called for—that is, one that is not in the response repertoire. While this contrast must sometimes be made, in naturalistic settings both modeling and operant conditioning are often employed together. The child observes a demonstration of a particular behavior, and when it is imitated, the child is reinforced for doing so.

Bandura (1965) and his associates have conducted numerous controlled experiments in an attempt to identify variables that enhance or detract from the effectiveness of a model. Among those variables that appear to be related are the following:

1. *Sex of the model:* Same-sex models enhance the learning.
2. *Consequences for behavior:* If the model is rewarded for the behavior, the observer is more likely to perform the behavior; if the model is punished, imitation is not as likely. Note that this does not affect whether learning has occurred, only whether it will be performed.
3. *Human and nonhuman models:* While live models work effectively, human subjects seen on films seem equally effective. But the use of nonhuman figures (e.g., puppets) diminishes the effectiveness. The extent to which nonhuman subjects detract from modeling is in direct relation to the extent to which they deviate from reality.

Modeling has been shown to affect various classes of responses. First, modeling can facilitate the acquisition of new or unique behaviors (*modeling effect*) such as learning to swing a baseball bat or, for a young child, learning to speak. These new behaviors are acquired through observation and imitation. Second, previously acquired responses can be inhibited or disinhibited (*inhibitory effect* or *disinhibitory effect*). If a child who fears snakes observes other children handling snakes, modeling has been shown to have a disinhibitory effect on the child's reticence to touch snakes. Finally, observation can serve to trigger a response that has been dormant in the response repertoire of the child. This *response facilitation effect* has been demonstrated in studies conducted by Bandura (1965) in which children observed aggressive behavior by models who were rewarded or punished for their aggressive acts.

Application to Mental Retardation. Ball (1970) traced the use of imitation training with the retarded back to such nineteenth-century pioneers as Itard and Seguin. Altman and Talkington (1971) contend that modeling should actually be enhanced for retarded persons, because they rely on external cues in problem solving (Turnure & Zigler 1964)—a quality known as *outerdirectedness*—and because they are willing to conform to maintain social contact (Balla & Zigler 1979). Altman and Talkington maintain that the orientation of the retarded to their immediate environment would facilitate the acquisition of modeled responses. The evidence indicates that the retarded are affected in the same way as normals by their observations of behavior. Edgerton and Dingman (1964b) observed that the institutionalized retarded frequently imitated the "hip" culture they observed before institutionalization—in dress, language, mannerism, and even tattooing. The literature suggests, however, that retarded persons are less efficient than normals in attention and incidental learning. If this is the case, it may be necessary to focus their attention on the salient dimensions of modeled behavior so that they will learn only what is intended, not unrelated peripheral aspects of the behavior. To date, little research on modeling with retarded subjects has been completed (Mercer & Snell 1977), but what has been done suggests the following conclusions: (1) association of rewards with the model facilitates imitation by retarded observers (Ross 1970), (2) the sex of the model is unrelated to the effectiveness of the modeling (Holt, Rickard, & Ellis 1972), and (3) retarded subjects were more inclined to model competent than incompetent models (Strichart 1974).

There is some literature on the effectiveness of imitation learning with the severely retarded. Semmel and Dolley (1971) found a relationship between IQ and the ability to learn through imitation. Altman, Talkington, and Cleland (1972) reported that imitation occurred only when modeling was combined with verbal instruction. Evidence indicates, however, that once imitation occurs it is generalized and maintained (Baer & Guess 1973). Techniques of imitation have been found to be effective in producing speech in previously mute children through the use of puppets as models (Baer, Peterson, & Sherman 1967), in teaching industrial-type motor tasks to the severely retarded (Bender 1972), and, when combined with reinforcement conditions, in promoting self-help skills in the severely retarded (Baer et al. 1967).

Assuming that modeling is an effective tool with the retarded, questions of a programmatic nature arise. Is placement in settings with only retarded peers (institutions, special classes) a desirable practice? Since segregated placement will expose children to peer behavior that is seldom much advanced beyond their own behavior, the behaviors they are likely to model are the very ones that led to their being classified as retarded. In mainstreamed educational settings, teachers must be cautious to apply appropriate consequences for behavior (both desirable and undesirable), recognizing that others in the class may observe a child winning the teacher's attention by a particular behavior. This may happen for reasons that observers may not fully understand, yet other children will imitate the behavior to obtain the same treatment (teacher attention). When a nonretarded child exhibits inappropriate behavior, the teacher should perhaps consider using a public display of disapproval instead of ignoring the behavior, since the retarded child may consider the behavior acceptable to the teacher if it is not punished.

Implications. One fact that can be counted on is that any behavior observed by a child, regardless of IQ, runs the risk of being modeled. This highlights the need for parents and teachers to be alert to their own behavior, for they as well as a child's peers serve as models. Emotional outbursts, foul language, verbal attacks on minority groups, and so on all set an example that can be, and all too often is, later imitated by children. There are some additional implications stemming from observational learning:

1. Teachers should call attention to students who are exhibiting desirable behaviors, singling them out as models to the rest of the class. A teacher can employ modeling by saying, "I like the way Daniel is working quietly," instead of citing those misbehaving ("John, sit down and be quiet.").
2. Teachers should remain alert to the possibility that because of their attempts to extinguish inappropriate behaviors (usually by ignoring them), others in the class may assume that the behavior being exhibited is acceptable. If others begin imitating the misbehavior, the teacher may find it advantageous to use punishment.
3. The literature on observational learning suggests that the media, in combination wtih live demonstrations, can be useful in instruction. A study by Litrownik (1972), for instance, indicated that retarded subjects attended to video tapes better than normals.

SUMMARY

In contrast to the situation in other areas in the field of retardation, there is a vast literature on the learning characteristics of the mentally retarded. Rather than trying to summarize all of this information, we have discussed some of the important trends.

The distinction between learning and performance is important, especially with the mentally retarded, whose performance is altered by many noncognitive factors—motivation, for example. Be careful to distinguish between what children have learned and what they are willing to perform.

The research on EMR subjects, at least, fails to demonstrate clear-cut qualitative differences between the way EMR subjects learn and the way nonretarded subjects learn. Hence it appears that the EMR population represents a downward extension of normal intellectual abilities. They use the same learning strategies as nonretarded subjects, albeit less efficiently.

The literature concerning the learning of school subjects (reading and arithmetic) supports the notion that the way in which mentally retarded children learn does not differ dramatically from that of the nonretarded. The research in these content areas fails to support the need for special instructional approaches for teaching reading and arithmetic to EMR children. The consideration of curricular emphasis for TMR students involves a question of time—that is, is it worth the time it would require to establish certain academic skills in TMR students, or would the time be better spent on social and vocational skills?

A review of the literature pertaining to specific learning characteristics reveals some behavioral characteristics that appear to impede the performance of mentally retarded students. Research on the cognition and learning of mentally retarded subjects indicates that they lack rehearsal strategies, or at least use them inefficiently. The problem is not that they cannot use rehearsal strategies, but that they seldom use them spontaneously. There is also some evidence that the retarded have difficulty in reasoning, that is, in selecting a strategy appropriate to the situation confronting them and spontaneously employing it. This finding is particularly evident in some of the recent research of Herman Spitz.

Language is an area of relative weakness for retarded individuals. In verbal functioning they use the same strategies as the nonretarded, but often they have to be prompted to do so.

Programs of instruction for retarded students would differ depending on the theoretical framework within which the teacher operates: operant behaviorism, cognitive-developmental theories, social learning theory, or observational learning.

CHAPTER 11

Noncognitive Characteristics

We know that retarded people differ from the nonretarded in intelligence and cognition, but do they also differ in noncognitive characteristics? If their noncognitive characteristics are different, are the differences a cause or an effect of the cognitive differences? Are the retarded more likely to be psychotic, neurotic, or criminal? Are there basic personality differences between retarded and nonretarded people, or do institutionalized and non-institutionalized retarded people differ from one another? If differences in noncognitive characteristics do exist, are they inherent in the retarded condition or are they the result of experiential differences?

We do not have conclusive answers to these questions. The evidence that suggests a higher prevalence of emotional disturbance and behavior disorders among the mentally retarded is based primarily on surveys of institutionalized retarded persons, leaving open the possibility that retarded persons in the community do not differ dramatically in personality from their nonretarded counterparts. A number of authors have bewailed the fact that less attention has been paid to the affective characteristics of retarded individuals than to their cognitive characteristics (Cromwell 1967; Heber 1964; Sarason & Gladwin 1958). And although a variety of studies of specific personality characteristics have been made, they form a patchwork of random observations with few attempts to tie them together into some unified theory (Bloom 1964).

There are two notable exceptions, two general theories that have stimulated considerable research. One is Lewin's (1935) dynamic theory of the feeble-minded, which postulated that there are personality differences inherent in mental retardation (a "difference" position). The other is Cromwell's (1963) application of Rotter's (1954) social learning theory to mental retardation. Cromwell, unlike Lewin, emphasizes the impact on personality of experiences encountered by retarded individuals. Certain forces such as failure and frustration are encountered more frequently and perhaps with greater potency by retarded than by nonhandicapped persons. According to Cromwell's logic, the consequences of these experiences could result in characteristic personality traits that differentiate the mentally retarded from their nonhandicapped peers.

THE IMPORTANCE OF NONCOGNITIVE FACTORS

Cognitive measures are those that predict school achievement. These measures, which are of such qualities as intellectual ability, information-processing skills, and achievement, reveal *aptitudes* that predict a child's ability to learn various skills. Messick (1979) refers to the many other attributes of personality that influence learning—affect, motivation, and related characteristics—as *noncognitive* characteristics. These attributes can facilitate or disrupt learning; they may explain why persons with comparable aptitudes sometimes learn differently. Two children with the same IQ, for example, may achieve differently because one of them has a low need for achievement. It is a mistake to assume that cognitive and noncognitive factors can be separated, however. Many noncognitive characteristics have important cognitive components. Individual differences in performance and personality are determined by a complex series of interactions between cognitive and noncognitive factors. To quote Messick (1979):

> It is clear that simple contrasts such as *cognitive* versus *noncognitive* are popularly embraced in spite of the dangers of stereotyping . . . *cognitive* does not imply *only* cognitive and . . . *noncognitive* does not imply the *absence* of cognition.

(p. 282)

In this chapter we will examine research dealing with personality factors—those that result from the interaction of cognitive and noncognitive factors. These factors are often overlooked in special education practice. Cromwell (1967) observed that ignoring personality factors in evaluating the mentally retarded is both unfortunate and paradoxical. He noted that in the certification of an individual as retarded, personality assessment often is not legally required. However, in most cases of mental retardation that are identified between the first year and enrollment in school, it is children's personalities that bring them to the attention of the specialists. These children evidence certain behaviors that concern their parents, so the parents try to find out what is wrong with them. When they take their child to a physician or psychologist, the professional will usually attempt to assess the physical or intellectual development of the child to make the diagnosis, instead of assessing the very dimension that led the parent to bring the child to them—personality. In the diagnosis and in subsequent treatment as well, assessment and treatment of the child's personality are relegated to secondary importance.

The paradox increases when we consider the frequency with which personality factors are involved in the disciplinary problems in residential facilities, the deportment problems in regular classrooms that often lead to a child's being referred for EMR workup, and the subsequent disciplinary problems in special classrooms, and the importance of personality attributes in the occupational adjustment of retarded persons. In each of these cases the personality of the retarded person is certainly as responsible for adjustment problems as the lowered intellect. Yet at the present time we know much less about the personality of retarded persons than we do about their learning.

Often the concerns expressed about labeling children as retarded or providing poor-quality services for them are stated in terms of concern about the impact on their personalities. For example, labeling is feared by some to lead to devaluation of the self, mortification of the self, lowered level of aspiration, stigmatization, and the like. Special classes for EMR children are alleged by some to lead to poorer self-concept, rejection by peers, and attempts to pass for normal (Edgerton 1967; Jones 1972; Mercer 1973a). With all the concern over the possible effects of various practices on personality, we have to conclude that the personality of retarded individuals is considered important, even if it is not very well understood.

RESEARCH LIMITATIONS

There are several reasons for the paucity of research on the personality of the mentally retarded. One major problem is that of measurement. If you consider the instruments and procedures used to assess personality in non-handicapped persons, it is apparent that they are not useful with a large segment of the mentally retarded population because they require considerable verbal skill. Bloom (1964) described the three commonly used sources of information on personality:

1. Others' perceptions of the individual, usually through observation

and then rating of the individual on pertinent factors (e.g., aggression, anxiety). This assessment can be obtained from parents, teachers, peers, and others, such as trained observers. Sometimes a sociometric instrument is used in which a child is asked to select other children with whom the child would want to interact in certain instances.

2. Unconscious self-revelation, through tests that attempt to limit the conscious control of the subject over responses. Included here are projective techniques (e.g., Rorschach Test, Thematic Apperception Test), drawing tests (Draw-A-Person), and certain unobtrusive measures of interests (e.g., number of books read in some period of time).

3. Self-reports, a method that often requires the subject to respond to a questionnaire. The major limitation of this approach is the conscious control the subject exerts over responses, which are easily faked.

These procedures have enough problems when used with nonhandicapped subjects, but the verbal limitations of the retarded compound these problems. The projective techniques are particularly subject to criticism when used with retarded subjects (Garfield 1963).

There have not been extensive attempts to develop personality tests for the retarded, probably in part because the classification requirements do not mandate such assessment in most states. Hence what we know about the personality of the mentally retarded comes in large part from clinical impressions and research that has employed procedures developed on the nonhandicapped.

Recent research on such noncognitive variables as self-concept, attitudes, and the effects of failure has also been limited by the establishment of human subjects committees. These committees screen research proposals and enforce informed consent requirements to ensure that persons serving as research subjects are not deceived and that they know what the research involves. These review committees have unquestionably affected the amount of research done on many of the variables reviewed in this chapter, to the extent that there is less new material on noncognitive characteristics than on any other subject covered in this book.

We will begin our examination of the research on noncognitive factors by considering the various approaches to studying personality.

THEORETICAL APPROACHES TO PERSONALITY

What do we mean by personality? Cromwell (1967) wrote that the term "refers to the recurring, long-term aspects of behavior that characterize individual differences among people" (p. 67). Note that the emphasis is on behaviors that persist as opposed to behaviors that may occasionally be emitted but are not characteristic of the individual.

Personality theories attempt to describe persistent characteristics and also to predict future behavior (How will the individual behave in a certain situation next week?). Attempts to develop theories of personality fall into roughly three groups: type theories, trait theories, and need theories.

The *type theory* approach classifies individuals into groups, such as introverts and extraverts. It assumes that there are *types* of personalities that can be differentiated. Individuals within each group will react similarly to one another, and as a group they will react differently from members of another type. The limitation to this approach is that it ignores individual variation within a type and fails to reflect the different degrees of types.

Rather than identifying the overriding type of personality that characterizes a person, the *trait theory* identifies a series of behaviors (honesty, compulsiveness, dependency) and then rates the individual on each of the traits of interest. The composite picture revealed by such measurement would characterize a given person's personality. The trait approach fractionates the total personality in order to obtain greater precision on selected characteristics, but it thereby fails to consider the global personality of the individual.

The *need theory* analyzes behavior in terms of goals that the individual approaches. The goals may reflect physiological needs (hunger) or psychological needs (such as the social interactions a person seeks). Personality is described on the basis of the relative importance a given individual places on various goals (such as affiliation, heterosexuality, achievement).

The model proposed by Cromwell (1967) suggests that personality can be studied from a number of interrelated angles. In addition to the constructs we have already mentioned—needs, traits, and types—he includes two theoretical constructs from the psychoanalytic framework: threats and defense mechanisms. These headings cover most of the theoretical constructs used in the study of personality. They also provide a framework within which we can consider what is known about the personality of the mentally retarded population or some of its subgroups.

Figure 11.1 shows a schematic presentation based on Cromwell's model. We will not try to describe it in detail here, since the rest of the chapter will be devoted to explaining the theories and evidence bearing on each part of it. But, in general, it demonstrates that an individual's personality may be affected by threats (on the left of the figure) and needs or goals (shown at the far right of the figure). To avoid perceived threats, such as fear of authority figures and fear of failure, the individual may use certain defense mechanisms to protect personal integrity. On the other side of the figure, the individual's goals are related to trait constructs. The traits can be characterized as goal-seeking behaviors, even though they are seldom tied to specific goals. At the middle in this diagram is typology, the global personality construct that is determined by the other four constructs. Our discussion will be organized according to Figure 11.1, taking in turn the various constructs that affect the typology of the personality.

FIGURE 11.1 Personality Constructs

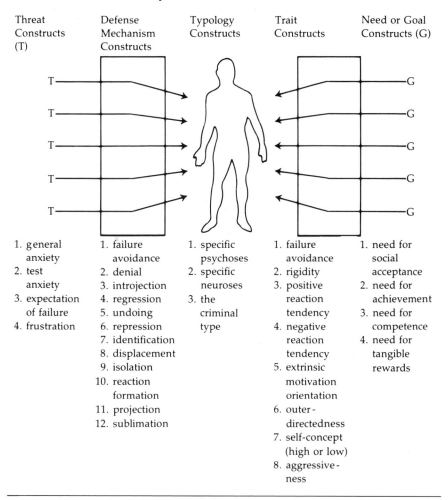

Threat Constructs (T)	Defense Mechanism Constructs	Typology Constructs	Trait Constructs	Need or Goal Constructs (G)
1. general anxiety	1. failure avoidance	1. specific psychoses	1. failure avoidance	1. need for social acceptance
2. test anxiety	2. denial	2. specific neuroses	2. rigidity	2. need for achievement
3. expectation of failure	3. introjection	3. the criminal type	3. positive reaction tendency	3. need for competence
4. frustration	4. regression		4. negative reaction tendency	4. need for tangible rewards
	5. undoing		5. extrinsic motivation orientation	
	6. repression		6. outer-directedness	
	7. identification		7. self-concept (high or low)	
	8. displacement		8. aggressive-ness	
	9. isolation			
	10. reaction formation			
	11. projection			
	12. sublimation			

This figure is based on Cromwell's original model in R. L. Cromwell, "Personality evaluation," A. A. Baumeister, ed., *Mental Retardation: Appraisal, Education, and Rehabilitation* (Chicago: Aldine, 1967).

In considering the discussion of each construct, we must be careful not to conclude that we know what the retarded personality is really like. As Heber cautioned:

> Textbooks are replete with statements describing the retarded as passive, anxious, impulsive, rigid, suggestible, lacking in persistence, immature, and withdrawn, and as having a low frustration tolerance and an unrealistic self-concept and level of aspiration. Yet not one of these purported attributes can be either substantiated or refuted on the basis of available research data.
>
> (p. 169)

Even the extant evidence is replete with methodological flaws that render the results questionable. Only the work of Zigler and his associates at Yale (Zigler 1966; Balla & Zigler 1979) and the research based on the application of social learning theory to the mentally retarded (Cromwell 1963) have tied the life experiences of the retarded to personal and motivational outcomes.

THREAT CONSTRUCTS

In describing an individual's interaction with the environment, the first step is to identify those events the individual perceives as threatening. Do the mentally retarded, as a group, show greater or lesser fear than normals of certain objects or events? If such differences exist, are they an inherent part of retardation or a result of experiences the retarded encounter?

There is no formalized system by which threatening objects or events can be analyzed (Cromwell 1967). But Garfield (1963) hypothesized that the higher incidence of emotional disturbance observed in retarded individuals is due to their more frequent rejection or the fact that they more frequently encounter frustration, failure, and ridicule, a point supported by an analysis of the literature (Robinson & Paseward 1951). A higher level of anxiety has also been postulated as a threat construct.

Anxiety

Although some retarded children may perceive specific things as threats, not much is known about this phenomenon. What has been researched is the degree to which they feel anxiety, a more vague kind of fear. Fear itself is related to something specific that is consciously known to the individual (e.g., a fear of snakes or heights). An anxiety reaction, on the other hand, elicits some of the same feelings as does fear but the individual may not know what specific stimulus arouses that set of feelings. Nevertheless, tension is felt. As the individual learns to anticipate dangers, a warning signal prompts a defensive reaction to guard against the threats and alleviate the tension.

In general, those who work with retarded children find them more anxious than normal children, a notion supported by clinical evidence (Heber 1964). Anxiety is usually assessed by one of the anxiety scales (Taylor Manifest Anxiety Scale or Children's Form of the Manifest Anxiety Scale). They indicate that anxiety improves test performance when the individual knows the correct response but hinders it when the answer involves complex learning in which the correct response is not dominant (Lipman 1960).

There is additional evidence that complex learning and academic achievement are adversely affected by high anxiety levels (Kitano 1960; Lipman & Griffith 1960; Malpass, Mark, & Palermo 1960). And limited evidence indicates that there may be social class differences in anxiety, with lower-class children scoring higher in manifest anxiety (Cochran & Cleland 1963; Feldhusen & Klausmeier 1962; Haywood & Dobbs 1964).

It has been found that retarded samples score higher than normals on general anxiety (Cochran & Cleland 1963; Lipman & Griffith 1960) and that the institutionalized retarded score higher on anxiety than noninstitutionalized retarded children (Malpass et al. 1960).

Anxiety may be caused by the test situation itself. High test anxiety has been reported to be highly related to poor test performance in mildly and moderately retarded subjects (Reger 1964; Silverstein 1966b). One study found that poor academic achievement in retarded males was related to high test anxiety but not to high general anxiety (Weiner, Crawford, & Snyder 1960).

General anxiety is difficult to measure since it may be covert rather than manifest. It is especially hard to measure in retarded individuals because the commonly used scales mentioned earlier have not been tested for their validity with retarded subjects (Sarason 1960). But by using a different procedure from the other studies—obtaining anxiety scores from the analysis of subjects' drawings of human figures—Snyder (1966) reported that in a sample of mildly retarded subjects, high academic achievement was related to low anxiety, and low achievement was related to high anxiety. Heber (1964), though, points out that while there is evidence of higher anxiety scores for retarded samples, anxiety itself has not been shown to be a major factor that limits performance.

Expectation of Failure

Because of their limited intellectual abilities, mentally retarded people do not compete favorably with their normal peers; as a result they encounter relatively few successes and many failures. This may be especially true of mildly retarded children struggling to keep up in a regular classroom. Many tasks that are presented to such children with histories of excessive failure may seem to pose threats to them. It is postulated that the threat of failure prompts the retarded child to exhibit defensive behavior designed to avoid failure.

According to the fear-of-failure hypothesis, mentally retarded individuals fail so often that, when presented with a new task, they often expect to fail before even attempting the task. Retarded children come to perceive certain events as threatening, events that are perceived by children with histories of success as neutral or even positive—as challenges. This is not to suggest that retarded children will have different perceptions because they are retarded per se, but rather that as a result of repeated failure, the number of threats they perceive in the environment is increased.

In seeking evidence to support this theory we must be careful not to assume automatically that certain situations pose a greater threat of failure for retarded children than for normal children. For example, Gardner (1958) speculated that his experimental failure had a greater magnitude for normal than for retarded children since it was unexpected for the normal children. Similarly, a given failure situation may have greater potency for children with histories of success; a child with a history of failure may find the current failure mild by comparison.

The assumption of failure has been tested in the social learning theory model postulated by Rotter (1954) and extended to mentally retarded individuals by Cromwell (1963). Rotter postulated that the probability of a behavior at any time is, in part, a function of the *situational* and *generalized* expectation that a particular reinforcement will occur because of that behavior. Situational expectation is related to the specific success and failure experiences the individual has had in the particular situation, whereas generalized expectation is related to a broad range of experiences the individual has had in a variety of situations. In extending Rotter's theory to the mentally retarded, Cromwell hypothesized that they would be lower than normals in generalized and situational expectation for success because of their general histories of failure.

Heber (1964) suggested that fear of failure becomes a vicious circle that results in a continual decrement in the performance of the retarded. He wrote:

> Since expectancy is one of the variables mediating behavior potential, the performance of the retarded child should show a further qualitative and quantitative decrement with the acquisition of a low expectancy for success. This reduction in performance efficiency would result in further failure leading to even lower expectancies and so on, in circular fashion.
>
> (pp. 165–166)

This line of reasoning suggests that a high expectancy for failure compounds the performance deficits of the mentally retarded below the level we would expect based on intellectual level alone.

There is little research evidence to confirm this theory. But findings in a recent study (MacMillan 1975b) suggest that situational expectation is altered by experimentally induced success and failure. Lower-class and minority children served as subjects for both retarded and nonretarded groups, and the groups did not differ on generalized expectation. The lack of difference may be explained by the possibility that the nonretarded children, despite adequately high IQ, encountered sufficient failure in school to lower generalized expectation for success in a manner similar to the EMR sample.

The reactions to expectation of failure will be considered later in the discussion of defense mechanism constructs. But, in general, there is concern that persistent failure will result in a lowered functioning level, diminished social and cognitive growth, devaluation of the feeling of self-worth (Cromwell 1967; MacMillan 1971b), and development of a sense of incompetence (Harter 1978).

Frustration

In addition to general anxiety and the fear of failure, a third kind of threat has been hypothesized to characterize the retarded—frustration.

Sources of possible frustration are common in institutions for retarded persons. Often institutional life signifies minimal privacy, few avenues by which patients can vent hostility, and a subservient status of being cared for. A study of frustration of the hunger drive (via restriction of diet) showed increased aggression in institutionalized patients (Talkington & Riley 1971). The inability to express their needs and to communicate with others has also been studied as a source of frustration for retarded subjects (Talkington, Hall, & Altman 1971). Such frustrations have been linked with aggression. Since the aggression shown was not directed towards *self* or *others* but was aimed at attention getting (tearing clothes, window breaking), the investigators suggested the following formula:

$$\text{frustration} \rightarrow \text{aggression} \rightarrow \text{attention}$$

in which attention getting is the goal of the aggression (Talkington & Hall 1969; Talkington & Riley 1971; Talkington et al. 1971). Other studies found that running away was a response to frustration generated from restrictions in the institution (Gothberg 1947; Thorne 1947).

Is frustration typical of retarded individuals in general or only of those who are subjected to institutional living conditions? Remarkably few studies have been conducted on frustration and its effects despite the common assumption that the mentally retarded tend to be subjected to more frustration than other individuals (Heber 1964). The available evidence shows a variety of presumed *reactions* to frustration, such as aggression. However, some of this aggressive behavior seen may have existed before the retarded individuals were institutionalized, with aggression more the cause than the result of the institutionalization.

Does frustration increase as IQ drops? Dollard, Doob, Miller, Mourer, and Sears (1939) speculated that the relationship between intelligence and frustration may not be so simple:

Not only would low intelligence seem likely to increase the amount of frustration experienced by an individual; it would also be expected to diminish the effectiveness of socializing forces in that it would imply a lowered capacity to appreciate the consequences of specific acts.

(p. 116)

A certain level of intelligence is necessary to comprehend that one has failed or that there are goals that are desired but unobtainable. So the same lowered intellect that would diminish accomplishment could also serve to lower the level of frustration that the retarded would experience as a result of lower accomplishment. We might therefore expect greater frustration in the mildly retarded than in the severely retarded.

The interesting theory proposed by Dollard and his associates has not been empirically verified, for attempts to study frustration have encountered problems in instrumentation. Several studies have employed a projective type of test developed by Rosenzweig (1945). Angelino and Shedd (1956) administered the test to mildly retarded children and found that they responded in the same manner as normals to the frustration. The only difference was in the timing of the normals' shift from aggression toward others (extrapunitive) to expressing aggression toward themselves. The retarded children reached the second stage at an age approximately two years older. Portnoy and Stacey (1954) used the same instrument with institutionalized retarded subjects and reported a higher than normal frequency of aggression directed toward others in both black and white subjects. However, Lipman's (1959) study raised serious quesions as to the validity of the Rosenzweig technique, as he found no differences on this test between a group of children with behavior problems and model students.

David (1968) tried using a physiological measure of galvanic skin response to compare frustration in mildly retarded persons and normals. He found no differences between the two groups.

DEFENSE MECHANISM CONSTRUCTS

When the individual perceives a threat and is unable to tolerate the anxiety or fear, the individual attempts to reduce the tension that results. This is usually accomplished in one of two ways: coping directly and realistically with the threat or coping indirectly by reducing the conflict via defense mechanisms. Although defense mechanisms seem to distort reality, they do serve to reduce the conflict. The goal of both coping and defense mechanisms is to return the organism to a state of equilibrium. If you look back at Figure 11.1 you will see that the arrows running from threats through defense mechanisms are directed toward the organism. Defensive behavior is not goal-directed, unless protecting the organism from threats can be interpreted as a goal.

Defense Mechanisms

As Cromwell (1967) noted, the work on defense mechanisms comes almost exclusively from psychoanalytic theory. Table 11.1 summarizes some hypothesized defense mechanisms and how they operate. Defense mechanisms are used by all people to some extent. But when used to excess they become dysfunctional, and this can lead to further maladaptive behavior on the part of the individual.

There is little empirical evidence bearing on the use of defense mechanisms by retarded individuals. There is speculation that retarded children have a greater need to employ defense mechanisms, presumably because of their relative inability to cope realistically with threats. At the same time, retarded individuals may be less successful than normals at using defense mechanisms. There is a clinical impression that retarded individuals use certain defense mechanisms more often than do normals of the same chronological age. Other defense mechanisms seem to be beyond the capacity of the retarded.

It is believed that the retarded child relies mostly on the more primitive defense mechanisms, such as denial, introjection, regression, undoing, and repression; retarded children use defenses such as projection, reaction formation, and isolation to a lesser degree.

Stephens (1953) studied defense mechanisms used by the retarded and reported that the main one used is denial. He attributes its primacy to the inability of retarded individuals to accept the reality of their retardation. He also reported the use of *identification:* the retarded child who has feelings of inadequacy identifies with someone else with whom the child has contact. This is a slight variation of introjection. Frequently, the individual identified with has capabilities far beyond those of the retarded person. This can lead to problems when retarded persons are unable to live up to the ideals incorporated as their own.

Flexibility is another way in which retarded individuals are thought to differ from normals in their use of defense mechanisms. The retarded tend to be less flexible than normals, using the same defense mechanisms over and over again, even when they have other, more appropriate defense mechanisms in their repertoire.

While these notions are based on extrapolation from theory or from clinical observation, anyone who has experienced the verbal behavior of institutionalized retarded persons can confirm these observations to some extent. For instance, it is not at all uncommon to find individuals in institutions denying their retardation and contending that if they could only

TABLE 11.1   Defense Mechanisms

Defense Mechanism	Definition	Example
1. Repression	Hostile feelings are forced from consciousness, making the individual unaware of them. They may surface in dreams, slips of tongue.	1. A child who hates a parent forces feeling to a subconscious level.
2. Denial	Feelings are actively denied but are still conscious to the individual.	2. An angry person says, "I'm not mad at him. He hasn't done anything to make me mad."
3. Regression	A more satisfying mode of behavior is resumed—usually a more infantile mode of behavior.	3. Thumb sucking or use of a bottle is resumed when a sibling is brought into family.
4. Displacement	The hostile feelings are transferred to a less threatening object.	4. A child picks a fight with a younger sibling when angry with the mother.
5. Isolation	The emotional components of a drive are separated from the content of the message or act itself.	5. A murderer confesses a heinous crime with no emotion, or a child says "I'd like to kill her" without emotion.

6. Undoing — An act is performed that is symbolically the opposite of a previous act in a subconscious attempt to nullify, or undo, the previous act.

7. Introjection — Attitudes or prohibitions from the outside are internalized and treated as though they were one's own ideas or beliefs.

8. Reaction formation — Behavior is exhibited that is exactly the opposite of what would be exhibited by an unacceptable drive.

9. Projection — One's own impulses, traits, or thoughts are attributed to another person.

10. Sublimation — The drive is satisfied in an indirect, socially acceptable manner.

6. A parent buys expensive toys for a child otherwise neglected and ignored.

7. A child behaves as though he wanted to do what the mother would insist that he do.

8. A person shows affection for someone she feels hostile toward.

9. A person says, "He is jealous of me" or "She hates me" when in fact the person is jealous of or hates that person to whom the feelings are attributed.

10. The sex drive is redirected toward work, dancing, or athletics.

get outside they would prove they were not retarded. In many cases they deny their retardation in the face of confirming evidence. According to psychoanalytic theory, they may be repressing the failure they experienced on the outside.

Sternlicht and Deutsch (1972) describe a situation in which the occurrence of denial, withdrawal, or both is associated with a pattern of depression. In this situation, the retarded person is preoccupied with feelings of inadequacy and failure. Those who use this defense mechanism feel inferior, worry about past failures, and anticipate future failures. Any successes experienced by these people are transitory. Failures assume an exaggerated meaning; they may be viewed as deserved because of the person's feelings of inadequacy.

There is a need for more systematic research on the use of defense mechanisms by retarded individuals. It seems oversimplistic to make blanket statements about how the retarded use defense mechanisms, or to state that sublimation is beyond their capacity. To do so ignores the vast heterogeneity within the retarded population and implies that severely retarded patients in institutions and mildly retarded children in EMR classes use the same defense mechanisms in the same inflexible manner. It seems more likely that the specific mechanisms used and the variability shown in their deployment would be a function of the degree of retardation, the past history of the individual, and the extent to which the environment is adapted to the individual's intellectual limitations.

Failure Avoidance

The expectation of failure—discussed earlier as a threat construct—can lead to defensive behaviors designed to avoid failure experiences. Normally, according to Cromwell (1963, 1967), personality develops through several motivational stages. In the second stage—the "Intact Hedonist"— the individual is motivated to achieve immediate gratification and avoid unpleasant circumstances. This stage of development is superseded by what Cromwell calls the "Conceptual Motivational System"; in it the child comes to respond to conceptual goals rather than immediate gratification. As children become more and more aware of the acceptability of their behavior (and able to conceptualize success and failure), they are motivated to approach success and avoid failure.

Several characteristics are noted in children functioning at this conceptual success-failure motivational level. First, they are more able to delay gratification instead of anticipating immediate hedonistic rewards. Second, frustration or failure is less anxiety producing; instead of giving up, they are thought to increase efforts to overcome failures and to correct the situation. Third, they are more inclined to see event outcomes and life circumstances as being determined by themselves (Bialer 1960). That is, they come to see that they can determine whether they succeed or fail, rather than assuming that such outcomes are the result of fate or circumstances beyond their control. This is the internal locus of control. Ultimately, the mature individual comes to operate in accordance with the "minimax theory," seeking solutions of maximal gain and minimal loss in a balance between striving for success and avoidance of failure (Cromwell 1967).

This normal development, according to Cromwell's theory (1967), can be thwarted by excessive failure. While small amounts of failure may inspire individuals to prove their ability, this behavior deteriorates when failure continues. The reactions of persons who often fail and seldom succeed may include depression, regression, and a decrease in effort. They may begin to believe that circumstances are beyond their control and that the best they can do is to avoid failure. In their preoccupation with avoiding failure they may become so attuned to cues that are related to failure that they fail to attend to cues that are relevant to success (Cromwell 1967).

Application of the Theory to Retarded Children. While some studies (Bialer & Cromwell 1965; McManis, Bell, & Pike 1969) have identified some retarded children as "success strivers," the majority of the studies have supported the notion that due to prolonged and consistent exposure to failure, retarded children are motivated primarily to avoid failure. Moss (1958) characterized retarded children as "failure avoiders" who are sensitive to cues associated with impending failure; because of their preoccupation with failure cues they are not alert to cues that are relevant to successful solutions. In contrast, children characterized as success strivers are alert to cues helpful to achieving success, sometimes overlooking cues that warn of impending failure.

Another hypothesized reaction of retarded children to repeated failure is the adoption of a very unstable level of aspiration (Cromwell 1967) or a lowered level of aspiration (Zigler 1968). Cromwell suggests that when retarded children expect to fail they will set goals so high that they are unattainable; following the anticipated failure they will establish extremely cautious goals that represent an attempt to prevent failure. Zigler observes that low aspiration levels can lead to great frustration on the part of those working with the retarded, particularly if they are below levels acceptable to a teacher, for example. When the child achieves the goal, the child is satisfied and cannot understand the teacher's dissatisfaction. These constructs, if valid, would pose serious barriers to school learning and personal growth. Both approaches to goal setting fail to achieve the match described as ideal by Hunt (1961). He contended that optimal growth results from goals set slightly beyond present levels of functioning, although they must be within the capabilities of the child. Goals that are very low require no growth, while goals that are unobtainable, since they are too high, lead to frustration, failure, and a decrease in effort.

The Research Evidence. Although these theories seem plausible to those who have worked with retarded children, they have been somewhat difficult to prove experimentally. One way to induce failure and then study its effects is the *interrupted task paradigm*. Children are given a series of tasks. On some they are interrupted prior to completion; on others they are allowed to complete the task. After working on the entire series of tasks, usually six or so, the children are told that they can now work on any of the tasks again. The tasks that were interrupted are presumed to represent failures and the completed ones success. For a detailed consideration of the theoretical issues in the interrupted task paradigm consult Butterfield (1964).

Research using the interrupted task paradigm (Bialer & Cromwell 1960; Butterfield 1964; MacMillan 1969a, 1969b; MacMillan & Keogh 1971; MacMillan & Knopf 1971; Miller 1961; Spradlin 1960) has consistently shown that brighter children and older mentally retarded children tend to choose to repeat the previously interrupted task. Bialer (1961), however, reported the choice of interrupted tasks to be related to higher mental age rather than chronological age. More recently we have found that retarded children seem to perceive interruption differently than nonretarded children (MacMillan 1975b). Because of their history of failure, the retarded children did in fact perceive interruption to be failure. This reaction was not found in children with histories of academic success.

Several studies conducted at George Peabody College exploring differing reactions of normal and retarded subjects to failure (Gardner 1958; Heber 1957; Ringelheim 1958) came up with somewhat conflicting results. Heber found that both normals and retarded subjects had terminal levels of performance that were higher after failure, although both showed a decrease in effort on trials late in the sequence. But Gardner reported that a greater proportion of normals than retarded increased their efforts following failure. And Ringelheim found an effect that was similar for retarded and normal subjects.

Balla and Zigler (1979) summarize a different line of research, in which the effects of success and failure on problem solving are considered. In this research, children were given an insoluble task that involved picking one of several stimuli. There was no completely correct choice, but one of the three choices was partially reinforced. Those who chose the partially reinforced stimulus are said to use a *maximizing strategy*, because they maximize their chances for reinforcement. At the same time, however, they minimize their chances of securing 100 percent success. Research indicates that nonretarded children try to achieve complete success and do not use a maximizing strategy. The retarded, however, do tend to opt for a maximizing strategy. These findings may indicate lower aspiration levels or need for achievement among those who adopt maximizing strategies and forego opportunities for complete success.

Few studies have examined the effects of prolonged failure. A notable exception is one by Zeaman and House (1963). They found that after a series of failure experiences, retarded children were unable to solve problems that they had been able to solve earlier.

Reversing the Failure Set. If retarded children use defensive behavior to avoid the threat of failure, they are avoiding the challenges necessary for cognitive and social growth. Their behavioral limitations as a result of lowered intellectual functioning may thus be compounded by their avoidance of situations that would promote growth.

It is important to reverse the failure set in retarded children in educational programing. There are indications that this is possible. For instance, Osler (1970) gave mentally retarded children a simple task that monkeys had learned in 35 to 40 trials. For the retarded subjects every correct response was rewarded with a piece of candy. After 150 to 200 trials they still had not solved the problem, but they were getting candy for about 50 percent of their responses, which were correct only by chance. At this point Osler considered the possibility that these children were satisfied with the 50 percent reinforcement they received for their random responding. She speculated that for some retarded children, being rewarded for being correct half the time was better than they had ever done and they were willing to settle for that; they did not aspire to 100 percent levels of performance. To see if she could change this low level of aspiration, Osler then told the children that from that point on they would have to return a piece of candy for every incorrect response. Subjects learned to solve the problem in two or three trials.

Although it will not always be possible to achieve such dramatic results in the classroom, the teacher should take the possible failure-avoidance defenses of retarded children into account. The teacher should be sensitive to retarded children's orientation to failure and assist them to work for success, possibly through focusing attention on successes and the cues that are relevant to the successful completion of tasks. Similarly, the teacher should watch for evidence of unrealistic aspirations of the child as a clue that the child may be experiencing excessive failure. And finally, the teacher must be very cautious to adapt the environment to the ability levels of the child, not expecting too much or too little, in order to avoid undue frustration or a lack of stimulation. Either might result in less than maximal growth.

NEED OR GOAL CONSTRUCTS

To approach the global personality from the right side of Cromwell's diagram (see Figure 11.1) instead of the left (the psychoanalytic constructs), we must figure out what kinds of needs or goals motivate retarded persons to behave the way they do. As we have already seen, one negative motivation may be the need to avoid failure. We will not review all that we have just said about failure avoidance, but it is important to remember that it can be included in the list of suspected goals and traits as well as the list of suspected defense mechanisms in retarded persons.

While it is possible to think of a number of need constructs on which retarded persons might differ from the nonretarded, many of the possibilities (such as need for affiliation, need for dependence, need for autonomy, and heterosexual needs) have not been studied systematically with retarded subjects. The constructs on which at least some work has been done with retarded samples include the need for social acceptance, the need for achievement, the need for competence, and the need for tangible versus intangible rewards.

Need for Social Acceptance

It has been suggested that because retarded individuals are often deprived of social acceptance and approval, they reflect a higher need for approval and acceptance than do nonretarded individuals. Even within the retarded population the need for acceptance might vary, with those who have the least social contact—the institutionalized—desiring it the most.

According to the social deprivation hypothesis (Stevenson & Cruse 1961; Stevenson & Fahel 1961; Stevenson & Knights 1961), institutionalized retarded children should persist longer on a task when given social reinforcement than normal children, since the former have been deprived of such interactions. The evidence seems to suggest that institutionalized retarded subjects do indeed find attention from the experimenter more reinforcing than do nonretarded children (Bijou & Oblinger 1960; Zigler, Hodgden, & Stevenson 1958). And some of the evidence reveals that the sex of the experimenter plays a role in determining how reinforcing the contact will be. A cross-sex situation is most effective (Stevenson 1961; Stevenson & Knights 1962).

As we will discuss in Chapter 14, Zigler and Balla (1977) have demonstrated that children coming from supportive homes to institutions are affected more adversely by institutionalization than those from deprived homes. Like other children, retarded children need social contact, approval, and love. When they are deprived of such support, they exhibit certain behavioral consequences. Retarded persons, for example, are likely to engage in repetitive behavior that appears monotonous and boring to the observer in attempts to maintain social interaction (Balla & Zigler 1979; Zigler 1968). In many situations, their tactics backfire and lead to rejection rather than acceptance. The important aspect of Zigler's observations is that these behavioral consequences of social deprivation are not inherent in the retarded condition; they are found among the retarded because they are more often socially deprived than the nonretarded. Nonretarded persons who are equally deprived of social contact and approval exhibit the same behavioral sequelae.

Need for Achievement

The extent to which retarded children are motivated by a need for achievement has not yet been conclusively demonstrated. When McClelland and his associates (McClelland, Atkinson, Clark, & Lowell 1953) identified the importance of the individual's need for achievement, they did show that it was related to intellectual ability. But this early research on the need for achievement was done on intellectually normal children. We might speculate that it is important for retarded children to develop a need for achievement, but little research has been done on this possible avenue to personal adjustment.

Tolman and Johnson (1958) contrasted institutionalized organic and familial retarded children on a projective test designed to tap achievement motivation. They found that familial retarded subjects tended to exhibit a higher need for achievement than those with organic problems. But in both groups the need for achievement dropped with length of institutionalization.

Does the child's community and family background have any effect on motivation to achieve? Although the vast majority of children from lower-class homes are not mentally retarded, studies have shown that as a group they are much lower in achievement motivation than their middle-class peers (Merbaum 1962; Rosen 1956; Veroff, Atkinson, Feld, & Gurin 1960). Tymchuk (1972) suggests that children coming from such backgrounds are ill-prepared to compete with middle-class children in whose homes language competence and achievement motivation are stressed. But whether mildly retarded children from such a background evidence any different need for achievement than those of normal intelligence from the same background remains unclear.

The motivation to achieve must have some bearing on how hard children try on tests. Much of the research evidence on learning reviewed in Chapter 10 was collected under conditions in which subjects were simply told to do their best. For many middle-class children of normal intelligence, such an incentive condition results in maximum effort. But there is evidence (Keogh

& MacMillan 1971) that lower-class EMR children put out less than their maximum effort under such incentives.

Need for Competence

White (1959, 1960) suggested that normal children are motivated to be competent or effective in dealing with their environment, a characteristic he labeled *competence motivation,* or *effectance motivation.* The existence of this motivation suggests that, after more basic needs such as hunger and thirst are met, children are continually manipulating their environment. Is the same need to be competent or effective in dealing with the environment found among mentally retarded children? Harter and Zigler (1974) concluded that mastery is pleasurable and that such pleasure is greatest when the task is challenging to the child. This notion is reminiscent of Hunt's (1961) suggestion that a match between a child's level of cognitive development and the demands of a task motivates the child to try to master the task. When Harter and Zigler compared nonretarded, noninstitutionalized retarded, and institutionalized retarded subjects, they found the highest degree of effectance motivation among the nonretarded. The next highest level occurred among the noninstitutionalized retarded, followed by the institutionalized retarded. The investigators hypothesized that retarded children, in general, become passive as a result of excessive failure. The institutionalized retarded are pressured to conform, which further diminishes their nonstriving orientation.

Harter (1978) has continued to study the effectance motivation of normal and retarded children. Her modification of White's original effectance motivation model is shown in Figure 11.2. In this figure, Harter considers the effects of failure as well as the effects of success. In an extremely well-conceived discussion, she explores the complexity of children's attempts at mastery and the factors that influence the ultimate effect of these attempts on effectance motivation.

As Figure 11.2 illustrates, Harter hypothesizes that children who attempt mastery and succeed experience a host of positive effects. The children are reinforced for trying new tasks, which diminishes the need for external approval and ultimately results in their becoming more independent. The children's sense of being in control of their fate (internal locus of control) also increases, which improves effectance motivation and increases the chances that the children will attempt subsequent mastery tasks. Conversely, when children make an attempt at mastery and fail, they are reinforced for dependency, which heightens reliance on external reinforcement or approval. Another result of failure is that children become less inclined to see themselves as in control of situations—their locus of control becomes more external—and ultimately their effectance motivation decreases.

FIGURE 11.2 Harter's Developmental Refinement and Extension of White's Model of Effectance Motivation

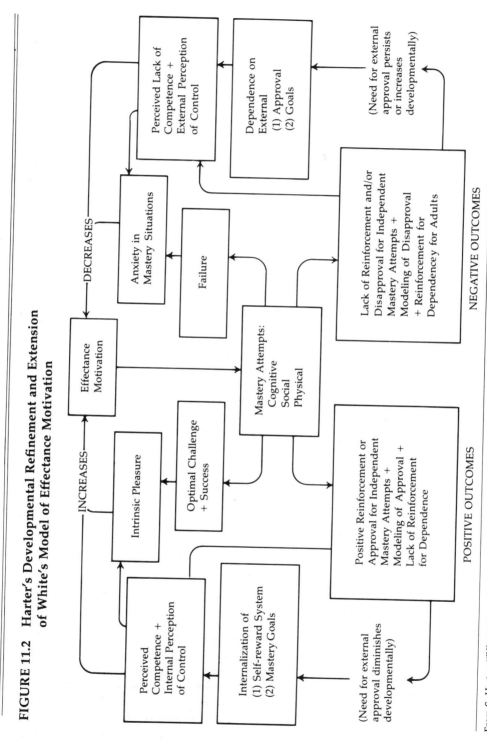

From S. Harter, "Effectance motivation reconsidered: Toward a developmental model," *Human Development*, 1978, **21**, 34–64.

Because retarded children experience excessive failure, the right side of the model is of interest here. The model explains the research findings that the mentally retarded tend to have an external locus of control and are relatively dependent on adults for social approval and judgments about what is correct and incorrect. Harter's findings suggest that programing success experiences for the retarded would reverse the trend toward lowered effectance motivation. It would be crucial to such programing that the retarded child regard tasks as attempts at mastery, not as easy exercises that require no effort. No sense of effectance or competence results from the successful completion of an unchallenging task.

Need for Tangible Rewards

Although they seem to need social acceptance and contact to a greater degree than normals, the needs of retarded persons may otherwise be more extrinsic or tangible in nature than intrinsic (Haywood 1968a). Zigler (1962) contends that retarded children may differ from normals in their preference for certain kinds of rewards or reinforcers. Although in many research studies employing incentives for correct responses all subjects receive the same incentive, Zigler suggested that being correct may not rank as high on the reinforcer hierarchy of retarded children as it does for normal children.

Some evidence is available on the reward hierarchy of mildly retarded children (Keogh & MacMillan 1971) and lower-class children (Terrell, Durkin, & Wiesley 1959) as compared with normal middle-class children. Differences in performance by the lower-class and EMR children were negated when the children were offered a tangible reward for correct performance. But when these children were performing under conditions in which they were simply told to do their best, their performance was significantly lower than that of normal middle-class children.

Heber (1964) reviewed the literature on the manipulation of tangible rewards and how it affected performance in the retarded. He concluded that the incentives used (peanuts, candy, cigarettes) were often of questionable reinforcing value. Heber (1959a) had the subjects themselves rank incentives from high to low and then had them perform under either high- or low-incentive conditions. He reported that their motor performance was facilitated when they performed for an incentive they ranked high as opposed to when they performed under low-incentive conditions.

There is an abundance of new evidence derived from behavior modification research that could bear on the responsiveness of retarded children to various consequences. In general it demonstrates that, like normal children, retarded children differ in terms of which specific stimuli are reinforcing and which are not. Since the principles of learning have been shown to work the same way with retarded children as with others, the key is to find the effective incentive for a specific child. Despite individual variations, at least one generalization about motivation seems safe: Because institutionalized retarded children are socially deprived, they tend to be more responsive to adult approval than do noninstitutionalized, nonretarded children.

TRAIT CONSTRUCTS

Individuals try to satisfy their needs by behaving in characteristic ways that we call *traits*. Persons who want to avoid failure, for instance, may exhibit behavior patterns typical of the failure-avoiding personality trait. As we have seen, they may set very low or unrealistically high goals for themselves, look for failure cues rather than success cues, inhibit their own growth by avoiding challenges, and feel incompetent and devalued as individuals.

Trait constructs have been studied far more in the mentally retarded than have the other constructs we have discussed. They are more easily measured than hypothesized threats, defenses, and motivations. Direct comparisons can be made between retarded and nonretarded samples or between different subgroups of retarded subjects to determine whether there are differences in the degree to which a given trait is exhibited by the different groups. We must be cautious, however, not to extrapolate too broadly from extant research, for a general trait is often inferred from a highly specific task or set of circumstances. The majority of research on the personality of the mentally retarded has been generated from three sources: the rigidity hypothesis of Lewin (1935) and Kounin (1941); social learning theory as applied to mental retardation (Cromwell 1963); and Zigler's (1966) motivational research.

Rigidity

One of the behavioral traits most commonly ascribed to mentally retarded individuals is that they exhibit rigid behaviors. Those who work with the retarded have often noticed in them a tendency to engage in repetitive, stereotyped behaviors and to develop abnormally fixated attachments to certain other people. Such observations led Lewin (1935) to postulate that rigidity was manifested as a result of qualitative differences in the thought processes of the retarded. Although his theory—"the dynamic theory of feeble-mindedness"—generated a good bit of research, it has not been conclusively proved, and rigidity has since been explained as a result of social deprivation and the need for social approval (Zigler 1962) rather than an organic defect, as we will see.

Even though it is only a theory, the rigidity hypothesis contributed to the belief that the retarded differ from normals in kind as well as degree. This belief, in turn, fostered the notion that the retarded must be taught differently and that the principles of learning that apply to normals do not necessarily apply to the mentally retarded. Traditional training programs in special education have thus consisted of courses that imply that there are unique teaching techniques and curricular approaches useful only with the mentally retarded (e.g., "Methods for Teaching Reading to the Educable Retarded").

Lewin's Theory and Kounin's Research.   Essentially, Lewin postulated that the cognitive structures of mentally retarded individuals have fewer regions and that the boundaries between regions are less fluid or permeable than is true for a normal individual of the same chronological age. Figure 11.3 shows his theoretical comparison of the brain structure of a normal child, a normal adult, and a retarded child of the same mental age as the normal child. Note the greater differentiation in the adult, and the greater permeability of the boundaries in the normal child.

To test the rigidity hypothesis, Kounin (1941) related this theoretical structural rigidity to behavioral rigidity. He suggested that if the hypothesis were valid, the same situations (or sets of stimuli) would be less stimulating for retarded persons than for normals because fewer cognitive areas would be activated. In addition, changes in one region would not affect other regions due to the impermeability of boundaries thought to be characteristic of the retarded.

To test these hypotheses generated from Lewin's theory, Kounin ran sev-

FIGURE 11.3   Schematic Representation of Comparative Differentiation and Permeability of Retarded and Normal Persons According to Lewin

normal child

normal adult

retarded person with mental age equal to a normal child

eral studies (1941). They consisted of a series of tasks that were performed until the subject *satiated* (refused to continue or stopped when asked if they would like to stop); the experiment was then switched to another task to determine the extent to which satiation on the first task, in theoretical region (1), affected the speed with which the subject would satiate on the second task, presumably in region (2). The prediction was that retarded subjects would persist longer on the second task because of the impermeability of the boundaries; satiating on task 1 should not affect task 2. He found that tasks that were facilitated by lack of communication between regions were indeed performed better by older retarded subjects and more severely retarded subjects, while normals performed better on tasks facilitated by such communication.

In his studies Kounin compared retarded subjects from institutions with normals, a lopsided sampling technique that introduced bias into his results. This and other methodological issues were raised in a series of criticisms that followed publication of Kounin's findings (Goldstein 1943; Plenderleith 1956; Stevenson & Zigler 1957; Werner 1946, 1948).

Zigler's Critique.   Zigler ran a very systematic research program (summarized in Zigler 1962) that he claimed demonstrated that the performance differences reported by Kounin were explained more parsimoniously by motivational differences than by the rigidity hypothesis.

Essentially, Zigler's criticism stemmed from his belief that retarded individuals in institutions are deprived of social contact with adults. He feels that they will engage in activities that appear quite monotonous just to maintain contact with an approving adult. In his experiments the differences in the length of time it took the institutionalized retarded subjects to stop the second task (and it usually was longer than for the nonretarded subjects) were true for institutionalized retarded subjects primarily when the experimenter was supportive during the time the subject worked on the task. In comparison, those institutionalized retarded subjects who performed the same task under a condition where the experimenter was not supportive did not persist as long.

In addition to the difference between retarded and nonretarded subjects in the time they would persist on the second task, a difference was also found among institutionalized retarded subjects according to the amount of social deprivation they had experienced. The group that had experienced more social deprivation was found to persist longer on the second task than were subjects who had experienced less social deprivation. A study by Green (1960) extended these findings. When he compared institutionalized retarded, noninstitutionalized retarded, and normals on a similar task, he reported that the institutionalized retarded subjects persisted on the second task to a greater degree than either of the other groups, neither of which were believed to have experienced as much social deprivation as the institutionalized retarded group. It was unclear whether the persistence was attributable to institutionalization per se, preinstitutionalization histories, or some interaction thereof. But Zigler's and Green's studies did invalidate the conclusions drawn by Kounin (1941) that mentally retarded children are more rigid in their cognitive structures than normal children.

Positive and Negative Reaction Tendencies

As we have seen, Zigler (1962) attributed to institutionalized retarded subjects the desire to interact and maintain contact with an approving adult, a trait that he felt was due to the social deprivation experienced by a sizeable proportion of institutionalized retarded children. But during his studies he encountered some retarded children who actually hesitated to interact. To accommodate this individual variation, Zigler (1962) labeled the desire to interact with an approving adult as the *positive reaction tendency* and labeled wariness of adults as the *negative reaction tendency*. He explained that a retarded child approaches an encounter with adults with a desire to interact because of deprivation from such contact and yet with a hesitancy to approach, resulting from numerous negative experiences with adults in the past (attendants, nurses, physicians). Whichever tendency is strongest determines the trait.

Although Zigler initially considered social deprivation a result of institutionalization, he later (1968) extended these constructs to children from impoverished backgrounds:

> Children who do not receive enough affection and attention from the important adults in their life space suffer in later years from an atypically high need for attention and affection. We find that such children, when faced with cognitive tasks, are not particularly motivated to solve the intellectual problems confronting them. Rather, those children employ their interactions with adults to satisfy their hunger for attention, affection, and yes, as unscientific as it might be, their need for love.
>
> (p. 21)

Harter (1967) demonstrated that if the need for attention and love is strong enough, it may even impair scholastic performance. She reported that children described as disadvantaged had more difficulty solving a problem when social interaction with an approving adult was possible than when such interaction was not possible.

The extension of the positive and negative reaction tendencies to the mildly retarded remains to be conclusively validated. Studies by Harter (1967) and Weaver (1966), however, seem to demonstrate the existence of positive and negative reaction tendencies in retarded children who are not institutionalized. Despite a dearth of confirming evidence, those working with mildly retarded children should be sensitive to the kinds of behaviors that may establish or undermine a sense of rapport with individual children.

We might anticipate that EMR children would evidence a high negative reaction tendency due to their history of negative interactions with teachers and others who have evaluated them in negative ways. In approaching such children the teacher might expect that while these children exhibit a wariness to interact, they may desire such interaction at the same time. The first few interactions may determine whether the child's desire for interaction or wariness of adults will come to the fore. Should the adult present an approachable image, the wariness may be overcome; a rejecting facade may have just the opposite effect.

If the EMR child does feel a precarious balance between a desire to interact with the teacher and a wariness of doing so, we should perhaps question the advice commonly offered to beginning teachers that you should be tough at the beginning of the year because you can never again establish control. Such teacher behavior might just tip the balance in such a child in favor of the defensive negative-reaction tendency.

Extrinsic Motivational Orientation

Another personality trait found in EMR children is their extrinsic motivational orientation (Tymchuk 1972), a trait particularly characteristic of retarded children from nondominant cultural backgrounds. Haywood and Dobbs (1964) described the extrinsically motivated child as interested in safety, comfort, and tangible or monetary rewards; this child tends to avoid tension-producing situations. In contrast, the intrinsically motivated child is inclined to be an overachiever in school.

Motivational orientation—intrinsic or extrinsic—has been shown to account for a considerable amount of the variance in scholastic achievement among EMR children (Haywood 1968a, 1968b; Haywood & Wachs 1966; Haywood & Weaver 1967). While the relationship between this trait and certain other variables is tenuous, extant evidence suggests that extrinsic motivational orientation has been related to high expectation of failure, low motivation, high anxiety, poor self-concept, and poor school performance.

Intrinsic and extrinsic motivation were also compared by Harter (1978). She defined intrinsic mastery motivation as "the desire to solve cognitively challenging problems for the gratification inherent in discovering the solution," while extrinsic motivation was defined as the need for approval or "the child's desire for adult praise" (p. 55). Using these definitions, Harter and Zigler (1974) reported that normal children were more oriented toward intrinsic mastery than were retarded children. Subsequent studies by Harter (1975a, 1975b) revealed a sex difference among normals, with older girls showing a greater extrinsic orientation than older boys.

Outerdirectedness

Two more behavioral traits that have often been noticed in retarded students are (1) their tendency to imitate the behavior of others and (2) their tendency to respond to cues that are emitted by others or that are available in their environment as to the correctness of their responses in problem solving. All of us on occasion make use of cues as to right and wrong, but the retarded seem to use them so much that their use may become detrimental. These behaviors, which are frequently observed in retarded children, have been labeled *outerdirectedness* by Zigler and his associates (Green & Zigler 1962; Turnure & Zigler 1964).

Zigler (1966) suggests that the retarded come to rely heavily on external cues because they are more conducive to successful problem solving than are their own poorly developed cognitive resources. In normal development, as children grow older and become more capable cognitively, they tend to rely increasingly on their own solutions. But as retarded persons attempt to solve problems through their own cognitive abilities, they learn that they are wrong more often than right. As a consequence they come to distrust their own abilities and the immature outerdirected style persists. Outerdirectedness in the mentally retarded is therefore thought to result from two factors: the child's lower mental age and the history of success and failure. Outerdirectedness is not found only among retarded children. Some children of normal intelligence with histories of academic failure manifested outerdirectedness similar to that of mentally retarded children described by Turnure and Zigler (1964) and Turnure (1970a, 1970b).

It has been somewhat hard to measure outerdirectedness variables because of the difficulty of distinguishing between a child who is simply not paying attention to the task and one who is actively seeking external cues to its solution (Turnure, Larsen, & Thurlow 1976). Most studies of outerdirectedness have looked for "glancing behavior" as a measure of the trait. But as Nakamura and Finck (1973) have pointed out, the child's looking at other people may serve social-interaction rather than task-solution purposes and in fact is completely unrelated to the solution of the task.

Despite methodological problems, it appears that children are most likely to use outerdirected behavior when they are unable to solve problems using their own resources. When the task confronting children is difficult for them they are more inclined to exhibit outerdirected behavior than they would in a situation when they felt in control. Two studies using retarded children (Balla, Styfco, & Zigler 1971; Yando & Zigler 1971) showed that the children most deficient in the tasks tended to evidence the most outerdirected problem-solving style.

It is important to note that outerdirectedness is not a trait inherent in mental retardation, nor is it invariably a handicap to the child. Sometimes it does pay off. Zigler (1966), however, contends that it tends to result in a lack of spontaneity and creativity. Children must rely on both external cues and their own cognitive resources to solve problems. It is possible that mentally retarded children become habitually dependent on external cues even when they are capable of solving problems by using their own cognitive resources.

Self-concept

In considering trait constructs, Carl Rogers (1951) suggests that it is important to understand the internal frame of reference by which individuals evaluate themselves. According to current personality theory, optimal personality development and adjustment require that the individual feel a sense of self-worth and that the "real self" and "ideal self" not be too discrepant. This dual requirement raises obvious problems for retarded individuals—they are damned if they do have a high self-concept and damned if they don't. For them an accurate self-perception would probably be negative—and according to current theory, a negative self-concept is a bad thing to have.

Despite the presumed importance of self-concept, this trait construct has received surprisingly little research attention. This is due in part to difficulties in assessing the self-concept of the retarded—most scales are verbal in nature or require skills beyond those of most retarded persons (Gardner 1966). Another problem, noted by Balla and Zigler (1979), is that there are almost as many measures of self-concept as there are reported studies. To further complicate comparisons of the results, some of the scales measure a unitary self-concept, whereas others break the construct down into academic, social, and other components.

Sternlicht and Deutsch (1972) suggested that retarded persons' conceptions of their own retardation is so emotionally laden that they are incapable of accepting their limitations and working within them. This notion is supported by Edgerton (1967) who noted that the retarded wrap themselves in a "cloak of competence" in their attempts to deny their retardation. This defensive behavior leads the retarded into situations they cannot cope with, which results in more failure and further attempts at denial. Sternlicht and Deutsch (1972) concluded that this sort of situation leads to feelings of inadequacy, self-denial, resentment, and frustration that others can sense. At the same time, retarded people may feel a need to protect themselves from their failures and from fears of negative evaluations by others and themselves. As you can see, there is ample reason for interpreting their responses on a self-concept measure cautiously.

There have been attempts to measure something akin to self-concept in many of the efficacy studies reviewed in Chapter 7. But the reasoning that was followed in those studies tends to emphasize the administrative arrangement as the variable that accounts for differences between groups of children equated on IQ, not the lowered intellect per se. In the present context, however, the question of interest is whether the retarded as a group tend to demonstrate lower or unrealistically higher self-concepts than do their normal peers.

The results of studies that have been made do not suggest any overall generalizations. One investigation (Guthrie, Butler, & Gorlow 1962) reported that institutionalized girls admitted fewer negative statements about themselves than did noninstitutionalized girls. But do these children actually have higher self-concepts, or are they more defensive about their limitations? Our inability to make this distinction is a major limitation of much of the self-concept research to date.

Ringness (1961) studied children's estimates of their achievement in eight different areas. Although the measure he used was more a measure of level of aspiration than of individuals' feelings about themselves (Heber 1964), Ringness concluded that (1) the retarded children tended to overestimate success as compared to brighter children; (2) the self-concepts of the retarded were less realistic than were those of brighter children; (3) ratings varied as a function of intelligence, sex, and the situation; and (4) self-ratings of the retarded children were less reliable than were those of brighter children.

But other studies have shown that within the retarded population, high self-concept is matched to relatively high ability. Hardy (1967) reported that adolescent EMRs who scored higher on a measure of self-concept were more efficient in learning paired associates than were classmates with less favorable self-concepts. In an institutionalized sample of retarded subjects, the group with higher self-concepts not only performed better on a learning task but also were able to handle better the effects of negative feedback (Wink 1963).

Bialer (1970) synthesized the available evidence as an indication that we cannot identify a single pattern that can be applied to all retarded subjects—some see themselves in extremely negative terms and others exhibit highly favorable self-perceptions. Also, there is a consistent tendency for intelligence level and self-appraisal to be positively related in both retarded and nonretarded groups. That is, the higher the IQ, the more favorable the self-appraisal is likely to be. Furthermore, there is a positive relationship between self-attitude and academic achievement, which is independent of IQ. And finally, there is a tendency for retarded subjects to overestimate themselves on current or future performance. When asked how well they will do on a task, retarded subjects tend to predict far greater success than they achieve when given a chance to perform.

We might speculate whether retarded subjects are simply unaware of their own limitations and thereby conclude that they will do extremely well, or whether the overestimation of their ability derives from a defensive response to feelings of inferiority. Several authors (Edgerton 1967; Guthrie,

Butler, Gorlow, & White 1964; Perron 1962) suggest that in the majority of instances a denial mechanism is operating with which retarded persons deny their inferiority or incompetence. An interesting study by Cleland, Patton, and Seitz (1967) suggests the vulnerability of the mentally retarded to their relatively low intellectual standing. A group of retarded subjects and a group of students attending business school were instructed to pretend to insult someone with whom they were angry. The retarded group generated insults that were commonly related to the intelligence of the person they were insulting, while the nonretarded sample generated insults aimed at the character of the person they wished to insult. It is not unreasonable to assume that such findings suggest that the retarded group perceived intellectual incompetence as a major area of vulnerability. But we do not yet know for sure whether this presumed feeling of vulnerability causes defensiveness in self-concept and whether it is felt by retarded people in general.

Aggressiveness

Are retarded people more likely to be aggressive than normals? Since frustration is one of the major causes of aggression, we should not be surprised to find frequent examples of aggressive behavior in the retarded since they are exposed to so much more frustration than are normals.

As we have seen, a number of studies show that institutional life can cause frustration and therefore aggression. For example, Talkington and Hall (1969) studied factors in institutions, such as having little privacy, being cared for, and having the conditions of life imposed by attendants, as contributors to aggression. In another study Talkington and Riley (1971) noted an increase in aggressive acts when patients were placed on restricted diets. Heber (1964) concluded that aggressiveness is well documented in institutionalized retarded persons; but he noted that this is not surprising, as aggressive behavior often leads to institutionalization.

A distinction can be made between overt aggression and fantasy aggression, which is not acted out but shows up in responses to tests such as the Thematic Apperception Test. One study (Sternlicht & Silverg 1965) found that there was no difference in fantasy aggression between institutionalized retarded groups and normals, although they did differ on overt aggression. Surveying penitentiaries, Silber and Courtless (1968) found that the most serious offenders (murder, rape, criminal assault) with IQ < 70 showed the least fantasy aggression. (These authors, incidentally, challenged the assumption that the retarded experience greater frustration.) This group, at least, had apparently acted out their aggressive feelings. Since some institutionalized retarded people become overtly aggressive and some do not, Heber (1964) concluded that, as in the nonretarded, the different manifestations of aggression serve different functions for different individuals.

One form of aggression that has been identified in institutionalized retarded patients is territoriality. Paluck and Esser (1971a) discovered that retarded patients in institutions establish spatial territories on wards, which they then protect. One group dominates certain areas, toys, tables, and so forth. Aggressive behavior was observed when a subject felt that a child from another group was threatening the territory. In a follow-up to their fascinating study Paluck and Esser (1971b) reported fights and other "aggressive territorial incidents" in which control of some areas of the experimental room was challenged, even though the children seemed to have established territorial boundaries in the earlier phase of the study.

Rago and his associates (Rago 1978; Rago, Parker, & Cleland 1978) continued this line of research in studies of profoundly retarded males in institutions. Rago (1978) reported the existence of a "dominance hierarchy" within groups. Any resident might be the victim of aggressive acts by the most dominant person in the group. The new members introduced to the group were not subjected to more aggressive behavior than the members they replaced, which suggests that they conformed to existing group standards. Rago et al. (1978) also reported that they were able to reduce significantly the number of aggressive behaviors by increasing (by 29 percent) the playroom space available to the group members.

As you may have noticed, the evidence on the greater prevalence of aggression in the retarded stems almost exclusively from research conducted on institutionalized populations. Since we know that aggression is a factor often leading to institutionalization, we must be extremely cautious in generalizing these findings to all retarded persons. Conditions in the institutions themselves, such as lack of privacy and territoriality, may contribute to aggressiveness. Other factors (e.g., communication deficits) may serve to limit the options of some retarded persons for venting frustration in socially acceptable ways, explaining in part the higher prevalence rates of overtly aggressive behavior noted in institutionalized retarded subjects.

Evidence on differential rates for mildly retarded subjects is woefully lacking. We might expect that EMR children integrated into regular classes would exhibit greater aggression than they would in self-contained special classrooms, since they would probably be more frustrated when the instruction is less adapted to their learning characteristics. But this remains to be investigated. What can be said is that the theory that frustration leads to aggression seems as applicable to retarded individuals as it is to the nonretarded.

TYPOLOGICAL CONSTRUCTS

When all their perceived threats, defense mechanisms, needs, and traits are taken into account, can retarded individuals be seen as people with generally disordered personalities? Are they usually psychotic, neurotic, or criminal? Attempts to sum up the types of people found in the retarded population present a garbled picture. Considerable attention has been paid to the prevalence of mental disorders within the mentally retarded population. There are extensive reviews of the evidence pertaining to behavior disorders or abnormal behavior in this population (see Beier 1964; Bialer 1970; Garfield 1963; Lang & Smirnoff 1970) as well as reviews of the use of psychotherapy in the treatment of such disorders (Bialer 1967; Gunzberg 1974; Sternlicht 1966).

Before considering the results of these studies, we should note that the terms *psychotic* and *neurotic* are used differently in different investigations and that the diagnostic criteria vary. As a result we cannot compare the results of such surveys with any degree of certainty (Garfield 1963). And in some cases it is difficult to determine whether a severely disturbed child is retarded or not. In autism, for instance, the emotional overlay is so great that it is difficult to determine whether the child would be mentally retarded were it not for the emotional disorder.

The prevailing opinion in texts on mental retardation is that there is a higher prevalence of behavior disorders in retarded persons than there is among the nonretarded population (Garfield 1963). But this generalization has been challenged (e.g., Rutter 1964). The evidence for such opinions tends to be taken from surveys, but Garfield (1963) argues that these surveys are too superficial to provide a clear picture of the extent of severe personality disorders. There are problems in diagnostic criteria and in sampling as well, for most of the surveys are based on institutionalized retarded populations. Efforts to obtain estimates on emotional problems among retarded persons coming to a diagnostic clinic (Philips 1966) or among preschool retarded children (Webster 1970) also reveal high frequencies of emotional disorders, yet these results cannot be generalized to the entire population of retarded persons. Children who are taken to a clinic or enrolled in a preschool program for retarded children are seldom uncomplicated cases of mental retardation; instead, they frequently evidence a compounding problem such as an emotional disorder.

Estimates of the frequency of emotional disorders among the mentally retarded range from 25 percent (Menolascino 1965) to 100 percent (Webster 1970). Some of these disorders are thought to predominate in the lower IQ ranges of the retarded population; stereotypic self-stimulatory movements and self-destructive behaviors, for instance, are found more frequently among the severely and profoundly retarded.

Psychoses

Although there is much overlap in the definitions used by various surveys, *psychosis* generally refers to the more severe mental disorders, characterized by the degeneration of social and cognitive functioning and by some degree of withdrawal from reality. Estimates of the prevalence of psychoses in retarded populations vary from 10 percent to 50 percent (Browne, Gunzberg, Johnston-Hannah, Maccoll, Oliver, & Thomas 1971; Craft 1959; Neuer 1947; Penrose 1954; Williams 1971; Wunsch 1951). These widely ranging estimates have all been drawn from institutional populations. The findings do seem to indicate, according to O'Connor and Tizard (1956), that "a higher figure for instability and emotional disturbance will be found in any defective population than for a normal population" (p. 66).

It is questionable how safe this generalization is, however. For one thing, it is unclear whether the institutional surveys are a fair indication of the prevalence of such disorders in the mentally retarded population at large, whether institutions in any way cause behavior disorders, or whether mentally retarded individuals who exhibit behavior disorders are more likely to be institutionalized than retarded persons without such disorders. The last alternative seems to represent the majority opinion (Beier 1964; Garfield 1963; Gunzberg 1974; Saenger 1960). Second, the prevalence figures are biased toward the more severely retarded since they tend to be institutionalized in greater numbers than the mildly retarded. This is particularly true today with the trend toward normalization. Third, there is some question as to the validity of the diagnosis of mental retardation. In one study (Craft 1960), four patients had IQs over 90 and in ten other cases the diagnoses were doubtful. The higher-functioning mentally retarded subjects available for study are probably those who get into trouble and are therefore institutionalized. Fourth, variability in criteria for psychoses also makes comparison difficult. Terminology in the various studies ranges from *psychiatric disorders, psychoses, major psychoses,* and *mental illness* to *minor psychoses* and *social adjustment problems.* These various degrees of disorder would obviously affect the prevalence figures obtained. Finally, the wide variation in prevalence figures itself makes generalizations difficult.

A few other studies have been conducted in an attempt to assess prevalence of behavior disorders among noninstitutionalized retarded persons. Some surveys of army populations and hospital outpatients have reported that almost half of those judged mentally retarded were also considered to be emotionally unstable (Dewan 1948), and that personality disorders are twice as prevalent among retarded individuals as among the nonretarded (Craft 1960). But a study by Weaver (1946) of 8000 mentally retarded members of the United States Army showed that the majority were reported to have made a satisfactory adjustment to military life; only 13 percent of the white subjects and 6.5 percent of the black subjects were given medical discharges because of severe psychiatric and physical conditions.

Surveys by Craft (1960) and Beier (1964) noted that retarded individuals rarely evidenced depression. And MacGillivray (1956) has made the provocative observation that as an IQ rises or as the retarded person gets older, the various forms of psychosis tend to separate out and become more clearly defined. But these surveys are all subject to the same kinds of criticisms made of institutional surveys (Garfield 1963).

In general, we can probably conclude that there is a reasonably high prevalence of severe personality disturbance in institutionalized retarded patients, but we must be extremely cautious in citing even a ball-park figure for this prevalence. The evidence on the prevalence of psychosis in the retarded population at large is even less satisfactory. There can be little doubt that retarded individuals do suffer from emotional disorders, but what is yet to be answered is whether it is their lowered mental ability or their experiences that make them more vulnerable to such disorders. Systematic research that is carefully controlled for criteria and sampling is still sorely needed.

Psychoneuroses

Compared to psychoses, neuroses are generally considered to be less crippling, minor maladjustments. The study of neuroses in retarded individuals is subject to the same criticism as that of psychoses: sampling bias and lack of precision in criteria. As Beier (1964) warned:

> In this area we have the alarmist approach which, in regard to maladjustments in the mentally retarded, finds maladjustment, not under every tree and bush, but under every leaf of every tree and bush.
>
> (p. 470)

The common assumption is that, due to their intellectual limitations, mentally retarded individuals encounter more adjustment problems than is the case for children of normal intelligence. Among the more common reasons suggested for maladjustment are rejection, overprotection, failure, and ridicule, which result in frustrations and strong feelings of guilt, shame, and inadequacy. Beier (1959) noted that because of their slower development, retarded children are slower to incorporate a sense of right and wrong, good and bad, into a value system. Internalization of control is thus slower to evolve, requiring longer and closer supervision. Because of this delay it is possible that observation of a retarded child might lead one to conclude that adjustment is maladaptive, when in fact it is the same type of behavior one would observe in a younger normal child.

Little is known for sure about the prevalence of neuroses in retarded individuals. In a survey of 3000 neurotic patients in the British military, Eysenck (1943) found a rather high percentage of both high- and low-intelligence subjects in the neurotic sample. But Craft's (1959) survey of residents of institutions found that as intellectual level increased, the prevalence of emotional instability decreased. These conflicting reports highlight the complexity of personality disorders and seem to indicate that the differences cannot be explained in terms of IQ differences alone.

If we are to understand the seemingly higher rates of emotional disturbance (assuming that this is verified by more rigorously controlled research), then the importance of rejection, overprotection, failure, ridicule, and other experiences often encountered by a large segment of the retarded population must be considered. There have been a few efforts in this direction. A study by Marcotte (1947) related certain factors to personality problems in the retarded; for instance, while mental ability was the factor most commonly related to behavior problems, family and school influences were also related. And Bourne (1955) reported that adverse home environments were found to have a negative effect on both intellectual and personality development of the child.

Some analysts feel that neurotic disturbance can depress intellectual functioning. If this were true it would compound the problems of retarded individuals. But this assumption has been challenged by a number of critics (Beier 1964; Bialer 1970) and researchers (Penrose 1963; Rabin 1967; Wolf 1965), who cite evidence that intellectual functioning is not adversely affected by neurotic disturbance. Bialer interpreted the evidence to mean the reverse. He hypothesized that lowered mental ability comes first, making the retarded person less able to cope with externally imposed stresses. The anxiety then manifested as a consequence of the inability to cope presumably leads to neurotic behavior.

In general, the evidence on prevalence of psychoses and psychoneuroses in the mentally retarded population cannot be explained in terms of the presence of retardation per se but must take into account the variability within the retarded population (O'Connor & Tizard 1956). Garfield (1963) concluded that the prevalence of emotional disturbance among the mentally retarded is not so high that we should associate one condition with the other. As a group, mentally retarded individuals represent a wide variety of personality types and the evidence to date does not warrant stereotypes of the group, or even of any subgroups.

Criminality

The last kind of personality construct we will consider for retarded persons is whether they are more likely than normals to become criminal types. Mentally retarded individuals, particularly those in the higher IQ strata, are certainly as capable of delinquent and criminal behavior as are their normal peers (Beier 1964). But in the first part of this century, some observers claimed that mental retardation was almost synonymous with criminal behavior. Palmer (1927), for instance, wrote:

> It is clearly established that the defective delinquent presents not only sub-normality of intelligence, but that he suffers from personality disorder and shows conduct deviation—that he occurs in the proportion of at least 35 in every 100 inmates of our correctional institutions and that because he is abnormal he is not susceptible to training intended for the normal.
>
> (Quoted in Beier 1964, p. 467)

In accounts published before 1930, the prevalence of sociopathic behavior among the retarded was estimated variously to be between 22 and 90 percent. An address by Walter E. Fernald, former superintendent of the Massachusetts School for the Feebleminded, exemplifies the prevalent attitude. In 1912, speaking before the Massachusetts Medical Society, he stated that:

> Every feebleminded person, especially the high grade imbecile, is a potential criminal needing only the proper environment and opportunity for the development and expression of his criminal tendencies. . . . Feebleminded women are almost invariably immoral. . . . It has been truly said that the feeblemindedness is the mother of crime, pauperism, and degeneracy.
>
> (Quoted in Wallin 1956, pp. 78–79)

After reviewing the early literature, however, Sternlicht and Deutsch (1972) concluded that when extraneous factors such as social class, age, and nationality are controlled, the differences in the frequency of delinquency among the retarded and the nonretarded are negligible.

Although the prevailing belief in the first half of this century was that retardation and criminality were intimately related, some investigators reported no differences in criminality between the retarded and the nonretarded, and others even suggested that there was a lower incidence of criminal behavior among the retarded (Zeleny 1933). Gradually, evidence began pointing to social factors that were related to delinquency and criminality, and the view that retarded individuals were a homogeneous group with criminal leanings subsided. Problems in the research that reported high prevalence rates of crime among the retarded were exposed, such as inaccurate diagnosis of retardation and the overlooking of significant social and environmental variables related to the criminal behavior (Garfield 1963).

There had been two studies that did carefully determine the accuracy of the diagnosis, and they showed a much lower prevalence than other early studies. Bromberg and Thompson (1937) evaluated 10,000 prisoners who came to the psychiatric clinic of a New York City court, and they found that only 2.4 percent of the prisoners were mentally retarded. Tulchin (1939) reported a similar figure in a survey of 10,000 inmates in Illinois prisons.

More recent studies have not pinned down the prevalence figure but they have contributed some interesting observations. Beier (1964), for instance, noticed that in terms of the types of crimes committed by retarded individuals, few are white-collar criminals. In a more significant observation, Beier noted that while retardation may not be a direct cause of delinquency, it well may be a complicating factor. Smith (1962), for example, noted that the retarded may become involved in crime because they do not have the insight or awareness of consequences of such behavior.

SUMMARY

Research on affective states in the mentally retarded is a critical area, since the adjustment of retarded individuals seems to hinge on characteristics closely related to personality. But the research evidence that does exist tends to suffer from several problems. First, much of it is based on work done with institutionalized subjects, whose personality problems may well have led to their being institutionalized. Furthermore, while this research provides us with some sense of the personality of institutionalized retarded persons, we are left with far less evidence on noninstitutionalized retarded persons. In all probability they differ from those in institutions, particularly on personality variables. In addition, there is a tendency for those writing in the field to consider lower-class children as synonymous with mildly retarded children (EMR). This tendency probably arises from the observation that disproportionate numbers of EMR children come from such backgrounds, but we must not draw conclusions about mildly retarded children based on this evidence no matter how frustrating is the paucity of evidence about actual EMR children.

Another series of problems with the evidence reviewed pertains to the instruments employed. In many cases the same instruments used to study a particular personality construct in nonhandicapped populations are used with retarded subjects, even though they often require reading ability or verbal comprehension skills in which the retarded are at a disadvantage. The reliability of these scales is therefore questionable.

Finally, remember that the development of personality theories was seldom done with the mentally retarded in mind (Lewin is one exception). Speculation as to whether the retarded move more slowly through the postulated stages or whether they never get to some of the higher stages is merely that—speculation—sometimes supported by clinical impression, but nevertheless of questionable validity.

In general, there is no support for the position that personality dynamics in the mentally retarded operate any differently than they do in nonretarded persons. What does stand out is that the retarded are often exposed to situations with which they are ill-prepared to deal. As a consequence they fail too often or are placed into environments that, independent of intellectual level, exert their own pressures on personalities, which results in differences of *degree,* not *kind.*

To consider specific personality constructs, we used Cromwell's division of current theories into threats, defenses, needs, traits, and types.

Since there is no good way to measure *threats,* they have been inferred from behavior. It was suggested that as a consequence of their histories of failure, retarded individuals may perceive as threats situations and events that would not be perceived that way by children with more successful histories. The retarded seem to exhibit a high expectation for failure, for they exhibit behaviors interpreted as defenses designed to protect themselves from additional failure or to escape the situation that is perceived as threatening. This response may compound the performance problems of the retarded, for it may direct them away from learning experiences that they are capable of mastering but that they do not attempt for fear that they will fail.

The evidence indicates that anxiety seems to operate similarly in the retarded as in normal persons; a high level of anxiety seems to facilitate performance on easy tasks and interfere with performance on complex learning tasks. But anxiety levels tend to be measured by paper-and-pencil tests of unknown validity for retarded subjects, so we do not yet know whether retarded children are more anxious or less anxious than normals. As for frustration, another presumed threat, the examination of the literature fails to support the notion that the retarded are inherently more frustrated than normals; in fact, it seems to reveal that frustration operates in the retarded the same way it does in normals. But it can be said that the conditions and practices in institutions seem to be a source of frustration to residents.

In considering *defense mechanisms,* we found that the mentally retarded child does appear to exhibit behavior whose function is to defend the self from threats. While none of the evidence indicates that the defensive behaviors exhibited by the retarded are unique to them, the retarded may use a greater proportion of their energy in defensive behavior because of the failure they encounter in social and learning situations.

The defense mechanisms derived from psychoanalytic theory are thought to be used less efficiently by mentally retarded individuals than by normals, primarily because of the lack of variation shown by the retarded in employing these mechanisms. Further, the retarded as a group are described as using the more primitive defense mechanisms, although this generalization may not be valid for all subgroups of retarded individuals. Actually, the use of defense mechanisms by the retarded has received only scant systematic attention and is based almost exclusively on clinical impressions and extrapolation from theoretical writings.

In terms of *needs* we found that retarded children seem to be motivated by the need for social acceptance as much as, or even more than, normal children. This need seems to be strongest in those who have been socially deprived by institutionalization. The need for achievement may not be as fully developed in retarded as in normal children, but this difference may be a result of social and family background rather than of retardation in itself. And retarded children seem to feel less need for competence than normal children, especially if they have been institutionalized. In test situations they may prefer either social contact with an approving adult or else tangible rewards to more intangible incentives, like being correct. But in their hierarchy of preferred rewards, retarded children show individual variations, just as normal children do.

The review of personality *traits* in retarded persons fails to reveal differences of kind and only serves to emphasize that the retarded are not a group apart from the nonretarded but rather part of a continuum. While there may be differences in the frequency with which the retarded exhibit certain traits, these differences can be explained by the different life experiences to which they are exposed (e.g., greater amounts of failure) and certainly cannot be interpreted as characteristics inherent in mental retardation.

In terms of global personality *types*, research findings indicate that the same disorders that are present in the population at large are also present in the mentally retarded population. There does appear to be a higher than normal prevalence of psychoses in the institutionalized retarded. But due to lack of evidence on the noninstitutionalized retarded population, generalizations must be restricted to that portion of the mentally retarded population who reside in institutions.

The notion that the retarded as a group suffer more mild personality disorders receives only minimal support from the extant research. The more recent studies that attempt to relate certain experiences (such as failure and ridicule) to the presence of psychoneuroses appear to be potentially more fruitful than the earlier attempts simply to ascribe these conditions to lowered intellect per se.

The claims of a high incidence of criminal behavior in the retarded population in the early 1900s have not been substantiated in more carefully controlled research. But although the notion of an inherent tendency toward crime and immorality among the retarded can be dispelled once and for all based on the evidence, lowered intellect may serve indirectly to make the retarded individual more vulnerable to committing criminal acts. The retarded individual may not consider the consequences of such actions and may be more easily convinced to perform them due to lesser reasoning powers.

PART VI

Education, Training, and Treatment

CHAPTER 12

Educational Programing

In this chapter, we will discuss the education of mentally retarded children—their diagnosis, classification, and placement having been discussed previously. Since the passage of PL 94-142 and state and local attempts to implement its provisions, it has been increasingly difficult to talk of *programs* or *administrative arrangements*. The essence of the law is that the education of handicapped children is to be prescribed individually and that the services are to be delivered in the least restrictive environment. These provisions have profoundly altered the educational programs for EMR children, and, to a slightly lesser extent, programs for TMR children as well. In addition, Meyers, MacMillan, and Zetlin (1978) noted that the law dramatically altered the meaning of the word *education*—it can now involve teaching such basic self-care skills as toileting, feeding, dressing, and talking. This change came about as a result of the "zero reject" provision whereby no child, regardless of the severity of handicap, can be denied a free and appropriate public education.

School districts vary in their ability to provide alternative placements for retarded children. Fully developed districts offer a wide array of alternatives, but others may offer only a few. The goal in educational placement and programing is to achieve the best match possible between a child's needs and the ability of an educational environment to meet them.

How important is the kind of placement to a retarded child's educational success? According to Bruininks and Rynders (1971), too much emphasis has been placed on administrative arrangements as compared to teaching methods, materials, and roles. As Figure 12.1 illustrates schematically, these forces should interact to achieve one goal of special education: to achieve differential instruction for children through the alteration of the curriculum or professional roles. Similarly, because there are various elements that go into an educational program (e.g., administrative arrangement, instructional strategies, materials), we must be careful to determine what proportion of the variation in student performance is accounted for by the administrative arrangement. And Smith (1974) has argued that a debate over the relative merits of the various placement alternatives for mentally retarded children misses the important question when it comes down to deciding on the placement for a given child. As he puts it, the central question should be: "Where within the existing resources of my school district can the individual educational plan required by each retarded child best be provided at the present time?" (p. 113).

On the other hand, there are aspects of the administrative arrangement that may have an important bearing on a retarded child's success. Careful placement decisions not only require an assessment of the child's educational needs, using data that are reliable and valid, and a thoughtful review

**FIGURE 12.1   Educational Influences of the Development
of the Retarded Child**

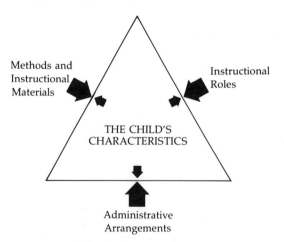

R. H. Bruininks, and J. E. Rynders, "Alternatives to special class placement for educable mentally retarded children," from *Focus on Exceptional Children*, 1971. Reprinted by permission of Love Publishing Company.

of how these needs can be matched with available educational options, but they also must consider the attitudes of a specific teacher or building principal, transportation requirements, and other factors outside the child that might determine the success of a given placement.

Despite pleas for de-emphasis of administrative arrangements, special educators have debated the placement of mildly retarded children extensively (Christophos & Renz 1969; Dunn 1968; Goldstein 1967; MacMillan 1971b; Meyers, MacMillan, & Yoshida 1980). The arguments and evidence pertaining to the advantages and disadvantages of special class placement for EMR children will be discussed later in this chapter.

We will first discuss traditional considerations in the education of EMR and TMR children. The education of SPMR children in the public schools, which is a relatively recent development, will also be considered later in the chapter.

TRADITIONAL SPECIAL EDUCATION FOR RETARDED CHILDREN

The diagnosis of EMR and TMR children was discussed in Chapter 6. It was noted there that educators were required to determine (1) the special needs of the child and (2) which existing program was most likely to meet these needs. Recently, there have been two basic programs in most school systems, an EMR and a TMR program. The administrative arrangements and curricula of these programs were predetermined and basically static—adjustments were not made for individual children, although variations did occur between school districts. The basic administrative arrangement for EMR students was a self-contained special class, usually with some integration into regular education. TMR children were frequently placed in special day schools or special classes for TMR children on the regular elementary school grounds.

CONTINUUM OF PLACEMENT ALTERNATIVES

Since the mentally retarded population is extremely heterogeneous with respect to virtually every attribute, various educational options are needed to provide a reasonably good fit with differing individual needs. Figure 12.2 and Table 12.1 show the complete range of placement alternatives (which would be found only in fully developed special educational systems).

Although various authors (e.g., Cruickshank & Johnson 1967; Deno 1972) have discussed the ways in which different kinds of placements vary, there

FIGURE 12.2   Deno's Cascade of Special Education Services

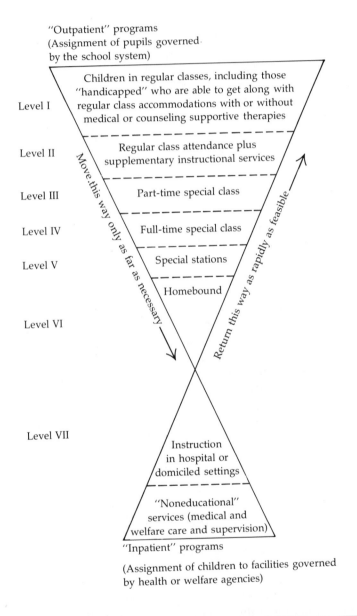

"Outpatient" programs
(Assignment of pupils governed
by the school system)

Level I — Children in regular classes, including those "handicapped" who are able to get along with regular class accommodations with or without medical or counseling supportive therapies

Level II — Regular class attendance plus supplementary instructional services

Level III — Part-time special class

Level IV — Full-time special class

Level V — Special stations

Homebound

Level VI

Move this way only as far as necessary

Return this way as rapidly as feasible

Level VII — Instruction in hospital or domiciled settings

"Noneducational" services (medical and welfare care and supervision)

"Inpatient" programs

(Assignment of children to facilities governed by health or welfare agencies)

TABLE 12.1   Administrative Options for Mentally Retarded Children

Administrative Arrangement	Subgroup Served	Corresponding Level on Deno's Cascade
1. Regular Class with:		
no ancillary services	EMR	Level I
itinerant teacher	EMR	Level II
resource room	EMR	Level II
2. Special Class	EMR, TMR	Levels III and IV
3. Special School	TMR	Level V
developmental center	SPMR	Level V
4. Special Residential School	TMR, SPMR	Level VII
5. Institution	SPMR	Level VII

is no consensus on the definitional parameters of each of Deno's levels. There are at least two possibilities. First, the points may represent differing degrees to which special services are concentrated. That is, in Deno's model (Figure 12.2) concentration of special services increases from Level I through Level VII; in Table 12.1, services increase from administrative arrangements 1 through 5. An alternative explanation for the continuum is that it represents the degree to which children are removed from contact with their nonretarded peers. From Levels I through VII in Deno's cascade and Levels 1 through 5 in Table 12.1, there is a gradual increase in the amount of time the retarded child is removed from contact with nonretarded children.

Before we consider the placement alternatives separately, there are two general points that should be remembered in considering where to place specific retarded children. One is the principle of *normalization*, which has received widespread support in special education circles. This philosophical principle, which came to us from the Scandinavian countries, means "making available to the mentally retarded patterns and conditions of everyday life which are as close as possible to the norms and patterns of the mainstream of society" (Nirje 1969, p. 181). When applied to the placement of mentally retarded children in programs, normalization means that (1) the child should be placed in the administrative arrangement closest to the regular class that the child's own needs and characteristics will allow and (2) the administrative arrangements should be as flexible as possible to allow as much meaningful integration of the mentally retarded into mainstream education as is beneficial, both for the retarded child and the nonretarded peers.

The second point is that no one placement should be considered to be appropriate for a prolonged period of time but only for the retarded child's *present* needs and characteristics. All programs must make provisions for periodic and short-term reevaluation of the child to determine the desirability of continuing with a particular placement or moving the child if the needs and characteristics have changed.

The Regular Class

Some children with IQs between 55 and 70, especially those with IQs in the high 60s, seem to profit from regular education. Others, however, have learning problems and require special attention (see Chapter 6 for a discussion of referral and placement of the EMR). Those who function fairly well in regular classes should not be designated EMR—the current definition states that mental retardation consists of both low intellectual functioning *and* problems in adaptive behavior. Those who can manage in the regular class usually remain there. But what about those who have persistent academic problems across most subject matter areas? Should they be left in the regular class to sink or swim?

To answer this question, we must consider the problems associated with inclusive definitions, which identify large numbers of children, and "restrictive" definitions, which identify relatively few. The use of an inclusive definition involves a risk of false positive identifications—labeling children who do not need services. Restrictive definitions may lead to false negatives—the failure to identify all of the children who need services. Concern about the failure to provide for the unmet needs of mildly handicapped children is clearly expressed in PL 94-142, which states that there are many handicapped school children throughout the United States participating in regular school programs who are prevented from having successful educational experiences because their handicaps go undetected (Section 601).

Many critics of special class placement advocate the return of EMR children to regular classes in the name of mainstreaming, citing efficacy studies interpreted as indicating that special class students have lower academic achievement than low-IQ subjects in regular classes. (For a discussion of these studies, see Goldstein 1967; Guskin & Spicker 1968; MacMillan 1971b; Meyers, MacMillan, & Yoshida 1980; Semmel, Gottlieb & Robinson 1979). The argument based on these studies usually runs like this: If the regular class subjects achieve academically as well as, or better than, special class subjects, then all EMR children can be placed in regular classes, and without ancillary support they will achieve as well as or better than they would if they were in a special class. But there are several problems with this line of reasoning. First, the comparison of EMR to equal-IQ children in regular classes implies that the equal-IQ children are also retarded. According to the dual criteria for diagnosis of mental retardation, this assumption is invalid. In some cases the regular class subjects in the efficacy studies were comparable in IQ to the special class subjects but had avoided being identified as mentally retarded because their academic achievement was *not* deficient.

A second line of reasoning for returning EMR children to regular classrooms, or for not separating them in the first place, seems to come from the legal actions and public concern over the effects of labeling children as mentally retarded. The court decisions (Gilhool 1973; Hall 1970; Kirp 1973, 1974b; Kirp, Buss, & Kuriloff 1974; Ross, DeYoung, & Cohen 1971), pieces of legislation, and professional literature have made the case that by attaching the label *mentally retarded* to children we depress their academic and social performance by triggering a "self-fulfilling prophecy." The rationale for placing these children in regular classes instead goes as follows: If one removes the label and returns the child to a regular class the problem will disappear, because it was the labeling or segregation that was causing the educational problem.

The oversimplistic nature of this rationale has been criticized for its apparent assumption that one can legislate away learning problems. We contend that if the children had problems in learning that led to their being classified as mentally retarded, then they are in need of some special assistance, regardless of what label is attached to them or the administrative arrangement in which they are placed.

If we do leave low-IQ children with academic problems in the regular class, either because of a lack of placement alternatives within a reasonable distance (Smith 1974) or because the option of special class placement has been blocked by legal action, we can anticipate certain problems. First, the research evidence on EMR children in the regular class (e.g., Johnson 1950; Johnson & Kirk 1950) indicated that EMR children were rejected by their nonretarded classmates not because of their lowered intellect but because of their behaviors. This problem is not likely to disappear. Another possibility is that retarded children will be unable to compete favorably with their more able classmates and will therefore experience undue failure and suffer a loss of self-esteem. Third, mildly retarded children left in regular classes have often received "social" promotions through the grades without learning much. When they leave school (through graduation or dropping out), we find that they have not begun to learn what should be expected of a child who has completed the same grades in school. And finally, at the risk of sounding "exclusionary," we must note that the retarded children may have a negative impact on the nonretarded children in the regular class. This concern always lurks in the background but it is seldom voiced and has not been systematically researched. Whether these four concerns can be accommodated in the regular classroom without loss to either the retarded children or the nonretarded children—since curriculum and instructional strategies might have to be altered—will depend on the teacher's inclinations and attitudes toward retarded children (Smith 1974).

Scholarly analyses of research on the efficacy of special versus regular class placement (e.g., Corman & Gottlieb 1979) do not indicate that one placement is superior to the other. As Semmel et al. (1979) put it, "The review provides no indication of differential achievement gains among EMR pupils as a function of regular or special class placement" (p. 247). Corman and Gottlieb also concluded that placing these children in regular classrooms does not improve their social adjustment. Clearly, the disenchantment with special classes is not derived from empirical evidence. Rather, philosophical, social, and legal considerations simply override research evidence in the courts (see Chapter 8). This leads to large-scale efforts to mainstream the mildly retarded, which will be discussed in detail in Chapter 13.

Regular Class with Itinerant Teacher or Resource Room

One way to sidestep some of these problems without sacrificing the presumed benefits of mainstreaming is to leave retarded children in the regular class for at least 50 percent of the school hours but have them tutored the rest of the time by an itinerant special teacher or a resource room teacher. As with regular class placement, this option is applicable only to EMR children, not to TMR or SPMR children.

There are some administrative differences between an itinerant teacher and a resource room teacher. Typically the itinerant teacher has responsibility only for children enrolled in that building. Both of these models have been used primarily with visually handicapped children and only recently have been adapted for learning-disabled and EMR children (Cruickshank & Johnson 1967). Cruickshank and Johnson claimed that the resource room model was inappropriate for EMR children; Dunn (1968) presented it as a viable alternative to the special class.

Hammill (1972) listed some advantages of the resource room that can probably be applied to the use of an itinerant teacher as well:

1. Students need not be labeled in order to receive assistance.
2. Resource rooms are less expensive to operate than are special classes.
3. Students can continue to be with their classmates who do not need assistance.
4. There will be a greater likelihood of a "multiplier effect" (more children can be served) than is true in the special class model.
5. Related to step 4 is the possibility that children who could not qualify for any of the special class categories can receive help as needed.

There has been considerable variability among programs as to what qualifications, background, and role are appropriate for a resource room or itinerant teacher. According to Reger and Koppman (1971) there is not universal understanding of the purpose of resource teachers. For example Smith (1974) portrays the resource teacher in the general role of a specialist in remedial instruction, while Reger (1972) lists three responsibilities of the resource room teacher: (1) offer direct services to children, (2) offer direct services to teachers, and (3) effect changes in the educational program through other teachers and administrators. Adelman (1972), on the other hand, sees resource room teachers primarily as inservice change-agents who work with staff teachers to change practices in the building. The fact that resource room teachers play different roles in different settings makes the model difficult to study and difficult to make predictions about.

Despite some variability in other responsibilities, the resource room teacher, or the itinerant teacher, *does* work with retarded children directly. In addition, the resource teacher *should* inform the regular teacher of the resource teacher's work with the child and offer assistance in terms of materials and techniques. To a great extent the resource teacher's effectiveness will probably depend on ability to get along with other teachers as well as with retarded children.

One would hope that consultative specialists, be they resource or itinerant teachers, would serve in a manner that would meet preventive as well as remedial goals. Particularly in the primary grades of school, children with slight learning problems might avoid the later need for remediation if steps could be taken to prevent them from becoming casualties of the regular educational system (Forness 1972). For an interesting exchange on the varied positions on the resource room, see the *Journal of Special Education* (1972).

Special Class

After World War II, concerns about the inability of teachers to meet the needs of retarded children in regular classrooms led to the establishment of large numbers of special full-time EMR classes. Despite their proliferation, special classes came under attack in the late 1960s and are now the subject of the hottest debates in special education circles.

The arguments that led to the large-scale creation of special classes were not sinister or exclusionary in nature as Mercer (1974b) claimed. In fact, the special class was thought to protect EMR children from undue failure, peer rejection, and loss of self-esteem. Placing them in a class with a smaller enrollment supposedly afforded them more individualized intruction and a curriculum that would prepare them for the kinds of occupations they were likely to enter upon leaving school. While the advent of special classes probably brought a sense of relief among regular teachers, who were frustrated in trying to teach these children because they met with little success, special classes were created with the primary intent of helping the children. This administrative arrangement may have been oversold by those who promised that it would result in better achievement, better adjustment, or the like. But we must keep in mind that the children identified as EMR are a hard-to-teach group, regardless of the administrative arrangement in which they are placed.

Despite the theoretically humane reasons for the creation of special classes for EMR children, this administrative arrangement ran into criticism from parents of minority children who were placed in special classes on grounds considered discriminatory. Some pointed to the disproportionate numbers of minority children in EMR classes and argued that special class placement represented a form of institutional racism—a contention agreed with by many critics (Dunn 1968; Johnson 1969; Mercer 1973a). Legal action has mandated modifications in the identification process, particularly the use of intelligence tests. A decision by Judge Wright against the tracking system of Washington, D.C., has been interpreted by many (e.g., Dunn 1968) to include special education, although Judge Wright apparently had no intention of including special education in his decision regarding tracking (Hall 1969).

Another source of criticism came from the ranks of higher education. While earlier papers had been published questioning the special class (e.g., Johnson 1962), an article by Dunn (1968) was the catalyst for serious challenges to the special class. Then followed many variations of Dunn's theme (Christophos & Renz 1969; Johnson 1969; Lilly 1970; Milazzo 1970; Sheila 1968). Very few voices were lifted to defend the special class or to challenge the evidence cited by the critics as proof that the special class had failed. But gradually a few educators began to speak for the other side (Kidd 1970; MacMillan 1971b; Nelson & Schmidt 1971). The arguments for and against special classes are nicely summarized by Bruininks and Rynders (1971) in Table 12.2.

To contend that any one administrative arrangement is the best for *all* EMR children, or, conversely, to argue that one is *bad* for all EMR children, is naive and ignores variation in individuals within the population of EMR. Over time educators came to think of the self-contained special class as *the* way to educate mildly retarded children; the fallacy in that line of reasoning has been exposed as it should have been. However, a cursory examination of current literature and conferences might lead one to the conclusion that the resource program or resource teacher is now being pushed as *the* best way to educate the same group of children. If this is the case, the notion that the resource teacher is the best arrangement for teaching mildly retarded children may become as inflexible as the earlier notion that special classes were the best solution.

TABLE 12.2   Selected Positions on Special Class Placement for EMR Children

Pros

1. Research evidence indicates that mentally retarded children in regular classrooms are usually rejected by more able classroom peers.

2. Mentally retarded children in regular classrooms experience loss of self-esteem because of their inability to compete with more able classroom peers.

3. It is logically absurd to assign children to instruction without considering differences in ability or achievement levels.

4. Evidence on the efficacy of special classes is inconclusive since most studies possess significant flaws in research design.

5. Criticisms of special classes are based ostensibly upon examples of poorly implemented programs.

6. The alternatives to present practices are less desirable and would lead to a return to "social" promotion as an approach to dealing with mildly retarded children.

7. Properly implemented special classes are optimally suited to deal with the major learning problems of retarded children.

8. Special class arrangements should not be unfairly indicted for mistakes in diagnosis and placement.

9. A democratic philosophy of education does not dictate that all children have the same educational experiences, but that all children receive an equal opportunity to learn according to their individual needs and abilities.

Cons

1. Special class placement isolates the retarded child from normal classroom peers.

2. Special class placement results in stigmatizing the retarded child, resulting in a loss of self-esteem and lowered acceptance by other children.

3. There is little evidence to support the practice of ability grouping for retarded or normal children.

4. Mildly retarded children make as much or more academic progress in regular classrooms as they do in special classrooms.

5. There is little point in investing further energy in improving special classes, since this arrangement poorly serves the social and educational needs of children.

6. Other more flexible administrative and curricular arrangements should be developed to supplement or supplant special classes.

7. Special class arrangements inappropriately place the responsibility for academic failure on children rather than upon schools or teachers.

8. The very existence of special classes encourages the misplacement of many children, particularly children from minority groups.

9. Special class placement is inconsistent with the tenets of a democratic philosophy of education because it isolates retarded from normal children, and vice versa.

R. H. Bruininks and J. E. Rynders, "Alternatives to special class placement for educable mentally retarded children," from *Focus on Exceptional Children*, 1971. Reprinted by permission of Love Publishing Company. Most of this table is based on articles by Dunn (1968), Milazzo (1970), Kidd (1970), Johnson (1962), Lilly (1970), and Christophos and Renz (1969).

In addition to the fact that there are great variations among children even though they may have the same IQ, there are also great variations between programs even though they have the same name. Special classes differ tremendously in practice; as with all administrative arrangements, one can find both good and bad examples. The curriculum, instructional strategies, and teacher qualifications vary from one special class to another. In a special class with an excellent teacher, a given EMR child is probably far better off than the same child would be in a regular class with a poor teacher, and vice versa. In all probability, too much importance is ascribed to the administrative arrangement in this debate (Vergason 1972) and too little emphasis on what is done once children are in an alternate placement (MacMillan 1971b).

At present, the debate over special versus class placement is largely irrelevant. First, PL 94-142 requires that children be placed in the least restrictive alternative possible. Regardless of the empirical evidence, it mandates that children be placed in regular classes whenever feasible. According to the least restrictive environment clause, placement in special classes does not mean that retarded children will be completely segregated from regular class children. Even before the push for mainstreaming, children in special classes were integrated into the regular program whenever possible. EMR children, for example, have typically taken nonacademic classes such as art, physical education, and music with regular class students.

Assuming that we still have a choice in the matter, we cannot rule out the possibility of special class placement. While there is an overriding desire to integrate EMR children into regular education programs and settings to the greatest degree possible, some children have significant learning problems across all subjects and problems in deportment and social behavior as well. For such children, placement in a special class on a full-time basis may be the best alternative. For others, integration into the regular classroom on a part-time basis with ancillary services may be the best option; still others may be capable of full-time regular class placement.

Even if special class placement seems best suited to some children's needs at one point in time, they should frequently be reevaluated. Such periodic evaluations keep the door open to alternate placements (such as part-time integration) if they have progressed to the point that the alternative to the special class is judged feasible and in their best interest.

This discussion has centered on EMR children, but special class placement is sometimes used for TMR children as well. Being in a special class within a regular school offers TMR children the advantages of contact with nonretarded peers with whom the retarded children can interact as their abilities allow. Smith (1974) has recommended a part-time special class for children who have more fundamental educational problems and need both a developmental and remedial program, since the resource room typically provides the remedial aspects. But whereas some EMR children may need a self-contained special class for only part of the school day, TMR children can usually be integrated with regular classes only on a highly selective basis for some nonacademic tasks.

Special Schools

The community special school is used rather frequently with TMR children for several reasons. First, in many communities there are simply not enough TMR children in an area served by a single school district to warrant the establishment of a special class for TMR children in one of their school buildings. In such a case a larger unit of organization (such as the county) may establish a school for TMR and possibly other handicapped children. It serves the children from several school districts that do not offer their own TMR program. Under these circumstances the consideration is largely an economic one. The cost required to provide the varied services—medical, speech, psychological, vocational, social welfare, and physical therapy—is considerable, making a centralized facility the most economically feasible alternative.

A second set of circumstances in which a special school is warranted occurs when a child is placed in a psychiatric treatment center on an outpatient basis. This is a fairly common placement for retarded children who have needs that require specialization beyond that which can be offered in a school with limited therapeutic services. University-based research centers on mental retardation and related aspects of human development have established educational programs in hospitals for research purposes. Children with multiple handicaps who live close to such facilities can usually be better served in the research center program than in the alternate community programs.

Recommendation for placement in a community special school comes usually for children with rather severe problems that require services of a team of specialists from different fields. For such children, community school placement has several advantages over residential institutions. Since the school is in the community the children are able to live at home. They therefore retain the support of their families and are able to have contact with nonhandicapped children in their neighborhoods, albeit probably on a limited basis. Another advantage over residential schools is that with good public relations the community school can attract a variety of first-rate consultative services; since special schools tend to be located in larger urban communities, these services can be plentiful. Furthermore, teachers in these special schools can continue their professional growth at colleges and universities, which are often located in the same general area.

Despite these advantages in comparison with institutionalization,

Cruickshank (1958) noted several disadvantages of the community special school in comparison with special class placement in public schools. Children in a special school interact with nonhandicapped peers very infrequently during the school day, a factor that he contends is not offset by the opportunity to play with their nonhandicapped peers in the neighborhood after school and on weekends. Another problem with special schools is the amount of time children spend traveling to and from the school; either the instructional program is shortened or the children do not have the time to interact with nonhandicapped children in their neighborhood. Finally, Cruickshank expressed concern that the very presence of special schools may cause general educators to ignore responsibility for handicapped children, a situation particularly distressing in cases where the child might have been able to attend a regular school. According to this logic, children may be referred to special schools merely because they are available. Such action is counter to Deno's (1972) cascade principle that children be placed in a setting that most closely approximates the regular class and yet meets their special needs.

It should be noted that there is variety in special schools, as in all administrative arrangements mentioned in this chapter. The most notable difference among special schools for the mentally retarded is that some serve only the mentally retarded while others serve different types of exceptional children (e.g., mentally retarded, physically handicapped, deaf, and blind) in one school. In the latter case children are usually grouped by disabilities, with classes for the mentally retarded containing only retarded children. When multihandicapped children (e.g., deaf mentally retarded children) are enrolled in a special school that serves children of varying handicapped conditions, a decision must be made as to which handicap is the child's primary handicap so that the child can be placed in the class that can best serve the combination and severity of handicaps.

In the past all classes for the TMR child, whether in a regular elementary school or a community special school, had certain prerequisites for admission. Usually these consisted in the child's being toilet-trained and able to communicate basic needs. But there was a segment of mentally retarded children who fell below that self-care level and were unacceptable to those running TMR programs. These children were called "subtrainable" or "custodial" and, until recently, were typically excluded from public education. But some parents who did not wish to institutionalize their subtrainable children and have kept them at home feel that, since they are taxpayers, their children should have educational opportunities equal in quality to those for any other child. They have gone to the courts to force the public educational agencies to provide for these children (see Chapter 8). One of the provisions that has been made for these children is the day activity center, in which subtrainable mentally retarded children are given training under the auspices of the state department of education.

Residential Schools and Institutions

The earliest programs for the mentally retarded were provided in residential institutions. They were frequently called "schools" even if their emphasis was on medical treatment (Eyman & Silverstein 1973). After World War II, in some of the institutions one could find children who would be classified today as borderline normal, EMR, or delinquent; they had been placed in these institutions for the mentally retarded for reasons other than impaired intellect (Tarjan 1972). However, since the establishment of the National Association for Retarded Citizens (NARC) there has been a drastic change in institutional programs (Roos 1970a). One such change is that the population being served in residential facilities has become a more disabled subset of the former population.

There is considerable variability in the nature of residential facilities. They range from medically oriented hospitals serving the profoundly retarded, in which the treatment is primarily medical in nature, to residential schools, in which the treatment consists of an educational program for children who do not need constant medical attention.

Retarded children who receive their instruction on an inpatient basis are usually in the TMR range or below. Often the educational component of the total treatment program is of secondary importance to medical or psychiatric components. Prior to the onset of the court cases discussed in Chapter 8, the educational programs offered in such institutions were under the authority of agencies other than education—for example, departments of mental hygiene, health, or welfare. However, states are increasingly giving state departments of education responsibility for instruction of all children, regardless of their degree of disability or whether they live at home or in an institution.

The major advantage claimed for residential programs is that services of several types (medical, psychological, social welfare, educational) can be concentrated at relatively few sites and yet benefit many retarded children. Hence the advantage is primarily an economic one.

The disadvantages are fairly numerous and widely cited (Cruickshank 1958). First, the children are removed from their homes and are thereby denied the benefit of their parents and siblings; at the same time they are denied an opportunity to have informal and spontaneous contact with nonretarded children who are their age or have similar interests. A second criticism is that there is often a stigma attached to the retarded school. Third, Cruickshank points out that seldom does a residential school have all the professional services that are available to a public school, so the quality of the teaching staff and curriculum development suffers. Furthermore, residential schools are frequently isolated geographically, limiting the opportunity for public involvement and professional growth for teachers and possibly making it more difficult to recruit qualified staff.

Despite these disadvantages, it should be noted that institutional placement for retarded children is often done following public school placement
in which the child's needs have not been met. Many of these retarded children are institutionalized for secondary problems—emotional problems,
home instability, multiple handicaps—that compound the mental retardation and necessitate an intensive treatment program.

CURRICULA

Mentally retarded children pose a unique problem to education, one not
presented by any other exceptionality. While the blind, deaf, or learning-
disabled require modifications in the way they are taught, mentally
retarded students require educators to decide *what* they should be taught.
Since their limited intellectual ability slows down the learning process, one
must consider the most efficient use of the time available for instruction
and determine what is going to be emphasized.

In this section, we will discuss curricular emphases in programs for EMR,
TMR, and SPMR children. Our discussion of EMR and TMR children examines the traditional emphases of standard curricula. Yet current practices
have changed dramatically for EMR children, and, to a lesser extent, for
TMR children as well, while programs for SPMR children are relatively
new.

Our review of curricula for the retarded cannot be comprehensive. An
extensive discussion would require an entire text. Those in training to be
teachers will consider curricula for the retarded in a separate course. Those
who wish to pursue the subject of curricula independently can consult Haring & Brown (1976), Kirk & Johnson (1951), Kolstoe (1976), Meyen & Horner (1976), Smith (1974), or Snell (1978).

Although the advent of special classes brought prescribed certification
standards for those who were to teach mentally retarded children in the
special classes (Bruininks & Rynders 1971), we might question the need for
specialized training, either in terms of courses taken or of competencies.
This question need not be restricted to special education but could be raised
for general education as well (Popham 1971). This does not mean, of course,
that teacher training per se is irrelevant but that what is being taught to
teachers must be evaluated in the light of what children need to learn to be
successful adults.

Although you might assume that specialized training would prepare a
special education teacher to use a specialized curriculum adapted to the
needs of retarded children, this assumption may be unfounded (Bruininks
& Rynders 1971). After reviewing 250 different curriculum guides, Simches
and Bohn (1963) concluded that there seldom were carefully sequenced cur-

ricula for mentally retarded learners. All the same, it is important to consider what skills are relevant for retarded students.

Keep in mind that the curricula we will consider were developed for an EMR and TMR population prior to the onset of litigation regarding placement. MacMillan and Borthwick (1980) indicate that the EMR population in California—a state with very low prevalence of school-age mentally retarded children—has changed drastically since that time. They also suggest that the current group is much more severely debilitated than the group enrolled in EMR programs around 1970, and that the vast majority of current EMRs could not be integrated with other children for any academic instruction. As a result, the entire EMR curriculum may have to be reconsidered in states with drastically reduced EMR enrollments, because the children for whom it was developed are no longer being served. In addition, we are told by school psychologists and special education teachers in California that the composition of the TMR program has also changed. It now includes many more children from what used to be considered the lower end of the TMR level. Hence, the appropriateness of the curricula we discuss should be considered in the context of the levels of functioning of the EMR and TMR children served in each state.

EMR Curriculum

A major problem in choosing a curriculum for EMR students is that they vary so widely that what would be appropriate for one is not appropriate for another. The mildly retarded population is quite heterogeneous with regard to all traits except IQ, which typically falls within the 50 to 70 range. And even with IQ, if we look beyond the full-scale score achieved we find variations in scores on different items of the Stanford-Binet and different subtests of the WISC. On the WISC, some EMR children achieve better scores on the performance items and others show greater relative strength on the verbal portion of the test (Berkson 1966; Bruininks & Rynders 1971).

EMR children vary not only in specific intellectual abilities but also in personality characteristics, cultural background, inheritance, and past histories. An EMR class might include bilingual children who are not genotypically retarded but simply have trouble with the language, children from impoverished environments who merely lack the background for school learning, children who have developed failure sets and have stopped trying, children of dull-normal ability whose emotional overlay depresses their academic performance, and children who received a poor genetic draw or suffered prenatal or postnatal brain damage. The special needs of these varying types of children obviously differ greatly.

On the other hand, EMR children do have one thing in common: they all encountered considerable difficulty in the regular classroom as inefficient learners of the material taught there. The program that is offered to EMR children has as its major goal that these children will as adults possess the skills and attitudes needed for successful living and working in the society. For EMR children to be capable of independent adult living that they will find satisfying, they will have to possess vocational, personal, and social skills. The EMR curriculum should be designed to achieve that goal in a sequential fashion.

Since there is no single EMR curriculum, the teacher can, and must, adapt any curriculum guide to fit the particular children and geographic setting served. The vocational skills taught in a rural setting, where most program graduates will seek employment in farm-related jobs, would be different from those that might be taught in a program whose graduates will work in an urban factory. Nevertheless, there are common elements that would appear in both programs.

Specific Objectives. The EMR curriculum typically is designed to develop competency in several areas. Kolstoe (1976) mentioned a variety of outcomes contained in various programs, including arithmetic competencies, social competencies, communicative skills, safety and health competencies, vocational competencies, motor and recreation skills, and avoidance of drug and alcohol abuse. These skills can probably be subsumed under the three major rubrics suggested by Kirk and Johnson (1951): occupational adequacy, social competence, and personal adequacy.

To elaborate, occupational success is important in order for the individual to be self-supporting. Success in unskilled and semiskilled positions will depend in large part on the individual's ability to be prompt, get along with coworkers, maintain good health, manage money, and display a number of habits and skills that are not specific to job performance. Development of these attitudes and habits is of paramount importance in EMR programs.

Since EMR students will, in most cases, live in the community as parents, neighbors, and citizens, it is also important that the EMR program develop the knowledge, skills, and attitudes that will enable them to be active members of the adult community. Kirk and Johnson (1951) described some of these skills as those required for establishing a home, raising children, getting along with neighbors, and respecting the rights of others.

The third objective, a sense of personal adequacy, is very difficult for retarded children to develop if they meet with constant frustration and failure. The emotional well-being of these children should be considered as they are educated, to help them develop a sense of belonging to the class and friendships with peers.

Organization. For purposes of instruction, general education groups children in grades K through 12. In the EMR program the organization usually consists instead of (1) primary class, (2) intermediate class, (3) secondary class (sometimes separated into *prevocational* and *vocational* programs), and (4) a postschool program. While it is common to find mention of preschool programs for EMR children, this assumes that EMR children can be identified during the preschool years, and the discussion in Chapter 6 reveals that this is not usually the case. Preschool programs exist only for children who are at risk of becoming EMR or in areas in which there is a high incidence of EMR children; these "early intervention" programs will be discussed in Chapter 13.

Figure 12.3 summarizes the curricular content emphasized at various levels of the EMR program. Note that during the elementary school years there is a relatively heavy emphasis on readiness and academic tool subjects and little emphasis on prevocational development. In the secondary school years this emphasis is reversed, as the program becomes increasingly weighted with vocational development and with a progressive lessening in the emphasis placed on the development of academic skills. What attention is given to academic skills tends to be applied to daily living situations. Also noteworthy is the fairly constant emphasis placed on areas II and III across all levels of the program.

Throughout the EMR program, attempts at teaching academic tool subjects stress the application of these skills to practical living and vocational situations. For example, social studies units tend to emphasize the specific local community on the assumption that most will reside close to the area in which they attend school.

The development of postschool programs is slow and apparently has been for some time (Kirk & Johnson 1951). Federal sponsorship for vocational rehabilitation services has resulted in some activity that is beneficial to mildly retarded persons (Morgenstern & Michal-Smith 1973). As society gets more and more complex, mildly retarded individuals will need more support and guidance to remain self-sufficient and employed.

TMR Curriculum

As we have seen, the TMR program traditionally included those retarded children below IQ 50 who are both toilet-trained and able to communicate their basic needs. Retarded children who did not meet these two criteria were denied admission to TMR programs. The term *trainable* was used to signify that TMR children were not amenable to education yet could be trained to master certain skills.

Certain assumptions permeate the TMR curriculum. First, TMR children are thought to be incapable of social or economic independence as adults. As adults it is expected they will be dependent upon others to a considerable degree. This is not to say they are unable to be gainfully employed or

FIGURE 12.3   Curricular Content Areas by Organizational Levels in EMR Programs

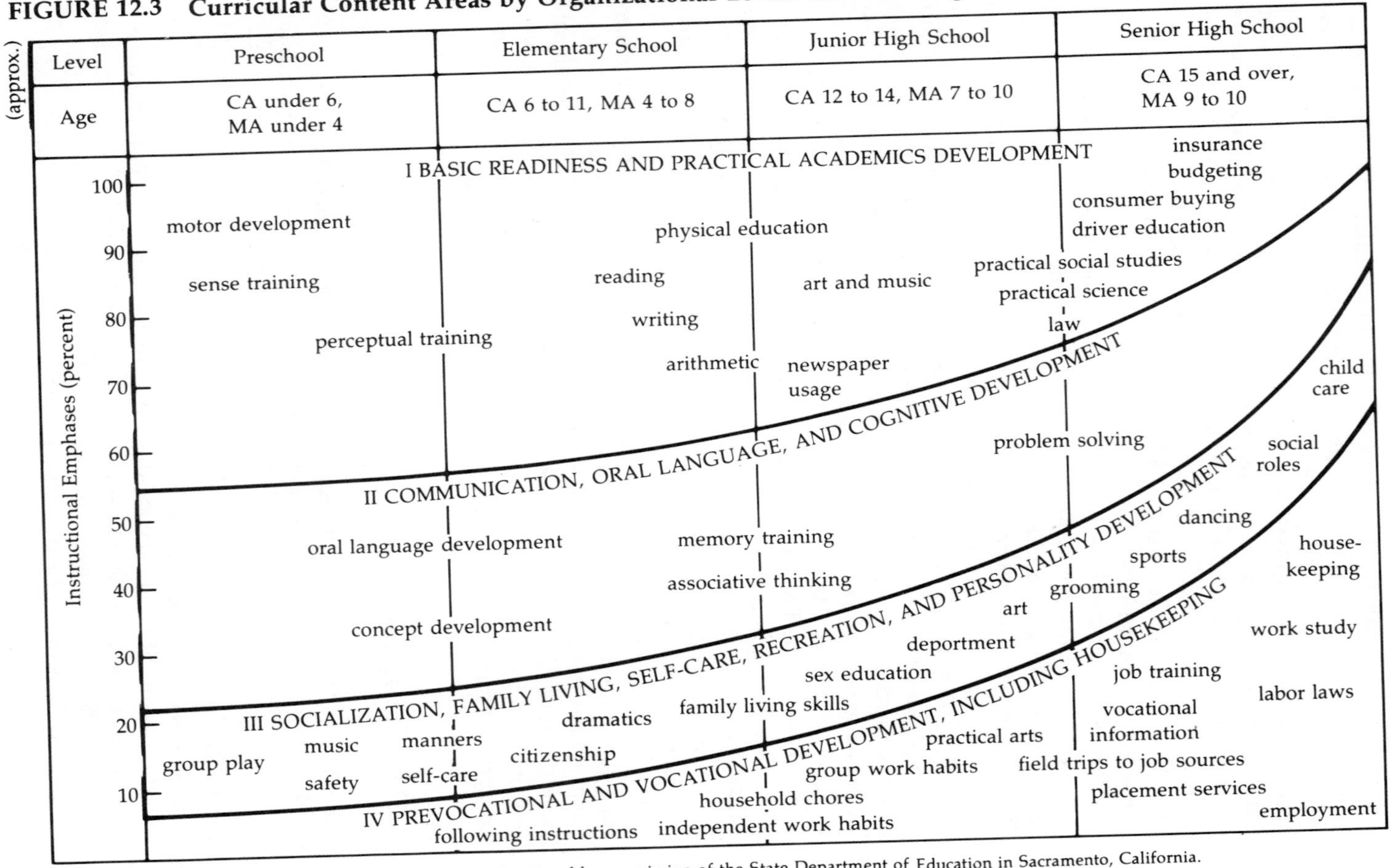

Level	Preschool	Elementary School	Junior High School	Senior High School
Age	CA under 6, MA under 4	CA 6 to 11, MA 4 to 8	CA 12 to 14, MA 7 to 10	CA 15 and over, MA 9 to 10

I BASIC READINESS AND PRACTICAL ACADEMICS DEVELOPMENT

- motor development
- sense training
- perceptual training
- physical education
- reading
- writing
- arithmetic
- art and music
- newspaper usage
- practical social studies
- practical science
- law
- insurance
- budgeting
- consumer buying
- driver education

II COMMUNICATION, ORAL LANGUAGE, AND COGNITIVE DEVELOPMENT

- oral language development
- concept development
- memory training
- associative thinking
- problem solving

III SOCIALIZATION, FAMILY LIVING, SELF-CARE, RECREATION, AND PERSONALITY DEVELOPMENT

- group play
- music
- safety
- manners
- self-care
- citizenship
- dramatics
- family living skills
- sex education
- deportment
- art
- grooming
- sports
- dancing
- social roles
- child care

IV PREVOCATIONAL AND VOCATIONAL DEVELOPMENT, INCLUDING HOUSEKEEPING

- following instructions
- independent work habits
- household chores
- group work habits
- practical arts
- field trips to job sources
- placement services
- job training
- vocational information
- labor laws
- work study
- house-keeping
- employment

Instructional Emphases (percent)

100
90
80
70
60
50
40
30
20
10

From L. W. Campbell, *Study of Curriculum Planning*, 1968. Reprinted by permission of the State Department of Education in Sacramento, California.

472

(approx.)

that they are unable to function socially, but they will always require some degree of assistance or supervision. Another assumption pertains to the rate of mental growth; based on IQ, it is estimated to proceed at approximately one-fourth to one-half of a year in any calendar year (Rosenzweig & Long 1960). At maturity, the dependent retarded individual is expected to attain the level of development achieved by a normal child of between four and eight years. But while these traditional assumptions may be valid for the vast majority of TMR children, they may serve to restrict the development of others who are capable of more independence than the norm. So in using a TMR curriculum we should be careful not to preclude the possibility that a TMR child can become independent. By the nature of what is taught and what is excluded, the TMR child may sometimes be prevented from achieving beyond what TMR children are generally expected to achieve.

Specific Objectives. There is a philosophical belief underlying TMR programs that a major goal of education is to enable individuals to develop whatever potentialities they have, regardless of how limited these potentialities may be in comparison to others. At the terminal stages of a TMR program, it is hoped that students will be able to engage in useful work and function in a social setting such as the family. To do so they must be able to care for their own bodily needs, dress and groom themselves, exhibit certain appropriate behaviors (e.g., manners, control of emotions), and perform certain routine chores (e.g., housekeeping chores). The TMR curriculum is designed to develop these skills and prepare students to lead a fulfilling life and achieve the degree of independence of which they are capable.

In addition to developing these skills, TMR programs have the side benefit of relieving parents of the constant attention these children require when they are at home. This relief may enable parents to establish a healthier relationship with these children and to develop realistic expectations for their development. Otherwise, with the child at home constantly, the care required can result in resentment or a lack of perspective on how the child's rate of development compares to that of nonhandicapped children.

Organization. TMR programs tend to be organized into primary classes, intermediate classes, and advanced classes. The approximate chronological ages corresponding to these class levels are shown in Figure 12.4. You will note that the diagram also includes a preprimary class for TMR children of preschool age. It is possible to initiate treatment for TMR children at an early age because they can be identified very early.

Note also in Figure 12.4 the relative emphasis placed on the four content areas at each of the program levels. There is a heavy emphasis on development of self-help skills (toileting, dressing, eating) during the early school years; training in the area of independent living continues through-

FIGURE 12.4   Curricular Content Areas by Organizational Levels in TMR Programs

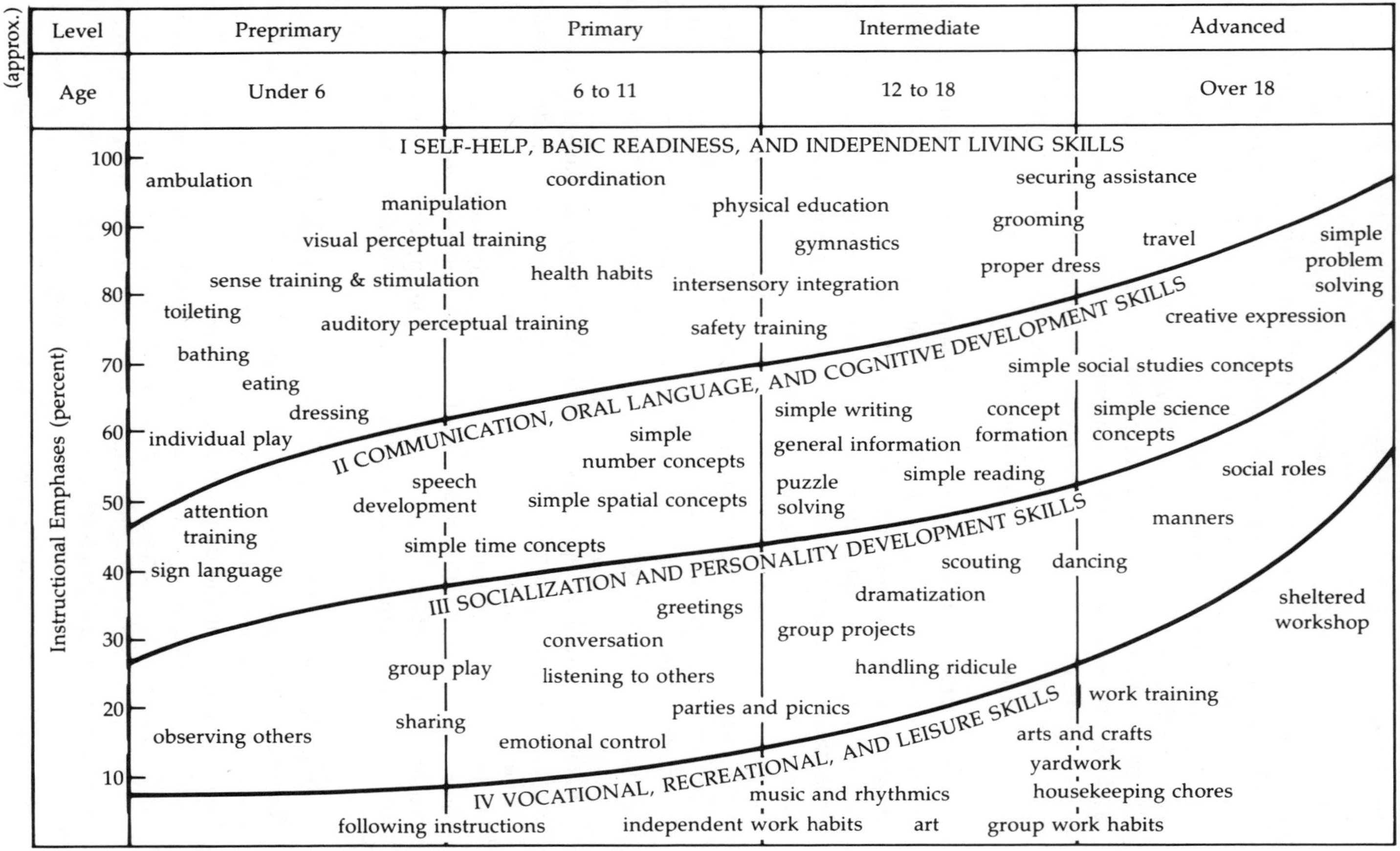

Level				
Age (approx.)	Preprimary	Primary	Intermediate	Advanced
	Under 6	6 to 11	12 to 18	Over 18

Instructional Emphases (percent): 10, 20, 30, 40, 50, 60, 70, 80, 90, 100

I SELF-HELP, BASIC READINESS, AND INDEPENDENT LIVING SKILLS

- ambulation
- coordination
- manipulation
- visual perceptual training
- physical education
- sense training & stimulation
- health habits
- gymnastics
- grooming
- travel
- simple problem solving
- toileting
- auditory perceptual training
- intersensory integration
- proper dress
- bathing
- safety training
- creative expression
- eating
- securing assistance
- dressing

II COMMUNICATION, ORAL LANGUAGE, AND COGNITIVE DEVELOPMENT SKILLS

- individual play
- speech development
- simple number concepts
- simple writing
- concept formation
- simple social studies concepts
- simple spatial concepts
- general information
- simple science concepts
- attention training
- simple time concepts
- puzzle solving
- simple reading
- social roles
- sign language

III SOCIALIZATION AND PERSONALITY DEVELOPMENT SKILLS

- group play
- greetings
- dramatization
- scouting
- dancing
- conversation
- group projects
- manners
- listening to others
- handling ridicule
- observing others
- sharing
- parties and picnics
- emotional control

IV VOCATIONAL, RECREATIONAL, AND LEISURE SKILLS

- following instructions
- independent work habits
- music and rhythmics
- art
- work training
- sheltered workshop
- arts and crafts
- yardwork
- housekeeping chores
- group work habits

From L. W. Campbell, *Study of Curriculum Planning,* 1968. Reprinted by permission of the State Department of Education in Sacramento, California.

out the educational program. Vocational skills are emphasized during the teen-age years, though to a lesser extent than was true for EMR children and toward a different end. TMR adults are unlikely to be employed in the kinds of jobs that will make them economically self-sufficient. But even though TMR adults are unlikely to be able to support themselves, Rosenzweig and Long (1960) recommend that their training should develop vocational skills that will enable them to make some contribution to society. The occupations for which TMR individuals will probably qualify include unskilled positions (e.g., household chores, messengers, unskilled factory work, or light assembly), assistance to skilled laborers, or work in sheltered workshops. Toward the goal of providing opportunities for employment for TMR and SPMR individuals, parents groups have created sheltered workshops, some of which have been taken over by nonprofit organizations. Workshop supervisors analyze the tasks and break them down into fairly simple components that can be mastered by the retarded employees, who as a group produce the product. The setting provides individuals with an opportunity to be productive, to interact socially, and to be paid for their work. Unfortunately, there is a need for many more sheltered workshops than currently exist if such opportunities are to be available to all retarded persons who are capable of some productivity but are unable to compete in the labor market.

The curriculum for TMR students emphasizes academic tool subjects (e.g., reading, arithmetic) only to the extent that such skills will be functionally useful to them. Certain words (e.g., stop, men, women, walk) must be recognized if any degree of independence is to be achieved. Similarly, the ability to make change and to count the number of items will be important skills in daily living and occupational functioning. Specific academic goals and standards must take into account individual capacity, for some TMR children will be capable of greater accomplishment than others.

The TMR program for social functioning is important because although social competence is one of the areas in which TMR children are notably deficient, later acceptance will depend in large part on social functioning. Regardless of the residential or vocational setting in which TMR persons function, their acceptance and success will depend on their ability to get along with others, control their emotions, be polite, follow rules, and assume appropriate social roles. As Figure 12.4 indicates, there is a gradual progression of social skills emphasized at different levels of the TMR program.

SPMR Programs

The severely and profoundly mentally retarded have long been considered to be primarily the responsibility of the medical profession. This belief relegated education or other forms of treatment to a position of secondary importance, and programs for the SPMR were essentially custodial. PL 94-142, however, has a provision for "zero reject," which requires that the severely handicapped not be denied educational services because they fail to meet criteria for school entry, such as toilet training. This legislation also stated that children currently receiving no educational services were the top priority, followed by those with the most severe handicaps in each disability area who were not receiving adequate education. A large percentage of both first- and second-priority children came from the same group—the severely handicapped.

Definitions of severe and profound retardation tend to emphasize IQ ranges (roughly IQ 0 to 40), but definitions of the severely handicapped tend to be much vaguer. How can one differentiate, for example, an autistic child from a retarded child, when they have so many characteristics in common? Wilcox (1979) pointed out that the one characteristic severely handicapped children share is their significantly discrepant behavior, which requires sustained, intensive intervention from the educational community. Wilcox offers this definition:

> The term "severely handicapped" will be used to collectively refer to students who have traditionally been labeled moderately, severely, or profoundly retarded; autistic, autistic-like, or severely emotionally disturbed; and multi-handicapped. . . . Students labeled severely handicapped may manifest sensory impairments, physical abnormalities, crippling conditions, or bizarre behavioral repertoires. They share no common etiology.
>
> (p. 140)

Others have emphasized these characteristics: (1) numerous physical defects, (2) absence of self-care skills, (3) behavior characteristics injurious to self or others, (4) mixed or multiple sensorimotor disabilities, (5) inadequate communication skills, and (6) related problems such as hyperactivity or convulsive disorders (Brown, Branston, Hamre-Nietupski, Johnson, Wilcox, & Gruenwald 1979).

Specific Objectives. The objectives for an SPMR educational program cannot be specified as can those for EMR and TMR programs, because they vary with the problems of the children in question. Behavioral assessment is important for educational programing because it determines the child's areas of greatest need. It involves assessing the child's gross motor development, communication skills, social and self-help skills, and cognitive and preacademic skills. Williams and Gotts (1977) observed that although developing a curriculum for the severely handicapped is currently an art rather than a science, there are several priorities for establishing content and strategies. The skills to be taught must be useful to the students and relevant to their daily functioning and should lead to increased independence. Brown,

Nietupski, and Hamre-Nietupski (1976) refer to these attributes as the "functionality" of skills—the extent to which the skills promote maximum independence and integration into the normal community.

The objectives of an educational program for SPMR children are often selected to achieve the prerequisites of entry into TMR programs. These objectives might include (1) activities of daily living such as self-feeding or self-toileting; (2) training in physical mobility and coordination—crawling, rolling, or walking; and (3) sensorimotor training—stimulation of sight, smell, touch, hearing, or muscular responses.

Organization. A variety of curriculum models for use with severely handicapped children have been proposed. One of the more popular is the *functional developmental behavioral approach* (Cohen, Gross, & Haring 1976; Williams & Gotts 1977), which emphasizes two elements: task analysis and skill sequences. In this technique, a skill needed by the child is broken into component parts through logical analysis. (This is not done according to any particular theory.) Then the various tasks involved in the skill are sequenced in the order they are to be taught. Williams and Gotts (1977) broke task analysis for the sequence of adaptive behavior skills into the following steps:

1. Delineate a behavioral objective.
2. Review the available resources.
3. Derive and sequence the component skills of the objective.
4. Eliminate unnecessary component skills.
5. Eliminate redundant component skills.
6. Determine what prerequisite skills are needed by the student.
7. Monitor the student's performance and revise the skill sequence accordingly.

An alternative curriculum model, derived from Piaget's work (Bricker & Bricker 1974; Robinson 1976; Stephens 1977), involves assessing the Piagetian level at which the SPMR child is functioning. This can present problems, because the scales used must be shown to be reliable with SPMR populations. Frequently, however, teachers must teach very basic skills before academic learning can be considered. A teacher might be concerned with getting the child to pay attention, motor skills, adaptive behaviors (including self-help skills), language skills, and, during later schooling, some prevocational training.

To teach skills such as these, the approach used most frequently is behavior modification. Behavior modification techniques have been used extensively for quite a few years to promote self-help skills such as toileting (Azrin & Foxx 1971: Mahoney, Van Wagenen, & Meyerson 1971), feeding (Azrin & Armstrong 1973; Barton, Guess, Garcia, & Baer 1970), grooming

(Hunt, Fitzhugh, & Fitzhugh 1968), and self-dressing (Karen & Maxwell 1967). These studies have demonstrated the effectiveness of techniques derived from learning principles for developing better adaptive skills.

Efforts to toilet train SPMR subjects have become increasingly sophisticated. They include the use of electric devices that signal when urination begins so that attendants can gradually assist the subject to associate bladder cues with going to the bathroom and eliminating (Van Wagenen, Myerson, Kerr, & Mahoney 1969). Physical and verbal prompts used initially in toilet-training programs can gradually be faded out. The program used by Azrin and his associates (Azrin & Armstrong 1971; Azrin & Foxx 1971) included positive reinforcement for urinating in the toilet (praise, hugs, candy) and punishment (spanking) for wetting one's pants, followed by a ten-minute time-out from reinforcement. Such techniques have met with considerable success in toilet training SPMR individuals who in the past were incontinent and believed to be incapable of bladder and bowel control. Similar techniques have been used by Azrin and Foxx (1971) in shaping appropriate undressing and dressing behavior.

Appropriate self-feeding behaviors in SPMR subjects have also been developed by various techniques. Some include physical prompts to place a spoon in the food and then put it in the mouth, with the assistant gradually requiring closer approximations to the appropriate behaviors. Some of the programs have used prosthetic utensils such as nonspill spoons to facilitate the teaching of appropriate feeding behaviors. And Barton and his colleagues (1970) succeeded in reducing inappropriate mealtime behaviors (e.g., fingering food, stealing food) by removing a subject's tray of food or removing the subject himself from the table.

Dressing behavior has been taught by means of breaking down the complex task into simpler elements; these elements are taught separately and then put into sequence. Special loose-fitting clothing with elastic waistbands or large buttons has been used in the early stages of such programs. For instructional purposes, Karen and Maxwell (1967) designed a special vest with varying size buttons.

These programs have demonstrated that SPMR individuals are often capable of developing many self-help skills. Development of the skills has not come easily—the behaviorists who have worked in these programs have used shaping techniques precisely. Progress has been achieved only after hard work and systematic programing. But once SPMR persons can care for themselves, they require less custodial supervision, and alternative residential, educational, and rehabilitative placements become possible.

Recent changes in the curriculum for SPMR children show that they can do more than merely acquire self-help skills. Today's curricular goals include working on a specific skill until it is mastered and then generalizing the skill to new settings. This change has resulted in part from the provision of PL 94-142 that requires an individualized education program (IEP) for each child. (We will discuss the development of IEPs in the following section.) Readers interested in more information about curricula for the severely handicapped are referred to Bender, Valetutti, and Bender (1976), Bigge and O'Donnell (1976), Billingsley and Neafsey (1978), Snell (1978), and publications of The Association for the Severely Handicapped (TASH) such as *TASH Review* and *Teaching the Severely Handicapped.*

PROVISIONS OF PL 94-142

PL 94-142 is based on six principles: (1) zero reject, (2) nondiscriminatory testing, (3) individualized education programs (IEPs), (4) least restrictive environment (LRE), (5) due process, and (6) parent participation. Zero reject was discussed in the preceding section; nondiscriminatory testing and due process considerations were discussed in Chapters 5 and 8, respectively. In this section, we will consider how the remaining elements of PL 94-142 have affected educational programing for mentally retarded children.

Since the passage of PL 94-142, traditional EMR and TMR programs have changed dramatically. Formerly, the EMR program took place in a self-contained special class, and all the children in the class took the same program with common objectives, materials, teaching strategies, and evaluative criteria. Today, programs must be designed to meet the needs of individual children. The setting of the program and the objectives, teaching strategies, and evaluative criteria must all be chosen on the basis of individual needs. This goal is accomplished in part through the elements of PL 94-142 that we have not yet discussed: the IEP, LRE, and parental participation requirements.

Individualized Education Programs

An IEP must be provided for every handicapped child receiving special education. Turnbull, Strickland, and Brantley (1978) observed that the IEP requirement ensures that education will be tailored to a child's individual needs; Meyers et al. (1978) noted that it ensures the accountability of those responsible for the education of the child.

Each IEP must include the following elements:

1. A documentation of the student's current level of educational performance.
2. Annual goals or the attainments expected by the end of the school year.
3. Short-term objectives, stated in instructional terms, which are the intermediate steps leading to the mastery of annual goals.
4. Documentation of the particular special education and related services which will be provided to the child.

5. An indication of the extent of time a child will participate in the regular education program.
6. Projected dates for initiating services and the anticipated duration of services.
7. Evaluation procedures and schedules for determining mastery of short-term objectives at least on an annual basis.

(Turnbull, Strickland, & Brantley 1978, p. 5)

The IEP is designed by the child's teacher, the parents, the children themselves (when appropriate), and a representative of the school or public agency involved, other than the child's teacher, who is qualified to provide, or supervise the provision of, special education. A sample IEP format and a sample total service plan and individual implementation plan are shown in Figures 12.5 and 12.6, respectively.

It is important to realize that although the IEP is an attempt to assure individualization, the IEP can become the "impossible education plan" without the necessary backup support (Turnbull, Strickland, & Hammer 1978). Violations of the intent of the provision have occurred. Several instances have been noted in which one IEP was developed and applied indiscriminately to all the members of a class. It is to be hoped that such cases are uncommon exceptions. We recommend the book by Turnbull, Strickland, and Brantley (1978) for a comprehensive review of the process of developing and implementing IEPs.

Least Restrictive Environment

The least restrictive environment clause of PL 94-142 requires that retarded children be educated with nonretarded children to the maximum extent appropriate in view of the child's strengths and weaknesses. The decision to place a child in a *more* restrictive environment is made by the committee members, who must state why the child cannot benefit from a less restrictive placement. The LRE is determined largely by the objectives and services outlined in the IEP, since the services must be available in whatever placement is recommended. Nevertheless, efforts must be made to ensure that retarded children receive services in the educational setting that allows them the most contact with nonretarded children.

It is important to realize that the LRE clause does not mean that all children will attend regular classes for the entire school day, although the legal preference is for regular class placement. The more severely retarded and those who have multiple problems may require services such as speech therapy, physical therapy, vocational training, and audiological services. In order for the staff to coordinate these services and implement the educational plan fully, the child may have to spend part of the day in a more restrictive setting. The IEP should, however, specify what percentage of

FIGURE 12.5 Sample IEP Format

Individual Education Plan (IEP)

Identification Information

Name _____

School _____

Birthdate _____ Grade _____

Parent's Name _____

Address _____

Phone: Home _____ Office _____

Continuum of Services

	Hours Per Week
Regular class	_____
Resource teacher in regular classroom	_____
Resource room	_____
Reading specialist	_____
Speech/language therapist	_____
Counselor	_____
Special class	_____
Transition class	_____
Others:	_____
	_____

Yearly Class Schedule

	Time	Subject	Teacher
1st semester			
2nd semester			

Testing Information

Test Name	Date Admin.	Interpretation

Checklist

_____ Referral by
_____ Parents informed of rights; permission obtained for evaluation
_____ Evaluation compiled
_____ Parents contacted
_____ Total Committee meets and subcommittee assigned
_____ IEP developed by subcommittee
_____ IEP approved by total committee

Committee Members

Teacher _____

Other LEA representative _____

Parents _____
_____

Date IEP initially approved _____

Health Information

Vision: _____
Hearing: _____
Physical: _____
Other: _____

481

FIGURE 12.5 cont'd.

Individual Education Plan (IEP)

Student's Name _____   Subject Area _____

Level of Performance _____   Teacher _____

Annual Goals   1. _____

2. _____

3. _____

Objectives	September	October	November	December	January
Materials					
Evaluation Agent					

From A. Turnbull, B. Strickland, and J. Brantley, *Developing and Implementing Individualized Education Programs*, 1978. © 1978 Bell & Howell Co. Reprinted by permission of Charles E. Merrill Publishing Co.

FIGURE 12.6 Sample Total Service Plan and Individual Implementation Plan

Individual Education Program: Total Service Plan

Child's Name_____

School_____

Date of Program Entry_____

Prioritized Long-term Goals:

_____

_____

_____

Summary of Present
Levels of Performance

_____

_____

_____

_____

Short-term Objectives	Specific Educational and/or Support Services	Person(s) Responsible	Percent of Time	Beginning and Ending Date	Review Date

Percent of Time in Regular Classroom

Placement Recommendation

Committee Members Present

_____

_____

_____

_____

Dates of Meeting_____

Committee Recommendations for Specific Procedures/Techniques, Material, Etc. (include information about learning style)

Objective Evaluation Criteria for Each Annual Goal Statement

FIGURE 12.6   cont'd.

Individual Education Program: Individual Implementation Plan

(Complete one of these for each goal statement specified on Total Service Plan)

Child's Name_____   Goal Statement:_____
School_____
Date of Program Entry_____   Short-term Instructional Objectives:
Projected Ending Date_____
Person(s) Completing Form_____   _____

Behavioral Objectives	Task Analysis of Objectives	Strategies and/or Techniques	Materials and/or Resources	Date Started	Date Ended	Comments

instructional time the retarded child should spend in the regular classroom (Turnbull, Strickland, & Brantley 1978).

It is also important to ensure that the handicapped will not be harmed by placement in a setting regarded as least restrictive. We must be sensitive to the possibility that placing the retarded with the nonretarded can lead to ridicule, failure, and self-depreciating experiences. The intent of LRE is not to expose any handicapped children to experiences that will adversely affect their development; but the hypothesis that contact with the non-handicapped promotes greater acceptance of the handicapped carries with it the possibility that such contact may well have negative consequences.

Parental Involvement

A major goal of PL 94-142 is to ensure that the parents of handicapped children participate in decisions about the education of their child. The law guarantees certain rights to parents (Turnbull et al. 1978), including the right to inspect school records and the right to request an explanation or interpretation of the records. If the records contain inaccurate or incomplete information, the parents have a right to request that the records be amended.

Parents play a variety of roles in the programing for their handicapped child at different stages of the process, according to Yoshida and Gottlieb (1977), who had extensive experience with program planning for handicapped children in Connecticut. In the early stages of referral and assessment, which they call the *input phase*, the committee in charge of certification and planning is concerned with gathering information to make decisions about eligibility and the need for special education. Yoshida and Gottlieb describe three possible parental roles at this stage. First, parents can be *permission-givers*, assenting to the assessment and testing of their child. During the assessment, parents can be *information-givers*, supplementing the information obtained by the psychologist through a battery of tests with information about the child's preschool medical and social history and information on the child's current behavior at home and in the neighborhood. Finally, during the input phase, when the committee is considering alternatives, parents can serve as *preference-givers*, stating in which program they would like to see their child enrolled.

Yoshida and Gottlieb also determined that parents play different roles in the committee meetings that are held to determine what level of special education the child needs, if any. Parents can choose to be *outsiders* and not attend conferences or offer any input. They can be *passive participants*, attending conferences and responding to questions by committee members but not offering suggestions or questioning the alternatives considered by the committee members. Parents can also be *active participants*, suggesting placements and instructional methods that seem appropriate to them or questioning the suitability of placements suggested by committee members. Parents who choose to be active participants have a voice equal to that of school personnel, whereas parents who choose to be passive participants voluntarily assume a lesser role.

Once recommendations have been made by the committee, the parents assume the role of *legitimizers*. In this capacity, they either accept or reject the recommendations of the committee. If the parents accept the recommendations, they legitimize the placement and IEP. If they reject the committee's recommendations, they begin the mandated process for a fair hearing, in which they can challenge the committee's decisions about eligibiltiy and program planning when they are in conflict with the parents' notions of appropriate action.

Throughout PL 94-142, there are provisions for parental involvement in decisions about their child's education. In the past, parents were often either excluded from the process altogether or required to play roles with which they were unfamiliar. Further study is necessary to determine how much they actually participate and what factors limit their participation.

SUMMARY

The mentally retarded have traditionally been educated in a variety of placements, including regular classes, resource rooms, special classes, special schools, and residential schools. Placement in these programs, however, was based not on individual differences, but on classifications of the mentally retarded as EMR, TMR, or SPMR. The diagnosis of a child as EMR often led automatically to placement in a special class, the implication being that EMR children were a homogeneous group with identical needs. This procedure led to the creation of a set curriculum for all EMR children. Assumptions about the homogeneity of the EMR and the wisdom of a set curriculum have since been rejected, and educational programing for the EMR (and the TMR, too, for that matter) has been individualized according to the provisions of PL 94-142.

An overview of traditional EMR and TMR curricula was also presented in this chapter. Unlike the curricula for other groups of exceptional children, curricula for the mentally retarded must take into account *what* should be taught in addition to *how* it should be taught.

The meaning of "education" was revolutionized by the "zero reject" provision of PL 94-142. SPMR children must now be given a free education that is appropriate to their needs, and education is now considered to involve the teaching of self-help skills, communication skills, and other skills previously assumed to be outside the realm of public education. Since the education and training of the SPMR has become the responsibility of the public education system, curricular models and specific teaching techniques have been developed to promote the development of basic skills and to encourage their generalization to everyday living situations. Most of these methods are based on the principles of operant behaviorism.

This chapter concludes with a discussion of three basic provisions of PL 94-142 that have altered educational programing for mentally retarded children: (1) individualized education programs, (2) least restrictive environment, and (3) parental participation. These provisions require that educational programs for mentally retarded children be based on individual needs. They have also influenced the settings in which needed services are delivered and have involved parents as equal participants in planning, implementing, and evaluating their child's program.

CHAPTER 13

New Directions in Treatment and Education

The treatment and education of mentally retarded children has changed as a result of the passage of PL 94-142, court cases, and the accumulating empirical evidence on the needs of the retarded. One major change has occurred in the treatment of SPMR children, a decreasing percentage of whom are being served in large state-sponsored institutions. This development will be discussed in detail in Chapter 14. Two other new directions in treatment and education are the increase in early intervention with retarded children and mainstreaming in the public schools. In this chapter, we will consider these two recent developments and the evidence on how they affect children.

PL 94-142 alludes to early intervention and mainstreaming, although the term *mainstreaming* does not appear in that document. The law required that by September 1, 1980, all handicapped children between the ages of three and twenty-one would be provided with a free appropriate public education. The law extended age limits in most states to include both younger and older children than were served formerly. State statutes vary somewhat in the mandated ages for handicapped children, as can be seen in Table 13.1. Notice the variations in lower and upper ages, permissive versus required services, and the provisions for program completion (or graduation) that constitute termination of responsibility.

The provision that children be educated in the least restrictive environment refers to what most educators call *mainstreaming*—educating children in the mainstream of public education whenever possible. We will discuss the similarities and differences between "least restrictive environment" (LRE) and mainstreaming later in this chapter.

In examining these new directions, you should consider why it is believed that providing services to children younger than age five and educating retarded children in classes with nonhandicapped children will ultimately benefit retarded children. You should also consider the extent to which the impetus behind these changes was social or philosophical rather than empirical. As we examine the literature on early intervention and mainstreaming, we will discuss the goals of these practices, how we attempt to meet them, and to what extent our efforts have succeeded. We will first consider early intervention. You should be aware that some early intervention actually takes the form of mainstreaming, in which young handicapped children are placed in preschool programs for the nonhandicapped, or "reverse mainstreaming," in which some nonhandicapped children are enrolled in preschool programs designed primarily to serve handicapped children.

EARLY INTERVENTION

Great emphasis has been placed on early identification and intervention in an effort to prevent milder cases of retardation and ameliorate cases of moderate and severe retardation. In this context early intervention is considered to refer to treatment programs initiated during the preschool years, with some being started during infancy. During the last fifteen years, early intervention has become one of the most heavily funded areas in the field of mental retardation. It has been the subject of many articles and a great deal of discussion. To understand the enthusiasm it has generated, one must be familiar with several basic concepts.

There have been two types of early intervention programs: (1) programs for the poor and (2) programs for the handicapped (Robinson 1976). Early programs such as Head Start were aimed at children from poor economic areas who were considered likely (or "at risk") to fail in school and later in their careers. The purpose of these programs was to prevent these children from eventually being labeled as retarded. More recently, early intervention programs have been implemented for children diagnosed as handicapped before entering school—the moderately and severely retarded (Guralnick 1978). For these children, prevention is impossible; the purpose of early intervention is to improve their ultimate level of achievement. The distinctions between the two programs are reflected in this chapter to help

TABLE 13.1   State Mandatory Ages for Handicapped

State	Ages	Exceptions/Clarifications*
Alabama	6 to 21	Permissive services for deaf and blind from 3 to 21. Education for 12 consecutive years starting at age 6. If school district offers kindergarten, then services required at 5.
Alaska	3 through 19	—
Arizona	Between 6 and 21	If kindergarten is maintained, then 5. 3–5 permissive.
Arkansas	6 through 21	If kindergarten program, then 5–21.
California	4 years/9 months through 18	3 to 4.9 intensive services; 19 through 21 if not graduated or completed course of study. 0–3 permissive under Master Plan.
Colorado	Between 5 and 21	Or until graduation; 3–5 permissive.
Connecticut	4 to 18	May serve only until graduation. Hearing-impaired beginning at age 3. Starting 9/80 serve until age 21 unless child graduates.
Delaware	Between 4 and 21	Allows services 0 to 21 for deaf/blind and hearing-impaired.
District of Columbia	Between 3 and 18; 3–21 by Fall 1979	—
Florida	5 through 17	Beginning at kindergarten and for 13 consecutive years. Permitted with state funds from age 3.
Georgia	5 through 18	0 through 4 and 19 through 21, permissive.
Hawaii	6 to 20	3 to 5 permissive.
Idaho	5 through 18	5 through 21 by 9/1/80; 0 through 4 at local discretion.
Illinois	3 through 18	3 through 21; 9/1/80.
Indiana	6 to 18	—
Iowa	Birth through 20	—
Kansas	5 to 21	Through school year during which reach 21 or until completed an appropriate curriculum, whichever occurs first. 0–5 permissive.
Kentucky	5 through 17	Permitted to 21.
Louisiana	3 through 21	—
Maine	5 to 20	—
Maryland	3 to 21	Birth to 21 beginning 9/80.
Massachusetts	3 through 21	—
Michigan	0 to 26	Who have not graduated from high school.
Minnesota	4 to 21	Or completion of secondary program.
Mississippi	6 through 18	6 through 20 by 9/1/80. No requirement and not usual to provide classes to 3–5.
Missouri	5 through 20	Allows districts to provide programs to 3 through 4.
Montana	6 through 18	3 through 21 by 9/80. Provides for services to 0–2 after 9/1/80 under certain circumstances; 3–5 and 19–21 currently under same circumstances.

State	Mandatory age range	Notes
Nebraska	0 to 21	From date of diagnosis or notification of district; voluntary as specified by parent—below 5.
Nevada	Between 6 and 18	Between 3 and 21 by 9/1/80. (Under 18) attendance excused when completed 12 grades. 3–5 is permissive.
New Hampshire	Between 3 and 21	—
New Jersey	5 to 21	Permissive below 5 and above 20.
New Mexico†	—	—
New York	5 through 17	0 through 4 and 18 through 21 permissive.
North Carolina	Between 5 and 21	0 to 6 permissive.
North Dakota	6 to 21	Do not actually say 5–21 is mandate.
Ohio	5–21‡	Except no set minimum age for visually impaired/hearing-impaired. 3 through 17 for severely multihandicapped, severely handicapped, minimum of 12 years of schooling.
Oklahoma	4 through 17	3–5 and 21 at local options.
Oregon	6 through 20	Permissive below 6. Virtually all districts provide kindergarten for 5-year-olds; therefore, must provide for handicapped at 5.
Pennsylvania	6–21‡	3–21 by 9/1/80 (until complete high school or reach age 21, whichever comes first).
Rhode Island	3–18‡	Hearing-impaired 4 to 21.
South Carolina	Between 5 and 21	—
South Dakota	0 through 21	Hearing-impaired and deaf 3 through 21.
Tennessee	4 through 21	—
Texas	Between 3 and 21	—
Utah	5 through 21	Or completion of high school, 3–5 as funds are available except all districts providing public kindergarten will serve 5-year-olds.
Vermont	6 to 21	—
Virginia	Between 2 and 21	Preschool permissive below 5 except if offer preschool as a part of regular program. Every handicapped of same age shall be provided same services. Eligibility ends when goals of IEP reached, at graduation, or at age 21. 3 and above at local discretion. Below 3 if multiple, gross-motor, sensory, moderate, or severe mental retardation.
Washington	5 to 21	—
West Virginia	Between 5 and 23	3 and 4 permissive.
Wisconsin	3 to 21	—
Wyoming	0 through 21	—

*Many states provide for permissive services at ages below 6 and above 17. For some states this may mean that state funds can be used, while for other states, this means that services are not prohibited for these children.

†This information was taken from Annual Program Plans submitted in accordance with PL 94-142. New Mexico has elected not to participate in this grant program during the current school year and, therefore, has submitted no plan.

‡These states did not provide information in their plans as to whether the age range was to, or through, the upper age figure.

the reader understand the differences between the two populations, their treatments, and their goals. You should realize, however, that the two groups overlap somewhat and can be regarded as occupying two positions on the same continuum.

Despite recent enthusiasm for the potential of early intervention, it is not a new idea. Caldwell (1974) stated that early childhood education was *rediscovered* in 1965, when Project Head Start was begun. Educational pioneers in Europe—Comenius, Rousseau, Pestalozzi, Froebel, Seguin, and Montessori—and G. Stanley Hall, whose work catalyzed the kindergarten movement in America, all contributed to the spread of nursery schools and preschool programs that took place in the 1920s. These early preschools tended to serve the more affluent families, however, and except in research programs at such schools as the University of California, the University of Iowa, and the University of Minnesota, the poor and the handicapped were simply unable to participate.

Concepts of Risk Status

Tjossem (1976) defined three categories of children at risk for delayed cognitive development and life adjustment; two of them are germane to our discussion. *Established risk* cases are those in which early aberrant development is related to a known medical etiology that permits prognosis to be made with some certainty. *Environmental risk* cases comprise children who appear biologically sound and have no major health problems, but who live in environments that are relatively likely to delay their development. Early intervention is directed primarily at these two groups. The third group, *biological risk* cases, are those in which the child's perinatal or postnatal history suggests that a biological insult may have occurred, but unlike established risk children, no specific problem can be discovered at the time. This group includes children who were born prematurely. Biological risk children are in need of close monitoring by physicians, and certainly parents should be sensitive to signs that educational problems are emerging. Should such problems arise during the preschool years, the child would be a candidate for early intervention. However, until biological risk children evidence problems, they would be treated as nonhandicapped children whose needs do not warrant special treatment.

Down's syndrome children are among those who would be placed in the established risk category, whereas children born and reared in poverty would be considered in the environmental risk category. Tjossem (1976) noted that these categories are not mutually exclusive. This is particularly true of environmental risk individuals, among whom a higher incidence of biological risk is found. Children born into very poor families, for example, are more likely to be born prematurely. Our purpose is served best by discussing the two categories separately, however.

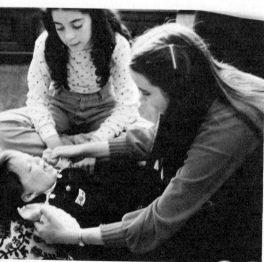

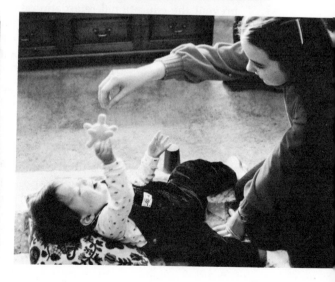

Why is it important to identify these children early in their lives and begin intervention? Does early intervention result in greater developmental and educational gains than beginning treatment when the child enters school? The answers to these questions are related to the rationale for special education, in general, and early intervention, in particular, which we shall now address.

Rationale for Early Intervention

Early identification and intervention are crucial in the prevention and treatment of certain types of mental retardation. For example, dietary treatment of PKU (see Chapter 4) is far more effective in minimizing developmental delays when started early. Prolonged delays result in progressively more serious damage. PKU, however, is a specific metabolic disturbance that can be diagnosed and treated with predictable effectiveness. In this chapter, we are discussing not medical treatments but educational, social, and psychological interventions, in which services are provided directly to a child or in which parents are trained as interventionists. Although accumulating evidence supports the effectiveness of various interventions, their benefits cannot be predicted with anything resembling the certainty with which the benefits of dietary treatment of PKU are predicted. Moreover, the intent for established risk children is not to prevent the retardation, but to enable these children to develop to the upper limit of their capabilities. Intervention with Down's syndrome children, for example, will not raise the IQ to 100 or enable them to attend college, but it may help these children achieve an IQ in the 60s rather than the 40s or 30s, which might have been the result without intervention. On the other hand, we do hope to prevent the educational retardation and related problems in learning and achievement frequently found among environmental risk children.

The rationale articulated by Caldwell (1974) applies primarily to environmental risk children, but professionals in other areas are also considering the benefits of early intervention. The prevailing sentiment, as reflected in federal funding priorities, professional literature, and topics at professional conferences, clearly favors early intervention. There are two contrasting positions regarding the relative importance of early years on development, which we shall now discuss.

Early Experience Position. Evans (1975) summarized five of the assumptions made by those who argue that the early years exert a disproportional influence on developmental outcomes:

1. Children are, by nature, malleable and their growth and development can be modified extensively in a variety of directions.
2. The earlier one can effect a plausible intervention, the better.

3. The manipulation of early experience will influence subsequent psychological functioning. This influence can be salutary or hindering. In either case,
   cumulative development is involved.
4. The provision of qualitatively sound experience can mollify or compensate
   for basic lacks in the child's environments. Such lacks define the basis on
   which experiences can be built. Furthermore, since the school's scholastic
   emphasis demands certain basic learning capabilities, such capabilities must
   become the focus for early intervention.
5. Children who fail to reap the benefits of planned intervention are likely to
   develop in ways that are counterproductive to extant social-educational
   conditions. Or, since a high level capacity for symbolic (cognitive) activity
   is one of man's greatest strengths, children who manifest disorders in cognitive performance are failing to achieve their human potential. Thus,
   resources must be marshalled to prevent or remediate such disorders.

(p. 6)

Beliefs about the importance of the preschool years are derived from several sources (Caldwell 1974; Goldhaber 1979; Hunt 1969). They are based on
the view that "the effects of cultural deprivation are analogous to the experimentally found effects of experiential deprivation in infancy" (Hunt 1969,
p. 47). Some of the experiments referred to have involved research on animals (e.g., Denenberg 1969; Harlow 1949; Riesen 1961). This research indicated that animals' experiences and the age at which they experience them
are crucial developmental variables. Much of this research entailed exposing young animals to very atypical early rearing experiences. Caldwell
(1974) observed that animal research consistently indicates that early
infancy is the crucial period during which experiences could accelerate or
retard development.

A second series of reports concerned children who had experienced
extreme social deprivation in early childhood. Research on infants exposed
to sterile institutional environments (Dennis & Dennis 1941; Goldfarb 1955)
and reports about children coming from a "culture of poverty" (Deutsch
1960; Lewis 1966) seem to indicate that the very early years are a period
during which irreversible harm can result from unstimulating environments. This position is supported in part by a third type of research, which
evaluated planned early interventions designed to provide the experiences
that were lacking in institutions (e.g., Skeels 1966; Skeels & Dye 1939; Spitz
1946a, 1946b) and low-income neighborhoods (Kirk 1958).

Another major impetus to early childhood intervention came from conceptual analyses of the role of experience in development. These writers
included Caldwell (1967) and Hebb (1949), but Hunt (1961, 1969) and
Bloom (1964) were primarily responsible for persuading politicians and the
academic community that (1) experience and environment are, if not the
most important, then certainly notable determinants of intelligence and (2)
environmental intervention will have its greatest impact before age four.
Hunt's and Bloom's reasoning, based on analysis of longitudinal evidence
(discussed in detail in Chapter 4), led to the belief that the influences on

children in these early years were disproportionately important in determining ultimate developmental levels. An important conclusion is
expressed by Bloom (1964): "In terms of intelligence measured at age 17,
about 50 percent of the development takes place between conception and
age 4, about 30 percent between ages 4 and 8, and about 20 percent between
ages 8 and 17" (p. 88).

Life Span Position.   A reexamination of the evidence presented above
has led to a reinterpretation of the position that the early years exert a disproportionate influence on subsequent development. Goldhaber (1979) has
called this alternative the "strong life span position." Advocates of this
position regard early experience as a necessary link in development, but
they do not necessarily assume that early experiences have long-term
effects on adult behavior. Instead, they argue that *continuing* influences are
important. Although they may have begun in the early years, these influences continue to affect development in the years long after early childhood. Goldhaber (1979) contrasts the two positions as follows:

> The strong early experience position views early experience as both a neces-
> sary and, in many instances, a sufficient condition for future development. The
> strong life span position views early experience as a necessary but not suffi-
> cient condition for future development. One should not interpret this strong
> life span view as implying that the early years are unimportant. To say that
> experiences during the early years are not sufficient for future development
> does not make these experiences any less necessary.
>
> (p. 119)

The life span position has been advocated most forcefully by the British
psychologists Clarke and Clarke (Clarke & Clarke 1972, 1976; Clarke,
Clarke, & Reiman 1958). In their book *Early Experience: Myth and Evidence,*
Clarke and Clarke (1976) provide a comprehensive review of such issues as
critical periods, the durability of early experiences, the reversibility of early
trauma, and the relevance of animal research to theories about the importance of early experience. They came to these conclusions:

1. The notion that a critical period of development exercises a powerful influence on later characteristics is not in accord with some evidence about the
   development of deprived children, specifically about those who later experienced significant environmental change.
2. Normally, for most children, environmental changes do not occur, so the
   outcome of later life may be a result not merely of early experience, but of
   continuing experiences.
3. The results of experimental studies of extreme deprivation in animals,
   although important, must be extrapolated to humans cautiously.
4. Important experiments about reversing the effects of early experiences in
   animals have yet to be carried out.

(p. 12)

The Clarkes' book contains chapters by Davis (1976) and Koluchova (1976a,b), who report on cases in which severe early isolation was followed by placement in homes that offered plenty of stimulation, firmness, and attention to the child. In these cases, the developmental lags were reversed. Few such studies exist, probably in part because a child severely delayed in development is difficult to place with those who could offer the necessary stimulation and time. Hence, earlier research reporting long-term effects of early isolation may actually reflect both early and later deprivation.

In addition, differences in the development of humans and lower animal species make direct extrapolations from animal research hazardous. Hebb (1949) observed that humans are capable of more complex associations at maturity and that initial learning is slower in higher species. Hence, even if a critical period of early experiences does exist in animals, the critical period for humans may extend well into adulthood.

The life span position offers a more optimistic outlook for children exposed to depriving conditions early in life. It suggests to the psychologist and educator that efforts to stimulate and educate such children should continue even after what is believed to be the critical period for intellectual development has passed. The interested reader should consult the book by Clarke and Clarke (1976) and the review by Goldhaber (1979) for a critical analysis of the vast literature that questions some of the assumptions about the importance of early experience.

Early Intervention Programs

Preschool education was revived during the Johnson Administration's War on Poverty, which provided funding for Head Start, a preschool education program designed to prepare children from impoverished homes for public school, thereby preventing school failure. Takanishi (1977) noted that Head Start had a variety of goals. The social and economic goal was to provide programs that dealt with societal conflicts about race and poverty in the context of urban unrest and minority militancy. Another goal was to improve the health and abilities of children, thereby encouraging their emotional and social development. A third goal was to help families relate to children's problems and otherwise serve children effectively. Ambitious as these goals were, Anastasiow (1978) wrote that no models existed for establishing complete programs; directors of Head Start programs had to search for models and techniques to serve these children. A similar problem was faced by directors of the original projects sponsored by the Handicapped Children's Early Education Program (HCEEP) of the Bureau of Education for the Handicapped.

Despite the lack of appropriate models for Head Start directors, within a few years several projects achieved high visibility, including the Perry

Preschool Project (Weikart 1967), the Indiana Project (Hodges, McCandless, & Spicker 1967), the Karnes Ameliorative Program (Karnes 1969), the Bereiter and Englemann (1966) project, and the Early Training Project (Gray & Klaus 1969). Each of these projects had to piece together a curriculum and develop teaching methods from sources other than previous preschool projects, since previous projects had not served children considered to be at risk (Anastasiow 1978; Spicker 1974). These projects varied in many ways—in the degree of home intervention, the age at which intervention was begun, and the duration of the intervention. These projects also served different types of children and employed different pedagogical approaches. For a detailed description of these projects, refer to the original writings mentioned above.

Head Start and other projects serving poor children could borrow to a certain extent from traditional nursery school programs and general developmental evidence, but they could not borrow from programs designed to serve impoverished children for the simple reason that none existed. Anastasiow (1978) concluded that this lack of precedent resulted in a "trial and error" approach, not only for Head Start but for its companion program, Follow Through (Klein 1976). (Follow Through was initiated to continue the stimulation and support initiated during the preschool years under the auspices of Head Start as the children entered regular elementary grades.) A similar problem later confronted developers of preschool programs for handicapped children, who could borrow from programs devised for impoverished children, but who had to recognize that handicapped children are a different population with different needs. Hence, they, too, had to improvise in setting up their programs.

Preschool Models Used with Handicapped and At Risk Children. Anastasiow (1978) described four models of preschool programs for handicapped children: (1) the normal developmental model, (2) the behavioral model, (3) the cognitive developmental model, and (4) the cognitive learning model. Programs derived from these models use different curricula.

The *normal developmental model* is the major model of public education. It uses large-group and small-group instruction. Appropriate learning tasks are derived from age-norms, which indicate what children at various ages should be accomplishing. Anastasiow (1978) contends that preschool programs derived from the normal developmental model are chiefly concerned with preparation. The activities provided before the child enters school are undertaken to prepare the child for the demands of regular education. A major activity in such preschool programs involves "readiness" for reading, arithmetic, and social control. Training in social control consists in taking turns, listening to oral instructions, sitting quietly, and controlling impulses. The child's progress or standing is determined through comparison with the group. These comparisons are the standard for assessing progress in grade-by-grade mean-level achievement. Anastasiow contends that a "hidden curriculum" exists in such programs, which requires that practices emulate what middle-class parents do with their children at home.

The appropriateness of the normal developmental model for handicapped children is questionable, since the age-norms provided are not applicable to the handicapped child. Moreover, group instruction with handicapped children may be inappropriate. For an example of the application of the normal developmental model to environmental risk children, the reader should consult descriptions of the Indiana Project (Hodges et al. 1967). When this project began, it reflected many characteristics of this model, but as the curriculum was developed and strategies for teaching evolved, areas of weakness in the model were rectified.

The *behavioral model* is based on the work of applied behaviorists, who translated operant principles into educational practice (see the discussion of operant theory in Chapter 10). Anastasiow (1978) evaluated the behavioral model and concluded that it was good for use with handicapped preschoolers because it emphasized individualized treatment. The behavioral model relies heavily on (1) observing and measuring behaviors, (2) constant recording of behavior to assess improvement, and (3) the systematic use of principles of learning either to modify existing behaviors that may impede school progress or to develop behaviors needed for success in the regular school program.

One popular early program based on a behavioral model was that of Bereiter and Englemann (1966), which originally served children who were economically or environmentally at risk. The program was highly structured according to learning principles such as positive reinforcement, extinction, and contingency management, which provided the basis for instructional practices designed to promote readiness and basic skills in reading, language arts, and writing. The behavioral model has also worked effectively with preschool children who have problems in deportment behaviors such as acting out, aggression, and difficulty in sitting still. These programs have decreased inappropriate behaviors—frequently through extinction—and increased the probability of desirable behaviors through reinforcement.

The *cognitive developmental model* is derived from Piaget's theory of cognitive development (see Chapter 10 for a discussion of Piaget's theory). According to Piaget, children develop through four stages—sensorimotor, preoperational, concrete operational, and abstract reasoning. Because we are interested in the preschool years, we will discuss only the first two stages here—the sensorimotor stage, which typically includes children from birth to age two, and the preoperational stage, which includes children from two to five years old. (These age ranges would have to be adjusted for children who are at risk or handicapped.)

The curriculum and teaching strategies derived from the cognitive developmental model emphasize determining the stage at which the child is functioning and then presenting the child with opportunities and materials to explore and experience the environment. During the sensorimotor stage, the child passes through six substages of learning how the world operates. Through exploration and experimentation, the child comes to understand causality, time, space, and certain basic physical laws such as conservation. During the preoperational stage, the child comes to understand reality through imitation, symbolic play, drawing, and verbalization. The teacher assesses the child's level of functioning and, viewing the child as an active learner who is motivated to learn, provides the materials, freedom, and guidance the child needs to have the experiences necessary for progress through the stages. Anastasiow (1978) notes that the English informal school is derived from a cognitive developmental model, but no preschool program for environmentally at risk or handicapped children is based exclusively on the cognitive developmental model.

Anastasiow (1978) calls the fourth model the *cognitive learning model.* Programs based on this model have been developed by Bricker and Bricker (1974) and Guralnick (1975). These programs use operant procedures for lesson strategies and remediation, but concepts from other theories—psycholinguistic, cognitive, perceptual, and information processing, among others—are used for assessment and instruction. Guralnick (1975), for example, used behavior analysis for instructional strategies and evaluation, but he relied heavily upon other theories and bodies of literature in designing his program for handicapped preschoolers.

Bricker and Bricker (1974), noting that the cognitive developmental model assumes that children initiate exploration behavior, stated that the model must be modified for handicapped children, who must be taught to explore. This exploration behavior can be encouraged and taught through a variety of strategies, including techniques derived from operant theory. In this area and others, the cognitive learning model relies heavily on operant theory for the basis of its diagnostic, teaching, and evaluation framework, but it also makes use of other theories when necessary to meet the needs of the handicapped child. If the child needs work in language, this model turns to psycholinguistic theory; when cognitive experiences are needed, it turns to a cognitive theory; and when perceptual training is called for, it relies on a perception theory for guidance.

It is important to realize that these models use different curricular designs and reflect different conceptions of the role of the learner. Although the normal developmental model was used in the early projects serving environmentally at risk children, Anastasiow's (1978) analysis led him to conclude it should not be used with at risk or handicapped children. Thus, just two models are currently being used with some success with at risk and handicapped children in early intervention projects: the behavioral model and the cognitive learning model. The cognitive developmental model is promising, but it has not yet been tested extensively with either at risk or handicapped children.

Two Total Intervention Programs. Space limitations preclude extensive discussion of specific projects, but several projects can be briefly described to provide examples of different child populations and different approaches to early intervention.

There are two major long-range studies concerning lower-class homes and children who are environmentally at risk for educational failure: The Milwaukee Project and the Abecedarian Project. These are both "total intervention" projects—in addition to educational help, they provide medical care, social work service, and techniques of parental involvement beginning at birth for children born in impoverished homes. Thus, they provide interventions across a broad front in an attempt to prevent the educational failure so frequently found among impoverished children, who are disproportionately represented in EMR classes.

The Milwaukee Project is headed by Rick Heber and his associates at the University of Wisconsin (Heber, Dever, & Conry 1968; Heber & Garber 1971; Heber, Garber, Harrington, Hoffman, & Falender 1972). This project is an ambitious undertaking, with the most extensive intervention program to date and the best experimental controls yet employed in such a project.

The experimenters first identified an area in Milwaukee that had the highest density of population in the city coupled with the lowest family income and the poorest housing conditions. Though only 5 percent of Milwaukee's population lived in the area, approximately one-third of the mentally retarded children in the public schools of Milwaukee came from there. The investigators then selected 88 consecutive births to mothers in the area who already had another child of age six. When intelligence tests were administered to the mothers and their six-year-olds, a strong relationship was found to exist between the child's IQ and that of the mother, as shown in Figure 13.1. Mothers with IQs lower than 80 (less than half of the mothers) accounted for approximately four-fifths of the children with IQs below 80. A fairly close relationship was also reported between the maternal and paternal IQs, suggesting that assortative mating (i.e., like attracts like) had occurred.

Switching to the infants, the investigators were able to plot, through repeated testings, the changes in IQ for those children of mothers with IQs above 80 (N = 48) and below 80 (N = 40). Figure 13.2 shows the progressive decline in IQ for the children whose mothers' IQs were below 80. Note that the two groups scored about the same on the infant test when it was administered initially. To test the effects of early intervention on this pattern of declining relative IQ the investigators selected 50 mothers scoring below 75 in IQ and assigned them to either experimental or control groups. Another group of mothers from the same area with IQs over 100 served as a comparison group.

FIGURE 13.1 IQs of Children as a Function of Maternal IQ

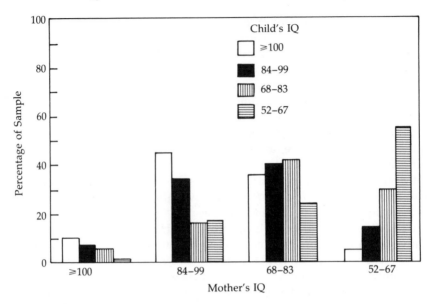

R. F. Heber, and R. B. Dever, "Research on education and habilitation of the mentally retarded," in H. C. Haywood, ed., *Social-Cultural Aspects of Mental Retardation*, p. 420. © 1970. Reprinted by permission of Prentice-Hall, Inc., Englewood Cliffs, New Jersey.

One component of the project is the infant stimulation program. A trained staff member was assigned to each mother in the experimental group. This assistant worked with the mother in establishing stimulation for the infant as soon as the two came home from the hospital. At age four months the child was taken to the Infant Education Center, where teachers tried to stimulate language and sensory development in the experimental infants. The educational program provided to the children was designed to prevent the language, problem-solving, and achievement motivation deficits so often noted in mildly retarded children. The approach used reflected no particular theoretical or curricular model; instead it used methods and materials that emphasized language and cognition.

A second component was designed to promote vocational skills or rehabilitation for the mothers with IQ < 75 in the experimental group. In addition to occupational training, these mothers were trained in homemaking and child care. While mothers received this training, any other preschool-age children they had were provided for in nursery school programs or day care facilities.

The children's progress was periodically evaluated while these two kinds of interventions were taking place. In the early phases of the project, gen-

FIGURE 13.2 IQ Scores of Children at Differing Ages as a Function of Maternal IQ above or below 80

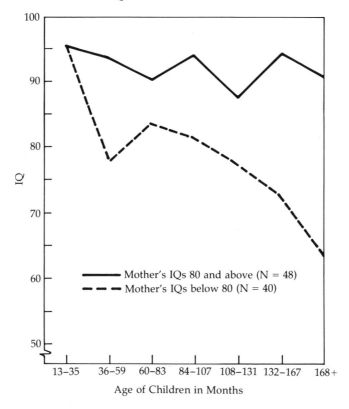

Mother's IQs 80 and above (N = 48)
Mother's IQs below 80 (N = 40)

Age of Children in Months

eral developmental scales (e.g., the Gesell Developmental Scale) were used; as the children grew older the experimenters switched to use of the Cattell, the Stanford-Binet, and the Wechsler Preschool and Primary Scale of Intelligence. Figure 13.3 shows the results of the IQ evaluations of the experimental and control groups. As you can see, these early returns looked very promising. At age sixty months there was a 26-point difference in the mean IQ for the two groups (Stanford-Binet IQ). Similar differences were apparent on other behavioral measures (e.g., Illinois Test of Psycholinguistic Abilities), with an apparent acceleration in the development of the experimental group children.

Early follow-up data (Heber et al. 1972) suggested a decline in the per-

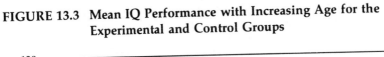

FIGURE 13.3   Mean IQ Performance with Increasing Age for the Experimental and Control Groups

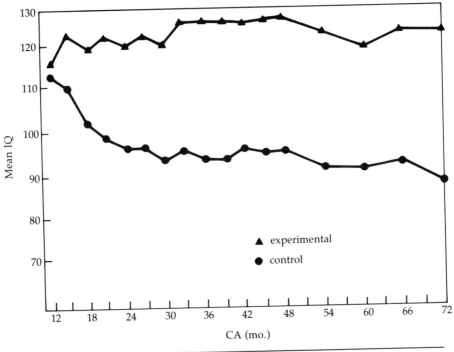

R. Heber, H. Garber, S. Harrington, C. Hoffman, and C. Falender, "Rehabilitation of families at risk for mental retardation—Progress report," 1972. Reprinted by permission of The Rehabilitation Research and Training Center in Mental Retardation at the University of Wisconsin.

formance of the experimental group, but a later report (Garber & Heber 1977) presented more positive findings. Possibly the most dramatic finding involved the differences between experimental and control mothers. The self-concepts and self-confidence of experimental mothers grew as a result of the treatment. They also became more responsive to their children and more verbal, which the authors considered a result of their changed perspective on their importance as parents. The experimental children scored higher than controls on language development, problem solving, and IQ. Experimental children did encounter some difficulty in school—they exhibited more behavior problems, in part because they were more verbal. Overall, however, the Milwaukee Project strongly suggests that an intensive intervention program can interrupt the vicious circle in which poverty leads to mild retardation, which leads to further poverty. The results emphasize the variability of children and families—some were helped more than others. The results were positive, however, and despite criticism of the project on technical grounds (Page 1972) it must be regarded as a success.

The Carolina Abecedarian Project (Ramey & Campbell 1977, 1979a, 1979b; Ramey & Smith 1977) was begun in 1972. Like the Milwaukee Project, it intervened in many areas. Children were randomly assigned to experimental and control groups. Both groups received the following services:

1. *Family support social work services:* These services, available on request, were designed to keep the family intact by providing legal aid, food, family planning information, and clothing.
2. *Nutritional supplements:* The experimental children received these supplements as part of their day care center program. Control families received unlimited free formula for the first fifteen months after their child was born.
3. *Medical care:* Pediatric care was provided for both experimental children (at the day care center) and control children (through a local clinic).
4. *Transportation:* Transportation was provided to and from the center where services were dispensed.
5. *Payment:* Families received payments for participating.

In addition, a program at a day care facility was initiated for experimental children beginning when they were between one and a half and three months old. The curriculum was designed to provide experiences in physical and motor development, perceptual and cognitive development, language development, and social development.

Figure 13.4 presents comparisons between experimental and control children at six-month intervals up to the age of thirty-six months. The results were obtained on either the Mental Developmental Index (MDI), which was used for younger children, or the Stanford-Binet IQ test. Note the decline in performance for the control group between twelve and eighteen months. This was a reliable difference. Ramey and Campbell (1977) interpreted these results as suggesting that intervention was preventing progressive developmental retardation among the experimental children, primarily because they had better language abilities.

Further data on the social consequences of the Abecedarian intervention were also favorable (Ramey & Campbell 1979a,b). The experimental group children were more socially confident and exhibited more goal-directed behavior than did control group children. The control children appeared more fearful in situations in which an examiner was testing them, which was interpreted to indicate that the experimental children were more socially confident when interacting with an unfamiliar adult.

The results of the Abecedarian Project support the promising results of

FIGURE 13.4   Mean Mental Development Index and IQ for High-Risk Experimental (Center) and Control (Home) Children in the Carolina Abecedarian Project

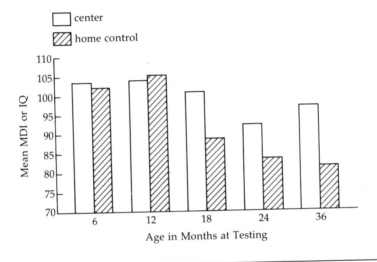

From C. T. Ramey and F. A. Campbell, "Prevention of developmental retardation in high risk children," in P. Mittler, ed., *Research to Practice in Mental Retardation: Care and Intervention*, Vol. 1. Reprinted by permission of the authors and the International Association for the Scientific Study of Mental Deficiency.

the Milwaukee Project, suggesting that the progressive deterioration of cognitive functioning in environmentally at risk children can be prevented. These projects offered intensive multidisciplinary interventions that provided much more than just preschool experiences. The success of these projects contradicts the conclusions of some critics of early intervention for environmentally at risk children. Jensen (1969), for example, concluded that the gains achieved in early intervention programs were unimpressive, writing that "compensatory education has been tried and it apparently has failed" (p. 2). Similarly, the U.S. Commission on Civil Rights (1967) reviewed compensatory education programs and reported the following:

> The Commission's analysis does not suggest that compensatory education is incapable of remedying the effects of poverty on the academic achievement of individual children. There is little question that school programs involving expenditures for cultural enrichment, better teaching, and other needed educational services can be helpful to disadvantaged children. The fact remains, however, that none of the programs appear to have raised significantly the achievement of participating pupils, as a group, within the period evaluated by the Commission.
>
> (p. 138)

Jensen (1969) criticized two notions that he saw underlying most compensatory education programs: (1) the "average child concept" and (2) the "social deprivation hypothesis." What he called the *average child concept* is the assumption that, except for major defects (such as neurological defects), all children are very similar in their mental development and capabilities; exposed to the same experiences, all would achieve at comparable levels. This position thus denies the possibility of individual differences. A related belief, the social deprivation hypothesis, holds that the reason children coming from low socioeconomic status backgrounds tend to achieve at a lower level than their middle-class peers is that they have not had the same experiences and therefore have not developed the skills prerequisite for successful school achievement. Jensen sees these two positions as invalid and yet persistent in the rationales behind most compensatory education programs.

As we saw in Chapter 3, Jensen feels that the effects of environment are best conceptualized as a threshold variable. He does not challenge the notion that extremely deprived environments can depress intelligence. The research evidence (e.g., Davis 1947; Koluchova 1972; Skeels & Dye 1939) clearly documents dramatic increments in development for children shifted from extremely disadvantaged environments to so-called normal environments. But Jensen feels that low socioeconomic status homes that merely lack middle-class amenities do not constitute extremely deprived environments.

While Jensen was skeptical of the ability of enrichment programs to change what he saw as basic individual differences, Vandenberg (1968) questioned the results of early intervention programs from another angle. If intervention programs boost IQ by only 10 points over a control group, he asked, will that increment be maintained or will the control group eventually catch up? He suggested that by analogy early intervention might have either a "hothouse" effect, forcing a "bloom" earlier than would otherwise have occurred, or a "fertilizer" effect, producing a bigger and better bloom. Advocates of early intervention would prefer to think that the extra attention would have a fertilizer effect rather than a short-range hothouse effect, but it is not clear what really happens. There is little doubt that children can be taught skills earlier than they would normally learn them, but does this mean that there will be less progress at the age when that specific learning would normally have occurred? If so, the experimental group would have no appreciable advantage over other children in the long run. But if the early advantage enables children to keep on moving more rapidly at subsequent stages of learning, the value of compensatory education would be irrefutable.

Although such concerns should be considered in the development of early intervention programs for environmentally at risk children, reports on the Milwaukee Project and Abecedarian Project suggest that intervention can be successful. It is important to consider the criteria by which such programs are evaluated. Thus far, great significance has been attached to changes in IQ—a not unreasonable practice, since IQ correlates with academic achievement, which we hope ultimately to affect. Zigler and Trickett (1978), however, warn against excessive reliance on IQ, suggesting that what we really hope to promote is broader gains in what they call *social competence*. They suggest several more molar outcomes that could be used in evaluations, such as (1) the incidence of juvenile delinquency, (2) the incidence of teen-age pregnancy, (3) the incidence of child abuse as either victim or perpetrator, (4) staying in school rather than dropping out, (5) being in the appropriate grade for age, (6) being in a regular classroom rather than a special education classroom, and (7) being self-supporting rather than on welfare (p. 796). Obviously, many of these outcomes cannot be determined until the child reaches a certain age. It is outcomes of this sort, however, that ultimately determine the worth of early intervention programs.

For further study of early intervention with environmentally at risk children, you should consult some of the original writings on specific projects. In addition to those already mentioned, Brofenbrenner (1975), Gordon and Guinagh (1974), and Lazar, Hubbell, Roshce, and Royce (1977) are valuable sources of information.

Exemplary Programs with Established Risk Children. The lion's share of attention and funding has gone to early intervention programs for disadvantaged children who are at risk of later being classified as mildly mentally retarded. However, there has also been some early intervention with children who fall into the moderate or severe categories of mental retardation and who are diagnosed as retarded very early in their lives. Obviously, early intervention with these children does not have as its goal the prevention of mental retardation, as is the case in the programs discussed in the previous section. Instead, the intervention is designed to prevent the deterioration that too often occurs with age. For example, Down's syndrome individuals have been found to evidence a progressive deterioration in cognition as they increase in age, particularly in the area of communication skills (Carr 1970b; Dameron 1963). The finding that Down's syndrome children reared at home tend to achieve better on tests of intelligence than do those placed in institutions (Centerwall & Centerwall 1960) has led to the belief that if the additional stimulation for Down's syndrome children in their natural homes benefits them intellectually, perhaps they can benefit from early intervention as well.

Guralnick (1978) has summarized a number of excellent projects dealing with moderately and severely retarded children, several of which involved integrating handicapped and nonhandicapped children in the same classes. The mainstreaming of preschool handicapped children will be discussed later in this chapter. Here we will consider the goals and program components of some preschool projects for the moderately and severely retarded.

One of the most systematic longitudinal studies on early intervention with Down's syndrome children is Project EDGE (Expanding Developmental Growth through Education), now being conducted at the University of Minnesota (Rynders & Horrobin 1975). Down's syndrome children and their mothers were enrolled in the program when the children were two and a half years old. Initially, a staff member assumed full responsibility for each child's daily instruction. But the parents were instructed to read to their child for thirty minutes a day at home, and the mothers were given six weeks of training in the use of the methods and materials for the stimulation program. Lessons were outlined in detail to give the mothers confidence to carry them out. Some materials were provided; other materials were objects commonly available in the home. The activities were designed to stimulate both sensorimotor and language development. After initial instruction of both the child and the mother by staff members, the mother gradually assumed more responsibility for the program. The special stimulation activities were continued until the children reached school age and were enrolled in the public school program.

When the subjects were five years of age, their IQs varied considerably. Of the thirty-five subjects, twenty achieved scores above 52, and four of these children scored over 68, which is, according to Grossman's AAMD standards, the upper limit for mental retardation. Seventeen subjects gained in IQ during the program, but Rynders, Spiker, and Horrobin (1978) reported that 45 percent of the control group also gained in IQ. (Many control children also were in some kind of preschool program.) Although Rynders and his associates (1978) interpret these results cautiously—their selection of children was not random—the results still appear promising.

Hayden and Haring (1976) developed another project dealing with Down's syndrome children at the University of Washington. The program was designed to promote greater educability in several curricular areas—cognition, self-help skills, and motor skills—through a behavior modification program. The sixty Down's syndrome children participating in the study came from diverse social and residential backgrounds and lived in their natural homes. These children performed very well on developmental screening tests at one year and five years of age, indicating that advantages found at age one were sustained until the children approached entry into the public schools. Rynders and his associates (1978) provide information on the IQs of eight of these children in kindergarten. Their IQs ranged from 61 to 105 with a mean of 83, well above the usual scores for Down's syndrome children.

Finally, we will consider the early intervention program of Bricker and Bricker (1974, 1976)—the Infant, Toddler, and Preschool Research and Intervention Project. Earlier in this chapter, the Brickers' approach was described as a cognitive learning model in that it used the behavioral approach and other techniques derived from Piaget and psycholinguistic theories. In the infant unit of the project, efforts were made to promote

Can Jane see Rex
Rex can see Ann play.
Look Jane, see Skip run.
Run Rex, Billy can play.

gross- and fine-motor skills, sensorimotor skills, and social and self-help skills. The unit for toddlers emphasized language training and, when necessary, individualized programing for gross- and fine-motor skills and cognitive skills such as concept formation and labeling, in preparation for the preschool unit. The preschool unit emphasized the skills needed for the child to be successful in early elementary educational programs.

Programs like the ones we have described have been successful in preparing established risk children to enter public school programs. Their goal has been not so much to make the children "normal," but to optimize their development through early stimulation. It is hoped that intervention will keep these children from being automatically excluded from public school programs because they behave in ways that are not tolerated, or because we failed to develop the abilities they were capable of developing. The preliminary finding—that these children are capable of higher levels of functioning than was formerly thought—indicates that early intervention holds some promise for established risk children.

Another approach to early intervention involves mainstreaming handicapped children with nonhandicapped children. Preschool mainstreaming of handicapped children—a forerunner to mainstreaming school-age handicapped children—is discussed in the next section.

MAINSTREAMING

Mainstreaming is the educational extension of the principle of *normalization* (see Chapter 14), which states that the handicapped should be treated in as normal a fashion as possible within the limits of their capabilities. The concept of mainstreaming is derived from the notion that the handicapped should be educated in the mainstream—the regular program—whenever possible. With regard to the mentally retarded, mainstreaming refers to the practice of integrating retarded children with nonretarded children whenever feasible. The most comprehensive definition of mainstreaming offered to date is that of Kaufman, Gottlieb, Agard, and Kukic (1975):

> Mainstreaming refers to the temporal, instructional, and social integration of eligible exceptional children with normal peers based on an ongoing, individually determined educational planning and programming process and requires clarification of responsibility among regular and special education administrative, instructional, and supportive personnel.
>
> (pp. 40–41)

The major components of the Kaufman et al. definition concern *where* the child is placed (with normal peers), for what length of time (temporal integration), what the child is doing (instructional integration), and with whom the child interacts during the school day (social integration). The definition also requires that the responsibilities of teachers and other educational personnel be specified to ensure that services will be coordinated. MacMillan and Semmel (1977) observed, however, that if all the elements of this definition must be present, "then no program to date constitutes mainstreaming" (p. 3). Most legislated and operational definitions emphasize that the child must be educated in a regular classroom for 50 percent or more of the school day. In practice, then, mainstreaming is defined in accordance with only the temporal aspect of the Kaufman et al. definition.

Today it is widely assumed that regular class placement is preferable to special class placement. Even when children need special help, they are kept in the regular educational program as much as possible, within the limits of their abilities and disabilities, and special help is provided in the context of the regular class when feasible. If, as Reynolds (1974) put it, school systems previously operated according to a kind of social Darwinism—the most fit were placed in regular classes and the others were consigned to special classes—mainstreaming reflects an important new philosophy.

Impetus for Mainstreaming

Mainstreaming developed from a number of different sources—legal and legislated mandates, philosophical and social forces, and some empirical evidence. When these forces coalesced, considerable pressure was exerted for the retarded and other handicapped children to be mainstreamed.

PL 94-142 never mentions mainstreaming by name, but it does refer to the "least restrictive environment." The definition in the *Federal Register* states:

1. That to the maximum extent appropriate, handicapped children, including children in public or private institutions or other care facilities, are educated with children who are not handicapped, and
2. That special classes, separate schooling or other removal of handicapped children from the regular educational environment occurs only when the nature or severity of the handicap is such that education in regular classes with the use of supplementary aids and services cannot be achieved satisfactorily.

(August 23, 1977, p. 42, 497)

In essence, the "burden of proof" has been shifted from the parents to the school. It is now the school's responsibility, not the parents', to justify why the child cannot remain in regular education.

Semmel, Gottlieb, and Robinson (1979) noted that some regard mainstreaming as the educational counterpart of the legal concept of least restriction, by which mainstreaming is associated with a continuum of placement options available to handicapped learners. The range of placement options can be ordered from the more restrictive to the less restrictive, as Lowenbraun and Affleck (1978) have done for the public schools:

1. *Special class placement:* The retarded child's primary assignment is to the special class, but the child could be integrated with nonhandicapped children for some school activities.
2. *Resource room placement:* The retarded child's primary assignment is to a regular classroom, but the child is given supplementary help outside the classroom for some part of the school day.
3. *Itinerant services placement:* The retarded child's primary assignment is to the regular class, but the child receives ancillary support from an itinerant teacher in the regular class on a one-to-one or small-group basis.
4. *In-class services placement:* The child's placement is in the regular class, and additional services are also provided within the regular class as part of the in-class support system, which might involve tutors, aides, or other help.
5. *Services to teacher placement:* The child's placement is in the regular class, and the teacher receives assistance in the form of materials and suggestions on instructional strategies and other programing to help the child achieve successfully.

The problem is in deciding when an option is too restrictive to be considered mainstreaming. The distinctions are not merely semantic—problems in determining whether or not a program is an example of mainstreaming are not at all unusual.

Other sources of the impetus for mainstreaming are more philosophical and social in nature. Turnbull and Blacher-Dixon (1981) noted that preschool mainstreaming apparently has a positive effect on both handicapped and nonhandicapped children, as well as on teachers and parents. Social contact with children who are different is assumed to increase understanding of individual differences and awareness of others. It should result in a more positive self-concept for the handicapped, possibly through identification with nonhandicapped children. Moreover, mainstreaming is simply good preparation for later adjustment, since the more able retarded children will live in the mainstream of society. Parental support for mainstreaming has been traced to their belief that mainstreaming results in social benefits for them and their child and that their child will model "normal" play and behavior rather than "deviant" models. These are logical possibilities, but they have not been confirmed empirically.

Another impetus for change was the interpretation of efficacy studies (see Chapters 7 and 12) as empirical evidence that mildly retarded children in special classes were worse off than those who remained in regular classes without support. Although the studies were flawed methodologically, a review by Semmel et al. (1979) provided no indication of differential achievement gains among EMR pupils as a function of regular or special class placement (p. 247). In other words, EMR children were no worse off in regular classes, which made it difficult to justify the small pupil/teacher ratios, extra cost, and specialized training for teachers of special classes. Mainstreaming was therefore mandated by the courts and legislatures in reaction to the philosophical and social belief that benefits would result from integrating handicapped with nonhandicapped children, and also because empirical evidence did not confirm the expected benefits of special classes. There was little empirical evidence that the retarded would peform *better* in mainstreamed settings, but the philosophical, social, and legal forces were too strong to be denied. As one professional put it, Lincoln did not need research to know that slavery was wrong, and we do not need empirical evidence to know that segregation of the handicapped is wrong. There is a different point of view, however. We would not want to deny children the protection of special classes and other presumably more restrictive settings if placement in the mainstream is going to be detrimental to them.

Although mainstreaming is relatively new, we have been using it long enough to have some experience with it and some empirical evidence about it. Our knowledge of mainstreaming is discussed below, first at the preschool level and then for the school years.

Preschool Mainstreaming

The 1972 Congressional mandate required that Head Start programs include 10 percent handicapped children. A handicapped preschool child was defined as any child under age six who exhibited a generally recognized and persistent physical or mental handicap that prevented the child from taking part freely in the activities important to all children (Lapides 1973). A summary of reports on Head Start efforts to integrate or mainstream handicapped children has been written by Turnbull and Blacher-Dixon (1981).

Projects like Head Start were originally designed to serve environmentally at risk children; the mainstreaming of *handicapped* children in such classes integrated environmentally at risk children with established risk children. Other programs (see Guralnick 1978) mainstreamed established risk children into preschool programs with children not considered to be at risk. Literature on the preschool mainstreaming of handicapped children frequently discusses projects that integrated children with varied handicaps—deafness, physical handicaps, mental retardation—into regular pre-school programs, which makes it difficult to determine how mainstreaming affected retarded children alone. Nevertheless, there is some information not only about different models and approaches for mainstreaming pre-school retarded children, but about program elements that appear to be related to successful outcomes and about potential problems.

Approaches to Preschool Mainstreaming. Turnbull and Blacher-Dixon (1981) describe the research on service delivery models as spotty and uncoordinated—program components are not clearly specified and have not yet been related to child outcomes. A distinction has been made between *traditional mainstreaming* and *reverse mainstreaming*. The traditional model involves placing handicapped children in preschool programs orig-inally developed for nonhandicapped children, whereas reverse main-streaming involves enrolling nonhandicapped children in a program orig-inally designed for handicapped children. Traditional mainstreaming is exemplified by the Head Start programs, which were required to enroll 10 percent handicapped children. The reverse mainstreaming model has been implemented primarily in the demonstration networks of the Handicapped Children's Early Education Program (HCEEP), in which approximately 30 out of a total of 200 programs enrolled nonhandicapped children (Turnbull & Blacher-Dixon 1980).

The ratio of handicapped to nonhandicapped children differs markedly in traditional and reverse mainstreaming. A handicapped child placed in a class of ten or fifteen nonhandicapped children may be affected very dif-ferently than a handicapped child placed in a program in which most of the students are handicapped. Evidence on the optimal ratio of handi-capped to nonhandicapped children is currently unavailable.

Preschool mainstreaming models also vary in the way they deliver ser-vices. After reviewing programs in the First Chance Network of HCEEP, Karnes and Zehrbach (1977) identified three major service-delivery types: home-based programs, combination home and center programs, and center-based programs. In home-based programs, a professional instructs a hand-icapped and a nonhandicapped child in the handicapped child's home. In the combination program, the handicapped child is initially served in the home and later enrolled in a center-based program in which handicapped and nonhandicapped children are integrated. The center-based program serves children in a classrom in which both handicapped and nonhandi-capped children are enrolled.

In traditional mainstreaming, the teacher is unlikely to have any background in the education of handicapped children, whereas the likeli-hood that the reverse mainstreaming teacher will have a background in spe-cial education is much greater. Although there is no evidence on the direct consequences of this difference in teacher training (Turnbull & Blacher-

Dixon 1980), it is logical to assume that it affects the handicapped child and the child's parents.

Successes in Preschool Mainstreaming.   Evidence indicates fairly consistently that the handicapped benefit from having nonhandicapped models of appropriate social behavior. Handicapped children appear to learn socially appropriate behaviors through modeling or imitating their nonhandicapped peers (Karnes & Zehrbach 1977; Peterson & Haralick 1977; Snyder, Apolloni, & Cooke 1977). In addition, social learning theory and behavioral models have been used to promote social interactions between handicapped and nonhandicapped children using the peer model approach, in which nonhandicapped children act as reinforcing agents (Guralnick 1978; Snyder et al. 1977).

Another benefit of preschool mainstreaming is that teachers and nonhandicapped children become more sensitive to the needs of handicapped children through interacting with them (Karnes & Zehrbach 1977; Snyder et al. 1977). Mainstreaming also results in more positive self-concepts among handicapped children (Turnbull & Blacher-Dixon 1980). In addition, interaction between the handicapped and the nonhandicapped presumably prepares the handicapped for public school mainstreaming and interactions with nonhandicapped children in other settings.

Another means of assessing the benefits of preschool mainstreaming is to examine the child's future class placement. If a mainstreamed preschool child needs to be placed in a special class or other restrictive environment upon reaching school age, the worth of preschool mainstreaming would be called into question. If the child can remain in the regular class for most of the school day, however, one might conclude that mainstreaming was beneficial. DeWeerd (1977) reported that the majority of handicapped children who participated in the First Chance projects entered regular school programs rather than special education programs. It is not clear whether this was a direct result of preschool mainstreaming experiences, but it does seem promising. As mentioned earlier, research has not yet determined specifically which elements of preschool mainstreaming programs are related to changes in child behavior, but some evidence suggests that certain elements are important. Turnbull and Blacher-Dixon (1980), for example, concluded that no one model appears superior to any other model, but teacher ability, teacher attitudes, and parental involvement are crucial to program success.

The willingness of preschool teachers to accept handicapped children in their classes is important in determining not just whether mainstreaming will be successful, but whether it will occur at all. A survey by Gorelick (1973) revealed that of children with various handicaps, preschool teachers were least inclined to work with the severely retarded and most inclined to work with partially deaf children. In addition to their own acceptance of handicapped children, teachers' attitudes are also critical in encouraging the nonhandicapped peer group to accept the handicapped child (Klein 1975). The attitudes of teachers who had received no training in working with handicapped preschoolers became more realistic after they had worked with handicapped children (Clark 1976). These teachers agreed that mainstreaming required modification of class routines and educational methodologies for individual exceptional children. They also recognized that the physically handicapped are not necessarily easier to mainstream than the mentally handicapped and that similar instructional techniques can be used with both normal and exceptional children.

It is crucial that parents become involved in preschool programs. Turnbull and Blacher-Dixon (1980) described the different roles parents could play in a preschool mainstreaming program. They can serve as educators trained to teach in the home, as counselors, as aides, and as decision-makers on advisory councils. Bronfenbrenner (1974) summarized the importance of parental involvement:

> The involvement of the child's family as an active participant is critical to the success of any intervention program. Without such family involvement, any effect of intervention ... appears to erode fairly rapidly once the program ends. In contrast, the involvement of the parents as partners in the enterprise provides an ongoing system which can reinforce the effects of the program while it is in operation and help to sustain them after the program ends.
>
> (p. 55)

Parental involvement in mainstreaming is not without its problems, however. Some of these problems are discussed below.

Impact on Parents. In a thought-provoking chapter, Turnbull and Blacher-Dixon (1980) summarized the research they conducted as part of the Carolina Institute for Research in Early Education of the Handicapped. They also provide anecdotal data on the problems faced by *some* parents of mainstreamed handicapped children. Often, when the focus is on the needs of the child, parental needs are relegated to the background. We have considered what the handicapped child gains by being mainstreamed. But how does the mainstreaming effort affect parents?

In Chapter 6, we discussed parental reactions to the birth of a severely retarded child and the stages they are believed to pass through before finally accepting the child. Turnbull and Blacher-Dixon (1980) point out that the effect of mainstreaming on the parent may be a function of the stage the parent is currently in. Parents who have accepted their retarded child may regard mainstreaming as a wonderful experience. Parents who are still emotionally disorganized, however, may feel additional conflict about mainstreaming placement. For these parents, it may not be the option of choice at that particular time. Turnbull and Blacher-Dixon listed the following possible problems for parents of mainstreamed retarded children:

(1) daily reminders of their child's developmental deficits from the child's associating with children who are developing normally, (2) the problem of shared stigma, (3) lack of common interests with parents of nonhandicapped children in the program, (4) addititional responsibilities for their child's educational and social adjustment, and (5) the increased likelihood that supportive services available through the preschool program are not suited to the needs of the handicapped child or the family. These problems are discussed in more detail below.

When retarded children are integrated with nonretarded children, their parents may suffer anxiety when they see their child struggling to master colors while other children are beginning to read or write their names. The constant reminder of how rapidly nonhandicapped children develop skills could detrimentally affect the parents' attitudes toward their child. In the segregated setting, such comparisons are less likely. Parents might prefer models who are handicapped themselves but who have overcome the handicap and adjusted well.

The concept of "shared stigma," derived from Goffman's work (1963), suggests that the relatives of stigmatized persons are forced to share the stigmatization. Shared stigmatization may cause the parents of the retarded to question their own identities. Goffman observed that stigmatized persons typically strive to present a more positive image. Turnbull and Blacher-Dixon (1980) relate the experience of the mother of a retarded girl going grocery shopping:

> When Beckie was little, such an excursion required only the extra energy needed to carry her on my hip and choose groceries one-handed and push the grocery cart with the other. But when she hit the teens, a completely new ingredient entered the challenge. I took her shopping with me only if I felt up to looking groomed, cheerful, competent and in command of any situation, so that when she bellowed and stamped with joy as she always did when we walked through the supermarket door, people who stared could quickly surmise that I would handle the situation, quiet my strange child, and get on with my shopping. To look tired and preoccupied with surviving as I so often felt would be to turn *both* of us into objects of pity, and that I clearly did not need. If I could not play the role of the coping, competent mother, I did better to stay at home and grocery shop after she went to bed, or ask one of the other children to come home early and "sit" for me, or leave the big shopping until another day and ask a neighbor to pick up a necessity or two for me, or make do with what I had until I felt more energetic, though chances were excellent that I wouldn't.
>
> (Morton 1978, pp. 144–145)

Efforts by parents of retarded children to prove themselves competent and in control can be trying if the child is mainstreamed.

Another problem is that the parents of the nonhandicapped do not share the feelings and concerns of the parents of retarded children. Parental support meetings are standard practice in preschool programs for handicapped children, but meetings with parents of normal children can be trying. One mother of a cerebral palsied and mentally retarded child related the following experience to Ann Turnbull: She attended a meeting of parents entitled "The Independent Three-Year-Old," and while the other parents lamented over their children's independence, temper, and energy, she stated that "she silently wept; yet wanted to scream out and let them know how she would give anything for similar problems" (Turnbull & Blacher-Dixon 1980, p. 38). Parents of handicapped children who need the support of parents in similar situations may not get it if their child is mainstreamed, which can exacerbate their problems. There has been little if any research on parents' need for support and how they can receive it in mainstreaming programs in which the other parents do not share similar problems or concerns.

Another potential problem is that the parents may need to be more involved in a mainstreaming program than they would if their child were in a preschool program exclusively for handicapped children. Turnbull and Blacher-Dixon (1980) note that parents of mainstreamed children may have to educate school personnel. They may have to explain their child's appearance and capabilities to other children in particular, because the staff may be uninformed about and uncomfortable with the handicapped child. The parents may have to assist the teacher, explaining the educational implications of the child's disability and suggesting adaptations of the curriculum or instructional activities to accommodate the child's disability. Thus, the parents of retarded children may have to be more involved in schooling than they would if their child were in a segregated program in which the teacher was trained specifically to work with retarded children. Parents who need support and respite may instead have to become more involved in the educational process to ensure that their child will be accommodated in the preschool mainstreaming program.

A final consideration is that in a segregated program, services such as physical therapy, language training, speech therapy, and respite care are usually within easy access. In a mainstreaming setting, however, such services may be unavailable. This places an additional burden on parents, who must locate services, transport the child to the service locations, and otherwise expend more time and energy than would be necessary in a segregated program. Turnbull and Blacher-Dixon (1980) expressed concern about the possibility that the parents may become angry and frustrated about having to serve as managers, which could adversely affect the parents' relations with the child.

Mainstreaming School-Age Children

PL 94-142 reversed the 75-year-old practice of placing the handicapped in special classes. Today, handicapped children are being dispersed throughout the school system. As noted previously, the impetus for main-streaming included social, philosophical, legal, and empirical forces. The first wave of mainstreamed children was met with enthusiasm by special education professors, lawyers, and others far from the classroom. Now that we have some perspective on mainstreaming, however, the enthusiasm has moderated somewhat (see Zigler & Muenchow 1979). We now realize that merely changing the placement will not guarantee success, and know that successful mainstreaming requires very hard work. As Zigler and Muen-chow (1979) put it, "Mainstreaming must not be allowed to proceed along the same lines as deinstitutionalization, which has often amounted to the trading of inferior care for no care at all" (p. 993). These authors go on to observe that the success of PL 94-142's push for mainstreaming will be determined by its implementation.

There is far too much information on mainstreaming available for us to discuss it all thoroughly. The reader is urged, however, to consult the thor-ough reviews of research on mainstreaming that have recently appeared (Corman & Gottlieb 1979; Gottlieb 1980; Meyers, MacMillan, & Morrison, in press; Meyers, MacMillan, & Yoshida 1980; Semmel, Gottlieb, & Robin-son 1979). These reviews all note that the studies vary greatly in what they consider mainstreaming; in fact, this body of research might more accu-rately be described as comparing integrated education for retarded learners to segregated education. The only element common to all the studies is that one group of children is assigned to regular classes, although they receive assistance elsewhere, while another group is assigned to a self-contained special class, although they may be integrated into regular classes for cer-tain activities.

Program Goals, Models, and Intended Outcomes. Special EMR classes usually operated on the assumption that educational programs for retarded children needed to be modified in terms of *what* they taught and *how* they taught. The pattern for the EMR program, frequently modeled after the *Illinois Curriculum Guide,* emphasized the development of social and voca-tional skills. Basic tool subjects such as math and social studies were pre-sented in a context resembling that in which the child was expected to apply these skills. In general, knowledge for knowledge's sake was empha-sized less than it was in the general curriculum. You will recall that in mainstreaming, the temporal dimension emphasizes where the child will be enrolled (preferably in the regular class), but the goals for the child are specified on the IEP (discussed in Chapter 12). The question confronting educators is how to achieve the goals on the IEP in the regular class, in which the curriculum for nonhandicapped children tends to emphasize academics. In mainstreaming, there are not program goals as in the old EMR programs or the standard elementary or secondary curriculum, but rather individually prescribed goals. Thus, the success of mainstreaming is deter-mined by the extent to which the individual goals specified on the IEP are achieved and by how well the retarded child masters whatever aspects of the standard curriculum the child is exposed to.

An issue to be considered in the development of the IEP is how the educational system is going to meet the special learning needs of retarded children in the regular program. Clearly, these children have special needs or they would not have been classified as retarded, for by definition retarded children were referred for assessment because they did not benefit from regular class instruction. Thus, these children cannot merely be exposed to the standard curriculum and be taught by standard teaching methods. Rather, special education must be provided for the children while they are enrolled in the regular educational program.

The literature offers several models for providing special education without segregating children in a special class:

1. *Resource room:* The child goes to a special education center in which a special education teacher works with small groups to meet the child's special needs.
2. *Consulting teacher:* The special teacher consults with the regular teacher and tries to help the regular teacher meet the retarded child's special needs.
3. *In-class services:* The child receives services in the regular class from aides, tutors, or therapists.

Other approaches have also been used. Haring and Krug (1975) gave students an intensive, highly structured program designed to improve reading and math rapidly in a special class setting. After this intensive remedial effort, the children were returned to the regular classroom, presumably with the academic skills needed to be successful. Other programs in California, called *transitional programs,* were designed to provide for the thousands of EMR children declared normal, as they made the transition from special EMR classes back into regular education. Meyers, MacMillan, and Yoshida (1975) found that in these programs, some children required no services at all, while others received assistance from a teacher's aide, and still others received services in a resource room.

The issue of precisely what we hope to accomplish through mainstreaming children has not been addressed extensively. MacMillan and Semmel (1977) noted that we cannot possibly select outcomes to measure in evaluating mainstreaming until we know what outcomes the program is designed to influence. Do we want higher academic achievement, better self-concepts, greater peer acceptance, more favorable attitudes toward school, lower dropout rates, greater economic independence as adults, or some other outcomes?

Once the desired outcomes are specified, they should be given priorities according to their relative importance. If outcomes are not ranked in order of importance, it would be impossible to determine whether a program that, say, improved academic achievement but resulted in lower self-concepts should be considered a success or a failure. The answer obviously depends on which outcome is considered the more important.

The empirical evidence on the relative merits of integrating retarded children and educating them in self-contained special classes is considered below. The evidence comes almost exclusively from research on EMR children. It tends to emphasize two outcomes: academic achievement and social adjustment.

Academic Achievement. Efficacy studies comparing EMR children in special classes with IQ-equal children in regular classes were discussed in Chapter 12. They bear on the present discussion to the extent that they show how low-IQ children (usually those without concomitant serious achievement deficits) perform in regular grades with *no ancillary services.* Semmel et al. (1979) reviewed ten efficacy studies and reported that five indicated that academic achievement was superior in regular classes and five indicated no reliable differences. That EMR children in special classes failed to show superior achievement was troubling to special educators, since special classes enrolled fewer students per class, spent more money for each child, and were taught by specially trained teachers.

Serious methodological problems with the efficacy studies have been exposed (Guskin & Spicker 1968; Kirk 1964; MacMillan 1971b). The most severe problem was the selective sampling bias favoring the regular class children. With only one exception (Goldstein, Moss, & Jordan 1965), the studies used samples that were not comparable—the regular class children were superior in achievement, despite having comparable IQs. Since these children were not assigned randomly, we must ask why one group of children with low IQs was left in regular classes (often without ever having been referred for evaluation) while another group with low IQs was placed in special classes. The most obvious answer is that the most severe cases of underachievement got the initial openings in special classes. Thus, the efficacy studies compared the achievement of higher-achieving low-IQ children with lower-achieving low-IQ children on achievement. It's not surprising that regular class children did better on achievement measures. Furthermore, the regular class curriculum stressed reading and math, whereas the special class curriculum stressed social skills, readiness activities, and prevocational skills. The reason for higher reading and math scores among the regular class students is obvious. It is like giving one group of college students a class on mental retardation and another a physics class and then giving them an exam about mental retardation. When the students who took physics do poorly on the exam, it is concluded that the physics course is less effective.

Research on mainstreaming has taken an approach similar to that of the efficacy studies—EMR students in a special class were typically compared with mainstreamed students who usually received resource room help. Walker (1974), for example, compared a resource room model with a special class model. The resource room children had significantly higher scores in vocabulary and word reading but were equal to special class students in arithmetic. The Walker results may have indicated a selective bias in sampling rather than a difference in the two models. Another study (Budoff and Gottlieb 1976) randomly assigned EMR children to either a resource room (45 to 60 minutes each day) or a special class. They found no significant differences between the two groups on either reading or math achievement.

In 1969, California initiated changes in special education in response to civil rights cases (see Chapter 8) over the disproportion of minority children in EMR programs. Although black and Hispanic children constituted 24 percent of the total California school population, they accounted for 55.3 percent of all EMR students (Simmons & Brinegar 1973). In an effort to correct this disproportion, the IQ cutoff was lowered from 85 to 70 and all children in EMR programs were required to be reassessed. All children who scored above IQ 70 on either the verbal *or* performance subtests of the WISC were to be provided with a transitional program to assist them to move back into the regular class (see Meyers, MacMillan, & Yoshida 1974, 1975; Yoshida, MacMillan, & Meyers 1976 for an extended discussion of the events that led to these changes in policy). As a result of these actions, EMR enrollments in California were reduced by between 11,000 and 18,000 cases in a few years.

This large-scale attempt at mainstreaming did not take place under ideal conditions. Careful consideration was not given to the appropriateness of the regular class curriculum for children formerly thought to be mildly retarded. Program elements needed much more refinement in terms of both *what* and *how* to teach these hard-to-teach children. The transition program was not well-crystallized. And, ironically, the IQ score—which had borne the brunt of the civil rights criticism that led to decertification—was itself used as a major index to determine which EMR children should be decertified and which should be retained in EMR classes.

Despite these flaws, a review of the California process and its consequences is still worth consideration. Our data are from a project funded by the Bureau of Education for the Handicapped (BEH, USOE) and undertaken to assess the plight of the decertified EMR children who were returned to regular classes. The project sought to determine the effects of the decertification process by contrasting the success of decertified EMR students (called the D group) relative to two other groups of children: (1) EMR students who were not decertified and remained in EMR programs (designated as EMR) and (2) a group of low-achieving regular class students (designated as RC) in classrooms in which decertified students were enrolled. In addition, information was sought that related to the process of decertification and transition—problems encountered, elements of the programs that worked well, the effect on the EMR program of removing the D children, and the effect on the regular program of introducing them into regular classes.

Academically, the D group of children were found to be achieving above the level of the EMR children who remained in the EMR program but below the level of their RC peers. Although comparison of the D and RC groups showed mean differences, it is noteworthy that there was considerable overlap in individual Metropolitan Achievement Test (MAT) scores in reading and arithmetic. In other words, some of the D sample were achieving at or above the level of a sizeable proportion of the RC sample. The D subjects were not achieving at the grade level in which they were enrolled (they achieved several years below grade level), but they were achieving at a level roughly comparable to that of the RC students. In classroom marks as well there was overlap in the distributions for the D and RC samples, suggesting that quite a few D children are escaping school failure.

A study by Haring and Krug (1975) suggests that an intensive special class program can be used to prepare handicapped children to function adequately in a regular class. These investigators used precision teaching and token reinforcement with low socioeconomic status children in special programs. The children assigned to the intensive program made dramatic gains in both reading and math compared to the control group. At the end of the year, 13 of the 24 intensive program students were recommended for regular class placement, whereas only 1 of the 24 control group children was placed in a regular class.

Semmel et al. (1979) have addressed the issue of comparing the achievement of children in regular and special programs:

> An examination of the data from the investigations reviewed reveals one marked fact: Regardless of class placement, mentally retarded children read exceedingly poorly. When differences between class placement do occur, these differences may be statistically significant but are probably trivial insofar as they affect retarded children's overall success in school. We note that in the investigations cited, mean reading scores of EMR pupils never reached a grade level of 4.0. These data suggest that the crucial need at present is to develop more appropriate instructional delivery systems for mentally retarded children. Instructional alternatives that have been offered to date have proven relatively ineffectual regardless of the environment in which these children are taught.
>
> (p. 237)

Project PRIME, a large-scale investigation conducted in Texas, provided some insights into the actual instructional process in regular and special education alternatives (Kaufman, Agard, & Semmel, in press). The investigators found that mainstreamed EMRs were the lowest achievers in their regular classes, achieving well below national norms. Their attention rate in the regular class was also lower than that of their normal peers, but it improved in the resource room, where there was a smaller ratio of pupils to teachers. The attention rate of the EMRs in self-contained special classes resembled that of the mainstreamed EMRs in resource rooms. The resource room and the special class also differed from the regular class in terms of (1) the availability of special support services, (2) the cognitive emphasis in instruction, and (3) the levels of cognitive demands placed on pupils. The special education settings provided access to support services, placed less emphasis on cognition, and made fewer cognitive demands. In addition, the special education settings offered more instructional differentiation, more small-group or individual instruction, and higher rates of verbal participation by students and teacher feedback.

Social Adjustment. We discussed the research on attitudes toward retarded children as a function of educational placement in Chapter 7, so we will not provide a detailed discussion here. One important finding is that research does not support the "contact hypothesis," which states that contact between the nonhandicapped and the retarded improves attitudes toward the retarded (Corman & Gottlieb 1979; Semmel et al. 1979). Studies indicate that the social status of EMR children in mainstreamed classes is lower than that of their nonhandicapped peers. [This finding is contradicted by Sheare (1974), who worked with secondary level students.] In fact, some of Gottlieb's work (1975b) suggests that in actual behavioral choices, nonhandicapped children prefer segregated EMRs, with whom they have had little if any contact, to the mainstreamed EMRs with whom they have had contact.

Two investigations have examined correlates of social status to discover what factors are related to the acceptance and rejection of EMR children. Gottlieb, Semmel, and Veldman (1978) found that the nonretarded peers in a mainstreaming setting respond to the behavior of the retarded child, rather than to the label itself. They reported that acceptance is determined by a variety of factors— for example, perceptions of the retarded child's academic competence —while rejection is related to misbehavior. This finding suggests that we can keep integrated EMRs from being rejected by reducing their misbehavior, but to encourage genuine acceptance, we will have to improve their academic performance in order to change peer perceptions of their academic competence. MacMillan and Morrison (1980), who also studied correlates of social status, found that the behaviors related to acceptance and rejection of EMRs in a special class were different from those of mainstreamed children. In the special class, teachers' perceptions of academic competence and misbehavior were each related to both acceptance and rejection. Thus, the most highly rated special class child will not necessarily be the best candidate for mainstreaming, because acceptance in the mainstreamed class may be determined by different factors.

Again, we must consider what we expect of mainstreamed EMR children in terms of social acceptance. Must they be at or above the mean of the nonhandicapped children in order for mainstreaming to be considered successful? We believe that this would be an unrealistic expectation and suggest that "tolerance" should be considered sufficient. Similarly, we are not convinced that the *number* of children who indicate that they accept a child is a valid indicator of acceptance. It may be more important to be accepted by one child whose acceptance is valued than to be accepted by twenty children whose acceptance is not valued.

Implementation of Mainstreaming. Although mainstreaming sounds fine in principle to many educators, implementation of the principle may be very complex. In addition to the general problem areas we have mentioned—possible resistance from regular teachers, the stigmatization that may accompany any kind of special attention, loss of self-respect with ability grouping, and potentially inappropriate curricula—the mechanics of returning formerly segregated EMR children to regular classrooms raises many unsolved questions. For instance:

1. Do you return the child to a class with age peers or to a class achieving academically at the same level (in which case the mainstreamed child will almost invariably be older)?
2. Is mainstreaming more successful in nongraded schools, where the problem posed in question 1 can be avoided?
3. In returning children to the regular class, should only one child be placed in a class or should several children be placed in a single class?
4. Should mainstreamed children be placed in classes where the modal achievement level is high, or is the effort more successful when the disparity between the child's achievement level and that of the class as a whole is minimized?
5. Should mainstreamed children be returned only to classes where the receiving teacher has a favorable attitude toward the program? Should the receiving teacher be informed about the child's former status as an EMR student at all?

Keep in mind that thus far educators have had little success with EMR children in any administrative arrangement. It is naive to assume that physical mainstreaming (the simple placement of the child in the class) will result in immediate success. These are hard-to-teach children, given the present structure of schools and the instructional techniques commonly employed. They will continue to pose a challenge to educators, in whatever educational arrangement they are served. However, we can hope that educators will accept the challenge and not resign themselves to a lack of achievement on the part of these children.

Although we do not yet know what *should* be done, evidence from Project PRIME and the California decertification study gives us an indication of what *is* being done (Meyers, MacMillan, and Yoshida 1975). An examination of the classes into which EMR children are mainstreamed reveals that the nonhandicapped peers are relatively low achievers. Similarly, PRIME findings indicated that the classes into which EMRs were mainstreamed were below average in both IQ and family socioeconomic status. In addition, Meyers et al. (1975) found that the classes in which the decertified EMRs were placed were among the lower-achieving tracks in the schools. Teachers indicated that over half of the children in the classes in which decertified children were placed were reading below grade level. It is also clear that mainstreamed children are old for the grades in which they are placed. Project PRIME (Kaufman et al., in press) found that mainstreamed EMRs were an average of one year older than their nonhandicapped class peers. Meyers et al. (1980) found that decertified children were enrolled in classes that placed them two years behind where they would have been if they had received the normal annual promotions. The possibility that being older impedes social acceptance or otherwise influences interactions has not been explored, but it does seem to be a characteristic pattern. Finally, findings indicate that clusters of EMRs tend to be integrated into the same class. Kaufman et al. (in press) reported that 19 percent of the classroom teachers they questioned reported six or more former EMR children in their classes. Thus, mainstreamed EMRs tend to be older than their classmates and are likely to be clustered into low-achieving classes. The placement of EMRs in low-achieving classes or tracks may be cause for some concern.

Ability grouping in regular classes is a common practice to increase the similarity of a group of students in one or more characteristics—intelligence, aptitude, or achievement. Given that, as Meyers et al. (1975) found, decertified EMRs achieved significantly lower than the lowest quartile of nonhandicapped children, it seems probable that mainstreamed EMRs will be placed in the lowest ability groups in a low-achieving class. The evidence indicates that ability grouping may have a negative effect on consequent achievement and feelings of self-worth. In a review of research on ability groupings, Esposito (1973) reported:

(a) Conflicting evidence in promoting scholastic achievement in the relatively high or superior groups; (b) almost uniformly unfavorable evidence for promoting scholastic achievement in average groups; and (c) almost uniformly unfavorable evidence for promoting scholastic achievement in relatively low ability groups.

(p. 167)

Furthermore, Esposito contended that students in the high-ability group tend to have an inflated sense of self-esteem, whereas those in average and low-ability groups tend to have a reduced sense of self-esteem. Since mainstreamed children are being assigned to low-ability groups, they may remain subject to the reduction in self-esteem formerly attributed to their EMR status (Dunn 1968; Mercer 1973a).

There are additional similarities between EMR status and placement in low-ability groups. Low-ability groups contain disproportionate numbers of low socioeconomic status children and minority children (Esposito 1973; Findlay & Bryan 1971). The charge of discrimination leveled at EMR special classes on these grounds seems equally applicable to low-ability groups in regular classes. We must be careful not to trade one set of problems for a different, equally serious one.

Teacher Attitudes.   The attitudes of regular class teachers are of great importance in determining the success of mainstreaming. Remember that these are the same teachers who initially referred the children for evaluation because they could not teach them successfully. In the name of mainstreaming, these children are now being returned to the regular class teacher's room, albeit with support services. We are telling these teachers that they can be successful with children they previously indicated they could not teach. An important distinction must be made here—the distinction between teachers' attitudes toward mainstreaming and their attitudes toward the children being mainstreamed.

There are several excellent reviews (Corman & Gottlieb 1979; Gottlieb 1975b; Semmel et al. 1979) on educators' attitudes toward mainstreaming. The general finding is that the regular teachers' attitudes toward receiving EMRs in their classes tend to range from neutral to negative. Melcher (1971) attributed this reaction to the fact that teachers who had had no training or practical experience with the retarded felt unprepared to work with them. Shotel, Iano, and McGettigan (1972) compared teachers' attitudes toward several disability groups—EMR, emotionally disturbed, and learning-disabled. The teachers expressed the most optimism about the integration of learning-disabled children and the least optimism about the integration of EMR children, even with resource room support. Similar findings were reported by Gickling and Theobald (1975), who found that 85 percent of the regular class teachers felt ill-equipped to deal with these children. Only Guerin and Szatlocky (1974) found that a majority of the teachers (62 percent) expressed positive attitudes. Semmel et al. (1979) noted that although differences were found across studies, teachers in the same school tended to have similar attitudes, which suggests that building principals and other administrative personnel play an important role in affecting the attitudes of teachers.

Payne and Murray (1974) found that 59 percent of the principals in suburban schools had favorable attitudes toward mainstreaming, while the fig-ure for principals of urban schools was only 46 percent. Vlasak (reported in Semmel et al. 1979) found that the longer a principal had had responsibility for the education of handicapped children, the less favorable were the atti-tudes of the teachers working in the principal's school. This finding contra-dicts that of Guerin and Szatlocky (1974), who found that the longer an administrator was involved in mainstreaming efforts, the more positive the attitude became.

Anxieties about mainstreaming tend to result in negative attitudes, which are further influenced by the behavior of specific EMR children who have been integrated into a teacher's class. Kaufman et al. (in press) reported that disciplinary problems in regular classes increased when EMR children were included. By contrast, Meyers et al. (1975) found that although regular class teachers in California did need to make some aca-demic accommodations for decertified children, very few reported that the students were disruptive or posed a deportment problem in class.

It is important to realize that many of these attitude studies were con-ducted when mainstreaming was in its infancy; procedures for facilitating the integration of EMR children into regular classes were unavailable or untried. It is not known whether these negative attitudes have persisted. It is to be hoped that regular teachers will realize that the question is not whether they will accept these children, but, according to the provisions of PL 94-142, how they can do so efficiently. More favorable attitudes may develop as a result of inservice training.

Emerging Issues in Mainstreaming

Like any other new endeavor in education, mainstreaming was thrust upon us rather suddenly, so the early programs were hastily conceived and implemented. We have considered the existing evidence on the impact of mainstreaming on EMR children; we have an improved understanding of some issues, and new issues have emerged. To understand these new issues, which are discussed in the remainder of this chapter, we are going to need more research.

Impact of Mainstreaming. The primary focus of research on main-streaming has been its impact on the mainstreamed EMR child. Much less attention has been devoted to its impact on the educational system as a whole and on the nonhandicapped children into whose classes EMR chil-dren are mainstreamed. We have seen that regular class teachers have neg-ative attitudes toward the process, but we do not understand whether this is because they think it makes their job more difficult or because they think mainstreaming impairs the quality of education they can give the nonhandicapped. We might speculate that nonhandicapped children are receiving less instructional attention than before if the regular class teacher has to provide more small-group or individual attention to EMR children.

Another question concerns the impact of mainstreaming on the composition of self-contained EMR classes and the educational process occurring in these classes. Meyers et al. (1975) found that teachers of self-contained EMR special classes thought that decertification had had a noticeable impact on their classes. The general level of ability, for example, was thought to be lower, as the more able EMR students were decertified. The remaining EMR students were considered a far more debilitated group than the previous population in EMR programs. This change necessitated more individual instruction because the children's learning problems were more severe. The teachers also noted that the decertified students had been their best in-class helpers. One subtle development was that teachers of special classes suddenly found themselves psychologically isolated—with fewer classes, there was often only one special education teacher in the school building, whereas previously there may have been two or three. Thus, there was no one with whom to share ideas or materials. Since the nature of the EMR population has changed dramatically (MacMillan & Borthwick 1980) as a result of the court cases and subsequent legislative changes, the appropriateness of the "EMR curriculum" for the current population should perhaps be reconsidered in some states.

Sidestepping Stigmatization. It appears that the principal model for delivering services to the former EMR child returned to the regular class is the use of a resource teacher. But singling out retarded children for any kind of different activities—even if they are no longer formally labeled retarded—may still result in stigmatization. If the children's peers see them cutting and pasting rather than reading and writing, they may make fun of them even if they carry no label. If so, then any service-delivery model that in any way designates the former EMR child as one who does different things than the majority of children may result in stigmatization. One way to get around this problem is to ensure that all children obtain individual help of some sort and that the resource teacher work at various times with all children, not only with problem learners.

Who Should Be Mainstreamed? The principle of least restriction does not imply that all retarded children should be mainstreamed. In our initial enthusiasm, some may have thought that special classes should be totally disbanded and that all retarded children should be mainstreamed. Special classes, like institutions, should be permitted to disappear when they are no longer needed; but it is clear that, at present, the regular educational system and our communities are unprepared to provide the services necessary for the more severely impaired to function in regular classes or in

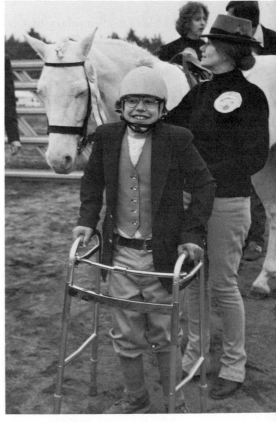

the community at large. Is mainstreaming appropriate for EMR children? The answer is probably that it is appropriate for some but inappropriate for others. The task facing us now is to determine which children it will benefit and which it will not.

Forness (1979) and his staff have developed clinical guidelines based on their many years of experience. He noted that decisions about mainstreaming must be made on an individual basis and suggests eight criteria that are helpful in deciding about the placement of individual children (see Table 13.2). Although no single criterion can be used to predict success or failure reliably and we do not know how many criteria should be met before a recommendation is made, the criteria are helpful in making decisions. Forness also mentions other factors—physical appearance, parental expecta-

TABLE 13.2   Summary of Criteria for Mainstreaming Decisions

A Child Should be Mainstreamed:	Caution Should be Used in Considering Mainstreaming:
1. If the child is young and the problem has been identified rather early in the school year.	1. If the child is older and the problem has continued unimproved for some time in the regular class.
2. If the child's problem is mild and not readily apparent outside of the school context.	2. If the child's problem is severe and pervades other areas of the child's life.
3. If the child's problem is limited to a single area of functioning.	3. If the child's problems are multiple (e.g., mild retardation *and* a behavior problem).
4. If remediation of the child's problem does not require complicated equipment or materials.	4. If the child's condition requires complicated remedial equipment or teaching methods.
5. If the child appears to have friends or the ability to develop supportive friendships with normal children.	5. If the child has had repeated difficulty in developing friendships with normal children.
6. If the regular classroom contains less than 25 or 30 children.	6. If the regular classroom contains more than 30 or 35 children.
7. If the child's regular class teacher appears knowledgeable and willing to deal with the child's problem.	7. If the child's teacher appears to be unwilling or grossly unable to continue working with the child.
8. If the child's family appears to be willing and able to deal effectively with his or her problem.	8. If the child's family appears to lack extensive support for dealing with his or her problem.

From S. R. Forness, "Clinical criteria for mainstreaming mildly handicapped children," *Psychology in the Schools,* 1979, **16,** 508–514. Reprinted by permission of the author.

tions for their child, racial balance in the classroom and race of the child—that may influence decisions.

Care must be exercised in extrapolating conclusions about children in one state to children in other states, because EMR enrollment varies considerably (see Table 2.5). MacMillan and Borthwick (1980), reporting on the amount of mainstreaming practiced over a two-year period in twenty-three California school districts, found that 80 percent of the EMR children were not integrated for academic subjects such as reading, language arts, and arithmetic. Less than 50 percent of the EMR children were integrated for nonacademic courses such as art, music, and vocational training. It should be noted that California was the site of the early court cases on EMR placement (*Diana, Larry P.*) It currently classifies few children as retarded in comparison to most other states. We doubt that schools in the state are resisting compliance with the principle of least restriction. We think, rather, that little integration occurs because California and other states with very low prevalence rates enroll more severely debilitated children in EMR classes than they did formerly. In the judgment of those responsible for IEP development, the vast majority of these children cannot be mainstreamed, so that special class placement for most of the day is considered the least restrictive environment. This finding points up the need to consider the worth of mainstreaming on a state-by-state basis. The possibility of successful mainstreaming is minimal when only the severely debilitated are classified as EMR. In states such as Alabama, where the prevalence of EMRs is high, a greater proportion of the EMR population can perhaps be mainstreamed successfully.

The findings of MacMillan and Borthwick (1980) raise another issue. When *Diana* and *Larry P.* were originally heard in court, an inclusive definition of mental retardation was in use. The definition used today is far more exclusive (see Chapter 2). Advocacy of mainstreaming may have been beneficial in the early 1970s when children with IQs up to 85 were enrolled in EMR classes, but we question the advisability of mainstreaming current California EMRs on a large scale, since today's EMRs are far more debilitated than the children enrolled in EMR programs in 1970. Even when the upper IQ limit is 70 or so, school personnel in California are reluctant to identify minority children as EMR. In addition, Meyen and Moran (1979) report that regular class teachers are reluctant to refer the mildly handicapped, for whom mainstreaming would be feasible, if in so doing the child must be labeled as handicapped. They noted that regular class teachers are not referring such children because of the extensive paperwork necessary to justify the referral and the lengthy conferences necessary to determine eligibility. Even if a child is found eligible, the child will probably remain in the teacher's class because it is the least restrictive environment. Thus, a teacher may have to do extensive paperwork and go to many conferences to develop an IEP, only to receive supplemental services that are not considered sufficiently helpful in the teacher's view. Our point is that the EMR population—the source of most candidates for mainstreaming—is changing; mainstreaming should therefore be discussed in relation to the type of children being identified as EMR in a given state.

SUMMARY

Two recent developments in the treatment and education of mentally retarded children are early intervention and mainstreaming. These new developments are currently being researched, and demonstration projects are providing new information about them. Retarded children are now receiving services *earlier* than they used to and in *settings* previously reserved for children considered "normal."

Early intervention has two major formats. Some programs are designed to prevent mild forms of retardation among children environmentally at risk. Others are directed toward established risk children. The latter type are designed, not to prevent retardation, but to ameliorate its effects and optimize the development of children in these programs.

Many programs for environmentally at risk children assume that the early years are a "critical period" for cognitive development, that the effects of early deprivation are irreversible, and that environmental effects in the early years are more significant than those that occur in later stages of development. Some scholars are beginning to question the validity of these assumptions. This is not to say that the early years are unimportant; rather, the disproportional influence of these early experiences on ultimate development is being questioned.

Two types of early intervention programs for environmentally at risk children were considered. Large-scale interventions such as the Milwaukee Project and the Abecedarian Project provided a broad spectrum of interventions, including parent training, preschool experiences, and health care. Other programs, such as Head Start, were essentially educational in nature. Although the emphases of these programs varied, they were generally designed to provide environmentally at risk children with experiences to improve their chances for success in the public schools.

Early intervention for established risk children typically involves parents in an effort to stimulate early development of language and other skills. Programs such as Project EDGE were designed to promote more rapid development in Down's syndrome children. The early evidence indicates that such efforts are successful.

In this chapter we also considered mainstreaming programs for preschool and school-age handicapped children. Two forms of preschool mainstreaming were described: traditional mainstreaming and reverse mainstreaming. Early results indicate that such efforts are very successful in promoting social behavior in retarded children, presumably because they provide the children with good models. It is becoming apparent, however, that preschool mainstreaming can pose problems for parents if they have not yet accepted that their child is handicapped. Traditional mainstreaming of the retarded child in preschool requires more parental effort and involvement than would special programs for the retarded, and denies parents the opportunity to place their child with a teacher and peers who understand the handicap.

The chapter concluded with a discussion of the mainstreaming of school-age children and a summary of existing research on that process. The academic achievement of EMR children appears to be slightly higher among those who are mainstreamed, but the influence of mainstreaming on ultimate levels of achievement has yet to be determined. Attempts to promote reading and arithmetic achievement in EMR children have been unsuccessful, regardless of labeling practices and the instructional setting. Findings suggest that we should concentrate on service-delivery models and instructional strategies. Preliminary findings about the social status of mainstreamed EMRs are not promising. The results indicate that nonretarded children do not accept integrated EMRs, but we questioned the methods used to assess acceptance. The success of mainstreaming seems to be determined by its implementation, but educators have been required to begin mainstreaming without ample opportunities for planning. A number of problems remain to be solved, including improving the attitudes of regular class teachers toward mainstreaming, designing nonstigmatizing service-delivery models, and assessing mainstreaming in the context of current educational practices such as ability grouping. Finally, the EMR population in some states is so severely debilitated that it cannot be mainstreamed.

CHAPTER 14

Residential Alternatives: Institutions and Community Residential Facilities

Today, the mildly retarded are seldom placed in residential institutions outside the natural home except in situations involving such factors as divorce or delinquency. The families of the severely retarded, however, are more often forced to decide whether to keep their retarded child at home or place the child elsewhere. As noted in Chapter 1, the only option available until quite recently was a large residential institution. More recently, however, other alternative placements have become available. These are generally referred to as *community residential facilities* (CRFs). In addition to questions about initial placements, some parents must decide whether to continue an institutional placement or seek CRF placement for a retarded person. Butterfield (1977) wrote of this development:

> We can see now what we could not see then; 1967 was a watershed year. Until then, the number of residents in public facilities for the mentally retarded increased steadily. Since 1967 the number has decreased. . . . The decrease in residential census is not the result of a decrease in admissions. Neither is it the result of increased deaths. . . . A dramatic upturn in the rate of release from public institutions began in 1965. By 1971, more people were released than were admitted. . . . The question must be asked, are these released people faring better outside than they were inside the institution? The easy response is that they must be; look how terribly our institutions have been run. But the fact that one kind of program was bad does not make another kind better.
>
> (p. 21)

In this chapter, we will examine the factors that determine whether a retarded child will be placed in an institution. It is extremely important to note that low IQ alone is not sufficient grounds for institutionalization. Some children are institutionalized because of certain family characteristics, which seem to predispose parents toward accepting this option.

Once thought to be benevolent, institutions have come under criticism in the past few decades. Critics such as Goffman (1957) point out that when institutions are big and concerned with efficiency, they may have dehumanizing effects on their residents. Although Goffman did not study institutions that housed mentally retarded persons, his investigation into other types of institutions revealed practices that resulted in "mortifications of the self." They were caused, Goffman said, by the mere situation of having large numbers of people living in the same institution under the supervision of a central authority. The potentially degrading experiences he described were extended to institutions for the mentally retarded and seen to fit those institutions as well. As we consider the evidence pertaining to the effects of institutions for the retarded on the residents, try to see if this criticism applies: specifically, does the largeness and impersonalization result in detrimental developmental outcomes?

Criticism of institutions has led to the adoption of the principle of *normalization*, which states that the retarded should be placed in environments that resemble, as closely as possible given the behavioral limitations of the individual, the environments in which the nonretarded live and work. Later in this chapter we will examine the literature on the extent to which alternative residences are "normalized" and whether they result in greater growth for their residents.

A HISTORY OF INSTITUTIONS

Institutionalization has undergone some interesting shifts in philosophy over the years. Before the first institutions for the mentally retarded were established in this country some 120 years ago, retarded persons were cared for by their families and in the community. Prior to the mid-1800s, home care was especially feasible with extended families in rural settings. Life expectancies for the more severely retarded were lower than they are now due to their greater susceptibility to respiratory and other ailments. There was also evidence of support for community assistance as far back as the mid-1600s. In some colonies, monies were provided to pay individuals to care for the "feeble-minded" in their homes. But whether they were cared for by members of the extended family or by other families, before 1850 the retarded remained close to their natural homes, either because it was believed to be advantageous or because no alternative placements were available.

By the mid-1800s there was a shift in attitude. In the belief that retardation could be cured, state legislatures provided support for institutions where the retarded could be housed and treated. Typically these institutions were small and were located close to population centers, providing families easy access to their retarded children. Residential placement was seen optimistically as a temporary arrangement in which retarded individuals were to be taught the necessary academic and social skills that would enable them to return to the community. Because of this positive outlook, the earliest residential institutions were regarded as schools where the retarded could be cured or rehabilitated.

This hopeful educational model was drastically modified as the hoped-for goals were not realized. By about 1880 the belief that institutions were to serve as temporary residences for the retarded had diminished, and the educational model was replaced by what Baumeister (1970) called a pessimistic "pity model" characterized by a pessimistic prognosis—sympathetic, but with the feeling that these individuals would never be able to function in society. Institutions became holding places whose prime function was to protect the retarded from the demands and requirements of society; programs were kind but custodial. Along with this shift in attitude, newly constructed institutions tended to be larger in size and located in out-of-the-way places (Hobbs 1975b). Moreover, responsibility for the retarded was shifted from the local and county levels to the state level (Farber 1968).

Distinct populations emerged in the institutions: (1) the feeble-minded, who were amenable to academic programs, and (2) the imbecile and idiot groups, who did not respond to rehabilitative programs. It became apparent that institutions could serve two major functions: rehabilitation and custodial care. Hence the institutions came to be departmentalized according to these functions and the populations of the institutions were grouped according to ability levels (Farber 1968).

In the early 1900s sentiment turned against the retarded (see Chapter 1). Accounts of the high rates of criminality, immorality, and pauperism said to exist among the retarded abounded. Coupled with high estimates of the prevalence of retardation, this line of reasoning crystallized into a eugenics scare movement. It was advocated that the retarded not be allowed to marry, that they be sterilized, and that they be segregated from the rest of society (Hobbs 1975b). As a consequence institutions were promoted to protect society from the retarded rather than to protect the retarded from society.

One outgrowth of the eugenics movement was that a new rationale was provided for locating institutions away from population centers—they were seen as a menace. Institutions were held accountable for their effectiveness in protecting society rather than for their effectiveness in rehabilitation. A new method of isolating the handicapped was the development of the colony system—retarded individuals were placed in special communities that were supposed to be self-sufficient. Many of these colonies were self-contained agricultural programs. But with mechanization and the application of scientific techniques to farming, the relative efficiency of the colonies declined. The proportion of the institutional population that could actually participate in farming was relatively small anyway, and overcrowding became a major problem. Political pressures as well forced institutions to rely on outside producers to supply food for the institutions (Farber 1968).

Fortunately, the eugenics scare was short-lived. But some argue that it has had an enduring effect on the lives of the retarded (Hobbs 1975b; Wolfensberger 1969). They point to the persistence of the image of the retarded as threatening and the continuing location of institutions in rural locations.

After the eugenics scare some residents were released and parole programs were established. By 1920 approximately twenty states had begun parole systems. Two consequences of the parole program were the necessity of adding social workers to the staffs of institutions and the creation of extramural services to ease the adjustment of the retarded to the community (Farber 1968).

By the 1940s and 1950s there was an emerging belief that the retarded and mentally ill had a right to treatment in their own community, a feeling that it should not be necessary to place an individual in a residential institution to obtain treatment (Grossman & Rowitz 1973). In an updated version of mid-1800 values, it was now argued that, if at all possible, the retarded person should be treated in the community and that only the most patently handicapped should be removed from the community. By the 1960s alternatives to inpatient care were being developed. Federal funding, matched by state funding, was made available for the construction and staffing of community facilities for the treatment of mental retardation. This move enabled families to maintain their retarded child in the home and still obtain needed services for the child. We have thus circled back to providing services in the community, with the new twist of state or federal funding for such programs.

Increasingly, alternatives are considered to placement in large residential institutions; but institutions are by no means going out of business. Edgerton, Eyman, & Silverstein (1975) reported that 75 percent of the retarded persons in this country are not in any form of residential facility for the retarded; the remaining 25 percent are in various institutional settings, including general hospitals, nursing hospitals, correctional institutions, and institutions for the mentally retarded and mentally ill. Increasingly, however, institutions are serving more debilitated clients than they were in the 1960s.

Scheerenberger's (1977) survey of public residential facilities revealed that progress is occurring in deinstitutionalization. He reported that 74 percent of the current residents of large institutions are severely and profoundly retarded, and that 65 percent are multiply handicapped. Bruininks, Hauber, and Kudla (1980) suggested that mentally retarded persons are now being placed in a wider variety of community-based facilities and rehabilitation programs that have grown out of the philosophical, legal, and legislative commitment to the principle of normalization. This transition has not been without problems, however. Conroy (1977) reported data from federal sources that indicate that readmissions to institutions have increased more rapidly than community placements. These data suggest that pressure from philosophical and legal sources may have forced institutions to release clients prematurely without sufficient attention to the quality of the community residential facilities available.

Approximately 10 percent of the mentally retarded, or 200,000 persons, reside in institutions for the retarded (U.S. Department of Health, Education, and Welfare 1972). Approximately 30 percent of these residents are children, and 81 percent have IQs below 50 (Hobbs 1975b). These 200,000 retarded persons live in 150 large public institutions, 500 private institutions, and a variety of smaller hostels, foster care homes, convalescent hospitals, and the like. The different types of residences vary tremendously in terms of the quality of life within them (Butterfield and Zigler 1965). In this chapter we will be talking mostly about the remaining large institutions, and then briefly about the recently emerging community residential facilities.

Although the large institution persists, forces are mobilizing against it as an acceptable facility for the residents. Despite the variability among institutions, the critics have generalized from deplorable conditions in some institutions that these conditions exist in *all* institutions (Blatt 1966; Rivera 1972). The current trend is clearly toward the policy of normalization, which for the moderately and severely retarded, means placement in smaller community-based facilities rather than in large institutions.

Before we examine the criticisms of large institutions we will look at the factors that influence which retarded people will be placed in institutions. We will then consider how institutions differ, how they may affect residents, and what quality of life exists inside them. The chapter will conclude with a discussion of normalization, a principle that suggests alternatives to institutional placement.

FACTORS RELATED TO INSTITUTIONALIZATION

Why is it that of two given retarded persons with the same IQ or the same clinical symptoms (such as Down's syndrome), one may be placed in an institution while the other is kept at home? According to Farber's synthesis of the results of two major studies (Farber, Jenne, & Toigo 1960; Saenger 1960):

Taken together, the Illinois and the New York City studies indicate that mental retardation alone is not a sufficient explanation for institutionalization. The mentally retarded individual must present some additional problems to either the family or the community which designate him as superfluous or threatening to social relationships.

(Farber 1968, p. 197)

To comprehend fully the factors related to the decision to institutionalize a retarded child we must consider the limitations of the particular child in question, the structure and dynamics of the family into which the child was born, and the outside forces impinging on that child and family. Although there is considerable overlap between these influences, for the sake of clarity we will try to divide the available data into child factors, family factors, and system and community factors.

Child Factors

One of the major factors found to influence the decision to institutionalize a retarded child is the degree of intellectual and physical impairment (Edgerton et al. 1975). As a group, children who are institutionalized score lower on tests of intelligence and evidence more physical impairments than do their noninstitutionalized retarded counterparts. Over half of those on the waiting lists for admission to Illinois institutions for the retarded had IQs below 20 (Farber 1968). The greater tendency to commit lower mental ability subjects to institutions has been reported with consistency (Eyman, Dingman & Sabagh 1966; Graliker, Koch, & Henderson 1965; Sabagh, Lei, & Eyman 1972; Saenger 1960).

When physical handicaps are present (visual, auditory, paralysis, convulsions, problems of ambulation), most studies have found that the likelihood of institutionalization is increased (Eyman, O'Connor, Tarjan, & Justice 1972; Sabagh et al. 1972). However, Saenger (1960) reported no differences between his institutional subjects and those at home in the number of physical handicaps.

IQ and the degree of physical handicap are not the only significant child factors. Eyman et al. (1972) concluded that, compared to the noninstitutionalized retarded, retarded individuals in institutions on the average (1) have IQs of less than 53, (2) are younger, (3) have more physical disabilities, (4) have more adaptive behavior failures, and (5) are white. (This study is a noteworthy exception to the fact that many such studies do not include families who are not receiving services and yet may need them.) If all five factors listed above are found in combination (i.e., IQ less than 53, under eight years of age, has twelve or more adaptive behavior failures, has three or more physical disabilities, and is white), there is a 90 percent probability that the individual will be institutionalized at some point in life.

Support for this list of significant factors comes from additional research studies (Farber 1968; Sabagh et al. 1972; Saenger 1960; Shellhaas & Nihira 1969). For instance, the assertion that age is a significant factor is backed up by Farber's (1968) report that the median age of those awaiting placement in the Illinois institutions was eight for males and six for females.

It seems clear that characteristics associated with retarded children influence whether they will be institutionalized. It is unclear, however, whether it is the child's status per se, that is influential, or the status as perceived by parents and others. McCarver and Craig (1974) concluded that most retarded persons are institutionalized because they exhibited behaviors that the community would not tolerate, because the family could not care for them, or because community services were not sufficiently developed to allow them to remain at home. These are perceptions held by parents or others—they are not inherent in the retarded person alone. Hence, it is possible that decisions are based on how the decision-makers (parents) perceive behavior, whether they can care for the child, and whether the community services are perceived as adequate.

Sex differences might be considered a significant factor, but they appear to exist in certain cases and not in others. At any rate, they are probably better understood in the context of the family, which is where we will consider them.

Family Factors

Admission to an institution for the mentally retarded is related to a number of family factors. As Farber (1968) noted, these factors have changed over time. During the time of the eugenics scare there was a greater tendency to institutionalize higher-functioning retarded children, a practice that had apparently been curtailed considerably by the late 1950s (Saenger 1960). It is predicted that the tendency to put all degrees of handicapped persons in institutions will be totally reversed over the next decade to the point that only the most debilitated individuals will be placed in institutions (Edgerton et al. 1975). This shift is a function of changes in family thinking rather than changes in child characteristics. It is not yet clear which kinds of factors—child or family—are most significant in the decision to institutionalize the child, for some investigators place greater importance on the child and others on the family (Shellhaas & Nihira 1969). But regardless of their relative importance, certain family variables have been isolated as determinants and warrant our attention.

Socioeconomic Class. Eyman et al. (1966) reported that the major factor associated with the rate of admission was the socioeconomic status of the family. Saenger (1960) found that, in general, institutionalized residents came from lower socioeconomic status homes, and Appell and Tisdall (1968) found that admitted patients were more likely to come from families on welfare than were retarded persons who were not institutionalized. In these studies social class was assessed in a variety of ways (e.g., income, father's education), yet this variable consistently emerged as one highly related to admission.

But social class per se may not be the critical factor. According to Farber and his associates (1960), higher and lower social class families institutionalize their retarded children under differing sets of circumstances, so the variables are actually more complex than mere social class differences. For example, Sabagh, Eyman, and Cogburn (1966) reported that in higher social class families, the parents' willingness to institutionalize their child was related directly to the number of normal children in the family. In lower-class homes, on the other hand, sex of the child was more important, with mothers more willing to institutionalize their retarded boys than their retarded girls (Farber et al. 1960). In addition to family size and sex of the child, another variable that becomes mixed in with social class differences is ethnic background. For example, there is evidence that middle-class Jewish families are very reluctant to institutionalize their retarded children (Farber et al. 1960; Saenger 1960).

Another way in which social class is related to admission is the age at which a child is placed. Downey (1965) found that parents with higher educational levels committed their retarded children at an earlier age. Their reason for placing the child was frequently related to concerns over the potential effect on other family members. Parents with lower educational levels were more likely to express concern over the child's trouble in the neighborhood and educational or vocational problems. To complicate matters further, it is also possible that the age factor may be explained by the greater likelihood that parents of high social class will have the retardation diagnosed at an earlier age, leading to earlier admission (Farber 1968).

Hence while there appears to be a greater proportion of institutionalized retarded children coming from lower socioeconomic status backgrounds, the dynamics behind this factor may be better understood in terms of other factors that interact with social class.

The interpretation of social class differences is also confusing. One might interpret these data as evidence that lower-class parents are more callous— that they feel less concern for their retarded child or are concerned that such a child will prove a hindrance to their upward social mobility. But the evidence on release of patients appears to contradict this kind of conclusion: lower-class parents tend to maintain contact with their institutionalized retarded children and in general look forward to their children's release more than middle-class parents do. It is possible that the greater admission rates from lower-class families may stem from real concern for the welfare of the child. In the natural homes of those admitted to institutions, there is often a lack of facilities for sleeping, working, and eliminating, and Shell-haas and Nihira (1969) have linked the factor of cultural deprivation with institutionalization. It may be that lower-class parents decide to commit their retarded children in the hope that they will be better off in the institution, feeling that they cannot provide adequately for them at home.

Family Disorganization. A high percentage of institutionalized retarded residents come from broken homes, the most obvious form of family disorganization. Studies consistently reveal that institutionalization is highly related to divorce in the family (Appell & Tisdall 1968; Farber 1968; Hobbs 1964; Saenger 1960; Shellhaas & Nihira 1969). Saenger (1960), for instance, reported that 90 percent of retarded children living at home lived with both parents, while only 40 percent of institutionalized residents lived with both parents prior to admission. Appell & Tisdall (1968) found that 37 percent of the residents were from broken homes as compared to 14 percent for the group not admitted.

Such data do not, however, reveal whether the divorce somehow leads to the decision to institutionalize the child or whether the debate over the decision somehow precipitates the divorce. Given the dependency of a severely retarded child on the parents, it is not surprising that when a couple separate or go through a divorce, or when one parent dies, the single parent may find it impossible to meet the needs of the retarded child, especially since the dependency may be prolonged. It is also possible to imagine situations in which the decision to institutionalize comes first, for the myriad emotions that emerge in deliberating about and finally deciding on institutionalization can irreparably damage a marriage. The point is that while a broken home is related to admission, we must be cautious about drawing causal inferences about the dynamics, for they will probably differ from one situation to another.

Though not so obvious as divorce or separation, a lack of marital integration can also be a form of family disorganization. Farber (1960a) wrote that marital integration included:

> (a) The consensus of husband and wife on domestic values and (b) the effective coordination of domestic roles assumes a consistence between means and ends.
>
> (p. 64)

When Farber analyzed his data he found no significant difference between families with a child at home as compared to those with a child in an institution in terms of the marital integration of the parents. Farber also broke his data down by social class. He found that in higher socioeconomic status families marital integration was not an important factor in the father's willingness to institutionalize the retarded child, but when marital integration was high in low socioeconomic status families, fathers were less willing to institutionalize their retarded children.

Normal Siblings. It appears that another factor that predisposes parents to institutionalize their retarded child is the number of normal children in the family. As we have seen, a major concern among parents of higher socioeconomic level is that a retarded child will have a detrimental effect on other family members, particularly on normal siblings. Appell and Tisdall (1968) reported that there was a greater number of siblings in the homes of retarded children admitted to an institution than in the homes of retarded children not admitted (see also Graliker et al. 1965). Farber (1968) noted that the concern over the effect on normal siblings is most pronounced when the retarded child is functioning at low mental levels.

After an extensive study of the impact of a severely retarded child on the family, Farber (1959a, 1960a) concluded that the two family factors that were most significant in determining whether the child would be kept at home or institutionalized were (1) the sex of the normal sibling and (2) the sibling's age relative to the age of the retarded child. He found that normal sisters showed more personality disorders when the retarded child was in the home than when the child was institutionalized, but that male siblings were adversely affected by the placement of a retarded child in the institution. His explanation for this sex difference was that for a boy having a retarded sibling at home meant that the mother was more likely to overlook his failings in her preoccupation with the retarded child. But girls, especially older sisters, are frequently expected to help care for the retarded child, so that having the child at home meant more rather than fewer demands on them (Farber 1959a).

In addition to the direct impact on siblings, the decision to—or not to—commit a retarded child may have a deleterious effect on a husband-wife relationship, the negative consequences of which could accrue indirectly to normal siblings. Hence Farber's findings regarding marital integration are also pertinent to the discussion of sibling factors. For example, Farber (1959a) found that normal sisters who interacted frequently with the retarded child tended to have more tense relationships with their mothers than did sisters who had less contact with their retarded sibling. Further, in families with low marital integration, parents who institutionalized their retarded child expressed dissatisfaction with their normal daughters, presumably because the daughters could not take over the care of the child (Farber et al. 1960).

Religion. There is some evidence on the role of religious affiliation as a determinant of institutionalization. Jewish parents, especially middle-class Jewish families, seem to be reluctant to institutionalize their seriously retarded children (Farber et al. 1960). In the case of children with IQs below

50, Saenger (1960) found that 1 out of every 10 white Protestant and Catholic families with a child functioning at this level admitted the child to an institution, while only 1 of every 20 Jewish families did so.

Another piece of information on this subject comes from Farber (1959a). He reported that placing a retarded son in an institution improved the relationship between a husband and wife if they were not Catholic. No beneficial effects were found in the case of Catholic parents.

Perception of the Child.   As we have indicated, attempts to ascertain which families will institutionalize their child have clearly pointed to the fact that mental retardation alone is not a sufficient explanation. In addition to the presence of mental retardation, the child must be perceived as "troublesome" (Farber 1968). The family may feel itself somehow disrupted by the child's presence, parents may see the retarded child as an impediment to the development of normal siblings, or the child may be labeled as a troublemaker when the child encounters problems outside the home.

Although it is hard now to study institutionalization of children with IQ > 50, since institutionalization of such children has been drastically reduced (Edgerton et al. 1975), the evidence on past practices suggests strongly that these individuals were institutionalized because of problems that occurred outside the home (Saenger 1960). Sexual problems almost invariably led to institutionalization, particularly for girls. Problems prevalent among higher-IQ children who were institutionalized in the Chicago area included stubbornness, temper tantrums, sexual problems, stealing, setting fires, entering other homes, and objectionable personal habits. In contrast, the problems mentioned for lower-ability children were restlessness or hyperactivity, self-destructiveness, and sleeplessness (Farber 1968). While the nature of the problem differs for higher and lower subgroups of institutionalized retarded children, the fact remains that they are perceived as posing a problem over and above being mentally retarded.

As for perception of how the child affects the family, over half of the parents asked in one study to give their reasons for committing a retarded family member stated that they believed that the retarded person had some harmful emotional effect on other family members (Illinois Department of Public Health 1965). A study by Appell and Tisdall (1968) of a number of families reported that 62 percent of the families who ultimately institutionalized their child rejected the child, and 57 percent of the families who decided not to institutionalize their child but to seek other services rejected their child as well.

In general, it appears that mentally retarded persons who are institutionalized differ from those who remain in the home. Whether this is due to real differences in their behavior or to family differences in perceptions of their behavior remains somewhat clouded. One methodological problem has been that most comparative studies have used families receiving services but have seldom included families who need services but are not receiving them or families who do not need such services (Eyman et al. 1972; Tarjan 1968).

System and Community Factors

In addition to child and family factors influencing institutionalization there are several outside factors to be considered. Appell and Tisdall (1968) reported that 87 percent of their sample who were admitted to an institution were reported to have caused concern in the community—either they were a general source of irritation or had come to the attention of authorities—compared to 44 percent of the retarded sample who were not admitted. Other factors, such as the availability of services in the community, orientation of professionals with whom the family has contact, economic conditions, and the prevailing sentiment toward mental retardation, all play a role in determining which retarded persons are placed in institutions.

Community Pressures. In some instances the retarded person is institutionalized because the family finally gives in to pressure exerted upon them by authorities. Appell and Tisdall (1968) reported that 82 percent of those admitted were referred with some degree of pressure exerted by law enforcement officials, professionals, and educators. A similar finding was reported by Garfield and Affleck (1960), who noted that definite pressures had been exerted to have the retarded individual removed from the community.

Sometimes community pressure is *against* admission of retarded people to institutions—parent groups, social welfare agencies, and others sometimes criticize what they see as indiscriminate admission policies. Goldstein (1957) was critical of either kind of extraneous pressures playing a role in deciding who would be institutionalized. He asserted that the individual cases should instead be decided in terms of what is in the best interest of a given retarded person and the person's family.

Services Available in the Community. The availability of services in the community and the satisfaction of parents with those services may be a decisive factor in whether or not a retarded person will be institutionalized (Eyman et al. 1972; McCarver & Craig 1974). Families living in communities in which services are of poor quality or are unavailable are more likely to institutionalize a child. If local physicians are unfamiliar with the unique health problems of the retarded or if special education or vocational training programs are poorly run or available only at a great distance, parents may feel that their child can be better cared for in an institution. Paren-

tal satisfaction with services may be as important as the availability of services—if the parents perceive available services as being of little or no
benefit, institutionalization is more likely than if parents are satisfied with
the quality of services.

Philosophy of Professionals Serving the Family.   In some cases the orientation of clinicians (physicians or psychologists) dealing with the families
of retarded persons may explain the inconsistent findings regarding the relative importance of child versus family factors in decisions to institutionalize. Eyman and his associates (1972) distinguish between two kinds of clinicians: *patient-oriented*   and   *family-oriented.*   The   patient-oriented
professional gives first priority to what is best for the retarded person in
the present context. This orientation could lead to a recommendation for
institutionalization, but it would come in the belief that it is the best alternative available for the retarded person. The family-oriented clinician, on
the other hand, bases recommendations on those variables believed to be in
the best interest of the family as a whole; they may not necessarily be of
maximum benefit to the retarded person.

Since chance factors often determine the clinician selected, it may be that
clinicians should clarify their bias to parents; perhaps parents should be
made aware that an equally competent clinician might make quite different
suggestions, depending on the orientation. It would be interesting to find
out whether parents shop for a recommendation that coincides with what
they have already decided or whether their decision is influenced by the
recommendation of the clinician.

Economic Conditions.   In his analysis of admission trends in the United
States between 1922 and 1963, Farber (1968) noted that admission rates for
the retarded with IQs above 50 have been sensitive to economic cycles of
prosperity and depression. The highest rate of admission for this upper
subgroup came during the Depression years of the 1930s; since World War
II the rate has declined. But this pattern has not been true for the severely
and profoundly retarded. For those with IQs between 25 and 50, the highest
admission rate came in the 1950s, and for those with IQ below 25, the proportion has increased since 1946, probably reflecting the availability of
space resulting from the decline in admission rates for the higher-functioning retarded since World War II.

Economic factors related to a family's social mobility may affect the decision to institutionalize. Culver (1967) found that families who keep the
retarded child at home were more likely to exhibit downward social mobility than were families who institutionalized their retarded child. Furthermore, parents who attended college were more likely to institutionalize
their retarded child than were parents who had terminated their education
at or before high school graduation. Farber (1968) interpreted these find-

ings as suggesting that when chances are high for upward social mobility, families tend to rid themselves of impediments to success; one manifestation of this is their willingness to institutionalize their severely retarded or even moderately retarded children.

Prevailing Public Sentiment toward the Retarded. As we noted at the beginning of this chapter, public sentiment toward retarded individuals as a group has shifted from time to time. Certain attitudes, such as those evident during the eugenics scare, are influential in pressuring for institutionalization. For instance, when the construction of public institutions was at a peak prior to World War II, public sentiment dictated institutionalization as a means of protecting society from the perceived threat of the mentally retarded.

Currently, public sentiment opposes institutionalization except in the most extreme cases. With normalization as the guiding principle, the movement today is toward removing residents from institutions and placing them in smaller community residences, which are regarded as more normalized and beneficial (Edgerton et al. 1975). Throne (1979) and others contend that although professionals and the public alike oppose large institutions, they are not united in favoring a single alternative—medium-size residences, group homes, foster homes, or some other arrangement. Crawford, Aiello, and Thompson (1979) correctly stated that the objective in selecting a placement is to provide the optimal balance between the client's behavioral competence and the sociophysical characteristics of the residential alternatives.

Regardless of the wisdom of large-scale deinstitutionalization and the problems involved in implementing it, large numbers of retarded persons are currently being moved into the community. Three consequences of this trend are already apparent: (1) a dramatic reduction in the rate of institutionalization of retarded persons with IQs above 50, (2) a higher rate of release from large institutions into smaller, community-based settings, and (3) a substantial number of cases in which the client must be readmitted to the large institution after failing in the community placement.

We will now discuss why large institutions were subjected to such severe criticism, which led to deinstitutionalization and the development of community residential facilities.

CRITICISMS OF INSTITUTIONS

The large residential institution has come under severe criticism in recent years. The trend toward normalization, coupled with court cases in which atrocities have been exposed, has served to mobilize strong opposition to institutions in general. It is important to note that the court cases have been extreme cases and must not be considered representative situations. But we must also acknowledge the lack of advocates on behalf of the institutionalized retarded; until recently their lot in life was not monitored carefully and they were unable to express grievances. Exposure of their sometimes deplorable circumstances has turned up horror stories like this one presented by the President's Committee on Mental Retardation (1973):

> The seclusion rooms are small cells with locked doors, barred windows, and are just large enough for one bed and a mattress on the floor. Residents are locked in these rooms without supervision and for long periods of time.
>
> One resident who was recently observed in a seclusion room had been there as long as the ward attendant had been assigned to that ward, which was six years. Physical restraints, including straight jackets, nylon stockings, rags as well as rope, are often used without physician's orders. One young girl was observed in a straight jacket, tied to a wooden bench. It was explained that she sucked her fingers and had been so restrained for nine years.
>
> (p. 24)

In Chapter 8, we discussed some of the court cases in which deplorable conditions and a lack of rehabilitation were exposed. Cases such as *Wyatt* have ended such abuses, at least temporarily. (It is to be hoped that the changes are permanent.) In the following sections, we will consider how institutions differ from one another—in size, quality of life, and administrative character—and how such differences affect residents.

Differences in Institutions

In trying to determine what effect institutions have upon their residents, researchers often lump together all institutions and contrast them to all noninstitutional settings in the hope that one category will prove superior to the other. But Butterfield and Zigler (1965) argued forcefully that institutions differ in their effects on their retarded residents.

There have been several attempts to identify the social-psychological factors within institutions that account for their differential effects. Bensberg and Barnett (1966) reported that the most significant factors were (1) personnel turnover, (2) attendant working conditions, (3) degree of modernity, (4) cost of operations, (5) rural versus urban settings, and (6) availability of professional services. Silverstein (1967) found that four slightly different factors best explained differential effects: (1) staffing adequacy of cottage and medical personnel, (2) staffing adequacy of teachers, psychologists, and social workers, (3) institution age, size, and crowding, and (4) resident competence.

Tizard and his associates (King & Raynes 1968; Raynes & King 1968;

Tizard 1960, 1964) studied four institutions in Great Britain. They reported that even though the two large hospitals they studied served different types of residents (physically handicapped, mentally retarded), they managed children in very similar ways. The two smaller hostel-type units (16 to 50 children) were characterized by more individual attention, greater amounts of personal liberties, and the possession of personal property. The major finding relative to the nature of care delivered was that the difference came not in the characteristics of the populations served but rather in the nature of the institution—large hospital or hostel. A follow-up study (Tizard 1970) compared various institutions serving severely retarded persons. The large hospitals were again found to be regimented and unstimulating, while the hostels provided greater individualization and flexibility. The large hospital pattern was institution-oriented while the hostel pattern was resident-oriented. But note that these are differences in organizational structure, not in child outcomes.

Klaber (1969, 1970) did relate differences in management practices to the abilities of residents, but he focused on the characteristics of ward personnel and their contact with residents. He found considerable differences in the quantity and quality of staff-resident interactions. He characterized "effective institutions" as those in which intellectual growth occurred and in which patients were happy and showed no excessive need for social reinforcement. According to this standard, the two institutions that emphasized efficiency and minimizing costs were rated "ineffective" in human terms. Of the institutions in which there was greater resident movement between units of the institution, one was small and used community resources to meet the needs of residents; Klaber rated it "effective." Klaber concluded that the difference came not so much in the nature of administrative arrangements but in the quality of the interaction between residents and the ward staff (Edgerton et al. 1975, p. 74).

Despite the inability of research to demonstrate direct beneficial consequences of certain management practices on behavioral outcomes (Edgerton et al. 1975), the literature is full of enthusiastic recommendations for improvements to the quality of life for institutional residents. There are obviously differences between institutions and they probably do affect the quality of patients' lives and their intellectual development. But the exact relationships have not yet been demonstrated.

Character of Institutions

The difference between effective and ineffective institutions probably involves a number of subtle factors, not just size. Farber (1968) has described the many forces that collectively shape the character of a residential institution. He notes that one fact that is often ignored is that political factors play a major role in the operation of the institution. Most large institutions employ large numbers of individuals with varying responsibilities. These individuals exert pressures on the institution and definitely shape the patient care program.

In addition to internal politics, institutions are shaped by their relationship to the surrounding community. Since institutions sometimes attempt to return some residents to the community, they cannot cut themselves off from the outside world. At the same time, institutions cannot allow excessive encroachment by the outside world, since this would have a disruptive effect on institutional routines and functioning. They must therefore maintain a delicate balance between openness and seclusion. Some believe that institutions have become too secluded. When the outside community does not know what goes on inside, there is no accountability for what is done in the institution.

Another character-shaping factor is the institution's mission or task. Sometimes this mission is perceived by those who work there as the need to preserve themselves rather than the need to serve the residents (Hobbs 1975b). Staff members decide on rules, establish routines, decide which behaviors will be rewarded and which punished, and establish dress codes. Critics of institutions argue that the guide to such decisions has too often been what will make life easier for the staff instead of what is best for the residents. Residents may be encouraged to be dependent and docile, when in fact such behaviors may impede their return to the community.

Few changes in institutional character have been brought about by parents. Those parents who maintain contact with their children after admission tend to be lower social class parents who have little influence and do not know how to bring about change. The middle-class parents who might pressure for change and know how to accomplish it are less prone to retain an active interest in their children once they are placed. Farber (1968) has found that middle-class families tend to institutionalize their severely retarded children early and then ignore their existence. Hence the parents who have contact with the institution are unable to effect change, and the character of the institution can continue to evolve for the benefit of the staff rather than the patients.

The character of institutions may also be negatively shaped by staffing problems, overcrowding, and underfinancing, discussed below.

Staffing.   Two functions are served by residential institutions for the retarded: (1) the custody of the retarded and (2) the return of some retarded persons to the community (Farber 1968). In most institutions these functions are served by different staffs. Those charged with custody are the ward attendants, nursing staff, and housekeeping staff; a different staff is maintained for rehabilitation, vocational training, and welfare (psychologists, teachers, and social workers). Farber observes that each of these staffs sees the residents in different settings—the custodial staff sees them on the wards and in job assignments in the institutions, while the professional staff charged with rehabilitation sees them in classrooms or offices. This appears to lead to the perception by the residents that the custodial staff has more direct authority over their lives.

Tension often arises between the two staffs because of differences in their backgrounds and responsibilities. In terms of education, the professional staff tends to be highly educated, while the custodial staff (with the exception of registered nurses) has far less formal education. Ward attendants average only a tenth-grade educational attainment (Cleland 1965). The activities of the professional staff may make the job of the custodial staff more difficult. The professionals may disrupt the routine and excite patients, making the running of the ward harder. The treatment orientation between the two staffs can be discrepant as well. A social worker may want to return to the community a resident whom a ward attendant uses as a helper in working with more disabled residents. As Farber (1968) put it, the custodial staff may use the patient population for their own convenience.

Understaffing is a problem in both custodial and professional positions. The custodial staffs have considerable turnover rates (Butterfield, Barnett, & Bensberg 1966), which have been related to the professional staff/attendant ratio. When there are many professionals the custodial staff turnover is high; when there are higher numbers of attendants per professional the turnover rate is lower. Farber (1968) suggests that this may be explained in terms of either the amount of supervision given attendants or the amount of attention required by the patient population. When there is a great deal of supervision the attendants are inclined to look elsewhere for work; or when the population of the institution is severely retarded, there are more professionals, and attendants look for work elsewhere because of the attention that must be given to patients. Turnover rates are also related to economic conditions in the surrounding community. There is a lower turnover when the unemployment rates are high, and higher turnover rates when more jobs are available. Farber concluded that the job of attendant is not attractive compared to other jobs and that the ideal attendant situation is one in which the patients are not in need of constant supervision and there is little professional supervision.

Problems exist in the recruitment of the professional staff as well. Prestige is low for professionals working in state institutions. As a group, the professionals who work in state hospitals have not aspired to national recognition among their peers, leading Farber to describe them as "locals" (professionals who evaluate their work from the viewpoint of people with whom they have day-to-day contact) as opposed to "cosmopolitans" (who evaluate their work from the viewpoint of professional peers all over). The implication is clear: professionals drawn to state hospitals for the mentally retarded are not often the elite of their respective professions.

Overcrowding. In many cases the demand for placement of retarded persons exceeds the official capacity of the institution, and the response has been to overadmit. As a result, institutions constructed to house 250 patients find themselves with 400 residents. Whether additional construction is considered or additional staff hired depends on the state legislature's willingness to allocate more money for the program. Often the money for extra construction and staffing has not been granted, leading to chronic overcrowding in many institutions. One consequence of overcrowding has been the placing of much responsibility and power in the hands of the attendants. The criticism leveled at this outcome has been that attendants have often been inclined to run the program with the intent of making life easy for themselves rather than running the program for the benefit of the residents. With attendants running a program under overcrowded conditions, ward status structures have often been created, with a subgroup of the patients being used to control and care for other patients.

Hobbs (1975b) reports that overcrowding is common, with many facilities having 25 to 50 percent more residents than they were designed to serve. Compounding the physical problems that overcrowding creates is the fact that the facilities are often old and in poor condition. Toilets do not work; there are unsanitary conditions where food is prepared; the wards are too cold in winter and hot and fly-infested in summer.

Underfinancing. A perpetual problem in administering institutions is the difficulty in obtaining adequate financing. Hobbs (1975b) found some dramatic examples of how little is spent on residents of institutions for the retarded:

> During 1966 and 1967 the per diem costs in United States institutions (except in Alaska) ranged from about $3 to $12 per person. In stark contrast, five of the largest United States zoos were spending, in a comparable period, an average of over $7 for their larger animals. Further, in 1966, general hospital care cost more than $40 per patient per day.
>
> (p. 127)

One result of underfinancing is that it aggravates staffing problems. Low salaries do not attract the best personnel, necessitating the hiring of unqualified personnel in some instances. Kugel (1969) reported that foreign-trained physicians who were unable to obtain state licenses have sometimes been hired.

Another result of underfinancing is institutional peonage, in which residents who might be able to succeed in the community are kept in the institution because they are needed to perform jobs there (Kugel 1969). If the residents were not available to perform the jobs it would be necessary to hire outside personnel, further increasing costs.

Effects of Institutions on Residents

There is a large body of research literature concerned with the effects of institutions on their residents. We will provide a brief discussion of the literature; readers interested in more extensive reviews are referred to Butterfield (1967), Edgerton et al. (1975), and Zigler and Balla (1977).

Mortality. In the mid-1970s the evidence indicated that institutionalized retarded persons had a shorter life expectancy than the general population. At that time, however, comparative figures about retarded persons living in the community were unavailable. The findings varied with age and degree of retardation, which led Edgerton and his associates (1975) to conclude that:

1. Young children (under six months), particularly those in the profoundly retarded range and with organic impairment, are more vulnerable and less adaptable to environmental changes.
2. When there are additional handicaps (such as epilepsy) or a lack of self-help skills (such as toileting), there is a higher mortality rate. This is particularly evident when mobility is impaired.
3. The most common causes of death are pulmonary diseases. This problem is particularly acute among the profoundly retarded. They are highly prone to infection. And due to their immobility there is a restriction of proper lung expansion, causing breathing problems when they eat.

Despite findings that age and degree of retardation are somehow linked to mortality, it is hard to pin down an exact cause-and-effect relationship. For instance, a study by McCurley, Mackay, and Scally (1972) reported much higher mortality rates for institutionalized retarded persons under age five than for retarded children of comparable age in the community. But such direct comparisons fail to clarify whether the institution *causes* higher mortality or whether retarded persons with greater susceptibility to fatal illnesses are placed in institutions for these very reasons.

If attempts are made to consider institutional differences as a factor in mortality, we may find that the size of the residential facility is of less importance than the quality of medical care delivered, particularly with respect to unique medical problems posed by the mentally retarded resident.

Miller (1975) examined mortality rates among the profoundly retarded in 1973, studying 3384 people with IQs under 20 who were living in institutions, convalescent hospitals, or community placements. The mortality rates for these three placements respectively were as follows: 19 in 1000, 36 in 1000, and 29 in 1000. The results indicate that moving the profoundly retarded to settings other than institutions does not reduce their mortality—in fact, it may increase it.

Intelligence.   Attempts to assess the effect of institutions on intellectual behavior have employed several different approaches, described in some detail by Butterfield (1967): (1) comparing institutionalized retarded subjects with those living at home, (2) comparing groups of institutionalized subjects who have been in an institution for varying lengths of time, and (3) periodic assessment of the same group of patients after different periods of time in an institution. Generally the findings of these studies suggest that institutions have an adverse effect on the intellectual development of retarded persons, although one of the better-controlled studies (Fisher & Zeaman 1970) reported no dramatic effects.

Butterfield (1967) noted many methodological flaws in the research to date on this topic. Particularly noteworthy is his observation that the effect of institutionalization interacts with variables such as diagnosis, preinstitutionalization history, and age at the time of placement. Nevertheless, several findings have emerged consistently enough to warrant attention:

1. The detrimental effects of institutions are more marked on verbal and abstract abilities than on performance tasks.
2. These detrimental effects are more pronounced for younger retarded persons and for retarded persons coming from more favorable home environments.
3. Retarded persons coming from adverse home environments may actually benefit from institutionalization.

Evidence for the third point comes from the work of the Clarkes (Clarke & Clarke 1953, 1954; Clarke, Clarke, & Reiman 1958), who followed a group of 59 retarded persons for six years from the time they were institutionalized. Subjects coming from adverse family backgrounds increased significantly more in IQ than did those coming from less adverse backgrounds.

While researchers have attempted to specify carefully the characteristics of the retarded subjects in this line of research, there has not been comparable care devoted to specifying the characteristics of the institutions in which they reside (Edgerton et al. 1975). For instance, we might interpret the findings that institutions have a depressing effect on verbal skills to reflect a fairly common characteristic of institutions—opportunities are limited for verbal expression by residents. Butterfield (1967) suggested that verbal stimulation does not necessitate great expertise and could be provided by means of a simple increase in the number of child care workers who would talk meaningfully, frequently, and directly to residents. Instead of recommending that all institutions be abandoned, we might better direct our attention to conditions such as the lack of verbalization in many institutions that should be modified.

Personality. Our earlier examination of personality variables (see Chapter 11) revealed that the institutionalized retarded tend to have more personality disorders than the noninstitutionalized retarded. These disorders, however, may be a cause of institutionalization, not a result of it. This selective bias hampers research on how institutionalization affects residents' personalities. Other problems in research in this area concern instrumentation (tests of personality are highly verbal) and the prevalent belief that the retarded are less variable in personality than normals.

The most extensive research program on the effects of institutions on personality has been carried out by Zigler and his associates (Zigler 1966; Zigler & Balla 1972, 1977). Zigler's work, which began in the late 1950s, indicates that several characteristics are more common among the institutionalized retarded than among the noninstitutionalized retarded:

1. An increased desire to interact with an approving adult, probably resulting from having been deprived of such contact. At the same time the individual is reluctant and wary to make contact, since in the past such attempts have often met with rejection.
2. A problem-solving strategy called *outerdirectedness*, characterized by a distrust of one's own solutions and a seeking of cues from the environment. This is a coping strategy resulting from excessive failure when retarded individuals attempt to rely on their own resources.
3. Differences in reinforcer hierarchy, as compared to normals, with tangible consequences being more effective than intangible consequences.
4. A high expectation of failure and a lower level of aspiration.

Another piece of evidence comes from the work of Stevenson and Knights (1961), who examined the desire of institution residents for social reinforcement after returning from summer vacations at home. Their results indicated that children had more intense feelings of deprivation immediately upon return to the institution, feelings that were reduced in intensity after the children readjusted to the institutional setting.

An impressive interpretation of the studies regarding the effects of institutionalization on the personality of the residents has been presented by Butterfield (1967). He hypothesizes that if children receive insufficient amounts of positive adult contact (which appears to be frequently the case for institutionalized retarded persons), they remain oriented toward receiving such attention. As a consequence these individuals do not make sufficient progress toward achieving independence. Instead they remain dependent, a condition that militates against satisfactory adjustment as an adult. This effect is compounded by their lowered intellect. It makes them incapable of meeting conventional behavioral standards, increasing the likelihood that they will receive insufficient positive attention.

Some twenty years of research by Zigler and his associates is nicely summarized in a paper by Zigler and Balla (1977), who point out that a retarded person's response to an institution depends on both the person's characteristics and the nature of the institution in which the person is placed. Preinstitutional experiences such as social deprivation, for example, influence the retarded person's response to being placed in an institution. Children from better homes, who were not socially deprived, exhibited a greater motivation for social reinforcement than residents coming from deprived homes. In other words, institutionalization was more socially depriving to children from relatively good homes than for those from deprived backgrounds. Similarly, children from better homes exhibited a decline in IQ, whereas those from deprived homes were more likely to increase in IQ. The point is that the relationship between institutionalization and behavioral outcomes is complex and cannot be understood by looking for a general pattern of individual preinstitutional experiences as well as individual experiences after placement.

Zigler and his associates also examined the effect on residents of the nature of the institution. In addition to the size of institutions, such variables as cost, ratio of staff to residents, and employee turnover were studied. McCormick, Balla, and Zigler (1975) found that only institution size and the level of retardation were related to care practices in the institution. Later studies, however, revealed that residents of larger living units were more wary of adults and exhibited a greater desire for adult approval. It was also found that residents living in situations that had high staff turnover rates exhibited a greater wariness of adults. The mental age of residents was found to be related to such effects—higher MA residents were less motivated to receive adult attention and support, were more wary of adults, and were less imitative.

The Zigler and Balla (1977) paper is important because it cautions us against making blanket statements about all institutions and all retarded residents. Both institutions and retarded residents vary considerably along a number of salient dimensions, which combine to determine the institution's effect on the individual resident. The paper also points out how social deprivation experienced relatively early in life can affect the behavior of retarded persons years later, a factor that must be considered in studies of the effects of institutions on their residents.

Conclusions.   The results bearing on the effects of institutions suggest that they do have certain detrimental effects on residents. But, in general, the research did not take into account the differences between institutions, so instead of pinpointing the effects of institutionalization per se, it points only to the effects of life in specific institutions. In some cases the factors causing the detrimental effects can be modified. For instance, the common finding that there is an apparent lack of verbal stimulation on institution wards could be remedied without shutting down the institutions. As normalization efforts are evaluated it will be important to assess the extent to which greater amounts of stimulation are provided to residents in smaller residential settings and the consequent effects this stimulation has on outcomes such as intelligence and personality.

Furthermore, future attempts at evaluating the quality of life in residential alternatives must be sensitive to forces within the alternatives (e.g., foster care homes) as well as differences between alternatives (e.g., foster care homes versus institutions). Anything less will mask the specific environmental forces that are significantly related to specific outcomes. We may find that the factors related to one outcome (e.g., intelligence) may be of little importance for a different outcome (e.g., mortality). Finally, care must be exercised in concluding that the effects of institutions are detrimental unless the experiences a child has had prior to institutionalization can be evaluated. In some cases the damage has been done before the child is placed.

LIFE IN AN INSTITUTION

Many of the investigations into what life in an institution is really like were made when facilities served a broader spectrum of the retarded population. In the past, institutions for the mentally retarded served children ranging from untestable cases below IQ 20 to children who were normal in intelligence but who had encountered problems with social agencies. At present the trend is toward placement of only the more severely disabled children of very low IQ, while less severely retarded children are being placed in alternative community placements (e.g., foster care homes) if they are removed from their natural homes.

"High-grades" and "Low-grades"

Some of the research suggests that certain unpleasant aspects of institutional life are imposed on the residents by the residents themselves. When children of more diverse ability ranges were residing in institutions there was a clear-cut distinction made between the more capable and less capable patients. This distinction was formalized in the vocabulary of the residents, which was apparently derived from terms the staff used to make similar distinctions (Edgerton 1963; Marden & Farber 1961). The resulting hierarchy seemed to be a source of tension.

Marden and Farber (1961) observed that boys on the wards labeled each other as *high-brows* (apparently an adaptation of "high-grade," used by the staff) or the derisive term *low-grades*, and these terms were understood by all boys on the ward. The high-grade group was further divided into *working* boys, who held jobs in institutional businesses, such as the bakery or the laundry, and *class* boys, who were designated by ward attendants to assist them in maintaining order among the other patients on the ward. Marden and Farber noted a constant conflict on the ward between working and class boys. Class boys often tried to get the working boys to violate the rules so that they would lose their working privileges, while the working boys frequently tried to defend the low-grade children from the class boys, who sometimes administered punishment to nonconformists. Such situations seem to mirror the conflicts between the custodial and rehabilitative staff of the institution. But in the case of residents, both higher-functioning roles were associated with high-brow status.

When they attempted to find out what factors led to classification as "high-grade," Marden and Farber found that residents cited the following criteria: (1) cleanliness, (2) conformity to rules (rule breaking was a criterion for low-grades), (3) display of power, and (4) behavior displays of privilege.

The "Hip" Elite

Edgerton's work (Edgerton 1963; Edgerton & Dingman 1964a, 1964b) parallels the Marden and Farber research except that it focused upon the "hip" elite group who were the institutional delinquents. In the institution Edgerton (1963) studied, the hip patients were often black and Mexican-American adolescents. Before admission to the institution these individuals were frequently on the periphery of a gang, sometimes as a scapegoat or butt of jokes. They were clearly more able than most children residing in institutions; they lacked physical handicaps and showed knowledge of hip teenage speech, dress, and behavior. Among this group sexuality was important, although there was apparently more discussion of sex than actual participation in it. New members were admitted only if they were sponsored by one of the group members.

Elite members opposed the regulations of the staff, but they did so by design, to test limits and to see what infractions would be tolerated. They were often used by attendants to perform supervisory jobs, such as to police the wards if they were relatively intelligent and tough.

In a related study Edgerton and Dingman (1964b) reported that the elite looked upon their lives in the institution as a game of cops-and-robbers in which they engaged in theft and vandalism to maintain the respect of other elite members. Over half of this elite group had a distinctive tattoo that served to mark them as tough guys. Boyfriend and girlfriend relationships were admired if each member tattooed the other's name on himself or herself. While others in the hospital were on occasion tattooed, tattooing was usually associated with elite status.

Farber (1968) suggests that among what he called the *high-grades* are the "hip" elite described by Edgerton and a "square" elite as well. The latter group is more prone to be conforming and is more actively engaged in rehabilitation. The hip elite scorn them, possibly reflecting the attitude of ward attendants. The hip elite boys provide services for attendants and in many cases come from similar social class backgrounds. The square high-grades may be more appreciated by the rehabilitation staff, since they exhibit behaviors that will enable them to return to the community.

Life for Low-functioning Residents

While for high-grade residents activities are scheduled for most of the day, they do have time slots in which they are able to avoid direct supervision. But the very low functioning patients are seldom out of the sight of either an attendant or a resident designated by the attendant to supervise the low-ability patients. Much of the day consists of routines of waking, toileting, dressing, and meals. The following selection by MacAndrew and Edgerton (1964) vividly portrays the routine in the daily lives of the profoundly retarded in an institution.

The Everyday Life of Institutionalized "Idiots"[1]

Craig MacAndrew and Robert Edgerton

It has been variously estimated that there are 100,000 idiots in the United States today. Because approximately half of these, including almost all of the adults, are in public institutions, common sense knowledge of idiots is typically both sketchy and ridden with clichés. Unfortunately, our scientific knowledge concerning idiots is not a great deal better. While there is a substantial, but spotty body of medical information at hand, detailed understanding of the psychological functioning of idiots is notably deficient[2] and knowledge of their social behavior is virtually nonexistent.[3]

[1]Craig MacAndrew and Robert Edgerton, "The Everyday Life of Institutionalized 'Idiots,'" from *Human Organization*, vol. 23, no. 4 (Winter 1964), pp. 312–318. Reproduced by permission of the Society for Applied Anthropology and the senior author. At the time of publication the authors acknowledged the possible offensiveness of the term "idiot," which had already been replaced by other terminology in the field of mental retardation. They decided to use it because it was more familiar and more specific in meaning to those working outside the field of mental retardation. Their use of the term is not in any way derogatory to the residents studied.

[2] G. A. Kelly, "The Theory and Technique of Assessment," *Annual Revue of Psychology*, IX (1958), 323–352.

[3] See S. B. Sarason and T. Gladwin, "Psychological and Cultural Problems in Mental Subnormality: A Review of Research," *American Journal of Mental Deficiency*, LXII (1958), 1115–1307.

There is a sense, of course, in which we know what idiots are: operationally, they are those who score less than 20 on a standard IQ test and who are judged to be organically incapable of scoring higher. They are, then, the most profound mental incompetents, as is indicated by the following typical professional definition:

> The idiot is . . . a person so deeply defective in mind from birth, or from an early age, as to be unable to guard himself against common physical danger.[4]

Specifically, we are instructed that:

> They have eyes but they see not; ears, but they hear not; they have no intelligence and no consciousness of pleasure or pain; in fact, their mental state is one entire negation.[5]

We are also advised that they are typically incapable of speech:

> Their utterances mostly consist of inarticulate grunts, screeches and discordant yells.[6]

Finally, we are informed that they are characteristically physically handicapped and frequently disfigured; references to their appearance often use words such as "stunted, misshapen, hideous, bestial," and the like. In a word, what we know—or at least what we think we know—about idiots is little more than a slightly elaborated set of first impressions.

Most importantly, we know practically nothing about their everyday *conduct*—about what they actually *do* in the course of living their lives in the institutions which are their typical abodes. In this article we attempt to provide a description of the everyday lives of institutionalized idiots as they are actually lived in one such institution. To our knowledge, the literature contains no such systematic description. In the discussion section we recommend the uniquely informing character of a detailed understanding of such profoundly retarded beings to certain of the perennial problems which are peculiar to a proper study of mankind—not the least of which is the elucidation of the very notion of "man" itself.

[4] A. F. Tredgold, *Mental Deficiency*, William Wood and Co., New York, 1956, p. 199.
[5] Ibid, p. 205.
[6] Ibid, p. 202.

The Physical Setting

Pacific State Hospital is a large state institution for the mentally retarded. Its 494 acre grounds are occupied by over 3000 patients and 1500 staff members who respectively live and work in an elaborate, self-contained complex of lawns, parks, roads, and some 70 major buildings. Located outside the city of Pomona, California, the hospital was founded in its present location in 1927 as Pacific Colony. While this location was characterized by rural seclusion at the time of its founding, it has since become increasingly surrounded by the expanding residential and commercial areas of the Southern California megalopolis and is now less than a mile from one of the major links in the greater Los Angeles freeway system. This agglutination process is pithily evidenced in the population statistics of the area: while the population of Pomona stood at 20,000 in 1927, it will soon top 100,000 and its rate of growth shows little sign of leveling off.

Accompanying this change in environs, at least equally dramatic changes have taken place in administrative philosophy. While the inmates of Pacific Colony once cultivated acres of farm land under a policy of primarily custodial care,[7] the custodial tradition was radically revised some ten years ago when the administrative orientation shifted to one of treatment and rehabilitation. In the process, the "colony" became a "hospital," the "cottages" became "wards," and the "inmates" became "patients."

Included in the hospital's 3000 resident mentally defective patients are approximately 900 idiots who are domiciled in various wards throughout the institution. The present paper is concerned with one such ward, a ward reserved for the most severely retarded ambulatory adult male patients (N = 82) in the hospital. Built in 1954, at a cost in excess of $210,000, Ward Y is a low, tile-roofed building separated from several other wards of similar design by stretches of lawns and shrubbery. While the ward is large and well constructed, both its design and detailing reflect the characteristic institutional stamp of

[7] That custodial care was the clear intent of the Legislature at the time of the Colony's founding is evidenced in the summary of the bill contained in the report of the California Committee on Mental Deficiency appointed by Act of the Legislature in 1915. "Purpose of the Institution: The institution should provide adequate custodial care and training for its inmates . . . provision should be made for the scientific study of the group of individuals thus gathered, with a view to discovering the best means of correcting the social conditions which make it necessary to maintain such institutions."

unimaginative drabness and of a grossly inadequate provision
for the entrance of natural light.

Patients and Staff

The 82 patients who reside in Ward Y range in age from 15
to 52; their average age is 27.1 (S.D. = 8.45). As for their measured intelligence, if we remove 8 patients—about whom more
in a moment—who comprise a clearly demarcated minor second mode in their IQ distribution, the mean IQ of the remaining 74 patients is 15.4 (S.D. = 9.05). In terms of the contemporary nomenclature, these remaining 74 patients are, without
exception, either severely or profoundly retarded. The 8 relatively high IQ patients have been assigned to Ward Y for
diverse reasons—as helpers, because they cannot get along on
the higher-grade wards, and so on. Most of them have come to
perform a number of assigned duties on the ward. In addition
to these 8 "in residence" helpers, 6 additional mildly retarded
patients are detailed to Ward Y to assist the staff during morning and afternoon hours.

The staff consists of from 11 to 13 male attendants and 3
female attendants, all of whom bear the title of psychiatric
technicians. Their work hours are set up on a standard three-
shift basis, with 7 on the day shift (6:30 A.M.–3:00 P.M.), 5 to 6
on the afternoon shift (2:45 P.M.–11:15 P.M.), and 2 to 3 on the
night shift (11:00 P.M.–7:00 A.M.).

First Impressions of Ward Y

Words, however well-chosen, cannot begin adequately to
convey the combined sights, sounds, and smells which initially
confront and affront the outsider on his first visit. What follows
is at best an approximation.

Despite the size of Ward Y, the simultaneous presence of its
82 patients evokes an immediate impression of overcrowding.
Additionally, most of the patients are marked by such obvious
malformations that their abnormal status appears evident at a
glance. One sees heads that are too large or too small, asymmet-
rical faces, distorted eyes, noses, and mouths, ears that are torn
or cauliflowered, and bodies that present every conceivable
sign of malproportion and malfunction. Most patients are barefooted, many are without shirts, and an occasional patient is—

at least momentarily—naked. What clothing is worn is often grossly ill-fitting. In a word, the first impression is that of a mass—a mass of undifferentiated, disabled, frequently grotesque caricatures of human beings.

Within moments, however, the mass begins to differentiate itself and individuals take form. A blond teen-ager flits about rapidly flapping his arms in a birdlike manner, emitting birdlike peeping sounds all the while. A large Buddhalike man sits motionless in a corner, staring straight ahead. A middle-aged man limps slowly in a circle, grunting, mumbling, and occasionally shaking his head violently. A shirtless patient lies quietly on a bench while a small patient circles about him furiously twirling a cloth with his left hand. A blind youngster sits quietly digging his index fingers into his eyes, twitching massively and finally resolving himself into motionless rigidity. A red-haired patient kneels and peers intently down a water drain. A portly patient sits off in a corner rocking. Another patient rocks from a position on all fours. Still another patient, lying supine, rolls first to one side then to the other. Several patients walk slowly and aimlessly around, as if in a trance, showing no recognition of anyone or anything. A microcephalic darts quickly about, grinning, drooling, and making unintelligible sounds. An early twentyish mongol wearing an oversized cowboy hat strides about with his hands firmly grasping the toy guns in his waistband holsters. Others smile emptily, many lie quietly, still others from time to time erupt into brief frenzies of motion or sound.

A few patients approach the newcomer to say, "Daddy," or "Wanna go home," or to give their name or to offer some paradoxical phrase such as "tapioca too, ooga, ooga." One or another patient may attempt to touch, pull, or grasp the stranger, but such attempts at interaction are usually of the most fleeting duration. Others may approach and observe from a distance before moving away. Most pay no attention to a new face.

In the background, strange and wondrous sounds originate from all sides. Few words can be distinguished (although many utterances, in their inflection, resemble English speech); rather, screams, howls, grunts, and cries predominate and reverberate in a cacophony of only sometimes human noise. At the same time, loud and rhythmic music is coming out of the loudspeaker system.

There are, finally, the odors. Although many patients are not toilet-trained, there is no strong fecal odor. Neither is there a distinct smell of sweat. Yet there is a peculiar smell of something indefinable. Perhaps it is a combination of institutional food and kitchen smells, soap, disinfectant, feces, urine, and the close confinement of many human bodies.

In sum, Ward Y and its inhabitants constitute a staggering visual, auditory and olfactory assault on the presupposedly invariant character of the natural normal world of everyday life. Here, to a monumental degree, things are different.

The Daily Routine

The day on Ward Y begins at 6:00 A.M. when the lights go on and the relatively high IQ helpers begin to get out of bed. By 6:15 these helpers are dressed and together with the employees they begin to rouse the more defective patients from their sleep. These patients are awakened in groups of 12, the number being determined by the number of toilets on the ward. With few exceptions, they sleep without clothing, and thus they are led, nude, into the bathroom where each is toileted. After they eliminate, helpers apply toilet paper appropriately, wash their hands, and lead them out of the washrooms. Each is then dressed in denim trousers with an elastic waistband and a shirt. This completed, they are permitted to go into the day hall where they mill about while the next group of 12 is awakened, toileted, washed, and dressed. As this is going on, one or two employees strip those beds which have been soiled during the night and helpers follow them making up all the beds.

By 7:15 A.M. most of the toileting, washing, and dressing has been completed and the most capable helpers are given their breakfasts in the dining room. No food is prepared on the ward; it all comes from a central kitchen and is delivered to the several wards by food truck. By 7:30, the helpers have finished and the 23 least capable patients—referred to by the staff as "the babies"—are led into the dining room. Since the babies are capable neither of carrying a tray nor of feeding themselves, they are individually led to a table, seated, and literally spoon-fed by an employee or a "detail." Feeding the 23 babies consumes about 30 minutes. Thus at about 8:00, the babies have finished their breakfast and are led out of the dining room and back to the bathroom where they are again toileted and washed before being led to the play yard where their incontinence is both less disturbing to, and more easily handled by, the staff. As the babies leave, the remaining 50-odd patients, most of whom have been standing in line in the corridor just outside the dining room, are allowed to enter. Just before the door is opened, those who have not been waiting outside are herded into this corridor by an employee whose job it is to check the entire ward for strays. Upon entering, they are led single file to a cafeterialike serving line where they pick up a tray and proceed along the counter. Both food and utensils are placed on the tray by employees or "details" as they move along. Some of these relatively more competent patients seem only dimly aware of what is happening and must be led by an employee both along the serving line and to a table. Others, however, exhibit great interest in the food, chatter excitedly, and once through the serving line walk off toward a table unaided and undirected.

As soon as all the patients have filed into the dining room, the door is locked. This measure is taken to prevent the premature exit of patients who might get into trouble if they were allowed to wander about the ward without supervision. In a very few minutes, all have been served and are seated, usually four to a table. Each has a spoon but no knife or fork. Their deportment at the table varies greatly. At some tables, the eating may proceed in a reasonably—indeed, remarkably—decorous fashion, but at other tables such is not at all the case. Whole hard-boiled eggs are eaten at a gulp, oatmeal with milk is eaten with the fingers, prunes drop to the floor, trays are overturned, neighbors have cups of milk poured or sloshed on them, and so on. While in the course of breakfast two or three arguments typically arise which on occasion lead to fights or tantrums, and while there are always some wanderers who leave their tables and stroll about, breakfast progresses, for the most part, with a significant semblance of order and propriety. Once breakfast is completed, about thirty minutes after commencement, these patients are led out of the dining room, leaving behind them an ample residue of spilled food and drink on tables, chairs, and floor. As they file out, helpers, details, and employees clean up behind them.

Leaving the dining room, these patients, like the babies, are led once more to the bathroom, where each is again undressed and toileted. Again, toilet paper is handled only by helpers and employees, for when left to their own devices, some have been known to flush entire rolls down the toilet—a sport which occasions major dislocations in the plumbing. After being toileted, each patient's hands are once again washed. Next comes toothbrushing; each patient has his own toothbrush identified by name, but only a few are capable of brushing their teeth unaided. Consequently, most patients, still undressed, wander about the bathroom waiting to have their teeth brushed by a helper or an employee. When a patient is finished, he files out of the bathroom where he is met at the door by another helper who wipes the excess toothpaste and saliva from his mouth with a cloth. This completed, he is once again dressed.

About 9:00 A.M.—some three hours after arising—all the patients are at last ready to meet the day. It is at this point that play activity, which for most patients is a euphemism for free time, begins. Just as in the case of the early activities—toileting, dressing, and feeding—the patients are again separated into competence groupings but now there is a territorial dimension to their division. The least competent patients, approximately 55 in number, go to the outside play yard (or in bad weather to the porch), while the more competent patients remain within the ward proper.

The play yard is a large asphalt-paved rectangle enclosed on two sides by the ward itself and on the other two sides by an 8½-ft.-high wire fence. Within the enclosure are several wooden benches, a tether ball, and two roofed structures which provide shade. Aside from the tether ball, which is typically not in use, the only objects provided for patients' amusement are balls of various sizes which an employee occasionally makes available. Employees and helpers sometimes attempt to induce organized activity by engaging a few of the relatively more able patients in throwing a ball back and forth. Such activity is never sustained for any length of time, however; few of the patients are interested in such activities and those who are interested can neither catch nor throw in any effective manner. Besides these natural handicaps, a few of the patients delight in capturing the ball and throwing or kicking it over the fence, whence the employee must retrieve it.

Thus, while the patients in the play yard are under constant supervision, they are in fact left almost entirely to their own singularly limited devices. At least 20 patients do nothing but sit, rock, or lie quietly. The activity of the remaining 30 or so consists of running, pacing, crying, or shouting, and this typically in a manner oblivious of their surroundings. Aside from an occasional ephemeral outburst when, for instance, two patients bump into each other or when one pushes or strikes another, there is little interaction between them. What interaction does occur is almost entirely limited to the tactual: there is occasional cuddling, stroking, huddling together, and amorphous, exploratory probing. These interactions have the quality of "pure happenings"; they are characteristically without relation either to past or future: in a word, they have the appearance of occurring outside of history. Occasionally one patient may approach another and launch into an outpouring of jibberish, gesturing frantically all the while, only to be met by a vacant stare or, contrariwise, he may stop in mid-passage as inexplicably as he began. Here, truly, one sees the in-vivo prototype of a "billiard-ball" theory of personality.

To the consternation of the staff, one activity which does occur with inexplicable frequency is spontaneous disrobing. A major task for the supervising employee and his two details consists in maintaining the minimal proprieties of everyday dress. While most patients are barefooted and while shirts are more often off than on, nothing whatsoever is done about the former and, except in case of sunburn, little, if anything is done about the latter. Trousers, however, are intimately involved with considerations of decency and their absence is quite another matter indeed. Trousers must be put back onto patients who simply remove them and they must be removed from patients who have soiled themselves. Approximately 25 patients on Ward Y are totally incontinent and another 25 are sometimes so. As has already been noted, virtually all of these are in the group sent to the play yard. There are two clothes hampers in the yard, one containing clean clothes and the other soiled clothes. As trousers are soiled, they are thrown into the one hamper and clean ones are taken from the other. Because trouser sizes are not marked, and because both patients and garments come in many sizes, one often sees some patients enshrouded by enormous pants and others constricted by tiny ones.

Inextricably combined with these matters of moral appropriateness is an imperative concern for the physical health of the patients. Enteric disease—especially bacillary dysentery and its complications—is an ever-present danger. Fecal matter is not always ignored by the incontinent idiot: it is sometimes smeared, played with, thrown, and even eaten. It is for these reasons, too, that incontinence is counted as a matter requiring urgent staff attention. Nor is every patient aware that all water is not fit to drink; some patients have been known to drink water out of the toilet bowls and from the shower room floors. There is, too, the constant danger that despite the plentiful administration of tranquilizers, certain of the patients might at any moment do grave physical damage to themselves or others.

Such outbursts are as a rule without apparent cause; a patient may bite, scratch, or gouge either himself or another patient. These occurrences are sufficiently frequent that periods of calm may correctly be seen as preceding the storms that will inevitably follow. There is, finally, the danger of accidental injury. Seizures occur unpredictably and handicapped patients such as these not infrequently slip and fall. The possibility of accidental injury is so great for some patients that the staff seldom permits them to enter the play yard because they feel a fall on its rough asphalt surface would be more likely to cause injury than would a similar fall on the polished cement floors of the ward.

Among the 25 or 30 patients who remain inside, the problems of incontinence and nudity are much less pressing. The demands for supervision are lessened by confining all patients to the dayroom and TV room, access between which is open at all times. Such confinement is accomplished by the simple policy of locking all other doors. Within the confines of these two rooms, then, the patients typically sit, sleep, watch TV, or pace about aimlessly; only rarely do they interact with one another. Their interaction with staff, too, is limited to brief encounters which more frequently than not consist of staff directives to refrain from doing one thing or another—to stay out of the office, to leave so-and-so alone, to stop masturbating, to stop hitting one's head against the wall, and so on. Much time is spent in staring intently at one or another staff member as he goes about his duties. In general the scene one confronts in the dayroom is not greatly different from that of the play yard.

From a pool of 20 select patients, rotating groups of 6 or 7 are daily given special training in the occupational therapy room. This training consists of such activities as coloring in coloring books, playing with plastic toys, listening to music, and practicing some elementary manipulative skills. Aside from this, those who remain inside the ward are, like their counterparts in the play yard, left for the most part to their own devices.

Throughout this period of play activity most of the staff is engaged in a variety of routine tasks. One employee, as we noted, supervises the play yard; another spends all or most of the day in the ward clinic dispensing medication and treating minor injuries or illnesses; another must supervise details and helpers in cleaning the dining room, bathroom, and the ward in general; one employee is required to be responsible for the patients who are in the occupational therapy room; another must each day take those patients who are scheduled for clinic appointments to the hospital. Finally, the ward charge must be on hand to meet the ward physician when he calls, must make out a number of written reports, and must oversee all activity on the ward.

At 11:00 A.M. play activity stops, and preparations for lunch begin. All patients are again toileted and washed, with the babies being undressed in order both to make toileting proceed more effectively and to insure against the stuffing of clothing into the toilets. The daily luncheon preparation occupies both patients and staff for the better part of an hour. Lunch itself begins around noon and follows the same pattern as breakfast: helpers first, babies next, then the rest of the patients. Following the meal, each patient is again toileted and washed. The entire luncheon operation lasts from 11:00 A.M. to about 1:30 P.M.

At 1:30, play activity is resumed. It follows the morning pattern in all major details and lasts until 4:00 P.M. On a nice day, 50 or more patients are usually taken to an open grassy area ("the park") about a quarter of a mile distant from the ward, where they are allowed to roam about. Little advantage is taken of this opportunity, however; the patients generally remain clustered together around the supervising staff members. Aside from this trip away from the ward, the afternoon activities parallel those of the morning.

At 4:00 P.M. toileting and washing begins again in preparation for the evening meal, which lasts from 5:00 to 6:00, once more along the same pattern. The evening meal too is followed by a brief toileting and washing, which is generally concluded by 6:30. This, in turn, is followed by the third play activity period of the day, which lasts until about 7:30. This time the porch replaces the play yard and the TV room tends to draw a larger audience than during the day. During this period, patients are frequently assembled and marched around the day hall for several minutes (ostensibly in order to work off unspent energy in preparation for bedtime).

The hour between 7:30 P.M. and 8:30 P.M. is devoted to bedtime preparation. After being toileted, each patient is directed under the shower, where employees apply soap here and there, supervise the rinsing, and then towel the patients dry. They are next inspected for cuts, bruises, rashes, and the like and following this they are at last sent off to bed. As noted earlier, almost all patients sleep without clothing. While the beds are labeled with the patient's names, none of the patients, of course, can read. Although some know their own bed, many do not and must be led there by staff. The beds of patients who characteristically get up during the night, of those given to nocturnal noise making, and of those subject to frequent convulsive seizures, are placed close to the office in order that night shift employees can observe them more closely and respond to them when necessary with minimal disturbance to the remaining patients.

While an occasional patient is simply unable to sleep, in which case he is typically dressed and brought into the day room where he sits silently, until morning, the most striking feature of the night is the ease with which it passes.

Periodically Recurring Events

There are other events in the lives of the idiots which, while they are no less constitutive of the routine of their institutional life, do not recur daily. In this category we include the weekly bath, the fortnightly pinworm inspection, the monthly weighing, the monthly haircut, and the aperiodic visits of relatives.

One night a week all patients are given baths. The procedure is as follows: the drain in the large shower room is plugged, the room is flooded and soap is liberally added to the water. Small groups of patients enter, sit on the floor, and soak themselves. Two male employees then strip to their shorts, wade into the now pondlike shower room, and scrub the patients. This completed, the patients are led under the showers to be rinsed and then are taken out of the shower room where they are dried. Following this, they are given their daily cut, bruise, and rash inspection and their fingernails and toenails are clipped as needed, while the next group of patients is being led in to soak.

Once every two weeks, all patients are inspected for pinworms. About midnight, after all have settled down, two employees enter the dormitory and turn the patients one by one onto their stomachs. The buttocks are then spread and with the aid of a flashlight the presence or absence of pinworms is determined. This seemingly bizarre practice is so routinized that little disturbance is created; in fact, many of the patients do not even awaken.

Once each month all patients are weighed. A large scale is set up in the day room and the patients are disrobed and lined up for weighing. If a patient cannot or will not stand quietly on the scale, an employee must hold him still until a reading is obtained. Not only is this weighing a part of standard records keeping, but the discovery of any marked changes in weight causes serious staff concern and typically leads to requests that patients evidencing these weight changes be examined medically.

A hospital barber spends one day a month on Ward Y and cuts as many patients' hair as he has time for. Those whom the barber misses—at least 20 and often many more than this— must be given haircuts by one or another employee. For reasons of efficiency, ease of care, and prevention of disease, patients are given crew cuts (the only patients exempted are those whose parents object to this kind of haircut). Patients are also shaved at least once a week. Shaving takes place in the ward barber shop and is ordinarily performed by a helper who uses an electric razor. Some patients, however, are frightened by the buzzing noise of the electric razor and must be shaved with a safety razor; in these cases, an employee does the shaving.

Patients on Ward Y received a total of 812 visits during the last year—an average of 15.6 visits per week. Although there is an occasional open house or family party, visits usually consist of one or both parents of a patient spending a part of the day with their son in the ward's reception room, on the hospital grounds, or off the grounds entirely. When patients are scheduled to receive visitors—and administrative efforts are made to schedule these visits in advance—they are bathed, shaved, and dressed in company clothes immediately prior to the appointed visit.

The round of life here described is notably bleak and impersonal in its objective characteristics. However, the attitude of the staff does much to balance this. Ward employees do, in fact, evince an entirely sincere interest in the patients and regularly display both kindness and sympathy toward them. Nor is either staff or administration content with merely guiding their charge through an endless succession of similar appearing days. For example, on Saturday nights one staff member often shows travelogues, cartoons, and home movies on the ward. These films are projected onto the wall of the day hall and are viewed by all patients. Also, on most Saturday afternoons there is a party. Girls for these occasions are provided by Ward Q, which houses equally retarded ambulatory female patients. One week the party is on Ward Y, the next week it is held on the female ward. Only the toilet-trained and better-behaved patients participate; the others remain on the porch or in the play yard, indifferent to the festivities. Party-going patients are dressed in their best clothing, the ward is decorated, refreshments are served, phonograph records are played, and dancing is attempted with at least an occasional semblance of partial success. It should also be noted that the hospital provides a variety of recreational activities in which varying numbers of patients from Ward Y sometimes participate. Thus, the more competent patients are frequently taken to the hospital canteen, and sometimes to the swimming pool or to listen to music. Once every month or so, some are taken off the hospital grounds to public parks, the beaches, restaurants, amusement parks, zoos, fairs, sport events, and the like. Needless to say, however, the participation of the least competent patients in these off-ward activities is of necessity strictly limited.

This said, it remains that these special events, while instantial of the good intentions of both staff and administration, stand in stark contrast to the mundane ward routine which *is* the patients' everyday life.

Discussion

At least one child out of every 1000 born in the United States will be an idiot—a person totally incapable throughout life of caring for his own needs. Many of these will be completely infirm and will live a vegetative existence, confined either to a hospital crib or to a wheelchair. Even those who are ambulatory, like the patients on Ward Y, will require institutional care of a most comprehensive nature. The preceding account of the institutional lives of the patients on Ward Y should have given some indication of the nature of the problems an institution faces in providing such care.

The cost of this care—roughly $300,000 per year for the 82 patients on Ward Y—is considerable. Not only is institutional care for the profoundly retarded costly, it is both practically and morally problematic, for it is subject to the vicissitudes of parental pressures, of state budgets, of administrative and legislative dicta, and of conflicting professional interests and circumstances. While students of social organization have directed much attention to institutions for the mentally ill, interest in institutions for the mentally retarded has been virtually nonexistent.

This singular neglect is the more curious when one considers the paradigmatic relevance of the mentally retarded to so many of social sciences' perennial issues. We invite, for instance, the consideration of the profoundly retarded as instructive examples of human beings whose capacity for culture is dramatically impaired. So construed, they stand on the threshold between man and not-man, and thus permit simultaneous inquiry into both the nature of man and the nature of culture-bearing animals.

Idiots' capacity for language is minimal (although it is greater than that of any of the nonhuman primates). This lack of language skills is, of course, related to their impoverished cultural and social behavior, but even the most rudimentary explication of the nature of this relationship awaits consideration. While they respond to some symbols, they create symbols only rarely if at all, they sustain little culture, develop few rules of their own, evidence relatively little exploratory curiosity, and their interaction with one another is both minimal and peculiarly ahistorical. In at least certain respects, then, they are less human than some infrahuman species. In short, the relationship between language, social interaction, and rule-oriented behavior is available here in vivo in a manner different from that found either among normal humans or normal nonhumans.

We recommend, too, that in the interaction between patients and staff it is possible to obtain a unique perspective on such concerns as responsibility, trust, competence, reciprocity, and the like—all of which have been from the beginning and remain quintessential to a proper study of mankind. Here such matters find a natural laboratory, for staff is necessarily concerned both with creating and sustaining the human character of its charge against a background of continually recurring evidence to the contrary.

In summary, the whole area of mental retardation is, for the social scientist, a research backwater; and profound mental retardation is totally ignored. The foregoing description of the everyday lives of institutionalized idiots is intended to provide an introduction to these profoundly incompetent beings. Our own research has already taken us into analyses of both the practical and theoretical problems posed by such as these. By describing what has previously not been recorded and by recommending its theoretical relevance, we would hope to interest others in similar inquiry.

NORMALIZATION

In recent years a radical shift in placement of the severely retarded has occurred, with a trend toward placement in facilities that are smaller in size and community-based. As Nirje (1969) describes it, "The normalization principle means making available to the mentally retarded patterns and conditions of everyday life which are as close as possible to the norms and patterns of the mainstream of society." This Scandinavian principle has widespread support throughout the United States, with its most ardent advocates portraying large institutions as unsalvageable. Wolfensberger (1971), for instance, called on superintendents of large institutions to do all in their power to phase out their institutions and promote new service-delivery models. But as Edgerton and his associates (1975) have noted, the claims that smaller programs are more humane, less expensive, and more individualized (and thereby superior) are simply not supported by extant research.

Butterfield (1977) concurred with Wolfensberger (1971) about the humanitarian goal of having retarded persons live in the least restrictive environment possible and about the importance of promoting behaviors that are as culturally normative as possible. He questioned, however, the wisdom of using the most culturally normative means possible to meet this end. In other words, the relative emphasis on normative means versus normative ends is debatable. In addition, Butterfield challenges the assumptions that no institution can be normative enough for any retarded person and that all institutions should be phased out and closed. As we will see later in this chapter, there is some doubt about the wisdom of placing profoundly retarded persons (and some severely retarded persons) in community residential facilities.

What Constitutes a Normalized Environment?

The most extensive efforts to provide normalized environments for retarded persons have been in Sweden and Denmark, but the literature describing these efforts is more programmatic than scientific (e.g., Bank-Mikkelson 1968; Dybwad 1970; Nirje 1969). And the efforts in the United States that have been reported only rarely specify what is meant by normalization.

A range of alternative residential placements for retarded persons has been described by various authors (Edgerton et al. 1975; Wolfensberger 1971). The two major dimensions on which they differ from large institutions are size and geographic location. Among the alternatives are home care facilities (hostels), family care facilities (Elliott & Mackay 1971; Justice, O'Connor, & Warren 1971), day care centers (Best 1965), sheltered workshops (Doll 1967), village communities (Forbes 1972), and halfway houses (Graebner 1969). But Edgerton and his associates (1975) complain about the lack of specificity of such models:

> Much is made of the shift from a large impersonal institution to a small family-model hostel. But what is meant by a family? Is it to be nuclear, extended, multigenerational? What qualities of life constitute a family? Are they purely affective, involving trust, love, and community; or are there essential structural and communicative features as well? Can a surrogate family ever succeed? Is there a model of "family" that they now share? Must these surrogate families always be one of "orientation"—based on a marital relationship and responsibilities to children? Needless to say, we do not know.
>
> (p.77)

Despite this uncertainty about the human factors in normalization, we can infer from the literature certain features of a normalized *physical* environment. Roos (1970b) described normalized environments as "homelike," including private bathrooms, small dining areas, lamps, carpeting or rugs, and the kinds of furniture found in typical homes. These characteristics are in contrast to the large institutional wards, where efficiency considerations have led to less privacy, tile floors, eating in common dining rooms, and so on. Since the size of living units is also of major concern to normalization advocates, newer state institutions are including smaller living units (fewer than 30 residents). But common bathing and eating facilities continue due to the ease of supervision and safety considerations.

In addition to their size and furnishings, it is thought that small living units should be located in or near population centers instead of being geographically isolated. They should provide opportunities for residents to become involved in the surrounding community through activities such as museum visits, hiking, and parties, or through working in the community when resident characteristics permit. According to the advocates of normalization, such physical changes should produce positive changes in the personalities and development of retarded persons. As Shapiro (1973) wrote, it is thought that life in a group home will give "the retarded adult dignity, identity, privacy, and motivation for community involvement" (p. 20). criticism:

But Edgerton and his associates (1975) question this assumption that normalization will improve the personal lives of retarded individuals. They ask whether retarded persons feel normalized, suggesting that it is possible that such arrangements make the retarded a part of the community physically but prohibit them from participating socially or psychologically. Their point is that physical placement may be far less important to the quality of a retarded person's life than social and psychological factors, which should receive serious consideration in normalization effects.

Early Attempts at Implementation

Early attempts to translate normalization principles into practice involved efforts to develop community alternatives to large institutions when out-of-home placement was necessary. These efforts (Scheerenberger 1974; Throne 1975) were not altogether successful; in fact, the evidence indicates that residents of institutions were prematurely placed in inappropriate, underprogramed community facilities. In evaluating the foster home program in Canada, Murphy, Rennee, and Luchins (1972) found that there was little interaction between residents and family, regimentation was common, and residents frequently had no interaction with the community.

These experiences are not typical, but we cite them as a reminder that retarded individuals are vulnerable to abuses in all programs. Regardless of the residential setting, care must be exercised to prevent violations of their rights. This concern is expressed in a statement by the National Association of Superintendents of Public Residential Facilities for the Mentally Retarded (1974):

> While the Association advocates without reservation the rights of the retarded to live in the least restrictive environment and to enjoy fully the benefits of a free and open society whenever possible, it does express concern over the manner in which this goal is being realized. First, the quality of community programs and services being offered to the mentally retarded and other developmentally disabled persons in many parts of the country is inadequate. All too often, "community back wards" and "closeting" [being shut up at home] are being substituted for institutional "warehousing." Neither community nor residential back wards or "closeting" are justified: the rights of the retarded must be respected wherever they reside.
>
> (pp. 2–3)

Normalization: Means or End?

In a provocative article, Throne (1975) accepts normalization as a goal toward which we should try to move the retarded but questions it as a means to achieve that goal. He points out that the fact that people are classified as mentally retarded is evidence that the normative environment did not foster normal development in them. Their retardation requires specialized techniques to promote more rapid development and help retarded persons to function at a normal level. As Fram (1974) has argued, we should not get carried away with treating retarded individuals as though they were normal; because they are retarded, they have a right to special services, which may not be altogether normal. According to Throne, normative procedures (efforts at making the environment more normal) work best for persons who are normal, but tend to be ineffective for persons who are retarded. Specialized procedures, he argues, should have priority over normative procedures if the retarded individual is to be maximally benefitted.

Community Residential Facilities

Early attempts to implement normalization have consisted largely in moving retarded persons out of institutions into community residential facilities (CRFs) of various types. CRFs differ from institutions in two important ways: they are smaller and they tend to be located in urban and residential areas. CRFs are regarded by most as an improvement over institutions, although large-scale deinstitutionalization without preplanning has been criticized by Throne (1979) and others. Wolfensberger (1972) is among those who have praised the move to deinstitutionalization. Like institutions, CRFs vary in their facilities, location, staff turnover, rehabilitation efforts, staff qualifications and attitudes, and a host of other factors, all of which influence the quality of life experienced by the residents. In the following sections, we will consider the various types of CRFs, who lives in them, whether they meet normalization criteria, and how they affect their residents. Extensive critical analyses of the research on CRFs is available in several excellent reviews (Bruininks, Thurlow, Thurman, & Fiorelli 1980; Butterfield 1977; Eyman, Silverstein, McLain, & Miller 1977; Heal, Sigelman, & Switzky 1978; Janicki 1981; O'Connor 1976).

The deinstitutionalization of retarded persons and their placement in CRFs has proceeded at an impressive rate. According to Bruininks, Hauber, & Kudla (1980), over 30,000 mentally retarded persons were shifted from state-operated facilities to community residences between 1960 and 1969. The major national demographic surveys (Bruininks, Hauber, & Kudla 1979; Scheerenberger 1979) support the observation that CRFs are being used increasingly. Bruininks et al. (1980) reported the year of opening of the 4290 CRFs in existence in 1977 (Figure 14.1). As you can see, the number has been increasing each year. Note that a rapid upswing in the opening of new CRFs started in 1968. The number of CRFs varies considerably from state to state, however; O'Connor (1976) found that nearly half of all CRFs were located in six states, whereas thirty states had fewer than eight facilities that met her definition of a CRF.

But what constitutes a community residence facility? Definitions vary considerably. Janicki (1981), for example, defined them as follows:

> A community residence is defined as a community-based residence facility that operates 24 hours a day to provide services to a small group of disabled people who are presently or potentially capable of functioning in a community setting with some degree of independence.
>
> (p. 60)

FIGURE 14.1   Year of Opening for 4290 Community Residential
Facilities in the United States in 1977 (87 percent
reporting)

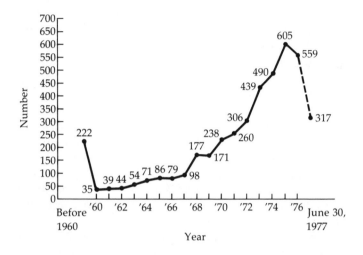

From R. H. Bruininks, F. A. Hauber, and M. J. Kudla, "National survey of community residential facilities:
A profile of facilities and residents in 1977," *American Journal of Mental Deficiency*, 1980, **84**, 470–478.
Reprinted by permission of the authors and the American Association on Mental Deficiency.

O'Connor (1976) altered this definition to exclude foster family placement
(which typically serves five or fewer persons), nursing homes, and other
facilities designed primarily to serve the health needs of their clients.
Eyman and Borthwick (1980) and others include convalescent hospitals,
since they are an alternative to institutionalization. It is important to realize
that CRFs vary in many ways—in the number of persons they serve, the
residential environment, the rehabilitative intent of the staff, the proximity
to community services, and the type of residents. The location of the facility
in a community is a prerequisite of normalization, but good location alone
is clearly not sufficient to ensure normalization.

Residents of CRFs.   Not everyone who requires out-of-home placement
is a likely candidate for CRF placement; neither are all retarded persons
candidates. As noted earlier, the institutionalized retarded differ in many
ways from the noninstitutionalized retarded, and any research comparing
the two must consider the influence of selective bias. Similarly, retarded
persons who live in large residential institutions differ from those who live
in CRFs of various kinds. Eyman and Borthwick (1980) found that retarded
persons living in community placements had an average IQ of 48, whereas

those living in institutions and convalescent hospitals had an average IQ of only 25. In addition, those living in community placements were better able to take care of themselves. Systematic differences were also found between residents of institutions and residents of convalescent hospitals. The institutionalized group had more severe behavioral problems in both personal and social areas, while convalescent hospital residents lacked basic self-help skills. These findings indicate that institutions, largely because the more able residents have been deinstitutionalized, have come to serve a severely debilitated population whose maladaptive behavior precludes the possibility of community placement, at least until their behaviors are modified. Similarly, convalescent hospital residents need better self-help skills before they can be considered for alternative community placement.

Surveys by O'Connor (1976) and Bruininks, Hauber, and Kudla (1980) indicate that the higher-level mentally retarded predominate in CRFs. O'Connor reported the following breakdown by level of retardation: (1) above IQ 70—22.6 percent, (2) mild—30.2 percent, (3) moderate—27.7 percent, (4) severe—17.1 percent, (5) profound—2.4 percent. Bruininks et al. (1980) reported this breakdown: (1) borderline—8.0 percent, (2) mild—22.4 percent, (3) moderate—35.3 percent, (4) severe—21.8 percent, (5) profound—10.6 percent, and (6) unknown—1.9 percent. There is little question that CRFs primarily serve mentally retarded subjects with IQs above 40 and serve relatively few severely and profoundly retarded residents. Janicki (1981) observed that community residences are an alternative for retarded persons who do not need the structure or restrictive services provided in institutions. Methods of determining who can prosper in CRFs deserve further study. It seems safe to say, however, that CRFs are not the answer for all retarded persons who cannot remain at home.

CRFs and Normalization.   Baroff (1980) suggests that smaller residential facilities should offer *individualization possibilities,* which are more difficult to implement in larger facilities. Small size alone, however, does not guarantee a more normalized environment—poorly run small residences can have environments just as impersonal and debilitating as institutions. Bjaanes, Butler, and Kelly (1980) suggest a distinction between *environmental* normalization and *client* normalization. Environmental normalization is the "process of developing culturally normative and appropriate residences and services, devoid of the dehumanizing stigma so often attached to being mentally retarded" (p. 2). Client normalization, on the other hand, is the "acquisition of necessary skills for . . . assuming culturally normative social roles and responsibilities" (p. 2).

Small size is often associated with effective normalization. The King and Raynes research reviewed earlier in the chapter (King & Raynes 1968; Raynes & King 1968; Tizard 1960, 1964) indicated that normalization is also influenced by the practices in different placements. *Institution-centered prac-*

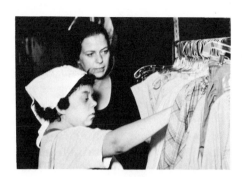

tices include rigid routines, regimentation of residents, depersonalization, and limited interaction between staff and residents. These practices are regarded by the staff as easing the operation of the residence. *Resident-oriented practices* include treating residents as individuals and giving them more autonomy in personal rights and choices. Presumably, resident-oriented practices are more likely to lead to a normalized environment.

O'Connor (1976) used several criteria to determine whether facilities were normalized: (1) the architecture of the building, (2) security features such as high fences, bars on windows, and locked areas, (3) personal effects in the sleeping area, (4) privacy in bathrooms and bedrooms, (5) characteristics of furniture (institutional or homelike), and (6) the interviewer's judgment of the general atmosphere and management of the facility. Applying these criteria to 611 facilities, she found that 69 percent were normalized. The large residences were less likely to be normalized; however, even though more than two-thirds of the *residences* were normalized, less than half of the *total population* in the facilities studied lived in normalized environments. Paradoxically, a high ratio of staff to residents was found to be associated with more normalized environments (a large staff is seen as likely to reduce the freedom of residents). It is possible that additional training in skills that promote independence compensated for the loss of freedom.

Certainly some CRFs are not normalized, as evidenced by the typology of Butler and Bjaanes (1977). These researchers divided community homes into three categories: custodial, therapeutic, and maintaining. Custodial homes provide little supervision and few activities and do not actively foster normalizing activities. Therapeutic environments actively support ongoing efforts to implement normalizing experiences. Maintaining environments fall in between, with residents maintaining their initial levels of competence. It is difficult, however, to make generalizations, even about a particular type of CRF, such as board-and-care or home care facilities. Bjaanes and Butler (1974) examined these two types of CRFs and found, contrary to their expectations, that larger facilities with thirty to fifty residents provided conditions more consistent with normalization criteria than smaller facilities with four to six residents. The two home care facilities, however, differed so much that generalizations were difficult to make.

Problems in Community Placements.   Although placement in the community affords retarded persons more normalized experiences and can foster more favorable attitudes in society, it also removes the protective aspect of institutions and exposes the retarded person to potentially damaging and sometimes even dangerous experiences. Nihira and Nihira (1975) conducted 109 interviews with caretakers to determine whether the community placement of formerly institutionalized residents increased the risk to residents or the citizens of the communities in which they were placed.

They reported 1252 instances of problem behavior, which they classified in three categories: (1) health and safety, (2) general welfare, or (3) the law. In 80 percent of the incidents, the danger was to the perpetrators themselves. Their fellow retarded residents were at risk in 12 percent of the incidents, and the general public in 9 percent. Danger to health and safety was by far the most frequent problem, constituting some 77 percent of the incidents. The incidents involved such problems as faulty eating habits, violence, getting lost, and sexual activities. Whether these problems would have been less severe in an institution is debatable; the point is that placement in the community is not without its risks.

Another problem to consider is why certain persons have to be returned to institutions. Gottesfeld's (1977) findings were consistent with those reviewed earlier—the major reason for rehospitalization of community-placed retarded persons was behavior that was bizarre, aggressive, or otherwise severely deviant. Crawford, Aiello, and Thompson (1979) concluded, after a review of the literature on reasons for readmission to hospitals or institutions, that failure of community adjustment is predicted best by maladaptive behavior. Characteristics such as IQ, age, sex, and functional skill levels were found to be inconsistently related to success or failure in the community.

Effects of CRFs on Resident Behavior.   Ultimately, the success or failure of community placement is determined by whether it benefits the retarded residents of these facilities. It is *assumed* that CRFs are better for their residents because they are more resident-oriented and more normalized and because they permit the residents to make use of community resources. To date, however, research examining the effects of CRF placement on retarded residents has been concerned primarily with other topics—mortality, adaptive behavior, and social behavior.

Miller's (1975) study of mortality rates among the profoundly retarded, mentioned previously, was designed to determine whether they should be deinstitutionalized. Based on his findings, Miller concluded that "shifting the burden of care to other facilities does not cause any reduction in mortality and more likely increases it" (p. 8). Miller and Eyman (1978) also studied mortality rates in institutions, convalescent hospitals, and community placements, but their study considered cases over a three-year period. They found similar mortality rates among those living in institutions and those living in other community placements. The mortality rate in convalescent hospitals was considerably higher than either group. One must consider, however, that other community placements generally served higher-level mentally retarded persons than convalescent hospitals or institutions. Another important factor is the role of ambulation (the ability to walk) in mortality. When the investigators controlled for ambulation, the mortality rates for institutions and convalescent hospitals were reduced considerably.

This reflects the fact that convalescent hospitals tend to draw more non-ambulatory cases and more persons with problems in self-help skills.

Some retarded persons placed in the community have unique medical problems (see Chapter 4), which raises the possibility that they will receive medical services from physicians unfamiliar with their medical needs. In this regard, it is reassuring to know that the severely and profoundly retarded, who are more likely to have these problems, are placed in CRFs relatively infrequently. Nevertheless, mortality rates should continue to be monitored to prevent serious problems in this area.

Efforts to relate residential arrangements to development have been limited by the complex problems involved in measuring important residential variables and relating them to change, which occurs slowly in retarded persons. The measurement of change is currently generating great controversy in the fields of psychology and education. Eyman et al. (1977) measured changes in personal self-sufficiency, community self-sufficiency, and personal and social responsibility among retarded persons living in institutions, convalescent hospitals, and other community facilities. This three-year study indicated that environmental characteristics were responsible for variations in growth in all three areas of development and in all three types of facilities. The foster care homes and board-and-care facilities promoted the most positive changes, and the less severely retarded subjects changed the most. Eyman, Demaine, and Lei (1979) found that the development of retarded persons was related to residential variables derived from the normalization principle, including administrative policies, environmental blending of the facility with the neighborhood, location and proximity of services, comfort, and appearance. The study also indicated that older and less retarded residents improved in overall adaptive behavior regardless of where they lived. Such findings are promising insofar as they indicate that normalization produces not merely cosmetic changes, but genuine developmental changes in retarded persons. It is to be hoped that normalization actually caused the beneficial effects.

Landesman-Dwyer and her associates (Landesman-Dwyer, Berkson, & Romer 1979; Landesman-Dwyer & Sackett 1978; Landesman-Dwyer, Sackett, & Kleinman 1980; Landesman-Dwyer, Stein, & Sackett 1978) have completed extensive observations of the mentally retarded in various living arrangements in an effort to relate factors such as size of facility and treatment patterns to various social behaviors. Observations were made in community residences ranging in size from six to twenty residents. This research failed to discover relationships between the factors studied and the daily activities of residents or the behavior of staff members. The investigators were able, however, to discern differences in the behavior of residents. Landesman-Dwyer et al. (1979) related size of the residence to the affiliative behavior of the residents. Residents in larger homes (eighteen to twenty residents) spent more time interacting with peers, associated with more peers in a day, and were more likely to have a "best friend" than residents of smaller homes (six to nine residents). The expected beneficial influence of smaller units on social behavior was not supported by these findings. In another paper, Landesman-Dwyer et al. (1980) speculated that very small CRFs have too few people in them to make it likely that many people would find a "best friend." These findings raise questions regarding the optimal size of a CRF, suggesting that some facilities may be too small to promote desirable social behaviors and affiliations. Another unexpected finding was that interactions between staff and residents did not vary with the size of facility—the presumed "opportunities for individualization" in smaller residences were not found to exist. Other researchers too have speculated that some facilities are too small (Janicki 1981); this issue should be addressed by more research. Since Landesman-Dwyer did not consider homes with more than twenty residents, the question of when increases in size begin to detract from the affiliative behavior of the residents remains to be answered.

Some evidence suggests that residents of CRFs who previously lived in institutions prefer their life-style in the community. Aninger and Bolinsky (1977) reported that residents of a community apartment program were quite happy in their residences. None of the eighteen subjects expressed a desire to return to the institution. Similarly, McDevitt, Smith, Schmidt, and Rosen (1978) and Scheerenberger and Felsenthal (1977) reported that interviews with former institutional residents indicated that they were content in their community residence and basically satisfied with their adjustment. In the McDevitt et al. study, the residents expressed pride in themselves and in their accomplishments in adjusting to the community.

SUMMARY

Institutions for retarded persons have not always met with the criticism heaped on them today. At first they were optimistic places where well-wishing families sent their retarded children to be cured. They didn't cure the retarded, though, and as the public became afraid of its retarded members, institutions turned into places where they could be excluded from society. Current institutions are large and located in sparsely inhabited out-of-the-way places; they continue to serve a portion of the retarded population, with varying degrees of humanity.

Today some parents send their severely retarded children to residential institutions and some keep them at home. In an attempt to discover what makes the difference, we found that the child's own characteristics are partly responsible. IQ, age, degree of physical handicaps, sex, and behaviors may all influence the parents' decision. Their decision is also subject to family factors, such as socioeconomic class, religion, whether the parents are divorced, whether there are normal children in the household, and whether the family or others in the community perceive the child as troublesome. Outside factors that have been identified include community pressures, whether services for retarded children are locally available, the attitude of physicians or psychologists serving the family, economic conditions, and trends in public attitudes toward retarded individuals.

Critics of institutions have found terrible conditions in some "human warehouses," but these conditions do not exist everywhere. Both good and bad practices can be found in small institutions as well as large ones. Among the specific factors that may have detrimental effects on residents are conflicts between the professional and custodial staffs, personnel who place their own interests before those of the residents, understaffing or the hiring of unqualified staff, overcrowding, and underfinancing. Patients themselves are often prevailed upon to help with routine chores, but whether this is altogether a bad practice is hard to say.

The evidence of direct ways in which institutions affect their residents is based on generalizations from samplings at certain institutions, which may or may not be representative of the range of variation among institutions. Institution residents tend to die young, but their premature deaths may be caused by their retardation rather than their institutionalization. Institutions seem to depress intellectual functioning, but this effect may be avoidable. If more attendants would engage residents in meaningful conversation, their verbal abilities might improve even within the institutional setting. A major effect of institutionalization on personality seems to be an abnormal need for contact with an approving adult, which may handicap the retarded person's growth. But whether this need is a symptom of the failure experiences associated with retardation or of impersonal institutional practices—and if so, whether they could be remedied—is not yet clear.

Life in an institution is at least partly affected by hierarchies formed by the residents themselves. Groups form according to degree of handicapping, knowledge of "hip" behavior from the outside, and amenability to rehabilitation, with resulting power struggles and alliances with ward attendants or therapeutic staff. But most descriptions of these groupings were written when institutions housed a broader variety of retarded people. Today it is only the more severely retarded who remain in institutions.

The trend toward normalization has been enthusiastically adopted in this country, although no one is really sure how to translate it into practice. Attempts at providing normalized environments as an alternative to large institutions have at least two things in common: they are smaller than institutions and less geographically isolated. But whether they make retarded individuals feel less isolated from the normal community is debatable. In some cases, small residential programs may meet the needs of residents no better than the much-criticized large institutions.

Attempts to normalize the living conditions of the retarded through the creation of CRFs have instigated many studies of the relative merits of CRFs and institutions. Thus far, it appears that small size alone does not assure a normalized environment, and some evidence suggests that when CRFs are too small the affiliative behavior of the residents is restricted. Generalization is difficult, however, because there are many differences among CRFs. Surprisingly, the behavior of the staff toward the residents does not seem to vary with the size of the residence, even though there are more opportunities for individualization in smaller residences. Although CRFs have failed to achieve all that was hoped of them, there is some evidence that these facilities, which reflect elements of the normalization principle, do promote improvements in adaptive behavior, with the greatest improvements occurring among the less severely retarded and older residents. Finally, CRF residents who formerly lived in institutions seem to enjoy their new residences and express no desire to return to the institution.

GLOSSARY

adaptive behavior: Exhibiting behaviors judged appropriate for an individual's age and cultural group to achieve personal independence and social responsibility. Three major aspects of these behaviors specified by the AAMD are maturation, learning, and social adjustment.

amniocentesis: A procedure in which a small amount of the amniotic fluid surrounding the fetus is drawn from the uterus and then subjected to cytogenetic or biochemical analysis.

anoxia: A blood condition in which the oxygen content is insufficient to maintain normal functioning of tissue. The tissue of the brain is particularly susceptible to this insufficiency.

aspiration level: Personally set performance objectives or goals against which the individual can evaluate subsequent performance.

associative learning: Learning in which the individual is required to recall one stimulus when presented with another (e.g., paired associates learning).

atrophy: A condition characterized by the deterioration or wasting of tissue, organs, or the entire body.

behavior modification: A generic term referring to a variety of techniques derived from various learning theories that are designed to alter existing behavior in some predetermined manner. These procedures all include common elements—especially the systematic arrangement of stimuli that are related to responses and the reliance on observable events. This generic term subsumes numerous concepts, including operant learning, respondent learning, observational learning, and contingency management.

birth injury: A trauma that occurs during the birth process that has either a temporary or a permanent effect.

chromosome abnormality: Any difference from what is normally found in the state or structure of the gene carriers of the cell nucleus.

congenital: Present at birth, including conditions that were either inherited or caused during gestation.

contingency management: The manipulation of environmental stimuli by specifying the conditions that behavior must meet before consequences will be forthcoming, with the aim of achieving specified behavioral goals.

cretinism: A condition resulting from a congenital thyroid deficiency that causes mental retardation. Symptoms include delayed skeletal development, large protruding tongue, and thick and dry skin.

cultural deprivation (cultural disadvantage): A constellation of environmental factors that collectively is considered to cause insufficient or inappropriate learning on the part of children reared under such conditions. These learning deficiencies are seen to interfere with educational and social adaptation, even though some of the learning is appropriate to the subculture.

cultural-familial retardation: Mild mental retardation with no known cause associated with a family history of low intellectual functioning. In cases of this type one must find at least one parent and sibling that are also retarded; such cases are found most commonly in low socioeconomic class families.

cytogenetics: A branch of biology concerned with the study of heredity that is relevant to the prevention of mental retardation in cases of inherited conditions or in analysis of fluid obtained through amniocentesis.

cytomegalic inclusion disease: A congenital infection characterized in the newborn by cells with inclusion bodies that can affect any organ system. In newborns this condition frequently involves the central nervous system and is potentially fatal; irreversible brain damage is found often in those who survive.

dependent mentally retarded: Those retarded persons requiring considerable direct supervision in social, academic, and daily living activities.

developmental disability: A disability originating prenatally or in the early years of life that is likely to persist. It can be a physical, mental, emotional, or speech disorder and can differ in the extent to which it handicaps individuals.

dominant inheritance: A pattern of inheritance in which a trait is determined by the dominant gene contributed by either parent. In such cases a dominant gene overrides the effect of the recessive gene contributed by the other parent and determines the phenotype. When one parent has the gene dominant for a trait there is a 50 percent chance of each offspring's manifesting that trait.

Down's syndrome (mongolism): A syndrome usually characterized by trisomy of chromosome 21. It accounts for the largest number of mentally retarded persons for whom etiology can be established. Mental retardation is accompanied by various clinical manifestations, among the most apparent of which are epicanthic folds, large tongue, broad and flat bridge of the nose, and poor muscle tone.

educable mentally retarded (EMR): That subgroup of retarded students capable of mastering fundamental academic skills such as reading and arithmetic. As adults, former EMR students are usually self-sufficient and independent. An approximate IQ range for this group is IQ 50 to 70; however, many students in this IQ range are never classified as EMR.

encephalitis: An inflammation of the brain caused by a response of tissue to toxins or infections.

etiology: The cause or origin of a condition or disease.

feeble-minded: A term no longer used, but that in the past referred to individuals with milder forms of retardation.

galactosemia: A congenital disorder causing elevated levels of galactose in the blood. This disorder can cause infant death or mental retardation.

genetic counseling: Counseling that interprets genetic information to parents; emphasis is commonly on the probabilities of their offspring's inheriting a genetically determined disorder.

genotype: The genetic makeup of an individual.

handicapped individual: A person significantly hindered in learning, social behavior, or occupational performance as a consequence of a physical, mental, emotional, or speech disability. Some developmentally disabled persons are not handicapped—and handicaps may either occur in only one area of performance (e.g., learning) or involve several areas of performance.

hemolytic disease of newborns: A blood disorder caused by maternal antibodies transferred through the placenta that destroys red blood cells in the fetus and causes oxygen deprivation. Among the factors causing this condition are Rh incompatibility and A or B incompatibility.

hostel: A relatively small, community-based group home providing supervision of residents' needs but allowing for community involvement to the maximum extent of the individual's capability.

hyperactivity: Excessive activity level for an individual of a particular age in a given setting; above-normal use of energy.

hypoactivity: Lower than normal use of energy for an individual of a particular age in a given setting—often described as sluggishness, listlessness, or slowness of movement.

idiot: An obsolete term used in the past to refer to an IQ level below 25 or 30; analogous to the SPMR.

imbecile: An obsolete term that in the past referred to the IQ level between 25 or 30 and 50 (approximately equivalent to the TMR range).

institution: Used in the text to refer to a public or private facility in which mentally retarded persons reside 24 hours a day and that provides services to them. Generally speaking, however, the term describes larger facilities, as contrasted to smaller hostels or foster care homes that depend on outside agencies for such services as medical care.

intelligence: A combination of abilities to perceive and understand relationships and carry on abstract reasoning, as well as one's total knowledge as measured by standardized tests such as the Stanford-Binet or Wechsler scales.

intelligence quotient (IQ): An index used to indicate an individual's relative level of performance on tests of intelligence. Formerly computed as mental age divided by chronological age times 100; now test manuals for major scales provide tables for converting scores to IQ in terms of standard scores.

karyotype: A photograph of a cell nucleus in which chromosome pairs are arranged systematically according to decreasing size and their structural characteristics (determined by the position of the centomere).

kernicterus: A blood condition in which the bilirubin level is abnormally high. The causes are several, but the condition can result in oxygen deficiency to the brain if not treated.

kwashiorkor: A condition resulting from severe protein deprivation despite reasonable caloric intake. It has several manifestations in children between the ages of four months and five years, including diarrhea, edema, and dermatitis.

lead poisoning: A poisoning of the central nervous system resulting from the ingestion of lead.

maladaptive behavior: Behavior judged as significantly below acceptable standards for a person's age and cultural peer group; the judgment is based on an evaluation of independent functioning and acceptance of social responsibility. In the behavioristic framework, the phrase refers to any behavior judged as inappropriate by the behavior analyst.

meningitis: Inflammation of the membranes of the brain or spinal cord that may have detrimental effects on hearing, intellectual functioning, or vision.

mental age (MA): A measured level of mental ability derived from a test of intelligence.

mental deficiency: A term sometimes used to designate that segment of the mentally retarded population whose intellectual deficits are due to organic causes. In other sources this term is used interchangeably with mental retardation.

mentally ill: A category that subsumes a variety of conditions in which the individual has personal problems or exhibits maladaptive behavior for reasons other than limited intellectual ability.

mental retardation: "Significantly subaverage general intellectual functioning existing concurrently with deficits in adaptive behavior, and manifested during the developmental period" (AAMD 1977).

metabolic disorder: Any condition that interferes with normal metabolic processes.

microcephaly: A condition characterized by a small head and mental retardation ranging in degree from moderate to profound. It can be transmitted genetically (primary microcephaly) or it may result from lesions due to prenatal infections, trauma, or birth injury.

moron: An obsolete term formerly used to designate that segment of the mentally retarded population with milder disabilities—roughly analogous to the EMR range.

mosaicism: A condition in which two or more "lines" of cells containing different genetic information are present in the same individual. All cells are not necessarily affected; individuals may possess some normal cells and some with trisomy 21, for example.

mutation: A condition in which a gene is changed in character, resulting in a new type of gene.

neurosis: A functional disorder less severe than psychosis that interferes with the adaptation of the person exhibiting behaviors judged abnormal. The general term subsumes various manifestations including anxiety, hysteria, obsessions, and phobias.

nondisjunction: An error caused by improper cell division resulting in a cell with an excess of one chromosome and another cell without that chromosome. This error accounts for the most common form of Down's syndrome, where there is an additional (or third) chromosome in what is normally the 21st pair.

normalization: A principle stating that services and treatment for disabled persons be provided to enable them to reside in a manner as close as possible to what is normal in a given society, based on the individual's capabilities.

perception: An awareness of neurologically transmitted stimuli, including visual, auditory, tactile, and kinesthetic sensations. As measured, perception includes both the awareness of the stimuli and the reaction or response made by the organism.

perseveration: A response pattern characterized by the involuntary continuation of a response beyond the point of being correct. Involves an inability or unwillingness to shift to a new response pattern or mental formation until the original pattern has run its temporal course.

phenotype: Those characteristics of the individual that can be observed or measured—one's appearance or abilities.

phenylketonuria (PKU): An inherited metabolic disorder that prevents proper metabolizing of a substance found in proteins (phenylalanine), resulting in high serum levels of phenyl-pyruvic acid. If untreated, the major consequence is almost always mental retardation, but this condition can be detected and treated by changing the diet, which minimizes the adverse consequences.

postmaturity: A gestation period exceeding the normal period by 7 days or more. The principle danger is that the placenta can degenerate, leading to a progressive reduction in the oxygen and nourishment reaching the fetus.

prematurity: A gestation period of less than 37 weeks. Newborns weighing 2500 grams or less have often been referred to as premature, but low birth weight can also be caused by a slower growth rate, so birth weight alone is an insufficient basis for inferring prematurity.

prenatal: Refers to the period before birth.

prognosis: A prediction of the future mental, physical, or social performance of an individual.

psychometrics: The measurement and evaluation of behavior; the aspect of behavior receiving the most attention has been intelligence.

recessive inheritance: A pattern of inheritance in which a trait is manifested only if both members of a chromosome pair carry the gene for that trait. If both parents carry the trait the probability that the child will manifest that trait is 25 percent; the probability that the child will not inherit a gene for that trait from either parent is 25 percent; and the probability that the child will be a carrier (an inheritor of only one gene for the trait) is 50 percent.

response: A unit into which behavior can be segmented, then observed and measured. Two kinds of responses are commonly distinguished; operant responses, which are voluntary and emitted, and respondent responses, which are involuntary and elicited by stimuli.

Rh incompatibility: This occurs when the mother has Rh negative blood and the fetus Rh positive. When blood leaks from the fetus into the mother's bloodstream, antibodies are produced that destroy Rh positive blood cells. This can cause abortions, stillbirth, kernicterus, or mental retardation. Procedures are available to prevent pathology.

rubella (German measles): A mild infection that, if contracted during the first trimester of the pregnancy, can cause deafness, cardiac malformations, or mental retardation in the child.

severe and profoundly mentally retarded (SPMR): That subset of mentally retarded persons of very low IQ (below 25 or 30) and requiring intensive supervision for academic and social functioning and daily living.

sheltered workshop: A structured program of activities, commonly used with TMR-level persons, designed to achieve placement in the competitive labor market. Employees are taught occupational skills as well as work-related attributes while functioning in this protective environment. They are paid for their work at a level consistent with limited production output.

slow learner: A term sometimes used to describe children whose academic, intellectual, and social behavior are below the mean for their peer group but above the cutoff for mental retardation (on IQ, it would be those cases between one and two standard deviations below the mean). In a few states this term has been used synonymously with EMR, but this is not common.

social responsibility: The ability of the individual to exhibit behaviors reflecting acceptance of accountability as a member of a social group. Behaviors indicating social responsibility include conformity, emotional maturity, and social adjustment. It is one component of adaptive behavior.

special class: A special education administrative arrangement characterized by a smaller pupil/teacher ratio to which children are assigned on the basis of a disability label (e.g., EMR, learning-disabled). Usually the age group is kept within a range of two or four years and the teacher has specialized training in instructing children with a specific disability.

stimulus: A unit into which the environment can be segmented, defined in terms of its function. Among the different types are eliciting stimuli, reinforcing stimuli, discriminative stimuli, and punishing stimuli.

Tay-Sachs disease: An inherited condition, transmitted by a recessive gene, that is largely restricted to children of Jewish ancestry from northeastern Europe. This condition results in progressive deterioration (paralysis, blindness) and finally in death.

toxoplasmosis: A condition resulting from an infection by an intestinal parasite; in its congenital form it is frequently manifested by a syndrome characterized by mental retardation, convulsions, and hydrocephalus or microcephaly.

trainable mentally retarded (TMR): That subgroup of retarded students who are capable only of very few basic academic skills. These students can profit from training in self-help skills, social behavior, and certain vocational skills. Approximate IQ guidelines for this group range from 25 or 30 to 50 or 55.

transfer of training: The facilitating or debilitating effect of learning one thing on learning something else. If the transfer is facilitative it is called *positive transfer;* if learning one thing interferes with learning something else it is called *negative transfer.*

translocation: A condition resulting from improper cell division, with all or a portion of one chromosome attaching itself onto another chromosome. Translocations occur most often in the 13 to 15 or 21 to 22 group of chromosomes, which constrict near the end of the chromosome. Though it accounts for some cases of Down's syndrome, translocation is not as common as nondisjunction.

trisomy 21: See Down's syndrome.

tuberous sclerosis: A syndrome caused by either dominant or recessive inheritance, often characterized by seizures and mental retardation.

X-linked inheritance: A pattern of maternally transmitted inheritance, with manifestation of a trait more common in males than females. In males, the Y chromosome lacks genetic information, so the trait carried on the X chromosome is manifested. Since a female offspring has two X chromosomes and the trait usually is not matched, there is a lower incidence among females.

BIBLIOGRAPHY

Abeson, A., Burgdorf, R. L., Casey, P. J., Kunz, J. W., & McNeil, W. Access to opportunity. In N. Hobbs (Ed.), *Issues in the classification of children.* Vol. 2, pp. 270–92. San Francisco: Jossey-Bass, 1975.

Abraham, W. *Barbara: A prologue.* New York: Holt, Rinehart, 1958.

Abramowicz, H. K., & Richardson, S. A. Epidemiology of severe mental retardation in children: Community studies. *American Journal of Mental Deficiency,* 1975, **80,** 18–39.

Abroms, K. I., & Bennett, J. W. Current genetic and demographic findings in Down's syndrome: How are they presented in college textbooks on exceptionality? *Mental Retardation,* 1980, **18,** 101–07.

Adelman, H. S. The resource concept: Bigger than a room. *Journal of Special Education,* 1972, **6,** 361–67.

Ad Hoc Committee on Educational Uses of Tests with Disadvantaged Students. Educational uses of tests with disadvantaged students. *American Psychologist,* 1975, **30,** 15–41.

Agard, J. A. Training conceptual organization in retarded children. Unpublished doctoral dissertation, University of Michigan, 1971.

Akers, R. Problems in the sociology of deviance: Social definitions and behavior. *Social Forces,* 1968, **46,** 455–65.

Allen, R. M., Cortazzo, A. D., & Toister, R. P. (Eds.) *Symposium on the role of genetics in mental retardation, Miami, 1970.* Coral Gables, Fla.: University of Miami Press, 1971.

Aloia, G. F. Effects of physical stigmata and labels. *Mental Retardation,* 1975, **13**(6), 17–21.

Alper, S., & Retish, P. M. A comparative study of the effects of student teaching on the attitudes of students in special education, elementary education, and secondary education. *Training School Bulletin,* 1972, **69,** 70–71.

Altman, R., & Talkington, L. W. Modeling: An alternative behavior modification approach for retardates. *Mental Retardation,* 1971, **9**(3), 20–23.

Altman, R., Talkington, L. W., & Cleland, C. C. Relative effectiveness of modeling and verbal instructions on severe retardates' gross motor performance. *Psychological Reports,* 1972, **31,** 695–98.

Anastasi, A. *Psychological testing.* (4th ed.) New York: Macmillan, 1976.

Anastasiow, N. J. Strategies and models for early childhood intervention programs in integrated settings. In M.J. Guralnick (Ed.), *Early intervention and the integration of handicapped and nonhandicapped children,* pp. 85–111. Baltimore: University Park Press, 1978.

Anderson, K. A. The "shopping" behavior of parents of mentally retarded children: The professional person's role. *Mental Retardation,* 1971, **9**(4), 3–5.

Anderson, V. E., Siegel, F. S., Tellegan, A., & Fisch, R. O. Manual dexterity in phenylketonuric children. *Perceptual and Motor Skills,* 1968, **26,** 827–34.

Angelino, H., & Shedd, C. L. A study of the reactions to "frustration" of a group of mentally retarded children by the Rosenzweig Picture-Frustration Study. *Psychological Newsletter,* 1956, **8,** 49–54.

Aninger, M., & Bolinsky, K. Levels of independent functioning of retarded adults in apartments. *Mental Retardation,* 1977, **15,** 12–13.

Appell, M. J., & Tisdall, W. J. Factors differentiating institutionalized from noninstitutionalized referred retardates. *American Journal of Mental Deficiency,* 1968, **73,** 424–32.

Armstrong, B. Illinois judge upholds IQ test use: Departs from *Larry P. APA Monitor,* 1980, **11**(11), 6–8.

Arreola v. Board of Education. Case 160–577 (Superior Court, Orange County, Calif.), 1968.

Ashurst, D. I., & Meyers, C. E. Social system and clinical model in school identification of the educable retarded. In R. K. Eyman, C. E. Meyers, & G. Tarjan (Eds.), Sociobehavioral studies in mental retardation. *Monographs of the American Association on Mental Deficiency,* 1973, No. 1, pp. 150–63.

Assali, N. S., Brinkman, C. R., III, & Nuwaybid, B. Uteroplacental circulation and respiratory gas exchange. In L. Gluck (Ed.), *Modern perinatal medicine,* pp. 67–81. Chicago: Yearbook, 1974.

Atchison, C. O. Use of the Wechsler Intelligence Scale for Children with eighty mentally defective Negro children. *American Journal of Mental Deficiency,* 1965, **60,** 378–79.

Atkinson, R. C., & Shiffrin, R. M. Human memory: A proposed system and its control processes. In K. W. Spence & J. T. Spence (Eds.), *The psychology of learning and motivation: Advances in research and theory.* Vol. 2., New York: Academic Press, 1968.

Atomic Energy Commission. Radiation protection: Implementation of NCRP recommendations for lower radiation exposure levels for fertile women. *Federal Register,* 1975, **40**(2), 779–80.

Auerbach, A. B. Group education for parents of the handicapped. *Children,* 1961, **8,** 135–40.

598

Ayrault, E. W. *You can raise your handicapped child.* New York: Putnam's Sons, 1964.

Azrin, N. H., & Armstrong, P. M. The "mini-meal"—A method for teaching eating skills to the profoundly retarded. *Mental Retardation,* 1973, **11**(1), 9–13.

Azrin, N. H., & Foxx, R. M. A rapid method of toilet training the institutionalized retarded. *Journal of Applied Behavior Analysis,* 1971, **4,** 89–99.

Babson, S. G., & Benson, R. C. *Primer on prematurity and high-risk pregnancy.* St. Louis: Mosby, 1966.

Bacher, J. H. The effect of special class placement on the self-concept of the adolescent mentally retarded in relation to certain groups of adolescents. *Dissertation Abstracts,* 1965, **25,** 2846–47.

Baer, D. M., & Guess, D. Teaching productive noun suffixes to severely retarded children. *American Journal of Mental Deficiency,* 1973, **77,** 498–505.

Baer, D. M., Peterson, R. F., & Sherman, J. A. The development of imitation by reinforcing behavioral similarity to a model. *Journal of Experimental Analysis of Behavior,* 1967, **10,** 405.

Ball, T. S. Training generalized imitation: Variations on an historical theme. *American Journal of Mental Deficiency,* 1970, **75,** 135–41.

Balla, D., Styfco, S. J., & Zigler, E. Use of the opposition concept and outerdirectedness in intellectually average, familial retarded, and organically retarded children. *American Journal of Mental Deficiency,* 1971, **75,** 663–80.

Balla, D., & Zigler, E. Personality development in retarded persons. In N. R. Ellis (Ed.), *Handbook of mental deficiency.* (2nd ed.), pp. 154–68. Hillsdale, N.J.: Lawrence Erlbaum, 1979.

Ballard, M., Corman, L., Gottlieb, J., & Kaufman, M. J. Improving the social status of mainstreamed retarded children. *Journal of Educational Psychology,* 1978, **69,** 605–11.

Baller, W. R. A study of the present social status of a group of adults who when they were in elementary schools were classified as mentally deficient. *Genetic Psychology Monographs,* 1936, **18,** 165–244.

Baller, W. R., Charles, D. C., & Miller, E. L. Mid-life attainment of the mentally retarded: A longitudinal study. *Genetic Psychology Monographs,* 1967, **75,** 235–329.

Bandura, A. Behavior modification through modeling procedures. In L.P. Ullman & L. Krasner (Eds.), *Research in behavior modification.* New York: Holt, Rinehart, and Winston, 1969.

Bank-Mikkelson, N. E. Services for mentally retarded children in Denmark. *Children,* 1968, 15, 198–200.

Baratz, S. S., & Baratz, J. C. Early childhood intervention: The social science base of institutionalized racism. *Harvard Educational Review,* 1970, **40,** 29–50.

Barnes, E. J. Cultural retardation or shortcomings of assessment techniques. In R. L. Jones & D. L. MacMillan (Eds.), *Special education in transition,* pp. 137–47. Boston: Allyn and Bacon, 1974.

Baroff, G. S. On "size" and the quality of residential care: A second look. *Mental Retardation,* 1980, **18,** 113–17.

Barr, M. W. *Mental defectives,* Ch. 2. Philadelphia: Blakiston, 1904.

Barton, E. S., Guess, D., Garcia, G., & Baer, D. Improvement on retardates' mealtime behaviors by time out procedures using multiple baseline techniques. *Journal of Applied Behavior Analysis,* 1970, **3,** 77–84.

Baumeister, A. A. Learning abilities of the mentally retarded. In A. A. Baumeister (Ed.), *Mental retardation: Appraisal, education, and rehabilitation,* pp. 181–211. Chicago: Aldine, 1967. (a)

Baumeister, A. A. Problems in comparative studies of mental retardates and normals. *American Journal of Mental Deficiency,* 1967, 71, 869–75. (b)

Baumeister, A. A. The American residential institution: Its history and character. In A. A. Baumeister & E. Butterfield (Eds.), *Residential facilities for the mentally retarded,* pp. 1–28. Chicago: Aldine, 1970.

Bayley, N. Consistency and variability in the growth of intelligence from birth to eighteen years. *Journal of Genetic Psychology,* 1949, **75,** 165–96.

Bayley, N. Some increasing parent-child similarities during the growth of children. *Journal of Educational Psychology,* 1954, **45,** 1–21.

Bayley, N. Cognition in aging. In K. W. Schaie (Ed.), *Theory and methods of research on aging,* pp. 97–119. Morgantown, W. Va.: West Virginia University Library, 1968.

Bayley, N., & Oden, M. H. The maintenance of intellectual ability in gifted adults. *Journal of Gerontology,* 1955, **10,** 91–107.

Beach, F. A. The individual from conception to conceptualization. In J. F. Rosenblith & W. Allinsmith (Eds.), *The causes of behavior,* pp. 35–44. Boston: Allyn and Bacon, 1966.

Beck, H. L. Counseling parents of retarded children. *Children,* 1959, **6,** 225–30.

Becker, H. S. *Outsiders: Studies in the sociology of deviance.* Glencoe, Ill.: Free Press, 1963.

Beez, W. V. Influence of biased psychological reports on teacher behavior and pupil performance. In M.B. Miles & W. W. Charters, Jr. (Eds.), *Learning and social settings: New readings in the social psychology of education,* pp. 328–34. Boston: Allyn and Bacon, 1970.

Behrman, R. (Ed.) *Neonatology: Diseases of the fetus and infant.* St. Louis: Mosby, 1973.

Beier, D. C. Factors in the management of mental retardation. *International Record of Medicine,* 1959, **172,** 155–61.

Beier, D. C. Behavioral disturbances in the mentally retarded. In H. A. Stevens & R. Heber (Eds.), *Mental retardation: A review of research,* pp. 453–87. Chicago: University of Chicago Press, 1964.

Belinkoff, C. Community attitudes toward mentally retarded. *American Journal of Mental Deficiency,* 1960, **65,** 221–26.

Bell, R. Q., & Harper, L. V. *Child effects on adults*. Hillsdale, N.J.: Lawrence Erlbaum, 1977.

Belmont, J. M. Long-term memory in mental retardation. In N. R. Ellis (Ed.), *International review of research in mental retardation*. Vol. 1, pp. 219–55. New York: Academic Press, 1966.

Belmont, J. M. Medical-behavioral research in retardation. In N. R. Ellis (Ed.), *International review of research in mental retardation*. Vol. 5, pp. 1–81. New York: Academic Press, 1971.

Belmont, J. M., & Butterfield, E. C. Learning strategies as determinants of memory deficiencies. *Cognitive Psychology*, 1971, **2**, 411–20.

Belmont, J. M., & Butterfield, E. C. The instructional approach to developmental cognitive research. In R.V. Kail & J. W. Hagen (Eds.), *Perspectives on the development of memory and cognition*. Hillsdale, N.J.: Lawrence Erlbaum, 1977.

Bender, M. An experiment using a visual method of instruction followed by imitation to teach selected industrial education psychomotor tasks to severely mentally retarded males. Doctoral dissertation, University of Maryland, 1971. *Dissertation Abstracts International*, 1972, **32**, 5004A–5005A.

Bender, M., Valetutti, P. J., & Bender, R. *Teaching the moderately and severely handicapped: Curriculum objectives, strategies, and activities*. Vols. I, II, & III. Baltimore: University Park Press, 1976.

Bensberg, G. J., & Barnett, C. D. *Attendant training in southern residential facilities for the mentally retarded: Report of the SREB attendant training project*. Atlanta: Southern Regional Education Board, 1966.

Bereiter, C., & Englemann, S. *Teaching disadvantaged children in the preschool*. Englewood Cliffs, N.J.: Prentice-Hall, 1966.

Berg, J. M., Gilderdale, S., & Way, J. On telling parents of a diagnosis of mongolism. *British Journal of Psychiatry*, 1969, **115**, 1195–96.

Bergsma, D. (Ed.) *Birth defects atlas and compendium*. Baltimore: Williams and Wilkins, 1973.

Berkson, G. When exceptions obscure the rule. *Mental Retardation*, 1966, **4**, 24–27.

Berkson, G., & Cantor, G. N. A note on method in comparisons of learning in normals and the mentally retarded. *American Journal of Mental Deficiency*, 1962, **67**, 475–77.

Berman, J. L. Phenylketonuria. *Practical Therapeutics*, 1971, **3**, 113–20.

Berman, J. L., & Ford, R. Intelligence quotients and intelligence loss in patients with phenylketonuria and some variant states. *Journal of Pediatrics*, 1970, **77**, 764–70.

Bernstein, B. Language and social class. *British Journal of Psychology*, 1960, **11**, 271–76.

Bernstein, B. Social structure, language, and learning. In A. H. Passow, M. Goldberg, & A. J. Tannenbaum (Eds.), *Education of the disadvantaged*, pp. 225–44. New York: Holt, Rinehart, and Winston, 1967.

Berry, H. K., Butcher, R. E., Brunner, R. L., Bray, N. W., Hunt, M. M., & Wharton, C. H. New approaches to treatment of phenylketonuria. In P. Mittler (Ed.), *Research to practice in mental retardation: Biomedical aspects*. Vol. III, pp. 229–39. Baltimore: University Park Press, 1977.

Berry, R. J. A., & Gordon, R. G. *The mental defective: A problem in social efficiency*. New York: McGraw-Hill, 1931.

Best, H. *Public provision for the mentally retarded in the United States*. Worcester, Mass.: Heffernan Press, 1965.

Bialer, I. *Conceptualization of success and failure in mentally retarded and normal children*. Ann Arbor, Mich.: University Microfilms, 1960.

Bialer, I. Conceptualization of success and failure in mentally retarded and normal children. *Journal of Personality*, 1961, **29**, 303–20.

Bialer, I. Psychotherapy and other adjustment techniques with the mentally retarded. In A. A. Baumeister (Ed.), *Mental retardation*, pp. 138–80. Chicago: Aldine, 1967.

Bialer, I. Relationship of mental retardation to emotional disturbance and physical disability. In H. C. Haywood (Ed.), *Social-cultural aspects of mental retardation*, pp. 607–60. New York: Appleton-Century-Crofts, 1970.

Bialer, I., & Cromwell, R. Task repetition in mental defectives as a function of chronological age and mental age. *American Journal of Mental Deficiency*, 1960, **65**, 265–68.

Bialer, I., & Cromwell, R. Failure as motivation with mentally retarded children. *American Journal of Mental Deficiency*, 1965, **69**, 680–84.

Bigge, J., & O'Donnell, P. *Teaching individuals with physical and mental disabilities*. Columbus, Ohio: Charles E. Merrill, 1976.

Bijou, S. W. A functional analysis of retarded development. In N. R. Ellis (Ed.), *International review of research in mental retardation*. Vol. 1, pp. 1–19. New York: Academic Press, 1966.

Bijou, S. W., & Baer, D. M. *Child development*. Vol. 1. New York: Appleton-Century-Crofts, 1961.

Bijou, S. W., & Oblinger, B. Responses of normal and retarded children as a function of the experimental situation. *Psychological Reports*, 1960, **6**, 447–54.

Billingsley, F. F., & Neafsey, S. S. Curriculum training guides: A survey of content and evaluation procedures. *AAESPH Review*, 1978, 3(1), 42–57.

Birch, H. B., Richardson, S. A., Baird, D., Horobin, G., & Illsley, R. *Mental subnormality in the community: A clinical and epidemiological study*. Baltimore: Williams and Wilkins, 1970.

Bjaanes, A. T., & Butler, E. W. Environmental variation in community care facilities for mentally retarded persons. *American Journal of Mental Deficiency*, 1974, **78**, 429–39.

Bjaanes, A. T., Butler, E. W., & Kelly, B. R. Placement type and client functional level factors in provision of sources aimed at increased adjustment. In R. Bruininks, C. E. Meyers, B. B. Sigford, & K. D. Lakin (Eds.), *Deinstitutionalization and community adjustment of developmentally disabled persons*. AAMD Monograph. Washington, D.C.: American Association on Mental Deficiency, 1980.

Blackman, L. S. An active-passive dimension in the definition of mental retardation. *Journal of Special Education*, 1972, **6**, 67–70.

Blatt, B. *Christmas in purgatory.* Boston: Allyn and Bacon, 1966.

Blatt, B. Introduction to symposium: The legal rights of the mentally retarded. *Syracuse Law Review*, 1972, **23**(4), 991–94.

Block, J., Block, J. H., & Harrington, D. M. Some misgivings about the Matching Familiar Figures Test as a measure of reflection-impulsivity. *Developmental Psychology*, 1974, **10**, 611–32.

Block, J., Block, J. H., & Harrington, D. M. Comment on the Kagan-Messer reply. *Developmental Psychology*, 1975, **11**, 249–52.

Blodgett, H. E. Counseling parents of mentally retarded children. *Minnesota Medicine*, 1957, **40**, 721–22, 730.

Bloom, B. S. *Stability and change in human characteristics.* New York: Wiley, 1964.

Bloom, B. S. Time and learning. *American Psychologist*, 1974, **29**, 682–88.

Blount, W. R. Concept usage research with the mentally retarded. *Psychological Bulletin*, 1968, **69**, 281–94. (a)

Blount, W. R. Language and the more severely retarded: A review. *American Journal of Mental Deficiency*, 1968, **73**, 21–29. (b)

Blount, W. R. Concept-usage performance: Abstraction ability, number of referents, and item familiarity. *American Journal of Mental Deficiency*, 1971, **76**, 125–29.

Boles, G. Personality factors in mothers of cerebral palsied children. *Genetic Psychology Monographs*, 1959, **59**, 159–218.

Borg, W. R. *Ability grouping in the schools.* Madison, Wisc.: Dembar Educational Research Services, 1966.

Bortner, M., & Birch, H. G. Cognitive capacity and cognitive competence. *American Journal of Mental Deficiency*, 1970, **75**, 735–44.

Bourne, H. Protophrenia: A study of perverted rearing and mental dwarfism. *Lancet*, 1955, **2**, 1156–63.

Bousfield, W. A. The occurrence of clustering in the recall of randomly arranged associates. *Journal of Genetic Psychology*, 1953, **49**, 229–40.

Boyd, D. The three stages in the growth of a parent of a mentally retarded child. *American Journal of Mental Deficiency*, 1951, **55**, 608–11.

Brakel, S. J., & Rock, R. S. (Eds.) *The mental disabled and the law.* (Rev. ed.) Chicago: University of Chicago Press, 1971.

Bricker, W., & Bricker, D. An early language training strategy. In R. Schiefelbusch & L. Lloyd (Eds.), *Language perspectives: Acquisition, retardation and intervention.* Baltimore: University Park Press, 1974.

Bricker, W. A. & Bricker, D. D. The infant, toddler, and preschool research and intervention project. In T. D. Tjossem (Ed.), *Early intervention strategies for high risk infants and young children*, pp. 545–72. Baltimore: University Park Press, 1976.

Brigham, C. C. *A study of American intelligence.* Princeton, N.J.: Princeton University Press, 1923.

Brigham, C. C. Value of tests in examination of immigrants. *Industrial Psychology*, 1926, **1**, 413–17.

Brigham, C. C. Intelligence tests of immigrant groups. *Psychological Review*, 1930, **37**, 158–65.

Brockopp, G. W. *The significance of selected variables on the prevalence of suspected mental retardates in the public schools of Indiana.* Ann Arbor, Mich.: University Microfilms, 1958.

Brofenbrenner, U. *A report on longitudinal evaluations of preschool programs.* Vol. 2, *Is early intervention effective?* Washington, D.C.: Department of Health, Education and Welfare, 1974.

Brofenbrenner, U. Is early intervention effective? In M. Guttentag & E. C. Struening (Eds.), *Handbook of evaluation research.* Beverly Hills, Calif.: Sage, 1975.

Brofenbrenner, U. Is early intervention effective? Facts and principles of early intervention: A summary. In A. M. Clarke & A. D. B. Clarke (Eds.), *Early experience: Myth and evidence*, pp. 247–56. New York: Free Press, 1976.

Bromberg, W., & Thompson, C. B. The relation of psychosis, mental defect, and personality types to crime. *Journal of Criminal Law and Criminology*, 1937, **28**, 70–89.

Brophy, J. E., & Good, T. L. Teacher's communication of differential expectations for children's classroom performance: Some behavioral data. *Journal of Educational Psychology*, 1970, **61**, 365–74.

Broverman, D. M. Cognitive styles and intra-individual variation in abilities. *Journal of Personality*, 1960, **28**, 240–56.

Brown, A. L. The role of strategic behavior in retardate memory. In N. R. Ellis (Ed.), *International review of research in mental retardation.* Vol. 7, pp. 55–111. New York: Academic Press, 1974.

Brown, A. L., Campione, J. C., & Murphy, M. D. Keeping track of changing variables: Long-term retention of a trained rehearsal strategy by retarded adolescents. *American Journal of Mental Deficiency*, 1974, **78**, 446–53.

Brown, L., Branston, M. B., Hamre-Nietupski, S., Johnson, F., Wilcox, B., & Gruenwald, L. A rationale for comprehensive longitudinal interactions between severely handicapped students and nonhandicapped students and other students. *AAESPH Review*, 1979, **4**(1), 3–14.

Brown, L., Nietupski, J., & Hamre-Nietupski, S. The criterion of ultimate functioning. In M. A. Thomas (Ed.), *Hey, don't forget about me!* Reston, Va.: Council for Exceptional Children, 1976.

Brown, R. I., & Dyer, L. Social arithmetic training for the subnormal: A comparison of two methods. *British Journal of Mental Subnormality*, 1963, **9**, 8–12.

Brown v. *Board of Education of Topeka.* 347 U.S. 483, 493, 1954.

Browne, R. A., Gunzberg, H. C., Johnston-Hannah, L. G. W., Maccoll, K., Oliver, B., & Thomas, A. The needs of patients in subnormality hospitals if discharged to community care. *British Journal of Mental Subnormality*, 1971, **17**, 7–24.

Bruininks, R. H. Physical and motor development of retarded persons. In N.R. Ellis (Ed.), *International review of research in mental retardation*. Vol. 7, pp. 209–61. New York: Academic Press, 1974.

Bruininks, R., Hauber, F., & Kudla, M. *National survey of community residential facilities: A profile of facilities and residents in 1977*. Developmental Disabilities Project on Residential Services and Community Adjustment. Minneapolis: University of Minnesota, 1979.

Bruininks, R. H., Hauber, F. A., & Kudla, M. J. National survey of community residential facilities: A profile of facilities and residents in 1977. *American Journal of Mental Deficiency*, 1980, **84**, 470–78.

Bruininks, R. H., & Rynders, J. E. Alternatives to special class placement for educable mentally retarded children. *Focus on Exceptional Children*, 1971, **3**(4), 1–12.

Bruininks, R. H., Rynders, J. E., & Gross, J. C. Social acceptance of mildly retarded pupils in resource rooms and regular classes. *American Journal of Mental Deficiency*, 1974, **78**, 377–83.

Bruininks, R. H., Thurlow, M., Thurman, S. K., & Fiorelli, J. S. Deinstitutionalization and community programs. In J. Wortis (Ed.), *Mental retardation and developmental disabilities: An annual review*. Vol. XI. New York: Brunner/Mazel, 1980.

Bruininks, R. H., & Warfield, G. The mentally retarded. In E. L. Meyen (Ed.), *Exceptional Children and Youth*. Denver: Love Publishing, 1978.

Bruner, J. S. *Toward a theory of instruction*. Cambridge, Mass.: Harvard University Press, 1966.

Bruner, J. S., Goodnow, J., & Austin, G. *A study of thinking*. New York: Wiley, 1956.

Bryant, K. N., & Hirschberg, J. C. Helping the parents of a retarded child. *American Journal of Disabled Children*, 1961, **102**, 52–66.

Bryant, K. N., & Hirschberg, J. C. Helping parents of a retarded child. *American Journal of Diseases of Children*, 1970, **102**, 52.

Bucky, S., & Banta, T. Racial factors in test performance. *Developmental Psychology*, 1972, **6**, 7–13.

Budoff, M. Learning potential among institutionalized young adult retardates. *American Journal of Mental Deficiency*, 1967, **72**, 404–11.

Budoff, M. Social and test data correlates of learning potential status in adolescent educable mental retardates. *Studies in Learning Potential*, 1970, **1**(3).

Budoff, M. & Gottlieb, J. Special class students mainstreamed: A study of an aptitude (learning potential) X treatment interaction. *American Journal of Mental Deficiency*, 1976, **81**, 1–11.

Budoff, M., Meskin, J., & Harrison, R. H. Educational test of the learning-potential hypothesis. *American Journal of Mental Deficiency*, 1971, **76**, 159–69.

Budoff, M., & Siperstein, G. N. Low-income children's attitudes toward mentally retarded children: Effects of labeling and academic behavior. *American Journal of Mental Deficiency*, 1978, **82**, 474–79.

Bunker, M. C., Morris, A. L., Lynch, H. T., Mickey, G. H., Roderick, T. H., Van Pelt, J. C., & Fornot, J. C. Will my baby be normal? *Patient Care*, 30 April 1972, pp. 18–47.

Burks, B. S. The relative influence of nature and nurture upon mental development: A comparative study of foster parent–foster child resemblance and true parent–true child resemblance. In *The 27th yearbook of the National Society for the Study of Education*. Part 1. Bloomington, Ind.: Public School Publishing, 1928.

Buros, O. K. *Seventh mental measurements yearbooks*. Vols. 1, 2. Highland Park, N.J.: Gryphon, 1972.

Burt, C. The evidence for the concept of intelligence. *British Journal of Educational Psychology*, 1955, **25**, 158–77.

Burt, C. The genetic determination of differences in intelligence: A study of monozygotic twins reared together and apart. *British Journal of Psychology*, 1966, **57**, 137–53.

Burt, C. Mental capacity and its critics. *Bulletin of the British Psychological Society*, 1968, **21**, 11–18.

Burt, C. Is intelligence distributed normally? In H.J. Eysenck (Ed.), *The measurement of intelligence*, pp. 62–77. Baltimore: Williams and Wilkens, 1973.

Burt, R. A. Judicial action to aid the retarded. In N. Hobbs (Ed.), *Issues in the classification of children*. Vol. 2, pp. 293–318. San Francisco: Jossey-Bass, 1975.

Butler, E. W., & Bjaanes, A. T. A typology of community care facilities and differential normalization outcomes. In P. Mittler (Ed.), *Research to practice in mental retardation*. Vol. 1, *Care and intervention*. Baltimore: University Park Press, 1977.

Butterfield, E. C. A provocative case of over-achievement by a mongoloid. *American Journal of Mental Deficiency*, 1961, **66**, 444–48.

Butterfield, E. C. The interruption of tasks: Methodological, factual, and theoretical issues. *Psychological Bulletin*, 1964, **62**, 309–22.

Butterfield, E. C. The role of environmental factors in the treatment of institutionalized mental retardates. In A. A. Baumeister (Ed.), *Mental retardation: Appraisal, education, and rehabilitation*, pp. 120–37. Chicago: Aldine, 1967.

Butterfield, E. C. Institutionalization and its alternatives for mentally retarded people in the United States. *International Journal of Mental Health*, 1977, **6**, 21–34.

Butterfield, E. C., Barnett, C. D., & Bensberg, G. J. Some objective characteristics of institutions for the mentally retarded: Implications for attendant turnover rate. *American Journal of Mental Deficiency*, 1966, **70**, 786–94.

Butterfield, E. C., & Belmont, J. M. Assessing and improving the executive cognitive functions of mentally retarded people. In I. Bialer & M. Sternlicht (Eds.), *The psychology of mental retardation*, pp. 277–318. New York: Psychological Dimensions, 1977.

Butterfield, E. C., Wambold, C., & Belmont, J. M. On theory and practice of improving short-term memory. *American Journal of Mental Deficiency*, 1973, **77**, 654–69.

Butterfield, E. C., & Zigler, E. The influence of differing institutional social climates on the effectiveness of social reinforcement in the mentally retarded. *American Journal of Mental Deficiency*, 1965, **70**, 48–56.

Cahn, E. Jurice prudince. *New York University Law Review*, 1955, **30**, 150–55.

Cain, L. F., Levine, S., & Elzey, E. F. *Manual for the Cain-Levine Social Competency Scale*. Palo Alto, Calif.: Consulting Psychologists, 1963.

Caldwell, B. M. What is the optimal learning environment for the young child? *American Journal of Orthopsychiatry*, 1967, **37**, 8–20.

Caldwell, B. M. The rationale for early intervention. In R. L. Jones & D. L. MacMillan (Eds.), *Special education in transition*, pp. 195–207. Boston: Allyn and Bacon, 1974.

Caldwell, B. M., & Richmond, J. B. Programmed day care for the very young child: A preliminary report. *Journal of Marriage and the Family.* 1964, **26**, 481–88.

Caldwell, B. M., & Smith, T. A. Intellectual structure of southern Negro children. *Psychological Reports*, 1968, **23**, 63–71.

California State Department of Education. *A master plan for special education in California*. Sacramento: California State Department of Education, 1973.

Calvin, K. Quest for the middle range. In G. C. Hazard (Ed.), *Law in a changing America*. Englewood Cliffs, N.J.: Prentice-Hall, 1968.

Campione, J. C., & Brown, A. L. Toward a theory of intelligence: Contributions from research with retarded children. *Intelligence*, 1978, **2**, 279–304.

Cantor, G. N., & Ryan, T. I. Retention of verbal paired-associates in normals and retardates. *American Journal of Mental Deficiency*, 1962, **66**, 861–65.

Carlson, J. S., & MacMillan, D. L. Comparison of probability judgments between EMR and nonretarded children. *American Journal of Mental Deficiency*, 1970, **74**, 697–700.

Carr, J. Mongolism: Telling the parents. *Developmental Medicine and Child Neurology*, 1970, **12**, 213–21. (a)

Carr, J. Mental and motor development in young mongol children. *Journal of Mental Deficiency Research*, 1970, **14**, 205–20. (b)

Carr, J. The effect of the severely subnormal on their families. In A. M. Clarke & A. D. B. Clarke (Eds.), *Mental deficiency: The changing outlook* (3rd. ed.), pp. 807–39. New York: Free Press, 1974.

Casarett, L. J., & Doull, J. (Eds.) *Toxicology, the basic science of poisons*. New York: Macmillan, 1975.

Casarett, M. G. Social poisons. In L. J. Casarett & J. Doull (Eds.), *Toxicology, the basic science of poisons*, pp. 627–56. New York: Macmillan, 1975.

Cattell, R. B. Theory of fluid and crystallized intelligence: A critical experiment. *Journal of Educational Psychology*, 1963, **54**, 1–22.

Catterall, C. D. Special education in transition: Implications for school psychology. *Journal of School Psychology*, 1972, **10**, 91–98.

Cavan, R. S. Subcultural variations and mobility. In H.T. Christensen (Ed.), *Handbook of marriage and the family*, pp. 535–81. Chicago: Rand McNally, 1964.

Cegelka, W. J., & Tyler, J. L. The efficacy of special class placement for the mentally retarded in proper perspective. *Training School Bulletin*, 1970, **65**, 33–68.

Centerwall, S., & Centerwall, W. A study of children with mongolism reared in the home compared to those reared away from the home. *Pediatrics*, 1960, **25**, 678–85.

Chall, J. S. *Learning to read: The great debate*. New York: McGraw-Hill, 1967.

Chapanis, A., & Williams, W. C. Results of a mental survey with the Kuhlman-Anderson intelligence tests in Williamson County, Tennessee. *Journal of Genetic Psychology*, 1945, **67**, 27–55.

Charles, D. C. Ability and accomplishment of persons earlier judged mentally deficient. *Genetic Psychology Monographs*, 1953, **47**, 3–71.

Charles, D. C. Adult adjustment of some deficient American children. *American Journal of Mental Deficiency*, 1957, **62**, 300–304.

Charles, D. C. Longitudinal follow-up studies of community adjustment. In S. G. DiMichael (Ed.), *New vocational pathways for the mentally retarded*. American Rehabilitation Counseling Association Symposium. Washington, D.C.: American Personnel and Guidance Association, 1966.

Chase, H. P., & Crnic, L. S. Undernutrition and human brain development. In P. Mittler (Ed.), *Research to practice in mental retardation: Biomedical aspects*. Vol. III, pp. 337–46. Baltimore: University Park Press, 1977.

Chennault, M. Improving the social acceptance of unpopular educable mentally retarded pupils in special classes. *American Journal of Mental Deficiency*, 1967, **72**, 455–58.

Chow, T. J., & Earl, J. L. Lead aerosols in the atmosphere: Increasing concentration. *Science*, 1970, **169**, 577.

Christophos, R., & Renz, P. A critical examination of special education programs. *Journal of Special Education*, 1969, **3**(4), 371–80.

Claiborn, W. L. Expectancy effects in the classroom: A failure to replicate. *Journal of Educational Psychology*, 1969, **60**, 377–83.

Clark, E. A. Teacher attitudes toward integration of children with handicaps. *Education and Training of the Mentally Retarded,* 1976, **11,** 333–35.

Clark, K. The social scientist, the *Brown* decision, and contemporary confusion. In L. Friedman (Ed.), *Argument.* New York: Chelsey House, 1969.

Clarke, A. D. B. The abilities and trainability of imbeciles. In A. D. B. Clarke & A. M. Clarke (Eds.), *Mental deficiency: The changing outlook.* Glencoe, Ill.: Free Press, 1958.

Clarke, A. D. B. Learning and human development. *British Journal of Psychiatry,* 1968, **114,** 1061–77.

Clarke, A. D. B., & Clarke, A.M. How constant is the IQ? *Lancet,* 1953, **2,** 877–80.

Clarke, A. D. B., & Clarke, A. M. Cognitive changes in the feeble-minded. *British Journal of Psychology,* 1954, **45,** 173–79.

Clarke, A. D. B., & Clarke, A. M. Recovery from the effects of deprivation. *Acta Psychologica,* 1959, **16,** 137–44.

Clarke, A. D. B., & Clarke, A. M. Recent advances in the study of deprivation. *Journal of Child Psychology and Psychiatry,* 1960, **1,** 26–36.

Clarke, A. D. B., & Clarke, A. M. Consistency and variability in the growth of human characteristics. In W. D. Wall & V. P. Varma (Eds.), *Advances in educational psychology.* Vol. 1. New York: Barnes & Noble, 1972.

Clarke, A. D. B., Clarke, A. M., & Reiman, S. Cognitive and social changes in the feeble-minded: Three further studies. *British Journal of Psychology,* 1958, **49,** 144–57.

Clarke, A. M., & Clarke, A. D. B. Genetic-environmental interactions in cognitive development. In A. M. Clarke & A. D. B. Clarke (Eds.), *Mental deficiency: The changing outlook* (3rd ed), pp. 164–205. New York: Free Press, 1974.

Clarke, A. M., & Clarke, A. D. B. (Eds.). *Early experience: Myth and evidence.* New York: Free Press, 1976.

Clausen, J. A. Mental deficiency: Development of a concept. *American Journal of Mental Deficiency,* 1967, **71,** 727–45.

Clausen, J. A. Quo Vadis, AAMD? *Journal of Special Education,* 1972, **6,** 51–60.

Clausen, J. A., & Williams, J. R. Sociological correlates of child behavior. In H. W. Stevenson (Ed.), *Child psychology.* Part 1, pp. 62–107. National Society for the Study of Education. Chicago: University of Chicago Press, 1963.

Cleary, T. A., Humphreys, L. G., Kendrick, S. A., & Wesman, A. Educational uses of tests with disadvantaged students. *American Psychologist,* 1975, **30,** 15–41.

Cleland, C. C. Evidence on the relationship between size and institutional effectiveness: A review and analysis. *American Journal of Mental Deficiency,* 1965, **70,** 423–31.

Cleland, C. C., & Chambers, I. L. The effect of institutional tours on attitudes of high school seniors. *American Journal of Mental Deficiency,* 1959, **64,** 124–30.

Cleland, C. C., Patton, W. F., & Seitz, S. The use of insult as an index of negative reference groups. *American Journal of Mental Deficiency,* 1967, **72,** 30–33.

Cochran, I. L., & Cleland, C. C. Manifest anxiety of retardates and normals matched as to academic achievement. *American Journal of Mental Deficiency,* 1963, **67,** 539–42.

Cohen, J. S. Employer attitudes toward hiring mentally retarded individuals. *American Journal of Mental Deficiency,* 1963, **67,** 705–12.

Cohen, J. S., & DeYoung, H. The role of litigation in the improvement of programming for the handicapped. In L. Mann & D. Sabatino (Eds.), *The first review of special education.* Vol. 2, pp. 261–86. Philadelphia: Journal of Special Education Press, 1973.

Cohen, M. A., Gross, P. G., & Haring, N. G. Developmental pinpoints. In N. G. Haring & L. J. Brown (Eds.), *Teaching the severely handicapped.* Vol. 1. New York: Grune & Stratton, 1976.

Cole, M., & Bruner, J. S. Cultural differences and inferences about psychological processes. *American Psychologist,* 1971, **26,** 867–76.

Coleman, J. S. *Equality of educational opportunity.* Washington, D. C.: U.S. Government Printing Office, 1966.

Collmann, R. D., & Newlyn, D. Employment success of mentally dull and intellectually normal ex-pupils in England. *American Journal of Mental Deficiency,* 1957, **61,** 484–90.

Collmann, R. D., & Newlyn, D. Changes in Terman-Merrill IQs of mentally retarded children. *American Journal of Mental Deficiency,* 1958, **63,** 308–11.

Committee on Nomenclature and Statistics. *Diagnostic and statistical manual: Mental disorders.* Washington, D.C.: American Psychiatric Association, 1952.

Conen, P. E., & Erkman, B. Combined mongolism and leukemia. *American Journal of Diseases in Children,* 1966, **112,** 429–43.

Conley, R. E. *The economics of mental retardation.* Baltimore: Johns Hopkins University Press, 1973.

Conroy, J. W. Trends in deinstitutionalization of the mentally retarded. *Mental Retardation,* 1977, **15,** 44–46.

Coop, R. H., & Sigel, I. E. Cognitive style: Implications for learning and instruction. In R. L. Jones & D. L. MacMillan (Eds.), *Special education in transition,* pp. 420–30. Boston: Allyn and Bacon, 1974.

Cooper, L. Z., & Krugman, S. Diagnosis and management: Congenital rubella. *Pediatrics,* 1966, **37,** 335.

Cooper, R., & Zubek, J. Effects of enriched and restricted early environments of the learning ability of bright and dull rats. *Canadian Journal of Psychology,* 1958, **12,** 159–64.

Corman, L., & Gottlieb, J. Mainstreaming mentally retarded children: A review of research. In N. R. Ellis

(Ed.), *International review of research in mental retardation.* Vol. 9, pp. 251–75. New York: Academic Press, 1979.

Cornblath, M. Neonatal hypoglycemia: A summons to action. *Hospital Practice,* 1967, **2**(5), 56–60.

Cornwell, A. C., & Birch, H. G. Psychological and social development in home-reared children with Down's syndrome (mongolism). *American Journal of Mental Deficiency,* 1969, **74,** 341–50.

Costello, H. M. The responses of mentally retarded children to specialized learning experiences in arithmetic. Unpublished doctoral dissertation, University of Pennsylvania, 1941.

Coulter, W. A., & Morrow, H. W. (Eds.) *Adaptive behavior: Concepts and measurements.* New York: Grune & Stratton, 1978.

Covarrubias v. San Diego Unified School District. Civil action 70–30d (S.D., Calif.), 1971.

Craft, M. Mental disorder in the defective: A psychiatric survey among in-patients. *American Journal of Mental Deficiency,* 1959, **63,** 829–34.

Craft, M. Mental disorder in a series of English out-patient defectives. *American Journal of Mental Deficiency,* 1960, **64,** 718–24.

Cranefield, P. F. Historical perspectives. In I. Phillips (Ed.), *Prevention and treatment of mental retardation,* pp. 3–14. New York: Basic Books, 1966.

Cranefield, P. F., & Federn, W. Paracelsus on goiter and cretinism: A translation and discussion of 'de struma, vulgo der kropf.' *Bulletin of the History of Medicine,* 1963, **37,** 463–71.

Cravioto, J., DeLicardie, E. R., & Birch, H. G. Nutrition, growth, and neuro-integrative development: An experimental and ecologic study. *Pediatrics,* 1966, **38** (supp. 2), 319.

Crawford, J. L., Aiello, J. R., & Thompson, D. E. Deinstitutionalization and community placement: Clinical and environmental factors. *Mental Retardation,* 1979, **17,** 59–63.

Crome, L., & Stern, J. *Pathology of mental retardation.* (2nd ed.) London: Edinburgh-Churchill-Livingstone, 1972.

Cromwell, R. L. A social learning approach to mental retardation. In N. R. Ellis (Ed.), *Handbook of mental deficiency,* pp. 41–91. New York: McGraw-Hill, 1963.

Cromwell, R. L. Personality evaluation. In A. A. Baumeister (Ed.), *Mental retardation: Appraisal, education, and rehabilitation,* pp. 66–85. Chicago: Aldine, 1967.

Cromwell, R. L., Blashfield, R. K., & Strauss, J. S. Criteria for classification systems. In N. Hobbs (Ed.), *Issues in the classification of children.* Vol. 1, pp. 4–25. San Francisco: Jossey-Bass, 1975.

Cronbach, L. J. Heredity, environment, and educational policy. *Harvard Educational Review,* 1969, **39**(2), 190–99.

Cronbach, L. J. *Essentials of psychological testing.* (3rd ed.) New York: Harper and Row, 1970.

Cronbach, L. J. Five decades of public controversy over mental testing. *American Psychologist,* 1975, **30,** 1–14.

Cruickshank, W. M. Arithmetic vocabulary of mentally retarded boys. *Exceptional Children,* 1946, **13,** 65–69.

Cruickshank, W. M. Arithmetic work habits of mentally retarded boys. *American Journal of Mental Deficiency,* 1948, **52,** 318–30. (a)

Cruickshank, W. M. Arithmetic ability of mentally retarded children, I. *Journal of Educational Research,* 1948, **42,** 161–70. (b)

Cruickshank, W. M. Arithmetic ability of mentally retarded children, II. *Journal of Educational Research,* 1948, **42,** 279–88. (c)

Cruickshank, W. M. Current educational practice with exceptional children. In W. M. Cruickshank & G. O. Johnson (Eds.), *Education of exceptional children and youth,* pp. 43–93. Englewood Cliffs, N.J.: Prentice-Hall, 1958.

Cruickshank, W. M., & Johnson, G. O. (Eds.) *Education of exceptional children and youth.* (2nd ed.) Englewood Cliffs, N.J.: Prentice-Hall, 1967.

Culver, M. Intergenerational social mobility among families with a severely mentally retarded child. Unpublished doctoral dissertation, University of Illinois, 1967.

Dailey, R. F. Dimensions and issues in '74: Tapping into the special education grapevine. *Exceptional Children,* 1974, **40,** 503–07.

Dalton, J., & Epstein, H. Counseling parents of mildly retarded children. *Social Casework,* 1963, **44,** 523–30.

Dameron, L. Development of intelligence of children with mongolism. *Child Development,* 1963, **34,** 733–38.

Dave, R. H. The identification and measurement of environmental process variables related to educational achievement. Unpublished doctoral dissertation, University of Chicago, 1963.

David, W. J. GSR study of frustration in retarded and average boys. *American Journal of Mental Deficiency,* 1968, **73,** 379–83.

Davies, S. P., & Ecob, K. G. *The mentally retarded in society.* New York: Columbia University Press, 1959.

Davis, K. Final note on a case of extreme isolation. *American Journal of Sociology,* 1947, **52,** 432–37.

Davis, N. J. Labeling theory in deviance research: A critique and reconsideration. *Sociological Quarterly,* 1972, **13,** 447–74.

Debus, R. L. Effects of brief observations of model behavior on conceptual tempo of impulsive children. *Developmental Psychology,* 1970, **2**(1), 22–32.

DeHirsch, K., Jansky, J. J., & Langford, W. S. *Predicting reading failure.* New York: Harper and Row, 1966.

DeLamater, J. On the nature of deviance. *Social Forces*, 1968, **46**, 445–55.

Demaine, G. C., & Silverstein, A. B. MA changes in institutionalized Down's syndrome persons: A semi-longitudinal approach. *American Journal of Mental Deficiency*, 1978, **82**, 429–32.

Denenberg, V. The effects of early experience. In E. S. E. Hofez (Ed.), *The behavior of domestic animals*. (2nd ed.) New York: Baillieu, Tindall, & Cox, 1969.

Dennis, W. A further analysis of reports of wild children. *Child Development*, 1951, **22**, 153–58.

Dennis, W. Causes of retardation among institutional children. *Journal of Genetic Psychology*, 1960, **96**, 47–59.

Dennis, W., & Dennis, M. G. Infant development under conditions of restricted practice and minimum social stimulation. *Genetic Psychology Monographs*, 1941, **23**, 149–55.

Denny, M. R. Research in learning and performance. In H. A. Stevens & R. Heber (Eds.), *Mental retardation: A review of research*, pp. 100–42. Chicago: University of Chicago Press, 1964.

Deno, E. Special education as developmental capital. *Exceptional Children*, 1972, **37**, 229–37.

Dentler, R. A., & Mackler, B. Ability and sociometric status among normal and retarded children: A review of the literature. *Psychological Bulletin*, 1962, **59**, 273–83.

Desmonts, G., & Couvreur, J. Congenital toxoplasmosis. *New England Journal of Medicine*, 1974, **290**, 1110–16.

Detterman, D. K. Memory in the mentally retarded. In N. R. Ellis (Ed.), *Handbook of mental deficiency*. (2nd. ed.), pp. 727–60. Hillsdale, N.J.: Lawrence Erlbaum, 1979.

Deutsch, C. P. Social class and child development. In B. M. Caldwell & H. N. Ricciuti (Eds.), *Review of child development research*. Vol. 3, pp. 233–82. Chicago: University of Chicago Press, 1973.

Deutsch, M. Minority group and class status as related to social and personality factors in scholastic achievement. *Society for Applied Anthropology*, 1960, No. 2.

Dewan, J. G. Intelligence and emotional stability. *American Journal of Psychiatry*, 1048, **104**, 548–54.

DeWeerd, J. Introduction. In J. B. Jordan, A. H. Hayden, M. B. Karnes, & M. M. Wood (Eds.), *Early education for exceptional children: A handbook of ideas and exemplary practices*. Reston, Va.: Council for Exceptional Children, 1977.

Dexter, L. A. Towards a sociology of the mentally defective. *American Journal of Mental Deficiency*, 1956, **61**, 10–16.

Dexter, L. A. A social theory of mental deficiency. *American Journal of Mental Deficiency*, 1958, **62**, 920–28.

Dexter, L. A. Research on problems of mental subnormality. *American Journal of Mental Deficiency*, 1960, **64**, 835–38.

Dexter, L. A. *The tyranny of schooling: An inquiry into the problem of "stupidity."* New York: Basic Books, 1964.

Diana v. State Board of Education. C–70–37 (RFP Dist. N. Calif.), 1970.

Dick, J. V. Equal protection and intelligence classifications. *Stanford Law Review*, 1974, **26**, 647–72.

Dinger, J. C. Former educable retarded pupils. *Exceptional Children*, 1961, **27**, 353–60.

Dingman, H. F. Social performance of the mentally retarded. In R. K. Eyman, C. E. Meyers, & G. Tarjan (Eds.), Sociobehavioral studies in mental retardation. *Monographs of the American Association on Mental Deficiency*, 1973, No. 1, pp. 87–90.

Dingman, H. F., & Tarjan, G. Mental retardation and the normal distribution curve. *American Journal of Mental Deficiency*, 1960, **64**, 991–94.

Dobson, J. C., Kushida, E., Williamson, M., & Friedman, E. G. Intellectual performance of 36 phenylketonuria patients and their nonaffected siblings. *Pediatrics*, 1976, **58**, 53–58.

Doe v. Board of School Directors of the City of Milwaukee. (U.S. Dist. Court, E.D., Wis.), 1970.

Doll, E. A. The essentials of an inclusive concept of mental deficiency. *American Journal of Mental Deficiency*, 1941, **46**, 214–19.

Doll, E. A. *Measurement of social competence: A manual for the Vineland social maturity scale*. Minneapolis: Educational Publishers, 1953.

Doll, E. E. A historical survey of research and management of mental retardation in the United States. In E. P. Trapp & P. Himelstein (Eds.), *Readings on the exceptional child*, pp. 21–68. New York: Appleton-Century-Crofts, 1962.

Doll, E. E. (Ed.) Historical review of mental retardation, 1800–1965: A symposium. *American Journal of Mental Deficiency*, 1967, **72**, 165–89.

Dollard, J., Doob, L. W., Miller, N. E., Mourer, D. H., & Sears, R. R. *Frustration and aggression*. New Haven, Conn.: Yale University Press, 1939.

Downey, K. J. Parents' reasons for institutionalizing severely mentally retarded children. *Journal of Health and Human Behavior*, 1965, **6**, 163–69.

Dreeben, R. The contribution of schooling to the learning of norms. *Harvard Educational Review*, 1967, **37**, 211–37.

Drews, E. M. The effectiveness of homogeneous and heterogeneous ability grouping in ninth grade English classes with slow, average, and superior students. Unpublished manuscript, Michigan State University, 1962.

Drillien, C. M., & Wilkinson, E. M. Mongolism: When should parents be told. *British Medical Journal*, 1964, **2**, 1306–07.

Duckworth, S. V., Ragland, G. G., Sommerfeld, R. E., & Wyne, M. D. Modification of conceptual impulsivity in retarded children. *American Journal of Mental Deficiency*, 1974, **79**, 59–63.

Dugdale, R. L. *The Jukes*. New York: Putnam, 1877.

Dunn, L. M. Special education for the mildly retarded: Is much of it justifiable? *Exceptional Children*, 1968, **35**, 5–22.

Dunn, L. M. (Ed.) *Exceptional children in the schools: Special education in transition*. (2nd ed.) New York: Holt, Rinehart, and Winston, 1973.

Dunn, L. M. & Capobianco, R. J. A comparison of the reading processes of mentally retarded and normal boys of the same mental age. *Monographs of the Society for Research in Child Development*, 1954, **19**, 7–99.

Dusek, J. B., & O'Connell, E. J. Teacher expectancy effects on the achievement test performance of elementary school children. *Journal of Educational Psychology*, 1973, **65**, 371–77.

Dybwad, G. Architecture's role in revitalizing the field of mental retardation. *Journal of Mental Subnormality*, 1970, **16**, 1.

Ebert, E., & Simmons, K. The Brush Foundation study of child growth and development: I. Psychometric tests. *Monographs of the Society for Research in Child Development*, 1943, **8**(35), 1.

Edgerton, R. B. A patient elite: Ethnography in a hospital for the mentally retarded. *American Journal of Mental Deficiency*, 1963, **68**, 383.

Edgerton, R. B. *The cloak of competence: Stigma in the lives of the mentally retarded*. Berkeley: University of California Press, 1967.

Edgerton, R. B., & Bercovici, S. M. The cloak of competence: Years later. *American Journal of Mental Deficiency*, 1976, **80**, 485–97.

Edgerton, R. B., & Dingman, H. F. Good reasons for bad supervision: "Dating" in a hospital for the mentally retarded. *The Psychiatric Quarterly Supplement*, 1964, Pt. 2, 1–13. (a)

Edgerton, R. B., & Dingman, H. F. Tattooing. *Abbottempo*, 1964, **2**(4), 23–25. (b)

Edgerton, R. B., Eyman, R. K., & Silverstein, A. B. Mental retardation system. In N. Hobbs (Ed.), *Issues in the classification of children*. Vol. 2, pp. 62–87. San Francisco: Jossey-Bass, 1975.

Edgerton, R. B., & Sabagh, G. From mortification to aggrandizement: Changing self conceptions in the careers of the mentally retarded. *Psychiatry*, 1962, **25**, 263–72.

Edgerton, R. B., Tarjan, G., & Dingman, H. F. Free enterprise in a captive society. *American Journal of Mental Deficiency*, 1961, **66**, 35–41.

Eells, K., Davis, A., Havighurst, R. J., Herrick, V. E., & Tyler, R. *Intelligence and cultural differences: A study of cultural learning and problem-solving*. Chicago: University of Chicago Press, 1951.

Efron, R. E., & Efron, H. Y. Measurement of attitudes toward the retarded and an application with educators. *American Journal of Mental Deficiency*, 1967, **72**, 100–107.

Egg, M. *When a child is different: A basic guide for parents and friends of mentally retarded children, giving practical suggestions on their education and training*. New York: John Day, 1964.

Elashoff, J. D., & Snow, R. E. *Pygmalion reconsidered*. Worthington, Ohio: C. A. Jones, 1971.

Elder, G. H., Jr. Adolescent socialization and development. In E. F. Borgatta & W. W. Lambert (Eds.), *Handbook of personality theory and research*, pp. 239–64. Chicago: Rand McNally, 1968.

Elliott, R., & Mackay, D. Social competence of subnormal and normal children living under different types of residential care. *Journal of Mental Subnormality*, 1971, **17**, 48–53.

Ellis, N. R. The stimulus trace and behavioral inadequacy. In N. R. Ellis (Ed.), *Handbook of mental deficiency*, pp. 134–58. New York: McGraw-Hill, 1963.

Ellis, N. R. A behavioral research strategy in mental retardation: Defense and critique. *American Journal of Mental Deficiency*, 1969, **73**, 557–66.

Ellis, N. R. Memory processes in retardates and normals. In N. R. Ellis (Ed.), *International review of research in mental retardation*. Vol. 4, pp. 1–32. New York: Academic Press, 1970.

Ellis, N. R. (Ed.) *Handbook of mental deficiency, psychological theory and research*. (2nd ed.) Hillsdale, N.J.: Lawrence Erlbaum, 1979.

Emde, R. N., & Brown, C. Adaptation to the birth of a Down's syndrome infant. *Journal of the American Academy of Child Psychiatry*, 1978, **17**, 299–323.

Erikson, K. T. Notes on the sociology of deviance. In H. S. Becker (Ed.), *The other side: Perspectives on deviance*, pp. 9–21. Glencoe, Ill.: Free Press, 1964.

Erlenmeyer-Kimling, L., & Jarvik, L. F. Genetics and intelligence: A review. *Science*, 1963, **142**, 1477–79.

Esposito, D. Homogeneous and heterogeneous ability grouping: Principal findings and implications for evaluating and designing more effective educational environments. *Review of Educational Research*, 1973, **42**(2), 163–79.

Evans, E. D. *Contemporary influences in early childhood education*. (2nd ed.) New York: Holt, Rinehart, & Winston, 1975.

Eyman, R. K. & Borthwick, S. A. Patterns of care for mentally retarded persons. *Mental Retardation*, 1980, **18**, 63–66.

Eyman, R. K., Demaine, G. C., & Lei, T. Relationship between community environments and resident changes in adaptive behavior: A path model. *American Journal of Mental Deficiency*, 1979, **83**, 330–38.

Eyman, R. K., Dingman, H., & Sabagh, G. Association of characteristics of retarded patients and their families with speed of institutionalization. *American Journal of Mental Deficiency*, 1966, **71**, 93–99.

Eyman, R. K., & Miller, C. A demographic overview of severe and profound mental retardation. In C. E. Meyers (Ed.), *Quality of life in severely and profoundly mentally retarded people: Research foundations for improvement*. *Monographs of the American Association on Mental Deficiency*, 1978, No. 3, ix–xii.

Eyman, R. K., O'Connor, G., Tarjan, G., & Justice, R. S. Factors determining residential placement of mentally retarded children. *American Journal of Mental Deficiency*, 1972, **76**, 692–98.

Eyman, R. K., & Silverstein, A. B. The history of patient management in institutions for the mentally retarded. In *Financial reporting plan for day and residential facilities for the mentally retarded*, pp. 12–25. Chicago: Division of Hospital Administrative Services, American Hospital Association, 1973.

Eyman, R. K., Silverstein, A. B., & McLain, R. Effects of treatment programs on the acquisition of basic skills. *American Journal of Mental Deficiency*, 1975, **79**, 573–82.

Eyman, R. K., Silverstein, A. B., McLain, R., & Miller, C. Effects of residential settings on development. In P. Mittler (Ed.), *Research to practice in mental retardation*. Vol. 1, Care and intervention. Baltimore: University Park Press, 1977.

Eysenck, H. J. Neurosis and intelligence. *Lancet*, 1943, **245**, 363.

Eysenck, H. J. *The measurement of intelligence*. Baltimore: Williams and Wilkins, 1973.

Fairbanks, R. The subnormal child seventeen years after. *Mental Hygiene*, 1933, **17**, 177–208.

Farber, B. Effects of a severely mentally retarded child on family integration. *Monographs of the Society for Research on Child Development*, 1959, **24**(2), Series No. 71. (a)

Farber, B. *Prevalence of exceptional children in Illinois in 1958*. Springfield, Ill.: Superintendent of Public Instruction, 1959. (b)

Farber, B. Family organization and crisis: Maintenance of integration in families with a severely mentally retarded child. *Monographs of the Society for Research in Child Development*, 1960, **25**(1), Series No. 75. (a)

Farber, B. Perceptions of crisis and related variables and the impact of a retarded child on the mother. *Journal of Health and Human Behavior*, 1960, **1**, 108–18. (b)

Farber, B. *Mental retardation: Its social context and social consequences*. Boston: Houghton Mifflin, 1968.

Farber B., Jenne, W. C., & Tiogo, R. Family crisis and the decision to institutionalize the retarded child. *Council for Exceptional Children, NEA Research Monographs*, 1960, No. 1 (Series A).

Faterson, H. F., & Witkin, H. A. Longitudinal study of development of body concept. *Developmental Psychology*, 1970, **2**(3), 429–38.

Feldhusen, J., & Klausmeier, H. Anxiety, intelligence, and achievement in children of low, average, and high intelligence. *Child Development*, 1962, **33**, 403–409.

Fernald, G. M. *Remedial techniques in basic school subjects*. New York: McGraw-Hill, 1943.

Fernald, W. E. After-care study of the patients discharged from Waverly for a period of twenty-five years. *Ungraded*, 1919, **5**, 25–31.

Findlay, W. G., & Bryan, M. M. *Ability grouping: 1970, status, impact, and alternatives*. Athens, Ga.: University of Georgia, Center for Educational Improvement, 1971.

Fisher, M. A., & Zeaman, D. Growth and decline of retardate intelligence. In N. R. Ellis (Ed.), *International review of research in mental retardation*. Vol. 4, pp. 151–91. New York: Academic Press, 1970.

Fisher, M. A., & Zeaman, D. An attention-retention theory of retardate discrimination learning. In N. R. Ellis (Ed.), *The international review of research in mental retardation*. Vol. 6. New York: Academic Press, 1973.

Flaugher, R. L. The many definitions of test bias. *American Psychologist*, 1978, **33**, 671–79.

Flavell, J. H. *The developmental psychology of Jean Piaget*. Princeton, N.J.: Van Nostrand, 1963.

Fleming, E. S., & Anttonen, R. G. Teacher expectancy or my fair lady. *American Educational Research Journal*, 1971, **8**, 241–52. (a)

Fleming, E. S., & Anttonen, R. G. Teacher expectancy as related to the academic and personal growth of primary-age children. *Monographs of the Society for Research in Child Development*, 1971, **36**(5). (b)

Foley, J. M. Effect of labeling and teacher behavior on children's attitudes. *American Journal of Mental Deficiency*, 1979, **83**, 380–84.

Foley, R. W. A study of patients discharged from the Rome State School for the 20 year period ending December 31, 1924. *Journal of Psycho-Asthenia*, 1929, **34**, 180–207.

Forbes, P. Caring for the mentally handicapped. *Social Service Quarterly*, 1972, **46**, 1.

Forness, S. The mildly retarded as casualties of the educational system. *Journal of School Psychology*, 1972, **10**, 117–25.

Forness, S. R. Clinical criteria for mainstreaming mildly handicapped children. *Psychology in the Schools*, 1979, **16**, 508–14.

Foster, G. G., Ysseldyke, J. E., & Reese, J. H. "I wouldn't have seen it if I hadn't believed it." *Exceptional Children*, 1975, **41**, 469–73.

Fram, J. The right to be retarded—normally. *Mental Retardation*, 1974, **12**(6), 32.

Frank, H. S., & Rabinovitch, M. S. Auditory short-term memory: Developmental changes in rehearsal. *Child Development*, 1974, **45**, 397–407.

Frank, J. P. *My son's story*. New York: Knopf, 1952.

Frostig, M., Lefever, D. W., & Whittlesey, J. R. B. *The Marianne Frostig Developmental Test of Visual Perception*. Palo Alto, Calif.: Consulting Psychologists, 1964.

Furth, H. G. *Piaget for teachers*. Englewood Cliffs, N.J.: Prentice-Hall, 1970.

Gabriel, R. S. Malformations of the nervous system. In J. H. Menkes (Ed.), *Textbook of child neurology*. Philadelphia: Lea and Febiger, 1974.

Gagne, R. M. *The conditions of learning*. New York: Holt, Rinehart, and Winston, 1965.

Gallagher, J. J. Educational research needs in the field of mental retardation. In H. C. Haywood (Ed.), *Social-cultural aspects of mental retardation*. New York: Appleton-Century-Crofts, 1970.

Gallagher, J. J., Forsythe, P., Ringelheim, D., & Weintraub, F. J. Funding patterns and labeling. In N. Hobbs (Ed.), *Issues in the classification of children.* Vol. 2, pp. 432–62. San Francisco: Jossey-Bass, 1975.

Garber, H. L. Intervention in infancy: A developmental approach. In M. J. Begab & S. A. Richardson (Eds.), *The mentally retarded and society,* pp. 287–303. Baltimore: University Park Press, 1975.

Garber, H., & Heber, R. F. The Milwaukee Project: Indications of the effectiveness of early intervention in preventing mental retardation. In P. Mittler (Ed.), *Research to practice in mental retardation: Care and intervention.* Vol. 1, pp. 119–27. Baltimore: University Park Press, 1977.

Gardner, G. E., Tarjan, G., & Richmond, J. B. *Mental retardation: A handbook for the primary physician.* Chicago: American Medical Association, 1965.

Gardner, R. W., Holzman, P. S., Klein, G., Linton, H., & Spence, D. S. Cognitive control: A study of individual consistencies in cognitive behavior. *Psychological Issues,* 1959, 1(4).

Gardner, R. W., & Moriarity, A. *Personality development at preadolescence: Explorations of structure formation.* Seattle: University of Washington Press, 1968.

Gardner, W. I. *Reactions of intellectually normal and retarded boys after experimentally induced failure: A social learning theory interpretation.* Doctoral dissertation, George Peabody College. Ann Arbor, Mich.: University Microfilms, 1958.

Gardner, W. I. Social and emotional adjustment of mildly retarded children and adolescents: Critical review. *Exceptional Children,* 1966, **33,** 97–105.

Gardner, W. I. *Behavior modification in mental retardation: The education and habilitation of the mentally retarded adolescent and adult.* Chicago: Aldine-Atherton, 1971.

Garfield, S. L. Abnormal behavior and mental deficiency. In N. R. Ellis (Ed.), *Handbook of mental deficiency,* pp. 574–601. New York: McGraw-Hill, 1963.

Garfield, S. L., & Affleck, D. Individuals committed to a state home who were later released. *American Journal of Mental Deficiency,* 1960, **64,** 907–15.

Gerard, H. B., & Miller, N. *School desegregation: A long-term study.* New York: Plenum, 1975.

Gerjuoy, I. R. Verbal learning. Paper presented at the annual meeting of the American Association on Mental Deficiency, Denver, May 1967.

Gerjuoy, I. R., & Spitz, H. H. Associative clustering in free recall: Intellectual and developmental variables. *American Journal of Mental Deficiency,* 1966, **70,** 918–27.

Gersh, K., & Jones, R. L. Children's perceptions of the trainable mentally retarded: An experimental analysis. Unpublished manuscript, Ohio State University, 1973.

Gibbons, F. X., & Gibbons, B. N. Effects of the institutional label on peer assessments of institutionalized EMR persons. *American Journal of Mental Deficiency,* 1980, **84,** 602–09.

Gibbons, F. X., Sawin, L. G., & Gibbons, B. N. Evaluations of mentally retarded persons: "Sympathy" or patronization? *American Journal of Mental Deficiency,* 1979, **84,** 124–31.

Gibbs, J. P. Conceptions of deviant behavior: the old & the new. *Pacific Sociological Review,* 1969, **9,** 9–14.

Gibson, D. *Down's syndrome: The psychology of mongolism.* London: Cambridge University Press, 1978.

Gickling, E., & Theobald, J. Mainstreaming: Affect or effect. *Journal of Special Education,* 1975, **9,** 317–28.

Gilhool, T. K. The uses of litigation: The right of retarded children to a free public education. *Peabody Journal of Education,* 1973, **50,** 120–217.

Ginzberg, E., & Bray, D. W. *The uneducated.* New York: Columbia University Press, 1953.

Girardeau, F. L. Cultural-familial retardation. In N. R. Ellis (Ed.), *International review of research in mental retardation.* Vol. 5, pp. 303–48. New York: Academic Press, 1971.

Glaser, D. *Social deviance.* Chicago: Markham, 1971.

Glidden, L. M. Training of learning and memory in retarded persons: Strategies, techniques, and teaching tools. In N. R. Ellis (Ed.), *Handbook of mental deficiency* (2nd ed.), pp. 619–57. Hillsdale, N.J.: Lawrence Erlbaum, 1979.

Goddard, H. H. Two thousand normal children measured by the Binet measuring scale of intelligence. *Pedagogical Seminary,* 1911, **18,** 231–58.

Goddard, H. H. *The Kallikak family: A study in the heredity of feeble-mindedness.* New York: Macmillan, 1912.

Goffman, E. On the characteristics of total institutions. In *Symposium on preventive and social psychiatry.* Washington, D.C.: U.S. Government Printing Office, 1957.

Goffman, E. *Stigma.* Englewood Cliffs, N.J.: Prentice-Hall, 1963.

Goldberg, M. L., Passow, A. H., & Justman, J. The effects of ability grouping. Unpublished manuscript, Columbia University, Teacher's College, 1961.

Goldfarb, W. Effects of psychological deprivation in infancy and subsequent stimulation. *American Journal of Psychiatry,* 1945, **102,** 18–33.

Goldfarb, W. Emotional and intellectual consequences of psychologic deprivation in infancy: A re-evaluation. In W. Hock & J. Zubin (Eds.), *Psychopathology of childhood,* pp. 105–19. New York: Grune & Stratton, 1955.

Goldhaber, D. Does the changing view of early experience imply a changing view of early development? In L. G. Katz (Ed.), *Current topics in early childhood education.* Vol. 2, pp. 117–40. Norwood, N.J.: Ablex Publishing, 1979.

Goldman, R. B, & Hartig, L. K. The WISC may not be a valid predictor of school performance for primary-grade minority children. *American Journal of Mental Deficiency,* 1976, **80,** 583–87.

Goldsmith, J. S., & Fry, E. The effect of a high prediction on reading achievement and IQ of students in grade 10. Paper presented at the meeting of the American Educational Research Association Annual Convention, New York, 1971.

Goldstein, H. Social aspects of mental retardation. Unpublished doctoral dissertation, University of Illinois, 1957.

Goldstein, H. Issues in the education of the educable mentally retarded. *Mental Retardation*, 1963, **1**, 10–12, 52–53.

Goldstein, H. Social and occupational adjustment. In H. A. Stevens & R. Heber (Eds.), *Mental retardation: A review of research.* Chicago: University of Chicago Press, 1964.

Goldstein, H. The efficacy of special classes and regular classes in the education of educable mentally retarded children. In J. Zubin & G. A. Jervis (Eds.), *Psychopathology of mental development*, pp. 580–602. New York: Grune and Stratton, 1967.

Goldstein, H., Moss, J. W., & Jordan, L. J. *The efficacy of special class training on the development of mentally retarded children.* Cooperative Research Project No. 619. U.S. Office of Education, 1965.

Goldstein, K. Concerning rigidity. *Character and Personality*, 1943, **11**, 209–26.

Good, T. I., Brophy, J. E. Behavioral expression of teacher attitudes. *Journal of Educational Psychology*, 1972, **63**, 617–24.

Goodenough, F. L. A critique of experiments on raising the IQ. *Educational Methods*, 1939, **19**, 73–79.

Goodenough, F. L. New evidence on environmental influence on intelligence. *National Society for the Study of Education Yearbook*, 1940, **39**, 307–65.

Goodman, H., Gottlieb, J., & Harrison, R. H. Social acceptance of EMRs integrated into a nongraded elementary school. *American Journal of Mental Deficiency*, 1972, **76**, 412–17.

Goodman, J. F. Aging and IQ change in institutionalized mentally retarded. *Psychological Reports*, 1976, **39**, 999–1006.

Goodman, J. F. The diagnostic fallacy: A critique of Jane Mercer's concept of mental retardation. *Journal of School Psychology*, 1977, **15**, 197–206. (a)

Goodman, J. F. IQ decline in mentally retarded adults: A matter of fact or methodological flaw. *Journal of Mental Deficiency Research*, 1977, **21**, 199–203. (b)

Goodman, J. F., & Cameron, J. The meaning of IQ constancy in young retarded children. *The Journal of Genetic Psychology*, 1978, **132**, 109–19.

Gordon, E. W., & Wilkerson, D. A. *Compensatory education for the disadvantaged.* New York: College Entrance Examination Board, 1966.

Gordon, I. J., & Guinagh, B. J. *A home learning center approach to early stimulation.* Gainesville, Fla.: Institute for Development of Human Resources, 1974.

Gordon, M. How to overcome. *Newsweek*, 1979 (Oct. 22), p. 27.

Gorelick, M. C. *Are preschools willing to integrate children with handicaps? Careers in integrated early childhood programs.* Northridge: California State University, Northridge, Home Economics Department, Social and Rehabilitation Service, 1973. (ERIC Document Reproduction Service No. ED-097-794)

Gothberg, L. C. A comparison of the personality of runaway girls with a control group as expressed in themas of Murray's thematic apperception test. *American Journal of Mental Deficiency*, 1947, **51**, 627–31.

Gotoff, S. P. Infections. In R. Behrman (Ed.), *Neonatology: Diseases of the fetus and infant*, pp. 129–68. St. Louis: Mosby, 1973.

Gottesfeld, H. *Alternatives to psychiatric hospitalization.* New York: Gardner Press, 1977.

Gottesman, I. Genetic aspects of intelligent behavior. In N. R. Ellis (Ed.), *Handbook of mental deficiency*, pp. 253–96. New York: McGraw-Hill, 1963.

Gottlieb, J. Bicultural study of attitude change and behavior towards retardates. Unpublished doctoral dissertation, Yeshiva University, 1972.

Gottlieb, J. Attitudes toward retarded children: Effects of labeling and academic performance. *Studies in Learning Potential*, 1974, **3**(67), 1–16.

Gottlieb, J. Progress report to Advisory Committee on BEH–USOE Intramural Research Program, Project PRIME. Washington, D.C., February 20, 1975. (a)

Gottlieb, J. Public, peer, and professional attitudes toward mentally retarded persons. In M. J. Begab & S. A. Richardson (Eds.), *The mentally retarded and society: A social science perspective*, pp. 99–125. Baltimore: University Park Press, 1975. (b)

Gottlieb, J. (Ed.) *Educating mentally retarded persons in the mainstream.* Baltimore: University Park Press, 1980.

Gottlieb, J., & Budoff, M. Social acceptability of retarded children in nongraded schools differing in architecture. *American Journal of Mental Deficiency*, 1973, **78**, 15–19.

Gottlieb, J., & Corman, L. Attitudes toward retarded children. In R. L. Jones (Ed.), *Attitude and attitude change in special education.* Reston, Va.: Council for Exceptional Children, in press.

Gottlieb, J., & Davis, J. E. Social acceptance of EMRs during overt behavioral interactions. *American Journal of Mental Deficiency*, 1973, **78**, 141–43.

Gottlieb, J., Hutton, L., & Budoff, M. A preliminary evaluation of the academic achievement and social adjustment of EMRs in a nongraded school placement. Unpublished manuscript, Research Institute for Educational Problems, Cambridge, Mass., 1972.

Gottlieb, J., & Leyser, Y. Developing friendships in mentally retarded children. Unpublished manuscript, Northern Illinois University, 1979.

Gottlieb, J., Semmel, M. I., & Veldman, D. J. Correlates of social status among mainstreamed mentally retarded children. *Journal of Educational Psychology*, 1978, **70**, 396–405.

Gottlieb, J., & Siperstein, G. N. Attitudes toward mentally retarded persons: Effects of attitude referent specificity. *American Journal of Mental Deficiency*, 1976, **80**, 376–81.

Gottwald, H. Public awareness about mental retardation. *Council for Exceptional Children Research Monograph*. Reston, Va.: Council for Exceptional Children, 1970.

Gove, W. R. Societal reaction as an explanation of mental illness: An evaluation. *American Sociological Review*, 1970, **35**, 873–83.

Gozali, J. Perceptions of the EMR special class by former students. *Mental Retardation*, 1972, **10**, 34–35.

Gozali, J., & Meyen, E. L. The influence of the teacher expectancy phenomenon on the academic performances of educable mentally retarded pupils in special classes. *Journal of Special Education*, 1970, **4**, 417–24.

Graebner, O. F. Post Oak Village Campus halfway cottages. *Training School Bulletin*, November 1969.

Graham, J. T., & Graham, L. W. Language behavior of the mentally retarded: Syntatic characteristics. *American Journal of Mental-Deficiency*, 1971, **75**, 623–29.

Graliker, B. V., Koch, R., & Henderson, R. A. A study of factors influencing placement of retarded children in a state residential institution. *American Journal of Mental Deficiency*, 1965, **69**, 553–59.

Graves, W. L., Freeman, M. G., & Thompson, J. D. Culturally related reproductive factors in mental retardation. In H. C. Haywood (Ed.), *Social-cultural aspects of mental retardation*, pp. 695–736. New York: Appleton-Century-Crofts, 1970.

Gray, S. W., & Klaus, R. A. *The early training project: A seventh year report*. Nashville, Tenn.: George Peabody College, Demonstration and Research Center in Early Education, 1969.

Grays, C. At the bedside: The pattern of acceptance in parents of the retarded child. *Tomorrow's Nurse*, 1963, 4(3), 30–34.

Grebler, A. M. Parental attitudes toward mentally retarded children. *American Journal of Mental Deficiency*, 1952, **56**, 475–83.

Green, C. Social interaction in feeble-minded children. Unpublished master's thesis, University of Missouri, 1960.

Green, C., & Zigler, E. Social deprivation and the performance of retarded and normal children on a satiation task. *Child Development*, 1962, **33**, 499–508.

Green, H. B. Infants of alcoholic mothers. *American Journal of Obstetrics and Gynecology*, 1974, **118**, 713–16.

Greenbaum, J. J., & Wang, D. D. A semantic-differential study of the concepts of mental retardation. *Journal of General Psychology*, 1965, **73**, 257–72.

Greenberg, J. Social scientists take the stand: A review and appraisal of their testimony and litigation. *Michigan Law Review*, 1956, **54**, 953–70.

Greene, M. A., & Retish, P. M. A comparative study of attitudes among students in special education and regular education. *Training School Bulletin*, 1973, **70**, 10–14.

Greer, B. G. On being the parent of a handicapped child. *Exceptional Children*, 1975, **41**, 519.

Grossman, H. J. (Ed.) *Manual on terminology and classification in mental retardation*. Washington, D.C.: American Association on Mental Deficiency, 1973.

Grossman, H. J. *Manual on terminology and classification in mental retardation*. Washington, D.C.: American Association on Mental Deficiency, 1977.

Grossman, H. J. (Ed.) *Manual on terminology and classification in mental retardation*. (3rd. rev.) Washington, D.C.: American Association on Mental Deficiency, in press.

Grossman, H. J., & Rowitz, L. A community approach to services for the retarded. In R. K. Eyman, C. E. Meyers, & G. Tarjan (Eds.), Sociobehavioral studies in mental retardation. *Monographs of the American Association on Mental Deficiency*, 1973, No. 1, pp. 248–58.

Group for the Advancement of Psychiatry. *Basic considerations in mental retardation: A preliminary report*, 1959, Report No. 43. New York: Group for the Advancement of Psychiatry, 1959.

Guadalupe v. Tempe Elementary School District. Civil action 71–435 (D. Ariz.), 1971.

Guerin, G., & Szatlocky, K. Integration programs for the mildly retarded. *Exceptional Children*, 1974, **41**, 173–79.

Guess, P. D., & Horner, R. D. The severely and profoundly handicapped. In E. L. Meyen (Ed.), *Exceptional children and youth: An introduction*. Denver: Love Publishing, 1978.

Guilford, J. P. The structure of intellect. *Psychological Bulletin*, 1956, **53**, 267–93.

Guilford, J. P. *The nature of human intelligence*. New York: McGraw-Hill, 1967.

Gunzburg, H. C. Educational problems in mental deficiency. In A. M. Clarke & A. D. B. Clarke (Eds.), *Mental deficiency: The changing outlook*. New York: Free Press, 1965.

Gunzburg, H. C. Pedagogy. In J. Wortis (Ed.), *Mental retardation: An annual review*. Vol. 2, pp. 117–31. New York: Grune and Stratton, 1970.

Gunzburg, H. C. Psychotherapy. In A. M. Clarke & A. D. B. Clarke (Eds.), *Mental deficiency: The changing outlook*. (3rd ed.), pp. 708–28. New York: Free Press, 1974.

Guralnick, M. J. Early classroom-based intervention and the role of organizational structure. *Exceptional Children*, 1975, **42**, 25–31.

Guralnick, M. J. Nonhandicapped peers as educational and therapeutic resources. In P. Mittler (Ed.),

Research to practice in mental retardation: Care and intervention, pp. 165–70. Baltimore: University Park Press, 1977.

Guralnick, M. J. (Ed.). *Early intervention and the integration of handicapped and nonhandicapped children*. Baltimore: University Park Press, 1978.

Guskin, S. L. The perception of subnormality in mentally defective children. *American Journal of Mental Deficiency*, 1962, **67**, 53–60.

Guskin, S. L. Measuring the strength of the stereotype of the mental defective. *American Journal of Mental Deficiency*, 1963, **67**, 569–75. (a)

Guskin, S. L. Social psychologies of mental deficiencies. In N. R. Ellis (Ed.), *Handbook of mental deficiency*, pp. 325–52. New York: McGraw-Hill, 1963. (b)

Guskin, S. L. Theoretical and empirical strategies for the study of the labeling of mentally retarded persons. In N. R. Ellis (Ed.), *International review of research in mental retardation*. Vol. 9, pp. 127–58. New York: Academic Press, 1978.

Guskin, S. L., Bartel, N. R., & MacMillan, D. L. Perspective of the labeled child. In N. Hobbs (Ed.), *Issues in the classification of children*. Vol. 2, pp. 189–212. San Francisco: Jossey-Bass, 1975.

Guskin, S. L., & Spicker, H. H. Educational research in mental retardation. In N. R. Ellis (Ed.), *International review of research in mental retardation*. Vol. 3, pp. 217–78. New York: Academic Press, 1968.

Guthrie, G. M., Butler, A., & Gorlow, L. Patterns of self-attitudes of retardates. *American Journal of Mental Deficiency*, 1962, **66**, 222–29.

Guthrie, G. M., Butler, A., Gorlow, L., & White, G. N. Non-verbal expression of self-attitudes in retardates. *American Journal of Mental Deficiency*, 1964, **69**, 42–49.

Hall, E. *The politics of special education: Inequality in education*. Cambridge, Mass.: Harvard Center for Law and Education, 1969.

Hall, E. On the road to educational failure: A lawyer's guide to tracking. *Inequality in Education*, 1970, **5**, 1–6.

Halpern, C. R. The right to habilitation. In M. Kindred, J. Cohen, D. Penrod, & T. Shaffer (Eds.), *The mentally retarded citizen and the law*, pp. 385–406. New York: Free Press, 1976.

Hammill, D. The resource-room model in special education. *Journal of Special Education*, 1972, **6**, 349–54.

Hansen, H. Specificity of phenylketonuria screening tests in newborns. In P. Mittler (Ed.), *Research to practice in mental retardation: Biomedical aspects*. Vol. III, pp. 115–23. Baltimore: University Park Press, 1977.

Hansen, H. Decline of Down's syndrome after abortion reform in New York state. *American Journal of Mental Deficiency*, 1978, **83**, 185–88.

Harasymiw, S. J. Relationship of certain demographic and psychological variables toward the disabled. *Research Development and Evaluation Bulletin*, Series 1: *Attitudes toward the disabled*, 1971.

Hardy, H. A. The relationship between self-attitudes and performance on a paired-associates learning task in educable retardates. *Dissertation Abstracts*, 1967, **27**, 1657.

Haring, N. G., & Brown, L. J. *Teaching the severely handicapped*. Vol. 1. New York: Grune & Stratton, 1976.

Haring, N. G., & Krug, D. Placement in regular programs: Procedures and results. *Exceptional Children*, 1975, **41**, 413–17.

Harlow, H. F. The formation of learning sets. *Psychological Review*, 1949, **56**, 51–65.

Harlow, H. F. Learning set and error factor theory. In S. Koch (Ed.), *Psychology: A study of a science*, pp. 492–537. New York: McGraw-Hill, 1959.

Harris, G. J. Input and output organization in short-term serial recall by retarded and nonretarded children. *American Journal of Mental Deficiency*, 1972, **76**, 423–26.

Harter, S. Mental age, IQ and motivational factors in the discrimination learning set performance of normal and retarded children. *Journal of Experimental Child Psychology*, 1967, **5**, 123–41.

Harter, S. Developmental differences in the manifestation of mastery motivation on problem-solving tasks. *Child Development*, 1975, **46**, 370–78. (a)

Harter, S. Mastery motivation and need for approval in older children and their relationship to social desirability response tendencies. *Developmental Psychology*, 1975, **11**, 186–96. (b)

Harter, S. Effectance motivation reconsidered: Toward a developmental model. *Human Development*, 1978, **21**, 34–64.

Harter, S., & Zigler, E. The assessment of effectance motivation in normal and retarded children. *Developmental Psychology*, 1974, **10**, 169–80.

Harvard Educational Review, 1973, 43(4).

Havighurst, R. J. *Developmental tasks and education*. (3rd ed.) New York: David McKay, 1972.

Hay, W. Mental retardation problems in different age groups. *American Journal of Mental Deficiency*, 1951, **55**, 191–97.

Hayden, A. H., & Haring, N. G. Early intervention for high risk infants and young children: Programs for Down's syndrome children. In T. D. Tjossem (Ed.), *Intervention strategies for high risk infants and young children*, pp. 573–607. Baltimore: University Park Press, 1976.

Haywood, H. C. Motivational orientation of overachieving and underachieving elementary school children. *American Journal of Mental Deficiency*, 1968, **72**, 662–67. (a)

Haywood, H. C. Psychometric motivation and the efficiency of learning and performance in the mentally retarded. In B. Rishards (Ed.), *Proceedings of the First Congress of the International Association for Scientific Study of Mental Deficiency*. Reigate, England: Michael Jackson, 1968. (b)

Haywood, H. C. Labeling: Efficacy, evils, and caveats. Paper presented at the Joseph P. Kennedy, Jr., Foundation International Symposium of Human Rights, Retardation, and Research. Washington, D.C., October 1971.

Haywood, H. C., & Dobbs, V. Motivation and anxiety in high school boys. *Journal of Personality*, 1964, **32**, 371-79.

Haywood, H. C., & Tapp, J. T. Experience and the development of adaptive behavior. In N. R. Ellis (Ed.), *International review of research in mental retardation*. Vol. 1, pp. 109-51. New York: Academic Press, 1966.

Haywood, H.C., & Wachs, T. Size discrimination learning as a function of motivation-hygiene orientation in adolescents. *Journal of Educational Psychology*, 1966, **57**, 279-86.

Haywood, H. C., & Weaver, S. Differential effects of motivational orientations and incentive conditions on motor performance in institutionalized retardates. *American Journal of Mental Deficiency*, 1967, **72**, 459-67.

Heal, L. W., Sigelman, C. K., & Switzky, H. N. Research on community alternatives for the mentally retarded. In N. R. Ellis (Ed.), *International review of research in mental retardation*, Vol. 9, pp. 209-49. New York: Academic Press, 1978.

Heatherington, E. M., & McIntyre, C. W. Developmental psychology. In M. R. Rozenzweig & L. W. Porter (Eds.), *Annual review of psychology*. Vol. 26, pp. 97-136. Palo Alto, Calif.: Annual Reviews, 1975.

Hebb, D. O. *Organization of behavior*. New York: Wiley, 1949.

Heber, R. F. The relation of intelligence and physical maturity to social status of children. *Journal of Educational Psychology*, 1956, **47**, 158-62.

Heber, R. F. *Expectancy and expectancy changes in normal and mentally retarded boys*. Doctoral dissertation, George Peabody College. Ann Arbor, Mich.: University Microfilms, 1957.

Heber, R. F. Motor task performance of high grade mentally retarded males as a function of magnitude of incentive. *American Journal of Mental Deficiency*, 1959, **63**, 667-71. (a)

Heber, R. F. A manual on terminology and classification in mental retardation. *American Journal of Mental Deficiency Monograph*, 1959 (Supp. 64). (b)

Heber, R. F. A manual on terminology and classification in mental retardation. (Rev. ed.) *American Journal of Mental Deficiency Monograph*, 1961 (Supp. 64).

Heber, R. F. Personality. In H. A. Stevens & R. Heber (Eds.), *Mental retardation: A review of research*, pp. 143-74. Chicago: University of Chicago Press, 1964.

Heber, R. F. Research on education and habilitation of the mentally retarded. Paper read at Conference on Sociocultural Aspects of Mental Retardation, George Peabody College, Nashville, June 1968.

Heber, R. F. *Epidemiology of mental retardation*. Springfield, Ill.: Thomas, 1970.

Heber, R. F., & Dever, R. B. Research on education and habilitation of the mentally retarded. In H. C. Haywood (Ed.), *Social-cultural aspects of mental retardation*, pp. 395-427. New York: Appleton-Century-Crofts, 1970.

Heber, R. F., Dever, R. B., & Conry, J. The influence of environmental and genetic variables on intellectual development. In H. H. Prehm, L. A. Hamerlynch, & J. E. Crossen (Eds.), *Behavioral research in mental retardation*, pp. 1-23. Eugene, Ore.: University of Oregon Press, 1968.

Heber, R. F., & Garber, H. An experiment in prevention of cultural-familial mental retardation. In D. A. Primrose (Ed.), *Proceedings of the Second Congress of the International Association for the Scientific Study of Mental Deficiency*. Warsaw: Polish Medical Publishers, 1971.

Heber, R. F., Garber, H., Harrington, S., Hoffman, C., & Falendar, C. *Rehabilitation of families at risk for mental retardation: Progress report*. Madison, Wisc.: University of Wisconsin, 1972.

Heffernan, H. Some solutions to problems of students of Mexican descent. *Bulletin of the National Association of Secondary School Principals*, 1955, **39**(209), 43-53.

Heintz, P., & Blackman, L. S. Psychoeducational considerations with the mentally retarded child. In I. Bialer & M. Sternlicht (Eds.), *The psychology of mental retardation*, pp. 321-64. New York: Psychological Dimensions, 1977.

Heller, C. S. *Mexican-American youth: Forgotten youth at the crossroads*. New York: Random House, 1966.

Hendrickson, K., & Doughty, R. Decelerating undesired mealtime behavior in a group of profoundly retarded boys. *American Journal of Mental Deficiency*, 1967, **72**, 40-44.

Hess, R. D., & Shipman, V. C. Early experience and the socialization of cognitive modes in children. *Child Development*, 1965, **36**, 869-86.

Hewett, F. M., & Forness, S. R. *Education of exceptional learners*. Boston: Allyn and Bacon, 1974.

Hewitt, P., & Massey, J. O. *Clinical cues from the WISC*. Palo Alto, Calif.: Consulting Psychologists, 1969.

Higgins, C., & Sivers, C. H. A comparison of Stanford-Binet and colored Raven Progressive Matrices IQs for children with low socioeconomic status. *Journal of Consulting Psychology*, 1958, **22**, 465-68.

Higgins, J. V., Reed, E. W., & Reed, S. C. Intelligence and family size: A paradox resolved. *Eugenics Quarterly*, 1962, **9**, 84-90.

Hinshaw, E. M., & Heal, L. W. Like and cross modality recognition in retardates. *American Journal of Mental Deficiency*, 1968, **72**, 798-802.

Hobbs, N. A comparison of institutionalized and noninstitutionalized mentally retarded. *American Journal of Mental Deficiency*, 1964, **69**, 206-10.

Hobbs, N. (Ed.) *Issues in the classification of children*. Vols. 1, 2. San Francisco: Jossey-Bass, 1975. (a)

Hobbs, N. *The futures of children*. San Francisco: Jossey-Bass, 1975. (b)

Hobson v. *Hansen.* 269 F. Supp. 401 (D.D.C.), 1967.

Hodges, W. L., McCandless, B. R., & Spicker, H. H. *The development and evaluation of a diagnostically based curriculum for preschool psychosocially deprived children.* Washington, D.C.: U.S. Department of Health, Education, and Welfare, 1967.

Hodges, W. L., McCandless, B. R., & Spicker, H. H. *Diagnostic teaching for preschool children.* Arlington, Va.: Council for Exceptional Children, 1971.

Hollinger, C. S., & Jones, R. L. Community attitudes toward slow learners and mental retardates: What's in a name? *Mental Retardation,* 1970, **8,** 19–23.

Hollingworth, L. S. *The psychology of subnormal children.* New York: Macmillan, 1926.

Holt, E. B. *Animal drive and the learning process.* Vol. 1. New York: Holt, 1931.

Holt, K. S. Home care of severely retarded children. *Pediatrics,* 1958, **22,** 744–55.

Holt, M. M., Rickard, H. C., & Ellis, N. R. A note on word modeling in retarded adolescents. *American Journal of Mental Deficiency,* 1972, **77,** 237–39.

Holtzman, N. A., Welcher, D. W., & Mellits, E. D. Termination of restricted diet in children with phenylketonuria: A randomized controlled study. *New England Journal of Medicine,* 1975, **293,** 1121–24.

Hon, E. H. Fetal heart monitoring. In L. Gluck (Ed.), *Modern perinatal medicine,* pp. 139–47. Chicago: Yearbook, 1974.

Honzik, M. P., Macfarlane, J. W., & Allen, L. The stability of mental test performance between two and eighteen years. *Journal of Experimental Education,* 1948, **17,** 309–14.

Horn, J. M., Loehlin, J. C., & Willerman, L. Intellectual resemblance among adoptive and biological relatives: The Texas Adoption Project. *Behavior Genetics,* 1979, **9,** 177–207.

House, B. J., & Zeaman, D. Visual discrimination learning in imbeciles. *American Journal of Mental Deficiency,* 1958, **63,** 447–52.

Howe, S. G. *On the causes of idiocy.* Edinburgh: McLacklan and Stewart, 1858.

Hsia, D. Y. Phenylketonuria. *Developmental Medicine and Child Neurology,* 1967, **9,** 531–40.

Hsia, D. Y. A critical evaluation of PKU screening. *Hospital Practice,* 1971, **6**(4), 101–12.

Hughes, R. B., & Lessler, K. A. A comparison of WISC and Peabody scores of Negro and white rural school children. *American Journal of Mental Deficiency,* 1965, **69,** 877–80.

Humphreys, L. G. Addendum. *American Psychologist,* 1975, **30,** 95–96.

Hunt, J. G., Fitzhugh, L. C., & Fitzhugh, K. B. Teaching "exit-ward" patients appropriate appearance behaviors by using reinforcement techniques. *American Journal of Mental Deficiency,* 1968, **73,** 41–45.

Hunt, J. M. *Intelligence and experience.* New York: Ronald Press, 1961.

Hunt, J. M. Environment, development, and scholastic achievement. In M. Deutsch, I. Katz, & A. R. Jensen (Eds.), *Social class, race, and psychological development,* pp. 293–336. New York: Holt, Rinehart, and Winston, 1968.

Hunt, J. M. *The challenge of incompetence and poverty.* Urbana, Ill.: University of Illinois Press, 1969.

Hunt, N. *The world of Nigel Hunt: The diary of a mongoloid youth.* New York: Garrett, 1967.

Hutton, L. V. Breaking the news. In *Stress on families of the mentally handicapped.* Third International Congress, International League of Societies for the Mentally Handicapped, 1966.

Iano, R. P., Ayers, D., Heller, H. B., McGettigan, J. F., & Walker, V. S. Sociometric status of retarded children in an integrated program. *Exceptional Children,* 1974, **40,** 267–71.

Illingworth, R. S. Delayed maturation in development. *Journal of Pediatrics,* 1961, **58,** 761.

Illingworth, R. S. *The development of the infant and young child.* Baltimore: Williams and Wilkins, 1966.

Illinois Department of Public Health. The waiting list: A study of the mentally retarded. Report to the Interdepartmental Committee on Mental Retardation, December 1965.

Illsley, R. The sociological study of reproduction and its outcome. In S. A. Richardson & A. F. Guttmacher (Eds.), *Childbearing: Its social and psychological aspects.* Baltimore: Williams and Wilkins, 1967.

Inhelder, B. *The diagnosis of reasoning in the mentally retarded.* New York: John Day, 1968.

Ireland, W. W. *On idiocy and imbecility.* London: Churchill, 1877.

Ireland, W. W. *The mental affections of children: Idiocy, imbecility, and insanity.* Philadelphia: Blakiston, 1900.

Jabbour, J. T., Danilo, A. D., Gilmartin, R. C., & Goulieb, M. I. *Pediatric neurology handbook.* Flushing, N.Y.: Medical Examination, 1973.

Jackson, G. D. Another psychological view from the Association of Black Psychologists. *American Psychologist.* 1975, **30,** 88–93.

Jaffe, J. Attitudes of adolescents toward the mentally retarded. *American Journal of Mental Deficiency,* 1966, **70,** 907–12.

Janicki, M. P. Personal growth and community residence environments: A review. In H. C. Haywood (Ed.), *Living environments for developmentally retarded persons,* pp. 59–101. Baltimore: University Park Press, 1981.

Jastak, J. F. Mental retardation. *Science,* 1967, **155,** 577–78.

Jensen, A. R. The clinical management of the mentally retarded child and the parents. *American Journal of Psychiatry,* 1950 **106,** 830–33.

Jensen, A. R. Learning abilities in retarded, average, and gifted children. *Merrill-Palmer Quarterly,* 1963, **9,** 123–40.

Jensen, A. R. Rote learning in retarded adults and normal children. *American Journal of Mental Deficiency,* 1965, **69,** 828–34.

Jensen, A. R. Social class, race, and genetics: Implications for education. *American Educational Research Journal*, 1968, **5**, 1–412.

Jensen, A. R. How much can we boost IQ and scholastic achievement? *Harvard Educational Review*, 1969, **39**, 1–123.

Jensen, A. R. Another look at culture-fair testing. In J. Hellmuth (Ed.), *Disadvantaged child*. Vol. 3. New York: Brunner/Mazel, 1970. (a)

Jensen, A. R. A theory of primary and secondary familial mental retardation. In N. R. Ellis (Ed.), *International review of research in mental retardation*. Vol. 4, pp. 33–105, New York: Academic Press, 1970. (b)

Jensen, A. R. g: Outmoded theory or unconquered frontier? *Creative Science and Technology*, 1979, **2**(3), 16–29.

Jensen, A. R. *Bias in mental testing*. New York: Free Press, 1980.

Jensen, A. R., & Rohwer, W. D., Jr. Verbal mediation in paired-associate and serial learning. *Journal of Learning and Verbal Behavior*, 1963, **1**, 346–52. (a)

Jensen, A. R., & Rohwer, W. D., Jr. The effect of verbal mediation on the learning and retention of paired-associates by retarded adults. *American Journal of Mental Deficiency*, 1963, **68**, 80–84. (b)

Jervis, G. A. The genetics of phenylpyruvic oligophrenia. *Journal of Mental Science*, 1939, **85**, 719.

Jervis, G. A. Medical aspects of mental deficiency. *American Journal of Mental Deficiency*, 1952, **57**, 175–88.

Johnson, G. O. A study of the social position of mentally handicapped children in the regular grades. *American Journal of Mental Deficiency*, 1950, **55**, 60–89.

Johnson, G. O. Special education for the mentally handicapped: A paradox. *Exceptional Children*, 1962, **19**, 62–69.

Johnson, G. O., & Kirk, S. A. Are mentally handicapped children segregated in the regular grades? *Exceptional Children*, 1950, **17**, 65–68.

Johnson, J. L. Special education and the inner city: A challenge for the future or another means for cooling the mark out? *Journal of Special Education*, 1969, **3**, 241–51.

Jones, K. L. Fetal alcohol syndrome. Orange County Chapter of the March of Dimes, Conference on Research, Irvine, Calif., May 31, 1980.

Jones, K. L., & Smith, D. W. Recognition of the fetal alcohol syndrome in early infancy. *Lancet*, 1974, **2**, 999–1001.

Jones, K. L., Smith, D. W., Streissguth, A. P., & Myrianthopoulos, N. C. Outcome in offspring of chronic alcoholic women. *Lancet*, 1974, **1**, 1076–78.

Jones, K. L., Smith, D. W., Ulleland, C. N., & Streissguth, A. P. Pattern of malformation in offspring of chronic alcoholic mothers. *Lancet*, 1973, **1**, 1267–71.

Jones, R. L. Research on the education of the mentally retarded. Cassette tape prepared for training of educational researchers. Project of the American Educational Association, 1971. (a)

Jones, R. L. Teacher management of stigma in classes for the educable mentally retarded. Paper presented at the annual meeting of the California Educational Research Association, San Diego, April 1971. (b)

Jones, R. L. Labels and stigma in special education. *Exceptional Children*, 1972, **38**, 553–64.

Jones, R. L. Educational alienation, fatalism, school achievement motivation, and self-concepts in mental retardates. Unpublished manuscript, University of California at Riverside, 1973. (a)

Jones, R. L. Special education and the minority child. In J. Magary & E. Williams (Eds.), *Eleventh annual distinguished lectures in special education and rehabilitation*. Los Angeles: University of Southern California Press, 1973. (b)

Jones, R. L., & Gottfried, N. W. The prestige of special education teaching. *Exceptional Children*, 1966, **32**, 465–68.

Jones, R. L., & MacMillan, D. L. *Special education in transition*. Boston: Allyn and Bacon, 1974.

Jordan, T. E. Language and mental retardation: A review of the literature. In R. L. Schiefelbusch, R. H. Copeland, & J. O. Smith (Eds.), *Language and mental retardation*, pp. 20–38. New York: Holt, Rinehart, and Winston, 1967.

Jose, J., & Cody, J. J. Teacher-pupil interaction as it related to attempted changes in teacher expectancy of academic ability and achievement. *American Educational Research Journal*, 1971, **8**, 39–49.

Journal of Special Education, 1972, **6**(4), 335–95.

Justice, R. S., O'Connor, G., & Warren, N. Problems reported by parents of mentally retarded children: Who helps? *American Journal of Mental Deficiency*, 1971, **75**, 685–91.

Kagan, J., & Kogan, N. Individuality and cognitive processes. In P. H. Mussen (Ed.), *Carmichael's handbook of child psychology*. (3rd ed.) Vol. 1, pp. 1273–1365. New York: Wiley, 1970.

Kagan, J., & Messer, S. B. A reply to "Some misgivings about the Matching Familiar Figures Test as a measure of reflection-impulsivity." *Developmental Psychology*, 1975, **11**, 244–48.

Kagan, J., Moss, H. A., & Sigel, I. E. Psychological significance of styles of conceptualization. In J. C. Wright & J. Kagan (Eds.), Basic cognitive processes in children. *Monographs of the Society for Research in Child Development*, 1963, **28**(2), Series No. 86.

Kagan, J., Pearson, L., & Welch, L. The modifiability of an impulsive tempo. *Journal of Educational Psychology*, 1966, **57**, 359–65.

Kagan, J., Rosman, B., Day, D., Albert, J., & Phillips, W. Information processing in the child: Significance of analytic and reflective attitudes. *Psychological Monographs*, 1964, **78**(1).

Kagan, J., Sontag, L. W., Baker, C. T., & Nelson, V. L. Personality and IQ change. *Journal of Abnormal and Social Psychology*, 1958, **56**, 261–66.

Kagan, S., & Madsen, M. C. Cooperation and competition of Mexican, Mexican-American, and Anglo-American children of two ages under four instructional sets. *Developmental Psychology*, 1971, **5**, 32–39.

Kanner, L. Miniature textbook of feeble-mindedness. *Child Care Monographs*, 1949, No. 1.

Kanner, L. Parents' feelings about retarded children. *American Journal of Mental Deficiency*, 1953, **57**, 375–83.

Kanner, L. Parent counseling. In J. Rothstein (Ed.), *Mental retardation: Readings and resources*. New York: Holt, Rinehart, and Winston, 1962.

Kanner, L. *A history of the care and study of the mentally retarded.* Springfield, Ill.: Thomas, 1964.

Kanner, L. Medicine in the history of mental retardation: 1800–1965. *American Journal of Mental Deficiency*, 1967, **72**, 165–70.

Kaplan, A. R. Genetics. In J. Wortis (Ed.), *Mental retardation and developmental disabilities*. Vol. 3, pp. 57–63. New York: Brunner/Mazel. 1971.

Karen, R. L., & Maxwell, S. J. Strengthening self-help behavior in the retardate. *American Journal of Mental Deficiency*, 1967, **71**, 546–50.

Karnes, M. B. *Research and developmental program on preschool disadvantaged children.* Final report. Vol. 1. University of Illinois. Contract OE-6-10-235, U.S. Office of Education, 1969.

Karnes, M. B., & Lee, R. C. Mainstreaming in the preschool. In L. G. Katz (Ed.), *Current topics in early childhood education*, Vol. 2, pp. 13–42. Norwood, N.J.: Ablex Publishing, 1979.

Karnes, M. B., & Zehrbach, R. R. Alternative models for delivering services to young handicapped children. In J. B. Jordan, A. H. Hayden, M. B. Karnes, & M. M. Woods (Eds.), *Early childhood education for exceptional children*. Reston, Va.: Council for Exceptional Children, 1977.

Katz, I. Review of evidence relating to effects of desegregation on the intellectual performance of Negroes. *American Psychologist*, 1964, **19**, 381–99.

Katz, I. Factors influencing Negro performance in the desegregated school. In M. Deutsch, I. Katz, & A. R. Jensen (Eds.), *Social class, race, and psychological development*, pp. 254–89. New York: Holt, Rinehart, and Winston, 1968.

Katz, I., Epps, E. C., & Benjamin, L. Effects of white authoritarianism in biracial work groups. *Journal of Abnormal and Social Psychology*, 1960, **61**, 448–56.

Katz, I., & Greenbaum, C. Effects of anxiety, threat, and racial environment on task performance of Negro college students. *Journal of Abnormal and Social Psychology*, 1963, **66**, 562–67.

Katz, I., Henchy, T., & Allen, H. Effects of race of tester, approval-disapproval, and need on Negro children's learning. *Journal of Personality and Social Psychology*, 1968, **8**, 34–42.

Katz, I., Roberts, S., & Robinson, J. Effects of task difficulty, race of administrator, and instruction upon the expression of hostility by Negro boys. *Journal of Personality and Social Psychology*, 1965, **2**, 53–59.

Katz, I., Robinson, J., Epps, E. C., & Waley, P. The influence of the race of the experimenter and instructions upon the expressions of hostility by Negro boys. *Journal of Social Issues*, 1964, **20**, 54–59.

Kaufman, M. E. The formation of a learning set in institutionalized and noninstitutionalized children. *American Journal of Mental Deficiency*, 1963, **67**, 601–05.

Kaufman, M. E., & Prehm, H. J. A review of research on learning sets and transfer of training in mental defectives. In N. R. Ellis (Ed.), *International review of research in mental retardation*. Vol. 2, pp. 123–49. New York: Academic Press, 1966.

Kaufman, M. J., Gottlieb, J., Agard, J. A., & Kukic, M. B. Mainstreaming: Toward an explication of the construct. In E. L. Meyen, G. A. Vergason, & R. J. Whelan (Eds.), *Alternatives for teaching exceptional children*, pp. 35–54. Denver: Love, 1975.

Keirn, W. C. Shopping parents: Patient problem or professional problem? *Mental Retardation*, 1971, **9**(4), 6–7.

Keller, F. S. *Learning: Reinforcement theory.* (2nd ed.) New York: Random House, 1969.

Kelman, H. R. The effect of a brain-damaged child on the family. In H. G. Birch (Ed.), *Brain-damage in children: The biological and social aspects*. Baltimore: Williams and Wilkins, 1964.

Kendler, T. S., & Kendler, H. H. Reversal and nonreversal shifts in kindergarten children. *Journal of Experimental Psychology*, 1959, **58**, 56–60.

Kennedy, R. J. R. *The social adjustment of morons in a Connecticut city.* Willport, Conn.: Commissions to Study Resources in Connecticut, 1948.

Kennedy, R. J. R. The social adjustment of morons in a Connecticut city: Summary and conclusions, and abstract of a Connecticut community revisited: A study of social adjustment of a group of mentally deficient adults in 1948 and 1960. In T. E. Jordan (Ed.), *Perspectives in mental retardation*. Carbondale, Ill.: Southern Illinois University Press, 1966.

Keogh, B. K. Perceptual and cognitive styles: Implications for special education. In L. Mann & D. A. Sabatino (Eds.), *The first review of special education*. Vol. 1, pp. 83–111. Philadelphia: Journal of Special Education Press, 1973.

Keogh, B. K., Levitt, M. L., & Robson, G. *Historical and legislative antecedents of decertification and transition programs in California public schools.* Technical Report SERP 74-A3. California State Department and University of California at Los Angeles Graduate School of Education, November 1974.

Keogh, B. K., & MacMillan, D. L. Effects of socioeconomic status, IQ, and motivation on children's serial learning. *American Educational Research Journal*, 1971, **8**, 27–38.

Keogh, B. K., & MacMillan, D. L. Issues in the education of exceptional children. Unpublished manuscript, University of California at Los Angeles, 1976.

Kester, S. W., & Letchworth, G. A. Communication of teacher expectations and their effects on achievement and attitudes of secondary school students. *Journal of Educational Research*, 1972, **66**, 51–55.

Keston, M. J., & Jiminez, C. A study of the performance on English and Spanish editions of the Stanford-Binet Intelligence Test by Spanish-American children. *Journal of Genetic Psychology*, 1954, **85**, 262–69.

Kidd, J. W. Toward a more precise definition of mental retardation. *Mental Retardation*, 1964, **2**, 209–12.

Kidd, J. W. Pro: The efficacy of special class placement for educable mental retardates. Paper presented at the 48th Annual Convention of the Council for Exceptional Children, Chicago, April 1970.

Kidd, J. W. A Committee praised . . .: An open letter to the Committee on Terminology and Classification of AAMD from the Committee on Definition and Terminology of CEC–MR. *Mental Retardation*, 1979, **17**, 96–97.

Kimbrell, D. L., & Luckey, R. E. Attitude change resulting from open-house guided tours in a state school for mental retardates. *American Journal of Mental Deficiency*, 1964, **69**, 21–22.

Kindred, M., Cohen, J., Penrod, D., & Shaffer, T. (Eds.), *The mentally retarded citizen and the law*. New York: Free Press, 1976.

King, R. D., & Raynes, N. V. Patterns of institutional care for the severely subnormal. *American Journal of Mental Deficiency*, 1968, **72**, 700–09.

Kirk, S. A. The influence of manual training on the learning of simple words in the case of subnormal boys. *Journal of Educational Psychology*, 1933, **24**, 525–35.

Kirk, S. A. *Teaching reading to slow learning children*. Boston: Houghton Mifflin, 1940.

Kirk, S. A. *Early education of the mentally retarded: An experimental study*. Urbana, Ill.: University of Illinois Press, 1958.

Kirk, S. A. Research in education. In H. A. Stevens & R. Heber (Eds.), *Mental retardation: A review of research*, pp. 57–99. Chicago: University of Chicago Press, 1964.

Kirk, S. A., & Johnson, G. O. *Educating the retarded child*. Cambridge, Mass.: Riverside Press, 1951.

Kirk, S. A., McCarthy, J., & Kirk, W. *Illinois Test of Psycholinguistic Abilities*. (Rev. ed.) Urbana, Ill.: University of Illinois Press, 1968.

Kirk, S. A., & Weiner, B. B. The Onondaga Census: Fact or artifact. *Exceptional Children*, 1959, **25**, 226–28, 230–31.

Kirman, B. H. Clinical aspects. In J. Wortis (Ed.), *Mental retardation*. Vol. 1, pp. 42–56. New York: Grune and Stratton, 1970. (a)

Kirman, B. H. Down's syndrome. In J. Wortis (Ed.), *Mental Retardation*. Vol. 1, pp. 57–74. New York: Grune and Stratton, 1970. (b)

Kirman, B. H. Clinical aspects. In J. Wortis (Ed.), *Mental retardation*, Vol. 3, pp. 1–20. New York: Grune & Stratton, 1971.

Kirp, D. L. Schools as sorters: The constitutional and policy implications of student classification. *University of Pennsylvania Law Review*, 1973, **121**(4), 705–97.

Kirp, D. L. On legal and educational questions of classification in students. *Harvard Educational Review*, 1974, **44**(1), 7–52. (a)

Kirp, D. L. Student classification, public policy, and the courts. *Harvard Educational Review*, 1974, **44**(1), 7–52. (b)

Kirp, D. L., Buss, W., & Kuriloff, P. J. Legal reform of special education: Empirical studies and procedural proposals. *California Law Review*, 1974, **62**(1), 40–155.

Kirp, D. L., Kuriloff, P. J., & Buss, W. C. Legal mandates and organizational change. In N. Hobbs (Ed.), *Issues in the classification of children*. Vol. 2, pp. 319–82. San Francisco: Jossey-Bass, 1975.

Kitano, H. H. L. Validity of the children's anxiety scale and the modified revised California inventory. *Child Development*, 1960, **31**, 67–72.

Kitsuse, J. I. 1962. Societal reaction to deviant behavior: Problems of theory and method. *Social Problems*, 1962, **9**, 247–56.

Klaber, M. M. A densely populated small state: Connecticut. In R. B. Kugel & W. Wolfensberger (Eds.), *Changing patterns in residential services for the mentally retarded*. Washington, D.C.: U.S. Government Printing Office, 1969.

Klaber, M. M. *Retardates in residence: A study of institutions*. West Hartford, Conn.: University of Hartford, 1970.

Klein, J. W. Mainstreaming the preschooler. *Young Children*, 1975, **30**, 317–26.

Klein, J. W. Comparison of model preschool programs. In K. F. Riegel & J. A. Meacham (Eds.), *The developing individual in a changing world*. The Hague: Mouton, 1976.

Knobloch, H., & Pasamanick, B. Seasonal variations in the births of the mentally deficient. *American Journal of Public Health*, 1958, **48**, 1201–08.

Knox, W. E. Phenylketonuria. In J. B. Stanbury, J. B. Wyngarten, & D. S. Frederickson (Eds.), *The metabolic basis of inherited disease*. New York: McGraw-Hill, 1972.

Koch, R., Graliker, B. V., Sands, R., & Parmalee, A. H. Attitude study of parents with mentally retarded children: I. Evaluation of parental satisfaction with medical care of a retarded child. *Pediatrics*, 1959, **23**, 582–84.

Koegler, S. J. The management of the retarded child in practice. *Canadian Medical Association Journal*, 1963, **89**, 1009–14.

Kohlberg, L., & Zigler, E. The impact of cognitive maturity on the development of sex-role attitude in the years 4 to 8. *Genetic Psychology Monographs*, 1967, **75**, 89–165.

Kolstoe, O. P. *Teaching educable mentally retarded children.* (2nd ed.) New York: Holt, Rinehart, and Winston, 1976.

Koluchova, J. Severe deprivation in twins: A case study. *Journal of Child Psychology and Psychiatry*, 1972, **13**, 107–14.

Koluchova, J. A report on the further development of twins after severe prolonged deprivation. In A. M. Clarke & A. D. B. Clarke (Eds.), *Early experience: Myth and evidence*, pp. 56–66. New York: Free Press, 1976. (a)

Koluchova, J. Severe deprivation in twins: A case study. In A. M. Clarke & A. D. B. Clarke (Eds.), *Early experience: Myth and evidence*, pp. 45–55. New York: Free Press, 1976. (b)

Korn, H. Law, fact, and science in the courts. *Columbia Law Review*, 1966, **66**, 1080–16.

Kounin, J. Experimental studies of rigidity. I. The measurement of rigidity in normal and feebleminded persons. *Character and Personality*, 1941, **9**, 251–73. (a)

Kounin, J. Experimental studies of rigidity. II. The explanatory power of the concept of rigidity as applied to feeblemindedness. *Character and Personality*, 1941, **9**, 273–82. (b)

Kounin, J. S. Intellectual development and rigidity. In R. G. Barker, J. S. Kounin, & H. F. Wright (Eds.), *Child behavior and development*, pp. 179–97. New York: McGraw-Hill, 1943.

Kramer, M. A discussion of the concepts of incidence and prevalence as related to epidemiologic studies of mental disorders. *American Journal of Public Health*, 1957, **47**, 826–40.

Kramm, E. R. *Families of mongoloid children.* Washington, D.C.: U.S. Government Printing Office, 1963.

Kranz, P. L., Weber, W. A., & Fishnell, K. N. The relationship between teacher perception of pupils and teacher behavior toward those pupils. Paper read at annual meeting of the American Education Research Association, Minneapolis, 1970.

Krugman, S. Present status of measles and rubella immunization in the United States: A medical progress report. *Journal of Pediatrics*, 1977, **90**, 1–12.

Kugel, R. B. Why innovative action? In R. B. Kugel & W. Wolfensberger (Eds.). *Changing patterns in residential services for the mentally retarded.* Washington, D. C.: U.S. Government Printing Office, 1969.

Kuhlman, F. Mental deficiency, feeble-mindedness, and defective delinquency. *American Association for the Study of the Feeble-minded*, 1924, **29**, 58–70.

Kuhlman, F. Definition of mental deficiency. *American Journal of Mental Deficiency*, 1941, **46**, 206–13.

Kurtz, P. S., Harrison, M., Neisworth, J. T., & Jones, R. T. Influence of "mentally retarded" label on teachers' nonverbal behavior toward preschool children. *American Journal of Mental Deficiency*, 1977, **82**, 204–06.

Labov, W. Academic ignorance and black intelligence. *The Atlantic Monthly*, 1971, **229** (6), 59–67.

Labov, W. The logic of nonstandard English. In P. P. Giglioli (Ed.), *Language and social context.* Harmondsworth, England: Penguin, 1972.

Lambert, N. M., Windmiller, M., Cole, L., & Figueroa, R. A. Standardization of a public school version of the AAMD Adaptive Behavior Scale. *Mental Retardation*, 1975, **13**(2), 3–7.

Landesman-Dwyer, S., Berkson, G., & Romer, D. Affiliation and friendship of mentally retarded residents in group homes. *American Journal of Mental Deficiency*, 1979, **83**, 571–80.

Landesman-Dwyer, S., Sackett, G. P., & Kleinman, J. S. Relationship of size to resident and staff behavior in small community residences. *American Journal of Mental Deficiency*, 1980, **85**, 6–17.

Landesman-Dwyer, S., & Sackett, G. P. Behavioral changes in nonambulatory, profoundly mentally retarded individuals. In C. E. Meyers (Ed.), Quality of life in severely and profoundly mentally retarded people: Research foundations for improvement. *Monographs of the American Association on Mental Deficiency*, 1978, No. 3., 55–144.

Landesman-Dwyer, S., Stein, J. G., & Sackett, G. P. A behavioral and ecological study of group homes. In G. P. Sackett (Ed.), *Observing behavior*, Vol. 1, Theory and applications in mental retardation. Baltimore: University Park Press, 1978.

Lang, J. L., & Smirnoff, V. N. Emotional disturbance in mental retardation: A review of recent research in France. In H. C. Haywood (Ed.), *Social-cultural aspects of mental retardation*, pp. 672–91. New York: Appleton-Century-Crofts, 1970.

Lapides, J. *Exceptional children in Head Start: Characteristics of preschool handicapped children.* ERIC Reproduction Service No. ED-089-844. College Park, Md.: Head Start Regional Resource and Training Center, 1973.

Lapp, E. R. A study of the social adjustment of slow-learning children who were assigned part-time to regular classes. *American Journal of Mental Deficiency*, 1957, **62**, 254–62.

Larry P. v. *Riles.* USLW 2033 (U.S. June 21), 1972.

Larsen, S. C. The influence of teacher expectations on school performance of handicapped children. *Focus on Exceptional Children*, 1975, **6**(8), 1–14.

Lazer, I., Hubbell, V. R., Roshce, M., & Royce, J. *The persistence of preschool effects: A long-term follow-up of fourteen infant and preschool experiments.* Ithaca, N.Y.: Cornell University, 1977.

Lazerson, M. Educational institutions and mental subnormality: Notes on writing a history. In M. J. Begab & S. A. Richardson (Eds.), *The Mentally retarded and society,* pp. 33–52. Baltimore: University Park Press, 1975.

Leahy, A. M. Nature-nurture and intelligence. *Genetic Psychology Monographs,* 1935, **17,** 236–308.

Leland, H. Testing the disadvantaged. In W. C. Rhodes (Chm.), *Use and misuse of standardized intelligence tests in psychological and educational research and practice.* Symposium presented at the American Psychological Association, Washington, D.C., September, 1971.

Leland, H. Mental retardation and adaptive behavior. *Journal of Special Education,* 1972, **6,** 71–80.

Leland, H. Adaptive behavior and mentally retarded behavior. In R. K. Eyman, C. E. Meyers, & G. Tarjan (Eds.), Sociobehavioral studies in mental retardation. *Monographs of the American Association of Mental Deficiency,* 1973, No. 1, pp. 91–100.

Leland, H., Nihira, K., Foster, R., Shellhaas, M., & Kagin, E. *Conference on the measurement of adaptive behavior.* Parsons, Kansas: Parsons State Hospital and Training Center, 1968.

Lemert, E. M. *Social pathology.* New York: McGraw-Hill, 1951.

Lemert, E. M. *Human deviance, social problems, and social control.* Englewood Cliffs, N.J.: Prentice-Hall, 1967; 2nd ed., 1972.

Lemkau, P. V., & Imre, P. D. Results of a field epidemiologic study. *American Journal of Mental Deficiency,* 1969, **73,** 858–63.

Lenneberg, E. H. *Biological foundations of language.* New York: Wiley, 1967.

Lenneberg, E. H., Nichols, I. A., & Rosenberger, E. F. Primitive stages of language development in mongolism. *Proceedings of the Association for Research in Nervous and Mental Diseases,* 1964, **42,** 119–37.

Levinson, E. J. *Retarded children in Maine: A survey and analysis.* Orono: University of Maine Press, 1962.

Lewin, K. *A dynamic theory of personality: Selected papers.* A. K. Adams & K. E. Zenner (Trans.). New York: McGraw-Hill, 1935.

Lewis, E. O. *Report on an investigation into the incidence of mental defect in six areas, 1925–1927.* Report of the Mental Deficiency Committee. Part 4. London: H. M. Stationery Office, 1929.

Lewis, E. O. Types of mental deficiency and their social significance. *Journal of Mental Science,* 1933, **79,** 298–304.

Lewis, O. The culture of poverty. *Scientific American,* 1966, **215,** 19–25.

Lewis, W. D. Some characteristics of children designated as mentally retarded, as problems, and as geniuses by teachers. *Journal of Genetic Psychology,* 1947, **70,** 29–51.

Lilly, M. S. Special education: A teapot in a tempest. *Exceptional Children,* 1970, **37**(1), 43–49.

Lilly, M. S. A training based model for special education. *Exceptional Children,* 1971, **37,** 747–49.

Lipman, R. S. Some test correlates of behavioral aggression in institutionalized retardates with particular reference to the Rosenzweig Picture-Frustration Study. *American Journal of Mental Deficiency,* 1959, **63,** 1038–45.

Lipman, R. S. Children's manifest anxiety in retardates and approximately equal MA normals. *American Journal of Mental Deficiency.* 1960, **64,** 1027–28.

Lipman, R. S., & Griffith, B. C. Effects of anxiety level on concept formation: A test of drive theory. *American Journal of Mental Deficiency,* 1960, **65,** 342–48.

Lipton, H. L., & Svarstad, B. Sources of variation in clinicians' communication to parents about mental retardation. *American Journal of Mental Deficiency,* 1977, **82,** 155–161.

Litrownik, A. J. Observational learning in retarded and normal children as a function of delay between observation and opportunity to perform. *Journal of Experimental Child Psychology,* 1972, **48,** 117–25.

Lochner, P. R., Jr. Some limits on the application of social science research in the legal process. *Arizona State Law Review,* 1973, **1973,** 815–62.

Lodge, A., & Kleinfeld, P. B. Early behavioral development in Down's syndrome. In M. Coleman (Ed.), *Serotonin in Down's syndrome.* London: North-Holland, 1973.

Lowenbraun, S., & Affleck, J. Q. *Least restrictive environment.* Seattle: University of Washington, 1978.

Lucas, C. The use and abuse of educational categories. In R. L. Jones & D. L. MacMillan (Eds.), *Special education in transition,* pp. 42–50. Boston: Allyn and Bacon, 1974.

Lucas, M. S. Assessment of coding behavior of trainable retardates. *American Journal of Mental Deficiency,* 1970, **75,** 309–15.

Ludlow, C. L. Children's language disorders: Recent research advances. *Annals of Neurology,* 1980, **7,** 497–507.

Luria, A. R. Experimental study of the higher nervous activity of the abnormal child. *Journal of Mental Deficiency Research,* 1959, **3,** 1–22.

Luria, A. R. *The role of speech in the regulation of normal and abnormal behavior.* New York: Liveright, 1961.

Luria, A. R. Psychological studies of mental deficiency in the Soviet Union. In N. R. Ellis (Ed.), *Handbook of mental deficiency,* pp. 353–87. New York: McGraw-Hill, 1963.

Luria, A. R., & Vinogradova, O. S. An objective investigation of the dynamics of semantic systems. *British Journal of Psychology,* 1959, **50,** 69–105.

Lyman, P. L. *Phenylketonuria.* Springfield, Ill.: Thomas, 1963

MacGillivray, R. C. The larval psychosis of idiocy. *American Journal of Mental Deficiency*, 1956, **60**, 570–74.

MacMillan, D. L. Motivational differences: Cultural-familial retardates vs. normal subjects on expectancy for failure. *American Journal of Mental Deficiency*, 1969, **74**, 254–58. (a)

MacMillan, D. L. Resumption of interrupted tasks by normal and educable mentally retarded subjects. *American Journal of Mental Deficiency*, 1969, **73**, 657–61.(b)

MacMillan, D. L. The problem of motivation in the education of the mentally retarded. *Exceptional Children*, 1971, **37**, 579–86.(a)

MacMillan, D. L. Special education for the mildly retarded: Servant or savant? *Focus on Exceptional Children*, 1971, **2**, 1–11.(b)

MacMillan, D. L. Facilitative effect on input organization as a function of verbal response to stimuli in EMR and nonretarded children. *American Journal of Mental Deficiency*, 1972, **76**, 408–11. (a)

MacMillan, D. L. Paired-associate learning as a function of explictness of mediational set by EMR and nonretarded children. *American Journal of Mental Deficiency*, 1972, **76**, 686–91. (b)

MacMillan, D. L. Decertification of EMRs: Problems and paradoxes. *Journal, California Council for Exceptional Children*, 1972, **21**(3), 3, 5–6, 8.(c)

MacMillan, D. L. *Behavior modification in education*. New York: MacMillan, 1973.(a)

MacMillan, D. L. Issues and trends in special education. *Mental Retardation*, 1973, **11**(2), 3–8.(b)

MacMillan, D. L. Mainstreaming: Implications for regular education. Speech delivered at the Special Study Institute, The Master Plan for Special Education: Implications for Teacher Education, California State University, Los Angeles, November 1974.(a)

MacMillan, D. L. Research on mainstreaming: Promise and reality. Paper read at Conference on Mainstreaming, sponsored by USOE and University of Miami, Fla., at San Diego, Calif., December 1974.(b)

MacMillan, D. L. Follow-up report on special education placement. Paper read at Conference on Mainstreaming sponsored by University of Connecticut, at New Orleans, February 1975.(a)

MacMillan D. L. The effect of experimental success and failure on the situational expectancy of EMR and nonretarded children. *American Journal of Mental Deficiency*, 1975, **80**, 90–95.(b)

MacMillan, D. L., & Borthwick, S. The new EMR population: Can they be mainstreamed? *Mental Retardation*, 1980, **18**, 155–158.

MacMillan, D. L., & Carlson, J. S. Probability judgments by EMR and nonretarded children. II: A replication and extension. *American Journal of Mental Deficiency*, 1971, **76**, 82–86.

MacMillan, D. L., Forness, S. R., & Trumbull, B. M. The role of punishment in the classroom. *Exceptional Children*, 1973, **40**, 85–96.

MacMillan, D. L., & Jones, R. L. Lions in search of more Christians. *Journal of Special Education*, 1972, **6**, 81–91.

MacMillan, D. L., Jones, R. L., & Aloia, G. F. The mentally retarded label: A theoretical analysis and review of research. *American Journal of Mental Deficiency*, 1974, **79**, 241–61.

MacMillan, D. L., Jones, R. L., & Meyers, C. E. Mainstreaming the mildly retarded: Some questions, cautions, and guidelines. *Mental Retardation*, 1976, **14**, 3–10.

MacMillan, D. L., & Keogh, B. K. Normal and retarded children's expectancy for failure. *Developmental Psychology*, 1971, **4**, 343–48.

MacMillan, D. L., & Knopf, E. P. Effects of instructional set on perceptions of event outcomes by EMR and nonretarded children. *American Journal of Mental Deficiency*, 1971, **76**, 185–89.

MacMillan, D. L., & Lucas, M. S. Probability judgment of EMR and nonretarded children. III: Motivational and methodological consideration. *American Journal of Mental Deficiency*, 1971, **76**, 87–91.

MacMillan, D. L., & Meyers, C. E. The nondiscriminatory testing provision of PL 94-142. *Viewpoints*, 1977, **53**(2), 39–56.

MacMillan, D. L., & Meyers, C. E. Educational labeling of handicapped learners. In D. C. Berliner (Ed.), *Review of research in education*, pp. 151–94. Washington, D.C.: American Educational Research Association, 1979.

MacMillan, D. L., & Meyers, C. E. *Larry P.:* An educational interpretation. *School Psychology Review*, 1980, **9**(2), 136–48.(a)

MacMillan, D. L., & Meyers, C. E. Molecular research and molar learning. Paper presented at NICHHD sponsored conference on "Cognition and Learning in the Mentally Retarded" at Vanderbilt University, Nashville, Tenn., 1980.(b)

MacMillan, D. L., Meyers, C. E., & Morrison, G. M. System-identification of mildly mentally retarded children: Implications for interpreting and conducting research. *American Journal of Mental Deficiency*, 1980, **85**, 108–15.

MacMillan, D. L., & Morrison, G. M. Educational programs. In H. C. Quay & J. S Werry (Eds.), *Psychopathological disorders of childhood* (2nd ed.), pp. 411–50. New York: Wiley, 1979.

MacMillan, D. L., & Morrison, G. M. Correlates of social status among mildly handicapped learners in self-contained special classes. *Journal of Educational Psychology*, 1980, **72**, 437–44.(a)

MacMillan, D. L., & Morrison, G. M. Evolution of behaviorism from the laboratory to special education settings. In B. K. Keogh (Ed.), *Advances in special education: Perspectives on applications*. Vol. 2, pp. 1–28. Greenwich, Conn.: JAI Press, 1980.(b)

MacMillan, D. L., & Morrison, G. M. Sociometric research in special education. In R. L. Jones (Ed.), *Attitude and attitude change in special education*. Reston, Va.: Council for Exceptional Children, in press.

MacMillan, D. L., & Semmel, M. I. Evaluation of mainstreaming programs. *Focus on Exceptional Children*, 1977, **9**, 1–14.

MacMillan, D. L., & Wright, D. L. Outerdirectedness in children of three ages as a function of experimentally induced success and failure. *Journal of Educational Psychology*, 1974, **66**, 919–25.

Madsen, M. C., & Shapira, A. Cooperative and competitive behavior of urban Afro-American, Anglo-American, Mexican-American and Mexican village children. *Developmental Psychology*, 1970, **3**, 16–20.

Madsen, W. *Mexican-Americans of South Texas*. New York: Holt, Rinehart, and Winston, 1964.

Mahoney, K., VanWagenen, R. K., & Meyerson, L. Toilet training on normal and retarded children. *Journal of Applied Behavior Analysis*, 1971, **4**, 173–81.

Malpass, L. F., Mark, S., & Palermo, D. S. Responses of retarded children to the Children's Manifest Anxiety Scale, *Journal of Educational Psychology*, 1960, **51**, 305–308.

Mankoff, M. L. Societal reaction and career deviance: A critical analysis. *Sociological Quarterly*, 1971, **12**, 204–18.

Mann, L. Psychometric phrenology and the new faculty psychology: The case against ability assessment and training. In R. L. Jones & D. L. MacMillan (Eds.) *Special education in transition*, pp. 160–73. Boston: Allyn and Bacon, 1974.

Mann, M. What does ability grouping do to the self-concept? *Childhood Education*, 1960, **26**, 357–60.

Manuel, H. T. *Spanish-speaking children of the Southwest: Their education and the public welfare.* Austin: University of Texas Press, 1965.

Marcotte, J. E. A. Mental deficiency in behavior problems. *American Journal of Mental Deficiency*, 1947, **51**, 407–19.

Marden, P. W., & Farber, B. High-brow versus low-grade status among institutionalized mentally retarded boys. *Social Problems*, 1961, **8**, 300–12.

Marlega v. *Board of School Directors of the City of Milwaukee.* Civil action 70–C–8 (E.D., Wis.), 1970.

Masland, R. L., Sarason, S. B., & Gladwin, T. *Mental subnormality.* New York: Basic Books, 1958.

Maslow, A. Cognition of the particular and of the generic. *Psychological Review*, 1948, **55**, 22–40.

Matarazzo, J. E. *Wechsler's measurement and appraisal of adult intelligence.* (5th ed.) Baltimore: Williams and Wilkins, 1972.

Matthews, M. One hundred institutionally trained male defectives in the community under supervision. *Mental Hygiene*, 1922, **6**, 332–42.

McAndrew, C., & Edgerton, R. B. The everyday life of institutionalized "idiots." *Human Organization*, 1964, **23**(4), 312–18.

McCall, R. B., Appelbaum, M. I., & Hogarty, P. S. Developmental changes in mental performance. *Monographs of the Society for Research in Child Development*, 1973, **38**. No. 3.

McCandless, B. R. Relation of environmental factors to intellectual functioning. In H. A. Stevens & R. F. Heber (Eds.), *Mental retardation: A review of research*, pp. 175–213. Chicago: University of Chicago Press, 1964.

McCarthy, J. J. Research on the linguistic problems of the mentally retarded. *Mental Retardation Abstracts*, 1964, **1**, 3–27.

McCarver, R. B., & Craig, E. M. Placement of the retarded in the community: Prognosis and outcome. In N. R. Ellis (Ed.), *International review of research in mental retardation.* Vol. 7, pp. 146–207. New York: Academic Press, 1974.

McClelland, D. C., Atkinson, J. W., Clark, R. A., & Lowell, E. L. *The achievement motive.* New York: Appleton-Century-Crofts, 1953.

McCormick, M., Balla, D., & Zigler, E. Resident-care practices in institutions for retarded persons: A cross-institutional, cross-cultural study. *American Journal of Mental Deficiency*, 1975, **80**, 1–17.

McCurley, R., Mackay, D. N., & Scally, B. G. The life expectation of the mentally subnormal under community and hospital care. *Journal of Mental Deficiency Research*, 1972, **16**, 57–66.

McDaniel, C. O., Jr. Participation in extracurricular activities, social acceptance, and social rejection among educable mentally retarded students. *Education and Training of the Mentally Retarded*, 1970, **5**, 4–14.

McDevitt, S. C., Smith, M. P., Schmidt, D. W., & Rosen, M. The deinstitutionalized citizen: Adjustment and quality of life. *Mental Retardation*, 1978, **16**, 22–24.

McIntosh, W. J. Follow-up study of 1000 nonacademic boys. *Journal of Exceptional Children*, 1949, **15**, 166–70.

McManis, D. L., Bell, D. R., & Pike, E. O. Performance of reward-seeking and punishment-avoiding retardates under reward and punishment. *American Journal of Mental Deficiency*, 1969, **73**, 906–11.

McNemar, Q. Critical examination of the University of Iowa studies of environmental influences upon the IQ. *Psychological Bulletin*, 1940, **37**, 63–92.

McNemar, Q. On so-called test bias. *American Psychologist*, 1975, **30**, 848–51.

Mealy, H. *The exceptional child: Your responsibility and mine.* Boston: Chapman & Grimes, 1940.

Meichenbaum, D. H., Bowers, K. S., & Ross, R. R. A behavioral analysis of teacher expectancy effect. *Journal of Personality and Social Psychology*, 1969, **13**, 306–16.

Melcher, J. W. Some questions from a school administrator. In E. L. Meyen (Ed.), *Proceedings of the Missouri Conference on the Categorical/Noncategorical Issue in Special Education*, pp. 33–38. Columbia: University of Missouri, 1971.

Mendels, G. E., & Flanders, J. P. Teacher expectations and pupil performance. *American Educational Research Journal*, 1973, **10**, 203–12.

Mendoza, S. M., Good, T. L., & Brophy, J. E. The communication of teacher expectations in a junior high school. Paper read at the annual meeting of the American Educational Research Association, New York, 1971.

Menkes, J. H. *Textbook of child neurology.* Philadelphia: Lea and Febiger, 1974.

Menolascino, F. J. Emotional disturbance and mental retardation. *American Journal of Mental Deficiency,* 1965, **70,** 248–56.

Merbaum, A. Need for achievement in Negro and white children. *Dissertation Abstracts,* 1962, **23,** 693–94.

Mercer, C. D., & Snell, M. E. *Learning theory research in mental retardation.* Columbus, Ohio: Merrill, 1977.

Mercer, J. R. Social system perspective and clinical perspective: Frames of reference for understanding career patterns of persons labelled as mentally retarded. *Social Problems,* 1965, **13,** 18–34.

Mercer, J. R. Who is normal? Two perspectives on mild mental retardation. In E. G. Jaco (Ed.), *Patients, physicians, and illness.* New York: Free Press, 1970.(a)

Mercer, J. R. Sociological perspectives on mild mental retardation. In H. C. Haywood (Ed.), *Social-cultural aspects of mental retardation,* pp. 378–91. New York: Appleton-Century-Crofts, 1970.(b)

Mercer, J. R. The labeling process. Paper presented at the Joseph P. Kennedy, Jr., Foundation International Symposium on Human Rights, Retardation, and Research, Washington, D.C., October 1971.(a)

Mercer, J. R. The meaning of mental retardation. In R. Koch & J. C. Dobson (Eds.), *The mentally retarded child and his family: A multidisciplinary handbook,* pp. 23–46. New York: Brunner/Mazel, 1971.(b)

Mercer, J. R. *Labeling the mentally retarded.* Berkeley: University of California Press, 1973.(a)

Mercer, J. R. The myth of 3% prevalence. In R. K. Eyman, C. E. Meyers & G. Tarjan (Eds.), Sociobehavioral studies in mental retardation, *Monographs of the American Association on Mental Deficiency,* 1973, No.1.(b)

Mercer, J. R. Sociocultural factors in educational labeling. Paper presented at NICHD Conference on "Current issues in mental retardation," Niles, Mich, April 18–20, 1974.(a)

Mercer, J. R. The who, why, and how of mainstreaming. Paper read at the Annual Convention of the American Association on Mental Deficiency, Toronto, June 1974.(b)

Mercer, J. R. *System of multicultural pluralistic assessment conceptual and technical manual.* Riverside: University of California at Riverside, 1977.

Mercer, J. R., & Lewis, J. *System of multicultural pluralistic assessment: Parent interview manual.* New York: Psychological Corporation, 1977.

Mercer, J. R., & Lewis, J. P. System of multicultural pluralistic assessment: Technical manual. Unpublished manuscript, University of California at Riverside, 1975.

Mercer, J. R., & Richardson, J. G. Mental retardation as a social problem. In N. Hobbs (Ed.), *Issues in the classification of children ,* Vol. 2, pp. 463–96. San Francisco: Jossey-Bass, 1975.

Merton, R. K. The self-fulfilling prophecy. *The Antioch Review,* 1948, **8,** 193–210.

Messé, L. A., Crano, W. D., Messé, S. R., & Rice, W. Evaluation of the predictive validity of tests of mental ability for classroom performance in elementary grades. *Journal of Educational Psychology,* 1979, **71,** 233–241.

Messick, S. Potential uses of noncognitive measurement in education. *Journal of Educational Psychology,* 1979, **71,** 281–92.

Meyen, E. L., & Horner, R. D. Curriculum development. In J. Wortis (Ed.), *Mental retardation and developmental disabilities.* Vol. 8, pp. 258–96. New York: Brunner/Mazel, 1976.

Meyen, E. L., & Moran, M. R. A perspective on the unserved mildly handicapped. *Exceptional Children,* 1979, **45,** 526–30.

Meyerowitz, J. H. Self-derogations in young retardates and special class placement. *Child Development,* 1962, **33,** 443–51.

Meyerowitz, J. H. Self-derogations in young retardates and special class placement, *Mental Retardation,* 1967, **5,** 23–26.

Meyers, C. E. Psychometrics. In J. Wortis (Ed.), *Mental retardation and developmental disabilities.* Vol. 5, pp. 25–54. New York: Brunner/Mazel, 1971.

Meyers, C. E. The school psychologist and mild retardation. *Mental Retardation,* 1973, **11**(1), 15–20.

Meyers, C. E. (Ed.) Quality of life in severely and profoundly mentally retarded people: Research foundations for improvement. *Monograph of the American Association on Mental Deficiency,* 1978, No. 3.

Meyers, C. E., & MacMillan, D. L. Utilization of learning principles in retardation. In R. Koch & J. Dobson (Eds.), *The mentally retarded child and his family: A multidisciplinary handbook,* (2nd ed.), pp. 339–67. New York: Brunner/Mazel, 1976.

Meyers, C. E., MacMillan, D. L., & Morrison, G. M. Effects of integrated vs. segregated education for the mildly impaired student. In M. Begab, R. Edgerton, & K. Kernan (Eds.), *Effects of different settings on the development of mentally retarded persons.* Baltimore: University Park Press, in press.

Meyers, C. E., MacMillan, D. L., & Yoshida, R. K. Preliminary findings on the decertification of inner city EMRs. Paper presented at the Annual Joint Convention, American Academy of Mental Retardation and the American Association on Mental Deficiency, Toronto, June 1974.

Meyers, C. E., MacMillan, D. L., & Yoshida, R. K. *Correlates of success in transition of MR to regular class.* Final report. Grant OEG-0-73-5263, The Psychiatric Institute, Pacific State Hospital Research Group, November 1975.

Meyers, C. E., MacMillan, D. L., & Yoshida, R. K. Regular class education of EMR students, from efficacy to mainstreaming: A review of issues and research. In J. Gottlieb (Ed.), *Educating mentally retarded persons in the mainstream*, pp. 176–206. Baltimore: University Park Press, 1980.

Meyers, C. E., MacMillan, D. L., & Zetlin, A. Education for all handicapped children. *Pediatric Annals*, 1978, **7,** 348–56.

Meyers, C. E., & Nihira, K. Development of adaptive behavior at home and school. Project in program project grant, "Program for the development of the mentally retarded," principal investigator, R. K. Eyman, 1975.

Meyers, C. E., Nihira, K., & Zetlin, A. The measurement of adaptive behavior. In N. R. Ellis (Ed.), *Handbook of mental deficiency: Psychological Theory and Research* (2nd ed.) pp. 431–81. Hillsdale, N.J.: Lawrence Erlbaum, 1979.

Meyers, C. E., Sitkei, E. G., & Watts, C. A. Attitudes toward special education and the handicapped in two community groups. *American Journal of Mental Deficiency*, 1966, **71,** 78–84.

Meyers, C. E., Sundstrom, P. E., & Yoshida, R. K. The school psychologist and assessment in special education. *School Psychology Monographs*, 1974, **2**(1), 3–57.

Michenbaum, D., & Goodman, J. Reflection-impulsivity and verbal control of motor behavior. *Child Development*, 1969, **40,** 785–97.

Milazzo, T. C. Special class placement or how to destroy in the name of help. Paper presented at the Forty-eighth Annual Convention of the Council for Exceptional Children, Chicago, April 1970.

Miles, T. R. On defining intelligence. *British Journal of Educational Psychology*, 1957, **27,** 153–65.

Milgram, N. A. The rationale and irrationale of Zigler's motivational approach to mental retardation. *American Journal of Mental Deficiency*, 1969, **73,** 527–32. (a)

Milgram, N. A. Retention of mediation set in paired-associate learning of normal and retarded children. *Journal of Experimental Child Psychology*, 1969, **5,** 341–49. (b)

Miller, C. Deinstitutionalization and mortality trends for the profoundly retarded. In C. Clelland & L. Talkington (Eds.), *Research with profoundly retarded: Conference proceedings*, pp. 1–8. Austin, Texas: Western Research Conference, 1975.

Miller, C., & Eyman, R. Hospital and community mortality rates among the retarded. *Journal of Mental Deficiency Research*, 1978, **22,** 127–45.

Miller, D. R., & Swanson, G. E. *Inner conflict and defense*. New York: Holt, Rinehart, and Winston, 1960.

Miller, E. L. Ability and social adjustment at midlife of persons earlier judged mentally deficient. *Genetic Psychology Monographs*, 1965, **72,** 139–98.

Miller, M. B. Rebelliousness and repetition choice in adolescent retardates. *American Journal of Mental Deficiency*, 1961, **66,** 428–34.

Miller, N. E., & Dollard, J. *Social learning and imitation*. New Haven, Conn: Yale University Press, 1941.

Miller, R. V. Social status and socioempathic differences among mentally superior, mentally typical, and mentally retarded children. *Exceptional Children*, 1956, **23,** 114–19.

Miller, W. A., & Erbe, R. Prenatal diagnosis of genetic disorders. *Southern Medical Journal*, 1978, **71,** 201–07.

Mills v. Board of Education of the District of Columbia. 348 F. Supp 866. (DDC), 1972.

Monahan, T. P. Premarital pregnancy in the United States. *Eugenics Quarterly*, 1960, **7,** 133–47.

Monson, L. B., Greenspan, S., & Simeonsson, R. J. Correlates of social competence in retarded children. *American Journal of Mental Deficiency*, 1979, **83,** 627–30.

Moore, T. Language and intelligence: A longitudinal study of the first eight years. I: Patterns of development in boys and girls. *Human Development*, 1967, **10,** 88–106.

Mordock, J. B. Paired associate learning in mental retardation. *American Journal of Mental Deficiency*, 1968, **72,** 857–65.

Morgenstern, M., & Michal-Smith, H. *Psychology in the vocational rehabilitation of the mentally retarded.* Springfield, Ill.: Thomas, 1973.

Morton, K. Identifying the enemy—A parent's complaint. In A. P. Turnbull & H. R. Turnbull (Eds.), *Parents speak out.* Columbus, Ohio: Merrill, 1978.

Morton, R. F., & Hebel, J. R. *A study guide to epidemiology and biostatistics.* Baltimore: University Park Press, 1979.

Moss, J. W. Failure-avoiding and success-striving behavior in mentally retarded and normal children. Unpublished doctoral dissertation. George Peabody College, 1958.

Mullen, F. A., & Nee, M. M. Distribution of mental retardation in an urban school population. *American Journal of Mental Deficiency*, 1952, **56,** 777–90.

Murphy, D. P. Ovarian irradiation: Its effect on the health of subsequent children. *Surgery, Gynecology, and Obstetrics*, 1928, **47,** 201–15.

Murphy, H., Rennee, B., & Luchins, D. Foster homes: The new back wards? *Canada's Mental Health Monograph*, 1972 (supp. 71).

Murphy, S. D. Pesticides. In L. J. Casarett & J. Doull (Eds.), *Toxicology, the basic science of poisons*, pp. 408–54. New York: Macmillan, 1975.

Mussen, P. H., Conger, J. J., & Kagan, J. *Child development and personality.* (3rd ed.) New York: Harper and Row, 1969.

Nagler, B. A change in terms or in concepts? A small step forward or a giant step backward? *Journal of Special Education*, 1972, **6**, 61–64.

Nakamura, C. Y., & Finsk, D. Effect of social or task orientation and evaluative or nonevaluative situations on performance. *Child Development*, 1973, **44**, 83–93.

National Association of Superintendents of Public Residential Facilities for the Mentally Retarded. *Contemporary issues in residential programming*. Washington, D.C.: President's Committee on Mental Retardation, 1974.

National Council on Radiation Protection and Measures, *Basic radiation protection criteria*. Report 39, January 15. Washington, D.C.: U.S. Government Printing Office, 1971.

National Foundation, March of Dimes. *Drugs causing fetal malformations in humans*. White Plains, N.Y., 1971.

National Foundation, March of Dimes. *Facts: 1975*. White Plains, N.Y., 1975.(a)

National Foundation, March of Dimes. *Genetic counseling*. White Plains, N.Y., 1975, No. 59–128A.(b)

National Research Council, National Academy of Sciences. *The effects on population of exposure to low levels of ionizing radiation*. Washington, D.C.: U.S. Government Printing Office, 1972.

Nelson, C. C., & Schmidt, L. J. The question of the efficacy of special classes. *Exceptional Children*, 1971, **37**(5), 381–84.

Neuer, H. The relationship between behavior disorders in children and the syndrome of mental deficiency. *American Journal of Mental Deficiency*, 1947, **52**, 143–47.

Newman, H. H., Freeman, F. N., & Holzinger, K. J. *Twins: A study of heredity and environment*. Chicago: University of Chicago Press, 1937.

New York State Association for Retarded Children Inc. v. *Rockefeller*. (U.S. Dist. Court, E.D., N.Y.), 1972.

New York State Department of Mental Hygiene. *Technical report of the Mental Health Research Unit, Syracuse*. New York: Syracuse University Press, 1955.

Nihira, K. Importance of environmental demands in the measurement of adaptive behavior. In R. K. Eyman, C. E. Meyers, & G. Tarjan (Eds.), Sociobehavioral studies in mental retardation. *Monographs of the American Association on Mental Deficiency*, 1973, No 1, pp. 101–12.

Nihira, K. Dimensions of adaptive behavior in institutionalized mentally retarded children and adults: Developmental perspective. *American Journal of Mental Deficiency*, 1976, **81**, 215–26.

Nihira, K., Foster R., Shellhaas, M., & Leland, H. *AAMD adaptive behavior scale*. Washington, D.C.: American Association on Mental Deficiency, 1969.

Nihira, K., & Shellhaas, M. Study of adaptive behavior: Its rationale, method, and implication in rehabilitation programs. *Mental Retardation*, 1970, **8**, 11–16.

Nihira, L., & Mayeda, T. *Tabulation of the California sample of the performance measure survey*. Report to the AAMD Ad Hoc Committee on the Use and Construction of Data Banks, January 1977.

Nihira, L., & Nihira, K. Jeopardy in community placement. *American Journal of Mental Deficiency*, 1975, **79**, 538–44.

Nirje, B. The normalization principle and its human management implications. In R. B. Kugel & W. Wolfensberger (Eds.), *Changing patterns in residential services for the mentally retarded*, pp. 179–88. Washington, D.C.: President's Committee on Mental Retardation, 1969.

Niswander, K. R., & Gordon, M. *The women and their pregnancies*. Vol. 1. Philadelphia: Saunders, 1972.

Norton, S. Toxicology of the central nervous system. In L. J.Casarett & J. Doull (Eds.), *Toxicology, the basic science of poisons*, pp. 527–54. New York: Macmillan, 1975.

Nowrey, J. E. A brief synopsis of mental deficiency. *American Journal of Mental Deficiency*, 1945, **49**, 319–57.

Oakland, T. An evaluation of the ABIC, pluralistic norms, and estimated learning potential. *Journal of School Psychology*, 1980, **18**, 3–11.

O'Connor, G. Home is a good place: A national perspective of community residential facilities for developmentally disabled persons. *Monographs of the American Association on Mental Deficiency*, 1976, No. 2.

O'Connor, N., & Hermelin, B. Discrimination and reversal learning in imbeciles, *Journal of Abnormal and Social Psychology*, 1959, **59**, 409–13.

O'Connor, N., & Hermelin, B. Like and cross modality recognition in subnormal children. *Quarterly Journal of Experimental Psychology*, 1961, **13**, 48–52.

O'Connor, N., & Hermelin, B. Recall in normals and subnormals of like mental age. *Journal of Abnormal and Social Psychology*,1963, **66**, 81–84.(a)

O'Connor, N., & Hermelin, B. *Speech and thought in severe subnormality*. New York: Pergamon, 1963.(b)

O'Connor N., & Tizard, J. *The social problem of mental deficiency*. New York: Pergamon, 1956.

Olson, D. Language acquisition and cognitive development. In H.C. Haywood (Ed.), *Social-cultural aspects of mental retardation*. New York: Appleton-Century-Crofts, 1970.

Olson, M. I., & Shaw, C. M. Presenile dementia and Alzheimer's disease in mongolism. *Brain*, 1969, **92**, 147–56.

Osler, S. Unpublished manuscript; personal communication, April,1970.

Ouelette, E. M., Rosett, H. L., Rosman, N. P., & Weiner, L. Adverse effects on offspring of maternal alcohol abuse during pregnancy. *The New England Journal of Medicine*, 1977, **297**, 528–30.

Page, E. B. Miracle in Milwaukee: Raising the IQ. *Educational Researcher*, 1972, **1**(10), 8–10, 15–16.

Palmer, L. J. The defective delinquent as a state problem. *Psychiatric Quarterly*, 1927, **1**, 91–95.

Paluck, R. J., & Esser, A. H. Controlled experiments modification of aggressive behavior in territories of severely retarded boys. *American Journal of Mental Deficiency*, 1971, **76**, 23–29.(a)

Paluck, R. J., & Esser, A. H. Territorial behavior as an indicator of changes in clinical condition of severely retarded boys. *American Journal of Mental Deficiency*, 1971, **76**, 284–90.(b)

Parsons, T. The school class as a social system: Some of its functions in American society. *Harvard Educational Review*, 1959, **29**, 297–318.

Payne, R., & Murray, C. Principals' attitudes toward integration of the handicapped. *Exceptional Children*, 1974, **41**, 123–25.

Peck, J. R., & Stephens, W. B. *Success of young adult male retardates*. Cooperative Research Project 1533. Austin: University of Texas, 1964.

Pennsylvania Association for Retarded Children v. *Commonwealth of Pennsylvania*. 343 F. Supp. 279 (E.D., Pa.), 1972.

Penrose, L. S. *The biology of mental defect*. New York: Grune and Stratton, 1949.

Penrose, L. S. *The biology of mental defect*. (Rev. ed.) London: Sidgwick and Jackson, 1954.

Penrose, L. S. *The biology of mental defect*. (3rd ed.) London: Sidgwick and Jackson, 1966.

Penrose, L. S. Mental deficiency. *Journal of Special Education*, 1972, **6**, 65–66.

People in Action on Special Education v. *Hannon*. (E.D., Ill.), 1980.

Perron, R. A. A priori estimation of success and feeling of personal worth among the mentally deficient. In B. W. Richards (Ed.) *Proceedings of the London Conference on the Scientific Study of Mental Deficiency*. Vol. 2. Dagenham, England: May and Baker, 1962.

Peterson, L., & Smith, L. The post-school adjustment of educable mentally retarded adults with that of adults of normal intelligence. *Exceptional Children*, 1960, **26**, 404–408.

Peterson, N. L., & Haralick, J. G. Integration of handicapped and nonhandicapped preschoolers: An analysis of play behavior and social interaction. *Education and Training of the Mentally Retarded*, 1977, **12**, 235–45.

Phelps, W. R. Attitudes related to the employment of mentally retarded. *American Journal of Mental Deficiency*, 1965, **69**, 575–85.

Philips, I. Children, mental retardation, and emotional disorder. In I. Philips (Ed.) *Prevention and treatment of mental retardation*. New York: Basic Books, 1966.

Piaget, J. *The psychology of intelligence*. New York: Harcourt, Brace, 1950.

Piaget, J., & Inhelder, B. *The psychology of the child*. New York: Basic Books, 1969.

Pitkin, W. B. *Twilight of the American mind*. New York: Simon and Schuster, 1928.

Plenderleith, M. Discrimination learning and discrimination reversal learning in normal and feeble-minded children. *Journal of Genetic Psychology*, 1956, **88**, 107–12.

Pope, L., & Haklay, A. Reading disability. In J. Wortis (Ed.), *Mental retardation: An annual review*. Vol. 2, pp. 132–49. New York: Grune and Stratton, 1970.

Popham, W. J. Performance tests of teaching proficiency: Rationale, development, and validation. *American Educational Research Journal*, 1971, **8**(1), 105–17.

Porter, R. B., & Milazzo, T.C. A comparison of mentally retarded adults who attended a special class with those who attended regular school classes. *Exceptional Children*, 1958, **24**, 410–12.

Portnoy, B., & Stacey, C. L. A comparative study of Negro and white subnormals on the children's form of the Rosenzweig Picture-Frustration Test. *American Journal of Mental Deficiency*, 1954, **59**, 272–78.

Potter, R. On the ethics of labeling. Paper presented at the Joseph P. Kennedy, Jr., Foundation International Symposium on Human Rights, Retardation, and Research, Washington, D.C., October 1971.

Prehm, H. J. Verbal learning research in mental retardation. *American Journal of Mental Deficiency*, 1966, **71**, 42–47.

Prehm, H. J., & Mayfield, S. Paired-associated learning and retention in retarded and nonretarded children. *American Journal of Mental Deficiency*, 1970, **74**, 622–25.

Premack, D. Toward empirical behavior laws. I: Positive reinforcement. *Psychological Review*, 1959, **66**, 219.

President's Committee on Mental Retardation. *Report to the president: A proposed program for national action to combat mental retardation*. Washington, D.C.: U.S. Government Printing Office, 1962.

President's Committee on Mental Retardation. *MR–67: A first report to the president on the nation's progress and remaining great needs in the campaign to combat mental retardation*. Washington, D.C.: U.S. Government Printing Office, 1967.

President's Committee on Mental Retardation. *MR–72: Islands of excellence*. Washington, D.C.: U.S. Government Printing Office, 1973.

President's Committee on Mental Retardation and Bureau of Education of the Handicapped. *The six-hour retarded child*. Washington, D.C.: U.S. Government Printing Office, 1969.

President's Task Force on the Mentally Handicapped. *Action against mental disability*. Washington, D.C.: U.S. Government Printing Office, 1970.

Pueschel, S. M., & Murphy, A. Assessment of counseling practices at the birth of a child with Down's syndrome. *American Journal of Mental Deficiency*, 1976, **81**, 325–30.

Quay, L.C. Academic skills. In N. R. Ellis (Ed.), *Handbook of mental deficiency*, pp. 664–90. New York: McGraw-Hill, 1963.

Quay, L. C. Language dialect, reinforcement, and the intelligence-test performance of Negro children. *Child Development*, 1971, **42**, 5–15.

Quay, L. C. Negro dialect and Binet performance in severely disadvantaged black four-year-old children. *Child Development*, 1972, **43**, 245–50.

Quay, L. C. Language dialect, age, and intelligence-test performance in disadvantaged black children. *Child Development*, 1974, **45**, 463–68.

Rabin, A. I. Assessment of abnormalities in intellectual development. In J. Zubin & G. A. Jervis (Eds.), *Psychopathology of mental development*. New York: Grune and Stratton, 1967.

Raech, H. A parent discusses initial counseling. *Mental Retardation*, 1966, **2**, 25–26.

Rago, W. V. Stability of territorial and aggressive behavior in profoundly retarded institutionalized male adults. *American Journal of Mental Deficiency*, 1978, **82**, 494–98.

Rago, W. V., Parker, R. M., & Cleland, C. C. Effect of increased space on the social behavior of institutionalized profoundly retarded male adults. *American Journal of Mental Deficiency*, 1978, **82**, 554–58.

Ramey, C. T., & Campbell, F. A. Prevention of developmental retardation in high risk children. In P. Mittler (Ed.), *Research to practice in mental retardation: Care and intervention*. Vol. 1, pp. 157–64. Baltimore: University Park Press, 1977.

Ramey, C. T., & Campbell, F. A. Compensatory education for disadvantaged children. *School Review*, 1979, **87**, 171–89.(a)

Ramey, C. T., & Campbell, F. A. Early childhood education for psychosocially disadvantaged children: Effects on psychological processes. *American Journal of Mental Deficiency*, 1979, **83**, 645–48.(b)

Ramey, C. T., & Smith, B. J. Assessing the intellectual consequences of early intervention with high-risk infants. *American Journal of Mental Deficiency*, 1977, **81**, 318–24.

Ramirez, M., & Gonzalez, A. Mexican-Americans and intelligence testing: Racism in the schools. Unpublished manuscript, University of California at Riverside, 1971.

Ramirez, M., Taylor, C., & Peterson, B. Mexican-American cultural membership and adjustment to school. *Developmental Psychology*, 1971, **4**, 141–48.

Raynes, N. V., & King, R. D. The measurement of child management in residential institutions for the retarded. In B. W. Richards (Ed.), *Proceedings of the First Congress of the International Association for the Scientific Study of Mental Deficiency*. Reigate, England: Michael Jackson, 1968.

Reed, E. W., & Reed, S. C. *Mental retardation: A family study*. Philadelphia: Saunders, 1965.

Reger, R. Reading ability and CMAD scores in educable mentally retarded boys. *American Journal of Mental Deficiency*, 1964, **68**, 652–55.

Reger, R. Resource rooms: Change agents or guardians of the status quo? *Journal of Special Education*, 1972, **6**, 355–59.

Reger, R., & Koppman, M. The child oriented resource room. *Exceptional Children*, 1971, **37**, 460–62.

Reschly, D. J. Nonbiased assessment. In G. Phye & D. Reschly (Eds.), *School psychology: Perspectives and issues*, pp. 215–53. New York: Academic Press, 1979.

Reynolds, G. S. *A primer of operant conditioning*. Glenview, Ill.: Scott, Foresman, 1968.

Reynolds, M.C. Models for coalitions in special education teacher training. In J. Creamer & J. Gilmore (Eds.), *Design for competency based education in special education*, pp. 11–26. Syracuse University School of Education, 1974.

Reynolds, M. C., & Balow, B. Categories and variables in special education. *Exceptional Children*, 1972, **38**, 357–66.

Ricci v. Greenblatt. Civil Action No. 72-496F (E.D., Mass.), 1972.

Rice, J. *Special education memorandum*. Sacramento: California Department of Education, August 31, 1971.

Richardson, S. A. Malnutrition and mental development: An ecological perspective. In P. Mittler (Ed.), *Research to practice in mental retardation: Biomedical aspects*, pp. 297–98. Baltimore: University Park Press, 1977.

Rieber, M. 1964. Verbal mediation in normal and retarded children. *American Journal of Mental Deficiency*, 1964, **68**, 634–41.

Riesen, A. H. Stimulation as a requirement for growth and function in behavioral development. In D. W. Fiske & S. R. Maddi (Eds.), *Functions of varied experience*. Homewood, Ill.: Dorsey, 1961.

Ring, E. N., & Palermo, D. S. 1961. Paired-associate learning of retarded and normal children. *American Journal of Mental Deficiency*, 1961, **66**, 100–107.

Ringelheim, D. Effects of internal and external reinforcements on expectancies of mentally retarded and normal boys. Unpublished doctoral dissertation, George Peabody College, 1958.

Ringness, T. A. Self-concept of children of low, average, and high intelligence. *American Journal of Mental Deficiency*, 1961, **65**, 453–62.

Riscalla, L. M. Mental retardation: Fact or conjecture? *Journal of Clinical Child Psychology*, 1974, **3**, 43–45.

Rivera, G. *Willowbrook: A report on how it is and why it doesn't have to be that way*. New York: Vintage Books, 1972.

Rivers, L. W., Henderson, D. M., Jones, R. L., Ladner, J. A., & Williams, R. L. Mosaic of labels for black children. In N. Hobbs (Ed.), *Issues in the classification of children*. Vol. 2, pp. 213–45. San Francisco: Jossey-Bass, 1975.

Robbins, R. C., Mercer, J. R., & Meyers, C. E. The school as a selecting-labeling system. *Journal of School Psychology*, 1967, **5**(4), 270–79.

Roberts, J. A. F. The genetics of mental deficiency. *Eugenics Review*. 1952, **44**, 71–83.

Roberts, S. O., Crump, E. P., Dickerson, A. E., & Horton, C. P. Longitudinal performance of Negro American children at 5 and 10 years on the Stanford-Binet. Paper presented at the meeting of the American Psychological Association, Chicago, September 1965.

Robinson, C. C. Application of Piagetian sensorimotor concepts of assessment and curriculum for severely handicapped children. *AAESPH Review*, 1976, **8**, 5–10.

Robinson, H. B., & Robinson, N. M. *The mentally retarded child: A psychological approach*. New York: McGraw-Hill, 1965.

Robinson, N. M. Prevention: The future society. The future of very early intervention and education. Paper read at the annual convention of The American Association on Mental Deficiency, June 1976.

Robinson, R. C., & Paseward, R. Behavior in intellectual deficit: A critical review of the literature. *American Journal of Mental Deficiency*, 1951, **55**, 598–607.

Rogers, C. R. *Client-centered therapy*. Boston: Houghton Mifflin, 1951.

Rohwer, W. D. Prime time for education: Early childhood or adolescence. *Harvard Educational Review*, 1971, **41**, 316–42.

Roith, A. J. The myth of parental attitudes. *Journal of Mental Subnormality*, 1963, **9**, 51–54.

Rondal, J. A. Maternal speech in normal and Down's syndrome children. In P. Mittler (Ed.), *Research to practice in mental retardation*. Vol. 2, pp. 239–43. Baltimore: University Park Press, 1977.

Rondal, J. A. Maternal speech to normal and Down's syndrome children matched for mean length of utterance. In C. E. Meyers (Ed.), Quality of life in severely and profoundly mentally retarded people: Research foundations for improvement. *Monographs of the American Association on Mental Deficiency*, 1978, No. 3, pp. 193–265.

Roos, P. Psychological counseling with parents of retarded children. *Mental Retardation*, 1963, **1**, 345–50.

Roos, P. Evolutionary changes of the residential facility. In A. A. Baumeister & E. Butterfield (Eds.), *Residential facilities for the mentally retarded*, pp. 29–58. Chicago: Aldine, 1970.(a)

Roos, P. Normalization, de-humanization, and conditioning: Conflict or harmony? *Mental Retardation*, 1970, **8**(4), 12–14.(b)

Roos, P. Parents and families of the mentally retarded. In J. M. Kauffman & J. S. Payne (Eds.), *Mental retardation: Introduction and personal perspectives*. Columbus, Ohio: Merrill, 1975.

Roos, P. Parents of mentally retarded children—misunderstood and mistreated. In A. P. Turnbull & H. R. Turnbull (Eds.), *Parents speak out*, pp. 12–27. Columbus: Merrill, 1978.

Rosen, B. The achievement syndrome. *American Sociological Review*, 1956, **21**, 203–11.

Rosen, L. Selected aspects in the development of the mother's understanding of her mentally retarded child. *American Journal of Mental Deficiency*, 1955, **59**, 522.

Rosenberg, S. Problems of language development in the retarded. In H. C. Haywood (Ed.), *Social-cultural aspects of mental retardation*, pp. 203–16. New York: Appleton-Century-Crofts, 1970.

Rosenthal, R., & Jacobson, L. *Pymalion in the classroom: Teacher expectation and pupils' intellectual development*. New York: Holt, Rinehart, and Winston, 1968.

Rosenzweig, L. E., & Long, J. *Understanding and teaching the dependent retarded child*. Darien, Conn.: Educational Publishing Corporation, 1960.

Rosenzweig, S. The picture-association method and its application in the study of reactions to frustration. *Journal of Personality*, 1945, **14**, 3–23.

Ross, A. O. *The exceptional child in the family*. New York: Grune and Stratton, 1964.

Ross, D. Effect on learning of psychological attachment to a film model. *American Journal of Mental Deficiency*, 1970, **74**, 701–07.

Ross, S. L., DeYoung, H. G., & Cohen, J. S. Confrontation: Special education placement and the law. *Exceptional Children*, 1971, **38**, 5–12.

Rossi, E. L., Associative clustering in normal and retarded children. *American Journal of Mental Deficiency*, 1963, **67**, 691–99.

Rothbart, M., Dalfen, S., & Barrett, R. Effects of teacher's expectancy on student-teacher interaction. *Journal of Educational Psychology*, 1971, **62**, 49–54.

Rotter, J. *Social learning and clinical psychology*. New York: Prentice-Hall, 1954.

Rowitz, L. Sociological perspective on labeling (a reaction to MacMillan, Jones, and Aloia). *American Journal of Mental Deficiency*, 1974, **79**, 265–67.

Royfe, E. H. A systems analysis of an historic mental retardation institution: A case study of Elwyn Institute, 1852–1970. Ed. D. dissertation, Temple University.

Rubington, E., & Weinberg, M. S. (Eds.) *Deviance: The interactionist perspective*. New York: Macmillan, 1968.

Rubovitz, P. C., & Maehr, M. L. Pygmalion analyzed: Toward an explanation of the Rosenthal-Jacobson findings. *Journal of Personality and Social Psychology*, 1971, **19**, 197–203.

Rucker, C. N., & Vincenzo, F. M. Maintaining social acceptance gains made by mentally retarded children. *Exceptional Children*, 1970, **36**, 679–80.

Rugh, R. X-irradiation effects on the human fetus. *Journal of Pediatrics*, 1958, **52**, 531–38.

Rutter, M. Intelligence and childhood psychiatric disorder. *British Journal of Social and Clinical Psychology*, 1964, **3**, 120–29.

Rutter, M. *Maternal deprivation reassessed*. Baltimore: Penguin, 1972.

Rynders, J. E., & Horrobin, J. M. Project EDGE: The University of Minnesota's communication stimulation program for Down's syndrome infants. In B. E. Friedlander (Ed.), *Exceptional infant*. Vol. 3, pp. 173–92. New York: Brunner/Mazel, 1975.

Rynders, J. E., Spiker, D., & Horrobin, J. M. Underestimating the educability of Down's syndrome children: Examination of methodological problems in recent literature. *American Journal of Mental Deficiency*, 1978, **82**, 440–48.

Sabagh, G., Eyman, R. K., & Cogburn, D. N. Speed of hospitalization: A study of a preadmission cohort in a hospital for the retarded. *Social Problems*, 1966, **14**, 119–28.

Sabagh, G., Lei, T., & Eyman, R. K. The speed of hospitalization revisited: A replication of a study of a preadmission waiting list cohort. *Social Problems*, 1972, **19**, 373–82.

Saenger, G. *The adjustment of severely retarded adults in the community*. Albany, N.Y.: Interdepartmental Health Resources Board, 1957.

Saenger, G. *Factors influencing the institutionalization of mentally retarded individuals in New York City*. Albany, N.Y.: Interdepartmental Health Resources Board, 1960.

Salvia, J., Clark, G. M., & Ysseldyke, J. E. Teacher retention of stereotypes of exceptionality. *Exceptional Children*, 1973, **29**, 651–52.

Samuda, R. J. *Psychological testing of American minorities*. New York: Dodd, Mead, 1975.

Sarason, I. G. Empirical findings and theoretical problems in the use of anxiety scales. *Psychological Bulletin*. 1960, **57**, 403–15.

Sarason, S. B. *Psychological problems in mental deficiency*. (2nd ed.) New York: Harper and Row, 1953.

Sarason, S. B., & Gladwin, T. Psychological and cultural problems in mental subnormality. In R. L. Masland, S. B. Sarason, & T. Gladwin (Eds.), *Mental subnormality*, pp. 145–400. New York: Basic Books, 1958.

Sattler, J. M. Racial "experimenter effects" in experimentation, testing, interviewing, and psycho-therapy. *Psychological Bulletin*, 1970, **73**, 137–60.

Sattler, J. M. Intelligence testing of ethnic-minority group and culturally disadvantaged children. In L. Mann & D. A. Sabatino (Eds.), *The first review of special education*. Vol. 2. Philadelphia: JSE Press, 1973.

Sattler, J. M. *Assessment of children's intelligence*. Philadelphia: Saunders, 1974.

Sattler, J. M. Intelligence tests on trial: *Larry P.* et al. vs. *Wilson Riles* et al. Paper presented at the Western Psychological Association, San Diego, Calif., 1979.

Scarr, S. From evolution to *Larry P.*, or what shall we do about IQ tests? *Intelligence*, 1978, **2**, 325–42.

Scarr, S., & Weinberg, R. A. The influence of "family background" on intellectual attainment. *American Sociological Review*, 1978, **43**, 674–92.

Scarr-Salapatek, S. Genetics and the development of intelligence. In F. D. Horowitz (Ed.), *Review of child development research*. Vol. 4, pp. 1–57. Chicago: University of Chicago Press, 1975.

Scheerenberger, R. *Public residential services for the mentally retarded*. National Association of Superintendents of Public Residential Facilities. Madison, Wisc.: 1979.

Scheerenberger, R. C. A model for deinstitutionalization. *Mental Retardation*, 1974, **12**(6), 3–7.

Scheerenberger, R. C. A study of public residential facilities. *Mental Retardation*, 1977, **15**, 58.

Scheerenberger, R. C., & Felsenthal, D. Community settings for MR persons: Satisfaction and activities. *Mental Retardation*, 1977, **15**, 3–7.

Schiefelbusch, R. L. Introduction. In R. L. Schiefelbusch, R. H. Copeland, & J. O. Smith (Eds.), *Language and mental retardation*, pp. 1–19. New York: Holt, Rinehart, and Winston, 1967.

Schild, S. Counseling with parents of retarded children living at home. *Social Work*, 1964, **9**, 86–91.

Schonebaum, R. M., & Zinober, J. W. Learning and memory in mental retardation: The defect-developmental distinction reevaluated. In I. Bialer & M. Sternlicht (Eds.), *The psychology of mental retardation*, pp. 243–74. New York: Psychological Dimensions, 1977.

School Psychology Digest, 1979, **8**(1).

Schroeder, S. R., Mulick, J. A., & Schroeder, C. S. Management of severe behavior problems of the retarded. In N. R. Ellis (Ed.), *Handbook of mental deficiency* (2nd ed.), pp. 341–66. Hillsdale, N.J.: Lawrence Erlbaum, 1979.

Schurr, K. T., Towne, R. C., & Joiner, L. M. Trends in self-concept of ability over 2 years of special class placement. *Journal of Special Education*, 1972, **6**, 161–66.

Schwebel, M., & Raph, J. *Piaget in the classroom*. New York: Basic Books, 1973.

Seagoe, M. V. *Yesterday was Tuesday, all night and all day*. Boston: Little, Brown, 1964.

Segal, R. M. (Ed.) *Advocacy for the legal and human rights of the mentally retarded*. Ann Arbor, Mich.: Institute for the Study of Mental Retardation and Related Disabilities, 1972.

Seguin, E. *Hygiène et éducation des idiots*. Paris: Balliére, 1843.

Seguin, E. *Idiocy: And its treatment by the physiological method*. New York: William Wood, 1866.

Seitz, S., & Geske, D. Mothers' and graduate trainees' judgments of children: Some effects of labeling. *American Journal of Mental Deficiency*, 1977, **81**, 362–70.

Sellin, D., & Mulehahay, R. The relationship of an institutional tour upon opinions about mental retardation. *American Journal of Mental Deficiency*, 1965, **70**, 408–12.

Sells, C. J., & Bennett, F. C. Prevention of mental retardation: The role of medicine. *American Journal of Mental Deficiency*, 1977, **82**, 117–29.

Semmel, M. I. Teacher attitudes and information pertaining to mental deficiency. *American Journal of Mental Deficiency*, 1959, **63**, 566–67.

Semmel, M. I. Language behavior of mentally retarded and culturally disadvantaged children. In J. F. Magary & R. B. McIntyre (Eds.), *Fifth annual distinguished lectures in special education and rehabilitation*. Los Angeles: University of Southern California Press, 1967.

Semmel, M. I. Competence vs. performance re language. In Performance vs. competence: A critical psychoeducational issue in mental retardation. Colloquium presented at the 93rd annual meeting of the American Association on Mental Deficiency, San Francisco, May 1969.

Semmel, M. I., Barritt, L. S., & Bennett, S. W. Performance of EMR and non-retarded children on a modified cloze task. *American Journal of Mental Deficiency*, 1970, **74**, 681–88.

Semmel, M. I., Barritt, L. S., Bennett, S. W., & Perfetti, C. A. Grammatical analysis of word associations of educable mentally retarded and normal children. *American Journal of Mental Deficiency*, 1968, 72, 567–76.

Semmel, M. I., & Bennett, S. W. Effects of linguistic structure and delay on memory span of EMR children. *American Journal of Mental Deficiency*, 1970, **74**, 674–80.

Semmel, M. I., & Dolley, D. G. Comprehension and imitation of sentences by Down's syndrome children as a function of transformational complexity. *American Journal of Mental Deficiency*, 1971, **75**, 739–45.

Semmel, M. I., Gottlieb, J., & Robinson, N. Mainstreaming: Perspectives on educating handicapped children in the public schools. In D. C. Berliner (Ed.), *Review of research in education*, pp. 223–79. Washington, D.C.: American Educational Research Association, 1979.

Semmel, M. I., & Heinmiller, J. I. (Eds.) The education for all handicapped children act (PL 94-142): Issues and implications. *Viewpoints*, 1977, **53**(2).

Sever, J. L. Infectious agents and fetal disease. In H. A. Weisman & G. R. Kerr (Eds.), *Fetal growth and development*. New York: McGraw-Hill, 1970.

Sever, J. L., & White, L. R. Intrauterine viral infections. *Annual Review of Medicine*, 1968, **19**, 471–86.

Severance, L. J., & Gasstrom, L. L. Effects of the label "mentally retarded" on causal explanations for success and failure outcomes. *American Journal of Mental Deficiency*, 1977, **81**, 547–55.

Shapiro, H. Circle of homes: Group homes for the retarded in Cuyahoga County. *Mental Retardation*, 1973, **11**(3), 19–21.

Sheare, J. B. Social acceptance of EMR adolescents in integrated programs. *American Journal of Mental Deficiency*, 1974, **78**, 678–82.

Sheila, M. When you wish upon a star: The self-fulfilling prophecy and special education. *Education and Training of the Mentally Retarded*, 1968, **3**, 189–93.

Sheimo, S. L. Problems in helping parents of mentally defective and handicapped children. *American Journal of Mental Deficiency*, 1951, **56**, 42–47.

Shellhaas, M. D., & Nihira, K. Factor analysis of reasons retardates are referred to an institution. *American Journal of Mental Deficiency*, 1969, **74**, 171–79.

Shif, Z. I. Development of children in schools for the mentally retarded. In M. Cole & I. Maltzman (Eds.), *A handbook of contemporary Soviet psychology*. New York: Basic Books, 1969.

Shotel, J. R., Iano, R. P., & McGettigan, J. F. Teacher attitudes associated with the integration of handicapped children. *Exceptional children*, 1972, **38**, 677–83.

Shuey, A. *The testing of Negro intelligence*. New York: Social Science Press, 1966.

Siegel, G. M. Interpersonal approaches to the study of communication disorders. *Journal of Speech and Hearing Disorders Monograph*, 1967, **32**, 112–20.

Sigel, I. E. *Cognitive style and personality dynamics*. Progress Report NIMH, 1961, No. M–2983.

Sigel, I. E. How intelligence tests limit understanding of intelligence. In I. J. Gordon (Ed.), *Human development: Readings in research*, pp. 287–97. Glenview, Ill.: Scott, Foresman, 1965.

Silber, D. E., & Courtless, T. F. Measures of fantasy aggression among mentally retarded offenders. *American Journal of Mental Deficiency*, 1968, **72**, 918–23.

Silberman, M. L. Behavioral expression of teacher's attitudes toward elementary school students. *Journal of Educational Psychology*, 1969, **60**, 402–07.

Silverstein, A. B. Mental growth in mongolism. *Child Development*, 1966, **37**, 725–29.(a)

Silverstein, A. B. Anxiety and the quality of human-figure drawings. *American Journal of Mental Deficiency*, 1966, **70**, 607–08.(b)

Silverstein, A. B. A dimensional analysis of institutional differences. *Training School Bulletin*, 1967, **64**, 102–03.

Silverstein, A. B. The measurement of intelligence. In N. R. Ellis (Ed.), *International review of research in mental retardation*. Vol. 4, pp. 194–227. New York: Academic Press, 1970.

Silverstein, A. B. Mental growth from six to sixty in an institutionalized mentally retarded sample. *Psychological Reports*, 1979, **45**, 643–46.

Silverstein, A. B., Auger, R., & Krudis, B. R. The meaning of indefinite number terms for mentally retarded children. *American Journal of Mental Deficiency*, 1964, **69**, 419–24.

Simches, G., & Bohn, R. Issues in curriculum: Research and responsibility. *Mental Retardation*, 1963, **1**, 84–87.

Simmons, A., & Brinegar, L. *Ethnic survey of EMR classes, 1973.* Sacramento: California State Department of Education, 1973.

Simmons, O. G. The mutual images and expectations of Anglo-Americans and Mexican-Americans. *Daedalus*, 1961, **90**, 286–99.

Siperstein, G. N., & Bak, J. J. Students' and teachers' perceptions of the mentally retarded child. In J. Gottlieb (Ed.), *Educating mentally retarded persons in the mainstream*, pp. 207–30. Baltimore: University Park Press, 1980.

Siperstein, G. N., Budoff, M., & Bak, J. J. Effects of the labels "mentally retarded" and "retard" on the social acceptability of mentally retarded children. *American Journal of Mental Deficiency*, 1980, **84**, 596–601.

Siperstein, G. N., & Gottlieb, J. Physical stigmata and academic performance as factors affecting children's first impressions of handicapped peers. *American Journal of Mental Deficiency*, 1977, **81**, 455–62.

Sitko, M. C., & Semmel, M. I. Effects of phrasal cueing on free recall of educable mentally retarded and nonretarded children. *American Educational Research Journal*, 1972, **9**, 217–29.

Sitko, M. C., & Semmel, M. I. Language and language behavior of the mentally retarded. In L. Mann & D. A. Sabatino (Eds.), *The first review of special education*. Vol. 1, pp. 203–59. Philadelphia: Journal of Special Education Press, 1973.

Skeels, H. M. Adult status of children with contrasting early life experiences: A follow-up study. *Monographs of the Society for Research in Child Development*, 1966, **31**(3), Series No. 105.

Skeels, H. M., & Dye, H. B. A study of the effects of differential stimulation on mentally retarded children. *Proceedings of the American Association on Mental Deficiency*, 1939, **44**, 114–36.

Skinner, B. F. *The behavior of organisms*. New York: Appleton-Century, 1938.

Skinner, B. F. *Science and human behavior*. New York: Macmillan, 1953.

Skodak, M. Adult status of individuals who experienced early intervention. In B. W. Richards (Ed.), *Proceedings of the 1st Congress of the Association for the Scientific Study of Mental Deficiency*, pp. 11–18. Reigate, England: Michael Jackson, 1968.

Sloan, W., & Harmon, H. H. Constancy of IQ in mental defectives. *Journal of Genetic Psychology*, 1947, **71**, 177–85.

Smith, D. W. *Recognizable patterns of human malformation*. Philadelphia: Saunders, 1970.

Smith, D. W., & Wilson, A. A. *The child with Down's syndrome (mongolism)*. Philadelphia: Saunders, 1973.

Smith, J. O. Criminality and mental retardation. *Training School Bulletin*, 1962, **59**, 74–80.

Smith, R. M. *Clinical teaching: Methods of instruction for the retarded*. New York: McGraw-Hill, 1974.

Snell, N. E. *Systematic instruction of the moderately and severely handicapped*. Columbus, Ohio: Merrill, 1978.

Snow, R. L. Unfinished pygmalion. *Contemporary Psychology*, 1969, **14**, 197–99.

Snyder, L., Apolloni, T., & Cooke, T. P. Integrated settings at the early childhood level: The role of nonretarded peers. *Exceptional Children*, 1977, **43**, 262–66.

Snyder, R. T. Personality adjustment, self-attitudes and anxiety differences in retarded adolescents. *American Journal of Mental Deficiency*, 1966, **71**, 33–41.

Sobel, W. E., Strazzulla, M., Sherman, B. S., Elkan, B., Morganstern, S. W., Marius, N., & Meisel, A. Vitamin A absorption and other blood composition studies in mongolism. *American Journal of Mental Deficiency*, 1958, **62**, 642–56.

Solnit, A. J., & Stark, M. H. Mourning and the birth of a defective child. *Psychoanalytic Study of the Child*, 1961, **16**, 523–37.

Sontag, L., Baker, C., & Nelson, V. Mental growth and personality: A longitudinal study. *Monographs of the Society for Research in Child Development*, 1958, **23**(2), 1–143.

Sorgen, M. S. Labeling and classification. In M. Kindred, et. al. (Eds.), *The mentally retarded citizen and the law*, pp. 214–44. New York: The Free Press, 1976.

Sorotzkin, F., Fleming, E. S., & Anttonen, R. G. Teacher knowledge of standardized test information and its effect on pupil IQ and achievement. *Journal of Experimental Education*, 1974, **43**, 79–85.

Soule, D. Teacher bias effects with severely retarded children. *American Journal of Mental Deficiency*, 1972, **77**, 208–11.

Spangler v. *Board of Education*. 311 F. Supp. 501 (Calif.), 1970.

Spearman, C. *The abilities of man*. New York: Macmillan, 1927.

Spicker, H. H. Intellectual development through early childhood education. In R. L. Jones & D. L. MacMillan (Eds.), *Special education in transition*, pp. 208–17. Boston: Allyn and Bacon, 1974.

Spitz, H. H. Field theory in mental deficiency. In N. R. Ellis (Ed.), *Handbook of mental deficiency*, pp. 11–40. New York: McGraw-Hill, 1963.

Spitz, H. H. The role of input organization in the learning and memory of mental retardates. In N. R. Ellis (Ed.), *International review of research in mental retardation*. Vol. 2, pp. 29–56. New York: Academic Press, 1966.

Spitz, H. H. The role of input organization in the learning and memory of mental retardates. In N. R. Ellis (Ed.), *International review of research in mental retardation*. Vol. 4. New York: Academic Press, 1970.

Spitz, H. H. Beyond field theory in the study of mental deficiency. In N. R. Ellis (Ed.), *Handbook of mental deficiency*. (2nd ed.), pp. 121–41. Hillsdale, N.J.: Erlbaum, 1979.

Spitz, R. A. Hospitalism: An inquiry into the genesis of psychiatric conditions in early childhood. *Psychoanalytic Study of the Child*, 1945, **1**, 53–74.

Spitz, R. A. Anaclitic depression. *Psychonalytic Study of the Child*, 1946, **2**, 313–42.(a)

Spitz, R. A. Hospitalism: A follow-up report. *Psychoanalytic Study of the Child*, 1946, **2**, 113–117.(b)

Spock, B. *On being a parent—of a handicapped child*. Chicago: National Society for Crippled Children and Adults, 1961.

Spradlin, J. E. Task resumption phenomena in mentally retarded Negro children. *Abstracts of Peabody Studies in Mental Retardation*, 1960, **1**(40).

Spradlin, J. E. Assessment of speech and language of retarded children: The Parsons language sample. *Journal of Speech and Hearing Disorders Monograph*, 1963 (Supp. 10).(a)

Spradlin, J. E. Language and communication of mental defectives. In N. R. Ellis (Ed.), *Handbook of mental deficiency*. New York: McGraw-Hill, 1963.(b)

Spradlin, J. E. Environmental factors and the language development of retarded children. In S. Rosenberg & J. H. Koplin (Eds.), *Developments in applied psycholinguistic research*. New York: Macmillan, 1968.

Spreen, O. Language functions in mental retardation: A review. *American Journal of Mental Deficiency*, 1965, **69**, 482–92.(a)

Spreen, O. Language functions in mental retardation: A review. *American Journal of Mental Deficiency*, 1965, **70**, 351–62.(b)

Standards for educational and psychological tests. Washington, D.C.: American Psychological Assoc., 1974.

Stedman, D. J. Associative clustering of semantic categories in normal and retarded subjects. *American Journal of Mental Deficiency*, 1963, **67**, 700–04.

Stein, Z. A., & Susser, M. Recent trends in Down's syndrome. In P. Mittler (Ed.), *Research to practice in mental retardation: Biomedical aspects*. Vol. III, pp. 45–54. Baltimore: University Park Press, 1977.

Stell v. *Savannah-Chatham County Board of Education*. 220 F. Supp. 667 (S.D., Ga.), 1963.

Stephens, B. A Piagetian approach to curriculum development. In E. Sontag (Ed.), *Educational programming for the severely and profoundly handicapped*. Reston, Va.: Council for Exceptional Children, 1977.

Stephens, B., Mahaney, E. J., & McLaughlin, J. A. Mental ages for achievement of Piagetian reasoning assessments. *Education and Training of the Mentally Retarded*, 1972, **7**, 124–28.

Stephens, B., McLaughlin, J. A., Hunt, J. M., Mahaney, E. J., Kohlberg, L., Moore, G., & Aronfreed, J. Symposium: Developmental gains in the reasoning, moral judgment, and moral conduct of retarded and nonretarded persons. *American Journal of Mental Deficiency*, 1974, **79**, 114–61.

Stephens, E. Defensive reactions of mentally retarded adults. *Social Casework*, 1953, **34**, 119–24.

Stephens, W. E. Category usage of normal and subnormal children on three types of categories. *American Journal of Mental Deficiency*, 1966, **71**, 266–73.(a)

Stephens, W. E. Category usage by normal and mentally retarded boys. *Child Development*, 1966, **37**, 355–61.(b)

Stephens, W. E. Equivalence formation by retarded and nonretarded children at different mental ages. *American Journal of Mental Deficiency*, 1972, **77**, 311–13.

Stephens, W. E. Equivalence formation by retarded and nonretarded children in structured and unstructured tasks. *American Journal of Mental Deficiency*, 1973, **77**, 445–50.

Stephens, W. E., Nopar, R., & Gillam, L. Equivalence formation by mentally retarded and nonretarded children using pictorial and printed work stimulus items. *American Journal of Mental Deficiency*, 1971, **76**, 252–56.

Stern, C. *Principles of human genetics*. (3rd ed.) San Francisco: Freeman, 1973.

Sternlicht, M. Psychotherapeutic procedure with the retarded. In N. R. Ellis (Ed.), *International review of research in mental retardation*. Vol. 2, pp. 279–354, New York: Academic Press, 1966.

Sternlicht, M., & Bialer, I. Psychological aspects of institutionalization in mental retardation. In I. Bialer & M. Sternlicht (Eds.), *The psychology of mental retardation*, pp. 603–44. New York: Psychological Dimensions, 1977.

Sternlicht, M., & Deutsch, M. R. *Personality development and social behavior in the mentally retarded*. Lexington, Mass.: Lexington Books, 1972.

Sternlicht, M., & Silverg, F. The relationship between fantasy aggression and overt hostility in mental retardates. *American Journal of Mental Deficiency*, 1965, **70**, 486–88.

Stevenson, H. W. Social reinforcement with children as a function of CA, sex of E, and sex of S. *Journal of Abnormal and Social Psychology*, 1961, **63**, 147–54.

Stevenson, H. W. *Children's learning*. New York: Appleton-Century-Crofts, 1972.

Stevenson, H. W., & Cruse, D. B. The effectiveness of social reinforcement with normal and feeble-minded children. *Journal of Personality*, 1961, **29**, 124–35.

Stevenson, H. W., & Fahel, L. S. The effect of social reinforcement on the performance of institutionalized and noninstitutionalized normal and feeble-minded children. *Journal of Personality*, 1961, **29**, 136–47.

Stevenson, H. W., & Knights, R. M. The effect of visual reinforcement with normal and feeble-minded children. *Journal of Personality*, 1961, **29**, 124–35.

Stevenson, H. W., & Knights, R. M. The effectiveness of social reinforcement after brief and extended institutionalization. *American Journal of Mental Deficiency*, 1962, **66**, 589–94.

Stevenson, H. W. & Zigler, E. F. Discrimination learning and rigidity in normal and feeble-minded individuals. *Journal of Personality*, 1957, **25**, 699–711.

Stewart, J. C. *Counseling parents of exceptional children*. Columbus, Ohio: Merrill, 1978.

Stewart v. Phillips. Civil action 70–1199F (D. Mass.), 1970.

Stoddard, G. D. *The meaning of intelligence*. New York: Macmillan, 1943.

Stoll, C. S. Images of man and social control. *Social Forces*, 1968, **47**, 119–27.

Storrs, H. C. A report on an investigation made of cases discharged from Letchworth Village, *Journal of Psycho-Asthenia*, 1924, **34**, 220–32.

Stott, D. H. Interaction of heredity and environment in regard to "measured intelligence." *British Journal of Educational Psychology*, 1960, **30**, 95–102.

Strauss, A. A., & Kephart, N. C. *Psychopathology and education of the brain-injured child*. Vol. 2. New York: Grune and Stratton, 1955.

Strauss, A. A., & Lehtinen, L. E. *Psychopathology and education of the brain-injured child*. Vol. 1. New York: Grune and Stratton, 1947.

Strichart, S. S. Effects of competence and nurturance on imitation of nonretarded peers by retarded adolescents. *American Journal of Mental Deficiency*, 1974, **78**, 665–73.

Strickland, O., & Arrell, V. Employment of the mentally retarded. *Exceptional Children*, 1967, **33**, 21–29.

Susser, M., Stein, Z. A., & Rush, D. Prenatal nutrition and subsequent development. In P. Mittler (Ed.), *Research to practice in mental retardation: Biomedical aspects*. Vol. III, pp. 311–26. Baltimore: University Park Press, 1977.

Taichert, L. C. Parental denial as a factor in the management of the severely retarded child. *Clinical Pediatrics*, 1975, **14**, 666–68.

Takanishi, R. Federal involvement in early education (1933–1973): The need for historical perspectives. In L. G. Katz (Ed.), *Current topics in early childhood education*. Vol. 1, pp. 139–63. Norwood, N.J.: Ablex Publishing, 1977.

Talbot, M. E. *Edouard Seguin: A study of an educational approach to the treatment of mentally defective children*. New York: Columbia University Press, 1964.

Talbot, M. E. Edouard Seguin. *American Journal of Mental Deficiency*, 1967, **72**, 184–89.

Talkington, L. W., & Hall, S. Hearing impairment and aggressiveness in the mentally retarded. *Perceptual and Motor Skills*, 1969, **28**, 303–06.

Talkington, L. W., Hall, S., & Altman, R. Communication deficits and aggression in the mentally retarded. *American Journal of Mental Deficiency*, 1971, **76**, 235–37.

Talkington, L. W., & Riley, J. B. Reduction diets and aggression in institutionalized mentally retarded patients. *American Journal of Mental Deficiency*, 1971, **76**, 370–72.

Tarjan, G. Some current issues in mental retardation. In A. Dorfman (Ed.), *Child care in health and disease: Symposium to dedicate the Silvain and Arma Wyler Children's Hospital and the Joseph P. Kennedy Mental Retardation Research Center*. Chicago: Yearbook, 1968.

Tarjan, G. Some thoughts on sociocultural retardation. In H. C. Haywood (Ed.), *Social-cultural aspects of mental retardation*. New York: Appleton-Century-Crofts, 1970.

Tarjan, G. Toward accelerated progress in mental retardation. Paper presented at the first convention of the Federación Venezolana de padres y amigos de niños excepcionales (FEVEPANE), Caracas, Venezuela, October 1972.

Tarjan, G., Eyman, R. K., & Dingman, H. F. Changes in patient population of a hospital for the mentally retarded. *American Journal of Mental Deficiency*, 1966, **70**, 529–41.

Tarjan, G., Wright, S.W., Eyman, R.K., & Keeran, C. V. Natural history of mental retardation: Some aspects of epidemiology. *American Journal of Mental Deficiency*, 1973, **77**, 369–79.

Taylor, A. M., Josberger, M., & Knowlton, J. Q. Mental elaboration and learning in EMR children. *American Journal of Mental Deficiency*, 1972, **77**, 69–76.

Teahan, J. E., & Drews, E. M. A comparison of northern and southern Negro children on the WISC. *Journal of Consulting Psychology*, 1962, **26**, 292.

Terman, L. M. Feeble-minded children in the public schools of California. *School and Society*, 1917, **5**, 161–65.

Terman, L. M. *The intelligence of school children*. Boston: Houghton Mifflin, 1919.

Terman, L. M., & Merrill, M. A. *Measuring intelligence: A guide to the administration of the new revised Stanford-Binet tests of intelligence*. Boston: Houghton Mifflin, 1937.

Terman, L. M., & Merrill, M. A. *Stanford-Binet Intelligence Scale: Manual for the third revision, Form L-M*. Boston: Houghton Mifflin, 1960.

Terman, L. M. & Merrill, M. A. *The Stanford-Binet Intelligence Scale, third revision* (with 1972 tables by R. L. Thorndike). Boston: Houghton Mifflin, 1973.

Terrell, G., Durkin, K., & Wiesley, M. Social class and the nature of the incentive in discrimination learning. *Journal of Abnormal and Social Psychology*, 1959, **59**, 270–72.

Teuber, H. L. Mental retardation after early trauma to the brain: Some issues in search of facts. In C. R. Angle & E. A. Bering, Jr. (Eds.), *Physical trauma as an etiological agent in mental retardation*. Washington, D.C.: U.S. Government Printing Office, 1970.

Thompson, J. J., & Thompson, M. W. *Genetics in medicine*. (2nd ed.) Philadelphia: Saunders, 1973.

Thorndike, E. L. *The measurement of intelligence*. New York: Columbia University Teachers College, 1925.

Thorndike, R. L. Review of R. Rosenthal and L. Jacobson, *Pygmalion in the classroom. American Educational Research Journal*, 1968, **5**, 708–11.

Thorne, F. C. The problems of institutional elopements. *American Journal of Mental Deficiency*, 1947, **51**, 637–43.

Throne, F. M., Schulman, J. L., & Kaspar, J. C. Reliability and stability of the Wechsler Intelligence Scale for Children for a group of mentally retarded boys. *American Journal of Mental Deficiency*, 1962, **67**, 455–57.

Throne, J. M. Normalization through the normalization principle: Right ends, wrong means. *Mental Retardation*, 1975, **13**(5), 23–25.

Throne, J. M. Deinstitutionalization: Too wide a swath. *Mental Retardation*, 1979, **17**, 171–75.

Thurstone, T. G. *An evaluation of educating mentally handicapped children in special classes and in regular grades.* U.S. Office of Education Cooperative Research Program Project OE–SAE-6452. Chapel Hill, N.C.: University of North Carolina, 1959.

Tisza, V. B. Management of the parents of the chronically ill child. *American Journal of Orthopsychiatry*, 1962, **32**, 53–59.

Tizard, J. The prevalence of mental subnormality, *Bulletin of the World Health Organization*, 1953, **9**, 423–40.

Tizard, J. Residential care of mentally handicapped children. *British Medical Journal*, 1960, **1**, 1041–46.

Tizard, J. *Community services for the mentally handicapped.* New York: Oxford University Press, 1964.

Tizard, J. The role of social institutions in the causation, prevention, and alleviation of mental retardation. In H. C. Haywood (Ed.), *Social-cultural aspects of mental retardation*, pp. 281–340. New York: Appleton-Century-Crofts, 1970.

Tizard, J., & Grad, J. C. *The mentally handicapped and their families.* London: Oxford University Press, 1961.

Tjossem, T. D. Early intervention: Issues and approaches. In T. D. Tjossem (Ed.), *Intervention strategies for high risk infants and young children*, pp. 3–33. Baltimore: University Park Press, 1976.

Tolman, N. G., & Johnson, A. P. Need for achievement as related to brain injury in mentally retarded children. *American Journal of Mental Deficiency*, 1958, **62**, 692–97.

Towne, R. C., Joiner, L. M., & Schurr, T. The effects of special classes on the self-concepts of academic ability of the educable mentally retarded: A time series experiment. Paper presented at the Forty-fifth Annual Council for Exceptional Children Convention, St. Louis, 1967.

Tredgold, A. F. *Mental deficiency*, London: Bailliera, Tindall, and Fox, 1908.

Tryon, W. W. The test-trait fallacy. *American Psychologist*, 1979, **34**, 402–06.

Tulchin, S. H. *Intelligence and crime.* Chicago: University of Chicago Press, 1939.

Turnbull, A. P., & Blacher-Dixon, J. Preschool mainstreaming: Impact on parents. In J. J. Gallagher (Ed.), *New directions for exceptional children*, pp. 25–46. San Francisco: Jossey Bass, 1980.

Turnbull, A. P., & Blacher-Dixon, J. Preschool mainstreaming: An empirical and conceptual review. In P. Strain & M. M. Kerr (Eds.), *Mainstreaming handicapped children: Research and instructional perspectives.* New York: Academic Press, 1981.

Turnbull, A. P., Strickland, B. B., & Brantley, J. C. *Developing and implementing individualized education programs.* Columbus, Ohio: Merrill, 1978.

Turnbull, A. P., Strickland, B., & Hammer, S. E. The individualized education program—Part 2: Translating law into practice. *Journal of Learning Disabilities*, 1978, **11**, 18–23.

Turnbull, A. P., & Turnbull, H. R. *Parents speak out.* Columbus, Ohio: Merrill, 1978.(a)

Turnbull, H. R., & Turnbull, A. *Free appropriate public education: Law and implementation.* Denver: Love Publishing Co., 1978.(b)

Turnure, J. E. Children's reactions to distractors in a learning situation. *Developmental Psychology*, 1970, **2**, 115–22.(a)

Turnure, J. E. Distractibility in the mentally retarded: Negative evidence for an orienting inadequacy. *Exceptional Children*, 1970, **37**, 181–86.(b)

Turnure, J. E., Larsen, S. N., & Thurlow, M. L. Effects of brain-injury and other subject characteristics on paired-associate performance under paragraph elaboration. *American Journal of Mental Deficiency*, 1973, **78**, 70–76.

Turnure, J. E., Larsen, S. N., & Thurlow, M. L. Outerdirectedness in retarded children as a function of sex of experimenter and sex of subject. *American Journal of Mental Deficiency*, 1976, **80**, 460–68.

Turnure, J. E., & Thurlow, M. L. Verbal elaboration and the promotion of transfer of training in educable mentally retarded children. *Journal of Experimental Child Psychology*, 1973, **15**, 137–48.

Turnure, J. E., & Thurlow, M. L. Effects of structural variations in elaboration on learning by EMR and nonretarded children. *American Journal of Mental Deficiency*, 1975, **79**, 632–39.

Turnure, J. E., & Walsh, M. K. Extended verbal mediation in the learning and reversal of paired-associates by EMR children. *American Journal of Mental Deficiency*, 1971, **76**, 60–67.

Turnure, J. E., & Zigler, E. Outerdirectedness in the problem-solving of normal and retarded children. *Journal of Abnormal and Social Psychology*, 1964, **69**, 427–36.

Tyler, L. E. *The psychology of human differences.* New York: Appleton-Century-Crofts, 1965.

Tymchuk, A. J. Personality and sociocultural retardation. *Exceptional Children*, 1972, **38**, 721–28.

U.S. Commission on Civil Rights. *Racial isolation in the public schools.* Vol. 1. Washington, D.C.: U.S. Government Printing Office, 1967.

U.S. Department of Health, Education, and Welfare. *Mental retardation source book.* Washington, D.C.: U.S. Government Printing Office, 1972.

U.S. Nuclear Regulatory Commission. *Office Regulatory Guide*, 1975, No. 8.13 (Rev. 1), pp. 1–2.

Uzgiris, I., & Hunt, J. M. *Assessment in infancy: Ordinal scales of psychological development*. Urbana: University of Illinois Press, 1975.

Vandenberg, S. G. The nature and nurture of intelligence. In D. C. Glass (Ed.), *Genetics*. New York: Rockefeller University Press, 1968.

Van Wagenen, R. K., Myerson, L., Kerr, N. J., & Mahoney, K. Field trials of a new procedure for toilet training. *Journal of Experimental Psychology*, 1969, **8**, 147–59.

Vergason, G. A. Retention in educable retarded and normal adolescent boys as a function of amount of original learning. Unpublished doctoral dissertation, George Peabody College, 1962.

Vergason, G. A. Instructional practices in special education. In E. L. Meyen, G. A. Vergason, & R. J. Whelan (Eds.), *Strategies for teaching exceptional children*, pp. 185–99. Denver: Love, 1972.

Vernon, M. Multiply handicapped deaf children: A study of significant problems and causes of the problem. *Council for Exceptional Children Research Monograph*, 1969.(a)

Vernon, M. Prenatal rubella and deafness. *Monograph of the National Association, March of Dimes*, 1969.(b)

Veroff, J., Atkinson, J., Feld, S., & Gurin, G. The use of thematic apperception to assess motivation in a nationwide interview study. *Psychological Monographs*, 1960, **74**(12), No. 449.

Vygotsky, L. S. *Thought and language*. Cambridge, Mass.: MIT Press, 1962.

Wachs, T. D., & DeRemer, P. Adaptive behavior and Uzgiris-Hunt Scale performance of young, developmentally disabled children. *American Journal of Mental Deficiency*, 1978, **83**, 171–76.

Walberg, H. J., & Marjoribanks, K. Family environment and cognitive development: Twelve analytic models. *Review of Educational Research*, 1976, **46**, 527–51.

Walker, V. The efficacy of the resource room for educating retarded children. *Exceptional Children*, 1974, **40**, 288–89.

Wallin, J. E. W. Mental deficiency: In relation to problems of genesis, social and occupational consequences, utilization, control, and prevention. *Journal of Clinical Psychology*, 1956, **15**, (200 pp.).

Wallin, J. E. W. Prevalence of mental retardates. *School and Society*, 1958, **86**, 55–56.

Wallin, J. E. W. Training of the severely retarded, viewed in historical perspective. *Journal of General Psychology*, 1966, **74**, 107–27.

Waltman, R., & Iniques, E. S. Placental transfer of ethanol and its elimination at term. *Obstetrics and Gynecology*, 1972, **40**, 180–85.

Wandersman, A., & Moos, R. H. Evaluating sheltered living environments for retarded people. In H. C. Haywood & J. R. Newbrough (Eds.), *Living environments for mentally retarded persons*. Baltimore: University Park Press, in press.

Warren, S. A. Psychological evaluation of the mentally retarded: A review of techniques. *Pediatric Clinics of North America*, 1968, **15**, 953–54.

Watson, L. S., Jr. Application of behavior-shaping devices to training severely and profoundly mentally retarded children in an institutional setting. Paper presented at the annual meeting of the Midwestern Psychological Association, at Chicago, May 1966.

Weaver, S. J. *Effects of motivation-hygiene orientations and interpersonal reaction tendencies in intellectually subnormal children*. Ann Arbor, Mich.: University Microfilms, 1966.

Weaver, T. R. The incidence of maladjustment among mental defectives in military environment. *American Journal of Mental Deficiency*, 1946, **51**, 238–46.

Webster, T. G. Unique aspects of emotional development in mentally retarded children. In F. T. Menolascino (Ed.), *Psychiatric approaches to mental retardation*. New York: Basic Books, 1970.

Wechsler, D. *Manual for the Wechsler Adult Intelligence Scale*. New York: Psychological Corporation, 1955.

Weikart, D. P. (Ed.) *Preschool intervention: A preliminary report of the Perry Preschool Project*. Ann Arbor, Mich.: Campus Publishers, 1967.

Weiner, B. A theory of motivation for some classroom experiences. *Journal of Educational Psychology*, 1979, **71**, 3–25.

Weiner, G., Crawford, E. E., & Snyder, R. T. Some correlates of overt anxiety in mildly retarded patients. *American Journal of Mental Deficiency*, 1960, **64**, 735–39.

Weintraub, F. J. Recent influences of law regarding the identification and educational placement of children. In E. L. Meyen, G. A. Vergason, & R. J. Whelan (Eds.), *Alternatives for teaching exceptional children*. Denver: Love, 1975.

Weir, M. Mental retardation. *Science*, 1967, **155**, 576–77.

Weisz, J. R., & Zigler, E. Cognitive development in retarded and nonretarded persons: Piagetian tests of the similar sequence hypothesis. *Psychological Bulletin*, 1979, **86**, 831–51.

Wellman, B. L., Skeels, H. M., & Skodak, M. Review of McNemar's critical examination of Iowa studies. *Psychological Bulletin*, 1940, **37**, 93–111.

Werner, J. Abnormal and subnormal rigidity. *Journal of Abnormal and Social Psychology*, 1946, **41**, 15–24.

Werner, J. The concept of rigidity: A critical review. *Psychological Review*, 1948, **53**, 43–52.

Wheeler, L. R. The intelligence of East Tennessee mountain children. *Journal of Educational Psychology*, 1932, **23**, 351–70.

White, R. W. Motivation reconsidered: The concept of competence. *Psychological Review*, 1959, **66**, 297–333.

White, R. W. Competence and the psychosexual stages of development. In M. R. Jones (Ed.), *Nebraska symposium on motivation*. Vol. 5. Lincoln, Neb.: University of Nebraska Press, 1960.

White, S. H. The learning theory tradition and child psychology. In P. H. Mussen (Ed.), *Carmichael's manual of child psychology* (3rd ed.), pp. 657–701. New York: Wiley, 1970.

Whitman, T. L., & Scibak, J. W. Behavior modification research with the severely and profoundly retarded. In N. R. Ellis (Ed.), *Handbook of mental deficiency* (2nd ed.), pp. 289–340. Hillsdale, N.J.: Lawrence Erlbaum, 1979.

Whitney, E. A. Mental deficiency in the 1880's and 1940's. *American Journal of Mental Deficiency,* 1949, **54,** 151–54.

Wilcox, B. Severe/profound handicapping conditions: Administrative considerations. In M. S. Lilly (Ed.), *Children with exceptional needs. A survey of special education.* New York: Holt, Rinehart, and Winston, 1979.

Willerman, L. Effects of families on intellectual development. *American Psychologist,* 1979, **34,** 923–29.

Willerman, L., & Churchill, J. A. Intelligence and birth weight in identical twins. *Child Development,* 1967, **38,** 623–29.

Williams, C. E. A study of the patients in a group of mental subnormality hospitals. *British Journal of Mental Subnormality,* 1971, **17,** 29–41.

Williams, R. L. Black pride, academic relevance, and individual achievement. *Counseling Psychologist,* 1970, **2,** 18–20.

Williams, R. L. Black intelligence test of cultural homogeneity. Unpublished manuscript, St. Louis, 1972.(a)

Williams, R. L. Problem of the match and mismatch of testing black children. Paper read at American Psychological Association meeting. Honolulu, September 1972.(b)

Williams, W., & Gotts, E. A. Selected considerations on developing curriculum for severely handicapped students. In E. Sontag (Ed.), *Educational programming for the severely and profoundly handicapped.* Reston, Va.: Council for Exceptional Children, 1977.

Wilson, J. B. Is the term "adaptive behavior" educationally relevant? *Journal of Special Education,* 1972, **6,** 93–95.

Wilson, J. G. *Environment and birth defects.* New York: Academic Press, 1973.

Wilson, J. G. Teralogic causation in man and its evaluation in nonhuman primates. In B. V. Beidel (Ed.), *Proceedings of the Fourth International Conference,* pp. 191–203. Dordrecht, Netherlands: Excerpta Medica, 1974.

Wilson, W. Social psychology and mental retardation. In N. R. Ellis (Ed.), *International review of research in mental retardation.* Vol. 4, pp. 229–62. New York: Academic Press, 1970.

Windle, C. Prognosis of mental subnormals. *American Journal of Mental Deficiency Monograph Supplement,* 1962, **66**(5).

Winick, M. Fetal malnutrition and growth process. *Hospital Practice,* 1970, **5**(5), 33–41.

Winick, M., & Rosso, P. Effects of malnutrition on brain development. *Biology of Brain Dysfunction,* 1973, **1,** 301–17.

Wink, C. F. Mental retardation and learning under symbolic reinforcement in view of self-acceptance. *Dissertation Abstracts,* 1963, **23,** 2430–31.

Winters, J. J. Methodological issues in psychological research with retarded persons. In I. Bialer & M. Sternlicht (Eds.), *The psychology of mental retardation,* pp. 185–240. New York: Psychological Dimensions, 1977.

Winthrop, H., & Taylor, H. An inquiry concerning the prevalence of popular misconceptions relating to mental deficiency. *American Journal of Mental Deficiency,* 1957, **62,** 344–48.

Witkin, H. A., Dyk, R., Faterson, H., Goodenough, D., & Karp, S. *Psychological differentiation.* New York: Wiley, 1962.

Witkin, H. A., Faterson, H. F., Goodenough, D. R., & Birnbaum, J. Cognitive patterning in mildly retarded boys. *Child Development,* 1966, **37,** 301–16.

Wolf, M. G. Effects of emotional disturbance in childhood on intelligence. *American Journal of Orthopsychiatry,* 1965, **35,** 906–08.

Wolf, R. M. The identification and measurement of environmental process variables related to intelligence. Unpublished doctoral dissertation, University of Chicago, 1964.

Wolfensberger, W. Construction of a table of the significance of the difference between verbal and performance IQ's on the WAIS and the Wechsler-Bellevue. *Journal of Clinical Psychology,* 1958, **14,** 92.

Wolfensberger, W. Counseling the parents of the retarded. In A. A. Baumeister (Ed.), *Mental retardation: Appraisal, education, and rehabilitation,* pp. 329–400. Chicago: Aldine, 1967.

Wolfensberger, W. The origin and nature of our institutional models. In R. B. Kugel & W. Wolfensberger (Eds.), *Changing patterns in residential services for the mentally retarded.* Washington, D.C.: U.S. Government Printing Office, 1969.

Wolfensberger, W. Will there always be an institution? II: The impact of new service models. *Mental Retardation,* 1971, **9**(6), 31–38.

Wolfensberger, W. *The principle of normalization in human services.* Toronto: National Institute on Mental Retardation, 1972.

Wolf v. Legislature of the State of Utah. Civil action 182646 (3rd Jud. Dist. Ct., Utah), 1969.

Wood, J. W., Johnson, K. G., & Omori, Y. In utero exposure to the Hiroshima atomic bomb. An evaluation of head size and mental retardation twenty years later. *Pediatrics,* 1967, **39,** 385–92.

Woodward, M. The application of Piaget's theory to research in mental deficiency. In N. R. Ellis (Ed.), *Handbook of mental deficiency,* pp. 297–324. New York: McGraw-Hill, 1963.

Woodward, W. M. Piaget's theory and the study of mental retardation. In N. R. Ellis (Ed.), *Handbook of mental deficiency*, pp. 169–95. Hillsdale, N.J.: Lawrence Erlbaum, 1979.

Woolf, L. I. Phenylketonuria and phenylalaninemia. In J. Wortis (Ed.), *Mental retardation*. Vol. 2, pp. 29–42. New York: Grune and Stratton, 1970.

World Health Organization. *The mentally subnormal child*. WHO Technical Reports Series, 1954, No. 75.

Wright, B. A. *Physical disability: A psychological approach*. New York: Harper and Row, 1960.

Wright, S. W., & Tarjan, G. Phenylketonuria. *American Journal of Diseases of Children*, 1957, **93**, 405–19.

Wright, S. W., & Tarjan, G. Mental retardation: A review for pediatricians. *American Journal of Diseases of Children*, 1963, **105**, 511–26.

Wunsch, W. L. The first complete tabulation of the Rhode Island Mental deficiency register. *American Journal of Mental Deficiency*, 1951, **55**, 293–312.

Wyatt v. Stickney. 325 F. Supp. 781 (M.D., Ala.), 1971.

Yando, R. M., & Kagan, J. The effect of teacher tempo on the child. *Child Development*, 1968, **39**, 27–34.

Yando, R. M., & Zigler, G. Outerdirectedness in the problem-solving of institutionalized normal and retarded children. *Developmental Psychology*, 1971, **4**, 277–88.

Yoshida, R. K. Effects of labeling on elementary and EMR teachers' expectancies for change in a student's performance. Unpublished doctoral dissertation, University of Southern California, 1974.

Yoshida, R. K., & Gottlieb, J. A model for parental participation in the pupil planning process. *Mental Retardation*, 1976, **15**(3), 17–20.

Yoshida, R. K., MacMillan, D. L., & Meyers, C. E. The decertification of minority group EMR students in California: Its historical background and assessment of student achievement and adjustment. In R. L. Jones (Ed.), *Mainstreaming and the minority child*, pp. 215–33. Minneapolis, Minn.: University of Minnesota, Leadership Training Institute, 1976.

Yoshida, R. K., & Meyers, C. E. Effects of labeling as EMR on teachers' expectancies for change in a student's performance. *Journal of Educational Psychology*, 1975, **67**, 521–27.

Zajonc, R. B. Family configuration and intelligence. *Science*, 1976, **19**, 227–36.

Zeaman, D., & House, B. J. Approach and avoidance in the discrimination learning of retardates. *Child Development*, 1962, **33**, 355–72.(a)

Zeaman, D., & House, B. J. Mongoloid MA is proportional to log CA. *Child Development*, 1962, **33**, 481–88.(b)

Zeaman, D., & House, B. J. The role of attention in retardate discrimination learning. In N. R. Ellis (Ed.), *Handbook of mental deficiency*, pp. 159–223. New York: McGraw-Hill, 1963.

Zeaman, D., & House, B. J. A review of attention theory. In N. R. Ellis (Ed.), *Handbook of mental deficiency* (2nd ed.) pp. 63–120. Hillsdale, N.J.: Lawrence Erlbaum, 1979.

Zeleny, L. D. Feeble-mindedness and criminal conduct. *American Journal of Sociology*, 1933, **38**, 564–76.

Zigler, E. Rigidity in the feeble-minded. In E. P. Trapp & P. Himelstein (Eds.), *Readings on the exceptional child*, pp. 141–62. New York: Appleton-Century-Crofts, 1962.

Zigler, E., Research on personality structure in the retardate. In N. R. Ellis (Ed.), *International review of research in mental retardation*. Vol. 1, pp. 77–108. New York: Academic Press, 1966.

Zigler, E. Familial mental retardation: A continuing dilemma. *Science*, 1967, **155**, 292–98.

Zigler, E. Training the intellect versus development of the child. Paper read at the annual meeting of the American Educational Research Association, Los Angeles, 1968.

Zigler, E. Developmental versus difference theories of mental retardation and the problem of motivation. *American Journal of Mental Deficiency*, 1969, **73**, 536–56.

Zigler, E. Social class and the socialization process. *Review of Educational Research*, 1970, **40**(1), 87–110.(a)

Zigler, E. The nature-nurture issue reconsidered. In H. C. Haywood (Ed.), *Social-cultural aspects of mental retardation*, pp. 81–106. New York: Appleton-Century-Crofts, 1970.(b)

Zigler, E. The retarded child as a whole person. In D. K. Routh (Ed.), *The experimental psychology of mental retardation*, pp. 267–73. Chicago: Aldine, 1973.

Zigler, E. Dealing with retardation. *Science*, 1977, **196**, 1192–94.

Zigler, E., & Balla, D. Developmental course of responsiveness to social reinforcement in normal children and institutionalized retarded children. *Developmental Psychology*, 1972, **6**, 66–73.

Zigler, E., & Balla, D. A. Impact of institutional experience on the behavior and development of retarded persons. *American Journal of Mental Deficiency*, 1977, **82**, 1–11.

Zigler, E., & Butterfield, E. C. Motivational aspects of changes in IQ test performance of culturally deprived nursery school children. *Child Development*, 1968, **39**, 1–14.

Zigler, E., Hodgden, L., & Stevenson, H. W. The effect of support and nonsupport on the performance of normal and feeble-minded children. *Journal of Personality*, 1958, **26**, 106–22.

Zigler, E., & Muenchow, S. Mainstreaming: The proof is in the implementation. *American Psychologist*, 1979, **34**, 993–96.

Zigler, E., & Phillips, L. Psychiatric diagnosis: A critique. *Journal of Abnormal and Social Psychology*, 1961, **63**, 607–18.

Zigler, E., & Trickett, P. K. IQ, social competence, and evaluation of early childhood intervention programs. *American Psychologist*, 1978, **33**, 789–98.

Zuk, G. H. The cultural dilemma and spiritual crisis of the family with a handicapped child. *Exceptional Children*, 1962, **28**, 405–08.

Zwerling, I. Initial counseling of parents with retarded children. *Journal of Pediatrics*, 1954, **44**, 469–79.

INDEX

AAMD. *See* American Association on
Mental Deficiency
AAMD Adaptive Behavior Scale (ABS),
331, 332, 334, 336–338, 341
Public School Version, 332, 338
standardization, 337–338
Abecedarian Project, 501–508
abortion laws, 123, 131
Abramowicz, H. K., 67, 68, 71, 74
Abroms, K. I., 124
abstract reasoning, 392
Down's syndrome and, 127
acceptance:
intelligence and, 273, 292–293
labeling and, 273–274, 526
need for social, 426–427
of the retarded, 288, 289, 292–295
accommodation, cognitive-developmental
theory, 397
achievement:
anxiety and, 415
early intervention and, 523–526
EMR, 435
low need for, 86, 205, 427
middle-class emphasis on, 98
need for, 427–428
predicting school, 170–171, 186
in reading, 388–389
acting out, as defense mechanism, 238
adaptability, and intelligence, 170
adaptive behavior:
assessing, 330–342
criticism of use, 44
in defining retardation, 41–42, 44, 58,
330, 331, 332
degree of deviation, 332, 337
development of, 341–342
Adaptive Behavior Inventory for Children
(ABIC), 234, 338
Adelman, H. S., 461
adjustment. *See* social adjustment
adoption, IQ and, 104–105
Affleck, D., 549
age:
and attitude toward retarded, 291
at diagnosis, 217
and effect of institutionalization, 557, 558
expectations re, 332, 334

mental/chronological and IQ, 175
at placement, 545
prevalence variations by, 67, 68–69
of siblings, 547
social class and maternal, 150
and variations in IQ, 179–180
aggression:
attention getting, 417
trait construct, 439–440
alcohol, harm to fetus, 60, 142–143, 148
Alpha/Beta tests, 30
Altman, R., 404–405
amentia, simple, 86
American Association on Mental
Deficiency (AAMD), 20, 40
on adaptive behavior, 330, 336, 338
classification system, 29
definitions of retardation, 37, 38, 40–44,
45, 48, 67, 75, 189, 338
on disease and retardation, 60–61
American Indians, infant mortality, 90
American Psychiatric Association, 58
amniocentesis, 11, 130, 137, 149, 152, 155
anaclitic depression, 101
analytic-descriptive, cognitive style, 212
Anastasiow, N. J., 497, 498, 499, 500
ancephaly, 149
Anderson, K. A., 249
anemia, 89, 140, 145
Angelino, H., 418
Aninger, M., 589
anoxia, 141, 151, 160
antibody titer, 144, 155
anxiety:
assessing, 414–415
during pregnancy, 89, 90
reaction to diagnosis, 236, 237–238,
243–244
in the retarded, 414–415
Appell, M. J., 545, 547, 548, 549
arithmetic, teaching, 390–392
articulation, 381
asbestos, hazard, 143
Ashurst, D. I., on diagnosis of EMR, 227–
228
asphyxia, 151–152, 158
assimilation, cognitive-developmental
theory, 397